Elements of Information Theory

WILEY SERIES IN TELECOMMUNICATIONS

Donald L. Schilling, Editor
City College of New York

Elements of Information Theory

THOMAS M. COVER

Stanford University
Stanford, California

JOY A. THOMAS

IBM T. J. Watson Research Center
Yorktown Heights, New York

A Wiley-Interscience Publication

JOHN WILEY & SONS, INC.

New York / Chichester / Brisbane / Toronto / Singapore

Library of Congress Cataloging in Publication Data:
Cover, T. M., 1938–
    Elements of Information theory / Thomas M. Cover, Joy A. Thomas.
      p. cm. -- (Wiley series in telecommunications)
    "A Wiley-Interscience publication."
    Includes bibliographical references and index.
    ISBN 0-471-06259-6
    1. Information theory. I. Thomas, Joy A. II. Title.
III. Series.
Q360.C68 1991
003'.54--dc20   90-45484
                                                      CIP

Printed in the United States of America

20 19 18 17 16 15 14 13 12

To my father
Tom Cover

To my parents
Joy Thomas

Preface

This is intended to be a simple and accessible book on information theory. As Einstein said, "*Everything should be made as simple as possible, but no simpler.*" Although we have not verified the quote (first found in a fortune cookie), this point of view drives our development throughout the book. There are a few key ideas and techniques that, when mastered, make the subject appear simple and provide great intuition on new questions.

This book has arisen from over ten years of lectures in a two-quarter sequence of a senior and first-year graduate level course in information theory, and is intended as an introduction to information theory for students of communication theory, computer science and statistics.

There are two points to be made about the simplicities inherent in information theory. First, certain quantities like entropy and mutual information arise as the answers to fundamental questions. For example, entropy is the minimum descriptive complexity of a random variable, and mutual information is the communication rate in the presence of noise. Also, as we shall point out, mutual information corresponds to the increase in the doubling rate of wealth given side information. Second, the answers to information theoretic questions have a natural algebraic structure. For example, there is a chain rule for entropies, and entropy and mutual information are related. Thus the answers to problems in data compression and communication admit extensive interpretation. We all know the feeling that follows when one investigates a problem, goes through a large amount of algebra and finally investigates the answer to find that the entire problem is illuminated, not by the analysis, but by the inspection of the answer. Perhaps the outstanding examples of this in physics are Newton's laws and

Schrödinger's wave equation. Who could have foreseen the awesome philosophical interpretations of Schrödinger's wave equation?

In the text we often investigate properties of the answer before we look at the question. For example, in Chapter 2, we define entropy, relative entropy and mutual information and study the relationships and a few interpretations of them, showing how the answers fit together in various ways. Along the way we speculate on the meaning of the second law of thermodynamics. Does entropy always increase? The answer is yes and no. This is the sort of result that should please experts in the area but might be overlooked as standard by the novice.

In fact, that brings up a point that often occurs in teaching. It is fun to find new proofs or slightly new results that no one else knows. When one presents these ideas along with the established material in class, the response is "sure, sure, sure." But the excitement of teaching the material is greatly enhanced. Thus we have derived great pleasure from investigating a number of new ideas in this text book.

Examples of some of the new material in this text include the chapter on the relationship of information theory to gambling, the work on the universality of the second law of thermodynamics in the context of Markov chains, the joint typicality proofs of the channel capacity theorem, the competitive optimality of Huffman codes and the proof of Burg's theorem on maximum entropy spectral density estimation. Also the chapter on Kolmogorov complexity has no counterpart in other information theory texts. We have also taken delight in relating Fisher information, mutual information, and the Brunn-Minkowski and entropy power inequalities. To our surprise, many of the classical results on determinant inequalities are most easily proved using information theory.

Even though the field of information theory has grown considerably since Shannon's original paper, we have strived to emphasize its coherence. While it is clear that Shannon was motivated by problems in communication theory when he developed information theory, we treat information theory as a field of its own with applications to communication theory and statistics.

We were drawn to the field of information theory from backgrounds in communication theory, probability theory and statistics, because of the apparent impossibility of capturing the intangible concept of information.

Since most of the results in the book are given as theorems and proofs, we expect the elegance of the results to speak for themselves. In many cases we actually describe the properties of the solutions before introducing the problems. Again, the properties are interesting in themselves and provide a natural rhythm for the proofs that follow.

One innovation in the presentation is our use of long chains of inequalities, with no intervening text, followed immediately by the explanations. By the time the reader comes to many of these proofs, we expect that he or she will be able to follow most of these steps without any explanation and will be able to pick out the needed explanations. These chains of inequalities serve as pop quizzes in which the reader can be reassured of having the knowledge needed to prove some important theorems. The natural flow of these proofs is so compelling that it prompted us to flout one of the cardinal rules of technical writing. And the absence of verbiage makes the logical necessity of the ideas evident and the key ideas perspicuous. We hope that by the end of the book the reader will share our appreciation of the elegance, simplicity and naturalness of information theory.

Throughout the book we use the method of weakly typical sequences, which has its origins in Shannon's original 1948 work but was formally developed in the early 1970s. The key idea here is the so-called asymptotic equipartition property, which can be roughly paraphrased as "Almost everything is almost equally probable."

Chapter 2, which is the true first chapter of the subject, includes the basic algebraic relationships of entropy, relative entropy and mutual information as well as a discussion of the second law of thermodynamics and sufficient statistics. The asymptotic equipartition property (AEP) is given central prominence in Chapter 3. This leads us to discuss the entropy rates of stochastic processes and data compression in Chapters 4 and 5. A gambling sojourn is taken in Chapter 6, where the duality of data compression and the growth rate of wealth is developed.

The fundamental idea of Kolmogorov complexity as an intellectual foundation for information theory is explored in Chapter 7. Here we replace the goal of finding a description that is good on the average with the goal of finding the universally shortest description. There is indeed a universal notion of the descriptive complexity of an object. Here also the wonderful number Ω is investigated. This number, which is the binary expansion of the probability that a Turing machine will halt, reveals many of the secrets of mathematics.

Channel capacity, which is the fundamental theorem in information theory, is established in Chapter 8. The necessary material on differential entropy is developed in Chapter 9, laying the groundwork for the extension of previous capacity theorems to continuous noise channels. The capacity of the fundamental Gaussian channel is investigated in Chapter 10.

The relationship between information theory and statistics, first studied by Kullback in the early 1950s, and relatively neglected since, is developed in Chapter 12. Rate distortion theory requires a little more background than its noiseless data compression counterpart, which accounts for its placement as late as Chapter 13 in the text.

The huge subject of network information theory, which is the study of the simultaneously achievable flows of information in the presence of noise and interference, is developed in Chapter 14. Many new ideas come into play in network information theory. The primary new ingredients are interference and feedback. Chapter 15 considers the stock market, which is the generalization of the gambling processes considered in Chapter 6, and shows again the close correspondence of information theory and gambling.

Chapter 16, on inequalities in information theory, gives us a chance to recapitulate the interesting inequalities strewn throughout the book, put them in a new framework and then add some interesting new inequalities on the entropy rates of randomly drawn subsets. The beautiful relationship of the Brunn-Minkowski inequality for volumes of set sums, the entropy power inequality for the effective variance of the sum of independent random variables and the Fisher information inequalities are made explicit here.

We have made an attempt to keep the theory at a consistent level. The mathematical level is a reasonably high one, probably senior year or first-year graduate level, with a background of at least one good semester course in probability and a solid background in mathematics. We have, however, been able to avoid the use of measure theory. Measure theory comes up only briefly in the proof of the AEP for ergodic processes in Chapter 15. This fits in with our belief that the fundamentals of information theory are orthogonal to the techniques required to bring them to their full generalization.

Each chapter ends with a brief telegraphic summary of the key results. These summaries, in equation form, do not include the qualifying conditions. At the end of each we have included a variety of problems followed by brief historical notes describing the origins of the main results. The bibliography at the end of the book includes many of the key papers in the area and pointers to other books and survey papers on the subject.

The essential vitamins are contained in Chapters 2, 3, 4, 5, 8, 9, 10, 12, 13 and 14. This subset of chapters can be read without reference to the others and makes a good core of understanding. In our opinion, Chapter 7 on Kolmogorov complexity is also essential for a deep understanding of information theory. The rest, ranging from gambling to inequalities, is part of the terrain illuminated by this coherent and beautiful subject.

Every course has its first lecture, in which a sneak preview and overview of ideas is presented. Chapter 1 plays this role.

TOM COVER
JOY THOMAS

Palo Alto, June 1991

Acknowledgments

We wish to thank everyone who helped make this book what it is. In particular, Toby Berger, Masoud Salehi, Alon Orlitsky, Jim Mazo and Andrew Barron have made detailed comments on various drafts of the book which guided us in our final choice of content. We would like to thank Bob Gallager for an initial reading of the manuscript and his encouragement to publish it. We were pleased to use twelve of his problems in the text. Aaron Wyner donated his new proof with Ziv on the convergence of the Lempel-Ziv algorithm. We would also like to thank Norman Abramson, Ed van der Meulen, Jack Salz and Raymond Yeung for their suggestions.

Certain key visitors and research associates contributed as well, including Amir Dembo, Paul Algoet, Hirosuke Yamamoto, Ben Kawabata, Makoto Shimizu and Yoichiro Watanabe. We benefited from the advice of John Gill when he used this text in his class. Abbas El Gamal made invaluable contributions and helped begin this book years ago when we planned to write a research monograph on multiple user information theory. We would also like to thank the Ph.D. students in information theory as the book was being written: Laura Ekroot, Will Equitz, Don Kimber, Mitchell Trott, Andrew Nobel, Jim Roche, Erik Ordentlich, Elza Erkip and Vittorio Castelli. Also Mitchell Oslick, Chien-Wen Tseng and Michael Morrell were among the most active students in contributing questions and suggestions to the text. Marc Goldberg and Anil Kaul helped us produce some of the figures. Finally we would like to thank Kirsten Goodell and Kathy Adams for their support and help in some of the aspects of the preparation of the manuscript.

Joy Thomas would also like to thank Peter Franaszek, Steve Lavenberg, Fred Jelinek, David Nahamoo and Lalit Bahl for their encouragement and support during the final stages of production of this book.

TOM COVER
JOY THOMAS

Contents

List of Figures

Elements of Information Theory

Chapter 1

Introduction and Preview

This "first and last lecture" chapter goes backwards and forwards through information theory and its naturally related ideas. The full definitions and study of the subject begin in Chapter 2.

Information theory answers two fundamental questions in communication theory: what is the ultimate data compression (answer: the entropy H), and what is the ultimate transmission rate of communication (answer: the channel capacity C). For this reason some consider information theory to be a subset of communication theory. We will argue that it is much more. Indeed, it has fundamental contributions to make in statistical physics (thermodynamics), computer science (Kolmogorov complexity or algorithmic complexity), statistical inference (Occam's Razor: "The simplest explanation is best") and to probability and statistics (error rates for optimal hypothesis testing and estimation).

Figure 1.1 illustrates the relationship of information theory to other fields. As the figure suggests, information theory intersects physics (statistical mechanics), mathematics (probability theory), electrical engineering (communication theory) and computer science (algorithmic complexity). We now describe the areas of intersection in greater detail:

Electrical Engineering (Communication Theory). In the early 1940s, it was thought that increasing the transmission rate of information over a communication channel increased the probability of error. Shannon surprised the communication theory community by proving that this was not true as long as the communication rate was below channel capacity. The capacity can be simply computed from the noise characteristics of the channel. Shannon further argued that random processes such as music and speech have an irreducible

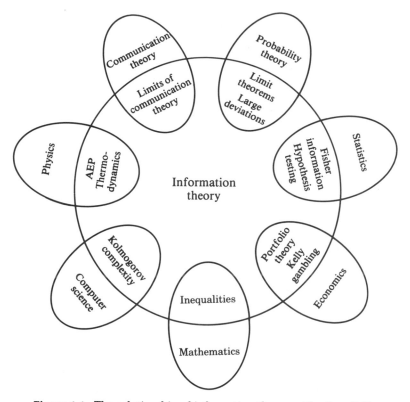

Figure 1.1. The relationship of information theory with other fields.

complexity below which the signal cannot be compressed. This he named the entropy, in deference to the parallel use of this word in thermodynamics, and argued that if the entropy of the source is less than the capacity of the channel, then asymptotically error free communication can be achieved.

Information theory today represents the extreme points of the set of all possible communication schemes, as shown in the fanciful Figure 1.2. The data compression minimum $I(X; \hat{X})$ lies at one extreme of the set of communication ideas. All data compression schemes require description rates at least equal to this minimum. At the other extreme is the data transmission maximum $I(X; Y)$, known as the channel capacity. Thus all

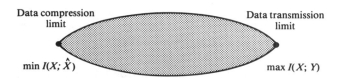

Figure 1.2. Information theoretic extreme points of communication theory.

modulation schemes and data compression schemes lie between these limits.

Information theory also suggests means of achieving these ultimate limits of communication. However, these theoretically optimal communication schemes, beautiful as they are, may turn out to be computationally impractical. It is only because of the computational feasibility of simple modulation and demodulation schemes that we use them rather than the random coding and nearest neighbor decoding rule suggested by Shannon's proof of the channel capacity theorem. Progress in integrated circuits and code design has enabled us to reap some of the gains suggested by Shannon's theory. A good example of an application of the ideas of information theory is the use of error correcting codes on compact discs.

Modern work on the communication aspects of information theory has concentrated on network information theory: the theory of the simultaneous rates of communication from many senders to many receivers in a communication network. Some of the trade-offs of rates between senders and receivers are unexpected, and all have a certain mathematical simplicity. A unifying theory, however, remains to be found.

Computer Science (Kolmogorov Complexity). Kolmogorov, Chaitin and Solomonoff put forth the idea that the complexity of a string of data can be defined by the length of the shortest binary program for computing the string. Thus the complexity is the minimal description length. This definition of complexity turns out to be universal, that is, computer independent, and is of fundamental importance. Thus Kolmogorov complexity lays the foundation for *the* theory of descriptive complexity. Gratifyingly, the Kolmogorov complexity K is approximately equal to the Shannon entropy H if the sequence is drawn at random from a distribution that has entropy H. So the tie-in between information theory and Kolmogorov complexity is perfect. Indeed, we consider Kolmogorov complexity to be more fundamental than Shannon entropy. It is the ultimate data compression and leads to a logically consistent procedure for inference.

There is a pleasing complementary relationship between algorithmic complexity and computational complexity. One can think about computational complexity (time complexity) and Kolmogorov complexity (program length or descriptive complexity) as two axes corresponding to program running time and program length. Kolmogorov complexity focuses on minimizing along the second axis, and computational complexity focuses on minimizing along the first axis. Little work has been done on the simultaneous minimization of the two.

Physics (Thermodynamics). Statistical mechanics is the birthplace of entropy and the second law of thermodynamics. Entropy always increases. Among other things, the second law allows one to dismiss any claims to perpetual motion machines. We briefly discuss the second law in Chapter 2.

Mathematics (Probability Theory and Statistics). The fundamental quantities of information theory—entropy, relative entropy and mutual information—are defined as functionals of probability distributions. In turn, they characterize the behavior of long sequences of random variables and allow us to estimate the probabilities of rare events (large deviation theory) and to find the best error exponent in hypothesis tests.

Philosophy of Science (Occam's Razor). William of Occam said "Causes shall not be multiplied beyond necessity," or to paraphrase it, "The simplest explanation is best". Solomonoff, and later Chaitin, argue persuasively that one gets a universally good prediction procedure if one takes a weighted combination of all programs that explain the data and observes what they print next. Moreover, this inference will work in many problems not handled by statistics. For example, this procedure will eventually predict the subsequent digits of π. When this procedure is applied to coin flips that come up heads with probability 0.7, this too will be inferred. When applied to the stock market, the procedure should essentially find all the "laws" of the stock market and extrapolate them optimally. In principle, such a procedure would have found Newton's laws of physics. Of course, such inference is highly impractical, because weeding out all computer programs that fail to generate existing data will take impossibly long. We would predict what happens tomorrow a hundred years from now.

Economics (Investment). Repeated investment in a stationary stock market results in an exponential growth of wealth. The growth rate of the wealth (called the doubling rate) is a dual of the entropy rate of the stock market. The parallels between the theory of optimal investment in the stock market and information theory are striking. We develop the theory of investment to explore this duality.

Computation vs. Communication. As we build larger computers out of smaller components, we encounter both a computation limit and a communication limit. Computation is communication limited and communication is computation limited. These become intertwined, and thus all of the developments in communication theory via information theory should have a direct impact on the theory of computation.

1.1 PREVIEW OF THE BOOK

The initial questions treated by information theory were in the areas of data compression and transmission. The answers are quantities like entropy and mutual information, which are functions of the probability distributions that underlie the process of communication. A few definitions will aid the initial discussion. We repeat these definitions in Chapter 2.

The entropy of a random variable X with a probability mass function $p(x)$ is defined by

$$H(X) = - \sum p(x) \log_2 p(x) . \tag{1.1}$$

We will use logarithms to base 2. The entropy will then be measured in bits. The entropy is a measure of the average uncertainty in the random variable. It is the number of bits on the average required to describe the random variable.

Example 1.1.1: Consider a random variable which has a uniform distribution over 32 outcomes. To identify an outcome, we need a label that takes on 32 different values. Thus 5-bit strings suffice as labels.

The entropy of this random variable is

$$H(X) = - \sum_{i=1}^{32} p(i) \log p(i) = - \sum_{i=1}^{32} \frac{1}{32} \log \frac{1}{32} = \log 32 = 5 \text{ bits} , \tag{1.2}$$

which agrees with the number of bits needed to describe X. In this case, all the outcomes have representations of the same length.

Now consider an example with a non-uniform distribution.

Example 1.1.2: Suppose we have a horse race with eight horses taking part. Assume that the probabilities of winning for the eight horses are $(\frac{1}{2}, \frac{1}{4}, \frac{1}{8}, \frac{1}{16}, \frac{1}{61}, \frac{1}{64}, \frac{1}{64}, \frac{1}{64})$. We can calculate the entropy of the horse race as

$$H(X) = - \frac{1}{2} \log \frac{1}{2} - \frac{1}{4} \log \frac{1}{4} - \frac{1}{8} \log \frac{1}{8} - \frac{1}{16} \log \frac{1}{16} - 4 \frac{1}{64} \log \frac{1}{64}$$

$$= 2 \text{ bits} . \tag{1.3}$$

Suppose that we wish to send a message to another person indicating which horse won the race. One alternative is to send the index of the winning horse. This description requires 3 bits for any of the horses. But the win probabilities are not uniform. It therefore makes sense to use shorter descriptions for the more probable horses, and longer descriptions for the less probable ones, so that we achieve a lower average description length. For example, we could use the following set of bit strings to represent the eight horses—0, 10, 110, 1110, 111100, 111101, 111110, 111111. The average description length in this case is 2 bits, as opposed to 3 bits for the uniform code. Notice that the average description length in this case is equal to the entropy. In Chapter 5, we show that the entropy of a random variable is a lower bound on the average number of bits required to represent the random variable and also on the average number of questions needed to identify the variable in a game of "twenty questions." We also show how to construct representations that have an average length within one bit of the entropy.

The concept of entropy in information theory is closely connected with the concept of entropy in statistical mechanics. If we draw a sequence of n independent and identically distributed (i.i.d.) random variables, we will show that the probability of a "typical" sequence is about $2^{-nH(X)}$ and that there are about $2^{nH(X)}$ such "typical" sequences. This property (known as the asymptotic equipartition property, or AEP) is the basis of many of the proofs in information theory. We later present other problems for which entropy arises as a natural answer (for example, the number of fair coin flips needed to generate a random variable).

The notion of descriptive complexity of a random variable can be extended to define the descriptive complexity of a single string. The Kolmogorov complexity of a binary string is defined as the length of the shortest computer program that prints out the string. It will turn out that if the string is indeed random, the Kolmogorov complexity is close to the entropy. Kolmogorov complexity is a natural framework in which to consider problems of statistical inference and modeling and leads to a clearer understanding of Occam's Razor "The simplest explanation is best." We describe some simple properties of Kolmogorov complexity in Chapter 7.

Entropy is the uncertainty of a single random variable. We can define conditional entropy, which is the entropy of a random variable, given another random variable. The reduction in uncertainty due to another random variable is called the mutual information. For two random variables X and Y this reduction is

$$I(X; Y) = H(X) - H(X|Y) = \sum_{x, y} p(x, y) \log \frac{p(x, y)}{p(x)p(y)} . \qquad (1.4)$$

The mutual information $I(X; Y)$ is a measure of the dependence between the two random variables. It is symmetric in X and Y and always non-negative.

A communication channel is a system in which the output depends probabilistically on its input. It is characterized by a probability transition matrix that determines the conditional distribution of the output given the input. For a communication channel with input X and output Y, we define the capacity C by

$$C = \max_{p(x)} I(X; Y) \,. \tag{1.5}$$

Later we show that the capacity is the maximum rate at which we can send information over the channel and recover the information at the output with a vanishingly low probability of error. We illustrate this with a few examples.

Example 1.1.3 (*Noiseless binary channel*): For this channel, the binary input is reproduced exactly at the output. This channel is illustrated in Figure 1.3. Here, any transmitted bit is received without error. Hence, in each transmission, we can send 1 bit reliably to the receiver, and the capacity is 1 bit. We can also calculate the information capacity $C = \max I(X; Y) = 1$ bit.

Example 1.1.4 (*Noisy four-symbol channel*): Consider the channel shown in Figure 1.4. In this channel, each input letter is received either as the same letter with probability $1/2$ or as the next letter with probability $1/2$. If we use all four input symbols, then inspection of the output would not reveal with certainty which input symbol was sent. If, on the other hand, we use only two of the inputs (1 and 3 say), then we can immediately tell from the output which input symbol was sent. This channel then acts like the noiseless channel of the previous example, and we can send 1 bit per transmission over this channel with no errors. We can calculate the channel capacity $C = \max I(X; Y)$ in this case, and it is equal to 1 bit per transmission, in agreement with the analysis above.

In general, communication channels do not have the simple structure of this example, so we cannot always identify a subset of the inputs to send information without error. But if we consider a sequence of transmissions, then all channels look like this example and we can then identify a subset of the input sequences (the codewords) which can be used to transmit information over the channel in such a way that the sets of possible output sequences associated with each of the codewords

Figure 1.3. Noiseless binary channel.

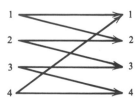

Figure 1.4. A noisy channel.

are approximately disjoint. We can then look at the output sequence and identify the input sequence with a vanishingly low probability of error.

Example 1.1.5 (*Binary symmetric channel*): This is the basic example of a noisy communication system. The channel is illustrated in Figure 1.5.

The channel has a binary input, and its output is equal to the input with probability $1 - p$. With probability p, on the other hand, a 0 is received as a 1, and vice versa.

In this case, the capacity of the channel can be calculated to be $C = 1 + p \log p + (1 - p) \log (1 - p)$ bits per transmission. However, it is no longer obvious how one can achieve this capacity. If we use the channel many times, however, the channel begins to look like the noisy four-symbol channel of the previous example, and we can send information at a rate C bits per transmission with an arbitrarily low probability of error.

The ultimate limit on the rate of communication of information over a channel is given by the channel capacity. The channel coding theorem shows that this limit can be achieved by using codes with a long block length. In practical communication systems, there are limitations on the complexity of the codes that we can use, and therefore we may not be able to achieve capacity.

Mutual information turns out to be a special case of a more general quantity called relative entropy $D(p\|q)$ which is a measure of the "distance" between two probability mass functions p and q. It is defined as

$$D(p\|q) = \sum_x p(x) \log \frac{p(x)}{q(x)} . \qquad (1.6)$$

Although relative entropy is not a true metric, it has some of the properties of a metric. In particular, it is always non-negative and is zero if and only if $p = q$. Relative entropy arises as the exponent in the

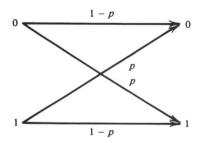

Figure 1.5. Binary symmetric channel.

probability of error in a hypothesis test between distributions p and q. Relative entropy can be used to define a geometry for probability distributions that allows us to interpret many of the results of large deviation theory.

There are a number of parallels between information theory and the theory of investment in a stock market. A stock market is defined by a random vector $\mathbf{X}$ whose elements are non-negative numbers equal to the ratio of the price of a stock at the end of a day to the price at the beginning of the day. For a stock market with distribution $F(x)$, we can define the doubling rate W as

$$W = \max_{\mathbf{b}:b_i \geq 0, \Sigma b_i = 1} \int \log \mathbf{b}^t \mathbf{x} \, dF(\mathbf{x}). \tag{1.7}$$

The doubling rate is the maximum asymptotic exponent in the growth of wealth. The doubling rate has a number of properties that parallel the properties of entropy. We explore some of these properties in Chapter 15.

The quantities H, I, C, D, K, W arise naturally in the following areas:

- *Data compression.* The entropy H of a random variable is a lower bound on the average length of the shortest description of the random variable. We can construct descriptions with average length within one bit of the entropy.

  If we relax the constraint of recovering the source perfectly, we can then ask what rates are required to describe the source up to distortion D? And what channel capacities are sufficient to enable the transmission of this source over the channel and its reconstruction with distortion less than or equal to D? This is the subject of rate distortion theory.

  When we try to formalize the notion of the shortest description for non-random objects, we are led to the definition of Kolmogorov complexity K. Later, we will show that Kolmogorov complexity is universal and satisfies many of the intuitive requirements for the theory of shortest descriptions.

- *Data transmission.* We consider the problem of transmitting information so that the receiver can decode the message with a small probability of error. Essentially, we wish to find codewords (sequences of input symbols to a channel) that are mutually far apart in the sense that their noisy versions (available at the output of the channel) are distinguishable. This is equivalent to sphere packing in high dimensional space. For any set of codewords it is possible to calculate the probability the receiver will make an error, i.e., make an incorrect decision as to which codeword was sent. However, in most cases, this calculation is tedious.

Using a randomly generated code, Shannon showed that one can send information at any rate below the capacity C of the channel with an arbitrarily low probability of error. The idea of a randomly generated code is very unusual. It provides the basis for a simple analysis of a very difficult problem. One of the key ideas in the proof is the concept of typical sequences.

- *Network information theory.* Each of the topics previously mentioned involves a single source or a single channel. What if one wishes simultaneously to compress many sources and then put the compressed descriptions together into a joint reconstruction of the sources? This problem is solved by the Slepian-Wolf theorem. Or what if one has many senders independently sending information to a common receiver? What is the channel capacity of this channel? This is the multiple access channel solved by Liao and Ahlswede. Or what if one has one sender and many receivers and wishes to simultaneously communicate (perhaps different) information to each of the receivers? This is the broadcast channel. Finally, what if one has an arbitrary number of senders and receivers in an environment of interference and noise. What is the capacity region of achievable rates from the various senders to the receivers? This is the general network information theory problem. All of the preceding problems fall into the general area of multiple-user or network information theory. Although hopes for a unified theory may be beyond current research techniques, there is still some hope that all the answers involve only elaborate forms of mutual information and relative entropy.

- *Ergodic theory.* The asymptotic equipartition theorem states that most sample n-sequences of an ergodic process have probability about 2^{-nH} and that there are about 2^{nH} such typical sequences.

- *Hypothesis testing.* The relative entropy D arises as the exponent in the probability of error in a hypothesis test between two distributions. It is a natural measure of distance between distributions.

- *Statistical mechanics.* The entropy H arises in statistical mechanics as a measure of uncertainty or disorganization in a physical system. The second law of thermodynamics says that the entropy of a closed system cannot decrease. Later we provide some interpretations of the second law.

- *Inference.* We can use the notion of Kolmogorov complexity K to find the shortest description of the data and use that as a model to predict what comes next. A model that maximizes the uncertainty or entropy yields the maximum entropy approach to inference.

- *Gambling and investment.* The optimal exponent in the growth rate of wealth is given by the doubling rate W. For a horse race with uniform odds, the sum of the doubling rate W and the entropy H is constant. The mutual information I between a horse race and some side information is an upper bound on the increase in the doubling rate due to the side information. Similar results hold for investment in a stock market.

- *Probability theory.* The asymptotic equipartition property (AEP) shows that most sequences are typical in that they have a sample entropy close to H. So attention can be restricted to these approximately 2^{nH} typical sequences. In large deviation theory, the probability of a set is approximately 2^{-nD}, where D is the relative entropy distance between the closest element in the set and the true distribution.

- *Complexity theory.* The Kolmogorov complexity K is a measure of the descriptive complexity of an object. It is related to, but different from, computational complexity, which measures the time or space required for a computation.

Information theoretic quantities like entropy and relative entropy arise again and again as the answers to the fundamental questions in communication and statistics. Before studying these questions, we shall study some of the properties of the answers. We begin in the next chapter with the definitions and the basic properties of entropy, relative entropy and mutual information.

Chapter 2

Entropy, Relative Entropy and Mutual Information

This chapter introduces most of the basic definitions required for the subsequent development of the theory. It is irresistible to play with their relationships and interpretations, taking faith in their later utility. After defining entropy and mutual information, we establish chain rules, the non-negativity of mutual information, the data processing inequality, and finally investigate the extent to which the second law of thermodynamics holds for Markov processes.

The concept of information is too broad to be captured completely by a single definition. However, for any probability distribution, we define a quantity called the *entropy*, which has many properties that agree with the intuitive notion of what a measure of information should be. This notion is extended to define *mutual information*, which is a measure of the amount of information one random variable contains about another. Entropy then becomes the self-information of a random variable. Mutual information is a special case of a more general quantity called *relative entropy*, which is a measure of the distance between two probability distributions. All these quantities are closely related and share a number of simple properties. We derive some of these properties in this chapter.

In later chapters, we show how these quantities arise as natural answers to a number of questions in communication, statistics, complexity and gambling. That will be the ultimate test of the value of these definitions.

2.1 ENTROPY

We will first introduce the concept of entropy, which is a measure of uncertainty of a random variable. Let X be a discrete random variable with alphabet $\mathscr{X}$ and probability mass function $p(x) = \Pr\{X = x\}$, $x \in \mathscr{X}$. We denote the probability mass function by $p(x)$ rather than $p_X(x)$ for convenience. Thus, $p(x)$ and $p(y)$ refer to two different random variables, and are in fact different probability mass functions, $p_X(x)$ and $p_Y(y)$ respectively.

Definition: The *entropy H(X)* of a discrete random variable X is defined by

$$H(X) = - \sum_{x \in \mathscr{X}} p(x) \log p(x). \qquad (2.1)$$

We also write $H(p)$ for the above quantity. The log is to the base 2 and entropy is expressed in bits. For example, the entropy of a fair coin toss is 1 bit. We will use the convention that $0 \log 0 = 0$, which is easily justified by continuity since $x \log x \to 0$ as $x \to 0$. Thus adding terms of zero probability does not change the entropy.

If the base of the logarithm is b, we will denote the entropy as $H_b(X)$. If the base of the logarithm is e, then the entropy is measured in *nats*. Unless otherwise specified, we will take all logarithms to base 2, and hence all the entropies will be measured in bits.

Note that entropy is a functional of the distribution of X. It does not depend on the actual values taken by the random variable X, but only on the probabilities.

We shall denote expectation by E. Thus if $X \sim p(x)$, then the expected value of the random variable $g(X)$ is written

$$E_p g(X) = \sum_{x \in \mathscr{X}} g(x) p(x), \qquad (2.2)$$

or more simply as $Eg(X)$ when the probability mass function is understood from the context.

We shall take a peculiar interest in the eerily self-referential expectation of $g(X)$ under $p(x)$ when $g(X) = \log \frac{1}{p(X)}$.

Remark: The entropy of X can also be interpreted as the expected value of $\log \frac{1}{p(X)}$, where X is drawn according to probability mass function $p(x)$. Thus

$$H(X) = E_p \log \frac{1}{p(X)}. \qquad (2.3)$$

This definition of entropy is related to the definition of entropy in thermodynamics; some of the connections will be explored later. It is possible to derive the definition of entropy axiomatically by defining certain properties that the entropy of a random variable must satisfy. This approach is illustrated in a problem at the end of the chapter. We will not use the axiomatic approach to justify the definition of entropy; instead, we will show that it arises as the answer to a number of natural questions such as "What is the average length of the shortest description of the random variable?" First, we derive some immediate consequences of the definition.

Lemma 2.1.1: $H(X) \geq 0$.

   Proof: $0 \leq p(x) \leq 1$ implies $\log(1/p(x)) \geq 0$. $\square$

Lemma 2.1.2: $H_b(X) = (\log_b a) H_a(X)$.

   Proof: $\log_b p = \log_b a \log_a p$. $\square$

The second property of entropy enables us to change the base of the logarithm in the definition. Entropy can be changed from one base to another by multiplying by the appropriate factor.

Example 2.1.1: Let

$$X = \begin{cases} 1 & \text{with probability } p, \\ 0 & \text{with probability } 1 - p. \end{cases} \tag{2.4}$$

Then

$$H(X) = -p \log p - (1 - p) \log(1 - p) \overset{\text{def}}{=} H(p). \tag{2.5}$$

In particular, $H(X) = 1$ bit when $p = 1/2$. The graph of the function $H(p)$ is shown in Figure 2.1. The figure illustrates some of the basic properties of entropy—it is a concave function of the distribution and equals 0 when $p = 0$ or 1. This makes sense, because when $p = 0$ or 1, the variable is not random and there is no uncertainty. Similarly, the uncertainty is maximum when $p = \frac{1}{2}$, which also corresponds to the maximum value of the entropy.

Example 2.1.2: Let

$$X = \begin{cases} a & \text{with probability } 1/2, \\ b & \text{with probability } 1/4, \\ c & \text{with probability } 1/8, \\ d & \text{with probability } 1/8. \end{cases} \tag{2.6}$$

The entropy of X is

$$H(X) = -\frac{1}{2} \log \frac{1}{2} - \frac{1}{4} \log \frac{1}{4} - \frac{1}{8} \log \frac{1}{8} - \frac{1}{8} \log \frac{1}{8} = \frac{7}{4} \text{ bits}. \tag{2.7}$$

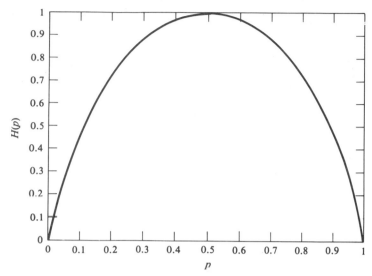

Figure 2.1. $H(p)$ versus p.

Suppose we wish to determine the value of X with the minimum number of binary questions. An efficient first question is "Is $X = a$?" This splits the probability in half. If the answer to the first question is no, then the second question can be "Is $X = b$?" The third question can be "Is $X = c$?" The resulting expected number of binary questions required is 1.75. This turns out to be the minimum expected number of binary questions required to determine the value of X. In Chapter 5, we show that the minimum expected number of binary questions required to determine X lies between $H(X)$ and $H(X) + 1$.

2.2   JOINT ENTROPY AND CONDITIONAL ENTROPY

We have defined the entropy of a single random variable in the previous section. We now extend the definition to a pair of random variables. There is nothing really new in this definition because (X, Y) can be considered to be a single vector-valued random variable.

Definition: The *joint entropy* $H(X, Y)$ of a pair of discrete random variables (X, Y) with a joint distribution $p(x, y)$ is defined as

$$H(X, Y) = - \sum_{x \in \mathscr{X}} \sum_{y \in \mathscr{Y}} p(x, y) \log p(x, y), \qquad (2.8)$$

which can also be expressed as

$$H(X, Y) = -E \log p(X, Y). \qquad (2.9)$$

We also define the conditional entropy of a random variable given another as the expected value of the entropies of the conditional distributions, averaged over the conditioning random variable.

Definition: If $(X, Y) \sim p(x, y)$, then the *conditional entropy* $H(Y|X)$ is defined as

$$H(Y|X) = \sum_{x \in \mathscr{X}} p(x) H(Y|X = x) \tag{2.10}$$

$$= - \sum_{x \in \mathscr{X}} p(x) \sum_{y \in \mathscr{Y}} p(y|x) \log p(y|x) \tag{2.11}$$

$$= - \sum_{x \in \mathscr{X}} \sum_{y \in \mathscr{Y}} p(x, y) \log p(y|x) \tag{2.12}$$

$$= - E_{p(x, y)} \log p(Y|X). \tag{2.13}$$

The naturalness of the definition of joint entropy and conditional entropy is exhibited by the fact that the entropy of a pair of random variables is the entropy of one plus the conditional entropy of the other. This is proved in the following theorem.

Theorem 2.2.1 *(Chain rule)*:

$$H(X, Y) = H(X) + H(Y|X). \tag{2.14}$$

Proof:

$$H(X, Y) = - \sum_{x \in \mathscr{X}} \sum_{y \in \mathscr{Y}} p(x, y) \log p(x, y) \tag{2.15}$$

$$= - \sum_{x \in \mathscr{X}} \sum_{y \in \mathscr{Y}} p(x, y) \log p(x) p(y|x) \tag{2.16}$$

$$= - \sum_{x \in \mathscr{X}} \sum_{y \in \mathscr{Y}} p(x, y) \log p(x) - \sum_{x \in \mathscr{X}} \sum_{y \in \mathscr{Y}} p(x, y) \log p(y|x) \tag{2.17}$$

$$= - \sum_{x \in \mathscr{X}} p(x) \log p(x) - \sum_{x \in \mathscr{X}} \sum_{y \in \mathscr{Y}} p(x, y) \log p(y|x) \tag{2.18}$$

$$= H(X) + H(Y|X). \tag{2.19}$$

Equivalently, we can write

$$\log p(X, Y) = \log p(X) + \log p(Y|X) \tag{2.20}$$

and take the expectation of both sides of the equation to obtain the theorem. $\square$

Corollary:

$$H(X, Y|Z) = H(X|Z) + H(Y|X, Z) . \qquad (2.21)$$

Proof: The proof follows along the same lines as the theorem.   □

Example 2.2.1: Let (X, Y) have the following joint distribution:

Y \ X	1	2	3	4
1	$\frac{1}{8}$	$\frac{1}{16}$	$\frac{1}{32}$	$\frac{1}{32}$
2	$\frac{1}{16}$	$\frac{1}{8}$	$\frac{1}{32}$	$\frac{1}{32}$
3	$\frac{1}{16}$	$\frac{1}{16}$	$\frac{1}{16}$	$\frac{1}{16}$
4	$\frac{1}{4}$	0	0	0

The marginal distribution of X is $(\frac{1}{2}, \frac{1}{4}, \frac{1}{8}, \frac{1}{8})$ and the marginal distribution of Y is $(\frac{1}{4}, \frac{1}{4}, \frac{1}{4}, \frac{1}{4})$, and hence $H(X) = 7/4$ bits and $H(Y) = 2$ bits. Also,

$$H(X|Y) = \sum_{i=1}^{4} p(Y = i)H(X|Y = i)$$

$$= \frac{1}{4} H\left(\frac{1}{2}, \frac{1}{4}, \frac{1}{8}, \frac{1}{8}\right) + \frac{1}{4} H\left(\frac{1}{4}, \frac{1}{2}, \frac{1}{8}, \frac{1}{8}\right) \qquad (2.22)$$

$$ \, \frac{1}{4} H\left(\frac{1}{4}, \frac{1}{4}, \frac{1}{4}, \frac{1}{4}\right) + \frac{1}{4} H(1, 0, 0, 0) \qquad (2.23)$$

$$= \frac{1}{4} \times \frac{7}{4} + \frac{1}{4} \times \frac{7}{4} + \frac{1}{4} \times 2 + \frac{1}{4} \times 0 \qquad (2.24)$$

$$= \frac{11}{8} \text{ bits} . \qquad (2.25)$$

Similarly $H(Y|X) = 13/8$ bits and $H(X, Y) = 27/8$ bits.

Remark: Note that $H(Y|X) \neq H(X|Y)$. However, $H(X) - H(X|Y) = H(Y) - H(Y|X)$, a property that we shall exploit later.

2.3   RELATIVE ENTROPY AND MUTUAL INFORMATION

The entropy of a random variable is a measure of the uncertainty of the random variable; it is a measure of the amount of information required on the average to describe the random variable. In this section, we introduce two related concepts: relative entropy and mutual information.

The relative entropy is a measure of the distance between two distributions. In statistics, it arises as an expected logarithm of the likelihood ratio. The relative entropy $D(p\|q)$ is a measure of the inefficiency of assuming that the distribution is q when the true distribution is p. For example, if we knew the true distribution of the random variable, then we could construct a code with average description length $H(p)$. If, instead, we used the code for a distribution q, we would need $H(p) + D(p\|q)$ bits on the average to describe the random variable.

Definition: The *relative entropy* or *Kullback Leibler distance* between two probability mass functions $p(x)$ and $q(x)$ is defined as

$$D(p\|q) = \sum_{x \in \mathcal{X}} p(x) \log \frac{p(x)}{q(x)} \qquad (2.26)$$

$$= E_p \log \frac{p(X)}{q(X)} . \qquad (2.27)$$

In the above definition, we use the convention (based on continuity arguments) that $0 \log \frac{0}{q} = 0$ and $p \log \frac{p}{0} = \infty$.

We will soon show that relative entropy is always non-negative and is zero if and only if $p = q$. However, it is not a true distance between distributions since it is not symmetric and does not satisfy the triangle inequality. Nonetheless, it is often useful to think of relative entropy as a "distance" between distributions.

We now introduce mutual information, which is a measure of the amount of information that one random variable contains about another random variable. It is the reduction in the uncertainty of one random variable due to the knowledge of the other.

Definition: Consider two random variables X and Y with a joint probability mass function $p(x, y)$ and marginal probability mass functions $p(x)$ and $p(y)$. The *mutual information* $I(X;Y)$ is the relative entropy between the joint distribution and the product distribution $p(x)p(y)$, i.e.,

$$I(X; Y) = \sum_{x \in \mathcal{X}} \sum_{y \in \mathcal{Y}} p(x, y) \log \frac{p(x, y)}{p(x)p(y)} \qquad (2.28)$$

$$= D(p(x, y) \| p(x)p(y)) \tag{2.29}$$

$$= E_{p(x, y)} \log \frac{p(X, Y)}{p(X)p(Y)} . \tag{2.30}$$

Example 2.3.1: Let $\mathcal{X} = \{0, 1\}$ and consider two distributions p and q on $\mathcal{X}$. Let $p(0) = 1 - r$, $p(1) = r$, and let $q(0) = 1 - s$, $q(1) = s$. Then

$$D(p \| q) = (1 - r) \log \frac{1 - r}{1 - s} + r \log \frac{r}{s} \tag{2.31}$$

and

$$D(q \| p) = (1 - s) \log \frac{1 - s}{1 - r} + s \log \frac{s}{r} . \tag{2.32}$$

If $r = s$, then $D(p \| q) = D(q \| p) = 0$. If $r = 1/2$, $s = 1/4$, then we can calculate

$$D(p \| q) = \frac{1}{2} \log \frac{\frac{1}{2}}{\frac{3}{4}} + \frac{1}{2} \log \frac{\frac{1}{2}}{\frac{1}{4}} = 1 - \frac{1}{2} \log 3 = 0.2075 \text{ bits}, \tag{2.33}$$

whereas

$$D(q \| p) = \frac{3}{4} \log \frac{\frac{3}{4}}{\frac{1}{2}} + \frac{1}{4} \log \frac{\frac{1}{4}}{\frac{1}{2}} = \frac{3}{4} \log 3 - 1 = 0.1887 \text{ bits}. \tag{2.34}$$

Note that $D(p \| q) \neq D(q \| p)$ in general.

2.4   RELATIONSHIP BETWEEN ENTROPY AND MUTUAL INFORMATION

We can rewrite the definition of mutual information $I(X; Y)$ as

$$I(X; Y) = \sum_{x, y} p(x, y) \log \frac{p(x, y)}{p(x)p(y)} \tag{2.35}$$

$$= \sum_{x, y} p(x, y) \log \frac{p(x|y)}{p(x)} \tag{2.36}$$

$$= -\sum_{x, y} p(x, y) \log p(x) + \sum_{x, y} p(x, y) \log p(x|y) \tag{2.37}$$

$$= -\sum_{x} p(x) \log p(x) - \left(-\sum_{x, y} p(x, y) \log p(x|y) \right) \tag{2.38}$$

$$= H(X) - H(X|Y). \tag{2.39}$$

Thus the mutual information $I(X; Y)$ is the reduction in the uncertainty of X due to the knowledge of Y.

By symmetry, it also follows that

$$I(X; Y) = H(Y) - H(Y|X) \,. \tag{2.40}$$

Thus X says as much about Y as Y says about X.

Since $H(X, Y) = H(X) + H(Y|X)$ as shown in Section 2.2, we have

$$I(X; Y) = H(X) + H(Y) - H(X, Y) \,. \tag{2.41}$$

Finally, we note that

$$I(X; X) = H(X) - H(X|X) = H(X) \,. \tag{2.42}$$

Thus the mutual information of a random variable with itself is the entropy of the random variable. This is the reason that entropy is sometimes referred to as *self-information*.

Collecting these results, we have the following theorem.

Theorem 2.4.1 (*Mutual information and entropy*):

$$I(X; Y) = H(X) - H(X|Y) \,, \tag{2.43}$$

$$I(X; Y) = H(Y) - H(Y|X) \,, \tag{2.44}$$

$$I(X; Y) = H(X) + H(Y) - H(X, Y) \,, \tag{2.45}$$

$$I(X; Y) = I(Y; X) \,, \tag{2.46}$$

$$I(X; X) = H(X) \,. \tag{2.47}$$

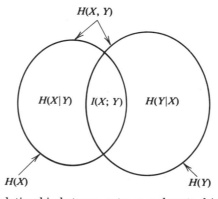

Figure 2.2. Relationship between entropy and mutual information.

The relationship between $H(X)$, $H(Y)$, $H(X, Y)$, $H(X|Y)$, $H(Y|X)$ and $I(X; Y)$ is expressed in a Venn diagram (Figure 2.2). Notice that the mutual information $I(X; Y)$ corresponds to the intersection of the information in X with the information in Y.

Example 2.4.1: For the joint distribution of example 2.2.1, it is easy to calculate the mutual information $I(X; Y) = H(X) - H(X|Y) = H(Y) - H(Y|X) = 0.375$ bits.

2.5   CHAIN RULES FOR ENTROPY, RELATIVE ENTROPY AND MUTUAL INFORMATION

We now show that the entropy of a collection of random variables is the sum of the conditional entropies.

Theorem 2.5.1 (*Chain rule for entropy*): *Let* $X_1, X_2, \ldots, X_n$ *be drawn according to* $p(x_1, x_2, \ldots, x_n)$. *Then*

$$H(X_1, X_2, \ldots, X_n) = \sum_{i=1}^{n} H(X_i | X_{i-1}, \ldots, X_1). \qquad (2.48)$$

Proof: By repeated application of the two-variable expansion rule for entropies, we have

$$H(X_1, X_2) = H(X_1) + H(X_2|X_1), \qquad (2.49)$$

$$H(X_1, X_2, X_3) = H(X_1) + H(X_2, X_3|X_1) \qquad (2.50)$$

$$= H(X_1) + H(X_2|X_1) + H(X_3|X_2, X_1), \qquad (2.51)$$

$$\vdots$$

$$H(X_1, X_2, \ldots, X_n) = H(X_1) + H(X_2|X_1) + \cdots + H(X_n|X_{n-1}, \ldots, X_1) \qquad (2.52)$$

$$= \sum_{i=1}^{n} H(X_i | X_{i-1}, \ldots, X_1). \qquad (2.53)$$

Alternative Proof: We write $p(x_1, \ldots, x_n) = \prod_{i=1}^{n} p(x_i | x_{i-1}, \ldots, x_1)$ and evaluate

$$H(X_1, X_2, \ldots, X_n)$$

$$= -\sum_{x_1, x_2, \ldots, x_n} p(x_1, x_2, \ldots, x_n) \log p(x_1, x_2, \ldots, x_n) \qquad (2.54)$$

$$= -\sum_{x_1, x_2, \ldots, x_n} p(x_1, x_2, \ldots, x_n) \log \prod_{i=1}^{n} p(x_i | x_{i-1}, \ldots, x_1) \qquad (2.55)$$

$$= -\sum_{x_1, x_2, \ldots, x_n} \sum_{i=1}^{n} p(x_1, x_2, \ldots, x_n) \log p(x_i | x_{i-1}, \ldots, x_1) \quad (2.56)$$

$$= -\sum_{i=1}^{n} \sum_{x_1, x_2, \ldots, x_n} p(x_1, x_2, \ldots, x_n) \log p(x_i | x_{i-1}, \ldots, x_1) \quad (2.57)$$

$$= -\sum_{i=1}^{n} \sum_{x_1, x_2, \ldots, x_i} p(x_1, x_2, \ldots, x_i) \log p(x_i | x_{i-1}, \ldots, x_1) \quad (2.58)$$

$$= \sum_{i=1}^{n} H(X_i | X_{i-1}, \ldots, X_1). \quad \square \quad (2.59)$$

We now define the conditional mutual information as the reduction in the uncertainty of X due to knowledge of Y when Z is given.

Definition: The *conditional mutual information* of random variables X and Y given Z is defined by

$$I(X; Y|Z) = H(X|Z) - H(X|Y, Z) \quad (2.60)$$

$$= E_{p(x, y, z)} \log \frac{p(X, Y|Z)}{p(X|Z)p(Y|Z)}. \quad (2.61)$$

Mutual information also satisfies a chain rule.

Theorem 2.5.2 (*Chain rule for information*):

$$I(X_1, X_2, \ldots, X_n; Y) = \sum_{i=1}^{n} I(X_i; Y | X_{i-1}, X_{i-2}, \ldots, X_1). \quad (2.62)$$

Proof:

$$I(X_1, X_2, \ldots, X_n; Y) = H(X_1, X_2, \ldots, X_n) - H(X_1, X_2, \ldots, X_n | Y) \quad (2.63)$$

$$= \sum_{i=1}^{n} H(X_i | X_{i-1}, \ldots, X_1) - \sum_{i=1}^{n} H(X_i | X_{i-1}, \ldots, X_1, Y)$$

$$= \sum_{i=1}^{n} I(X_i; Y | X_1, X_2, \ldots, X_{i-1}). \quad \square \quad (2.64)$$

We define a conditional version of the relative entropy.

Definition: The *conditional relative entropy* $D(p(y|x)\|q(y|x))$ is the average of the relative entropies between the conditional probability mass functions $p(y|x)$ and $q(y|x)$ averaged over the probability mass function $p(x)$. More precisely,

$$D(p(y|x)\|q(y|x)) = \sum_{x} p(x) \sum_{y} p(y|x) \log \frac{p(y|x)}{q(y|x)} \quad (2.65)$$

$$= E_{p(x,\,y)} \log \frac{p(Y|X)}{q(Y|X)}. \tag{2.66}$$

The notation for conditional relative entropy is not explicit since it omits mention of the distribution $p(x)$ of the conditioning random variable. However, it is normally understood from the context.

The relative entropy between two joint distributions on a pair of random variables can be expanded as the sum of a relative entropy and a conditional relative entropy. The chain rule for relative entropy will be used in Section 2.9 to prove a version of the second law of thermodynamics.

Theorem 2.5.3 (*Chain rule for relative entropy*):

$$D(p(x, y)\|q(x, y)) = D(p(x)\|q(x)) + D(p(y|x)\|q(y|x)). \tag{2.67}$$

Proof:

$$D(p(x, y)\|q(x, y)) = \sum_{x} \sum_{y} p(x, y) \log \frac{p(x, y)}{q(x, y)} \tag{2.68}$$

$$= \sum_{x} \sum_{y} p(x, y) \log \frac{p(x)p(y|x)}{q(x)q(y|x)} \tag{2.69}$$

$$= \sum_{x} \sum_{y} p(x, y) \log \frac{p(x)}{q(x)} + \sum_{x} \sum_{y} p(x, y) \log \frac{p(y|x)}{q(y|x)} \tag{2.70}$$

$$- D(p(x)\|q(x)) + D(p(y|x)\|q(y|x)). \quad \square \tag{2.71}$$

2.6   JENSEN'S INEQUALITY AND ITS CONSEQUENCES

In this section, we shall prove some simple properties of the quantities defined earlier. We begin with the properties of convex functions.

Definition: A function $f(x)$ is said to be *convex* over an interval (a, b) if for every $x_1, x_2 \in (a, b)$ and $0 \le \lambda \le 1$,

$$f(\lambda x_1 + (1 - \lambda)x_2) \le \lambda f(x_1) + (1 - \lambda)f(x_2). \tag{2.72}$$

A function f is said to be *strictly convex* if equality holds only if $\lambda = 0$ or $\lambda = 1$.

Definition: A function f is *concave* if $-f$ is convex.

A function is convex if it always lies below any chord. A function is concave if it always lies above any chord.

  Examples of convex functions include x^2, $|x|$, e^x, $x \log x$ (for $x \geq 0$), etc. Examples of concave functions include $\log x$ and $\sqrt{x}$ for $x \geq 0$. Figure 2.3 shows some examples of convex and concave functions. Note that linear functions $ax + b$ are both convex and concave. Convexity underlies many of the basic properties of information theoretic quantities like entropy and mutual information. Before we prove some of these properties, we derive some simple results for convex functions.

Theorem 2.6.1: *If the function f has a second derivative which is non-negative (positive) everywhere, then the function is convex (strictly convex).*

  Proof: We use the Taylor series expansion of the function around x_0, i.e.,

$$f(x) = f(x_0) + f'(x_0)(x - x_0) + \frac{f''(x^*)}{2}(x - x_0)^2 \tag{2.73}$$

where x^* lies between x_0 and x. By hypothesis, $f''(x^*) \geq 0$, and thus the last term is always non-negative for all x.

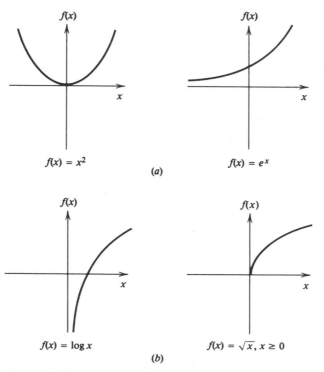

$f(x) = x^2$ $f(x) = e^x$

(a)

$f(x) = \log x$ $f(x) = \sqrt{x}, x \geq 0$

(b)

Figure 2.3. Examples of (a) convex and (b) concave functions.

We let $x_0 = \lambda x_1 + (1 - \lambda)x_2$ and take $x = x_1$ to obtain

$$f(x_1) \geq f(x_0) + f'(x_0)[(1 - \lambda)(x_1 - x_2)]. \tag{2.74}$$

Similarly, taking $x = x_2$, we obtain

$$f(x_2) \geq f(x_0) + f'(x_0)[\lambda(x_2 - x_1)]. \tag{2.75}$$

Multiplying (2.74) by λ and (2.75) by $1 - \lambda$ and adding, we obtain (2.72). The proof for strict convexity proceeds along the same lines. $\square$

Theorem 2.6.1 allows us to immediately verify the strict convexity of x^2, e^x and $x \log x$ for $x \geq 0$, and the strict concavity of $\log x$ and $\sqrt{x}$ for $x \geq 0$.

Let E denote expectation. Thus $EX = \Sigma_{x \in \mathscr{X}} \, p(x)x$ in the discrete case and $EX = \int xf(x) \, dx$ in the continuous case.

The next inequality is one of the most widely used in mathematics and one that underlies many of the basic results in information theory.

Theorem 2.6.2 (*Jensen's inequality*): *If f is a convex function and X is a random variable, then*

$$Ef(X) \geq f(EX). \tag{2.76}$$

Moreover, if f is strictly convex, then equality in (2.76) implies that $X = EX$ with probability 1, i.e., X is a constant.

Proof: We prove this for discrete distributions by induction on the number of mass points. The proof of conditions for equality when f is strictly convex will be left to the reader.

For a two mass point distribution, the inequality becomes

$$p_1 f(x_1) + p_2 f(x_2) \geq f(p_1 x_1 + p_2 x_2), \tag{2.77}$$

which follows directly from the definition of convex functions. Suppose the theorem is true for distributions with $k - 1$ mass points. Then writing $p_i' = p_i/(1 - p_k)$ for $i = 1, 2, \ldots, k - 1$, we have

$$\sum_{i=1}^{k} p_i f(x_i) = p_k f(x_k) + (1 - p_k) \sum_{i=1}^{k-1} p_i' f(x_i) \tag{2.78}$$

$$\geq p_k f(x_k) + (1 - p_k) f\left(\sum_{i=1}^{k-1} p_i' x_i\right) \tag{2.79}$$

$$\geq f\left(p_k x_k + (1 - p_k) \sum_{i=1}^{k-1} p_i' x_i\right) \tag{2.80}$$

$$= f\left(\sum_{i=1}^{k} p_i x_i\right),$$ (2.81)

where the first inequality follows from the induction hypothesis and the second follows from the definition of convexity.

The proof can be extended to continuous distributions by continuity arguments. $\square$

We now use these results to prove some of the properties of entropy and relative entropy. The following theorem is of fundamental importance.

Theorem 2.6.3 (*Information inequality*): *Let $p(x)$, $q(x)$, $x \in \mathcal{X}$, be two probability mass functions. Then*

$$D(p\|q) \geq 0$$ (2.82)

with equality if and only if

$$p(x) = q(x) \quad \text{for all } x.$$ (2.83)

Proof: Let $A = \{x : p(x) > 0\}$ be the support set of $p(x)$. Then

$$-D(p\|q) = -\sum_{x \in A} p(x) \log \frac{p(x)}{q(x)}$$ (2.84)

$$= \sum_{x \in A} p(x) \log \frac{q(x)}{p(x)}$$ (2.85)

$$\leq \log \sum_{x \in A} p(x) \frac{q(x)}{p(x)}$$ (2.86)

$$= \log \sum_{x \in A} q(x)$$ (2.87)

$$\leq \log \sum_{x \in \mathcal{X}} q(x)$$ (2.88)

$$= \log 1$$ (2.89)

$$= 0,$$ (2.90)

where (2.86) follows from Jensen's inequality. Since $\log t$ is a strictly concave function of t, we have equality in (2.86) if and only if $q(x)/p(x) = 1$ everywhere, i.e., $p(x) = q(x)$. Hence we have $D(p\|q) = 0$ if and only if $p(x) = q(x)$ for all x. $\square$

Corollary (*Non-negativity of mutual information*): *For any two random variables, X, Y,*

$$I(X; Y) \geq 0 , \qquad (2.91)$$

with equality if and only if X and Y are independent.

Proof: $I(X; Y) = D(p(x, y) \| p(x) p(y)) \geq 0$, with equality if and only if $p(x, y) = p(x) p(y)$, i.e., X and Y are independent. $\square$

Corollary:

$$D(p(y|x) \| q(y|x)) \geq 0 , \qquad (2.92)$$

with equality if and only if $p(y|x) - q(y|x)$ for all y and x with $p(x) > 0$.

Corollary:

$$I(X; Y|Z) \geq 0 , \qquad (2.93)$$

with equality if and only if X and Y are conditionally independent given Z.

We now show that the uniform distribution over the range $\mathscr{X}$ is the maximum entropy distribution over this range. It follows that any random variable with this range has an entropy no greater than $\log |\mathscr{X}|$.

Theorem 2.6.4: $H(X) \leq \log|\mathscr{X}|$, *where $|\mathscr{X}|$ denotes the number of elements in the range of X, with equality if and only if X has a uniform distribution over $\mathscr{X}$.*

Proof: Let $u(x) = \frac{1}{|\mathscr{X}|}$ be the uniform probability mass function over $\mathscr{X}$, and let $p(x)$ be the probability mass function for X. Then

$$D(p\|u) = \sum p(x) \log \frac{p(x)}{u(x)} = \log|\mathscr{X}| - H(X) . \qquad (2.94)$$

Hence by the non-negativity of relative entropy,

$$0 \leq D(p\|u) = \log |\mathscr{X}| - H(X) . \quad \square \qquad (2.95)$$

Theorem 2.6.5 (*Conditioning reduces entropy*):

$$H(X|Y) \leq H(X) \qquad (2.96)$$

with equality if and only if X and Y are independent.

Proof: $0 \le I(X; Y) = H(X) - H(X|Y)$. □

Intuitively, the theorem says that knowing another random variable Y can only reduce the uncertainty in X. Note that this is true only on the average. Specifically, $H(X|Y = y)$ may be greater than or less than or equal to $H(X)$, but on the average $H(X|Y) = \Sigma_y\, p(y)H(X|Y = y) \le H(X)$. For example, in a court case, specific new evidence might increase uncertainty, but on the average evidence decreases uncertainty.

Example 2.6.1: Let (X, Y) have the following joint distribution:

	X	
Y	1	2
1	0	$\frac{3}{4}$
2	$\frac{1}{8}$	$\frac{1}{8}$

Then $H(X) = H(\frac{1}{8}, \frac{7}{8}) = 0.544$ bits, $H(X|Y = 1) = 0$ bits and $H(X|Y = 2) = 1$ bit. We calculate $H(X|Y) = \frac{3}{4}H(X|Y = 1) + \frac{1}{4}H(X|Y = 2) = 0.25$ bits. Thus the uncertainty in X is increased if $Y = 2$ is observed and decreased if $Y = 1$ is observed, but uncertainty decreases on the average.

Theorem 2.6.6 (*Independence bound on entropy*): *Let* $X_1, X_2, \ldots, X_n$ *be drawn according to* $p(x_1, x_2, \ldots, x_n)$. *Then*

$$H(X_1, X_2, \ldots, X_n) \le \sum_{i=1}^{n} H(X_i) \tag{2.97}$$

with equality if and only if the X_i *are independent.*

Proof: By the chain rule for entropies,

$$H(X_1, X_2, \ldots, X_n) = \sum_{i=1}^{n} H(X_i|X_{i-1}, \ldots, X_1) \tag{2.98}$$

$$\le \sum_{i=1}^{n} H(X_i), \tag{2.99}$$

where the inequality follows directly from the previous theorem. We have equality if and only if X_i is independent of $X_{i-1}, \ldots, X_1$ for all i, i.e., if and only if the X_i's are independent. □

2.7   THE LOG SUM INEQUALITY AND ITS APPLICATIONS

We now prove a simple consequence of the concavity of the logarithm, which will be used to prove some concavity results for the entropy.

Theorem 2.7.1 (*Log sum inequality*): *For non-negative numbers, a_1, $a_2, \ldots, a_n$ and $b_1, b_2, \ldots, b_n$,*

$$\sum_{i=1}^{n} a_i \log \frac{a_i}{b_i} \geq \left(\sum_{i=1}^{n} a_i \right) \log \frac{\sum_{i=1}^{n} a_i}{\sum_{i=1}^{n} b_i} \qquad (2.100)$$

with equality if and only if $\frac{a_i}{b_i} = const.$

We again use the convention that $0 \log 0 = 0$, $a \log \frac{a}{0} = \infty$ if $a > 0$ and $0 \log \frac{0}{0} = 0$. These follow easily from continuity.

   Proof: Assume without loss of generality that $a_i > 0$ and $b_i > 0$.
   The function $f(t) = t \log t$ is strictly convex, since $f''(t) = \frac{1}{t} \log e > 0$ for all positive t. Hence by Jensen's inequality, we have

$$\sum \alpha_i f(t_i) \geq f\left(\sum \alpha_i t_i \right) \qquad (2.101)$$

for $\alpha_i \geq 0$, $\sum_i \alpha_i = 1$. Setting $\alpha_i = b_i/\sum_{j=1}^{n} b_j$ and $t_i = a_i/b_i$, we obtain

$$\sum \frac{a_i}{\sum b_j} \log \frac{a_i}{b_i} \geq \sum \frac{a_i}{\sum b_j} \log \sum \frac{a_i}{\sum b_j}, \qquad (2.102)$$

which is the log sum inequality.   ⊔

   We now use the log sum inequality to prove various convexity results. We begin by reproving Theorem 2.6.3, which states that $D(p\|q) \geq 0$ with equality if and only if $p(x) = q(x)$.
   By the log sum inequality,

$$D(p\|q) = \sum p(x) \log \frac{p(x)}{q(x)} \qquad (2.103)$$

$$\geq \left(\sum p(x) \right) \log \frac{(\sum p(x))}{(\sum q(x))} \qquad (2.104)$$

$$= 1 \log \frac{1}{1} = 0 \qquad (2.105)$$

with equality if and only if $p(x)/q(x) = c$. Since both p and q are probability mass functions, $c = 1$, and hence we have $D(p\|q) = 0$ if and only if $p(x) = q(x)$ for all x.

Theorem 2.7.2: $D(p\|q)$ is convex in the pair (p, q), i.e., if (p_1, q_1) and (p_2, q_2) are two pairs of probability mass functions, then

$$D(\lambda p_1 + (1 - \lambda)p_2 \| \lambda q_1 + (1 - \lambda)q_2) \leq \lambda D(p_1\|q_1) + (1 - \lambda)D(p_2\|q_2)$$

(2.106)

for all $0 \leq \lambda \leq 1$.

Proof: We apply the log sum inequality to a term on the left hand side of (2.106), i.e.,

$$(\lambda p_1(x) + (1 - \lambda)p_2(x)) \log \frac{\lambda p_1(x) + (1 - \lambda)p_2(x)}{\lambda q_1(x) + (1 - \lambda)q_2(x)}$$

$$\leq \lambda p_1(x) \log \frac{\lambda p_1(x)}{\lambda q_1(x)} + (1 - \lambda)p_2(x) \log \frac{(1 - \lambda)p_2(x)}{(1 - \lambda)q_2(x)}. \quad (2.107)$$

Summing this over all x, we obtain the desired property. $\square$

Theorem 2.7.3 (*Concavity of entropy*): $H(p)$ is a concave function of p.

Proof:

$$H(p) = \log |\mathscr{X}| - D(p\|u), \quad (2.108)$$

where u is the uniform distribution on $|\mathscr{X}|$ outcomes. The concavity of H then follows directly from the convexity of D.

Alternative Proof: Let X_1 be a random variable with distribution p_1 taking on values in a set A. Let X_2 be another random variable with distribution p_2 on the same set. Let

$$\theta = \begin{cases} 1 & \text{with probability } \lambda \\ 2 & \text{with probability } 1 - \lambda \end{cases} \quad (2.109)$$

Let $Z = X_\theta$. Then the distribution of Z is $\lambda p_1 + (1 - \lambda)p_2$. Now since conditioning reduces entropy, we have

$$H(Z) \geq H(Z|\theta), \quad (2.110)$$

or equivalently,

$$H(\lambda p_1 + (1 - \lambda)p_2) \geq \lambda H(p_1) + (1 - \lambda)H(p_2), \quad (2.111)$$

which proves the concavity of the entropy as a function of the distribution. $\square$

One of the consequences of the concavity of entropy is that mixing two gases of equal entropy results in a gas with higher entropy.

Theorem 2.7.4: Let $(X, Y) \sim p(x, y) = p(x)p(y|x)$. The mutual information $I(X; Y)$ is a concave function of $p(x)$ for fixed $p(y|x)$ and a convex function of $p(y|x)$ for fixed $p(x)$.

Proof: To prove the first part, we expand the mutual information

$$I(X; Y) = H(Y) - H(Y|X) = H(Y) - \sum_x p(x)H(Y|X = x). \quad (2.112)$$

If $p(y|x)$ is fixed, then $p(y)$ is a linear function of $p(x)$. Hence $H(Y)$, which is a concave function of $p(y)$, is a concave function of $p(x)$. The second term is a linear function of $p(x)$. Hence the difference is a concave function of $p(x)$.

To prove the second part, we fix $p(x)$ and consider two different conditional distributions $p_1(y|x)$ and $p_2(y|x)$. The corresponding joint distributions are $p_1(x, y) = p(x) \, p_1(y|x)$ and $p_2(x, y) = p(x) \, p_2(y|x)$, and their respective marginals are $p(x)$, $p_1(y)$ and $p(x)$, $p_2(y)$. Consider a conditional distribution

$$p_\lambda(y|x) = \lambda p_1(y|x) + (1 - \lambda)p_2(y|x) \quad (2.113)$$

that is a mixture of $p_1(y|x)$ and $p_2(y|x)$. The corresponding joint distribution is also a mixture of the corresponding joint distributions,

$$p_\lambda(x, y) = \lambda p_1(x, y) + (1 - \lambda)p_2(x, y), \quad (2.114)$$

and the distribution of Y is also a mixture

$$p_\lambda(y) = \lambda p_1(y) + (1 - \lambda)p_2(y). \quad (2.115)$$

Hence if we let $q_\lambda(x, y) = p(x)p_\lambda(y)$ be the product of the marginal distributions, we have

$$q_\lambda(x, y) = \lambda q_1(x, y) + (1 - \lambda)q_2(x, y). \quad (2.116)$$

Since the mutual information is the relative entropy between the joint distribution and the product of the marginals, i.e.,

$$I(X; Y) = D(p_\lambda \| q_\lambda), \quad (2.117)$$

and relative entropy $D(p\|q)$ is a convex function of (p, q), it follows that the mutual information is a convex function of the conditional distribution. $\square$

2.8   DATA PROCESSING INEQUALITY

The data processing inequality can be used to show that no clever manipulation of the data can improve the inferences that can be made from the data.

Definition: Random variables X, Y, Z are said to *form a Markov chain in that order* (denoted by $X \to Y \to Z$) if the conditional distribution of Z depends only on Y and is conditionally independent of X. Specifically, X, Y and Z form a Markov chain $X \to Y \to Z$ if the joint probability mass function can be written as

$$p(x, y, z) = p(x)p(y|x)p(z|y). \tag{2.118}$$

Some simple consequences are as follows:

- $X \to Y \to Z$ if and only if X and Z are conditionally independent given Y. Markovity implies conditional independence because

$$p(x, z|y) = \frac{p(x, y, z)}{p(y)} = \frac{p(x, y)p(z|y)}{p(y)} = p(x|y)p(z|y). \tag{2.119}$$

This is the characterization of Markov chains that can be extended to define Markov fields, which are n-dimensional random processes in which the interior and exterior are independent given the values on the boundary.
- $X \to Y \to Z$ implies that $Z \to Y \to X$. Thus the condition is sometimes written $X \leftrightarrow Y \leftrightarrow Z$.
- If $Z = f(Y)$, then $X \to Y \to Z$.

We can now prove an important and useful theorem demonstrating that no processing of Y, deterministic or random, can increase the information that Y contains about X.

Theorem 2.8.1 (*Data processing inequality*): If $X \to Y \to Z$, then $I(X; Y) \geq I(X; Z)$.

Proof: By the chain rule, we can expand mutual information in two different ways.

$$I(X; Y, Z) = I(X; Z) + I(X; Y|Z) \tag{2.120}$$

$$= I(X; Y) + I(X; Z|Y). \tag{2.121}$$

Since X and Z are conditionally independent given Y, we have $I(X; Z|Y) = 0$. Since $I(X; Y|Z) \geq 0$, we have

$$I(X; Y) \geq I(X; Z) . \qquad (2.122)$$

We have equality if and only if $I(X; Y|Z) = 0$, i.e., $X \to Z \to Y$ forms a Markov chain. Similarly, one can prove that $I(Y; Z) \geq I(X; Z)$. ☐

Corollary: *In particular, if $Z = g(Y)$, we have $I(X; Y) \geq I(X; g(Y))$.*

Proof: $X \to Y \to g(Y)$ forms a Markov chain. ☐

Thus functions of the data Y cannot increase the information about X.

Corollary: *If $X \to Y \to Z$, then $I(X; Y|Z) \leq I(X; Y)$.*

Proof: From (2.120) and (2.121), and using the fact that $I(X; Z|Y) = 0$ by Markovity and $I(X; Z) \geq 0$, we have

$$I(X; Y|Z) \leq I(X; Y) . \quad ☐ \qquad (2.123)$$

Thus the dependence of X and Y is decreased (or remains unchanged) by the observation of a "downstream" random variable Z.

Note that it is also possible that $I(X; Y|Z) > I(X; Y)$ when X, Y and Z do not form a Markov chain. For example, let X and Y be independent fair binary random variables, and let $Z = X + Y$. Then $I(X; Y) = 0$, but $I(X; Y|Z) = H(X|Z) - H(X|Y, Z) = H(X|Z) = P(Z = 1) H(X|Z = 1) = \frac{1}{2}$ bit.

2.9 THE SECOND LAW OF THERMODYNAMICS

One of the basic laws of physics, the second law of thermodynamics, states that the entropy of an isolated system is non-decreasing. We now explore the relationship between the second law and the entropy function that we have defined earlier in this chapter.

In statistical thermodynamics, entropy is often defined as the log of the number of microstates in the system. This corresponds exactly to our notion of entropy if all the states are equally likely. But why does the entropy increase?

We model the isolated system as a Markov chain (see Chapter 4) with transitions obeying the physical laws governing the system. Implicit in this assumption is the notion of an overall state of the system and the fact that, knowing the present state, the future of the system is independent of the past. In such a system, we can find four different interpretations of the second law. It may come as a shock to find that the entropy does not always increase. However, *relative* entropy always decreases.

1. *Relative entropy $D(\mu_n \| \mu_n')$ decreases with n.* Let μ_n and μ_n' be two probability distributions on the state space of a Markov chain at time n, and let μ_{n+1} and μ_{n+1}' be the corresponding distributions at time $n + 1$. Let the corresponding joint mass functions be denoted by p and q. Thus $p(x_n, x_{n+1}) = p(x_n) \, r(x_{n+1} | x_n)$ and $q(x_n, x_{n+1}) = q(x_n) \, r(x_{n+1} | x_n)$, where $r(\cdot | \cdot)$ is the probability transition function for the Markov chain. Then by the chain rule for relative entropy, we have two expansions:

$$
\begin{aligned}
D(p(x_n, x_{n+1}) &\| q(x_n, x_{n+1})) \\
&= D(p(x_n) \| q(x_n)) + D(p(x_{n+1} | x_n) \| q(x_{n+1} | x_n)) \\
&= D(p(x_{n+1}) \| q(x_{n+1})) + D(p(x_n | x_{n+1}) \| q(x_n | x_{n+1})).
\end{aligned}
$$

Since both p and q are derived from the Markov chain, the conditional probability mass functions $p(x_{n+1} | x_n)$ and $q(x_{n+1} | x_n)$ are equal to $r(x_{n+1} | x_n)$ and hence $D(p(x_{n+1} | x_n) \| q(x_{n+1} | x_n)) = 0$. Now using the non-negativity of $D(p(x_n | x_{n+1}) \| q(x_n | x_{n+1}))$ (Corollary to Theorem 2.6.3), we have

$$
D(p(x_n) \| q(x_n)) \geq D(p(x_{n+1}) \| q(x_{n+1})) \tag{2.124}
$$

or

$$
D(\mu_n \| \mu_n') \geq D(\mu_{n+1} \| \mu_{n+1}'). \tag{2.125}
$$

Consequently, the distance between the probability mass functions is decreasing with time n for any Markov chain.

An example of one interpretation of the preceding inequality is to suppose that the tax system for the redistribution of wealth is the same in Canada and in England. Then if μ_n and μ_n' represent the distributions of wealth among individuals in the two countries, this inequality shows that the relative entropy distance between the two distributions decreases with time. The wealth distributions in Canada and England will become more similar.

2. *Relative entropy $D(\mu_n \| \mu)$ between a distribution μ_n on the states at time n and a stationary distribution μ decreases with n.* In (2.125), μ_n' is any distribution on the states at time n. If we let μ_n' be any stationary distribution μ, then μ_{n+1}' is the same stationary distribution. Hence

$$
D(\mu_n \| \mu) \geq D(\mu_{n+1} \| \mu), \tag{2.126}
$$

which implies that any state distribution gets closer and closer to each stationary distribution as time passes. The sequence $D(\mu_n \| \mu)$ is a monotonically non-increasing non-negative sequence and must therefore have a limit. The limit is actually 0 if the stationary distribution is unique, but this is more difficult to prove.

3. *Entropy increases if the stationary distribution is uniform.* In general, the fact that the relative entropy decreases does not imply that the entropy increases. A simple counterexample is provided by any Markov chain with a non-uniform stationary distribution. If we start this Markov chain from the uniform distribution, which already is the maximum entropy distribution, the distribution will tend to the stationary distribution, which has a lower entropy than the uniform. Hence the entropy decreases with time rather than increases.

   If, however, the stationary distribution is the uniform distribution, then we can express the relative entropy as

$$D(\mu_n \| \mu) = \log |\mathcal{X}| - H(\mu_n) = \log |\mathcal{X}| - H(X_n). \quad (2.127)$$

In this case the monotonic decrease in relative entropy implies a monotonic increase in entropy. This is the explanation that ties in most closely with statistical thermodynamics, where all the microstates are equally likely. We now characterize processes having a uniform stationary distribution.

Definition: A probability transition matrix $[P_{ij}]$, $P_{ij} = \Pr\{X_{n+1} = j | X_n = i\}$ is called *doubly stochastic* if

$$\sum_i P_{ij} = 1, \quad j = 1, 2, \ldots \quad (2.128)$$

and

$$\sum_j P_{ij} = 1, \quad i = 1, 2, \ldots \quad (2.129)$$

Remark: The uniform distribution is a stationary distribution of P if and only if the probability transition matrix is doubly stochastic. See Problem 1 in Chapter 4.

4. *The conditional entropy $H(X_n | X_1)$ increases with n for a stationary Markov process.* If the Markov process is stationary, then $H(X_n)$ is constant. So the entropy is nonincreasing. However, we will prove that $H(X_n | X_1)$ increases with n. Thus the conditional uncertainty of the future increases. We give two alternative proofs of this result. First, we use the properties of entropy,

$$H(X_n|X_1) \geq H(X_n|X_1, X_2) \quad \text{(conditioning reduces entropy) (2.130)}$$

$$= H(X_n|X_2) \quad \text{(by Markovity)} \quad (2.131)$$

$$= H(X_{n-1}|X_1) \quad \text{(by stationarity)}. \quad (2.132)$$

Alternatively, by an application of the data processing inequality to the Markov chain $X_1 \rightarrow X_{n-1} \rightarrow X_n$, we have

$$I(X_1; X_{n-1}) \geq I(X_1; X_n). \quad (2.133)$$

Expanding the mutual informations in terms of entropies, we have

$$H(X_{n-1}) - H(X_{n-1}|X_1) \geq H(X_n) - H(X_n|X_1). \quad (2.134)$$

By stationarity, $H(X_{n-1}) = H(X_n)$, and hence we have

$$H(X_{n-1}|X_1) \leq H(X_n|X_1). \quad (2.135)$$

(These techniques can also be used to show that $H(X_0|X_n)$ is increasing in n for any Markov chain. See problem 35.)

5. *Shuffles increase entropy.* If T is a shuffle (permutation) of a deck of cards and X is the initial (random) position of the cards in the deck and if the choice of the shuffle T is independent of X, then

$$H(TX) \geq H(X), \quad (2.136)$$

where TX is the permutation of the deck induced by the shuffle T on the initial permutation X. Problem 31 outlines a proof.

2.10 SUFFICIENT STATISTICS

This section is a sidelight showing the power of the data processing inequality in clarifying an important idea in statistics. Suppose we have a family of probability mass functions $\{f_\theta(x)\}$ indexed by θ, and let X be a sample from a distribution in this family. Let $T(X)$ be any statistic (function of the sample) like the sample mean or sample variance. Then $\theta \rightarrow X \rightarrow T(X)$, and by the data processing inequality, we have

$$I(\theta; T(X)) \leq I(\theta; X) \quad (2.137)$$

for any distribution on θ. However, if equality holds, no information is lost.

A statistic $T(X)$ is called sufficient for θ if it contains all the information in X about θ.

Definition: A function $T(X)$ is said to be a *sufficient statistic* relative to the family $\{f_\theta(x)\}$ if X is independent of θ given $T(X)$, i.e., $\theta \to T(X) \to X$ forms a Markov chain.

This is the same as the condition for equality in the data processing inequality,

$$I(\theta; X) = I(\theta; T(X)) \tag{2.138}$$

for all distributions on θ. Hence sufficient statistics preserve mutual information and conversely.

Here are some examples of sufficient statistics:

1. Let $X_1, X_2, \ldots, X_n, X_i \in \{0, 1\}$, be an independent and identically distributed (i.i.d.) sequence of coin tosses of a coin with unknown parameter $\theta = \Pr(X_i = 1)$. Given n, the number of 1's is a sufficient statistic for θ. Here $T(X_1, X_2, \ldots, X_n) = \sum_{i=1}^n X_i$. In fact, we can show that given T, all sequences having that many 1's are equally likely and independent of the parameter θ. Specifically,

$$\Pr\left\{(X_1, X_2, \ldots, X_n) = (x_1, x_2, \ldots, x_n) \middle| \sum_{i=1}^n X_i = k\right\}$$

$$= \begin{cases} \dfrac{1}{\binom{n}{k}} & \text{if } \sum x_i = k, \\ 0 & \text{otherwise}. \end{cases} \tag{2.139}$$

Thus $\theta \to \sum X_i \to (X_1, X_2, \ldots, X_n)$ forms a Markov chain, and T is a sufficient statistic for θ.

The next two examples involve probability densities instead of probability mass functions, but the theory still applies. We define entropy and mutual information for continuous random variables in Chapter 9.

2. If X is normally distributed with mean θ and variance 1, i.e., if

$$f_\theta(x) = \frac{1}{\sqrt{2\pi}} e^{-(x-\theta)^2/2} = \mathcal{N}(\theta, 1), \tag{2.140}$$

and $X_1, X_2, \ldots, X_n$ are drawn independently according to this distribution, then a sufficient statistic for θ is $\overline{X}_n = \frac{1}{n} \sum_{i=1}^n X_i$. It can be verified that the conditional distribution of $X_1, X_2, \ldots, X_n$, conditioned on $\overline{X}_n$ and n does not depend on θ.

3. If $f_\theta = \text{Uniform}(\theta, \theta + 1)$, then a sufficient statistic for θ is

$$T(X_1, X_2, \ldots, X_n) = (\max\{X_1, X_2, \ldots, X_n\}, \min\{X_1, X_2, \ldots, X_n\}).$$
$$(2.141)$$

The proof of this is slightly more complicated, but again one can show that the distribution of the data is independent of the parameter given the statistic T.

The minimal sufficient statistic is a sufficient statistic that is a function of all other sufficient statistics.

Definition: A statistic $T(X)$ is a *minimal sufficient statistic* relative to $\{f_\theta(x)\}$ if it is a function of every other sufficient statistic U. Interpreting this in terms of the data processing inequality, this implies that

$$\theta \to T(X) \to U(X) \to X.$$
$$(2.142)$$

Hence a minimal sufficient statistic maximally compresses the information about θ in the sample. Other sufficient statistics may contain additional irrelevant information. For example, for a normal distribution with mean θ, the pair of functions giving the mean of all odd samples and the mean of all even samples is a sufficient statistic, but not a minimal sufficient statistic. In the preceding examples, the sufficient statistics are also minimal.

2.11 FANO'S INEQUALITY

Suppose we know a random variable Y and we wish to guess the value of a correlated random variable X. Fano's inequality relates the probability of error in guessing the random variable X to its conditional entropy $H(X|Y)$. It will be crucial in proving the converse to Shannon's second theorem in Chapter 8. From the problems at the end of the chapter, we know that the conditional entropy of a random variable X given another random variable Y is zero if and only if X is a function of Y. Hence we can estimate X from Y with zero probability of error if and only if $H(X|Y) = 0$.

Extending this argument, we expect to be able to estimate X with a low probability of error only if the conditional entropy $H(X|Y)$ is small. Fano's inequality quantifies this idea. Suppose we wish to estimate a random variable X with a distribution $p(x)$. We observe a random variable Y which is related to X by the conditional distribution $p(y|x)$. From Y, we calculate a function $g(Y) =$

$\hat{X}$, which is an estimate of X. We wish to bound the probability that $\hat{X} \neq X$. We observe that $X \rightarrow Y \rightarrow \hat{X}$ forms a Markov chain. Define the probability of error

$$P_e = \Pr\{\hat{X} \neq X\}. \tag{2.143}$$

Theorem 2.11.1 (*Fano's inequality*):

$$H(P_e) + P_e \log(|\mathscr{X}| - 1) \geq H(X|Y). \tag{2.144}$$

This inequality can be weakened to

$$1 + P_e \log|\mathscr{X}| \geq H(X|Y) \tag{2.145}$$

or

$$P_e \geq \frac{H(X|Y) - 1}{\log|\mathscr{X}|}. \tag{2.146}$$

Remark: Note that $P_e = 0$ implies that $H(X|Y) = 0$, as intuition suggests.

Proof: Define an error random variable,

$$E = \begin{cases} 1 & \text{if } \hat{X} \neq X, \\ 0 & \text{if } \hat{X} = X. \end{cases} \tag{2.147}$$

Then, using the chain rule for entropies to expand $H(E, X|Y)$ in two different ways, we have

$$H(E, X|Y) = H(X|Y) + \underbrace{H(E|X, Y)}_{=0} \tag{2.148}$$

$$= \underbrace{H(E|Y)}_{\leq H(P_e)} + \underbrace{H(X|E, Y)}_{\leq P_e \log(|\mathscr{X}|-1)}. \tag{2.149}$$

Since conditioning reduces entropy, $H(E|Y) \leq H(E) = H(P_e)$. Now since E is a function of X and $g(Y)$, the conditional entropy $H(E|X, Y)$ is equal to 0. Also, since E is a binary-valued random variable, $H(E) = H(P_e)$. The remaining term, $H(X|E, Y)$, can be bounded as follows:

$$H(X|E, Y) = \Pr(E = 0)H(X|Y, E = 0) + \Pr(E = 1)H(X|Y, E = 1) \tag{2.150}$$

$$\leq (1 - P_e)0 + P_e \log(|\mathscr{X}| - 1), \tag{2.151}$$

since given $E = 0$, $X = g(Y)$, and given $E = 1$, we can upper bound the conditional entropy by the log of the number of remaining outcomes ($|\mathscr{X}| - 1$ if $g(Y) \in \mathscr{X}$, else $|\mathscr{X}|$). Combining these results, we obtain Fano's inequality. □

Remark: Suppose that there is no knowledge of Y. Thus X must be guessed without any information. Let $X \in \{1, 2, \ldots, m\}$ and $p_1 \geq p_2 \geq \cdots \geq p_m$. Then the best guess of X is $\hat{X} = 1$ and the resulting probability of error is $P_e = 1 - p_1$. Fano's inequality becomes

$$H(P_e) + P_e \log(m - 1) \geq H(X). \qquad (2.152)$$

The probability mass function

$$(p_1, p_2, \ldots, p_m) = \left(1 - P_e, \frac{P_e}{m - 1}, \ldots, \frac{P_e}{m - 1}\right) \qquad (2.153)$$

achieves this bound with equality. Thus Fano's inequality is sharp.

The following telegraphic summary omits qualifying conditions.

SUMMARY OF CHAPTER 2

Definition: The *entropy* $H(X)$ of a discrete random variable X is defined by

$$H(X) = - \sum_{x \in \mathscr{X}} p(x) \log p(x). \qquad (2.154)$$

Properties of H:

1. $H(X) \geq 0$.
2. $H_b(X) = (\log_b a) H_a(X)$.
3. (*Conditioning reduces entropy*) For any two random variables, X and Y, we have

$$H(X|Y) \leq H(X) \qquad (2.155)$$

    with equality if and only if X and Y are independent.
4. $H(X_1, X_2, \ldots, X_n) \leq \sum_{i=1}^n H(X_i)$, with equality if and only if the random variables X_i are independent.
5. $H(X) \leq \log |\mathscr{X}|$ with equality if and only if X is uniformly distributed over $\mathscr{X}$.
6. $H(p)$ is concave in p.

Definition: The *relative entropy* $D(p\|q)$ of the probability mass function p with respect to the probability mass function q is defined by

$$D(p\|q) = \sum_x p(x) \log \frac{p(x)}{q(x)}. \qquad (2.156)$$

Definition: The *mutual information* between two random variables X and Y is defined as

$$I(X; Y) = \sum_{x \in \mathcal{X}} \sum_{y \in \mathcal{Y}} p(x, y) \log \frac{p(x, y)}{p(x)p(y)}. \qquad (2.157)$$

Alternative expressions:

$$H(X) = E_p \log \frac{1}{p(X)} \qquad (2.158)$$

$$H(X, Y) = E_p \log \frac{1}{p(X, Y)} \qquad (2.159)$$

$$H(X|Y) = E_p \log \frac{1}{p(X|Y)} \qquad (2.160)$$

$$I(X; Y) = E_p \log \frac{p(X, Y)}{p(X)p(Y)} \qquad (2.161)$$

$$D(p\|q) = E_p \log \frac{p(X)}{q(X)} \qquad (2.162)$$

Properties of D and I:

1. $I(X; Y) = H(X) - H(X|Y) = H(Y) - H(Y|X) = H(X) + H(Y) - H(X, Y)$.
2. $D(p\|q) \geq 0$ with equality if and only if $p(x) = q(x)$, for all $x \in \mathcal{X}$.
3. $I(X; Y) = D(p(x, y)\| p(x)p(y)) \geq 0$, with equality if and only if $p(x, y) = p(x)p(y)$, i.e., X and Y are independent.
4. If $|\mathcal{X}| = m$, and u is the uniform distribution over $\mathcal{X}$, then $D(p\|u) = \log m - H(p)$.
5. $D(p\|q)$ is convex in the pair (p, q).

Chain rules

Entropy: $H(X_1, X_2, \ldots, X_n) = \sum_{i=1}^n H(X_i|X_{i-1}, \ldots, X_1)$.

Mutual
information: $I(X_1, X_2, \ldots, X_n; Y) = \sum_{i=1}^n I(X_i; Y|X_1, X_2, \ldots, X_{i-1})$.

Relative entropy: $D(p(x, y)\|q(x, y)) = D(p(x)\|q(x)) + D(p(y|x)\|q(y|x))$.

Jensen's inequality: If f is a convex function, then $Ef(X) \geq f(EX)$.

Log sum inequality: For n positive numbers, $a_1, a_2, \ldots, a_n$ and $b_1, b_2, \ldots, b_n$,

$$\sum_{i=1}^n a_i \log \frac{a_i}{b_i} \geq \left(\sum_{i=1}^n a_i\right) \log \frac{\sum_{i=1}^n a_i}{\sum_{i=1}^n b_i} \qquad (2.163)$$

with equality if and only if $a_i/b_i = $ constant.

Data processing inequality: If $X \to Y \to Z$ forms a Markov chain, then $I(X; Y) \geq I(X; Z)$

Second law of thermodynamics: For a Markov chain,

1. Relative entropy $D(\mu_n \| \mu'_n)$ decreases with time.
2. Relative entropy $D(\mu_n \| \mu)$ between a distribution and the stationary distribution decreases with time.
3. Entropy $H(X_n)$ increases if the stationary distribution is uniform.
4. The conditional entropy $H(X_n | X_1)$ increases with time for a stationary Markov chain.
5. The conditional entropy $H(X_0 | X_n)$ of the initial condition X_0 increases for any Markov chain.

Sufficient statistic: $T(X)$ is sufficient relative to $\{f_\theta(x)\}$ if and only if $I(\theta; X) = I(\theta; T(X))$ for all distributions on θ.

Fano's inequality: Let $P_e = \Pr\{g(Y) \neq X\}$, where g is any function of Y. Then

$$H(P_e) + P_e \log(|\mathcal{X}| - 1) \geq H(X|Y). \qquad (2.164)$$

PROBLEMS FOR CHAPTER 2

1. *Coin flips.* A fair coin is flipped until the first head occurs. Let X denote the number of flips required.
   (a) Find the entropy $H(X)$ in bits. The following expressions may be useful:

   $$\sum_{n=1}^{\infty} r^n = \frac{r}{1-r}, \qquad \sum_{n=1}^{\infty} nr^n = \frac{r}{(1-r)^2}.$$

   (b) A random variable X is drawn according to this distribution. Find an "efficient" sequence of yes-no questions of the form, "Is X contained in the set S?" Compare $H(X)$ to the expected number of questions required to determine X.

2. *Entropy of functions.* Let X be a random variable taking on a finite number of values. What is the (general) inequality relationship of $H(X)$ and $H(Y)$ if
   (a) $Y = 2^X$?
   (b) $Y = \cos X$?

3. *Minimum entropy.* What is the minimum value of $H(p_1, \ldots, p_n) = H(\mathbf{p})$ as $\mathbf{p}$ ranges over the set of n-dimensional probability vectors? Find all $\mathbf{p}$'s which achieve this minimum.

4. *Axiomatic definition of entropy.* If we assume certain axioms for our measure of information, then we will be forced to use a logarithmic

measure like entropy. Shannon used this to justify his initial definition of entropy. In this book, we will rely more on the other properties
of entropy rather than its axiomatic derivation to justify its use. The
following problem is considerably more difficult than the other problems in this section.

If a sequence of symmetric functions $H_m(p_1, p_2, \ldots, p_m)$ satisfies
the following properties,

- Normalization: $H_2(\frac{1}{2}, \frac{1}{2}) = 1$,
- Continuity: $H_2(p, 1 - p)$ is a continuous function of p,
- Grouping: $H_m(p_1, p_2, \ldots, p_m) = H_{m-1}(p_1 + p_2, p_3, \ldots, p_m) +$
$(p_1 + p_2) H_2(\frac{p_1}{p_1 + p_2}, \frac{p_2}{p_1 + p_2})$,

prove that H_m must be of the form

$$H_m(p_1, p_2, \ldots, p_m) = - \sum_{i=1}^{m} p_i \log p_i, \qquad m = 2, 3, \ldots .$$

(2.165)

There are various other axiomatic formulations which also result in
the same definition of entropy. See, for example, the book by Csiszár
and Körner [83].

5.   *Entropy of functions of a random variable.* Let X be a discrete random
variable. Show that the entropy of a function of X is less than or
equal to the entropy of X by justifying the following steps:

$$H(X, g(X)) \overset{(a)}{=} H(X) + H(g(X)|X)$$

(2.166)

$$\overset{(b)}{=} H(X);$$

(2.167)

$$H(X, g(X)) \overset{(c)}{=} H(g(X)) + H(X|g(X))$$

(2.168)

$$\overset{(d)}{\geq} H(g(X)).$$

(2.169)

Thus $H(g(X)) \leq H(X)$.

6.   *Zero conditional entropy.* Show that if $H(Y|X) = 0$, then Y is a function
of X, i.e., for all x with $p(x) > 0$, there is only one possible value of y
with $p(x, y) > 0$.

7.   *Pure randomness and bent coins.* Let $X_1, X_2, \ldots, X_n$ denote the outcomes of independent flips of a *bent* coin. Thus $\Pr\{X_i = 1\} = p$,
$\Pr\{X_i = 0\} = 1 - p$, where p is unknown. We wish to obtain a sequence $Z_1, Z_2, \ldots, Z_K$ of *fair* coin flips from $X_1, X_2, \ldots, X_n$. Toward
this end let $f : \mathscr{X}^n \to \{0, 1\}^*$ (where $\{0, 1\}^* = \{\Lambda, 0, 1, 00, 01, \ldots\}$ is
the set of all finite length binary sequences) be a mapping
$f(X_1, X_2, \ldots, X_n) = (Z_1, Z_2, \ldots, Z_K)$, where $Z_i \sim$ Bernoulli $(\frac{1}{2})$, and K
may depend on $(X_1, \ldots, X_n)$. In order that the sequence $Z_1, Z_2, \ldots$

appear to be fair coin flips, the map f from bent coin flips to fair flips must have the property that all 2^k sequences $(Z_1, Z_2, \ldots, Z_k)$ of a given length k have equal probability (possibly 0), for $k = 1, 2, \ldots$. For example, for $n = 2$, the map $f(01) = 0$, $f(10) = 1$, $f(00) = f(11) = \Lambda$ (the null string), has the property that $\Pr\{Z_1 = 1 | K = 1\} = \Pr\{Z_1 = 0 | K = 1\} = \frac{1}{2}$.

Give reasons for the following inequalities:

$$nH(p) \overset{(a)}{=} H(X_1, \ldots, X_n)$$

$$\overset{(b)}{\geq} H(Z_1, Z_2, \ldots, Z_K, K)$$

$$\overset{(c)}{=} H(K) + H(Z_1, \ldots, Z_K | K)$$

$$\overset{(d)}{=} H(K) + E(K)$$

$$\overset{(e)}{\geq} EK.$$

Thus no more than $nH(p)$ fair coin tosses can be derived from $(X_1, \ldots, X_n)$, on the average.

(f) Exhibit a good map f on sequences of length 4.

8. *World Series.* The World Series is a seven-game series that terminates as soon as either team wins four games. Let X be the random variable that represents the outcome of a World Series between teams A and B; possible values of X are AAAA, BABABAB, and BBBAAAA. Let Y be the number of games played, which ranges from 4 to 7. Assuming that A and B are equally matched and that the games are independent, calculate $H(X)$, $H(Y)$, $H(Y|X)$, and $H(X|Y)$.

9. *Infinite entropy.* This problem shows that the entropy of a discrete random variable can be infinite. Let $A = \sum_{n=2}^{\infty} (n \log^2 n)^{-1}$. (It is easy to show that A is finite by bounding the infinite sum by the integral of $(x \log^2 x)^{-1}$.) Show that the integer-valued random variable X defined by $\Pr(X = n) = (An \log^2 n)^{-1}$ for $n = 2, 3, \ldots$ has $H(X) = +\infty$.

10. *Conditional mutual information vs. unconditional mutual information.* Give examples of joint random variables X, Y and Z such that
   (a) $I(X; Y|Z) < I(X; Y)$,
   (b) $I(X; Y|Z) > I(X; Y)$.

11. *Average entropy.* Let $H(p) = -p \log_2 p - (1 - p) \log_2(1 - p)$ be the binary entropy function.
   (a) Evaluate $H(1/4)$ using the fact that $\log_2 3 \approx 1.584$. *Hint:* Consider an experiment with four equally likely outcomes, one of which is more interesting than the others.
   (b) Calculate the average entropy $H(p)$ when the probability p is chosen uniformly in the range $0 \leq p \leq 1$.

(c) (*Optional*) Calculate the average entropy $H(p_1, p_2, p_3)$ where (p_1, p_2, p_3) is a uniformly distributed probability vector. Generalize to dimension n.

12. *Venn diagrams.* Using Venn diagrams, we can see that the mutual information common to three random variables X, Y and Z should be defined by

$$I(X; Y; Z) = I(X; Y) - I(X; Y|Z).$$

This quantity is symmetric in X, Y and Z, despite the preceding asymmetric definition. Unfortunately, $I(X; Y; Z)$ is not necessarily nonnegative. Find X, Y and Z such that $I(X; Y; Z) < 0$, and prove the following two identities:

$$I(X; Y; Z) = H(X, Y, Z) - H(X) - H(Y) - H(Z) + I(X; Y) + I(Y; Z)$$
$$+ I(Z; X)$$
$$I(X; Y; Z) = H(X, Y, Z) - H(X, Y) - H(Y, Z) - H(Z, X)$$
$$+ H(X) + H(Y) + H(Z)$$

The first identity can be understood using the Venn diagram analogy for entropy and mutual information. The second identity follows easily from the first.

13. *Coin weighing.* Suppose one has n coins, among which there may or may not be one counterfeit coin. If there is a counterfeit coin, it may be either heavier or lighter than the other coins. The coins are to be weighed by a balance.
    (a) Find an upper bound on the number of coins n so that k weighings will find the counterfeit coin (if any) and correctly declare it to be heavier or lighter.
    (b) (*Difficult*) What is the coin weighing strategy for $k = 3$ weighings and 12 coins?

14. *Drawing with and without replacement.* An urn contains r red, w white, and b black balls. Which has higher entropy, drawing $k \geq 2$ balls from the urn with replacement or without replacement? Set it up and show why. (There is both a hard way and a relatively simple way to do this.)

15. *A metric.* A function $\rho(x, y)$ is a metric if for all x, y,
    - $\rho(x, y) \geq 0$
    - $\rho(x, y) = \rho(y, x)$
    - $\rho(x, y) = 0$ if and only if $x = y$
    - $\rho(x, y) + \rho(y, z) \geq \rho(x, z).$

(a) Show that $\rho(X, Y) = H(X|Y) + H(Y|X)$ satisfies the first, second and fourth properties above. If we say that $X = Y$ if there is a one-to-one function mapping X to Y, then the third property is also satisfied, and $\rho(X, Y)$ is a metric.

(b) Verify that $\rho(X, Y)$ can also be expressed as

$$\rho(X, Y) = H(X) + H(Y) - 2I(X; Y) \qquad (2.170)$$

$$= H(X, Y) - I(X; Y) \qquad (2.171)$$

$$= 2H(X, Y) - H(X) - H(Y). \qquad (2.172)$$

16. *Example of joint entropy.* Let $p(x, y)$ be given by

X \ Y	0	1
0	$\frac{1}{3}$	$\frac{1}{3}$
1	0	$\frac{1}{3}$

Find

(a) $H(X)$, $H(Y)$.

(b) $H(X|Y)$, $H(Y|X)$.

(c) $H(X, Y)$.

(d) $H(Y) - H(Y|X)$.

(e) $I(X; Y)$.

(f) Draw a Venn diagram for the quantities in (a) through (e).

17. *Inequality.* Show $\ln x \geq 1 - \frac{1}{x}$ for $x > 0$.

18. *Entropy of a sum.* Let X and Y be random variables that take on values $x_1, x_2, \ldots, x_r$ and $y_1, y_2, \ldots, y_s$, respectively. Let $Z = X + Y$.

(a) Show that $H(Z|X) = H(Y|X)$. Argue that if X, Y are independent, then $H(Y) \leq H(Z)$ and $H(X) \leq H(Z)$. Thus the addition of *independent* random variables adds uncertainty.

(b) Give an example (of necessarily dependent random variables) in which $H(X) > H(Z)$ and $H(Y) > H(Z)$.

(c) Under what conditions does $H(Z) = H(X) + H(Y)$?

19. *Entropy of a disjoint mixture.* Let X_1 and X_2 be discrete random variables drawn according to probability mass functions $p_1(\cdot)$ and $p_2(\cdot)$ over the respective alphabets $\mathcal{X}_1 = \{1, 2, \ldots, m\}$ and $\mathcal{X}_2 = \{m + 1, \ldots, n\}$. Let

$$X = \begin{cases} X_1, & \text{with probability } \alpha, \\ X_2, & \text{with probability } 1 - \alpha. \end{cases}$$

(a) Find $H(X)$ in terms of $H(X_1)$ and $H(X_2)$ and α.

(b) Maximize over α to show that $2^{H(X)} \leq 2^{H(X_1)} + 2^{H(X_2)}$ and interpret using the notion that $2^{H(X)}$ is the effective alphabet size.

20. *A measure of correlation.* Let X_1 and X_2 be identically distributed, but not necessarily independent. Let

$$\rho = 1 - \frac{H(X_2|X_1)}{H(X_1)} \; .$$

(a) Show $\rho = I(X_1; X_2)/H(X_1)$.
(b) Show $0 \le \rho \le 1$.
(c) When is $\rho = 0$?
(d) When is $\rho = 1$?

21. *Data processing.* Let $X_1 \to X_2 \to X_3 \to \cdots \to X_n$ form a Markov chain in this order; i.e., let

$$p(x_1, x_2, \ldots, x_n) = p(x_1)p(x_2|x_1) \cdots p(x_n|x_{n-1}) \; .$$

Reduce $I(X_1; X_2, \ldots, X_n)$ to its simplest form.

22. *Bottleneck.* Suppose a (non-stationary) Markov chain starts in one of n states, necks down to $k < n$ states, and then fans back to $m > k$ states. Thus $X_1 \to X_2 \to X_3$, $X_1 \in \{1, 2, \ldots, n\}$, $X_2 \in \{1, 2, \ldots, k\}$, $X_3 \in \{1, 2, \ldots, m\}$.
(a) Show that the dependence of X_1 and X_3 is limited by the bottleneck by proving that $I(X_1; X_3) \le \log k$.
(b) Evaluate $I(X_1; X_3)$ for $k = 1$, and conclude that no dependence can survive such a bottleneck.

23. *Run length coding.* Let $X_1, X_2, \ldots, X_n$ be (possibly dependent) binary random variables. Suppose one calculates the run lengths $\mathbf{R} = (R_1, R_2, \ldots)$ of this sequence (in order as they occur). For example, the sequence $\mathbf{x} = 0001100100$ yields run lengths $\mathbf{R} = (3, 2, 2, 1, 2)$. Compare $H(X_1, X_2, \ldots, X_n)$, $H(\mathbf{R})$ and $H(X_n, \mathbf{R})$. Show all equalities and inequalities, and bound all the differences.

24. *Markov's inequality for probabilities.* Let $p(x)$ be a probability mass function. Prove, for all $d \ge 0$,

$$\Pr\{p(X) \le d\} \log\left(\frac{1}{d}\right) \le H(X) \; . \tag{2.173}$$

25. *Logical order of ideas.* Ideas have been developed in order of need, and then generalized if necessary. Reorder the following ideas, strongest first, implications following:
(a) Chain rule for $I(X_1, \ldots, X_n; Y)$, chain rule for $D(p(x_1, \ldots, x_n) \| q(x_1, x_2, \ldots, x_n))$, and chain rule for $H(X_1, X_2, \ldots, X_n)$.
(b) $D(f \| g) \ge 0$, Jensen's inequality, $I(X; Y) \ge 0$.

26. *Second law of thermodynamics.* Let $X_1, X_2, X_3 \ldots$ be a stationary first-order Markov chain. In Section 2.9, it was shown that $H(X_n|X_1) \ge H(X_{n-1}|X_1)$ for $n = 2, 3, \ldots$. Thus conditional uncertainty about the future grows with time. This is true although the unconditional uncertainty $H(X_n)$ remains constant. However, show by example that $H(X_n|X_1 = x_1)$ does not necessarily grow with n for every x_1.

27. *Conditional mutual information.* Consider a sequence of n binary random variables $X_1, X_2, \ldots, X_n$. Each sequence with an even number of 1's has probability $2^{-(n-1)}$ and each sequence with an odd number of 1's has probability 0. Find the mutual informations

$$I(X_1; X_2), I(X_2; X_3|X_1), \ldots, I(X_{n-1}; X_n|X_1, \ldots, X_{n-2}).$$

28. *Mixing increases entropy.* Show that the entropy of the probability distribution, $(p_1, \ldots, p_i, \ldots, p_j, \ldots, p_m)$, is less than the entropy of the distribution $(p_1, \ldots, \frac{p_i + p_j}{2}, \ldots, \frac{p_i + p_j}{2}, \ldots, p_m)$. Show that in general any transfer of probability that makes the distribution more uniform increases the entropy.

29. *Inequalities.* Let X, Y and Z be joint random variables. Prove the following inequalities and find conditions for equality.
    (a) $H(X, Y|Z) \geq H(X|Z)$.
    (b) $I(X, Y; Z) \geq I(X; Z)$.
    (c) $H(X, Y, Z) - H(X, Y) \leq H(X, Z) - H(X)$.
    (d) $I(X; Z|Y) \geq I(Z; Y|X) - I(Z; Y) + I(X; Z)$.

30. *Maximum entropy.* Find the probability mass function $p(x)$ that maximizes the entropy $H(X)$ of a non-negative integer-valued random variable X subject to the constraint

$$EX = \sum_{n=0}^{\infty} np(n) = A$$

for a fixed value $A > 0$. Evaluate this maximum $H(X)$.

31. *Shuffles increase entropy.* Argue that for any distribution on shuffles T and any distribution on card positions X that

$$H(TX) \geq H(TX|T) \tag{2.174}$$

$$= H(T^{-1}TX|T) \tag{2.175}$$

$$= H(X|T) \tag{2.176}$$

$$= H(X), \tag{2.177}$$

if X and T are independent.

32. *Conditional entropy.* Under what conditions does $H(X|g(Y)) = H(X|Y)$?

33. *Fano's inequality.* Let $\Pr(X = i) = p_i$, $i = 1, 2, \ldots, m$ and let $p_1 \geq p_2 \geq p_3 \geq \cdots \geq p_m$. The minimal probability of error predictor of X is $\hat{X} = 1$, with resulting probability of error $P_e = 1 - p_1$. Maximize $H(\mathbf{p})$ subject to the constraint $1 - p_1 = P_e$ to find a bound on P_e in terms of H. This is Fano's inequality in the absence of conditioning.

34. *Monotonic convergence of the empirical distribution.* Let $\hat{p}_n$ denote the empirical probability mass function corresponding to $X_1, X_2, \ldots, X_n$ i.i.d. $\sim p(x)$, $x \in \mathcal{X}$. Specifically,

$$\hat{p}_n(x) = \frac{1}{n} \sum_{i=1}^{n} I(X_i = x) \tag{2.178}$$

is the proportion of times that $X_i = x$ in the first n samples, where I is an indicator function.

(a) Show for $\mathcal{X}$ binary that

$$ED(\hat{p}_{2n} \| p) \leq ED(\hat{p}_n \| p). \tag{2.179}$$

Thus the expected relative entropy "distance" from the empirical distribution to the true distribution decreases with sample size. *Hint*: Write $\hat{p}_{2n} = \frac{1}{2}\hat{p}_n + \frac{1}{2}\hat{p}'_n$ and use the convexity of D.

(b) Show for an arbitrary discrete $\mathcal{X}$ that

$$ED(\hat{p}_n \| p) \leq ED(\hat{p}_{n-1} \| p). \tag{2.180}$$

35. *Entropy of initial conditions.* Prove that $H(X_0 | X_n)$ is non-decreasing with n for any Markov chain.

HISTORICAL NOTES

The concept of entropy was first introduced in thermodynamics, where it was used to provide a statement of the second law of thermodynamics. Later, statistical mechanics provided a connection between the macroscopic property of entropy and the microscopic state of the system. This work was the crowning achievement of Boltzmann, who had the equation $S = k \ln W$ inscribed as the epitaph on his gravestone.

In the 1930s, Hartley introduced a logarithmic measure of information for communication. His measure was essentially the logarithm of the alphabet size. Shannon [238] was the first to define entropy and mutual information as defined in this chapter. Relative entropy was first defined by Kullback and Leibler [167]. It is known under a variety of names, including the Kullback Leibler distance, cross entropy, information divergence and information for discrimination, and has been studied in detail by Csiszár [78] and Amari [10].

Many of the simple properties of these quantities were developed by Shannon. Fano's inequality was proved in Fano [105]. The notion of sufficient statistic was defined by Fisher [111], and the notion of the minimal sufficient statistic was introduced by Lehmann and Scheffé [174]. The relationship of mutual information and sufficiency is due to Kullback [165].

The relationship between information theory and thermodynamics has been discussed extensively by Brillouin [46] and Jaynes [143]. Although the basic theorems of information theory were originally derived for a communication system, attempts have been made to compare these theorems with the fundamental laws of physics. There have also been attempts to determine whether there are any fundamental physical limits to computation, including work by Bennett [24] and Bennett and Landauer [25].

Chapter 3

The Asymptotic Equipartition Property

In information theory, the analog of the law of large numbers is the Asymptotic Equipartition Property (AEP). It is a direct consequence of the weak law of large numbers. The law of large numbers states that for independent, identically distributed (i.i.d.) random variables, $\frac{1}{n} \sum_{i=1}^{n} X_i$ is close to its expected value EX for large values of n. The AEP states that $\frac{1}{n} \log \frac{1}{p(X_1, X_2, \ldots, X_n)}$ is close to the entropy H, where $X_1, X_2, \ldots, X_n$ are i.i.d. random variables and $p(X_1, X_2, \ldots, X_n)$ is the probability of observing the sequence $X_1, X_2, \ldots, X_n$. Thus the probability $p(X_1, X_2, \ldots, X_n)$ assigned to an observed sequence will be close to 2^{-nH}.

This enables us to divide the set of all sequences into two sets, the *typical set*, where the sample entropy is close to the true entropy, and the non-typical set, which contains the other sequences. Most of our attention will be on the typical sequences. Any property that is proved for the typical sequences will then be true with high probability and will determine the average behavior of a large sample.

First, an example. Let the random variable $X \in \{0, 1\}$ have a probability mass function defined by $p(1) = p$ and $p(0) = q$. If $X_1, X_2, \ldots, X_n$ are i.i.d. according to $p(x)$, then the probability of a sequence $x_1, x_2, \ldots, x_n$ is $\prod_{i=1}^{n} p(x_i)$. For example, the probability of the sequence $(1, 0, 1, 1, 0, 1)$ is $p^{\sum X_i} q^{n - \sum X_i} = p^4 q^2$. Clearly, it is not true that all 2^n sequences of length n have the same probability.

However, we might be able to predict the probability of the sequence that we actually observe. We ask for the probability $p(X_1, X_2, \ldots, X_n)$ of the outcomes $X_1, X_2, \ldots, X_n$, where $X_1, X_2, \ldots$ are i.i.d. $\sim p(x)$. This is insidiously self-referential, but well defined nonetheless. Apparently, we are asking for the probability of an event drawn according to the same probability distribution. Here it turns out that $p(X_1, X_2, \ldots, X_n)$ is close to 2^{-nH} with high probability.

We summarize this by saying, "Almost all events are almost equally surprising." This is a way of saying that

$$\Pr\{(X_1, X_2, \ldots, X_n): p(X_1, X_2, \ldots, X_n) = 2^{-n(H \pm \epsilon)}\} \approx 1, \qquad (3.1)$$

if $X_1, X_2, \ldots, X_n$ are i.i.d. $\sim p(x)$.

In the example just given, where $p(X_1, X_2, \ldots, X_n) = p^{\Sigma X_i} q^{n - \Sigma X_i}$, we are simply saying that the number of 1's in the sequence is close to np (with high probability), and all such sequences have (roughly) the same probability $2^{-nH(p)}$.

3.1   THE AEP

The asymptotic equipartition property is formalized in the following theorem:

Theorem 3.1.1 (*AEP*): *If* $X_1, X_2, \ldots$ *are i.i.d.* $\sim p(x)$, *then*

$$-\frac{1}{n} \log p(X_1, X_2, \ldots, X_n) \rightarrow H(X) \qquad in\ probability. \qquad (3.2)$$

Proof: Functions of independent random variables are also independent random variables. Thus, since the X_i are i.i.d., so are $\log p(X_i)$. Hence by the weak law of large numbers,

$$-\frac{1}{n} \log p(X_1, X_2, \ldots, X_n) = -\frac{1}{n} \sum_i \log p(X_i) \qquad (3.3)$$

$$\rightarrow -E \log p(X) \quad in\ probability \qquad (3.4)$$

$$= H(X), \qquad (3.5)$$

which proves the theorem. $\square$

Definition: The *typical set* $A_\epsilon^{(n)}$ with respect to $p(x)$ is the set of sequences $(x_1, x_2, \ldots, x_n) \in \mathcal{X}^n$ with the following property:

$$2^{-n(H(X)+\epsilon)} \leq p(x_1, x_2, \ldots, x_n) \leq 2^{-n(H(X)-\epsilon)} . \qquad (3.6)$$

As a consequence of the AEP, we can show that the set $A_\epsilon^{(n)}$ has the following properties:

Theorem 3.1.2:

1. If $(x_1, x_2, \ldots, x_n) \in A_\epsilon^{(n)}$, then $H(X) - \epsilon \leq -\frac{1}{n} \log p(x_1, x_2, \ldots, x_n) \leq H(X) + \epsilon$.

2. $\Pr\{A_\epsilon^{(n)}\} > 1 - \epsilon$ *for n sufficiently large.*
3. $|A_\epsilon^{(n)}| \leq 2^{n(H(X)+\epsilon)}$, *where $|A|$ denotes the number of elements in the set A.*
4. $|A_\epsilon^{(n)}| \geq (1 - \epsilon)2^{n(H(X)-\epsilon)}$ *for n sufficiently large.*

Thus the typical set has probability nearly 1, all elements of the typical set are nearly equiprobable, and the number of elements in the typical set is nearly 2^{nH}.

Proof: The proof of property (1) is immediate from the definition of $A_\epsilon^{(n)}$. The second property follows directly from Theorem 3.1.1, since the probability of the event $(X_1, X_2, \ldots, X_n) \in A_\epsilon^{(n)}$ tends to 1 as $n \to \infty$. Thus for any $\delta > 0$, there exists an n_0, such that for all $n \geq n_0$, we have

$$\Pr\left\{ \left| -\frac{1}{n} \log p(X_1, X_2, \ldots, X_n) - H(X) \right| < \epsilon \right\} > 1 - \delta . \tag{3.7}$$

Setting $\delta = \epsilon$, we obtain the second part of the theorem. Note that we are using ϵ for two purposes rather than using both ϵ and δ. The identification of $\delta = \epsilon$ will conveniently simplify notation later.

To prove property (3), we write

$$1 = \sum_{\mathbf{x} \in \mathscr{X}^n} p(\mathbf{x}) \tag{3.8}$$

$$\geq \sum_{\mathbf{x} \in A_\epsilon^{(n)}} p(\mathbf{x}) \tag{3.9}$$

$$\geq \sum_{\mathbf{x} \in A_\epsilon^{(n)}} 2^{-n(H(X)+\epsilon)} \tag{3.10}$$

$$= 2^{-n(H(X)+\epsilon)} |A_\epsilon^{(n)}| , \tag{3.11}$$

where the second inequality follows from (3.6). Hence

$$|A_\epsilon^{(n)}| \leq 2^{n(H(X)+\epsilon)} . \tag{3.12}$$

Finally, for sufficiently large n, $\Pr\{A_\epsilon^{(n)}\} > 1 - \epsilon$, so that

$$1 - \epsilon < \Pr\{A_\epsilon^{(n)}\} \tag{3.13}$$

$$\leq \sum_{\mathbf{x} \in A_\epsilon^{(n)}} 2^{-n(H(X)-\epsilon)} \tag{3.14}$$

$$= 2^{-n(H(X)-\epsilon)} |A_\epsilon^{(n)}| , \tag{3.15}$$

where the second inequality follows from (3.6). Hence

$$|A_\epsilon^{(n)}| \ge (1 - \epsilon)2^{n(H(X)-\epsilon)} . \qquad (3.16)$$

which completes the proof of the properties of $A_\epsilon^{(n)}$. $\square$

3.2 CONSEQUENCES OF THE AEP: DATA COMPRESSION

Let $X_1, X_2, \ldots, X_n$ be independent identically distributed random variables drawn from the probability mass function $p(x)$. We wish to find short descriptions for such sequences of random variables. We divide all sequences in $\mathcal{X}^n$ into two sets: the typical set $A_\epsilon^{(n)}$ and its complement, as shown in Figure 3.1.

We order all elements in each set according to some order (say lexicographic order). Then we can represent each sequence of $A_\epsilon^{(n)}$ by giving the index of the sequence in the set. Since there are $\le 2^{n(H+\epsilon)}$ sequences in $A_\epsilon^{(n)}$, the indexing requires no more than $n(H + \epsilon) + 1$ bits. (The extra bit may be necessary because $n(H + \epsilon)$ may not be an integer.) We prefix all these sequences by a 0, giving a total length of $\le n(H + \epsilon) + 2$ bits to represent each sequence in $A_\epsilon^{(n)}$. See Figure 3.2.

Similarly, we can index each sequence not in $A_\epsilon^{(n)}$ by using not more than $n \log |\mathcal{X}| + 1$ bits. Prefixing these indices by 1, we have a code for all the sequences in $\mathcal{X}^n$.

Note the following features of the above coding scheme.

- The code is one-to-one and easily decodable. The initial bit acts as a flag bit to indicate the length of the codeword that follows.
- We have used a brute force enumeration of the atypical set $A_\epsilon^{(n)c}$ without taking into account the fact that the number of elements in $A_\epsilon^{(n)c}$ is less than the number of elements in $\mathcal{X}^n$. Surprisingly, this is good enough to yield an efficient description.
- The typical sequences have short descriptions of length $\approx nH$.

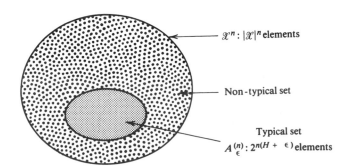

$\mathcal{X}^n : |\mathcal{X}|^n$ elements

Non-typical set

Typical set
$A_\epsilon^{(n)} : 2^{n(H + \epsilon)}$ elements

Figure 3.1. Typical sets and source coding.

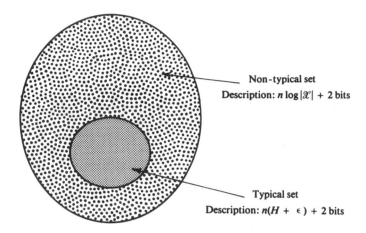

Figure 3.2. Source code using the typical set.

We will use the notation x^n to denote a sequence $x_1, x_2, \ldots, x_n$. Let $l(x^n)$ be the length of the codeword corresponding to x^n. If n is sufficiently large so that $\Pr\{A_\epsilon^{(n)}\} \geq 1 - \epsilon$, then the expected length of the codeword is

$$E(l(X^n)) = \sum_{x^n} p(x^n)l(x^n) \tag{3.17}$$

$$= \sum_{x^n \in A_\epsilon^{(n)}} p(x^n)l(x^n) + \sum_{x^n \in A_\epsilon^{(n)c}} p(x^n)l(x^n) \tag{3.18}$$

$$\leq \sum_{x^n \in A_\epsilon^{(n)}} p(x^n)[n(H + \epsilon) + 2] + \sum_{x^n \in A_\epsilon^{(n)c}} p(x^n)(n \log |\mathscr{X}| + 2) \tag{3.19}$$

$$= \Pr\{A_\epsilon^{(n)}\}[n(H + \epsilon) + 2] + \Pr\{A_\epsilon^{(n)c}\}(n \log |\mathscr{X}| + 2) \tag{3.20}$$

$$\leq n(H + \epsilon) + \epsilon n(\log|\mathscr{X}|) + 2 \tag{3.21}$$

$$= n(H + \epsilon'), \tag{3.22}$$

where $\epsilon' = \epsilon + \epsilon \log |\mathscr{X}| + \frac{2}{n}$ can be made arbitrarily small by an appropriate choice of ϵ followed by an appropriate choice of n. Hence we have proved the following theorem.

Theorem 3.2.1: Let X^n be i.i.d. $\sim p(x)$. Let $\epsilon > 0$. Then there exists a code which maps sequences x^n of length n into binary strings such that the mapping is one-to-one (and therefore invertible) and

$$E\left[\frac{1}{n} l(X^n)\right] \le H(X) + \epsilon , \tag{3.23}$$

for n sufficiently large.

Thus we can represent sequences X^n using $nH(X)$ bits on the average.

3.3 HIGH PROBABILITY SETS AND THE TYPICAL SET

From the definition of $A_\epsilon^{(n)}$, it is clear that $A_\epsilon^{(n)}$ is a fairly small set that contains most of the probability. But from the definition it is not clear whether it is the smallest such set. We will prove that the typical set has essentially the same number of elements as the smallest set, to first order in the exponent.

Definition: For each $n = 1, 2, \ldots$, let $B_\delta^{(n)} \subset \mathscr{X}^n$ be any set with

$$\Pr\{B_\delta^{(n)}\} \ge 1 - \delta . \tag{3.24}$$

We argue that $B_\delta^{(n)}$ must have significant intersection with $A_\epsilon^{(n)}$ and therefore must have about as many elements. In problem 7, we outline the proof of the following theorem:

Theorem 3.3.1: *Let $X_1, X_2, \ldots, X_n$ be i.i.d. $\sim p(x)$. For $\delta < \frac{1}{2}$ and any $\delta' > 0$, if $\Pr\{B_\delta^{(n)}\} > 1 - \delta$, then*

$$\frac{1}{n} \log|B_\delta^{(n)}| > H - \delta' \quad \text{for n sufficiently large} . \tag{3.25}$$

Thus $B_\delta^{(n)}$ must have at least 2^{nH} elements, to first order in the exponent. But $A_\epsilon^{(n)}$ has $2^{n(H \pm \epsilon)}$ elements. Therefore, $A_\epsilon^{(n)}$ is about the same size as the smallest high probability set.

We will now define some new notation to express equality to first order in the exponent.

Definition: The notation $a_n \doteq b_n$ means

$$\lim_{n \to \infty} \frac{1}{n} \log \frac{a_n}{b_n} = 0 . \tag{3.26}$$

Thus $a_n \doteq b_n$ implies that a_n and b_n are equal to the first order in the exponent.

We can now restate the above results as

$$|B_\delta^{(n)}| \doteq |A_\epsilon^{(n)}| \doteq 2^{nH} . \tag{3.27}$$

To illustrate the difference between $A_\epsilon^{(n)}$ and $B_\delta^{(n)}$, let us consider a Bernoulli sequence $X_1, X_2, \ldots, X_n$ with parameter $p = 0.9$. (A Bernoulli(θ) random variable is a binary random variable with takes on the value 1 with probability θ.) The typical sequences in this case are the sequences in which the proportion of 1's is close to 0.9. However, this does not include the most likely single sequence, which is the sequence of all 1's. The set $B_\delta^{(n)}$ includes all the most probable sequences, and therefore includes the sequence of all 1's. Theorem 3.3.1 implies that $A_\epsilon^{(n)}$ and $B_\delta^{(n)}$ must both contain the sequences that have about 90% 1's and the two sets are almost equal in size.

SUMMARY OF CHAPTER 3

AEP (*"Almost all events are almost equally surprising"*): Specifically, if $X_1, X_2, \ldots$ are i.i.d. $\sim p(x)$, then

$$-\frac{1}{n} \log p(X_1, X_2, \ldots, X_n) \to H(X) \text{ in probability} . \tag{3.28}$$

Definition: The *typical set* $A_\epsilon^{(n)}$ is the set of sequences $x_1, x_2, \ldots, x_n$ satisfying:

$$2^{-n(H(X)+\epsilon)} \leq p(x_1, x_2, \ldots, x_n) \leq 2^{-n(H(X)-\epsilon)} . \tag{3.29}$$

Properties of the typical set:

1. If $(x_1, x_2, \ldots, x_n) \in A_\epsilon^{(n)}$, then $p(x_1, x_2, \ldots, x_n) = 2^{-n(H \pm \epsilon)}$.
2. $\Pr\{A_\epsilon^{(n)}\} > 1 - \epsilon$, for n sufficiently large.
3. $|A_\epsilon^{(n)}| \leq 2^{n(H(X)+\epsilon)}$, where $|A|$ denotes the number of elements in set A.

Definition: $a_n \doteq b_n$ means $\frac{1}{n} \log \frac{a_n}{b_n} \to 0$ as $n \to \infty$.

Definition: Let $B_\delta^{(n)} \subset \mathcal{X}^n$ be the smallest set such that $\Pr\{B_\delta^{(n)}\} \geq 1 - \delta$, where $X_1, X_2, \ldots, X_n$ are i.i.d. $\sim p(x)$.

Smallest probable set: For $\delta < \frac{1}{2}$,

$$|B_\delta^{(n)}| \doteq 2^{nH} . \tag{3.30}$$

PROBLEMS FOR CHAPTER 3

1. *Markov's inequality and Chebyshev's inequality.*
   (a) (*Markov's inequality*) For any non-negative random variable X and any $\delta > 0$, show that

   $$\Pr\{X \geq \delta\} \leq \frac{EX}{\delta} . \qquad (3.31)$$

   Exhibit a random variable that achieves this inequality with equality.

   (b) (*Chebyshev's inequality*) Let Y be a random variable with mean μ and variance σ^2. By letting $X = (Y - \mu)^2$, show that for any $\epsilon > 0$,

   $$\Pr\{|Y - \mu| > \epsilon\} \leq \frac{\sigma^2}{\epsilon^2} . \qquad (3.32)$$

   (c) (*The weak law of large numbers*) Let $Z_1, Z_2, \ldots, Z_n$ be a sequence of i.i.d. random variables with mean μ and variance σ^2. Let $\bar{Z}_n = \frac{1}{n} \sum_{i=1}^{n} Z_i$ be the sample mean. Show that

   $$\Pr\{|\bar{Z}_n - \mu| > \epsilon\} \leq \frac{\sigma^2}{n\epsilon^2} . \qquad (3.33)$$

   Thus $\Pr\{|\bar{Z}_n - \mu| > \epsilon\} \to 0$ as $n \to \infty$. This is known as the weak law of large numbers.

2. *An AEP-like limit.* Let $X_1, X_2, \ldots$ be i.i.d. drawn according to probability mass function $p(x)$. Find

   $$\lim_{n \to \infty} [p(X_1, X_2, \ldots, X_n)]^{1/n} .$$

3. *The AEP and source coding.* A discrete memoryless source emits a sequence of statistically independent binary digits with probabilities $p(1) = 0.005$ and $p(0) = 0.995$. The digits are taken 100 at a time and a binary codeword is provided for every sequence of 100 digits containing three or fewer ones.
   (a) Assuming that all codewords are the same length, find the minimum length required to provide codewords for all sequences with three or fewer ones.
   (b) Calculate the probability of observing a source sequence for which no codeword has been assigned.
   (c) Use Chebyshev's inequality to bound the probability of observing a source sequence for which no codeword has been assigned. Compare this bound with the actual probability computed in part (b).

4. *Products.* Let

$$X = \begin{cases} 1, & \frac{1}{2} \\ 2, & \frac{1}{4} \\ 3, & \frac{1}{4} \end{cases}$$

Let $X_1, X_2, \ldots$ be drawn i.i.d. according to this distribution. Find the limiting behavior of the product

$$(X_1 X_2 \cdots X_n)^{1/n}.$$

5. *AEP.* Let $X_1, X_2, \ldots$ be independent identically distributed random variables drawn according to the probability mass function $p(x)$, $x \in \{1, 2, \ldots, m\}$. Thus $p(x_1, x_2, \ldots, x_n) = \prod_{i=1}^{n} p(x_i)$. We know that $-\frac{1}{n} \log p(X_1, X_2, \ldots, X_n) \to H(X)$ in probability. Let $q(x_1, x_2, \ldots, x_n) = \prod_{i=1}^{n} q(x_i)$, where q is another probability mass function on $\{1, 2, \ldots, m\}$.

    (a) Evaluate $\lim -\frac{1}{n} \log q(X_1, X_2, \ldots, X_n)$, where $X_1, X_2, \ldots$ are i.i.d. $\sim p(x)$.

    (b) Now evaluate the limit of the log likelihood ratio $\frac{1}{n} \log \frac{q(X_1, \ldots, X_n)}{p(X_1, \ldots, X_n)}$ when $X_1, X_2, \ldots$ are i.i.d. $\sim p(x)$. Thus the odds favoring q are exponentially small when p is true.

6. *Random box size.* An n-dimensional rectangular box with sides $X_1, X_2, X_3, \ldots, X_n$ is to be constructed. The volume is $V_n = \prod_{i=1}^{n} X_i$. The edge length l of a n-cube with the same volume as the random box is $l = V_n^{1/n}$. Let $X_1, X_2, \ldots$ be i.i.d. uniform random variables over the unit interval $[0, 1]$. Find $\lim_{n \to \infty} V_n^{1/n}$, and compare to $(EV_n)^{1/n}$. Clearly the expected edge length does not capture the idea of the volume of the box.

7. *Proof of Theorem 3.3.1.* Let $X_1, X_2, \ldots, X_n$ be i.i.d. $\sim p(x)$. Let $B_\delta^{(n)} \subset \mathcal{X}^n$ such that $\Pr(B_\delta^{(n)}) > 1 - \delta$. Fix $\epsilon < \frac{1}{2}$.

    (a) Given any two sets A, B such that $\Pr(A) > 1 - \epsilon_1$ and $\Pr(B) > 1 - \epsilon_2$, show that $\Pr(A \cap B) > 1 - \epsilon_1 - \epsilon_2$. Hence $\Pr(A_\epsilon^{(n)} \cap B_\delta^{(n)}) \geq 1 - \epsilon - \delta$.

    (b) Justify the steps in the chain of inequalities

$$1 - \epsilon - \delta \leq \Pr(A_\epsilon^{(n)} \cap B_\delta^{(n)}) \tag{3.34}$$

$$= \sum_{A_\epsilon^{(n)} \cap B_\delta^{(n)}} p(x^n) \tag{3.35}$$

$$\leq \sum_{A_\epsilon^{(n)} \cap B_\delta^{(n)}} 2^{-n(H-\epsilon)} \tag{3.36}$$

$$= |A_\epsilon^{(n)} \cap B_\delta^{(n)}| 2^{-n(H-\epsilon)} \tag{3.37}$$

$$\leq |B_\delta^{(n)}| 2^{-n(H-\epsilon)}. \tag{3.38}$$

    (c) Complete the proof of the theorem.

HISTORICAL NOTES

The Asymptotic Equipartition Property (AEP) was first stated by Shannon in his original 1948 paper [238], where he proved the result for i.i.d. processes and stated the result for stationary ergodic processes. McMillan [192] and Breiman [44] proved the AEP for ergodic finite alphabet sources. Chung [57] extended the theorem to the case of countable alphabets and Moy [197], Perez [208] and Kieffer [154] proved the $\mathscr{L}_1$ convergence when $\{X_i\}$ is continuous valued and ergodic. Barron [18] and Orey [202] proved almost sure convergence for continuous valued ergodic processes; a simple sandwich argument (Algoet and Cover [8]) will be used in Section 15.7 to prove the general AEP.

Chapter 4

Entropy Rates of a Stochastic Process

The asymptotic equipartition property in Chapter 3 establishes that $nH(X)$ bits suffice on the average to describe n independent and identically distributed random variables. But what if the random variables are dependent? In particular, what if the random variables form a stationary process? We will show, just as in the i.i.d. case, that the entropy $H(X_1, X_2, \ldots, X_n)$ grows (asymptotically) linearly with n at a rate $H(\mathcal{X})$, which we will call the *entropy rate* of the process. The interpretation of $H(\mathcal{X})$ as the best achievable data compression will await the analysis in Chapter 5.

4.1 MARKOV CHAINS

A stochastic process is an indexed sequence of random variables. In general, there can be an arbitrary dependence among the random variables. The process is characterized by the joint probability mass functions $\Pr\{(X_1, X_2, \ldots, X_n) = (x_1, x_2, \ldots, x_n)\} = p(x_1, x_2, \ldots, x_n)$, $(x_1, x_2, \ldots, x_n) \in \mathcal{X}^n$ for $n = 1, 2, \ldots$.

Definition: A stochastic process is said to be *stationary* if the joint distribution of any subset of the sequence of random variables is invariant with respect to shifts in the time index, i.e.,

$$\Pr\{X_1 = x_1, X_2 = x_2, \ldots, X_n = x_n\}$$
$$= \Pr\{X_{1+l} = x_1, X_{2+l} = x_2, \ldots, X_{n+l} = x_n\} \tag{4.1}$$

for every shift l and for all $x_1, x_2, \ldots, x_n \in \mathcal{X}$.

A simple example of a stochastic process with dependence is one in which each random variable depends on the one preceding it and is *conditionally* independent of all the other preceding random variables. Such a process is said to be Markov.

Definition: A discrete stochastic process $X_1, X_2, \ldots$ is said to be a *Markov chain* or a *Markov process* if, for $n = 1, 2, \ldots$,

$$\Pr(X_{n+1} = x_{n+1} | X_n = x_n, X_{n-1} = x_{n-1}, \ldots, X_1 = x_1)$$

$$= \Pr(X_{n+1} = x_{n+1} | X_n = x_n) \qquad\qquad (4.2)$$

for all $x_1, x_2, \ldots, x_n, x_{n+1} \in \mathcal{X}$.

In this case, the joint probability mass function of the random variables can be written as

$$p(x_1, x_2, \ldots, x_n) = p(x_1) p(x_2 | x_1) p(x_3 | x_2) \cdots p(x_n | x_{n-1}). \qquad (4.3)$$

Definition: The Markov chain is said to be *time invariant* if the conditional probability $p(x_{n+1} | x_n)$ does not depend on n, i.e., for $n = 1, 2, \ldots$

$$\Pr\{X_{n+1} = b | X_n = a\} = \Pr\{X_2 = b | X_1 = a\}, \quad \text{for all } a, b \in \mathcal{X}. \quad (4.4)$$

We will assume that the Markov chain is time invariant unless otherwise stated.

If $\{X_i\}$ is a Markov chain, then X_n is called the *state* at time n. A time invariant Markov chain is characterized by its initial state and a *probability transition matrix* $P = [P_{ij}]$, $i, j \in \{1, 2, \ldots, m\}$, where $P_{ij} = \Pr\{X_{n+1} = j | X_n = i\}$.

If it is possible to go with positive probability from any state of the Markov chain to any other state in a finite number of steps, then the Markov chain is said to be *irreducible*.

If the probability mass function of the random variable at time n is $p(x_n)$, then the probability mass function at time $n + 1$ is

$$p(x_{n+1}) = \sum_{x_n} p(x_n) P_{x_n x_{n+1}}. \qquad\qquad (4.5)$$

A distribution on the states such that the distribution at time $n + 1$ is the same as the distribution at time n is called a *stationary distribution*. The stationary distribution is so called because if the initial state of a Markov chain is drawn according to a stationary distribution, then the Markov chain forms a stationary process.

If the finite state Markov chain is irreducible and aperiodic, then the stationary distribution is unique, and from any starting distribution, the distribution of X_n tends to the stationary distribution as $n \to \infty$.

Example 4.1.1: Consider a two-state Markov chain with a probability transition matrix

$$P = \begin{bmatrix} 1 - \alpha & \alpha \\ \beta & 1 - \beta \end{bmatrix} \qquad (4.6)$$

as shown in Figure 4.1.

Let the stationary distribution be represented by a vector μ whose components are the stationary probabilities of state 1 and state 2, respectively. Then the stationary probability can be found by solving the equation $\mu P = \mu$ or, more simply, by balancing probabilities. For the stationary distribution, the net probability flow across any cut-set in the state transition graph is 0. Applying this to Figure 4.1, we obtain

$$\mu_1 \alpha = \mu_2 \beta . \qquad (4.7)$$

Since $\mu_1 + \mu_2 = 1$, the stationary distribution is

$$\mu_1 = \frac{\beta}{\alpha + \beta}, \qquad \mu_2 = \frac{\alpha}{\alpha + \beta} . \qquad (4.8)$$

If the Markov chain has an initial state drawn according to the stationary distribution, the resulting process will be stationary. The entropy of the state X_n at time n is

$$H(X_n) = H\left(\frac{\beta}{\alpha + \beta}, \frac{\alpha}{\alpha + \beta}\right). \qquad (4.9)$$

However, this is not the rate at which entropy grows for $H(X_1, X_2, \ldots, X_n)$. The dependence among the X_i's will take a steady toll.

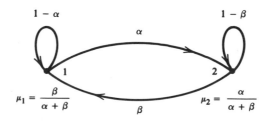

Figure 4.1. Two-state Markov chain.

4.2   ENTROPY RATE

If we have a sequence of n random variables, a natural question to ask is "how does the entropy of the sequence grow with n." We define the *entropy rate* as this rate of growth as follows.

Definition: The *entropy rate* of a stochastic process $\{X_i\}$ is defined by

$$H(\mathcal{X}) = \lim_{n \to \infty} \frac{1}{n} H(X_1, X_2, \ldots, X_n) \qquad (4.10)$$

when the limit exists.

We now consider some simple examples of stochastic processes and their corresponding entropy rates.

1. *Typewriter.* Consider the case of a typewriter that has m equally likely output letters. The typewriter can produce m^n sequences of length n, all of them equally likely. Hence $H(X_1, X_2, \ldots, X_n) = \log m^n$ and the entropy rate is $H(\mathcal{X}) = \log m$ bits per symbol.

2. $X_1, X_2, \ldots$ *are i.i.d. random variables.* Then

$$H(\mathcal{X}) = \lim \frac{H(X_1, X_2, \ldots, X_n)}{n} = \lim \frac{nH(X_1)}{n} = H(X_1), \quad (4.11)$$

   which is what one would expect for the entropy rate per symbol.

3. *Sequence of independent, but not identically distributed random variables.* In this case,

$$H(X_1, X_2, \ldots, X_n) = \sum_{i=1}^{n} H(X_i) \qquad (4.12)$$

   but the $H(X_i)$'s are all not equal. We can choose a sequence of distributions on $X_1, X_2, \ldots$ such that the limit of $\frac{1}{n} \sum H(X_i)$ does not exist. An example of such a sequence is a random binary sequence where $p_i = P(X_i = 1)$ is not constant, but a function of i, chosen carefully so that the limit in (4.10) does not exist. For example, let

$$p_i = \begin{cases} 0.5 & \text{if } 2k < \log \log i \le 2k + 1, \\ 0 & \text{if } 2k + 1 < \log \log i \le 2k + 2 \end{cases} \qquad (4.13)$$

   for $k = 0, 1, 2, \ldots$. Then there are arbitrarily long stretches where $H(X_i) = 1$, followed by exponentially longer segments where $H(X_i) = 0$. Hence the running average of the $H(X_i)$ will oscillate between 0 and 1 and will not have a limit. Thus $H(\mathcal{X})$ is not defined for this process.

We can also define a related quantity for entropy rate:

$$H'(\mathcal{X}) = \lim_{n \to \infty} H(X_n | X_{n-1}, X_{n-2}, \dots, X_1), \qquad (4.14)$$

when the limit exists.

The two quantities $H(\mathcal{X})$ and $H'(\mathcal{X})$ correspond to two different notions of entropy rate. The first is the per symbol entropy of the n random variables, and the second is the conditional entropy of the last random variable given the past. We will now prove the important result that for stationary processes both the limits exist and are equal.

Theorem 4.2.1: *For a stationary stochastic process, the limits in (4.10) and (4.14) exist and are equal, i.e.,*

$$H(\mathcal{X}) = H'(\mathcal{X}). \qquad (4.15)$$

We will first prove that $\lim H(X_n | X_{n-1}, \dots, X_1)$ exists.

Theorem 4.2.2: *For a stationary stochastic process, $H(X_n | X_{n-1}, \dots, X_1)$ is decreasing in n and has a limit $H'(\mathcal{X})$.*

Proof:

$$H(X_{n+1} | X_1, X_2, \dots, X_n) \le H(X_{n+1} | X_n, \dots, X_2) \qquad (4.16)$$

$$= H(X_n | X_{n-1}, \dots, X_1), \qquad (4.17)$$

where the inequality follows from the fact that conditioning reduces entropy and the equality follows from the stationarity of the process. Since $H(X_n | X_{n-1}, \dots, X_1)$ is a decreasing sequence of non-negative numbers, it has a limit, $H'(\mathcal{X})$. $\square$

We now use the following simple result from analysis.

Theorem 4.2.3 (*Cesáro mean*): *If $a_n \to a$ and $b_n = \frac{1}{n} \sum_{i=1}^{n} a_i$, then $b_n \to a$.*

Proof (*Informal outline*): Since most of the terms in the sequence $\{a_k\}$ are eventually close to a, then b_n, which is the average of the first n terms, is also eventually close to a.

Formal proof: Since $a_n \to a$, there exists a number $N(\epsilon)$ such that $|a_n - a| \le \epsilon$ for all $n \ge N(\epsilon)$. Hence

$$|b_n - a| = \left| \frac{1}{n} \sum_{i=1}^{n} (a_i - a) \right| \qquad (4.18)$$

$$\leq \frac{1}{n} \sum_{i=1}^{n} |(a_i - a)| \tag{4.19}$$

$$\leq \frac{1}{n} \sum_{i=1}^{N(\epsilon)} |a_i - a| + \frac{n - N(\epsilon)}{n} \epsilon \tag{4.20}$$

$$\leq \frac{1}{n} \sum_{i=1}^{N(\epsilon)} |a_i - a| + \epsilon , \tag{4.21}$$

for all $n \geq N(\epsilon)$. Since the first term goes to 0 as $n \to \infty$, we can make $|b_n - a| \leq 2\epsilon$ by taking n large enough. Hence $b_n \to a$ as $n \to \infty$. $\square$

Proof of Theorem 4.2.1: By the chain rule,

$$\frac{H(X_1, X_2, \ldots, X_n)}{n} = \frac{1}{n} \sum_{i=1}^{n} H(X_i | X_{i-1}, \ldots, X_1), \tag{4.22}$$

i.e., the entropy rate is the time average of the conditional entropies. But we know that the conditional entropies tend to a limit $H'(\mathcal{X})$. Hence, by Theorem 4.2.3, their running average has a limit, which is equal to the limit $H'(\mathcal{X})$ of the terms.

Thus, by Theorem 4.2.2.,

$$H(\mathcal{X}) = \lim \frac{H(X_1, X_2, \ldots, X_n)}{n} = \lim H(X_n | X_{n-1}, \ldots, X_1) = H'(\mathcal{X}) . \quad \square \tag{4.23}$$

The significance of the entropy rate of a stochastic process arises from the AEP for a stationary ergodic process. We will prove the general AEP in Section 15.7, where we will show that for any stationary ergodic process,

$$-\frac{1}{n} \log p(X_1, X_2, \ldots, X_n) \to H(\mathcal{X}), \tag{4.24}$$

with probability 1. Using this, the theorems of Chapter 3 can be easily extended to a general stationary ergodic process. We can define a typical set in the same way as we did for the i.i.d. case in Chapter 3. By the same arguments, we can show that the typical set has a probability close to 1, and that there are about $2^{nH(\mathcal{X})}$ typical sequences of length n, each with probability about $2^{-nH(\mathcal{X})}$. We can therefore represent the typical sequences of length n using approximately $nH(\mathcal{X})$ bits. This shows the significance of the entropy rate as the average description length for a stationary ergodic process.

The entropy rate is well defined for all stationary processes. The entropy rate is particularly easy to calculate for Markov chains.

Markov Chains: *For a stationary Markov chain, the entropy rate is given by*

$$H(\mathcal{X}) = H'(\mathcal{X}) = \lim H(X_n | X_{n-1}, \ldots, X_1) = \lim H(X_n | X_{n-1}) = H(X_2 | X_1),$$
$$(4.25)$$

where the conditional entropy is calculated using the given stationary distribution. We express this result explicitly in the following theorem:

Theorem 4.2.4: *Let $\{X_i\}$ be a stationary Markov chain with stationary distribution μ and transition matrix P. Then the entropy rate is*

$$H(\mathcal{X}) = -\sum_{ij} \mu_i P_{ij} \log P_{ij} \qquad (4.26)$$

Proof: $H(\mathcal{X}) = H(X_2 | X_1) = \Sigma_i \, \mu_i (\Sigma_j - P_{ij} \log P_{ij}). \quad \square$

Example 4.2.1 (*Two-state Markov chain*): The entropy rate of the two-state Markov chain in Figure 4.1 is

$$H(\mathcal{X}) = H(X_2 | X_1) = \frac{\beta}{\alpha + \beta} H(\alpha) + \frac{\alpha}{\alpha + \beta} H(\beta). \qquad (4.27)$$

Remark: If the Markov chain is irreducible and aperiodic, then it has a unique stationary distribution on the states, and any initial distribution tends to the stationary distribution as $n \to \infty$. In this case, even though the initial distribution is not the stationary distribution, the entropy rate, which is defined in terms of long term behavior, is $H(\mathcal{X})$ as defined in (4.25) and (4.26).

4.3   EXAMPLE: ENTROPY RATE OF A RANDOM WALK ON A WEIGHTED GRAPH

As an example of a stochastic process, let us consider a random walk on a connected graph (Figure 4.2). Consider a graph with m nodes labeled $\{1, 2, \ldots, m\}$, with weight $W_{ij} \geq 0$ on the edge joining node i to node j.

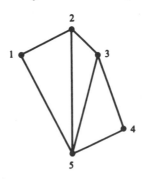

Figure 4.2. Random walk on a graph.

(The graph is assumed to be undirected, so that $W_{ij} = W_{ji}$. We set $W_{ij} = 0$ if the pair of nodes i and j are not connected.)

A particle randomly walks from node to node in this graph. The random walk $\{X_n\}$, $X_n \in \{1, 2, \ldots, m\}$ is a sequence of vertices of the graph. Given $X_n = i$, the next vertex j is chosen from among the nodes connected to node i with a probability proportional to the weight of the edge connecting i to j. Thus $P_{ij} = W_{ij}/\sum_k W_{ik}$.

In this case, the stationary distribution has a surprisingly simple form which we will guess and verify. The stationary distribution for this Markov chain assigns probability to node i proportional to the total weight of the edges emanating from node i. Let

$$W_i = \sum_j W_{ij} \tag{4.28}$$

be the total weight of edges emanating from node i and let

$$W = \sum_{i, j: j > i} W_{ij} \tag{4.29}$$

be the sum of the weights of all the edges. Then $\sum_i W_i = 2W$. We now guess that the stationary distribution is

$$\mu_i = \frac{W_i}{2W}. \tag{4.30}$$

We verify that this is the stationary distribution by checking that $\mu P = \mu$. Here

$$\sum_i \mu_i P_{ij} = \sum_i \frac{W_i}{2W} \frac{W_{ij}}{W_i} \tag{4.31}$$

$$= \sum_i \frac{1}{2W} W_{ij} \tag{4.32}$$

$$= \frac{W_j}{2W} \tag{4.33}$$

$$= \mu_j. \tag{4.34}$$

Thus the stationary probability of state i is proportional to the weight of edges emanating from node i. This stationary distribution has an interesting property of locality: it depends only on the total weight and the weight of edges connected to the node and hence does not change if the weights in some other part of the graph are changed while keeping the total weight constant.

We can now calculate the entropy rate as

$$H(\mathcal{X}) = H(X_2|X_1) \tag{4.35}$$

$$= -\sum_i \mu_i \sum_j P_{ij} \log P_{ij} \tag{4.36}$$

$$= -\sum_i \frac{W_i}{2W} \sum_j \frac{W_{ij}}{W_i} \log \frac{W_{ij}}{W_i} \tag{4.37}$$

$$= -\sum_i \sum_j \frac{W_{ij}}{2W} \log \frac{W_{ij}}{W_i} \tag{4.38}$$

$$= -\sum_i \sum_j \frac{W_{ij}}{2W} \log \frac{W_{ij}}{2W} + \sum_i \sum_j \frac{W_{ij}}{2W} \log \frac{W_i}{2W} \tag{4.39}$$

$$= H\left(\ldots, \frac{W_{ij}}{2W}, \ldots\right) - H\left(\ldots, \frac{W_i}{2W}, \ldots\right). \tag{4.40}$$

If all the edges have equal weight, the stationary distribution puts weight $E_i/2E$ on node i, where E_i is the number of edges emanating from node i and E is the total number of edges in the graph. In this case, the entropy rate of the random walk is

$$H(\mathscr{X}) = \log(2E) - H\left(\frac{E_1}{2E}, \frac{E_2}{2E}, \ldots, \frac{E_m}{2E}\right) \tag{4.41}$$

This answer for the entropy rate is so simple that it is almost misleading. Apparently, the entropy rate, which is the average transition entropy, depends only on the entropy of the stationary distribution and the total number of edges.

Example 4.3.1 (*Random walk on a chessboard*): Let a king move at random on an 8×8 chessboard. The king has 8 moves in the interior, 5 moves at the edges and 3 moves at the corners. Using this and the preceding results, the stationary probabilities are respectively $\frac{8}{420}$, $\frac{5}{420}$ and $\frac{3}{420}$, and the entropy rate is $0.92 \log 8$. The factor of 0.92 is due to edge effects; we would have an entropy rate of $\log 8$ on an infinite chessboard.

Similarly, we can find the entropy rate of rooks ($\log 14$ bits, since the rook always has 14 possible moves), bishops and queens. The queen combines the moves of a rook and a bishop. Does the queen have more or less freedom than the pair?

Remark: It is easy to see that a stationary random walk on a graph is *time-reversible*, that is, the probability of any sequence of states is the same forward or backward:

$$\Pr(X_1 = x_1, X_2 = x_2, \ldots, X_n = x_n) = \Pr(X_n = x_1, X_{n-1} = x_2, \ldots, X_1 = x_n). \tag{4.42}$$

Rather surprisingly, the converse is also true, that is, any time-reversible Markov chain can be represented as a random walk on an undirected weighted graph.

4.4   HIDDEN MARKOV MODELS

Here is an example that can be very difficult if done the wrong way. It illustrates the power of the techniques developed so far. Let X_1, $X_2, \ldots, X_n, \ldots$ be a stationary Markov chain, and let $Y_i = \phi(X_i)$ be a process, each term of which is a function of the corresponding state in the Markov chain. Such functions of Markov chains occur often in practice. In many situations, one has only partial information about the state of the system. It would simplify matters greatly if $Y_1, Y_2, \ldots, Y_n$ also formed a Markov chain, but in many cases this is not true. However, since the Markov chain is stationary, so is $Y_1, Y_2, \ldots, Y_n$, and the entropy rate is well defined. However, if we wish to compute $H(\mathcal{Y})$, we might compute $H(Y_n | Y_{n-1}, \ldots, Y_1)$ for each n and find the limit. Since the convergence can be arbitrarily slow, we will never know how close we are to the limit; we will not know when to stop. (We can't look at the change between the values at n and $n+1$, since this difference may be small even when we are far away from the limit—consider, for example, $\Sigma \frac{1}{n}$.)

It would be useful computationally to have upper and lower bounds converging to the limit from above and below. We can halt the computation when the difference between the upper bound and the lower bound is small, and we will then have a good estimate of the limit.

We already know that $H(Y_n | Y_{n-1}, \ldots, Y_1)$ converges monotonically to $H(\mathcal{Y})$ from above. For a lower bound, we will use $H(Y_n | Y_{n-1}, \ldots, Y_2, X_1)$. This is a neat trick based on the idea that X_1 contains as much information about Y_n as $Y_1, Y_0, Y_{-1}, \ldots$.

Lemma 4.4.1:

$$H(Y_n | Y_{n-1}, \ldots, Y_2, X_1) \le H(\mathcal{Y}) \tag{4.43}$$

Proof: We have, for $k = 1, 2, \ldots$,

$$H(Y_n | Y_{n-1}, \ldots, Y_2, X_1)$$

$$\stackrel{(a)}{=} H(Y_n | Y_{n-1}, \ldots, Y_2, Y_1, X_1) \tag{4.44}$$

$$\stackrel{(b)}{=} H(Y_n | Y_{n-1}, \ldots, Y_1, X_1, X_0, X_{-1}, \ldots, X_{-k}) \tag{4.45}$$

$$\stackrel{(c)}{=} H(Y_n | Y_{n-1}, \ldots, Y_1, X_1, X_0, X_{-1}, \ldots, X_{-k}, Y_0, \ldots, Y_{-k}) \tag{4.46}$$

$$\overset{(d)}{\le} H(Y_n | Y_{n-1}, \ldots, Y_1, Y_0, \ldots, Y_{-k}) \tag{4.47}$$

$$\overset{(e)}{=} H(Y_{n+k+1} | Y_{n+k}, \ldots, Y_1), \tag{4.48}$$

where (a) follows from that fact that Y_1 is a function of X_1, and (b) follows from the Markovity of X, (c) from the fact that Y_i is a function of X_i, (d) from the fact that conditioning reduces entropy, and (e) by stationarity. Since the inequality is true for all k, it is true in the limit. Thus

$$H(Y_n | Y_{n-1}, \ldots, Y_1, X_1) \le \lim_k H(Y_{n+k+1} | Y_{n+k}, \ldots, Y_1) \tag{4.49}$$

$$= H(\mathcal{Y}). \quad \square \tag{4.50}$$

The next lemma shows that the interval between the upper and the lower bounds decreases in length.

Lemma 4.4.2:

$$H(Y_n | Y_{n-1}, \ldots, Y_1) - H(Y_n | Y_{n-1}, \ldots, Y_1, X_1) \to 0. \tag{4.51}$$

Proof: The interval length can be rewritten as

$$H(Y_n | Y_{n-1}, \ldots, Y_1) - H(Y_n | Y_{n-1}, \ldots, Y_1, X_1) = I(X_1; Y_n | Y_{n-1}, \ldots, Y_1). \tag{4.52}$$

By the properties of mutual information,

$$I(X_1; Y_1, Y_2, \ldots, Y_n) \le H(X_1), \tag{4.53}$$

and hence

$$\lim_{n \to \infty} I(X_1; Y_1, Y_2, \ldots, Y_n) \le H(X_1). \tag{4.54}$$

By the chain rule,

$$\lim_{n \to \infty} I(X_1; Y_1, Y_2, \ldots, Y_n) = \lim_{n \to \infty} \sum_{i=1}^n I(X_1; Y_i | Y_{i-1}, \ldots, Y_1) \tag{4.55}$$

$$= \sum_{i=1}^{\infty} I(X_1; Y_i | Y_{i-1}, \ldots, Y_1). \tag{4.56}$$

Since this infinite sum is finite and the terms are non-negative, the terms must tend to 0, i.e.,

$$\lim I(X_1; Y_n | Y_{n-1}, \ldots, Y_1) = 0, \tag{4.57}$$

which proves the lemma. $\square$

Combining the previous two lemmas, we have the following theorem:

Theorem 4.4.1: *If* $X_1, X_2, \ldots, X_n$ *form a stationary Markov chain, and* $Y_i = \phi(X_i)$, *then*

$$H(Y_n | Y_{n-1}, \ldots, Y_1, X_1) \le H(\mathcal{Y}) \le H(Y_n | Y_{n-1}, \ldots, Y_1) \tag{4.58}$$

and

$$\lim H(Y_n | Y_{n-1}, \ldots, Y_1, X_1) = H(\mathcal{Y}) = \lim H(Y_n | Y_{n-1}, \ldots, Y_1). \tag{4.59}$$

SUMMARY OF CHAPTER 4

Entropy rate: Two definitions of entropy rate for a stochastic process are

$$H(\mathcal{X}) = \lim_{n \to \infty} \frac{1}{n} H(X_1, X_2, \ldots, X_n), \tag{4.60}$$

$$H'(\mathcal{X}) = \lim_{n \to \infty} H(X_n | X_{n-1}, X_{n-2}, \ldots, X_1). \tag{4.61}$$

For a stationary stochastic process,

$$H(\mathcal{X}) = H'(\mathcal{X}). \tag{4.62}$$

Entropy rate of a stationary Markov chain:

$$H(\mathcal{X}) = -\sum_{ij} \mu_i P_{ij} \log P_{ij}. \tag{4.63}$$

Functions of a Markov chain: If $X_1, X_2, \ldots, X_n$ form a Markov chain and $Y_i = \phi(X_i)$, then

$$H(Y_n | Y_{n-1}, \ldots, Y_1, X_1) \le H(\mathcal{Y}) \le H(Y_n | Y_{n-1}, \ldots, Y_1) \tag{4.64}$$

and

$$\lim_{n \to \infty} H(Y_n | Y_{n-1}, \ldots, Y_1, X_1) = H(\mathcal{Y}) = \lim_{n \to \infty} H(Y_n | Y_{n-1}, \ldots, Y_1). \tag{4.65}$$

PROBLEMS FOR CHAPTER 4

1. *Doubly stochastic matrices.* An $n \times n$ matrix $P = [P_{ij}]$ is said to be *doubly stochastic* if $P_{ij} \geq 0$ and $\Sigma_j P_{ij} = 1$ for all i and $\Sigma_i P_{ij} = 1$ for all j. An $n \times n$ matrix P is said to be a *permutation* matrix if it is doubly stochastic and there is precisely one $P_{ij} = 1$ in each row and each column.

    It can be shown that every doubly stochastic matrix can be written as the convex combination of permutation matrices.

    (a) Let $\mathbf{a}^t = (a_1, a_2, \ldots, a_n)$, $a_i \geq 0$, $\Sigma a_i = 1$, be a probability vector. Let $\mathbf{b} = \mathbf{a}P$, where P is doubly stochastic. Show that $\mathbf{b}$ is a probability vector and that $H(b_1, b_2, \ldots, b_n) \geq H(a_1, a_2, \ldots, a_n)$. Thus stochastic mixing increases entropy.

    (b) Show that a stationary distribution μ for a doubly stochastic matrix P is the uniform distribution.

    (c) Conversely, prove that if the uniform distribution is a stationary distribution for a Markov transition matrix P, then P is doubly stochastic.

2. *Time's arrow.* Let $\{X_i\}_{i=-\infty}^{\infty}$ be a stationary stochastic process. Prove that

    $$H(X_0 | X_{-1}, X_{-2}, \ldots, X_{-n}) = H(X_0 | X_1, X_2, \ldots, X_n).$$

    In other words, the present has a conditional entropy given the past equal to the conditional entropy given the future.

    This is true even though it is quite easy to concoct stationary random processes for which the flow into the future looks quite different from the flow into the past. That is to say, one can determine the direction of time by looking at a sample function of the process. Nonetheless, given the present state, the conditional uncertainty of the next symbol in the future is equal to the conditional uncertainty of the previous symbol in the past.

3. *Entropy of a random tree.* Consider the following method of generating a random tree with n nodes. First expand the root node:

    Then expand one of the two terminal nodes at random:

    At time k, choose one of the $k - 1$ terminal nodes according to a uniform distribution and expand it. Continue until n terminal nodes have been generated. Thus a sequence leading to a five node tree might look like this:

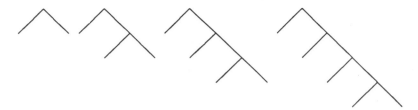

Surprisingly, the following method of generating random trees yields the same probability distribution on trees with n terminal nodes. First choose an integer N_1 uniformly distributed on $\{1, 2, \ldots, n-1\}$. We then have the picture.

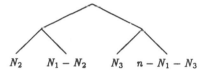

Then choose an integer N_2 uniformly distributed over $\{1, 2, \ldots, N_1 - 1\}$, and independently choose another integer N_3 uniformly over $\{1, 2, \ldots, (n - N_1) - 1\}$. The picture is now:

Continue the process until no further subdivision can be made. (The equivalence of these two tree generation schemes follows, for example, from Polya's urn model.)

Now let T_n denote a random n-node tree generated as described. The probability distribution on such trees seems difficult to describe, but we can find the entropy of this distribution in recursive form.

First some examples. For $n = 2$, we have only one tree. Thus $H(T_2) = 0$. For $n = 3$, we have two equally probable trees:

Thus $H(T_3) = \log 2$. For $n = 4$, we have five possible trees, with probabilities $1/3, 1/6, 1/6, 1/6, 1/6$.

Now for the recurrence relation. Let $N_1(T_n)$ denote the number of terminal nodes of T_n in the right half of the tree. Justify each of the steps in the following:

$$H(T_n) \overset{(a)}{=} H(N_1, T_n) \tag{4.66}$$

$$\overset{(b)}{=} H(N_1) + H(T_n | N_1) \tag{4.67}$$

$$\overset{(c)}{=} \log(n-1) + H(T_n | N_1) \tag{4.68}$$

$$\overset{(d)}{=} \log(n-1) + \frac{1}{n-1} \sum_{k=1}^{n-1} [H(T_k) + H(T_{n-k})] \tag{4.69}$$

$$\overset{(e)}{=} \log(n-1) + \frac{2}{n-1} \sum_{k=1}^{n-1} H(T_k) . \tag{4.70}$$

$$= \log(n-1) + \frac{2}{n-1} \sum_{k=1}^{n-1} H_k . \tag{4.71}$$

(f) Use this to show that

$$(n-1)H_n = nH_{n-1} + (n-1)\log(n-1) - (n-2)\log(n-2), \tag{4.72}$$

or

$$\frac{H_n}{n} = \frac{H_{n-1}}{n-1} + c_n , \tag{4.73}$$

for appropriately defined c_n. Since $\Sigma c_n = c < \infty$, you have proved that $\frac{1}{n}H(T_n)$ converges to a constant. Thus the expected number of bits necessary to describe the random tree T_n grows linearly with n.

4. *Monotonicity of entropy per element.* For a stationary stochastic process $X_1, X_2, \ldots, X_n$, show that

(a)
$$\frac{H(X_1, X_2, \ldots, X_n)}{n} \leq \frac{H(X_1, X_2, \ldots, X_{n-1})}{n-1} . \tag{4.74}$$

(b)
$$\frac{H(X_1, X_2, \ldots, X_n)}{n} \geq H(X_n | X_{n-1}, \ldots, X_1) . \tag{4.75}$$

5. *Entropy rates of Markov chains.*

(a) Find the entropy rate of the two-state Markov chain with transition matrix

$$P = \begin{bmatrix} 1 - p_{01} & p_{01} \\ p_{10} & 1 - p_{10} \end{bmatrix}.$$

(b) What values of p_{01}, p_{10} maximize the rate of part (a)?

(c) Find the entropy rate of the two-state Markov chain with transition matrix

$$P = \begin{bmatrix} 1 - p & p \\ 1 & 0 \end{bmatrix}.$$

(d) Find the maximum value of the entropy rate of the Markov chain of part (c). We expect that the maximizing value of p should be less than $1/2$, since the 0 state permits more information to be generated than the 1 state.

(e) Let $N(t)$ be the number of allowable state sequences of length t for the Markov chain of part (c). Find $N(t)$ and calculate

$$H_0 = \lim_{t \to \infty} \frac{1}{t} \log N(t).$$

Hint: Find a linear recurrence that expresses $N(t)$ in terms of $N(t-1)$ and $N(t-2)$. Why is H_0 an upper bound on the entropy rate of the Markov chain? Compare H_0 with the maximum entropy found in part (d).

6. *Maximum entropy process.* A discrete memoryless source has alphabet $\{1, 2\}$ where the symbol 1 has duration 1 and the symbol 2 has duration 2. The probabilities of 1 and 2 are p_1 and p_2, respectively. Find the value of p_1 that maximizes the source entropy per unit time $H(X)/El_X$. What is the maximum value H?

7. *Initial conditions.* Show, for a Markov chain, that

$$H(X_0|X_n) \geq H(X_0|X_{n-1}).$$

Thus initial conditions X_0 become more difficult to recover as the future X_n unfolds.

8. *Pairwise independence.* Let $X_1, X_2, \ldots, X_{n-1}$ be i.i.d. random variables taking values in $\{0, 1\}$, with $\Pr\{X_i = 1\} = \frac{1}{2}$. Let $X_n = 1$ if $\sum_{i=1}^{n-1} X_i$ is odd and $X_n = 0$ otherwise. Let $n \geq 3$.
   (a) Show that X_i and X_j are independent, for $i \neq j$, $i, j \in \{1, 2, \ldots, n\}$.
   (b) Find $H(X_i, X_j)$, for $i \neq j$.
   (c) Find $H(X_1, X_2, \ldots, X_n)$. Is this equal to $nH(X_1)$?

9. *Stationary processes.* Let $\ldots, X_{-1}, X_0, X_1, \ldots$ be a stationary (not necessarily Markov) stochastic process. Which of the following statements are true? State true or false. Then either prove or provide a counterexample. Warning: At least one answer is false.
   (a) $H(X_n|X_0) = H(X_{-n}|X_0)$.
   (b) $H(X_n|X_0) \geq H(X_{n-1}|X_0)$.
   (c) $H(X_n|X_1^{n-1}, X_{n+1})$ is nonincreasing in n.

10. *The entropy rate of a dog looking for a bone.* A dog walks on the integers, possibly reversing direction at each step with probability $p = .1$. Let $X_0 = 0$. The first step is equally likely to be positive or negative. A typical walk might look like this:

$$(X_0, X_1, \ldots) = (0, -1, -2, -3, -4, -3, -2, -1, 0, 1, \ldots).$$

   (a) Find $H(X_1, X_2, \ldots, X_n)$.
   (b) Find the entropy rate of this browsing dog.
   (c) What is the expected number of steps the dog takes before reversing direction?

11. *Random walk on chessboard.* Find the entropy rate of the Markov chain associated with a random walk of a king on the 3×3 chessboard

1	2	3
4	5	6
7	8	9

What about the entropy rate of rooks, bishops and queens? There are two types of bishops.

12. *Entropy rate.* Let $\{X_i\}$ be a discrete stationary stochastic process with entropy rate $H(\mathcal{X})$. Show

$$\frac{1}{n}H(X_n, \ldots, X_1 | X_0, X_{-1}, \ldots, X_{-k}) \to H(\mathcal{X}), \qquad (4.76)$$

for $k = 1, 2, \ldots$.

13. *Entropy rate of constrained sequences.* In magnetic recording, the mechanism of recording and reading the bits imposes constraints on the sequences of bits that can be recorded. For example, to ensure proper synchronization, it is often necessary to limit the length of runs of 0's between two 1's. Also to reduce intersymbol interference, it may be necessary to require at least one 0 between any two 1's. We will consider a simple example of such a constraint.

Suppose that we are required to have at least one 0 and at most two 0's between any pair of 1's in a sequences. Thus, sequences like 101001 and 0101001 are valid sequences, but 0110010 and 0000101 are not. We wish to calculate the number of valid sequences of length n.

(a) Show that the set of constrained sequences is the same as the set of allowed paths on the following state diagram:

(b) Let $X_i(n)$ be the number of valid paths of length n ending at state i. Argue that $\mathbf{X}(n) = [X_1(n) \ X_2(n) \ X_3(n)]^T$ satisfies the following recursion:

$$\begin{bmatrix} X_1(n) \\ X_2(n) \\ X_3(n) \end{bmatrix} = \begin{bmatrix} 0 & 1 & 1 \\ 1 & 0 & 0 \\ 0 & 1 & 0 \end{bmatrix} \begin{bmatrix} X_1(n-1) \\ X_2(n-1) \\ X_3(n-1) \end{bmatrix} = A\mathbf{X}(n-1) \qquad (4.77)$$

with initial conditions $\mathbf{X}(1) = [1 \ 1 \ 0]^T$.

(c) Then we have by induction

$$\mathbf{X}(n) = A\mathbf{X}(n-1) = A^2\mathbf{X}(n-2) = \cdots = A^{n-1}\mathbf{X}(1). \qquad (4.78)$$

Using the eigenvalue decomposition of A for the case of distinct eigenvalues, we can write $A = U^{-1} \Lambda U$, where Λ is the diagonal matrix of eigenvalues. Then $A^{n-1} = U^{-1} \Lambda^{n-1} U$. Show that we can write

$$\mathbf{X}(n) = \lambda_1^{n-1}\mathbf{Y}_1 + \lambda_2^{n-1}\mathbf{Y}_2 + \lambda_3^{n-1}\mathbf{Y}_3 , \qquad (4.79)$$

where $\mathbf{Y}_1$, $\mathbf{Y}_2$, $\mathbf{Y}_3$ do not depend on n. For large n, this sum is dominated by the largest term. Therefore argue that for $i = 1, 2, 3$, we have

$$\frac{1}{n} \log X_i(n) \to \log \lambda , \qquad (4.80)$$

where λ is the largest (positive) eigenvalue. Thus the number of sequences of length n grows as λ^n for large n. Calculate λ for the matrix A above. (The case when the eigenvalues are not distinct can be handled in a similar manner.)

(d) We will now take a different approach. Consider a Markov chain whose state diagram is the one given in part (a), but with arbitrary transition probabilities. Therefore the probability transition matrix of this Markov chain is

$$P = \begin{bmatrix} 0 & \alpha & 1 \\ 1 & 0 & 0 \\ 0 & 1-\alpha & 0 \end{bmatrix}. \qquad (4.81)$$

Show that the stationary distribution of this Markov chain is

$$\mu = \left[\frac{1}{3-\alpha}, \frac{1}{3-\alpha}, \frac{1-\alpha}{3-\alpha} \right]^T . \qquad (4.82)$$

(e) Maximize the entropy rate of the Markov chain over choices of α. What is the maximum entropy rate of the chain?

(f) Compare the maximum entropy rate in part (e) with $\log \lambda$ in part (c). Why are the two answers the same?

14. *Waiting times are insensitive to distributions.* Let $X_0, X_1, X_2, \ldots$ be drawn i.i.d. $\sim p(x)$, $x \in \mathcal{X} = \{1, 2, \ldots, m\}$ and let N be the waiting time to the next occurrence of X_0, where $N = \min_n \{X_n = X_0\}$.

(a) Show that $EN = m$.

(b) Show that $E \log N \le H(X)$.

(c) (Optional) Prove part (a) for $\{X_i\}$ stationary and ergodic.

HISTORICAL NOTES

The entropy rate of a stochastic process was introduced by Shannon [238], who also explored some of the connections between the entropy rate of the process and the number of possible sequences generated by the process. Since Shannon, there have been a number of results extending the basic theorems of information theory to general stochastic processes.

Chapter 5

Data Compression

We now put content in the definition of entropy by establishing the fundamental limit for the compression of information. Data compression can be achieved by assigning short descriptions to the most frequent outcomes of the data source and necessarily longer descriptions to the less frequent outcomes. For example, in Morse code, the most frequent symbol is represented by a single dot. In this chapter we find the shortest average description length of a random variable.

We first define the notion of an instantaneous code and then prove the important Kraft inequality, which asserts that the exponentiated codeword length assignments must look like a probability mass function. Simple calculus then shows that the expected description length must be greater than or equal to the entropy, the first main result. Then Shannon's simple construction shows that the expected description length can achieve this bound asymptotically for repeated descriptions. This establishes the entropy as a natural measure of efficient description length. The famous Huffman coding procedure for finding minimum expected description length assignments is provided. Finally, we show that Huffman codes are competitively optimal and that it requires roughly H fair coin flips to generate a sample of a random variable having entropy H.

Thus the entropy is the data compression limit as well as the number of bits needed in random number generation. And codes achieving H turn out to be optimal from many points of view.

5.1 EXAMPLES OF CODES

Definition: A *source code* C for a random variable X is a mapping from $\mathscr{X}$, the range of X, to $\mathscr{D}^*$, the set of finite length strings of symbols from a D-ary alphabet. Let $C(x)$ denote the codeword corresponding to x and let $l(x)$ denote the length of $C(x)$.

For example, $C(\text{Red}) = 00$, $C(\text{Blue}) = 11$ is a source code for $\mathscr{X} = \{\text{Red, Blue}\}$ with alphabet $\mathscr{D} = \{0, 1\}$.

Definition: The *expected length* $L(C)$ of a source code $C(x)$ for a random variable X with probability mass function $p(x)$ is given by

$$L(C) = \sum_{x \in \mathscr{X}} p(x)l(x), \tag{5.1}$$

where $l(x)$ is the length of the codeword associated with x.

Without loss of generality, we can assume that the D-ary alphabet is $\mathscr{D} = \{0, 1, \ldots, D-1\}$.
Some examples of codes follow.

Example 5.1.1: Let X be a random variable with the following distribution and codeword assignment:

$$
\begin{array}{llll}
\Pr(X=1) = 1/2, & \text{codeword} & C(1) = 0 & \\
\Pr(X=2) = 1/4, & \text{codeword} & C(2) = 10 & \\
\Pr(X=3) = 1/8, & \text{codeword} & C(3) = 110 & (5.2) \\
\Pr(X=4) = 1/8, & \text{codeword} & C(4) = 111 . &
\end{array}
$$

The entropy $H(X)$ of X is 1.75 bits, and the expected length $L(C) = El(X)$ of this code is also 1.75 bits. Here we have a code that has the same average length as the entropy. We note that any sequence of bits can be uniquely decoded into a sequence of symbols of X. For example, the bit string 0110111100110 is decoded as 134213.

Example 5.1.2: Consider another simple example of a code for a random variable:

$$
\begin{array}{llll}
\Pr(X=1) = 1/3, & \text{codeword} & C(1) = 0 & \\
\Pr(X=2) = 1/3, & \text{codeword} & C(2) = 10 & (5.3) \\
\Pr(X=3) = 1/3, & \text{codeword} & C(3) = 11 . &
\end{array}
$$

Just as in the previous case, the code is uniquely decodable. However, in this case the entropy is $\log 3 = 1.58$ bits, while the average length of the encoding is 1.66 bits. Here $El(X) > H(X)$.

Example 5.1.3 (*Morse code*): The Morse code is a reasonably efficient code for the English alphabet using an alphabet of four symbols: a dot, a dash, a letter space and a word space. Short sequences represent frequent letters (e.g., a single dot represents E) and long sequences represent infrequent letters (e.g., Q is represented by "dash, dash, dot, dash"). This is not the optimal representation for the alphabet in four symbols—in fact, many possible codewords are not utilized because the codewords for letters do not contain spaces except for a letter space at the end of every codeword and no space can follow another space. It is an interesting problem to calculate the number of sequences that can be constructed under these constraints. The problem was solved by Shannon in his original 1948 paper. The problem is also related to coding for magnetic recording, where long strings of 0's are prohibited [2], [184].

We now define increasingly more stringent conditions on codes. Let x^n denote $(x_1, x_2, \ldots, x_n)$.

Definition: A code is said to be *non-singular* if every element of the range of X maps into a different string in $\mathscr{D}^*$, i.e.,

$$x_i \neq x_j \Rightarrow C(x_i) \neq C(x_j). \tag{5.4}$$

Non-singularity suffices for an unambiguous description of a single value of X. But we usually wish to send a sequence of values of X. In such cases, we can ensure decodability by adding a special symbol (a "comma") between any two codewords. But this is an inefficient use of the special symbol; we can do better by developing the idea of self-punctuating or instantaneous codes. Motivated by the necessity to send sequences of symbols X, we define the extension of a code as follows:

Definition: The *extension* C^* of a code C is the mapping from finite length strings of $\mathscr{X}$ to finite length strings of $\mathscr{D}$, defined by

$$C(x_1 x_2 \cdots x_n) = C(x_1)C(x_2) \cdots C(x_n), \tag{5.5}$$

where $C(x_1)C(x_2) \cdots C(x_n)$ indicates concatenation of the corresponding codewords.

Example 5.1.4: If $C(x_1) = 00$ and $C(x_2) = 11$, then $C(x_1 x_2) = 0011$.

Definition: A code is called *uniquely decodable* if its extension is non-singular.

In other words, any encoded string in a uniquely decodable code has only one possible source string producing it. However, one may have to look at the entire string to determine even the first symbol in the corresponding source string.

Definition: A code is called a *prefix code* or an *instantaneous code* if no codeword is a prefix of any other codeword.

An instantaneous code can be decoded without reference to the future codewords since the end of a codeword is immediately recognizable. Hence, for an instantaneous code, the symbol x_i can be decoded as soon as we come to the end of the codeword corresponding to it. We need not wait to see the codewords that come later. An instantaneous code is a "self-punctuating" code; we can look down the sequence of code symbols and add the commas to separate the codewords without looking at later symbols. For example, the binary string 01011111010 produced by the code of Example 5.1.1 is parsed as 0, 10, 111, 110, 10.

The nesting of these definitions is shown in Figure 5.1. To illustrate the differences between the various kinds of codes, consider the following examples of codeword assignments $C(x)$ to $x \in \mathscr{X}$ in Table 5.1.

For the non-singular code, the code string 010 has three possible source sequences: 2 or 14 or 31, and hence the code is not uniquely decodable.

The uniquely decodable code is not prefix free and is hence not instantaneous. To see that it is uniquely decodable, take any code string and start from the beginning. If the first two bits are 00 or 10, they can be decoded immediately. If the first two bits are 11, then we must look at the following bits. If the next bit is a 1, then the first source symbol is a 3. If the length of the string of 0's immediately following the 11 is odd, then the first codeword must be 110 and the first source symbol must be

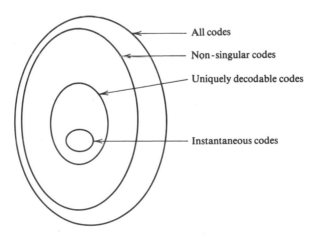

Figure 5.1. Classes of codes.

TABLE 5.1. Classes of Codes

X	Singular	Non-singular, but not uniquely decodable	Uniquely decodable, but not instantaneous	Instantaneous
1	0	0	10	0
2	0	010	00	10
3	0	01	11	110
4	0	10	110	111

4; if the length of the string of 0's is even, then the first source symbol is a 3. By repeating this argument, we can see that this code is uniquely decodable. Sardinas and Patterson have devised a finite test for unique decodability, which involves forming sets of possible suffixes to the codewords and systematically eliminating them. The test is described more fully in Problem 24 at the end of the chapter.

The fact that the last code in Table 5.1 is instantaneous is obvious since no codeword is a prefix of any other.

5.2 KRAFT INEQUALITY

We wish to construct instantaneous codes of minimum expected length to describe a given source. It is clear that we cannot assign short codewords to all source symbols and still be prefix free. The set of codeword lengths possible for instantaneous codes is limited by the following inequality:

Theorem 5.2.1 (*Kraft inequality*): *For any instantaneous code (prefix code) over an alphabet of size D, the codeword lengths $l_1, l_2, \ldots, l_m$ must satisfy the inequality*

$$\sum_i D^{-l_i} \le 1 .\qquad (5.6)$$

Conversely, given a set of codeword lengths that satisfy this inequality, there exists an instantaneous code with these word lengths.

Proof: Consider a D-ary tree in which each node has D children. Let the branches of the tree represent the symbols of the codeword. For example, the D branches arising from the root node represent the D possible values of the first symbol of the codeword. Then each codeword is represented by a leaf on the tree. The path from the root traces out the symbols of the codeword. A binary example of such a tree is shown in Figure 5.2.

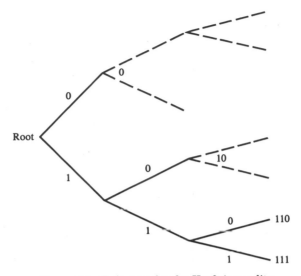

Figure 5.2. Code tree for the Kraft inequality.

The prefix condition on the codewords implies that no codeword is an ancestor of any other codeword on the tree. Hence, each codeword eliminates its descendants as possible codewords.

Let $l_{\max}$ be the length of the longest codeword of the set of codewords. Consider all nodes of the tree at level $l_{\max}$. Some of them are codewords, some are descendants of codewords, and some are neither. A codeword at level l_i has $D^{l_{\max}-l_i}$ descendants at level $l_{\max}$. Each of these descendant sets must be disjoint. Also, the total number of nodes in these sets must be less than or equal to $D^{l_{\max}}$. Hence, summing over all the codewords, we have

$$\sum D^{l_{\max}-l_i} \le D^{l_{\max}} \tag{5.7}$$

or

$$\sum D^{-l_i} \le 1, \tag{5.8}$$

which is the Kraft inequality.

Conversely, given any set of codeword lengths $l_1, l_2, \ldots, l_m$ which satisfy the Kraft inequality, we can always construct a tree like the one in Figure 5.2. Label the first node (lexicographically) of depth l_1 as codeword 1, and remove its descendants from the tree. Then label the first remaining node of depth l_2 as codeword 2, etc. Proceeding this way, we construct a prefix code with the specified $l_1, l_2, \ldots, l_m$. $\square$

We now show that an infinite prefix code also satisfies the Kraft inequality.

Theorem 5.2.2 (*Extended Kraft Inequality*): *For any countably infinite set of codewords that form a prefix code, the codeword lengths satisfy the extended Kraft inequality,*

$$\sum_{i=1}^{\infty} D^{-l_i} \le 1. \tag{5.9}$$

Conversely, given any $l_1, l_2, \ldots$ *satisfying the extended Kraft inequality, we can construct a prefix code with these codeword lengths.*

Proof: Let the D-ary alphabet be $\{0, 1, \ldots, D-1\}$. Consider the ith codeword $y_1 y_2 \ldots y_{l_i}$. Let $0.y_1 y_2 \cdots y_{l_i}$ be the real number given by the D-ary expansion

$$0.y_1 y_2 \cdots y_{l_i} = \sum_{j=1}^{l_i} y_j D^{-j}. \tag{5.10}$$

This codeword corresponds to the interval

$$\left(0.y_1 y_2 \cdots y_{l_i}, 0.y_1 y_2 \cdots y_{l_i} + \frac{1}{D^{l_i}} \right), \tag{5.11}$$

the set of all real numbers whose D-ary expansion begins with $0.y_1 y_2 \cdots y_{l_i}$. This is a subinterval of the unit interval $[0, 1]$. By the prefix condition, these intervals are disjoint. Hence the sum of their lengths has to be less than or equal to 1.

This proves that

$$\sum_{i=1}^{\infty} D^{-l_i} \le 1. \tag{5.12}$$

Just as in the finite case, we can reverse the proof to construct the code for a given $l_1, l_2, \ldots$ that satisfies the Kraft inequality. First reorder the indexing so that $l_1 \ge l_2 \ge \ldots$. Then simply assign the intervals in order from the low end of the unit interval. $\square$

In Section 5.5, we will show that the lengths of codewords for a uniquely decodable code also satisfy the Kraft inequality. Before we do that, we consider the problem of finding the shortest instantaneous code.

5.3 OPTIMAL CODES

In the previous section, we proved that any codeword set that satisfies the prefix condition has to satisfy the Kraft inequality and that the

Kraft inequality is a sufficient condition for the existence of a codeword set with the specified set of codeword lengths. We now consider the problem of finding the prefix code with the minimum expected length. From the results of the previous section, this is equivalent to finding the set of lengths $l_1, l_2, \ldots, l_m$ satisfying the Kraft inequality and whose expected length $L = \sum p_i l_i$ is less than the expected length of any other prefix code. This is a standard optimization problem: Minimize

$$L = \sum p_i l_i \tag{5.13}$$

over all integers $l_1, l_2, \ldots, l_m$ satisfying

$$\sum D^{-l_i} \leq 1. \tag{5.14}$$

A simple analysis by calculus suggests the form of the minimizing l_i^*. We neglect the integer constraint on l_i and assume equality in the constraint. Hence, we can write the constrained minimization using Lagrange multipliers as the minimization of

$$J = \sum p_i l_i + \lambda \left(\sum D^{-l_i} \right). \tag{5.15}$$

Differentiating with respect to l_i, we obtain

$$\frac{\partial J}{\partial l_i} = p_i - \lambda D^{-l_i} \log_e D. \tag{5.16}$$

Setting the derivative to 0, we obtain

$$D^{-l_i} = \frac{p_i}{\lambda \log_e D}. \tag{5.17}$$

Substituting this in the constraint to find λ, we find $\lambda = 1/\log_e D$ and hence

$$p_i = D^{-l_i}, \tag{5.18}$$

yielding optimal codelengths

$$l_i^* = -\log_D p_i. \tag{5.19}$$

This non-integer choice of codeword lengths yields expected codeword length

$$L^* = \sum p_i l_i^* = -\sum p_i \log_D p_i = H_D(X). \tag{5.20}$$

But since the l_i must be integers, we will not always be able to set the codeword lengths as in (5.19). Instead, we should choose a set of codeword lengths l_i "close" to the optimal set. Rather than demonstrate by calculus that $l_i^* = -\log_D p_i$ is a global minimum, we will verify optimality directly in the proof of the following theorem.

Theorem 5.3.1: *The expected length L of any instantaneous D-ary code for a random variable X is greater than or equal to the entropy $H_D(X)$, i.e.,*

$$L \geq H_D(X) \tag{5.21}$$

with equality iff $D^{-l_i} = p_i$.

Proof: We can write the difference between the expected length and the entropy as

$$L - H_D(X) = \sum p_i l_i - \sum p_i \log_D \frac{1}{p_i} \tag{5.22}$$

$$= -\sum p_i \log_D D^{-l_i} + \sum p_i \log_D p_i . \tag{5.23}$$

Letting $r_i = D^{-l_i}/\sum_j D^{-l_j}$ and $c = \sum D^{-l_i}$, we obtain

$$L - H = \sum p_i \log_D \frac{p_i}{r_i} - \log_D c \tag{5.24}$$

$$= D(\mathbf{p}\|\mathbf{r}) + \log_D \frac{1}{c} \tag{5.25}$$

$$\geq 0 \tag{5.26}$$

by the non-negativity of relative entropy and the fact (Kraft inequality) that $c \leq 1$. Hence $L \geq H$ with equality iff $p_i = D^{-l_i}$, i.e., iff $-\log_D p_i$ is an integer for all i. $\square$

Definition: A probability distribution is called *D-adic* with respect to D if each of the probabilities is equal to D^{-n} for some n.

Thus we have equality in the theorem if and only if the distribution of X is D-adic.

The preceding proof also indicates a procedure for finding an optimal code: find the D-adic distribution that is closest (in the relative entropy sense) to the distribution of X. This distribution provides the set of codeword lengths. Construct the code by choosing the first available node as in the proof of the Kraft inequality. We then have an optimal code for X.

However, this procedure is not easy, since the search for the closest D-adic distribution is not obvious. In the next section, we give a good suboptimal procedure (Shannon-Fano coding). In Section 5.6, we describe a simple procedure (Huffman coding) for actually finding the optimal code.

5.4   BOUNDS ON THE OPTIMAL CODELENGTH

We now demonstrate a code that achieves an expected description length L within 1 bit of the lower bound, that is,

$$H(X) \le L < H(X) + 1 .\tag{5.27}$$

Recall the setup of the last section: we wish to minimize $L = \sum p_i l_i$ subject to the constraint that $l_1, l_2, \ldots, l_m$ are integers and $\sum D^{-l_i} \le 1$. We proved that the optimal codeword lengths can be found by finding the D-adic probability distribution closest to the distribution of X in relative entropy i.e., finding the D-adic $\mathbf{r}$ $(r_i = D^{-l_i}/\sum_j D^{-l_j})$ minimizing

$$L - H_D = D(\mathbf{p}\|\mathbf{r}) - \log\left(\sum D^{-l_i}\right) \ge 0 .\tag{5.28}$$

The choice of word lengths $l_i = \log_D \frac{1}{p_i}$ yields $L = H$. Since $\log_D \frac{1}{p_i}$ may not equal an integer, we round it up to give integer word length assignments,

$$l_i = \left\lceil \log_D\left(\frac{1}{p_i}\right)\right\rceil ,\tag{5.29}$$

where $\lceil x \rceil$ is the smallest integer $\ge x$. These lengths satisfy the Kraft inequality since

$$\sum D^{-\left\lceil \log \frac{1}{p_i}\right\rceil} \le \sum D^{-\log \frac{1}{p_i}} = \sum p_i = 1 .\tag{5.30}$$

This choice of codeword lengths satisfies

$$\log_D \frac{1}{p_i} \le l_i < \log_D \frac{1}{p_i} + 1 .\tag{5.31}$$

Multiplying by p_i and summing over i, we obtain

$$H_D(X) \le L < H_D(X) + 1 .\tag{5.32}$$

Since the optimal code can only be better than this code, we have the following theorem:

Theorem 5.4.1: *Let $l_1^*, l_2^*, \ldots, l_m^*$ be the optimal codeword lengths for a source distribution $\mathbf{p}$ and a D-ary alphabet, and let L^* be the associated expected length of the optimal code $(L^* = \Sigma \, p_i l_i^*)$. Then*

$$H_D(X) \le L^* < H_D(X) + 1 . \tag{5.33}$$

Proof: Let $l_i = \lceil \log_D \frac{1}{p_i} \rceil$. Then l_i satisfies the Kraft inequality and from (5.32) we have

$$H_D(X) \le L = \sum p_i l_i < H_D(X) + 1 . \tag{5.34}$$

But since L^*, the expected length of the optimal code, is less than $L = \Sigma \, p_i l_i$, and since $L^* \ge H_D$ from Theorem 5.3.1, we have the theorem. $\square$

In the preceding theorem, there is an overhead which is at most 1 bit, due to the fact that $\log \frac{1}{p_i}$ is not always an integer. We can reduce the overhead per symbol by spreading it out over many symbols. With this in mind, let us consider a system in which we send a sequence of n symbols from X. The symbols are assumed to be drawn i.i.d. according to $p(x)$. We can consider these n symbols to be a supersymbol from the alphabet $\mathcal{X}^n$.

Define L_n to be the expected codeword length per input symbol, i.e., if $l(x_1, x_2, \ldots, x_n)$ is the length of the codeword associated with $(x_1, x_2, \ldots, x_n)$, then

$$L_n = \frac{1}{n} \sum p(x_1, x_2, \ldots, x_n) l(x_1, x_2, \ldots, x_n) = \frac{1}{n} \, El(X_1, X_2, \ldots, X_n) . \tag{5.35}$$

We can now apply the bounds derived above to the code:

$$H(X_1, X_2, \ldots, X_n) \le El(X_1, X_2, \ldots, X_n) < H(X_1, X_2, \ldots, X_n) + 1 . \tag{5.36}$$

Since $X_1, X_2, \ldots, X_n$ are i.i.d., $H(X_1, X_2, \ldots, X_n) = \Sigma \, H(X_i) = nH(X)$. Dividing (5.36) by n, we obtain

$$H(X) \le L_n < H(X) + \frac{1}{n} . \tag{5.37}$$

Hence by using large block lengths we can achieve an expected codelength per symbol arbitrarily close to the entropy.

We can also use the same argument for a sequence of symbols from a stochastic process that is not necessarily i.i.d. In this case, we still have the bound

$$H(X_1, X_2, \ldots, X_n) \le El(X_1, X_2, \ldots, X_n) < H(X_1, X_2, \ldots, X_n) + 1 .$$

$$(5.38)$$

Dividing by n again and defining L_n to be the expected description length per symbol, we obtain

$$\frac{H(X_1, X_2, \ldots, X_n)}{n} \le L_n < \frac{H(X_1, X_2, \ldots, X_n)}{n} + \frac{1}{n} . \qquad (5.39)$$

If the stochastic process is stationary, then $H(X_1, X_2, \ldots, X_n)/n \to H(\mathcal{X})$, and the expected description length tends to the entropy rate as $n \to \infty$. Thus we have the following theorem:

Theorem 5.4.2: *The minimum expected codeword length per symbol satisfies*

$$\frac{H(X_1, X_2, \ldots, X_n)}{n} \le L_n^* < \frac{H(X_1, X_2, \ldots, X_n)}{n} + \frac{1}{n} . \qquad (5.40)$$

Moreover, if $X_1, X_2, \ldots, X_n$ is a stationary stochastic process,

$$L_n^* \to H(\mathcal{X}) , \qquad (5.41)$$

where $H(\mathcal{X})$ is the entropy rate of the process.

This theorem provides another justification for the definition of entropy rate—it is the expected number of bits per symbol required to describe the process.

Finally, we ask what happens to the expected description length if the code is designed for the wrong distribution. For example, the wrong distribution may be the best estimate that we can make of the unknown true distribution.

We consider the Shannon code assignment $l(x) = \lceil \log \frac{1}{q(x)} \rceil$ designed for the probability mass function $q(x)$. Suppose the true probability mass function is $p(x)$. Thus we will not achieve expected length $L \approx H(p) = -\sum p(x) \log p(x)$. We now show that the increase in expected description length due to the incorrect distribution is the relative entropy $D(p \| q)$. Thus $D(p \| q)$ has a concrete interpretation as the increase in descriptive complexity due to incorrect information.

Theorem 5.4.3: *The expected length under $p(x)$ of the code assignment $l(x) = \lceil \log \frac{1}{q(x)} \rceil$ satisfies*

$$H(p) + D(p \| q) \le E_p l(X) < H(p) + D(p \| q) + 1 . \qquad (5.42)$$

Proof: The expected codelength is

$$El(X) = \sum_x p(x) \left\lceil \log \frac{1}{q(x)} \right\rceil \tag{5.43}$$

$$< \sum_x p(x) \left(\log \frac{1}{q(x)} + 1 \right) \tag{5.44}$$

$$= \sum_x p(x) \log \frac{p(x)}{q(x)} \frac{1}{p(x)} + 1 \tag{5.45}$$

$$= \sum_x p(x) \log \frac{p(x)}{q(x)} + \sum_x p(x) \log \frac{1}{p(x)} + 1 \tag{5.46}$$

$$= D(p\|q) + H(p) + 1. \tag{5.47}$$

The lower bound can be derived similarly. $\square$

Thus using the wrong distribution incurs a penalty of $D(p\|q)$ in the average description length.

5.5 KRAFT INEQUALITY FOR UNIQUELY DECODABLE CODES

We have proved that any instantaneous code must satisfy the Kraft inequality. The class of uniquely decodable codes is larger than the class of instantaneous codes, so one expects to achieve a lower expected codeword length if L is minimized over all uniquely decodable codes. In this section, we prove that the class of uniquely decodable codes does not offer any further possibilities for the set of codeword lengths than do instantaneous codes. We now give Karush's elegant proof of the following theorem.

Theorem 5.5.1 (*McMillan*): *The codeword lengths of any uniquely decodable code must satisfy the Kraft inequality*

$$\sum D^{-l_i} \le 1. \tag{5.48}$$

Conversely, given a set of codeword lengths that satisfy this inequality, it is possible to construct a uniquely decodable code with these codeword lengths.

Proof: Consider C^k, the kth extension of the code, i.e., the code formed by the concatenation of k repetitions of the given uniquely decodable code C. By the definition of unique decodability, the kth extension of the code is non-singular. Since there are only D^n different D-ary strings of length n, unique decodability implies that the number of code sequences of length n in the kth extension of the code must be no greater than D^n. We now use this observation to prove the Kraft inequality.

Let the codeword lengths of the symbols $x \in \mathscr{X}$ be denoted by $l(x)$. For the extension code, the length of the code-sequence is

$$l(x_1, x_2, \ldots, x_k) = \sum_{i=1}^{k} l(x_i). \qquad (5.49)$$

The inequality that we wish to prove is

$$\sum_{x \in \mathscr{X}} D^{-l(x)} \leq 1. \qquad (5.50)$$

The trick is to consider the kth power of this quantity. Thus

$$\left(\sum_{x \in \mathscr{X}} D^{-l(x)} \right)^k = \sum_{x_1 \in \mathscr{X}} \sum_{x_2 \in \mathscr{X}} \cdots \sum_{x_k \in \mathscr{X}} D^{-l(x_1)} D^{-l(x_2)} \cdots D^{-l(x_k)} \qquad (5.51)$$

$$= \sum_{x_1, x_2, \ldots, x_k \in \mathscr{X}^k} D^{-l(x_1)} D^{-l(x_2)} \cdots D^{-l(x_k)} \qquad (5.52)$$

$$= \sum_{x^k \in \mathscr{X}^k} D^{-l(x^k)}, \qquad (5.53)$$

by (5.49). We now gather the terms by word lengths to obtain

$$\sum_{x^k \in \mathscr{X}^k} D^{-l(x^k)} = \sum_{m=1}^{kl_{\max}} a(m) D^{-m}, \qquad (5.54)$$

where $l_{\max}$ is the maximum codeword length and $a(m)$ is the number of source sequences x^k mapping into codewords of length m. But the code is uniquely decodable, so there is at most one sequence mapping into each code m-sequence and there are at most D^m code m-sequences. Thus $a(m) \leq D^m$, and we have

$$\left(\sum_{x \in \mathscr{X}} D^{-l(x)} \right)^k = \sum_{m=1}^{kl_{\max}} a(m) D^{-m} \qquad (5.55)$$

$$\leq \sum_{m=1}^{kl_{\max}} D^m D^{-m} \qquad (5.56)$$

$$= kl_{\max} \qquad (5.57)$$

and hence

$$\sum_{j} D^{-l_j} \leq \left(kl_{\max} \right)^{1/k}. \qquad (5.58)$$

Since this inequality is true for all k, it is true in the limit as $k \to \infty$. Since $(k l_{max})^{1/k} \to 1$, we have

$$\sum_j D^{-l_j} \le 1 , \tag{5.59}$$

which is the Kraft inequality.

Conversely, given any set of $l_1, l_2, \ldots, l_m$ satisfying the Kraft inequality, we can construct an instantaneous code as proved in Section 5.2. Since every instantaneous code is uniquely decodable, we have also constructed a uniquely decodable code. ☐

Corollary: *A uniquely decodable code for an infinite source alphabet $\mathcal{X}$ also satisfies the Kraft inequality.*

Proof: The point at which the preceding proof breaks down for infinite $|\mathcal{X}|$ is at (5.58), since for an infinite code l_{max} is infinite. But there is a simple fix to the proof. Any subset of a uniquely decodable code is also uniquely decodable; hence, any finite subset of the infinite set of codewords satisfies the Kraft inequality. Hence,

$$\sum_{i=1}^{\infty} D^{-l_i} = \lim_{N \to \infty} \sum_{i=1}^{N} D^{-l_i} \le 1 . \tag{5.60}$$

Given a set of word lengths $l_1, l_2, \ldots$ that satisfy the Kraft inequality, we can construct an instantaneous code as in the last section. Since instantaneous codes are uniquely decodable, we have constructed a uniquely decodable code with an infinite number of codewords. So the McMillan theorem also applies to infinite alphabets. ☐

The theorem implies a rather surprising result—that the class of uniquely decodable codes does not offer any further choices for the set of codeword lengths than the class of prefix codes. The set of achievable codeword lengths is the same for uniquely decodable and instantaneous codes. Hence the bounds derived on the optimal codeword lengths continue to hold even when we expand the class of allowed codes to the class of all uniquely decodable codes.

5.6 HUFFMAN CODES

An optimal (shortest expected length) prefix code for a given distribution can be constructed by a simple algorithm discovered by Huffman [138]. We will prove that any other code for the same alphabet cannot have a lower expected length than the code constructed by the algorithm. Before we give any formal proofs, let us introduce Huffman codes with some examples:

Example 5.6.1: Consider a random variable X taking values in the set $\mathscr{X} = \{1, 2, 3, 4, 5\}$ with probabilities 0.25, 0.25, 0.2, 0.15, 0.15, respectively. We expect the optimal binary code for X to have the longest codewords assigned to the symbols 4 and 5. Both these lengths must be equal, since otherwise we can delete a bit from the longer codeword and still have a prefix code, but with a shorter expected length. In general, we can construct a code in which the two longest codewords differ only in the last bit. For this code, we can combine the symbols 4 and 5 together into a single source symbol, with a probability assignment 0.30. Proceeding this way, combining the two least likely symbols into one symbol, until we are finally left with only one symbol, and then assigning codewords to the symbols, we obtain the following table:

Codeword length	Codeword	X	Probability			
2	01	1	0.25	0.3	0.45	0.55 ⟶ 1
2	10	2	0.25	0.25	0.3	0.45
2	11	3	0.2	0.25	0.25	
3	000	4	0.15	0.2		
3	001	5	0.15			

This code has average length 2.3 bits.

Example 5.6.2: Consider a ternary code for the same random variable. Now we combine the three least likely symbols into one supersymbol and obtain the following table:

Codeword	X	Probability		
1	1	0.25	0.5 ⟶ 1
2	2	0.25	0.25
00	3	0.2	0.25
01	4	0.15	
02	5	0.15	

This code has an average length of 1.5 ternary digits.

Example 5.6.3: If $D \geq 3$, we may not have a sufficient number of symbols so that we can combine them D at a time. In such a case, we add dummy symbols to the end of the set of symbols. The dummy symbols have probability 0 and are inserted to fill the tree. Since at each stage of the reduction, the number of symbols is reduced by $D - 1$, we want the total number of symbols to be $1 + k(D - 1)$, where k is the number of levels in the tree. Hence, we add enough dummy symbols so that the total number of symbols is of this form. For example:

Codeword	X	Probability			
1	1	0.25	0.25	0.5	1.0
2	2	0.25	0.25	0.25	
01	3	0.2	0.2	0.25	
02	4	0.1	0.2		
000	5	0.1	0.1		
001	6	0.1			
002	Dummy	0.0			

This code has an average length of 1.7 ternary digits.

A proof of the optimality of Huffman coding will be given in Section 5.8.

5.7 SOME COMMENTS ON HUFFMAN CODES

1. **Equivalence of source coding and 20 questions.** We now digress to show the equivalence of coding and the game of 20 questions.

    Supposing we wish to find the most efficient series of yes-no questions to determine an object from a class of objects. Assuming we know the probability distribution on the objects, can we find the most efficient sequence of questions?

    We first show that a sequence of questions is equivalent to a code for the object. Any question depends only on the answers to the questions before it. Since the sequence of answers uniquely determines the object, each object has a different sequence of answers, and if we represent the yes-no answers by 0's and 1's, we have a binary code for the set of objects. The average length of this code is the average number of questions for the questioning scheme.

    Also, from a binary code for the set of objects, we can find a sequence of questions that correspond to the code, with the average number of questions equal to the expected codeword length of the code. The first question in this scheme becomes "Is the first bit equal to 1 in the object's codeword?"

    Since the Huffman code is the best source code for a random variable, the optimal series of questions is that determined by the Huffman code. In Example 5.6.1, the optimal first question is "Is X

equal to 2 or 3?" The answer to this determines the first bit of the Huffman code. Assuming the answer to the first question is "Yes," the next question should be "Is X equal to 3?" which determines the second bit. However, we need not wait for the answer to the first question to ask the second. We can ask as our second question "Is X equal to 1 or 3?" determining the second bit of the Huffman code independently of the first.

The expected number of questions EQ in this optimal scheme satisfies

$$H(X) \le EQ < H(X) + 1 . \tag{5.61}$$

2. **Huffman coding for weighted codewords.** Huffman's algorithm for minimizing $\Sigma \, p_i l_i$ can be applied to any set of numbers $p_i \ge 0$, regardless of $\Sigma \, p_i$. In this case, the Huffman code minimizes the sum of weighted codelengths $\Sigma \, w_i l_i$ rather than the average codelength.

Example 5.7.1: We perform the weighted minimization using the same algorithm.

X	Codeword	Weights
1	00	5 ⟋ 8 ⟋ 10 — 18
2	01	5 ⟍ 5 ⟍ 8
3	10	4 ⟋ 5
4	11	4

In this case the code minimizes the weighted sum of the codeword lengths, and the minimum weighted sum is 36.

3. **Huffman coding and "slice" questions.** We have described the equivalence of source coding with the game of 20 questions. The optimal sequence of questions corresponds to an optimal source code for the random variable. However, Huffman codes ask arbitrary questions of the form "Is $X \in A$?" for any set $A \subseteq \{1, 2, \ldots, m\}$.

Now we consider the game of 20 questions with a restricted set of questions. Specifically, we assume that the elements of $\mathscr{X} = \{1, 2, \ldots, m\}$ are ordered so that $p_1 \ge p_2 \ge \cdots \ge p_m$ and that the only questions allowed are of the form "Is $X > a$?" for some a.

The Huffman code constructed by the Huffman algorithm may not correspond to "slices" (sets of the form $\{x : x < a\}$). If we take the codeword lengths $(l_1 \le l_2 \le \cdots \le l_m$, by Lemma 5.8.1) derived from the Huffman code and use them to assign the symbols to the code tree by taking the first available node at the corresponding level, we will construct another optimal code. However, unlike the Huffman code itself, this code is a "slice" code, since each question (each bit of the code) splits the tree into sets of the form $\{x : x > a\}$ and $\{x : x < a\}$.

We illustrate this with an example.

Example 5.7.2: Consider the first example of Section 5.6. The code that was constructed by the Huffman coding procedure is not a "slice" code. But using the codeword lengths from the Huffman procedure, namely, $\{2, 2, 2, 3, 3\}$, and assigning the symbols to the first available node on the tree, we obtain the following code for this random variable:

$$1 \rightarrow 00, \quad 2 \rightarrow 01, \quad 3 \rightarrow 10, \quad 4 \rightarrow 110, \quad 5 \rightarrow 111$$

It can be verified that this code is a "slice" code. These "slice" codes are known as *alphabetic codes* because the codewords are alphabetically ordered.

4. **Huffman codes and Shannon codes.** Using codeword lengths of $\lceil \log \frac{1}{p_i} \rceil$ (which is called Shannon coding) may be much worse than the optimal code for some particular symbol. For example, consider two symbols, one of which occurs with probability 0.9999 and the other with probability 0.0001. Then using codeword lengths of $\lceil \log \frac{1}{p_i} \rceil$ implies using codeword lengths of 1 bit and 14 bits respectively. The optimal codeword length is obviously 1 bit for both symbols. Hence, the code for the infrequent symbol is much longer in the Shannon code than in the optimal code.

Is it true that the codeword lengths for an optimal code are always less than $\lceil \log \frac{1}{p_i} \rceil$? The following example illustrates that this is not always true.

Example 5.7.3: Consider a random variable X with a distribution $(\frac{1}{3}, \frac{1}{3}, \frac{1}{4}, \frac{1}{12})$. The Huffman coding procedure results in codeword lengths of $(2, 2, 2, 2)$ or $(1, 2, 3, 3)$ (depending on where one puts the merged probabilities, as the reader can verify). Both these codes achieve the same expected codeword length. In the second code, the third symbol has length 3, which is greater than $\lceil \log \frac{1}{p_3} \rceil$. Thus the codeword length for a Shannon code could be less than the codeword length of the corresponding symbol of an optimal (Huffman) code.

This example also illustrates the fact that the set of codeword lengths for an optimal code is not unique (there may be more than one set of lengths with the same expected value).

Although either the Shannon code or the Huffman code can be shorter for individual symbols, the Huffman code is shorter on the average. Also, the Shannon code and the Huffman code differ by less than one bit in expected codelength (since both lie between H and $H + 1$.)

5. **Fano codes.** Fano proposed a suboptimal procedure for constructing a source code, which is similar to the idea of slice codes. In his method, we first order the probabilities in decreasing order. Then we choose k such that $|\Sigma_{i=1}^k p_i - \Sigma_{i=k+1}^m p_i|$ is minimized. This point divides the source symbols into two sets of almost equal probability. Assign 0 for the first bit of the upper set and 1 for the lower set. Repeat this process for each subset. By this recursive procedure, we obtain a code for each source symbol. This scheme, though not optimal in general, achieves $L(C) \le H(X) + 2$. (See [137].)

5.8   OPTIMALITY OF HUFFMAN CODES

We prove by induction that the binary Huffman code is optimal. It is important to remember that there are many optimal codes: inverting all the bits or exchanging two codewords of the same length will give another optimal code. The Huffman procedure constructs one such optimal code. To prove the optimality of Huffman codes, we first prove some properties of a particular optimal code.

Without loss of generality, we will assume that the probability masses are ordered, so that $p_1 \ge p_2 \ge \cdots > p_m$. Recall that a code is optimal if $\Sigma\, p_i l_i$ is minimal.

Lemma 5.8.1: *For any distribution, there exists an optimal instantaneous code (with minimum expected length) that satisfies the following properties:*

1. *If $p_j > p_k$, then $l_j \le l_k$.*
2. *The two longest codewords have the same length.*
3. *The two longest codewords differ only in the last bit and correspond to the two least likely symbols.*

Proof: The proof amounts to swapping, trimming and rearranging, as shown in Figure 5.3. Consider an optimal code C_m:

- *If $p_j > p_k$, then $l_j \le l_k$.* Here we swap codewords.
  Consider C'_m, with the codewords j and k of C_m interchanged. Then

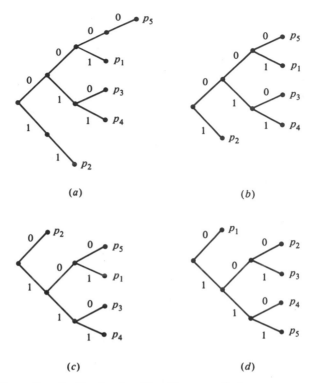

Figure 5.3. Properties of optimal codes. We will assume that $p_1 \geq p_2 \geq \cdots \geq p_m$. A possible instantaneous code is given in (a). By trimming branches without siblings, we improve the code to (b). We now rearrange the tree as shown in (c) so that the word lengths are ordered by increasing length from top to bottom. Finally, we swap probability assignments to improve the expected depth of the tree as shown in (d). Thus every optimal code can be rearranged and swapped into the canonical form (d). Note that $l_1 \leq l_2 \leq \cdots \leq l_m$, that $l_{m-1} = l_m$, and the last two codewords differ only in the last bit.

$$L(C_m') - L(C_m) = \sum p_i l_i' - \sum p_i l_i \qquad (5.62)$$

$$= p_j l_k + p_k l_j - p_j l_j - p_k l_k \qquad (5.63)$$

$$= (p_j - p_k)(l_k - l_j). \qquad (5.64)$$

But $p_j - p_k > 0$, and since C_m is optimal, $L(C_m') - L(C_m) \geq 0$. Hence we must have $l_k \geq l_j$. Thus C_m itself satisfies property 1.

- *The two longest codewords are of the same length.* Here we trim the codewords.

  If the two longest codewords are not of the same length, then one can delete the last bit of the longer one, preserving the prefix property and achieving lower expected codeword length. Hence the two longest codewords must have the same length. By property 1, the longest codewords must belong to the least probable source symbols.

- *The two longest codewords differ only in the last bit and correspond to the two least likely symbols.* Not all optimal codes satisfy this property, but by rearranging, we can find a code that does.

If there is a maximal length codeword without a sibling, then we can delete the last bit of the codeword and still satisfy the prefix property. This reduces the average codeword length and contradicts the optimality of the code. Hence every maximal length codeword in any optimal code has a sibling.

Now we can exchange the longest length codewords so the two lowest probability source symbols are associated with two siblings on the tree. This does not change the expected length $\Sigma\, p_i l_i$. Thus the codewords for the two lowest probability source symbols have maximal length and agree in all but the last bit.

Summarizing, we have shown that if $p_1 \geq p_2 \geq \cdots \geq p_m$, then there exists an optimal code with $l_1 \leq l_2 \leq \cdots \leq l_{m-1} = l_m$, and codewords $C(x_{m-1})$ and $C(x_m)$ that differ only in the last bit. $\square$

Thus we have shown that there exists an optimal code satisfying the properties of the lemma. We can now restrict our search to codes that satisfy these properties.

For a code C_m satisfying the properties of the lemma, we now define a "merged" code C_{m-1} for $m-1$ symbols as follows: take the common prefix of the two longest codewords (corresponding to the two least likely symbols), and allot it to a symbol with probability $p_{m-1} + p_m$. All the other codewords remain the same. The correspondence is shown in the following:

$$
\begin{array}{ccccc}
 & \multicolumn{2}{c}{C_{m-1}} & \multicolumn{2}{c}{C_m} \\
p_1 & w_1' & l_1' & w_1 = w_1' & l_1 = l_1' \\
p_2 & w_2' & l_2' & w_2 = w_2' & l_2 = l_2' \\
\vdots & \vdots & \vdots & \vdots & \vdots \\
p_{m-2} & w_{m-2}' & l_{m-2}' & w_{m-2} = w_{m-2}' & l_{m-2} = l_{m-2}' \\
p_{m-1} + p_m & w_{m-1}' & l_{m-1}' & w_{m-1} = w_{m-1}'0 & l_{m-1} = l_{m-1}' + 1 \\
 & & & w_m = w_{m-1}'1 & l_m = l_{m-1}' + 1
\end{array}
\tag{5.65}
$$

where w denotes a binary codeword and l denotes its length. The expected length of the code C_m is

$$
L(C_m) = \sum_{i=1}^{m} p_i l_i
\tag{5.66}
$$

$$= \sum_{i=1}^{m-2} p_i l_i' + p_{m-1}(l_{m-1}' + 1) + p_m(l_{m-1}' + 1) \tag{5.67}$$

$$= \sum_{i=1}^{m-1} p_i l_i' + p_{m-1} + p_m \tag{5.68}$$

$$= L(C_{m-1}) + p_{m-1} + p_m . \tag{5.69}$$

Thus the expected length of the code C_m differs from the expected length of C_{m-1} by a fixed amount independent of C_{m-1}. Thus minimizing the expected length $L(C_m)$ is equivalent to minimizing $L(C_{m-1})$. Thus we have reduced the problem to one with $m-1$ symbols and probability masses $(p_1, p_2, \ldots, p_{m-2}, p_{m-1} + p_m)$. This step is illustrated in Figure 5.4. We again look for a code which satisfies the properties of Lemma 5.8.1 for these $m-1$ symbols and then reduce the problem to finding the optimal code for $m-2$ symbols with the appropriate probability masses obtained by merging the two lowest probabilities on the previous merged list. Proceeding this way, we finally reduce the problem to two symbols, for which the solution is obvious, i.e., allot 0 for one of the symbols and 1 for the other. Since we have maintained optimality at

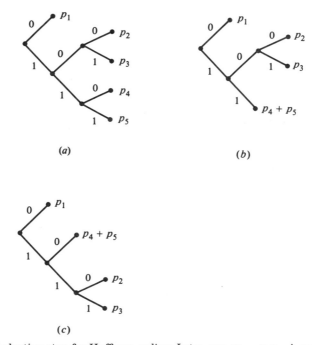

(a)   (b)

(c)

Figure 5.4. Induction step for Huffman coding. Let $p_1 \geq p_1 \geq \cdots \geq p_5$. A canonical optimal code is illustrated in (a). Combining the two lowest probabilities, we obtain the code in (b). Rearranging the probabilities in decreasing order, we obtain the canonical code in (c) for $m-1$ symbols.

every stage in the reduction, the code constructed for m symbols is optimal. Thus we have proved the following theorem for binary alphabets.

Theorem 5.8.1: *Huffman coding is optimal, i.e., if C^* is the Huffman code and C' is any other code, then $L(C^*) \leq L(C')$.*

Although we have proved the theorem for a binary alphabet, the proof can be extended to establishing optimality of the Huffman coding algorithm for a D-ary alphabet as well. Incidentally, we should remark that Huffman coding is a "greedy" algorithm in that it coalesces the two least likely symbols at each stage. The above proof shows that this local optimality ensures a global optimality of the final code.

5.9   SHANNON-FANO-ELIAS CODING

In Section 5.4, we showed that the set of lengths $l(x) = \lceil \log \frac{1}{p(x)} \rceil$ satisfies the Kraft inequality and can therefore be used to construct a uniquely decodable code for the source. In this section, we describe a simple constructive procedure which uses the cumulative distribution function to allot codewords.

Without loss of generality we can take $\mathcal{X} = \{1, 2, \ldots, m\}$. Assume $p(x) > 0$ for all x. The cumulative distribution function $F(x)$ is defined as

$$F(x) = \sum_{a \leq x} p(a) . \tag{5.70}$$

This function is illustrated in Figure 5.5. Consider the modified cumulative distribution function

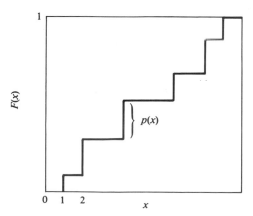

Figure 5.5. Cumulative distribution function and Shannon-Fano-Elias coding.

$$\bar{F}(x) = \sum_{a<x} p(a) + \frac{1}{2} p(x), \qquad (5.71)$$

where $\bar{F}(x)$ denotes the sum of the probabilities of all symbols less than x plus half the probability of the symbol x. Since the random variable is discrete, the cumulative distribution function consists of steps of size $p(x)$. The value of the function $\bar{F}(x)$ is the midpoint of the step corresponding to x.

Since all the probabilities are positive, $F(a) \neq F(b)$ if $a \neq b$, and hence we can determine x if we know $\bar{F}(x)$. Merely look at the graph of the cumulative distribution function and find the corresponding x. Thus the value of $\bar{F}(x)$ can be used as a code for x.

But in general $\bar{F}(x)$ is a real number expressible only by an infinite number of bits. So it is not efficient to use the exact value of $\bar{F}(x)$ as a code for x. If we use an approximate value, what is the required accuracy?

Assume that we round off $\bar{F}(x)$ to $l(x)$ bits (denoted by $\lfloor \bar{F}(x) \rfloor_{l(x)}$). Thus we use the first $l(x)$ bits of $\bar{F}(x)$ as a code for x. By definition of rounding off, we have

$$\bar{F}(x) - \lfloor \bar{F}(x) \rfloor_{l(x)} < \frac{1}{2^{l(x)}}. \qquad (5.72)$$

If $l(x) = \lceil \log \frac{1}{p(x)} \rceil + 1$, then

$$\frac{1}{2^{l(x)}} < \frac{p(x)}{2} = \bar{F}(x) - F(x-1), \qquad (5.73)$$

and therefore $\lfloor \bar{F}(x) \rfloor_{l(x)}$ lies within the step corresponding to x. Thus $l(x)$ bits suffice to describe x.

In addition to requiring that the codeword identify the corresponding symbol, we also require the set of codewords to be prefix-free. To check whether the code is prefix-free, we consider each codeword $z_1 z_2 \ldots z_l$ to represent not a point but the interval $[0.z_1 z_2 \ldots z_l, 0.z_1 z_2 \ldots z_l + \frac{1}{2^l}]$. The code is prefix-free if and only if the intervals corresponding to codewords are disjoint.

We now verify that the code above is prefix-free. The interval corresponding to any codeword has length $2^{-l(x)}$, which is less than half the height of the step corresponding to x by (5.73). The lower end of the interval is in the lower half of the step. Thus the upper end of the interval lies below the top of the step, and the interval corresponding to any codeword lies entirely within the step corresponding to that symbol in the cumulative distribution function. Therefore the intervals corresponding to different codewords are disjoint and the code is prefix-free.

Note that this procedure does not require the symbols to be ordered in terms of probability. Another procedure that uses the ordered probabilities is described in Problem 25 at the end of the chapter.

Since we use $l(x) = \lceil \log \frac{1}{p(x)} \rceil + 1$ bits to represent x, the expected length of this code is

$$L = \sum_x p(x)l(x) = \sum_x p(x)\left(\left\lceil \log \frac{1}{p(x)} \right\rceil + 1\right) < H(X) + 2 . \qquad (5.74)$$

Thus this coding scheme achieves an average codeword length that is within two bits of the entropy.

Example 5.9.1: We first consider an example where all the probabilities are dyadic. We construct the code in the following table:

x	$p(x)$	$F(x)$	$\bar{F}(x)$	$\bar{F}(x)$ in binary	$l(x) = \lceil \log \frac{1}{p(x)} \rceil + 1$	Codeword
1	0.25	0.25	0.125	0.001	3	001
2	0.5	0.75	0.5	0.10	2	10
3	0.125	0.875	0.8125	0.1101	4	1101
4	0.125	1.0	0.9375	0.1111	4	1111

In this case, the average codeword length is 2.75 bits while the entropy is 1.75 bits. The Huffman code for this case achieves the entropy bound. Looking at the codewords, it is obvious that there is some inefficiency—for example, the last bit of the last two codewords can be omitted. But if we remove the last bit from all the codewords, the code is no longer prefix free.

Example 5.9.2: We now give another example for the construction for the Shannon-Fano-Elias code. In this case, since the distribution is not dyadic, the representation of $F(x)$ in binary may have an infinite number of bits. We denote 0.01010101 ... by $0.\overline{01}$.

We construct the code in the following table:

x	$p(x)$	$F(x)$	$\bar{F}(x)$	$\bar{F}(x)$ in binary	$l(x) = \left\lceil \log \frac{1}{p(x)} \right\rceil + 1$	Codeword
1	0.25	0.25	0.125	0.001	3	001
2	0.25	0.5	0.375	0.011	3	011
3	0.2	0.7	0.6	0.10$\overline{011}$	4	1001
4	0.15	0.85	0.775	0.110$\overline{0011}$	4	1100
5	0.15	1.0	0.925	0.1110$\overline{110}$	4	1110

The above code is 1.2 bits longer on the average than the Huffman code for this source (Example 5.6.1).

In the next section, we extend the concept of Shannon-Fano-Elias coding and describe a computationally efficient algorithm for encoding and decoding called arithmetic coding.

5.10 ARITHMETIC CODING

From the discussion of the previous sections, it is apparent that using a codeword length of $\log \frac{1}{p(x)}$ for the codeword corresponding to x is nearly optimal in that it has an expected length within 1 bit of the entropy. The optimal codes are Huffman codes, and these can be constructed by the procedure described in Section 5.6.

For small source alphabets, though, we have efficient coding only if we use long blocks of source symbols. For example, if the source is binary, and we code each symbol separately, we must use 1 bit per symbol irrespective of the entropy of the source. If we use long blocks, we can achieve an expected length per symbol close to the entropy rate of the source.

It is therefore desirable to have an efficient coding procedure that works for long blocks of source symbols. Huffman coding is not ideal for this situation, since it is a bottom-up procedure that requires the calculation of the probabilities of all source sequences of a particular block length and the construction of the corresponding complete code tree. We are then limited to using that block length. A better scheme is one which can be easily extended to longer block lengths without having to redo all the calculations. Arithmetic coding, a direct extension of the Shannon-Fano-Elias coding scheme of the last section, achieves this goal.

The essential idea of arithmetic coding is to efficiently calculate the probability mass function $p(x^n)$ and the cumulative distribution function $F(x^n)$ for the source sequence x^n. Using the ideas of Shannon-Fano-Elias coding, we can use a number in the interval $(F(x^n) - p(x^n), F(x^n)]$ as the code for x^n. For example, expressing $F(x^n)$ to an accuracy of $\lceil \log \frac{1}{p(x^n)} \rceil$ will give us a code for the source. Using the same arguments as in the discussion of the Shannon-Fano-Elias code, it follows that the codeword corresponding to any sequence lies within the step in the cumulative distribution function (Figure 5.5) corresponding to that sequence. So the codewords for different sequences of length n are different. However, the procedure does *not* guarantee that the set of codewords is prefix-free. We can construct a prefix-free set by using $\bar{F}(x)$ rounded off to $\lceil \log \frac{1}{p(x)} \rceil + 1$ bits as in Section 5.9. In the algorithm described below, we will keep track of both $F(x^n)$ and $p(x^n)$ in the course of the algorithm, so we can calculate $\bar{F}(x)$ easily at any stage.

We now describe a simplified version of the arithmetic coding algorithm to illustrate some of the important ideas. We assume that we have a fixed block length n that is known to both the encoder and the decoder. With a small loss of generality, we will assume that the source alphabet is binary. We assume that we have a simple procedure to calculate $p(x_1, x_2, \ldots, x_n)$ for any string $x_1, x_2, \ldots, x_n$. We will use the natural lexicographic order on strings, so that a string x is greater than a string y if $x_i = 1$, $y_i = 0$ for the first i such that $x_i \neq y_i$. Equivalently, $x > y$ if $\Sigma_i x_i 2^{-i} > \Sigma_i y_i 2^{-i}$, i.e., if the corresponding binary numbers satisfy $0.x > 0.y$. We can arrange the strings as the leaves of a tree of depth n, where each level of the tree corresponds to one bit. Such a tree is illustrated in Figure 5.6. In this figure, the ordering $x > y$ corresponds to the fact that x is to the right of y on the same level of the tree.

From the discussion of the last section, it appears that we need to find $p(y^n)$ for all $y^n \leq x^n$ and use that to calculate $F(x^n)$. Looking at the tree, we might suspect that we need to calculate the probabilities of all the leaves to the left of x^n to find $F(x^n)$. The sum of these probabilities is the sum of the probabilities of all the subtrees to the left of x^n. Let $T_{x_1 x_2 \cdots x_{k-1} 0}$ be a subtree starting with $x_1 x_2 \cdots x_{k-1} 0$. The probability of this subtree is

$$p(T_{x_1 x_2 \cdots x_{k-1} 0}) = \sum_{y_{k+1} \cdots y_n} p(x_1 x_2 \cdots x_{k-1} 0 y_{k+1} \cdots y_n) \qquad (5.75)$$

$$= p(x_1 x_2 \cdots x_{k-1} 0), \qquad (5.76)$$

and hence can be calculated easily. Therefore we can rewrite $F(x^n)$ as

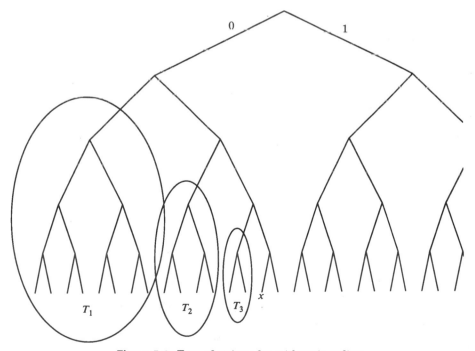

Figure 5.6. Tree of strings for arithmetic coding.

$$F(x^n) = \sum_{y^n \leq x^n} p(y^n) \tag{5.77}$$

$$= \sum_{T \,:\, T \text{ is to the left of } x^n} p(T) \tag{5.78}$$

$$= \sum_{k \,:\, x_k = 1} p(x_1 x_2 \cdots x_{k-1} 0). \tag{5.79}$$

Thus we can calculate $F(x^n)$ quickly from $p(x^n)$.

Example 5.10.1: If $X_1, X_2, \ldots, X_n$ are Bernoulli(θ) in Figure 5.6, then

$$F(01110) = p(T_1) + p(T_2) + p(T_3) = p(00) + p(010) + p(0110) \tag{5.80}$$

$$= (1 - \theta)^2 + \theta(1 - \theta)^2 + \theta^2(1 - \theta)^2. \tag{5.81}$$

Note that these terms can be calculated recursively. For example, $\theta^3(1 - \theta)^3 = (\theta^2(1 - \theta)^2)\theta(1 - \theta)$.

To encode the next bit of the source sequence, we need only calculate $p(x^i x_{i+1})$ and update $F(x^i x_{i+1})$ using the above scheme. Encoding can therefore be done sequentially, by looking at the bits as they come in.

To decode the sequence, we use the same procedure to calculate the cumulative distribution function and check whether it exceeds the value corresponding to the codeword. We then use the tree in Figure 5.6 as a decision tree. At the top node, we check to see if the received codeword $F(x^n)$ is greater than $p(0)$. If it is, then the subtree starting with 0 is to the left of x^n and hence $x_1 = 1$. Continuing this process down the tree, we can decode the bits in sequence. Thus we can compress and decompress a source sequence in a sequential manner.

The above procedure depends on a model for which we can easily compute $p(x^n)$. Two examples of such models are i.i.d. sources, where

$$p(x^n) = \prod_{i=1}^{n} p(x_i). \tag{5.82}$$

and Markov sources, where

$$p(x^n) = p(x_1) \prod_{i=2}^{n} p(x_i | x_{i-1}). \tag{5.83}$$

In both cases, we can easily calculate $p(x^n x_{n+1})$ from $p(x^n)$.

Note that it is not essential that the probabilities used in the encoding be equal to the true distribution of the source. In some cases, such as in image compression, it is difficult to describe a "true" distribution for the source. Even then, it is possible to apply the above arithmetic coding procedure. The procedure will be efficient only if the model distribution is close to the empirical distribution of the source (Theorem 5.4.3). A more sophisticated use of arithmetic coding is to change the model dynamically to adapt to the source. Adaptive models work well for large classes of sources. The adaptive version of arithmetic coding is a simple example of a universal code, that is, a code that is designed to work with an arbitrary source distribution. Another example is the Lempel-Ziv code, which is discussed in Section 12.10.

The foregoing discussion of arithmetic coding has avoided discussion of the difficult implementation issues of computational accuracy, buffer sizes, etc. An introduction to some of these issues can be found in the tutorial introduction to arithmetic coding by Langdon [170].

5.11   COMPETITIVE OPTIMALITY OF THE SHANNON CODE

We have shown that Huffman coding is optimal in that it has minimum expected length. But what does that say about its performance on any particular sequence? For example, is it always better than any other code for all sequences? Obviously not, since there are codes which assign short codewords to infrequent source symbols. Such codes will be better than the Huffman code on those source symbols.

To formalize the question of competitive optimality, consider the following two-person zero sum game: Two people are given a probability distribution and are asked to design an instantaneous code for the distribution. Then a source symbol is drawn from this distribution and the payoff to player A is 1 or -1 depending on whether the codeword of player A is shorter or longer than the codeword of player B. The payoff is 0 for ties.

Dealing with Huffman codelengths is difficult, since there is no explicit expression for the codeword lengths. Instead, we will consider the Shannon code with codeword lengths $l(x) = \lceil \log \frac{1}{p(x)} \rceil$. In this case, we have the following theorem:

Theorem 5.11.1: *Let $l(x)$ be the codeword lengths associated with the Shannon code and let $l'(x)$ be the codeword lengths associated with any other code. Then*

$$\Pr(l(X) \geq l'(X) + c) \leq \frac{1}{2^{c-1}} . \tag{5.84}$$

Thus, for example, the probability that $l'(X)$ is 5 or more bits shorter than $l(X)$ is less than $\frac{1}{16}$.

Proof:

$$\Pr(l(X) \geq l'(X) + c) = \Pr\left(\left\lceil \log \frac{1}{p(X)} \right\rceil \geq l'(X) + c\right) \quad (5.85)$$

$$\leq \Pr\left(\log \frac{1}{p(X)} \geq l'(X) + c - 1\right) \quad (5.86)$$

$$= \Pr(p(X) \leq 2^{-l'(X)-c+1}) \quad (5.87)$$

$$= \sum_{x \,:\, p(x) \leq 2^{-l'(x)-c+1}} p(x) \quad (5.88)$$

$$\leq \sum_{x \,:\, p(x) \leq 2^{-l'(x)-c+1}} 2^{-l'(x)-(c-1)} \quad (5.89)$$

$$\leq \sum_x 2^{-l'(x)} 2^{-(c-1)} \quad (5.90)$$

$$\leq 2^{-(c-1)}, \quad (5.91)$$

since $\sum 2^{-l'(x)} \leq 1$ by the Kraft inequality. $\square$

Hence, no other code can do much better than the Shannon code most of the time.

We now strengthen this result in two ways. First, there is the term $+1$ that has been added, which makes the result non-symmetric. Also, in a game theoretic setting, one would like to ensure that $l(x) < l'(x)$ more often than $l(x) > l'(x)$. The fact that $l(x) \leq l'(x) + 1$ with probability $\geq \frac{1}{2}$ does not ensure this. We now show that even under this stricter criterion, Shannon coding is optimal. Recall that the probability mass function $p(x)$ is dyadic if $\log \frac{1}{p(x)}$ is an integer for all x.

Theorem 5.11.2: *For a dyadic probability mass function $p(x)$, let $l(x) = \log \frac{1}{p(x)}$ be the word lengths of the binary Shannon code for the source, and let $l'(x)$ be the lengths of any other uniquely decodable binary code for the source. Then*

$$\Pr(l(X) < l'(X)) \geq \Pr(l(X) > l'(X)), \quad (5.92)$$

with equality iff $l'(x) = l(x)$ for all x. Thus the code length assignment $l(x) = \log \frac{1}{p(x)}$ is uniquely competitively optimal.

Proof: Define the function sgn(t) as follows:

$$\text{sgn}(t) = \begin{cases} 1 & \text{if } t > 0 \\ 0 & \text{if } t = 0 \\ -1 & \text{if } t < 0 \end{cases}. \quad (5.93)$$

Then it is easy to see from Figure 5.7 that

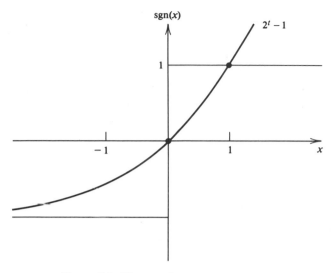

Figure 5.7. The sgn function and a bound.

$$\text{sgn}(t) \leq 2^t - 1 \quad \text{for } t = 0, \pm 1, \pm 2, \ldots . \tag{5.94}$$

Note that though this inequality is not satisfied for all t, it is satisfied at all integer values of t.

We can now write

$$\Pr(l'(X) < l(X)) - \Pr(l'(X) > l(X)) = \sum_{x : l'(x) < l(x)} p(x) - \sum_{x : l'(x) > l(x)} p(x) \tag{5.95}$$

$$= \sum_{x} p(x) \, \text{sgn}(l(x) - l'(x)) \tag{5.96}$$

$$= E \, \text{sgn}(l(X) - l'(X)) \tag{5.97}$$

$$\overset{(a)}{\leq} \sum_{x} p(x)(2^{l(x)-l'(x)} - 1) \tag{5.98}$$

$$= \sum_{x} 2^{-l(x)}(2^{l(x)-l'(x)} - 1) \tag{5.99}$$

$$= \sum_{x} 2^{-l'(x)} - \sum_{x} 2^{-l(x)} \tag{5.100}$$

$$= \sum_{x} 2^{-l'(x)} - 1 \tag{5.101}$$

$$\overset{(b)}{\leq} 1 - 1 \tag{5.102}$$

$$= 0, \tag{5.103}$$

where (a) follows from the bound on sgn(x) and (b) follows from the fact that $l'(x)$ satisfies the Kraft inequality.

We have equality in the above chain only if we have equality in (a) and (b). We have equality in the bound for sgn(t) only if t is 0 or 1, i.e., $l(x) = l'(x)$ or $l(x) = l'(x) + 1$. Equality in (b) implies that $l'(x)$ satisfy the Kraft inequality with equality. Combining these two facts implies that $l'(x) = l(x)$ for all x. $\square$

Corollary: *For non-dyadic probability mass functions,*

$$E \, \text{sgn}(l(X) - l'(X) - 1) \le 0 \tag{5.104}$$

where $l(x) = \lceil \log \frac{1}{p(x)} \rceil$ and $l'(x)$ is any other code for the source.

Proof: Along the same lines as the preceding proof. $\square$

Hence we have shown that Shannon coding is optimal under a variety of criteria; it is robust with respect to the payoff function. In particular, for dyadic p, $E(l - l') \le 0$, $E \, \text{sgn}(l - l') \le 0$, and by use of inequality (5.94), $Ef(l - l') \le 0$, for any function f satisfying $f(t) \le 2^t - 1$, $t = 0, \pm 1, \pm 2, \ldots$.

5.12 GENERATION OF DISCRETE DISTRIBUTIONS FROM FAIR COINS

In the early sections of this chapter, we considered the problem of representing a random variable by a sequence of bits such that the expected length of the representation was minimized. It can be argued (Problem 26) that the encoded sequence is essentially incompressible, and therefore has an entropy rate close to 1 bit per symbol. Therefore the bits of the encoded sequence are essentially fair coin flips.

In this section, we will take a slight detour from our discussion of source coding and consider the dual question. How many fair coin flips does it take to generate a random variable X drawn according to some specified probability mass function **p**? We first consider a simple example:

Example 5.12.1: Given a sequence of fair coin tosses (fair bits), suppose we wish to generate a random variable X with distribution

$$X = \begin{cases} a & \text{with probability } \frac{1}{2}, \\ b & \text{with probability } \frac{1}{4}, \\ c & \text{with probability } \frac{1}{4}. \end{cases} \tag{5.105}$$

It is easy to guess the answer. If the first bit is 0, we let $X = a$. If the first two bits are 10, we let $X = b$. If we see 11, we let $X = c$. It is clear that X has the desired distribution.

We calculate the average number of fair bits required for generating the random variable in this case as $\frac{1}{2}1 + \frac{1}{4}2 + \frac{1}{4}2 = 1.5$ bits. This is also the entropy of the distribution. Is this unusual? No, as the results of this section indicate.

The general problem can now be formulated as follows. We are given a sequence of fair coin tosses $Z_1, Z_2, \ldots$, and we wish to generate a discrete random variable $X \in \mathcal{X} = \{1, 2, \ldots, m\}$ with probability mass function $\mathbf{p} = (p_1, p_2, \ldots, p_m)$. Let the random variable T denote the number of coin flips used in the algorithm.

We can describe the algorithm mapping strings of bits $Z_1, Z_2, \ldots$, to possible outcomes X by a binary tree. The leaves of the tree are marked by output symbols X and the path to the leaves is given by the sequence of bits produced by the fair coin. For example, the tree for the distribution $(\frac{1}{2}, \frac{1}{4}, \frac{1}{4})$ is shown in Figure 5.8.

The tree representing the algorithm must satisfy certain properties:

1. The tree should be complete, i.e., every node is either a leaf or has two descendants in the tree. The tree may be infinite, as we will see in some examples.
2. The probability of a leaf at depth k is 2^{-k}. Many leaves may be labeled with the same output symbol—the total probability of all these leaves should equal the desired probability of the output symbol.
3. The expected number of fair bits ET required to generate X is equal to the expected depth of this tree.

There are many possible algorithms that generate the same output distribution. For example, the mapping: $00 \rightarrow a, 01 \rightarrow b, 10 \rightarrow c, 11 \rightarrow a$ also yields the distribution $(\frac{1}{2}, \frac{1}{4}, \frac{1}{4})$. However, this algorithm uses two fair bits to generate each sample, and is therefore not as efficient as the mapping given earlier, which used only 1.5 bits per sample. This brings up the question: What is the most efficient algorithm to generate a given distribution and how is this related to the entropy of the distribution?

Figure 5.8. Tree for generation of the distribution $(\frac{1}{2}, \frac{1}{4}, \frac{1}{4})$.

We expect that we need at least as much randomness in the fair bits as we produce in the output samples. Since entropy is a measure of randomness, and each fair bit has an entropy of 1 bit, we expect that the number of fair bits used will be at least equal to the entropy of the output. This is proved in the following theorem.

We will need a simple lemma about trees in the proof of the theorem. Let $\mathcal{Y}$ denote the set of leaves of a complete tree. Consider a distribution on the leaves, such that the probability of a leaf at depth k on the tree is 2^{-k}. Let Y be a random variable with this distribution. Then we have the following lemma:

Lemma 5.12.1: *For any complete tree, consider a probability distribution on the leaves, such that the probability of a leaf at depth k is 2^{-k}. Then the expected depth of the tree is equal to the entropy of this distribution.*

Proof: The expected depth of the tree

$$ET = \sum_{y \in \mathcal{Y}} k(y) 2^{-k(y)} \tag{5.106}$$

and the entropy of the distribution of Y is

$$H(Y) = - \sum_{y \in \mathcal{Y}} \frac{1}{2^{k(y)}} \log \frac{1}{2^{k(y)}} \tag{5.107}$$

$$= \sum_{y \in \mathcal{Y}} k(y) 2^{-k(y)}, \tag{5.108}$$

where $k(y)$ denotes the depth of leaf y. Thus

$$H(Y) = ET . \quad \square \tag{5.109}$$

Theorem 5.12.1: *For any algorithm generating X, the expected number of fair bits used is greater than the entropy $H(X)$, i.e.,*

$$ET \geq H(X) . \tag{5.110}$$

Proof: Any algorithm generating X from fair bits can be represented by a binary tree. Label all the leaves of this tree by distinct symbols $y \in \mathcal{Y} = \{1, 2, \dots \}$. If the tree is infinite, the alphabet $\mathcal{Y}$ is also infinite.

Now consider the random variable Y defined on the leaves of the tree, such that for any leaf y at depth k, the probability that $Y = y$ is 2^{-k}. By Lemma 5.12.1, the expected depth of this tree is equal to the entropy of Y, i.e.,

$$ET = H(Y) . \tag{5.111}$$

Now the random variable X is a function of Y (one or more leaves map onto an output symbol), and hence by the result of Problem 5 in Chapter 2, we have

$$H(X) \leq H(Y).$$ (5.112)

Thus for any algorithm generating the random variable X, we have

$$H(X) \leq ET. \quad \square$$ (5.113)

The same argument answers the question of optimality for a dyadic distribution.

Theorem 5.12.2: *Let the random variable X have a dyadic distribution. The optimal algorithm to generate X from fair coin flips requires an expected number of coin tosses precisely equal to the entropy, i.e.,*

$$ET = H(X).$$ (5.114)

Proof: The previous theorem shows that we need at least $H(X)$ bits to generate X.

For the constructive part, we use the Huffman code tree for X as the tree to generate the random variable. For a dyadic distribution, the Huffman code is the same as the Shannon code and achieves the entropy bound. For any $x \in \mathcal{X}$, the depth of the leaf in the code tree corresponding to x is the length of the corresponding codeword, which is $\log \frac{1}{p(x)}$. Hence when this code tree is used to generate X, the leaf will have a probability $2^{-\log(1/p(x))} = p(x)$.

The expected number of coin flips is the expected depth of the tree, which is equal to the entropy (because the distribution is dyadic). Hence for a dyadic distribution, the optimal generating algorithm achieves

$$ET = H(X). \quad \square$$ (5.115)

What if the distribution is not dyadic? In this case, we cannot use the same idea, since the code tree for the Huffman code will generate a dyadic distribution on the leaves, not the distribution with which we started. Since all the leaves of the tree have probabilities of the form 2^{-k}, it follows that we should split any probability p_i that is not of this form into atoms of this form. We can then allot these atoms to leaves on the tree.

To minimize the expected depth of the tree, we should use atoms with as large a probability as possible. So given a probability p_i, we find the largest atom of the form 2^{-k} that is less than p_i, and allot this atom to the tree. Then we calculate the remainder and find that largest atom that will fit in the remainder. Continuing this process, we can split all the probabilities into dyadic atoms. This process is equivalent to finding the binary expansions of the probabilities. Let the binary expansion of the probability p_i be

$$p_i = \sum_{j \geq 1} p_i^{(j)}, \tag{5.116}$$

where $p_i^{(j)} = 2^{-j}$ or 0. Then the atoms of the expansion are the $\{p_i^{(j)} : i = 1, 2, \ldots, m, j \geq 1\}$.

Since $\Sigma_i \, p_i = 1$, the sum of the probabilities of these atoms is 1. We will allot an atom of probability 2^{-j} to a leaf at depth j on the tree. The depths of the atoms satisfy the Kraft inequality, and hence by Theorem 5.2.1, we can always construct such a tree with all the atoms at the right depths.

We illustrate this procedure with an example:

Example 5.12.2: Let X have the distribution

$$X = \begin{cases} a & \text{with probability } \frac{2}{3}, \\ b & \text{with probability } \frac{1}{3}. \end{cases} \tag{5.117}$$

We find the binary expansions of these probabilities:

$$\frac{2}{3} = 0.10101010 \ldots {}_2 \tag{5.118}$$

$$\frac{1}{3} = 0.01010101 \ldots {}_2 \tag{5.119}$$

Hence the atoms for the expansion are

$$\frac{2}{3} \rightarrow \left(\frac{1}{2}, \frac{1}{8}, \frac{1}{32}, \ldots \right) \tag{5.120}$$

$$\frac{1}{3} \rightarrow \left(\frac{1}{4}, \frac{1}{16}, \frac{1}{64}, \ldots \right) \tag{5.121}$$

These can be allotted to a tree as shown in Figure 5.9.

This procedure yields a tree that generates the random variable X. We have argued that this procedure is optimal (gives a tree of minimum

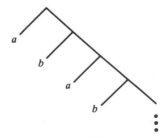

Figure 5.9. Tree to generate a $(\frac{2}{3}, \frac{1}{3})$ distribution.

expected depth), but we will not give a formal proof. Instead, we bound the expected depth of the tree generated by this procedure.

Theorem 5.12.3: *The expected number of fair bits required by the optimal algorithm to generate a random variable X lies between H(X) and H(X) + 2, i.e.,*

$$H(X) \le ET < H(X) + 2 . \tag{5.122}$$

Proof: The lower bound on the expected number of coin tosses is proved in Theorem 5.12.1.

For the upper bound, we write down an explicit expression for the expected number of coin tosses required for the procedure described above. We split all the probabilities $(p_1, p_2, \ldots, p_m)$ into dyadic atoms, e.g.,

$$p_1 \to (p_1^{(1)}, p_1^{(2)}, \ldots), \tag{5.123}$$

etc. Using these atoms (which form a dyadic distribution), we construct a tree with leaves corresponding to each of these atoms. The number of coin tosses required to generate each atom is its depth in the tree, and therefore the expected number of coin tosses is the expected depth of the tree, which is equal to the entropy of the dyadic distribution of the atoms. Hence

$$ET = H(Y), \tag{5.124}$$

where Y has the distribution, $(p_1^{(1)}, p_1^{(2)}, \ldots, p_2^{(1)}, p_2^{(2)}, \ldots, p_m^{(1)}, p_m^{(2)}, \ldots)$. Now since X is a function of Y, we have

$$H(Y) = H(Y, X) = H(X) + H(Y|X), \tag{5.125}$$

and our objective is to show that $H(Y|X) < 2$. We now give an algebraic proof of this result. Expanding the entropy of Y, we have

$$H(Y) = - \sum_{i=1}^{m} \sum_{j \ge 1} p_i^{(j)} \log p_i^{(j)} \tag{5.126}$$

$$= \sum_{i=1}^{m} \sum_{j : p_i^{(j)} > 0} j 2^{-j}, \tag{5.127}$$

since each of the atoms is either 0 or 2^{-k} for some k. Now consider the term in the expansion corresponding to each i, which we shall call T_i, i.e.,

$$T_i = \sum_{j : p_i^{(j)} > 0} j 2^{-j} . \tag{5.128}$$

We can find an n such that $2^{-(n-1)} > p_i \ge 2^{-n}$, or

$$n - 1 < -\log p_i \le n. \tag{5.129}$$

Then it follows that $p_i^{(j)} > 0$ only if $j \ge n$, so that we can rewrite (5.128) as

$$T_i = \sum_{j:j \ge n,\, p_i^{(j)} > 0} j 2^{-j}. \tag{5.130}$$

We use the definition of the atom to write p_i as

$$p_i = \sum_{j:j \ge n,\, p_i^{(j)} > 0} 2^{-j}. \tag{5.131}$$

In order to prove the upper bound, we first show that $T_i < -p_i \log p_i + 2p_i$. Consider the difference

$$T_i + p_i \log p_i - 2p_i \overset{(a)}{<} T_i - p_i(n - 1) - 2p_i \tag{5.132}$$

$$= T_i - (n - 1 + 2)p_i \tag{5.133}$$

$$= \sum_{j:j \ge n,\, p_i^{(j)} > 0} j 2^{-j} - (n + 1) \sum_{j:j \ge n,\, p_i^{(j)} > 0} 2^{-j} \tag{5.134}$$

$$= \sum_{j:j \ge n,\, p_i^{(j)} > 0} (j - n - 1)2^{-j} \tag{5.135}$$

$$= -2^{-n} + 0 + \sum_{j:j \ge n + 2,\, p_i^{(j)} > 0} (j - n - 1)2^{-j} \tag{5.136}$$

$$\overset{(b)}{=} -2^{-n} + \sum_{k:k \ge 1,\, p_i^{(k+n+1)} > 0} k 2^{-(k+n+1)} \tag{5.137}$$

$$\overset{(c)}{\le} -2^{-n} + \sum_{k:k \ge 1} k 2^{-(k+n+1)} \tag{5.138}$$

$$= -2^{-n} + 2^{-(n+1)}2 \tag{5.139}$$

$$= 0, \tag{5.140}$$

where (a) follows from (5.129), (b) from a change of variables for the summation and (c) from increasing the range of the summation. Hence we have shown that

$$T_i < -p_i \log p_i + 2p_i. \tag{5.141}$$

Since $ET = \Sigma_i T_i$, it follows immediately that

$$ET < -\sum_i p_i \log p_i + 2 \sum_i p_i = H(X) + 2 \tag{5.142}$$

completing the proof of the theorem. $\square$

SUMMARY OF CHAPTER 5

Kraft inequality: Instantaneous codes $\Leftrightarrow \Sigma D^{-l_i} \le 1$

McMillan inequality: Uniquely decodable codes $\Leftrightarrow \Sigma D^{-l_i} \le 1$

Entropy bound on data compression (*Lower bound*):

$$L \overset{\triangle}{=} \sum p_i l_i \ge H_D(X). \tag{5.143}$$

Shannon code:

$$l_i = \left\lceil \log_D \frac{1}{p_i} \right\rceil \tag{5.144}$$

$$L < H_D(X) + 1. \tag{5.145}$$

Huffman code:

$$L^* = \min_{\Sigma D^{-l_i} \le 1} \sum p_i l_i. \tag{5.146}$$

$$H_D(X) \le L^* < H_D(X) + 1. \tag{5.147}$$

Wrong code: $X \sim p(x)$, $l(x) = \lceil \log \frac{1}{q(x)} \rceil$, $L = \Sigma p(x)l(x)$:

$$H(p) + D(p\|q) < L < H(p) + D(p\|q) + 1. \tag{5.148}$$

Stochastic processes:

$$\frac{H(X_1, X_2, \ldots, X_n)}{n} \le L_n < \frac{H(X_1, X_2, \ldots, X_n)}{n} + \frac{1}{n}. \tag{5.149}$$

Stationary processes:

$$L_n \to H(\mathscr{X}). \tag{5.150}$$

Competitive optimality: $l(x) = \lceil \log \frac{1}{p(x)} \rceil$ (Shannon code) versus any other code $l'(x)$:

$$\Pr(l(X) \ge l'(X) + c) \le \frac{1}{2^{c-1}}. \tag{5.151}$$

Generation of random variables:

$$H(X) \le ET < H(X) + 2. \tag{5.152}$$

PROBLEMS FOR CHAPTER 5

1. *Uniquely decodable and instantaneous codes.* Let $L = \sum_{i=1}^{m} p_i l_i^{100}$ be the expected value of the 100th power of the word lengths associated with an encoding of the random variable X. Let $L_1 = \min L$ over all instantaneous codes; and let $L_2 = \min L$ over all uniquely decodable codes. What inequality relationship exists between L_1 and L_2?

2. *How many fingers has a Martian?* Let

$$S = \begin{pmatrix} S_1, \ldots, S_m \\ p_1, \ldots, p_m \end{pmatrix}.$$

The S_i's are encoded into strings from a D-symbol output alphabet in a uniquely decodable manner. If $m = 6$ and the codeword lengths are $(l_1, l_2, \ldots, l_6) = (1, 1, 2, 3, 2, 3)$, find a good lower bound on D. You may wish to explain the title of the problem.

3. *Slackness in the Kraft inequality.* An instantaneous code has word lengths $l_1, l_2, \ldots, l_m$ which satisfy the strict inequality

$$\sum_{i=1}^{m} D^{-l_i} < 1.$$

The code alphabet is $\mathscr{D} = \{0, 1, 2, \ldots, D - 1\}$. Show that there exist arbitrarily long sequences of code symbols in $\mathscr{D}^*$ which cannot be decoded into sequences of codewords.

4. *Huffman coding.* Consider the random variable

$$X = \begin{pmatrix} x_1 & x_2 & x_3 & x_4 & x_5 & x_6 & x_7 \\ 0.49 & 0.26 & 0.12 & 0.04 & 0.04 & 0.03 & 0.02 \end{pmatrix}$$

   (a) Find a binary Huffman code for X.
   (b) Find the expected codelength for this encoding.
   (c) Find a ternary Huffman code for X.

5. *More Huffman codes.* Find the binary Huffman code for the source with probabilities (1/3, 1/5, 1/5, 2/15, 2/15). Argue that this code is also optimal for the source with probabilities (1/5, 1/5, 1/5, 1/5, 1/5).

6. *Bad codes.* Which of these codes cannot be Huffman codes for any probability assignment?
   (a) $\{0, 10, 11\}$.
   (b) $\{00, 01, 10, 110\}$.
   (c) $\{01, 10\}$.

7. *Huffman 20 Questions.* Consider a set of n objects. Let $X_i = 1$ or 0 accordingly as the i-th object is good or defective. Let $X_1, X_2, \ldots, X_n$ be independent with $\Pr\{X_i = 1\} = p_i$; and $p_1 > p_2 > \ldots > p_n > 1/2$. We are asked to determine the set of all defective objects. Any yes-no question you can think of is admissible.

(a) Give a good lower bound on the minimum average number of questions required.

(b) If the longest sequence of questions is required by nature's answers to our questions, what (in words) is the last question we should ask? And what two sets are we distinguishing with this question? Assume a compact (minimum average length) sequence of questions.

(c) Give an upper bound (within 1 question) on the minimum average number of questions required.

8. *Simple optimum compression of a Markov source.* Consider the 3-state Markov process $U_1, U_2, \ldots$ having transition matrix

U_{n-1} \\ U_n	S_1	S_2	S_3
S_1	1/2	1/4	1/4
S_2	1/4	1/2	1/4
S_3	0	1/2	1/2

Thus the probability that S_1 follows S_3 is equal to zero. Design 3 codes C_1, C_2, C_3 (one for each state S_1, S_2, S_3), each code mapping elements of the set of S_i's into sequences of 0's and 1's, such that this Markov process can be sent with maximal compression by the following scheme:

(a) Note the present symbol S_i.

(b) Select code C_i.

(c) Note the next symbol S_j and send the codeword in C_i corresponding to S_j.

(d) Repeat for the next symbol.

What is the average message length of the next symbol conditioned on the previous state $S = S_i$ using this coding scheme? What is the unconditional average number of bits per source symbol? Relate this to the entropy rate $H(\mathcal{U})$ of the Markov chain.

9. *Optimal code lengths that require one bit above entropy.* The source coding theorem shows that the optimal code for a random variable X has an expected length less than $H(X) + 1$. Give an example of a random variable for which the expected length of the optimal code is close to $H(X) + 1$, i.e., for any $\epsilon > 0$, construct a distribution for which the optimal code has $L > H(X) + 1 - \epsilon$.

10. *Ternary codes that achieve the entropy bound.* A random variable X takes on m values and has entropy $H(X)$. An instantaneous ternary code is found for this source, with average length

$$L = \frac{H(X)}{\log_2 3} = H_3(X) . \qquad (5.153)$$

(a) Show that each symbol of X has a probability of the form 3^{-i} for some i.

(b) Show that m is odd.

11. *Suffix condition.* Consider codes that satisfy the suffix condition, which says that no codeword is a suffix of any other codeword. Show that a suffix condition code is uniquely decodable, and show that the minimum average length over all codes satisfying the suffix condition is the same as the average length of the Huffman code for that random variable.

12. *Shannon codes and Huffman codes.* Consider a random variable X which takes on four values with probabilities $(\frac{1}{3}, \frac{1}{3}, \frac{1}{4}, \frac{1}{12})$.

(a) Construct a Huffman code for this random variable.

(b) Show that there exist two different sets of optimal lengths for the codewords, namely, show that codeword length assignments $(1, 2, 3, 3)$ and $(2, 2, 2, 2)$ are both optimal.

(c) Conclude that there are optimal codes with codeword lengths for some symbols that exceed the Shannon code length $\lceil \log \frac{1}{p(x)} \rceil$.

13. *Twenty questions.* Player A chooses some object in the universe, and player B attempts to identify the object with a series of yes-no questions. Suppose that player B is clever enough to use the code achieving the minimal expected length with respect to player A's distribution. We observe that player B requires an average of 38.5 questions to determine the object. Find a rough lower bound to the number of objects in the universe.

14. *Huffman code.* Find the (a) *binary* and (b) *ternary* Huffman codes for the random variable X with probabilities

$$p = \left(\frac{1}{21}, \frac{2}{21}, \frac{3}{21}, \frac{4}{21}, \frac{5}{21}, \frac{6}{21} \right).$$

(c) Calculate $L = \Sigma \, p_i l_i$ in each case.

15. *Classes of codes.* Consider the code $\{0, 01\}$

(a) Is it instantaneous?

(b) Is it uniquely decodable?

(c) Is it nonsingular?

16. *The game of Hi-Lo.*

(a) A computer generates a number X according to a known probability mass function $p(x), x \in \{1, 2, \ldots, 100\}$. The player asks a question, "Is $X = i$?" and is told "Yes", "You're too high," or "You're too low." He continues for a total of six questions. If he is right (i.e. he receives the answer "Yes") during this sequence, he receives a prize of value $v(X)$. How should the player proceed to maximize his expected winnings?

(b) The above doesn't have much to do with information theory. Consider the following variation: $X \sim p(x)$, prize $= v(x)$, $p(x)$

known, as before. But *arbitrary* Yes–No questions are asked sequentially until X is determined. ("Determined" doesn't mean that a "Yes" answer is received.) Questions cost one unit each. How should the player proceed? What is his expected return?

(c) Continuing (b), what if $v(x)$ is fixed, but $p(x)$ can be chosen by the computer (and then announced to the player)? The computer wishes to minimize the player's expected return. What should $p(x)$ be? What is the expected return to the player?

17. *Huffman codes with costs.* Words like Run! Help! and Fire! are short, not because they are frequently used, but perhaps because time is precious in the situations in which these words are required. Suppose that $X = i$ with probability p_i, $i = 1, 2, \ldots, m$. Let l_i be the number of binary symbols in the codeword associated with $X = i$, and let c_i denote the cost per letter of the codeword when $X = i$. Thus the average cost C of the description of X is $C = \sum_{i=1}^{m} p_i c_i l_i$.

(a) Minimize C over all $l_1, l_2, \ldots, l_m$ such that $\sum 2^{-l_i} \le 1$. Ignore any implied integer constraints on l_i. Exhibit the minimizing $l_1^*, l_2^*, \ldots, l_m^*$ and the associated minimum value C^*.

(b) How would you use the Huffman code procedure to minimize C over all uniquely decodable codes? Let C_{Huffman} denote this minimum.

(c) Can you show that

$$C^* \le C_{\text{Huffman}} \le C^* + \sum_{i=1}^{m} p_i c_i ?$$

18. *Conditions for unique decodability.* Prove that a code C is uniquely decodable if (and only if) the extension

$$C^k(x_1, x_2, \ldots, x_k) = C(x_1)C(x_2) \cdots C(x_k)$$

is a one-to-one mapping from $\mathscr{X}^k$ to D^* for every $k \ge 1$. (The only if part is obvious.)

19. *Average length of an optimal code.* Prove that $L(p_1, \ldots, p_m)$, the average codeword length for an optimal D-ary prefix code for probabilities $\{p_1, \ldots, p_m\}$, is a continuous function of $p_1, \ldots, p_m$. This is true even though the optimal code changes discontinuously as the probabilities vary.

20. *Unused code sequences.* Let C be a variable length code that satisfies the Kraft inequality with equality but does *not* satisfy the prefix condition.

(a) Prove that some finite sequence of code alphabet symbols is not the prefix of any sequence of codewords.

(b) (Optional) Prove or disprove: C has infinite decoding delay.

21. *Optimal codes for uniform distributions.* Consider a random variable with m equiprobable outcomes. The entropy of this information source is obviously $\log_2 m$ bits.

(a) Describe the optimal instantaneous binary code for this source and compute the average codeword length L_m.

(b) For what values of m does the average codeword length L_m equal the entropy $H = \log_2 m$?

(c) We know that $L < H + 1$ for any probability distribution. The *redundancy* of a variable length code is defined to be $\rho = L - H$. For what value(s) of m, where $2^k \leq m \leq 2^{k+1}$, is the redundancy of the code maximized? What is the limiting value of this worst case redundancy as $m \to \infty$?

22. *Optimal codeword lengths.* Although the codeword lengths of an optimal variable length code are complicated functions of the message probabilities $\{p_1, p_2, \ldots, p_m\}$, it can be said that less probable symbols are encoded into longer codewords. Suppose that the message probabilities are given in decreasing order $p_1 > p_2 \geq \cdots \geq p_m$.

(a) Prove that for any binary Huffman code, if the most probable message symbol has probability $p_1 > 2/5$, then that symbol must be assigned a codeword of length 1.

(b) Prove that for any binary Huffman code, if the most probable message symbol has probability $p_1 < 1/3$, then that symbol must be assigned a codeword of length ≥ 2.

23. *Merges.* Companies with values $W_1, W_2, \ldots, W_m$ are merged as follows. The two least valuable companies are merged, thus forming a list of $m - 1$ companies. The *value of the merge* is the sum of the values of the two merged companies. This continues until one supercompany remains. Let V equal the sum of the values of the merges. Thus V represents the total reported dollar volume of the merges. For example, if $\mathbf{W} = (3, 3, 2, 2)$, the merges yield $(3, 3, 2, 2) \to (4, 3, 3) \to (6, 4) \to (10)$, and $V = 4 + 6 + 10 = 20$.

(a) Argue that V is the minimum volume achievable by sequences of pair-wise merges terminating in one supercompany. (*Hint*: Compare to Huffman coding.)

(b) Let $W = \Sigma\, W_i$, $\tilde{W}_i = W_i / W$, and show that the minimum merge volume V satisfies

$$WH(\tilde{\mathbf{W}}) \leq V \leq WH(\tilde{\mathbf{W}}) + W. \tag{5.154}$$

24. *The Sardinas-Patterson test for unique decodability.* A code is not uniquely decodable iff there exists a finite sequence of code symbols which can be resolved in two different ways into sequences of codewords. That is, a situation such as

A_1		A_2		A_3	$\cdots$	A_m	
B_1	B_2		B_3		$\cdots$	B_n	

must occur where each A_i and each B_i is a codeword. Note that B_1 must be a prefix of A_1 with some resulting "dangling suffix." Each dangling suffix must in turn be either a prefix of a codeword or have another codeword as its prefix, resulting in another dangling suffix. Finally, the last dangling suffix in the sequence must also be a codeword. Thus one can set up a test for unique decodability (which is essentially the Sardinas-Patterson test [228]) in the following way: Construct a set S of all possible dangling suffixes. The code is uniquely decodable iff S contains no codeword.

(a) State the precise rules for building the set S.

(b) Suppose the codeword lengths are l_i, $i = 1, 2, \ldots, m$. Find a good upper bound on the number of elements in the set S.

(c) Determine which of the following codes is uniquely decodable:

     i. $\{0, 10, 11\}$.

     ii. $\{0, 01, 11\}$.

     iii. $\{0, 01, 10\}$.

     iv. $\{0, 01\}$.

     v. $\{00, 01, 10, 11\}$.

     vi. $\{110, 11, 10\}$.

     vii. $\{110, 11, 100, 00, 10\}$.

(d) For each uniquely decodable code in part (c), construct, if possible, an infinite encoded sequence with a known starting point, such that it can be resolved into codewords in two different ways. (This illustrates that unique decodability does not imply finite decodability.) Prove that such a sequence cannot arise in a prefix code.

25. *Shannon code.* Consider the following method for generating a code for a random variable X which takes on m values $\{1, 2, \ldots, m\}$ with probabilities $p_1, p_2, \ldots, p_m$. Assume that the probabilities are ordered so that $p_1 \geq p_2 \geq \cdots \geq p_m$. Define

$$F_i = \sum_{k=1}^{i-1} p_i \, , \tag{5.155}$$

the sum of the probabilities of all symbols less than i. Then the codeword for i is the number $F_i \in [0, 1]$ rounded off to l_i bits, where $l_i = \lceil \log \frac{1}{p_i} \rceil$.

(a) Show that the code constructed by this process is prefix-free and the average length satisfies

$$H(X) \leq L < H(X) + 1 \, . \tag{5.156}$$

(b) Construct the code for the probability distribution (0.5, 0.25, 0.125, 0.125).

26. *Optimal codes for dyadic distributions.* For a Huffman code tree, define the probability of a node as the sum of the probabilities of all the leaves under that node. Let the random variable X be drawn from a dyadic distribution, i.e., $p(x) = 2^{-i}$, for some i, for all $x \in \mathscr{X}$. Now consider a binary Huffman code for this distribution.

(a) Argue that for any node in the tree, the probability of the left child is equal to the probability of the right child.

(b) Let $X_1, X_2, \ldots, X_n$ be drawn i.i.d. $\sim p(x)$. Using the Huffman code for $p(x)$, we map $X_1, X_2, \ldots, X_n$ to a sequence of bits $Y_1, Y_2, \ldots, Y_{k(X_1, X_2, \ldots, X_n)}$. (The length of this sequence will depend on the outcome $X_1, X_2, \ldots, X_n$.) Use part (a) to argue that the sequence $Y_1, Y_2, \ldots,$ forms a sequence of fair coin flips, i.e., that $\Pr\{Y_i = 0\} = \Pr\{Y_i = 1\} = \frac{1}{2}$, independent of $Y_1, Y_2, \ldots, Y_{i-1}$. Thus the entropy rate of the coded sequence is 1 bit/symbol.

(c) Give a heuristic argument why the encoded sequence of bits for any code that achieves the entropy bound cannot be compressible and therefore should have an entropy rate of 1 bit per symbol.

HISTORICAL NOTES

The foundations for the material in this chapter can be found in Shannon's original paper [238], in which Shannon stated the source coding theorem and gave simple examples of codes. He described a simple code construction procedure (described in Problem 25), which he attributed to Fano. This method is now called the Shannon-Fano code construction procedure.

The Kraft inequality for uniquely decodable codes was first proved by McMillan [193]; the proof given here is due to Karush [149]. The Huffman coding procedure was first exhibited and proved to be optimal by Huffman [138].

In recent years, there has been considerable interest in designing source codes that are matched to particular applications such as magnetic recording. In these cases, the objective is to design codes so that the output sequences satisfy certain properties. Some of the results for this problem are described by Franaszek [116], Adler, Coppersmith and Hassner [2] and Marcus [184].

The arithmetic coding procedure has its roots in the Shannon-Fano code developed by Elias (unpublished), which was analyzed by Jelinek [146]. The procedure for the construction of a prefix-free code described in the text is due to Gilbert and Moore [121]. Arithmetic coding itself was developed by Rissanen [217] and Pasco [207]; it was generalized by Rissanen and Langdon [171]. See also the enumerative methods in Cover [61]. Tutorial introductions to arithmetic coding can be found in Langdon [170] and Witten, Neal and Cleary [275]. We will discuss universal source coding algorithms in Chapter 12, where we will describe the popular Lempel-Ziv algorithm.

Section 5.12 on the generation of discrete distributions from fair coin flips follows the work of Knuth and Yao [155].

Chapter 6

Gambling and Data Compression

At first sight, information theory and gambling seem to be unrelated. But as we shall see, there is strong duality between the growth rate of investment in a horse race and the entropy rate of the horse race. Indeed the sum of the growth rate and the entropy rate is a constant. In the process of proving this, we shall argue that the financial value of side information is equal to the mutual information between the horse race and the side information.

We also show how to use a pair of identical gamblers to compress a sequence of random variables by an amount equal to the growth rate of wealth on that sequence. Finally, we use these gambling techniques to estimate the entropy rate of English.

The horse race is a special case of investment in the stock market, studied in Chapter 15.

6.1 THE HORSE RACE

Assume that m horses run in a race. Let the ith horse win with probability p_i. If horse i wins, the payoff is o_i for 1, i.e., an investment of one dollar on horse i results in o_i dollars if horse i wins and 0 dollars if horse i loses.

There are two ways of describing odds: a-for-1 and b-to-1. The first refers to an exchange that takes place before the race—the gambler puts down one dollar before the race and at a-for-1 odds will receive a dollars after the race if his horse wins, and will receive nothing otherwise. The second refers to an exchange after the race—at b-to-1 odds, the gambler will pay one dollar after the race if his horse loses and will pick up b

dollars after the race if his horse wins. Thus a bet at b-to-1 odds is equivalent to a bet at a-for-1 odds if $b = a - 1$.

We assume that the gambler distributes all of his wealth across the horses. Let b_i be the fraction of the gambler's wealth invested in horse i, where $b_i \geq 0$ and $\Sigma\, b_i = 1$. Then if horse i wins the race, the gambler will receive o_i times the amount of wealth bet on horse i. All the other bets are lost. Thus at the end of the race, the gambler will have multiplied his wealth by a factor $b_i o_i$ if horse i wins, and this will happen with probability p_i. For notational convenience, we use $b(i)$ and b_i interchangeably throughout this chapter.

The wealth at the end of the race is a random variable, and the gambler wishes to "maximize" the value of this random variable. It is tempting to bet everything on the horse that has the maximum expected return, i.e., the one with the maximum $p_i o_i$. But this is clearly risky, since all the money could be lost.

Some clarity results from considering repeated gambles on this race. Now since the gambler can reinvest his money, his wealth is the product of the gains for each race. Let S_n be the gambler's wealth after n races. Then

$$S_n = \prod_{i=1}^{n} S(X_i), \qquad (6.1)$$

where $S(X) = b(X)o(X)$ is the factor by which the gambler's wealth is multiplied when horse X wins.

Definition: The *wealth relative* $S(X) = b(X)o(X)$ is the factor by which the gambler's wealth grows if horse X wins the race.

Definition: The *doubling rate* of a horse race is

$$W(\mathbf{b}, \mathbf{p}) = E(\log S(X)) = \sum_{k=1}^{m} p_k \log b_k o_k. \qquad (6.2)$$

The definition of doubling rate is justified by the following theorem.

Theorem 6.1.1: *Let the race outcomes $X_1, X_2, \ldots, X_n$ be i.i.d. $\sim p(x)$. Then the wealth of the gambler using betting strategy $\mathbf{b}$ grows exponentially at rate $W(\mathbf{b}, \mathbf{p})$, i.e.,*

$$S_n \doteq 2^{nW(\mathbf{b},\, \mathbf{p})}. \qquad (6.3)$$

Proof: Functions of independent random variables are also independent, and hence $\log S(X_1), \log S(X_2), \ldots, \log S(X_n)$ are i.i.d. Then, by the weak law of large numbers,

$$\frac{1}{n} \log S_n = \frac{1}{n} \sum_{i=1}^{n} \log S(X_i) \rightarrow E(\log S(X)) \quad \text{in probability}. \quad (6.4)$$

Thus

$$S_n \doteq 2^{nW(\mathbf{b}, \mathbf{p})}. \quad \square \quad (6.5)$$

Now since the gambler's wealth grows as $2^{nW(\mathbf{b}, \mathbf{p})}$, we seek to maximize the exponent $W(\mathbf{b}, \mathbf{p})$ over all choices of the portfolio $\mathbf{b}$.

Definition: The optimum doubling rate $W^*(\mathbf{p})$ is the maximum doubling rate over all choices of the portfolio $\mathbf{b}$, i.e.,

$$W^*(\mathbf{p}) = \max_{\mathbf{b}} W(\mathbf{b}, \mathbf{p}) = \max_{\mathbf{b}: b_i \geq 0, \Sigma_i b_i = 1} \sum_{i=1}^{m} p_i \log b_i o_i. \quad (6.6)$$

We maximize $W(\mathbf{b}, \mathbf{p})$ as a function of $\mathbf{b}$ subject to the constraint $\Sigma b_i = 1$. Writing the functional with a Lagrange multiplier, we have

$$J(\mathbf{b}) = \sum p_i \log b_i o_i + \lambda \sum b_i. \quad (6.7)$$

Differentiating this with respect to b_i yields

$$\frac{\partial J}{\partial b_i} = \frac{p_i}{b_i} + \lambda, \quad i = 1, 2, \ldots, m. \quad (6.8)$$

Setting the partial derivative equal to 0 for a maximum, we have

$$b_i = -\frac{p_i}{\lambda}. \quad (6.9)$$

Substituting this in the constraint $\Sigma b_i = 1$ yields $\lambda = -1$ and $b_i = p_i$. Hence, we can conclude that $\mathbf{b} = \mathbf{p}$ is a stationary point of the function $J(\mathbf{b})$. To prove that this is actually a maximum is tedious if we take second derivatives. Instead, we use a method that works for many such problems: guess and verify. We verify that proportional gambling $\mathbf{b} = \mathbf{p}$ is optimal in the following theorem.

Theorem 6.1.2 (*Proportional gambling is log-optimal*): *The optimum doubling rate is given by*

$$W^*(\mathbf{p}) = \sum p_i \log o_i - H(\mathbf{p}) \quad (6.10)$$

and is achieved by the proportional gambling scheme $\mathbf{b}^* = \mathbf{p}$.

Proof: We rewrite the function $W(\mathbf{b}, \mathbf{p})$ in a form in which the maximum is obvious:

$$W(\mathbf{b}, \mathbf{p}) = \sum p_i \log b_i o_i \tag{6.11}$$

$$= \sum p_i \log\left(\frac{b_i}{p_i} p_i o_i\right) \tag{6.12}$$

$$= \sum p_i \log o_i - H(\mathbf{p}) - D(\mathbf{p}\|\mathbf{b}) \tag{6.13}$$

$$\leq \sum p_i \log o_i - H(\mathbf{p}), \tag{6.14}$$

with equality iff $\mathbf{p} = \mathbf{b}$, i.e., the gambler bets on each horse in proportion to its probability of winning. □

Example 6.1.1: Consider a case with two horses, where horse 1 wins with probability p_1 and horse 2 wins with probability p_2. Assume even odds (2-for-1 on both horses). Then the optimal bet is proportional betting, i.e., $b_1 = p_1$, $b_2 = p_2$. The optimal doubling rate is $W^*(\mathbf{p}) = \sum p_i \log o_i - H(\mathbf{p}) = 1 - H(\mathbf{p})$, and the resulting wealth grows to infinity at this rate, i.e.,

$$S_n \doteq 2^{n(1-H(\mathbf{p}))}. \tag{6.15}$$

Thus, we have shown that proportional betting is growth rate optimal for a sequence of i.i.d. horse races if the gambler can reinvest his wealth and if there is no alternative of keeping some of the wealth in cash.

We now consider a special case when the odds are fair with respect to some distribution, i.e., there is no track take and $\sum \frac{1}{o_i} = 1$. In this case, we write $r_i = \frac{1}{o_i}$, where r_i can be interpreted as a probability mass function over the horses. (This is the bookie's estimate of the win probabilities.) With this definition, we can write the doubling rate as

$$W(\mathbf{b}, \mathbf{p}) = \sum p_i \log b_i o_i \tag{6.16}$$

$$= \sum p_i \log\left(\frac{b_i}{p_i} \frac{p_i}{r_i}\right) \tag{6.17}$$

$$= D(\mathbf{p}\|\mathbf{r}) - D(\mathbf{p}\|\mathbf{b}). \tag{6.18}$$

This equation gives another interpretation for the relative entropy "distance": the doubling rate is the difference between the distance of the bookie's estimate from the true distribution and the distance of the gambler's estimate from the true distribution. Hence the gambler can make money only if his estimate (as expressed by $\mathbf{b}$) is better than the bookie's.

An even more special case is when the odds are m-for-1 on each horse. In this case, the odds are fair with respect to the uniform distribution and the optimum doubling rate is

$$W^*(\mathbf{p}) = D\left(\mathbf{p} \| \frac{1}{m}\right) = \log m - H(\mathbf{p}) . \tag{6.19}$$

In this case we can clearly see the duality between data compression and the doubling rate:

Theorem 6.1.3 (*Conservation theorem*): *For uniform fair odds,*

$$W^*(\mathbf{p}) + H(\mathbf{p}) = \log m . \tag{6.20}$$

Thus the sum of the doubling rate and the entropy rate is a constant.

Every bit of entropy decrease doubles the gambler's wealth. Low entropy races are the most profitable.

In the above analysis, we assumed that the gambler was fully invested. In general, we should allow the gambler the option of retaining some of his wealth as cash. Let $b(0)$ be the proportion of wealth held out as cash, and $b(1), b(2), \ldots, b(m)$ be the proportions bet on the various horses. Then at the end of a race, the ratio of final wealth to initial wealth (the *wealth relative*) is

$$S(X) = b(0) + b(X)o(X) . \tag{6.21}$$

Now the optimum strategy may depend on the odds and will not necessarily have the simple form of proportional gambling. We distinguish three subcases:

1. *Fair odds with respect to some distribution.* $\sum \frac{1}{o_i} = 1$. For fair odds, the option of withholding cash does not change the analysis. This is because we can get the effect of withholding cash by betting $b_i = \frac{1}{o_i}$ on the ith horse, $i = 1, 2, \ldots, m$. Then $S(X) = 1$ irrespective of which horse wins. Thus whatever money the gambler keeps aside as cash can equally well be distributed over the horses, and the assumption that the gambler must invest all his money does not change the analysis. Proportional betting is optimal.

2. *Superfair odds.* $\sum \frac{1}{o_i} < 1$. In this case, the odds are even better than fair odds, so one would always want to put all one's wealth into the race rather than leave it as cash. In this race too the optimum strategy is proportional betting. However, it is possible to choose $\mathbf{b}$ so as to form a "Dutch book" by choosing $b_i = \frac{1}{o_i}$, to get $o_i b_i = 1$ irrespective of which horse wins. With this allotment, there will be $1 - \sum \frac{1}{o_i}$ left over as cash, so that at the end of the race, one has wealth $1 + (1 - \sum \frac{1}{o_i}) > 1$ with probability 1, i.e., no risk. Needless to say, one seldom finds such odds in real life. Incidentally, a Dutch book, though risk-free, does not optimize the doubling rate.

3. *Subfair odds* $\Sigma \frac{1}{o_i} > 1$. This is more representative of real life. The organizers of the race track take a cut of all the bets. In this case, it is usually desirable to bet only some of the money and leave the rest aside as cash. Proportional gambling is no longer log-optimal.

6.2 GAMBLING AND SIDE INFORMATION

Suppose the gambler has some information that is relevant to the outcome of the gamble. For example, the gambler may have some information about the performance of the horses in previous races. What is the value of this side information?

One definition of the financial value of such information is the increase in wealth that results from that information. In the setting described in the previous section, the measure of the value of information is the increase in the doubling rate due to that information. We will now derive a connection between mutual information and the increase in the doubling rate.

To formalize the notion, let horse $X \in \{1, 2, \ldots, m\}$ win the race with probability $p(x)$ and pay odds of $o(x)$ for 1. Let (X, Y) have joint probability mass function $p(x, y)$. Let $b(x|y) \geq 0$, $\Sigma_x b(x|y) = 1$ be an arbitrary conditional betting strategy depending on the side information Y, where $b(x|y)$ is the proportion of wealth bet on horse x when y is observed. As before, let $b(x) \geq 0$, $\Sigma b(x) = 1$ denote the unconditional betting scheme.

Let the unconditional and the conditional doubling rates be

$$W^*(X) = \max_{\mathbf{b}(x)} \sum_x p(x) \log b(x)o(x), \tag{6.22}$$

$$W^*(X|Y) = \max_{\mathbf{b}(x|y)} \sum_{x, y} p(x, y) \log b(x|y)o(x) \tag{6.23}$$

and let

$$\Delta W = W^*(X|Y) - W^*(X). \tag{6.24}$$

We observe that for (X_i, Y_i) i.i.d. horse races, wealth grows like $2^{nW^*(X|Y)}$ with side information and like $2^{nW^*(X)}$ without side information.

Theorem 6.2.1: *The increase ΔW in doubling rate due to side information Y for a horse race X is*

$$\Delta W = I(X; Y). \tag{6.25}$$

Proof: With side information, the maximum value of $W^*(X|Y)$ with side information Y is achieved by conditionally proportional gambling, i.e., $\mathbf{b}^*(x|y) = p(x|y)$. Thus

$$W^*(X|Y) = \max_{\mathbf{b}(x|y)} E[\log S] = \max_{\mathbf{b}(x|y)} \sum p(x, y) \log o(x)b(x|y) \quad (6.26)$$

$$= \sum p(x, y) \log o(x)p(x|y) \quad (6.27)$$

$$= \sum p(x) \log o(x) - H(X|Y). \quad (6.28)$$

Without side information, the optimal doubling rate is

$$W^*(X) = \sum p(x) \log o(x) - H(X). \quad (6.29)$$

Thus the increase in doubling rate due to the presence of side information Y is

$$\Delta W = W^*(X|Y) - W^*(X) = H(X) - H(X|Y) = I(X; Y). \quad \square \quad (6.30)$$

Hence the increase in doubling rate is equal to the mutual information between the side information and the horse race. Not surprisingly, independent side information does not increase the doubling rate.

This relationship can also be extended to the general stock market (Chapter 15). In this case, however, one can only show the inequality $\Delta W \leq I$, with equality if and only if the market is a horse race.

6.3   DEPENDENT HORSE RACES AND ENTROPY RATE

The most common example of side information for a horse race is the past performance of the horses. If the horse races are independent, this information will be useless. If we assume that there is dependence among the races, we can calculate the effective doubling rate if we are allowed to use the results of the previous races to determine the strategy for the next race.

Suppose the sequence $\{X_k\}$ of horse race outcomes forms a stochastic process. Let the strategy for each race depend on the results of the previous races. In this case, the optimal doubling rate for uniform fair odds is

$$W^*(X_k|X_{k-1}, X_{k-2}, \ldots, X_1)$$

$$= E\left[\max_{\mathbf{b}(\cdot|X_{k-1}, X_{k-2}, \ldots, X_1)} E[\log S(X_k)|X_{k-1}, X_{k-2}, \ldots, X_1]\right]$$

$$= \log m - H(X_k|X_{k-1}, X_{k-2}, \ldots, X_1), \quad (6.31)$$

which is achieved by $b^*(x_k|x_{k-1}, \ldots, x_1) = p(x_k|x_{k-1}, \ldots, x_1)$.

At the end of n races, the gambler's wealth is

$$S_n = \prod_{i=1}^{n} S(X_i), \tag{6.32}$$

and the exponent in the growth rate (assuming m for 1 odds) is

$$\frac{1}{n} E \log S_n = \frac{1}{n} \sum E \log S(X_i) \tag{6.33}$$

$$= \frac{1}{n} \sum \left(\log m - H(X_i | X_{i-1}, X_{i-2}, \ldots, X_1) \right) \tag{6.34}$$

$$= \log m - \frac{H(X_1, X_2, \ldots, X_n)}{n}. \tag{6.35}$$

The quantity $\frac{1}{n} H(X_1, X_2, \ldots, X_n)$ is the average entropy per race. For a stationary process with entropy rate $H(\mathcal{X})$, the limit in (6.35) yields

$$\lim_{n \to \infty} \frac{1}{n} E \log S_n + H(\mathcal{X}) = \log m. \tag{6.36}$$

Again, we have the result that the entropy rate plus the doubling rate is a constant.

The expectation in (6.36) can be removed if the process is ergodic. It will be shown in Chapter 15 that for an ergodic sequence of horse races,

$$S_n \doteq 2^{nW}, \quad \text{with probability 1}, \tag{6.37}$$

where $W = \log m - H(\mathcal{X})$ and

$$H(\mathcal{X}) = \lim \frac{1}{n} H(X_1, X_2, \ldots, X_n). \tag{6.38}$$

Example 6.3.1 (*Red and Black*): In this example, cards replace horses and the outcomes become more predictable as time goes on.

Consider the case of betting on the color of the next card in a deck of 26 red and 26 black cards. Bets are placed on whether the next card will be red or black, as we go through the deck. We also assume the game pays 2-for-1, that is, the gambler gets back twice what he bets on the right color. These are fair odds if red and black are equally probable.

We consider two alternative betting schemes:

1. If we bet sequentially, we can calculate the conditional probability of the next card and bet proportionally. Thus we should bet $(\frac{1}{2}, \frac{1}{2})$ on (red, black) for the first card, and $(\frac{26}{51}, \frac{25}{51})$ for the second card, if the first card is black, etc.

2. Alternatively, we can bet on the entire sequence of 52 cards at once. There are $\binom{52}{26}$ possible sequences of 26 red and 26 black cards, all of them equally likely. Thus proportional betting implies that we put $1/\binom{52}{26}$ of our money on each of these sequences and let each bet "ride."

We will argue that these procedures are equivalent. For example, half the sequences of 52 cards start with red, and so the proportion of money bet on sequences that start with red in scheme 2 is also one half, agreeing with the proportion used in the first scheme. In general, we can verify that betting $1/(\genfrac{}{}{0pt}{}{52}{26})$ of the money on each of the possible outcomes will at each stage give bets that are proportional to the probability of red and black at that stage. Since we bet $1/(\genfrac{}{}{0pt}{}{52}{26})$ of the wealth on each possible output sequence, and a bet on a sequence increases wealth by a factor of 2^{52} on the observed sequence and 0 on all the others, the resulting wealth is

$$S_{52}^{*} = \frac{2^{52}}{(\genfrac{}{}{0pt}{}{52}{26})} = 9.08 \, . \tag{6.39}$$

Rather interestingly, the return does not depend on the actual sequence. This is like the AEP in that the return is the same for all sequences. All sequences are typical in this sense.

6.4   THE ENTROPY OF ENGLISH

An important example of an information source is English text. It is not immediately obvious whether English is a stationary ergodic process. Probably not! Nonetheless, we will be interested in the entropy rate of English. We will discuss various stochastic approximations to English. As we increase the complexity of the model, we can generate text that looks like English. The stochastic models can be used to compress English text. The better the stochastic approximation, the better the compression.

For the purposes of discussion, we will assume that the alphabet of English consists of 26 letters and the space symbol. We therefore ignore punctuation and the difference between upper and lower case letters. We construct models for English using empirical distributions collected from samples of text. The frequency of letters in English is far from uniform. The most common letter E has a frequency of about 13% while the least common letters, Q and Z, occur with a frequency of about 0.1%. The letter E is so common that it is rare to find a sentence of any length that does not contain the letter. (A surprising exception to this is the 267 page novel, *"Gadsby"*, by Ernest Vincent Wright, in which the author deliberately makes no use of the letter E.)

The frequency of pairs of letters is also far from uniform. For example, the letter Q is always followed by a U. The most frequent pair is TH, which occurs normally with a frequency of about 3.7%. We can use the frequency of the pairs to estimate the probability that a letter follows any other letter. Proceeding this way, we can also estimate higher order conditional probabilities and build more complex models for the language. However, we soon run out of data. For example, to build a third order Markov approximation, we must estimate the values of $p(x_i | x_{i-1} x_{i-2} x_{i-3})$. There are $27^4 = 531441$ entries in this table, and we would need to process millions of letters to make accurate estimates of these probabilities.

The conditional probability estimates can be used to generate random samples of letters drawn according to these distributions (using a random number generator). But there is a simpler method to simulate randomness using a sample of text (a book, say). For example, to construct the second order model, open the book at random and choose a letter at random on the page. This will be the first letter. For the next letter, again open the book at random and starting at a random point, read until the first letter is encountered again. Then take the letter after that as the second letter. We repeat this process by opening to another page, searching for the second letter, and taking the letter after that as the third letter. Proceeding this way, we can generate text that simulates the second-order statistics of the English text.

Here are some examples of Markov approximations to English from Shannon's original paper [138]:

1. *Zero-order approximation.* (The symbols are independent and equiprobable.)

   XFOML RXKHRJFFJUJ ZLPWCFWKCYJ

   FFJEYVKCQSGXYD QPAAMKBZAACIBZLHJQD

2. *First-order approximation.* (The symbols are independent. Frequency of letters matches English text.)

   OCRO HLI RGWR NMIELWIS EU LL NBNESEBYA TH EEI

   ALHENHTTPA OOBTTVA NAH BRL

3. *Second-order approximation.* (The frequency of pairs of letters matches English text.)

   ON IE ANTSOUTINYS ARE T INCTORE ST BE S DEAMY

   ACHIN D ILONASIVE TUCOOWE AT TEASONARE FUSO

   TIZIN ANDY TOBE SEACE CTISBE

4. *Third-order approximation.* (The frequency of triplets of letters matches English text.)

   IN NO IST LAT WHEY CRATICT FROURE BERS GROCID

   PONDENOME OF DEMONSTURES OF THE REPTAGIN IS

   REGOACTIONA OF CRE

5. *Fourth-order approximation.* (The frequency of quadruplets of letters matches English text. Each letter depends on the previous three letters. This sentence is from Lucky's book, *Silicon Dreams* [183].)

THE GENERATED JOB PROVIDUAL BETTER TRAND THE

DISPLAYED CODE, ABOVERY UPONDULTS WELL THE

CODERST IN THESTICAL IT DO HOCK BOTHE MERG.

(INSTATES CONS ERATION. NEVER ANY OF PUBLE AND TO

THEORY. EVENTIAL CALLEGAND TO ELAST BENERATED IN

WITH PIES AS IS WITH THE)

Instead of continuing with the letter models, we jump to word models.

6. *First-order word model.* (The words are chosen independently but with frequencies as in English.)

REPRESENTING AND SPEEDILY IS AN GOOD APT OR COME

CAN DIFFERENT NATURAL HERE HE THE A IN CAME THE TO

OF TO EXPERT GRAY COME TO FURNISHES THE LINE

MESSAGE HAD BE THESE.

7. *Second-order word model.* (The word transition probabilities match English text.)

THE HEAD AND IN FRONTAL ATTACK ON AN ENGLISH

WRITER THAT THE CHARACTER OF THIS POINT IS

THEREFORE ANOTHER METHOD FOR THE LETTERS THAT THE

TIME OF WHO EVER TOLD THE PROBLEM FOR AN

UNEXPECTED

The approximations get closer and closer to resembling English. For example, long phrases of the last approximation could have easily occurred in a real English sentence. It appears that we could get a very good approximation by using a more complex model.

These approximations can be used to estimate the entropy of English. For example, the entropy of the zeroth-order model is $\log 27 = 4.76$ bits per letter. As we increase the complexity of the model, we capture more of the structure of English and the conditional uncertainty of the next letter is reduced. The first-order model gives an estimate of the entropy of 4.03 bits per letter, while the fourth-order model gives an estimate of

2.8 bits per letter. But even the fourth-order model does not capture all the structure of English. In Section 6.6, we describe alternative methods for estimating the entropy of English.

The statistics of English are useful in decoding encrypted English text. For example, a simple substitution cipher (where each letter is replaced by some other letter) can be solved by looking for the most frequent letter and guessing that it is the substitute for E, etc. The redundancy in English can be used to fill in some of the missing letters after the other letters are decrypted. For example,

TH_R_ _S _NLY _N_ W_Y T_ F_LL _N TH_ V_W_LS _N TH_S S_NT_NC_.

Some of the inspiration for Shannon's original work on information theory came out of his work in cryptography during World War II. The mathematical theory of cryptography and its relationship to the entropy of language is developed in Shannon [241].

Stochastic models of language also play a key role in some speech recognition systems. A commonly used model is the trigram (second-order Markov) word model, which estimates the probability of the next word given the previous two words. The information from the speech signal is combined with the model to produce an estimate of the most likely word that could have produced the observed speech. Random models do surprisingly well in speech recognition, even when they do not explicitly incorporate the complex rules of grammar that govern natural languages like English.

We can apply the techniques of this section to estimate the entropy rate of other information sources like speech and images. A fascinating non-technical introduction to these issues can be found in the book by Lucky [183].

6.5 DATA COMPRESSION AND GAMBLING

We now show a direct connection between gambling and data compression, by showing that a good gambler is also a good data compressor. Any sequence on which a gambler makes a large amount of money is also a sequence that can be compressed by a large factor.

The idea of using the gambler as a data compressor is based on the fact that the gambler's bets can be considered to be his estimate of the probability distribution of the data. A good gambler will make a good estimate of the probability distribution. We can use this estimate of the distribution to do arithmetic coding (Section 5.10). This is the essential idea of the scheme described below.

We assume that the gambler has a mechanically identical twin, who will be used for the data decompression. The identical twin will place the same bets on possible sequences of outcomes as the original gambler (and will therefore make the same amount of money). The cumulative amount of money that the gambler would have made on all sequences that are lexicographically less than the given sequence will be used as a code for the sequence. The decoder will use the identical twin to gamble on all sequences, and look for the sequence for which the same cumulative amount of money is made. This sequence will be chosen as the decoded sequence.

Let $X_1, X_2, \ldots, X_n$ be a sequence of random variables that we wish to compress. Without loss of generality, we will assume that the random variables are binary. Gambling on this sequence will be defined by a sequence of bets

$$b(x_{k+1}|x_1, x_2, \ldots, x_k) \geq 0, \quad \sum_{x_{k+1}} b(x_{k+1}|x_1, x_2, \ldots, x_k) = 1, \quad (6.40)$$

where $b(x_{k+1}|x_1, x_2, \ldots, x_k)$ is the proportion of money bet at time k on the event that $X_{k+1} = x_{k+1}$ given the observed past $x_1, x_2, \ldots, x_k$. Bets are paid at uniform odds (2-for-1). Thus the wealth S_n at the end of the sequence is given by

$$S_n = 2^n \prod_{k=1}^{n} b(x_k|x_1, \ldots, x_{k-1}) \qquad (6.41)$$

$$= 2^n b(x_1, x_2, \ldots, x_n), \qquad (6.42)$$

where

$$b(x_1, x_2, \ldots, x_n) = \prod_{k=1}^{n} b(x_k|x_{k-1}, \ldots, x_1). \qquad (6.43)$$

So sequential gambling can also be considered as an assignment of probabilities (or bets) $b(x_1, x_2, \ldots, x_n) \geq 0$, $\sum_{x_1, \ldots, x_n} b(x_1, \ldots, x_n) = 1$, on the 2^n possible sequences.

This gambling elicits both an estimate of the true probability of the text sequence ($\hat{p}(x_1, \ldots, x_n) = S_n/2^n$) as well as an estimate of the entropy ($\hat{H} = -\frac{1}{n} \log \hat{p}$) of the text from which the sequence was drawn. We now wish to show that high values of wealth S_n lead to high data compression. Specifically, we shall argue that if the text in question results in wealth S_n, then $\log S_n$ bits can be saved in a naturally associated deterministic data compression scheme. We shall further assert that if the gambling is log optimal, then the data compression achieves the Shannon limit H.

Consider the following data compression algorithm that maps the text $\mathbf{x} = x_1 x_2 \ldots x_n \in \{0, 1\}^n$ into a code sequences $c_1 c_2 \ldots c_k, c_i \in \{0, 1\}$. Both the compressor and the decompressor know n. Let the 2^n text sequences be arranged in lexicographical order. Thus, for example, $0100101 < 0101101$. The encoder observes the sequence $x^n = (x_1, x_2, \ldots, x_n)$. He then calculates what his wealth $S_n(x'(n))$ would have been on all sequences $x'(n) \leq x(n)$ and calculates $F(x(n)) = \sum_{x'(n) \leq x(n)} 2^{-n} S_n(x'(n))$. Clearly, $F(x(n)) \in [0, 1]$. Let $k = \lceil n - \log S_n(x(n)) \rceil$. Now express $F(x(n))$ as a binary decimal to k place accuracy: $\lfloor F(x(n)) \rfloor = .c_1 c_2 \ldots c_k$. The sequence $c(k) = (c_1, c_2, \ldots, c_k)$ is transmitted to the decoder.

The decoder twin can calculate the precise value $S(x'(n))$ associated with each of the 2^n sequences $x'(n)$. He thus knows the cumulative sum of $2^{-n} S(x'(n))$ up through any sequence $x(n)$. He tediously calculates this sum until it first exceeds $.c(k)$. The first sequence $x(n)$ such that the cumulative sum falls in the interval $[.c_1 \ldots c_k, .c_1 \ldots c_k + (1/2)^k]$ is uniquely defined, and the size of $S(x(n))/2^n$ guarantees that this sequence will be precisely the encoded $x(n)$.

Thus the twin uniquely recovers $x(n)$. The number of bits required is $k = \lceil n - \log S(x(n)) \rceil$. The number of bits saved is $n - k = \lfloor \log S(x(n)) \rfloor$. For proportional gambling, $S(x(n)) = 2^n p(x(n))$. Thus the expected number of bits is $Ek = \sum p(x(n)) \lceil -\log p(x(n)) \rceil \leq H(X_1, \ldots, X_n) + 1$.

We see that if the betting operation is deterministic and is known both to the encoder and the decoder, then the number of bits necessary to encode $x_1, \ldots, x_n$ is less than $n - \log S_n + 1$. Moreover, if $p(x)$ is known, and if proportional gambling is used, then the expected description length is $E(n - \log S_n) \leq H(X_1, \ldots, X_n) + 1$. Thus the gambling results correspond precisely to the data compression that would have been achieved by the given human encoder-decoder identical twin pair.

The data compression scheme using a gambler is similar to the idea of arithmetic coding (Section 5.10) using a distribution $b(x_1, x_2, \ldots, x_n)$ rather than the true distribution. The above procedure brings out the duality between gambling and data compression. Both involve estimation of the true distribution. The better the estimate, the greater the growth rate of the gambler's wealth and the better the data compression.

6.6 GAMBLING ESTIMATE OF THE ENTROPY OF ENGLISH

We now estimate the entropy rate for English using a human gambler to estimate probabilities. We assume that English consists of 27 characters (26 letters and a space symbol). We therefore ignore punctuation and case of letters. Two different approaches have been proposed to estimate the entropy of English.

1. *Shannon guessing game.* In this approach, the human subject is given a sample of English text and asked to guess the next letter.

An optimal subject will estimate the probabilities of the next letter and guess the most probable letter first, then the second most probable letter next, etc. The experimenter records the number of guesses required to guess the next letter. The subject proceeds this way through a fairly large sample of text. We can then calculate the empirical frequency distribution of the number of guesses required to guess the next letter. Many of the letters will require only one guess; but a large number of guesses will usually be needed at the beginning of words or sentences.

Now let us assume that the subject can be modeled as a computer making a deterministic choice of guesses given the past text. Then if we have the same machine, and the sequence of guess numbers, we can reconstruct the English text. Just let the machine run, and if the number of guesses at any position is k, choose the kth guess of the machine as the next letter. Hence the amount of information in the sequence of guess numbers is the same as the English text. The entropy of the guess sequence is the entropy of English text. We can bound the entropy of the guess sequence by assuming that the samples are independent. Hence the entropy of the guess sequence is bounded above by the entropy of the histogram in the experiment.

The experiment was conducted by Shannon [242] in 1950, who obtained a value of 1.3 bits per symbol for the entropy of English.

2. *Gambling estimate.* In this approach, we let a human subject gamble on the next letter in a sample of English text. This allows finer gradations of judgement than does guessing. As in the case of a horse race, the optimal bet is proportional to the conditional probability of the next letter. The payoff is 27-for-1 on the correct letter.

Since sequential betting is equivalent to betting on the entire sequence, we can write the payoff after n letters as

$$S_n = (27)^n b(X_1, X_2, \ldots, X_n). \qquad (6.44)$$

Thus after n rounds of betting, the expected log wealth satisfies

$$E \frac{1}{n} \log S_n = \log 27 + \frac{1}{n} E \log b(X_1, X_2, \ldots, X_n) \qquad (6.45)$$

$$= \log 27 + \frac{1}{n} \sum_{x^n} p(x^n) \log b(x^n) \qquad (6.46)$$

$$= \log 27 - \frac{1}{n} \sum_{x^n} p(x^n) \log \frac{p(x^n)}{b(x^n)} + \frac{1}{n} \sum_{x^n} p(x^n) \log p(x^n)$$

$$(6.47)$$

$$= \log 27 - \frac{1}{n} D(p(x^n) \| b(x^n)) - \frac{1}{n} H(X_1, X_2, \ldots, X_n)$$

$$\text{(6.48)}$$

$$\leq \log 27 - \frac{1}{n} H(X_1, X_2, \ldots, X_n) \qquad\qquad \text{(6.49)}$$

$$\leq \log 27 - H(\mathscr{X}), \qquad\qquad\qquad\qquad \text{(6.50)}$$

where $H(\mathscr{X})$ is the entropy rate of English. Thus $\log 27 - E\frac{1}{n} \log S_n$ is an upper bound on the entropy rate of English. The upper bound estimate, $\hat{H} = \log 27 - \frac{1}{n} \log S_n$ converges to H with probability one if English is ergodic and the gambler uses $b(x^n) = p(x^n)$.

An experiment [72] with 12 subjects and a sample of 75 letters from the book *Jefferson the Virginian* by Dumas Malone (the same source used by Shannon) resulted in an estimate of 1.34 bits per letter for the entropy of English.

SUMMARY OF CHAPTER 6

Doubling rate: $W(\mathbf{b}, \mathbf{p}) = E(\log S(X)) = \sum_{k=1}^{m} p_k \log b_k o_k$.

Optimal doubling rate: $W^*(\mathbf{p}) = \max_{\mathbf{b}} W(\mathbf{b}, \mathbf{p})$.

Proportional gambling is log-optimal:

$$W^*(\mathbf{p}) = \max_{\mathbf{b}} W(\mathbf{b}, \mathbf{p}) = \sum p_i \log o_i - H(\mathbf{p}) \qquad \text{(6.51)}$$

is achieved by $\mathbf{b}^* = \mathbf{p}$.

Growth rate: Wealth grows as $S_n \doteq 2^{nW^*(\mathbf{p})}$.

Conservation law: For uniform fair odds,

$$H(\mathbf{p}) + W^*(\mathbf{p}) = \log m . \qquad\qquad \text{(6.52)}$$

Side information: In a horse race X, the increase ΔW in doubling rate due to side information Y is

$$\Delta W = I(X; Y) . \qquad\qquad\qquad \text{(6.53)}$$

PROBLEMS FOR CHAPTER 6

1. *Horse race.* Three horses run a race. A gambler offers 3-for-1 odds on each of the horses. These are fair odds under the assumption that all horses are equally likely to win the race. The true win probabilities are known to be

$$\mathbf{p} = (p_1, p_2, p_3) = \left(\frac{1}{2}, \frac{1}{4}, \frac{1}{4}\right). \tag{6.54}$$

Let $\mathbf{b} = (b_1, b_2, b_3)$, $b_i \geq 0$, $\Sigma\, b_i = 1$, be the amount invested on each of the horses. The expected log wealth is thus

$$W(\mathbf{b}) = \sum_{i=1}^{3} p_i \log 3b_i. \tag{6.55}$$

   (a) Maximize this over $\mathbf{b}$ to find $\mathbf{b}^*$ and W^*. Thus the wealth achieved in repeated horse races should grow to infinity like 2^{nW^*} with probability one.
   (b) Show that if instead we put all of our money on horse 1, the most likely winner, we will eventually go broke with probability one.

2. *Horse race with unfair odds.* If the odds are bad (due to a track take) the gambler may wish to keep money in his pocket. Let $b(0)$ be the amount in his pocket and let $b(1), b(2), \ldots, b(m)$ be the amount bet on horses $1, 2, \ldots, m$, with odds $o(1), o(2), \ldots, o(m)$, and win probabilities $p(1), p(2), \ldots, p(m)$. Thus the resulting wealth is $S(x) = b(0) + b(x)o(x)$, with probability $p(x)$, $x = 1, 2, \ldots, m$.
   (a) Find $\mathbf{b}^*$ maximizing $E \log S$ if $\Sigma\, 1/o(i) < 1$.
   (b) Discuss $\mathbf{b}^*$ if $\Sigma\, 1/o(i) > 1$. (There isn't an easy closed form solution in this case, but a "water-filling" solution results from the application of the Kuhn-Tucker conditions.)

3. *Cards.* An ordinary deck of cards containing 26 red cards and 26 black cards is shuffled and dealt out one card at at time without replacement. Let X_i be the color of the ith card.
   (a) Determine $H(X_1)$.
   (b) Determine $H(X_2)$.
   (c) Does $H(X_k|X_1, X_2, \ldots, X_{k-1})$ increase or decrease?
   (d) Determine $H(X_1, X_2, \ldots, X_{52})$.

4. *Beating the public odds.* Consider a 3 horse race with win probabilities

$$(p_1, p_2, p_3) = \left(\frac{1}{2}, \frac{1}{4}, \frac{1}{4}\right)$$

and fair odds with respect to the (false) distribution

$$(r_1, r_2, r_3) = \left(\frac{1}{4}, \frac{1}{4}, \frac{1}{2}\right).$$

Thus the odds are

$$(o_1, o_2, o_3) = (4, 4, 2).$$

(a) What is the entropy of the race?

(b) Find the set of bets (b_1, b_2, b_3) such that the compounded wealth in repeated plays will grow to infinity.

5. A 3 horse race has win probabilities $\mathbf{p} = (p_1, p_2, p_3)$, and odds $\mathbf{o} = (1, 1, 1)$. The gambler places bets $\mathbf{b} = (b_1, b_2, b_3)$, $b_i \geq 0$, $\Sigma \, b_i = 1$, where b_i denotes the proportion on wealth bet on horse i. These odds are very bad. The gambler gets his money back on the winning horse and loses the other bets. Thus the wealth S_n at time n resulting from independent gambles goes exponentially to zero.

(a) Find the exponent.

(b) Find the optimal gambling scheme $\mathbf{b}$.

(c) Assuming $\mathbf{b}$ is chosen as in (b), what distribution $\mathbf{p}$ causes S_n to go to zero at the fastest rate?

6. *Gambling.* Suppose one gambles sequentially on the card outcomes in Problem 3. Even odds of 2-for-1 are paid. Thus the wealth S_n at time n is $S_n = 2^n b(x_1, x_2, \ldots, x_n)$, where $b(x_1, x_2, \ldots, x_n)$ is the proportion of wealth bet on $x_1, x_2, \ldots, x_n$. Find $\max_{b(\cdot)} E \log S_{52}$.

7. *The St. Petersburg paradox.* Many years ago in St. Petersburg the following gambling proposition caused great consternation. For an entry fee of c units, a gambler receives a payoff of 2^k units with probability 2^{-k}, $k = 1, 2, \ldots$.

(a) Show that the expected payoff for this game is infinite. For this reason, it was argued that $c = \infty$ was a "fair" price to pay to play this game. Most people find this answer absurd.

(b) Suppose that the gambler can buy a share of the game. For example, if he invests $c/2$ units in the game, he receives $1/2$ a share and a return $X/2$, where $\Pr(X = 2^k) = 2^{-k}$, $k = 1, 2, \ldots$. Suppose $X_1, X_2, \ldots$ are i.i.d. according to this distribution and the gambler reinvests all his wealth each time. Thus his wealth S_n at time n is given by

$$S_n = \prod_{i=1}^{n} \frac{X_i}{c}. \qquad (6.56)$$

Show that this limit is ∞ or 0, with probability one, accordingly as $c < c^*$ or $c > c^*$. Identify the "fair" entry fee c^*.

More realistically, the gambler should be allowed to keep a proportion $\bar{b} = 1 - b$ of his money in his pocket and invest the rest in the St. Petersburg game. His wealth at time n is then

$$S_n = \prod_{i=1}^{n} \left(\bar{b} + \frac{bX_i}{c} \right). \qquad (6.57)$$

Let

$$W(b, c) = \sum_{k=1}^{\infty} 2^{-k} \log\left(1 - b + \frac{b2^k}{c}\right).$$ (6.58)

We have

$$S_n \doteq 2^{nW(b, c)}.$$ (6.59)

Let

$$W^*(c) = \max_{0 \le b \le 1} W(b, c).$$ (6.60)

Here are some questions about $W^*(c)$.

(c) For what value of the entry fee c does the optimizing value b^* drop below 1?

(d) How does b^* vary with c?

(e) How does $W^*(c)$ fall off with c?

Note that since $W^*(c) > 0$, for all c , we can conclude that any entry fee c is fair.

8. *Super St. Petersburg.* Finally, we have the super St. Petersburg paradox, where $\Pr(X = 2^{2^k}) = 2^{-k}, k = 1, 2, \ldots$. Here the expected log wealth is infinite for all $b > 0$, for all c, and the gambler's wealth grows to infinity faster than exponentially for any $b > 0$. But that doesn't mean all investment ratios b are equally good. To see this, we wish to maximize the relative growth rate with respect to some other portfolio, say, $\mathbf{b} = (\frac{1}{2}, \frac{1}{2})$. Show that there exists a unique b maximizing

$$E \ln \frac{(\bar{b} + bX/c)}{(\frac{1}{2} + \frac{1}{2}X/c)}$$

and interpret the answer.

HISTORICAL NOTES

The original treatment of gambling on a horse race is due to Kelly [150], who found $\Delta W = I$. Log optimal portfolios go back to the work of Bernoulli, Kelly [150] and Latané [172, 173]. Proportional gambling is sometimes referred to as the Kelly gambling scheme.

Shannon studied stochastic models for English in his original paper [238]. His guessing game for estimating the entropy rate of English is described in [242]. Cover and King [72] described the gambling estimate for the entropy of English. The analysis of the St. Petersburg paradox is from Bell and Cover [20]. An alternative analysis can be found in Feller [110].

Chapter 7

Kolmogorov Complexity

The great mathematican Kolmogorov culminated a lifetime of research in mathematics, complexity and information theory with his definition in 1965 of the intrinsic descriptive complexity of an object. In our treatment so far, the object X has been a random variable drawn according to a probability mass function $p(x)$. If X is random, there is a sense in which the descriptive complexity of the event $X = x$ is $\log \frac{1}{p(x)}$, because $\lceil \log \frac{1}{p(x)} \rceil$ is the number of bits required to describe x by a Shannon code. One notes immediately that the descriptive complexity of such an object depends on the probability distribution.

Kolmogorov went further. He defined the algorithmic (descriptive) complexity of an object to be the length of the shortest binary computer program that describes the object. (Apparently a computer, the most general form of data decompressor, will use this description to exhibit the described object after a finite amount of computation.) Thus the Kolmogorov complexity of an object dispenses with the probability distribution. Kolmogorov made the crucial observation that the definition of complexity is essentially computer independent. It is an amazing fact that the expected length of the shortest binary computer description of a random variable is approximately equal to its entropy. Thus the shortest computer description acts as a universal code which is uniformly good for all probability distributions. In this sense, algorithmic complexity is a conceptual precursor to entropy.

This chapter is intellectually more demanding than the others in this book, and indeed, it can be omitted in a first course on information theory. Perhaps a proper point of view of the role of this chapter is to consider Kolmogorov complexity as a way to think. One does not use the shortest computer program in practice because it may take infinitely long to find such a minimal program. But one can use very short, not necessarily minimal, programs in practice. And the idea of finding such short programs leads to universal codes, a good basis for inductive inference, a formalization of Occam's Razor ("The simplest explanation is best") and to clarity of thought in physics, computer science, and communication theory.

Before formalizing the notion of Kolmogorov complexity, let us give three strings as examples. They are

1. 0101010101010101010101010101010101010101010101010101010-
   101010101
2. 0110101000001001111001100110011111110011101111001100100-
   100001000
3. 1101111001110101111101101011111011101011011111000101110010-
   100111011

What are the shortest binary computer programs for each of these sequences? The first sequence is definitely simple. It consists of thirty-two 01's. The second sequence looks random and passes most tests for randomness, but it is in fact the binary expansion of $\sqrt{2} - 1$. Again, this is a simple sequence. The third again looks random, except that the proportion of 1's is not near $1/2$. We shall assume that it is otherwise random. It turns out that by describing the number k of 1's in the sequence, then giving the index of the sequence in a lexicographic ordering of those with this number of 1's, one can give a description of the sequence in roughly $\log n + nH(\frac{k}{n})$ bits. This again is substantially less than the n bits in the sequence. Again, we conclude that the sequence, random though it is, is simple. In this case, however, it is not as simple as the other two sequences, which have constant length programs. In fact, its complexity is proportional to n. Finally, we can imagine a truly random sequence generated by pure coin flips. There are 2^n such sequences and they are all equally probable. It is highly likely that such a random sequence cannot be compressed, i.e., there is no better program for such a sequence than simply saying "Print the following: 0101100111010 ... 0." The reason for this is that there are not enough short programs to go around. Thus the descriptive complexity of a truly random binary sequence is as long as the sequence itself.

These are the basic ideas. It will remain to be shown that this notion of intrinsic complexity is computer independent, i.e., that the length of the shortest program does not depend on the computer. At first, this seems like nonsense. But it turns out to be true, up to an additive constant. And for long sequences of high complexity, this additive constant (which is the length of the pre-program that allows one computer to mimic the other) is negligible.

7.1 MODELS OF COMPUTATION

To formalize the notions of algorithmic complexity, we first discuss acceptable models for computers. All but the most trivial computers are universal, in the sense that they can mimic the actions of other computers. We will briefly touch on a certain canonical universal computer, the universal Turing machine. The universal Turing machine is the conceptually simplest universal computer.

In 1936, Turing was obsessed with the question of whether the thoughts in a living brain could equally well be held by a collection of inanimate parts. In short, could a machine think? By analyzing the human computational process, he posited some constraints on such a computer. Apparently, a human thinks, writes, thinks some more, writes, and so on. Consider a computer as a finite state machine operating on a finite symbol set. (The symbols in an infinite symbol set cannot be distinguished in finite space.) A program tape, on which a binary program is written, is fed left to right into this finite state machine. At each unit of time, the machine inspects the program tape, writes some symbols on a work tape, changes its state according to its transition table and calls for more program. The operations of such a machine can be described by a finite list of transitions. Turing argued that this machine could mimic the computational ability of a human being.

After Turing's work, it turned out that every new computational system could be reduced to a Turing machine, and conversely. In particular, the familiar digital computer with its CPU, memory and input output devices could be simulated by and could simulate a Turing machine. This led Church to state what is now known as Church's thesis, which states that all (sufficiently complex) computational models are equivalent in the sense that they can compute the same family of functions. The class of functions they can compute agrees with our intuitive notion of effectively computable functions, that is, functions for which there is a finite prescription or program that will lead in a finite number of mechanically specified computational steps to the desired computational result.

We shall have in mind throughout this chapter the computer illustrated in Figure 7.1. At each step of the computation, the computer reads a symbol from the input tape, changes state according to its state transition table, possibly writes something on the work tape or output tape, and moves the program read head to the next cell of the program read tape. This machine reads the program from right to left only, never going back, and therefore the programs form a prefix-free set. No program leading to a halting computation can be the prefix of another such program. The restriction to prefix-free programs leads immediately to a theory of Kolmogorov complexity which is formally analogous to information theory.

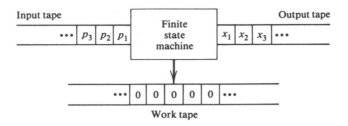

Figure 7.1. A Turing machine.

We can view the Turing machine as a map from a set of finite length binary strings to the set of finite or infinite length binary strings. In some cases, the computation does not halt, and in such cases the value of the function is said to be undefined. The set of functions $f:\{0,1\}^* \rightarrow \{0,1\}^* \cup \{0,1\}^\infty$ computable by Turing machines is called the set of *partial recursive functions*.

7.2   KOLMOGOROV COMPLEXITY: DEFINITIONS AND EXAMPLES

Let x be a finite length binary string and let $\mathcal{U}$ be a universal computer. Let $l(x)$ denote the length of the string x. Let $\mathcal{U}(p)$ denote the output of the computer $\mathcal{U}$ when presented with a program p.

We define the Kolmogorov (or algorithmic) complexity of a string x as the minimal description length of x.

Definition: The *Kolmogorov complexity* $K_{\mathcal{U}}(x)$ of a string x with respect to a universal computer $\mathcal{U}$ is defined as

$$K_{\mathcal{U}}(x) = \min_{p\,:\,\mathcal{U}(p)=x} l(p), \tag{7.1}$$

the minimum length over all programs that print x and halt. Thus $K_{\mathcal{U}}(x)$ is the shortest description length of x over all descriptions interpreted by computer $\mathcal{U}$.

An important technique for thinking about Kolmogorov complexity is the following—if one person can describe a sequence to another person in such a manner as to lead unambiguously to a computation of that sequence in a finite amount of time, then the number of bits in that communication is an upper bound on the Kolmogorov complexity. For example, one can say "Print out the first 1,239,875,981,825,931 bits of the square root of e." Allowing 8 bits per character (ASCII), we see that the above unambiguous 73 symbol program demonstrates that the Kolmogorov complexity of this huge number is no greater than $(8)(73) = 584$ bits. Most numbers of this length have a Kolmogorov complexity of

1,239,875,981,825,931 bits. The fact that there is a simple algorithm to calculate the square root of e provides the saving in descriptive complexity.

In the above definition, we have not mentioned anything about the length of x. If we assume that the computer already knows the length of x, then we can define the *conditional Kolmogorov complexity* knowing $l(x)$ as

$$K_{\mathcal{U}}(x|l(x)) = \min_{p\,:\,\mathcal{U}(p,\,l(x))=x} l(p). \qquad (7.2)$$

This is the shortest description length if the computer $\mathcal{U}$ has the length of x made available to it.

It should be noted that $K_{\mathcal{U}}(x|y)$ is usually defined as $K_{\mathcal{U}}(x|y, y^*)$, where y^* is the shortest program for y. This is to avoid certain slight asymmetries in chain rules like $K(x, y) = K(x) + K(y|x) \approx K(y) + K(x|y)$, but we will not use this definition here.

We first prove some of the basic properties of Kolmogorov complexity and then consider various examples.

Theorem 7.2.1 (*Universality of Kolmogorov complexity*): *If $\mathcal{U}$ is a universal computer, then for any other computer $\mathcal{A}$,*

$$K_{\mathcal{U}}(x) \le K_{\mathcal{A}}(x) + c_{\mathcal{A}} \qquad (7.3)$$

for all strings $x \in \{0, 1\}^*$, where the constant $c_{\mathcal{A}}$ does not depend on x.

Proof: Assume that we have a program $p_{\mathcal{A}}$ for computer $\mathcal{A}$ to print x. Thus $\mathcal{A}(p_{\mathcal{A}}) = x$. We can precede this program by a simulation program $s_{\mathcal{A}}$ which tells computer $\mathcal{U}$ how to simulate computer $\mathcal{A}$. The computer $\mathcal{U}$ will then interpret the instructions in the program for $\mathcal{A}$, perform the corresponding calculations and print out x. The program for $\mathcal{U}$ is $p = s_{\mathcal{A}}p_{\mathcal{A}}$ and its length is

$$l(p) = l(s_{\mathcal{A}}) + l(p_{\mathcal{A}}) = c_{\mathcal{A}} + l(p_{\mathcal{A}}), \qquad (7.4)$$

where $c_{\mathcal{A}}$ is the length of the simulation program. Hence,

$$K_{\mathcal{U}}(x) = \min_{p\,:\,\mathcal{U}(p)=x} l(p) \le \min_{p\,:\,\mathcal{A}(p)=x} (l(p) + c_{\mathcal{A}}) = K_{\mathcal{A}}(x) + c_{\mathcal{A}} \qquad (7.5)$$

for all strings x. $\square$

The constant $c_{\mathcal{A}}$ in the theorem may be very large. For example, $\mathcal{A}$ may be a large computer with a large number of functions built into the system. The computer $\mathcal{U}$ can be a simple microprocessor. The simulation program will contain the details of the implementation of all these functions, in fact, all the software available on the large computer. The crucial point is that the length of this simulation program is independent of the length of x, the string to be compressed. For sufficiently long x, the length of this simulation program can be neglected, and we can discuss Kolmogorov complexity without talking about the constants.

If $\mathscr{A}$ and $\mathscr{U}$ are both universal, then we have

$$|K_{\mathscr{U}}(x) - K_{\mathscr{A}}(x)| < c \tag{7.6}$$

for all x. Hence we will drop all mention of $\mathscr{U}$ in all further definitions. We will assume that the unspecified computer $\mathscr{U}$ is a fixed universal computer.

Theorem 7.2.2 (*Conditional complexity is less than the length of the sequence*):

$$K(x|l(x)) \leq l(x) + c . \tag{7.7}$$

Proof: We can exhibit the string x in the program. The program is self-delimiting because $l(x)$ is provided and the end of the program is thus clearly defined. A program for printing x is

```
Print the following l-bit sequence: x₁x₂...x_{l(x)} .
```

Note that no bits are required to describe l since l is given. The length of this program is $l(x) + c$. □

Without knowledge of the length of the string, we will need an additional stop symbol or we can use a self-punctuating scheme like the one described in the proof of the next theorem.

Theorem 7.2.3 (*Upper bound on Kolmogorov complexity*):

$$K(x) \leq K(x|l(x)) + 2 \log l(x) + c . \tag{7.8}$$

Proof: If the computer does not know $l(x)$, the method of Theorem 7.2.2 does not apply. We must have some way of informing the computer when it has come to the end of the string of bits that describes the sequence. We describe a simple but inefficient method which uses a sequence 01 as a "comma."

Suppose $l(x) = n$. To describe $l(x)$, repeat every bit of the binary expansion of n twice; then end the description with a 01 so that the computer knows that it has come to the end of the description of n. For example, the number 5 (binary 101) will be described as 11001101. This description requires $2\lceil \log n \rceil + 2$ bits.

Thus, inclusion of the binary representation of $l(x)$ does not add more than $2 \log l(x) + c$ bits to the length of the program, and we have the bound in the theorem. $\square$

A more efficient method for describing n is to do so recursively. We first specify the number ($\log n$) of bits in the binary representation of n, and then specify the actual bits of n. To specify $\log n$, the length of the binary representation of n, we can use the inefficient method ($2 \log \log n$) or the efficient method ($\log \log n + \cdots$). If we use the efficient method at each level, until we have a small number to specify, we can describe n in $\log n + \log \log n + \log \log \log n + \cdots$ bits, where we continue the sum until the last positive term. This sum of iterated logarithms is sometimes written $\log^* n$. Thus Theorem 7.2.3 can be improved to

$$K(x) \le K(x|l(x)) + \log^* l(x) + c. \tag{7.9}$$

We now prove that there are very few sequences with low complexity.

Theorem 7.2.4 (*Lower bound on Kolmogorov complexity*): *The number of strings x with complexity $K(x) < k$ satisfies*

$$|\{x \in \{0,1\}^* : K(x) < k\}| < 2^k. \tag{7.10}$$

Proof: There are not very many short programs. If we list all the programs of length $< k$, we have

$$\underbrace{\Lambda}_{1}, \underbrace{0, 1}_{2}, \underbrace{00, 01, 10, 11}_{4}, \ldots, \underbrace{\ldots, \overbrace{11 \ldots 1}^{k-1}}_{2^{k-1}} \tag{7.11}$$

and the total number of such programs is

$$1 + 2 + 4 + \cdots + 2^{k-1} = 2^k - 1 < 2^k. \tag{7.12}$$

Since each program can produce only one possible output sequence, the number of sequences with complexity $< k$ is less than 2^k. $\square$

To avoid confusion and to facilitate exposition in the rest of this chapter, we shall need to introduce a special notation for the *binary entropy function*

$$H_0(p) = -p \log p - (1-p) \log(1-p). \tag{7.13}$$

Thus, when we write $H_0(\frac{1}{n} \Sigma_{i=1}^n X_i)$, we will mean $-\bar{X}_n \log \bar{X}_n - (1 - \bar{X}_n) \log(1 - \bar{X}_n)$ and not the entropy of random variable $\bar{X}_n$. When there is no confusion, we shall simply write $H(p)$ for $H_0(p)$.

Now let us consider various examples of Kolmogorov complexity. The complexity will depend on the computer, but only up to an additive constant. To be specific, we consider a computer that can accept unambiguous commands in English (with numbers given in binary notation). We will assume the inequality

$$\frac{1}{n+1} 2^{nH(\frac{k}{n})} \le \binom{n}{k} \le 2^{nH(\frac{k}{n})} , \tag{7.14}$$

which can be easily proved using Stirling's formula [110]. An alternative proof can be found in Example 12.1.3.

Example 7.2.1 (*A sequence of n zeroes*): If we assume that the computer knows n, then a short program to print this string is

```
Print the specified number of zeroes.
```

The length of this program is a constant number of bits. This program length does not depend on n. Hence the Kolmogorov complexity of this sequence is c, and

$$K(000 \ldots 0|n) = c \quad \text{for all } n . \tag{7.15}$$

Example 7.2.2 (*Kolmogorov complexity of π*): The first n bits of π can be calculated using a simple series expression. This program has a small constant length, if the computer already knows n. Hence

$$K(\pi_1 \pi_2 \ldots \pi_n|n) = c . \tag{7.16}$$

Example 7.2.3 (*Gotham weather*): Suppose we want the computer to print out the weather in Gotham for n days. We can write a program that contains the entire sequence $x - x_1 x_2 \ldots x_n$, where $x_i = 1$ indicates rain on day i. But this is inefficient, since the weather is quite dependent. We can devise various coding schemes for the sequence to take the dependence into account. A simple one is to find a Markov model to approximate the sequence (using the empirical transition probabilities) and then code the sequence using the Shannon code for this probability distribution. We can describe the empirical Markov transitions in $O(\log n)$ bits, and then use $\log \frac{1}{p(x)}$ bits to describe x, where p is the specified Markov probability. Assuming that the entropy of the weather is 1/5 bits per day, we can describe the weather for n days using about $n/5$ bits, and hence

$$K(\text{Gotham weather}|n) \approx \frac{n}{5} + O(\log n) + c . \tag{7.17}$$

Example 7.2.4 (*A repeating sequence of the form 01010101 ... 01*): A short program suffices. Simply print the specified number of 01 pairs. Hence

$$K(010101010 \ldots 01 | n) = c. \tag{7.18}$$

Example 7.2.5 (*A fractal*): The fractal on the cover is part of the Mandelbrot set, and is generated by a simple computer program. For different points c in the complex plane, one calculates the number of iterations of the map $z_{n+1} = z_n^2 + c$ (starting with $z_0 = 0$) needed for $|z|$ to cross a particular threshold. The point c is then colored according to the number of iterations needed.

Thus the fractal is an example of an object that looks very complex but is essentially very simple. Its Kolmogorov complexity is nearly zero.

Example 7.2.6 (*The Mona Lisa*): We can make use of the many structures and dependencies in the painting. We can probably compress the image by a factor of 3 or so by using some existing easily described image compression algorithm. Hence, if n is the number of pixels in the image of the Mona Lisa,

$$K(\text{Mona Lisa} | n) \le \frac{n}{3} + c. \tag{7.19}$$

Example 7.2.7 (*An integer n*): If the computer knows the number of bits in the binary representation of the integer, then we need only provide the values of these bits. This program will have length $c + \log n$.

In general the computer will not know the length of the binary representation of the integer. So we must inform the computer in some way when the description ends. Using the method to describe integers used to derive (7.9), we see that the Kolmogorov complexity of an integer is bounded by

$$K(n) \le \log^* n + c. \tag{7.20}$$

Example 7.2.8 (*A sequence of n bits with k ones*): Can we compress a sequence of n bits with k ones?

Our first guess is no, since we have a series of bits that must be reproduced exactly. But consider the following program:

```
Generate, in lexicographic order, all sequences with k ones;
    Of these sequences, print the ith sequence.
```

This program will print out the required sequence. The only variables in the program are k (with range $\{0, 1, \ldots, n\}$) and i (with conditional range $\binom{n}{k}$). The total length of this program is

$$l(p) = c + \underbrace{\frac{2\log k}{\text{to express } k}} + \underbrace{\frac{\log\binom{n}{k}}{\text{to express } i}} \qquad (7.21)$$

$$\leq c + 2\log k + nH_0\left(\frac{k}{n}\right), \qquad (7.22)$$

since $\binom{n}{k} \leq 2^{nH_0\left(\frac{k}{n}\right)}$ by (7.14). We have used $2\log k + 2$ bits to represent k by the inefficient method described in the proof of Theorem 7.2.3. Thus if $\sum_{i=1}^{n} x_i = k$, then

$$K(x_1, x_2, \ldots, x_n \mid n) \leq nH\left(\frac{k}{n}\right) + 2\log k + c. \qquad (7.23)$$

We can summarize the last example in the following theorem:

Theorem 7.2.5: *The Kolmogorov complexity of a binary string x is bounded by*

$$K(x_1 x_2 \ldots x_n \mid n) \leq nH_0\left(\frac{1}{n}\sum_{i=1}^{n} x_i\right) + 2\log n + c. \qquad (7.24)$$

Proof: Use the program described in the last example. $\square$

Remark: Let $x \in \{0,1\}^*$ be the data we wish to compress, and consider the program p to be the compressed data. We will have succeeded in compressing the data only if $l(p) < l(x)$, or

$$K(x) < l(x). \qquad (7.25)$$

In general, when the length $l(x)$ of the sequence x is small, the constants that appear in the expressions for the Kolmogorov complexity will overwhelm the contributions due to $l(x)$. Hence the theory is useful primarily when $l(x)$ is very large. In such cases, we can safely neglect the constants that do not depend on $l(x)$.

7.3   KOLMOGOROV COMPLEXITY AND ENTROPY

We now consider the relationship between the Kolmogorov complexity of a sequence of random variables and its entropy. In general, we show that the expected value of the Kolmogorov complexity of a random sequence is close to the Shannon entropy. First, we prove that the program lengths satisfy the Kraft inequality:

Lemma 7.3.1: *For any computer* $\mathcal{U}$,

$$\sum_{p\,:\,\mathcal{U}(p)\text{ halts}} 2^{-l(p)} \leq 1 \,. \tag{7.26}$$

Proof: If the computer halts on any program, it does not look any further for input. Hence, there cannot be any other halting program with this program as a prefix. Thus the halting programs form a prefix-free set, and their lengths satisfy the Kraft inequality (Theorem 5.2.1). $\square$

We now show that $\frac{1}{n}EK(X^n|n) \approx H(X)$ for i.i.d. processes with a finite alphabet.

Theorem 7.3.1 (*Relationship of Kolmogorov complexity and entropy*): *Let the stochastic process* $\{X_i\}$ *be drawn i.i.d. according to the probability mass function* $f(x)$, $x \in \mathcal{X}$, *where* $\mathcal{X}$ *is a finite alphabet. Let* $f(x^n) = \prod_{i=1}^{n} f(x_i)$. *Then there exists a constant* c *such that*

$$H(X) \leq \frac{1}{n} \sum_{x^n} f(x^n) K(x^n|n) \leq H(X) + \frac{|\mathcal{X}|\log n}{n} + \frac{c}{n} \tag{7.27}$$

for all n. *Thus*

$$E\,\frac{1}{n}K(X^n|n) \to H(X)\,. \tag{7.28}$$

Proof: Consider the lower bound. The allowed programs satisfy the prefix property, and thus their lengths satisfy the Kraft inequality. We assign to each x^n the length of the shortest program p such that $\mathcal{U}(p, n) = x^n$. These shortest programs also satisfy the Kraft inequality. We know from the theory of source coding that the expected codeword length must be greater than the entropy. Hence

$$\sum_{x^n} f(x^n) K(x^n|n) \geq H(X_1, X_2, \ldots, X_n) = nH(X)\,. \tag{7.29}$$

We first prove the upper bound when $\mathcal{X}$ is binary, i.e., $X_1, X_2, \ldots, X_n$ are i.i.d. $\sim$ Bernoulli(θ). Using the method of Theorem 7.2.5, we can bound the complexity of a binary string by

$$K(x_1 x_2 \ldots x_n|n) \leq nH_0\left(\frac{1}{n}\sum_{i=1}^{n} x_i\right) + 2\log n + c\,. \tag{7.30}$$

Hence

$$EK(X_1 X_2 \ldots X_n|n) \leq nEH_0\left(\frac{1}{n}\sum_{i=1}^{n} X_i\right) + 2\log n + c \tag{7.31}$$

$$\overset{(a)}{\le} nH_0\left(\frac{1}{n}\sum_{i=1}^{n} EX_i\right) + 2\log n + c \tag{7.32}$$

$$= nH_0(\theta) + 2\log n + c\,, \tag{7.33}$$

where (a) follows from Jensen's inequality and the concavity of the entropy. Thus we have proved the upper bound in the theorem for binary processes.

We can use the same technique for the case of a non-binary finite alphabet. We first describe the type of the sequence (the empirical frequency of occurrence of each of the alphabet symbols as defined in Section 12.1) using $|\mathscr{X}|\log n$ bits. Then we describe the index of the sequence within the set of all sequences having the same type. The type class has less than $2^{nH(P_{x^n})}$ elements (where P_{x^n} is the type of the sequence x^n), and therefore the two-stage description of a string x^n has length

$$K(x^n|n) \le nH(P_{x^n}) + |\mathscr{X}|\log n + c\,. \tag{7.34}$$

Again, taking the expectation and applying Jensen's inequality as in the binary case, we obtain

$$EK(X^n|n) \le nH(X) + |\mathscr{X}|\log n + c\,. \tag{7.35}$$

Dividing this by n yields the upper bound of the theorem. $\square$

7.4   KOLMOGOROV COMPLEXITY OF INTEGERS

In the last section, we defined the Kolmogorov complexity of a binary string as the length of the shortest program for a universal computer that prints out that string. We can extend that definition to define the Kolmogorov complexity of an integer to be the Kolmogorov complexity of the corresponding binary string.

Definition: The *Kolmogorov complexity of an integer n* is defined as

$$K(n) = \min_{p\,:\,\mathscr{U}(p)=n} l(p)\,. \tag{7.36}$$

The properties of the Kolmogorov complexity of integers are very similar to those of the Kolmogorov complexity of bit strings. The following properties are immediate consequences of the corresponding properties for strings.

Theorem 7.4.1: *For universal computers $\mathscr{A}$ and $\mathscr{U}$,*

$$K_{\mathcal{U}}(n) \le K_{\mathcal{A}}(n) + c_{\mathcal{A}} \, . \tag{7.37}$$

Also, since any number can be specified by its binary expansion, we have the following theorem.

Theorem 7.4.2:

$$K(n) \le \log^* n + c \, . \tag{7.38}$$

Theorem 7.4.3: *There are an infinite number of integers n such that $K(n) > \log n$.*

   Proof: We know from Lemma 7.3.1 that

$$\sum_n 2^{-K(n)} \le 1 \, , \tag{7.39}$$

and

$$\sum_n 2^{-\log n} = \sum_n \frac{1}{n} = \infty \, . \tag{7.40}$$

But if $K(n) < \log n$ for all $n > n_0$, then

$$\sum_{n=n_0}^{\infty} 2^{-K(n)} > \sum_{n=n_0}^{\infty} 2^{-\log n} = \infty \, , \tag{7.41}$$

which is a contradiction. $\square$

7.5 ALGORITHMICALLY RANDOM AND INCOMPRESSIBLE SEQUENCES

From the examples in Section 7.2, it is clear that there are some long sequences that are simple to describe, like the first million bits of π. By the same token, there are also large integers that are simple to describe, such as

$$2^{2^{2^{2^{2^{2^{2}}}}}}$$

or $(100!)!$.
   We now show that although there are some simple sequences, most sequences do not have simple descriptions. Similarly, most integers are not simple. Hence if we draw a sequence at random, we are likely to draw a complex sequence. The next theorem shows that the probability that a sequence can be compressed by more than k bits is no greater than 2^{-k}.

Theorem 7.5.1: Let $X_1, X_2, \ldots, X_n$ be drawn according to a Bernoulli($\frac{1}{2}$) process. Then

$$P(K(X_1 X_2 \ldots X_n | n) < n - k) < 2^{-k}. \tag{7.42}$$

Proof:

$$P(K(X_1 X_2 \ldots X_n | n) < n - k)$$

$$= \sum_{x_1, x_2, \ldots, x_n : K(x_1 x_2 \ldots x_n | n) < n - k} p(x_1, x_2, \ldots, x_n) \tag{7.43}$$

$$= \sum_{x_1, x_2, \ldots, x_n : K(x_1 x_2 \ldots x_n | n) < n - k} 2^{-n} \tag{7.44}$$

$$= |\{x_1, x_2, \ldots, x_n : K(x_1 x_2 \ldots x_n | n) < n - k\}| 2^{-n}$$

$$< 2^{n-k} 2^{-n} \quad \text{(by Theorem 7.2.4)} \tag{7.45}$$

$$= 2^{-k}. \quad \square \tag{7.46}$$

Thus most sequences have a complexity close to their length. For example, the fraction of sequences of length n that have complexity less than $n - 5$ is less than $1/32$. This motivates the following definition:

Definition: A sequence $x_1, x_2, \ldots, x_n$ is said to be *algorithmically random* if

$$K(x_1 x_2 \ldots x_n | n) \geq n. \tag{7.47}$$

Note that by the counting argument, there exists, for each n, at least one sequence x^n such that

$$K(x^n | n) \geq n. \tag{7.48}$$

Definition: We call an infinite string x *incompressible* if

$$\lim_{n \to \infty} \frac{K(x_1 x_2 x_3 \ldots x_n | n)}{n} = 1. \tag{7.49}$$

Theorem 7.5.2 (*Strong law of large numbers for incompressible sequences*): If a string $x_1 x_2 \ldots$ is incompressible, then it satisfies the law of large numbers in the sense that

$$\frac{1}{n} \sum_{i=1}^{n} x_i \to \frac{1}{2}. \tag{7.50}$$

Hence the proportions of 0's and 1's in any incompressible string are almost equal.

Proof: Let $\theta_n = \frac{1}{n} \sum_{i=1}^{n} x_i$ denote the proportion of 1's in $x_1, x_2, \ldots, x_n$. Then using the method of Example 7.2 of Section 7.2, one can write a program of length $nH_0(\theta_n) + 2 \log(n\theta_n) + c$ to print x^n. By the incompressibility assumption, we also have the lower bound,

$$n - c_n \le K(x^n | n) \le nH_0(\theta_n) + 2 \log n + c' . \tag{7.51}$$

where $c_n/n \to 0$ and c' does not depend on n. Thus

$$H_0(\theta_n) > 1 - \frac{2 \log n + c_n + c'}{n} . \tag{7.52}$$

Inspection of the graph of $H_0(p)$ (Figure 7.2) shows that θ_n is close to $\frac{1}{2}$ for large n. Specifically, the above inequality implies that

$$\theta_n \in \left(\frac{1}{2} - \delta_n, \frac{1}{2} + \delta_n \right), \tag{7.53}$$

where δ_n is chosen so that

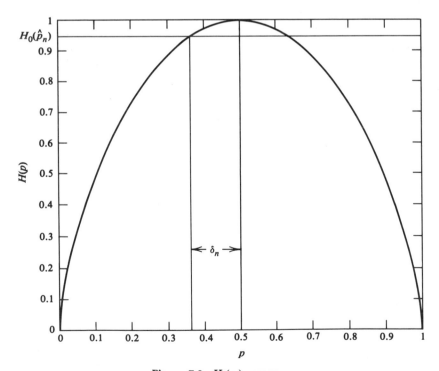

Figure 7.2. $H_0(p)$ versus p.

$$H_0\left(\frac{1}{2} - \delta_n\right) = 1 - \frac{2 \log n + c_n + c'}{n} , \tag{7.54}$$

which implies that $\delta_n \to 0$ as $n \to \infty$. Thus $\frac{1}{n} \Sigma x_i \to \frac{1}{2}$ as $n \to \infty$. $\square$

We have now proved that incompressible sequences look random in the sense that the proportion of 0's and 1's are almost equal. In general, we can show that if a sequence is incompressible, it will satisfy all computable statistical tests for randomness. (Otherwise, identification of the test that x fails will reduce the descriptive complexity of x, yielding a contradiction.) In this sense, the algorithmic test for randomness is the ultimate test, including within it all other computable tests for randomness.

We now prove a related law of large numbers for the Kolmogorov complexity of Bernoulli(θ) sequences. The Kolmogorov complexity of a sequence of binary random variables drawn i.i.d. according to a Bernoulli(θ) process is close to the entropy $H_0(\theta)$.

Theorem 7.5.3: *Let $X_1, X_2, \ldots, X_n$ be drawn i.i.d. $\sim$ Bernoulli(θ). Then*

$$\frac{1}{n} K(X_1, X_2, \ldots, X_n | n) \to H_0(\theta) \quad \text{in probability} . \tag{7.55}$$

Proof: Let $\bar{X}_n = \frac{1}{n} \Sigma X_i$ be the proportion of 1's in $X_1, X_2, \ldots, X_n$. Then using the method described in (7.23), we have

$$K(X_1, X_2, \ldots, X_n | n) \le nH_0(\bar{X}_n) + 2 \log n + c , \tag{7.56}$$

and since by the weak law of large numbers, $\bar{X}_n \to \theta$ in probability, we have

$$\Pr\left\{\frac{1}{n} K(X_1, X_2, \ldots, X_n | n) - H_0(\theta) \ge \epsilon\right\} \to 0 . \tag{7.57}$$

Conversely, we can bound the number of sequences with complexity significantly lower than the entropy. From the AEP, we can divide the set of sequences into the typical set and the non-typical set. There are at least $(1 - \epsilon)2^{n(H_0(\theta) - \epsilon)}$ sequences in the typical set. At most $2^{n(H_0(\theta) - c)}$ of these typical sequences can have a complexity less than $n(H_0(\theta) - c)$. The probability that the complexity of the random sequence is less than $n(H_0(\theta) - c)$ is

$$\Pr(K(X^n | n) < n(H_0(\theta) - c))$$

$$\le \Pr(X^n \notin A_\epsilon^{(n)}) + \Pr(X^n \in A_\epsilon^{(n)}, K(X^n | n) < n(H_0(\theta) - c))$$

$$\leq \epsilon + \sum_{x^n \in A_\epsilon^{(n)}, \, K(x^n|n) < n(H_0(\theta) - c)} p(x^n) \tag{7.58}$$

$$\leq \epsilon + \sum_{x^n \in A_\epsilon^{(n)}, \, K(x^n|n) < n(H_0(\theta) - c)} 2^{-n(H_0(\theta) - \epsilon)} \tag{7.59}$$

$$\leq \epsilon + 2^{n(H_0(\theta) - c)} \, 2^{-n(H_0(\theta) - \epsilon)} \tag{7.60}$$

$$= \epsilon + 2^{-n(c - \epsilon)}, \tag{7.61}$$

which is arbitrarily small for appropriate choice of ϵ, n and c. Hence with high probability, the Kolmogorov complexity of the random sequence is close to the entropy, and we have

$$\frac{K(X_1, X_2, \ldots, X_n | n)}{n} \to H_0(\theta) \quad \text{in probability.} \quad \square \tag{7.62}$$

7.6 UNIVERSAL PROBABILITY

Suppose that a computer is fed a random program. Imagine a monkey sitting at a keyboard and typing the keys at random. Equivalently, feed a series of fair coin flips into a universal Turing machine. In either case, most strings will not make sense to the computer. If a person sits at a terminal and types keys at random, he will probably get an error message, i.e., the computer will print the null string and halt. But with a certain probability he will hit on something that makes sense. The computer will then print out something meaningful. Will this output sequence look random?

From our earlier discussions, it is clear that most sequences of length n have complexity close to n. Since the probability of an input program p is $2^{-l(p)}$, shorter programs are much more probable than longer ones. And shorter programs, when they produce long strings, do not produce random strings; they produce strings with simply described structure.

The probability distribution on the output strings is far from uniform. Under the computer induced distribution, simple strings are more likely than complicated strings of the same length. This motivates us to define a universal probability distribution on strings as follows:

Definition: The *universal probability* of a string x is

$$P_\mathcal{U}(x) = \sum_{p \, : \, \mathcal{U}(p) = x} 2^{-l(p)} = \Pr(\mathcal{U}(p) = x), \tag{7.63}$$

which is the probability that a program randomly drawn as a sequence of fair coin flips $p_1, p_2, \ldots$ will print out the string x.

This probability is universal in many senses. We can consider it as the probability of observing such a string in nature; the implicit belief is that simpler strings are more likely than complicated strings. For example, if we wish to describe the laws of physics, we might consider the simplest string describing the laws as the most likely. This principle is known as "Occam's Razor", and has been a general principle guiding scientific research for centuries—if there are many explanations consistent with the observed data, choose the simplest. In our framework, Occam's Razor is equivalent to choosing the shortest program that produces a given string.

This probability mass function is called universal because of the following theorem:

Theorem 7.6.1: *For every computer* $\mathcal{A}$,

$$P_{\mathcal{U}}(x) \geq c'_{\mathcal{A}} P_{\mathcal{A}}(x) \tag{7.64}$$

for every string $x \in \{0, 1\}^*$, *where the constant* $c'_{\mathcal{A}}$ *depends only on* $\mathcal{U}$ *and* $\mathcal{A}$.

Proof: From the discussion of Section 7.2, we recall that for every program p' for $\mathcal{A}$ that prints x, there exists a program p for $\mathcal{U}$ of length not more than $l(p') + c_{\mathcal{A}}$ produced by prefixing a simulation program for $\mathcal{A}$. Hence

$$P_{\mathcal{U}}(x) = \sum_{p\,:\,\mathcal{U}(p)=x} 2^{-l(p)} \geq \sum_{p'\,:\,\mathcal{A}(p')=x} 2^{-l(p')-c_{\mathcal{A}}} = c'_{\mathcal{A}} P_{\mathcal{A}}(x). \quad \square \tag{7.65}$$

Any sequence drawn according to a computable probability mass function on binary strings can be considered to be produced by some computer $\mathcal{A}$ acting on a random input (via the probability inverse transformation acting on a random input). Hence the universal probability distribution includes a mixture of all computable probability distributions.

Remark (*Bounded likelihood ratio*): In particular, Theorem 7.6.1 guarantees that a likelihood ratio test of the hypothesis that X is drawn according to $P_{\mathcal{U}}$ versus the hypothesis that it is drawn according to $P_{\mathcal{A}}$ will have bounded likelihood ratio. If $\mathcal{U}$ and $\mathcal{A}$ are universal, then $P_{\mathcal{U}}(x)/P_{\mathcal{A}}(x)$ is bounded away from zero and infinity for all x. This is in contrast to other simple hypothesis testing problems (like Bernoulli(θ_1) versus Bernoulli(θ_2)) where the likelihood ratio goes to 0 or ∞ as the sample size goes to infinity. Apparently $P_{\mathcal{U}}$ can never be completely rejected as the true distribution of any data drawn according to some computable probability distribution. In that sense, we cannot reject the possibility that the universe is the output of monkeys typing at a computer.

In Section 7.11 we will prove that

$$P_{\mathcal{U}}(x) \approx 2^{-K(x)} , \tag{7.66}$$

thus showing that $K(x)$ and $\log \frac{1}{P_{\mathcal{U}}(x)}$ have equal status as universal algorithmic complexity measures.

We will conclude this section with an example of a monkey at a typewriter vs. a monkey at a computer keyboard. If the monkey types at random on a typewriter, the probability that it types out all the works of Shakespeare (assuming the text is 1 million bits long) is $2^{-1,000,000}$. If the monkey sits at a computer terminal, however, the probability that it types out Shakespeare is now $2^{-K(\text{Shakespeare})} \approx 2^{-250,000}$, which though extremely small is still exponentially more likely than when the monkey sits at a dumb typewriter.

The example indicates that a random input to a computer is much more likely to produce "interesting" outputs than a random input to a typewriter. We all know that a computer is an intelligence amplifier. Apparently it creates sense from nonsense as well.

7.7   THE HALTING PROBLEM AND THE NON-COMPUTABILITY OF KOLMOGOROV COMPLEXITY

Consider the following paradoxical statement:

This statement is false.

This paradox is sometimes stated in a two-statement form:

The next statement is false.

The preceding statement is true.

These paradoxes are versions of what is called the Epimenides Liar Paradox, and it illustrates the pitfalls involved in self-reference. In 1931, Gödel used this idea of self-reference to show that any interesting system of mathematics is not complete; there are statements in the system that are true but which cannot be proved within the system. To accomplish this, he translated theorems and proofs into integers, and constructed a statement of the above form, which can therefore not be proved true or false.

The halting problem in computer science is very closely connected with Gödel's incompleteness theorem. In essence, it states that for any computational model, there is no general algorithm to decide whether a program will halt or not (go on forever). Note that it is not a statement about any specific program. Quite clearly, there are many programs that can be easily shown to halt or go on forever. The halting problem says that we cannot answer this question for all programs. The reason for this is again the idea of self-reference.

To a practical person, the halting problem may not be of any immediate significance, but it has great theoretical importance as the dividing line between things that can be done on a computer (given unbounded memory and time) and things that cannot be done at all (such as proving all true statements in number theory). Gödel's incompleteness theorem is one of the most important mathematical results of this century, and its consequences are still being explored. The halting problem is an essential example of Gödel's incompleteness theorem.

One of the consequences of the non-existence of an algorithm for the halting problem is the non-computability of Kolmogorov complexity. The only way to find the shortest program in general is to try all short programs and see which of them can do the job. However, at any time some of the short programs may not have halted and there is no effective (finite mechanical) way to tell whether they will halt or not and what they will print out. Hence, there is no effective way to find the shortest program to print a given string.

The non-computability of Kolmogorov complexity is an example of the Berry paradox. The Berry paradox asks for "the shortest number not nameable in under ten words." No number like 1,101,121 can be a solution since the defining expression itself is less than ten words long. This illustrates the problems with the terms nameable and describable; they are too powerful to be used without a strict meaning. If we restrict ourselves to the meaning "can be described for printing out on a computer," then we can resolve Berry's paradox by saying that the smallest number not describable in less than ten words exists, but is not computable. This so-called "description" is not a program for computing the number. E. F. Beckenbach pointed out a similar problem in the classification of numbers as dull or interesting; the smallest dull number must be interesting.

As stated at the beginning of the chapter, one does not really anticipate that practitioners will find the shortest computer program for a given string. The shortest program is not computable, although as more and more programs are shown to produce the string, the estimates from above of the Kolmogorov complexity converge to the true Kolmogorov complexity. (The problem, of course, is that one may have found the shortest program and never know that no shorter program exists.) Even though Kolmogorov complexity is not computable, it provides a framework within which to consider questions of randomness and inference.

7.8 Ω

In this section, we introduce Chaitin's mystical, magical number Ω, which has some extremely interesting properties.

Definition:

$$\Omega = \sum_{p\,:\,\mathcal{U}(p)\,\text{halts}} 2^{-l(p)} . \tag{7.67}$$

Note that $\Omega = \text{Pr}(\mathcal{U}(p)$ halts), the probability that the given universal computer halts when the input to the computer is a binary string drawn according to a Bernoulli($\frac{1}{2}$) process.

Since the programs that halt are prefix-free, their lengths satisfy the Kraft inequality, and hence the above sum is always between 0 and 1. Let $\Omega_n = .\omega_1 \omega_2 \ldots \omega_n$ denote the first n bits of Ω.

Properties of Ω:

1. Ω *is non-computable.* There is no effective (finite, mechanical) way to check whether arbitrary programs halt (the halting problem), so there is no effective way to compute Ω.

2. Ω *is a "Philosopher's Stone".* Knowing Ω to an accuracy of n bits will enable us to decide the truth of any provable or finitely refutable mathematical theorem that can be written in less than n bits. Actually all that this means is that given n bits of Ω, there is an effective procedure to decide the truth of n-bit theorems; the procedure may take an arbitrarily long (but finite) time. Of course, without knowing Ω, it is not possible to check the truth or falsity of every theorem by an effective procedure (Gödel's incompleteness theorem).

   The basic idea of the procedure using n bits of Ω is simple: we run all programs until the sum of the masses $2^{-l(p)}$ contributed by programs that halt equals or exceeds Ω_n, the truncated version of Ω that we are given. Then, since

$$\Omega - \Omega_n < 2^{-n} , \tag{7.68}$$

   we know that the length of all further contributions of the form $2^{-l(p)}$ to Ω from programs that halt must also be less than 2^{-n}. This implies that no program of length $\leq n$ that has not yet halted will ever halt, which enables us to decide the halting or non-halting of all programs of length $\leq n$.

   To complete the proof, we must show that it is possible for a computer to run all possible programs in "parallel" in such a way that any program that halts will eventually be found to halt. First, list all possible programs, starting with the null program, Λ:

$$\Lambda, 0, 1, 00, 01, 10, 11, 000, 001, 010, 011, \ldots \qquad (7.69)$$

Then let the computer execute one clock cycle of Λ for the first cycle. In the next cycle, let the computer execute two clock cycles of Λ and two clock cycles of the program 0. In the third cycle, let it execute three clock cycles of each of the first three programs, and so on. In this way, the computer will eventually run all possible programs and run them for longer and longer times, so that if any program halts, it will eventually be discovered to halt. The computer keeps track of which program is being executed and the cycle number so that it can produce a list of all the programs that halt. This enables the computer to find any proof of the theorem or a counterexample to the theorem if the theorem can be stated in less than n bits. Knowledge of Ω turns previously unprovable theorems into provable theorems. Here Ω acts as an oracle.

Though Ω seems magical in this respect, there are other numbers that carry the same information. For example, if we take the list of programs and construct a real number in which the ith bit indicates whether program i halts, then this number also can be used to decide any finitely refutable question in mathematics. This number is very dilute (in information content) because one needs approximately 2^n bits of this indicator function to decide whether an n-bit program halts or not. Given 2^n bits, one can tell immediately without any computation whether any program of length less than n halts or not. However, Ω is the most compact representation of this information since it is algorithmically random and incompressible.

What are some of the questions that we can resolve using Ω? Many of the interesting problems in number theory can be stated as a search for a counterexample. For example, it is straightforward to write a program that searches over the integers x, y, z and n and halts only if it finds a counterexample to Fermat's last theorem, which states that

$$x^n + y^n = z^n \qquad (7.70)$$

has no solution in integers for $n \geq 3$. Another example is Goldbach's conjecture, which states that any even number is a sum of two primes. Our program would search through all the even numbers starting with 2, check all prime numbers less than it and find a decomposition as a sum of two primes. It will halt if it comes across an even number that does not have such a decomposition.

Knowing whether this program halts is equivalent to knowing the truth of Goldbach's conjecture.

We can also design a program that searches through all proofs and halts only when it finds a proof of the required theorem. This program will eventually halt if the theorem has a finite proof. Hence knowing n bits of Ω, we can find the truth or falsity of all theorems that have a finite proof or are finitely refutable and which can be stated in less than n bits.

3. Ω *is algorithmically random.*

Theorem 7.8.1: Ω *cannot be compressed by more than a constant, i.e., there exists a constant c such that*

$$K(\omega_1 \omega_2 \ldots \omega_n) \geq n - c, \quad \text{for all } n. \tag{7.71}$$

Proof: We know that if we are given n bits of Ω, we can determine whether or not any program of length $\leq n$ halts. Using $K(\omega_1 \omega_2 \ldots \omega_n)$ bits, we can calculate n bits of Ω, and then we can generate a list of all programs of length $\leq n$ that halt, together with their corresponding outputs. We find the first string x_0 that is not on this list. The string x_0 is then the shortest string with Kolmogorov complexity $K(x_0) > n$. The complexity of this program to print x_0 is $K(\Omega_n) + c$, which must be at least as long as the shortest program for x_0. Consequently,

$$K(\Omega_n) + c \geq K(x_0) > n, \tag{7.72}$$

for all n. Thus $K(\omega_1 \omega_2 \ldots \omega_n) > n - c$, and Ω cannot be compressed by more than a constant. ∎

7.9 UNIVERSAL GAMBLING

Suppose a gambler is asked to gamble sequentially on sequences $x \in \{0, 1\}^*$. He has no idea of the origin of the sequence. He is given fair odds (2-for-1) on each bit. How should he gamble?

If he knew the distribution of the elements of the string, then he might use proportional betting because of its optimal growth-rate properties, as shown in Chapter 6. If he believes that the string occurred naturally, then it seems intuitive that simpler strings are more likely than complex ones. Hence, if he were to extend the idea of proportional betting, he might bet according to the universal probability of the string. For reference, note that if the gambler knows the string x in advance, then he can increase his wealth by a factor of $2^{l(x)}$ simply by betting all his wealth each time on the next symbol of x. Let the wealth $S(x)$ associated with betting scheme $b(x)$, $\Sigma \, b(x) = 1$, be given by

$$S(x) = 2^{l(x)}b(x) . \qquad (7.73)$$

Suppose the gambler bets $b(x) = 2^{-K(x)}$ on a string x. This betting strategy can be called *universal gambling*. We note that the sum of the bets

$$\sum_x b(x) = \sum_x 2^{-K(x)} \le \sum_{p:p \text{ halts}} 2^{-l(p)} = \Omega \le 1 , \qquad (7.74)$$

and he will not have used all his money. For simplicity, let us assume that he throws the rest away. For example, the amount of wealth resulting from a bet $b(0110)$ on a sequence $x = 0110$ is $2^{l(x)}b(x) = 2^4 b(0110)$ plus the amount won on all bets $b(0110 \ldots)$ on sequences consistent with x.

Then we have the following theorem:

Theorem 7.9.1: *The logarithm of the amount of money a gambler achieves on a sequence using universal gambling plus the complexity of the sequence is no smaller than the length of the sequence, or*

$$\log S(x) + K(x) \ge l(x) . \qquad (7.75)$$

Remark: This is the counterpart of the gambling conservation theorem $W^* + H = \log m$ from Chapter 6.

Proof: The proof follows directly from the universal gambling scheme, $b(x) = 2^{-K(x)}$, since

$$S(x) = \sum_{x' \sqsupseteq x} 2^{l(x')}b(x') \ge 2^{l(x)}2^{-K(x)} , \qquad (7.76)$$

where $x' \sqsupseteq x$ means that x is a prefix of x'. Taking logarithms establishes the theorem. $\square$

The result can be understood in many ways. For sequences with finite Kolmogorov complexity,

$$S(x) \ge 2^{l(x)-K(x)} = 2^{l(x)-c} \qquad (7.77)$$

for all x. Since $2^{l(x)}$ is the most that can be won in $l(x)$ gambles at fair odds, this scheme does asymptotically as well as the scheme based on knowing the sequence in advance. Thus, for example, if $x = $

$\pi_1 \pi_2 \ldots \pi_n \ldots$, the digits in the expansion of π, then the wealth at time n will be $S_n = S(x^n) \geq 2^{n-c}$ for all n.

If the string is actually generated by a Bernoulli process with parameter p, then

$$S(X_1 \ldots X_n) \geq 2^{n - nH_0(\bar{X}_n) - 2\log n - c} \approx 2^{n\left(1 - H_0(p) - 2\frac{\log n}{n} - \frac{c}{n}\right)}, \quad (7.78)$$

which is the same to first order as the rate achieved when the gambler knows the distribution in advance, as in Chapter 6.

From the examples, we see that the universal gambling scheme on a random sequence does asymptotically as well as a scheme which uses prior knowledge of the true distribution.

7.10   OCCAM'S RAZOR

In many areas of scientific research, it is important to choose among various explanations of observed data. And after choosing the explanation, we wish to assign a confidence level to the predictions that ensue from the laws that have been deduced.

For example, Laplace considered the probability that the sun will rise again tomorrow, given that it has risen every day in recorded history. Laplace's solution was to assume that the rising of the sun was a Bernoulli(θ) process with unknown parameter θ. He assumed that θ was uniformly distributed on the unit interval. Using the observed data, he calculated the posterior probability that the sun will rise again tomorrow and found that it was

$$P(X_{n+1} = 1 | X_n = 1, X_{n-1} = 1, \ldots, X_1 = 1)$$

$$= \frac{P(X_{n+1} = 1, X_n = 1, X_{n-1} = 1, \ldots, X_1 = 1)}{P(X_n = 1, X_{n-1} = 1, \ldots, X_1 = 1)}$$

$$= \frac{\int_0^1 \theta^{n+1} \, d\theta}{\int_0^1 \theta^n \, d\theta} \quad (7.79)$$

$$= \frac{n+1}{n+2}, \quad (7.80)$$

which he put forward as the probability that the sun will rise on day $n+1$ given that it has risen on days 1 through n.

Using the ideas of Kolmogorov complexity and universal probability, we can provide an alternative approach to the problem. Under the universal probability, let us calculate the probability of seeing a 1 next after having observed n 1's in the sequence so far. The conditional probability that the next symbol is a 1 is the ratio of the probability of all sequences with initial segment 1^n and next bit equal to 1 to the probability of all sequences with initial segment 1^n. The simplest programs carry most of the probability, hence we can approximate the probability that the next bit is a 1 with the probability of the program that says "Print 1's forever". Thus

$$\sum_y p(1^n 1y) \approx p(1^\infty) = c > 0 . \tag{7.81}$$

Estimating the probability that the next bit is 0 is more difficult. Since any program that prints $1^n 0 \ldots$ yields a description of n, its length should at least be $K(n)$, which for most n is about $\log n + O(\log \log n)$, and hence ignoring second-order terms, we have

$$\sum_y p(1^n 0y) \approx p(1^n 0) \approx 2^{-\log n} \approx \frac{1}{n} . \tag{7.82}$$

Hence the conditional probability of observing a 0 next is

$$p(0|1^n) = \frac{p(1^n 0)}{p(1^n 0) + p(1^\infty)} \approx \frac{1}{cn + 1} \tag{7.83}$$

which is similar to the result $p(0|1^n) = 1/(n+1)$ derived by Laplace.

This type of argument is a special case of "Occam's Razor", which is a general principle governing scientific research, weighting possible explanations by their complexity. William of Occam said "Nunquam ponenda est pluralitas sine necesitate", i.e., explanations should not be multiplied beyond necessity [259]. In the end, we choose the simplest explanation that is consistent with the observed data. For example, it is easier to accept the general theory of relativity than it is to accept a correction factor of c/r^3 to the gravitational law to explain the precession of the perihelion of Mercury, since the general theory explains more with fewer assumptions than does a "patched" Newtonian theory.

7.11 KOLMOGOROV COMPLEXITY AND UNIVERSAL PROBABILITY

We now prove an equivalence between Kolmogorov complexity and universal probability. We begin by repeating the basic definitions.

$$K(x) = \min_{p : \mathcal{U}(p) = x} l(p) . \tag{7.84}$$

$$P_\mathcal{U}(x) = \sum_{p : \mathcal{U}(p) = x} 2^{-l(p)} . \tag{7.85}$$

Theorem 7.11.1 (*Equivalence of $K(x)$ and $\log \frac{1}{P_{\mathcal{U}}(x)}$*): *There exists a constant c, independent of x, such that*

$$2^{-K(x)} \le P_{\mathcal{U}}(x) \le c 2^{-K(x)} \qquad (7.86)$$

for all strings x. Thus the universal probability of a string x is essentially determined by its Kolmogorov complexity.

Remark: This implies that $K(x)$ and $\log \frac{1}{P_{\mathcal{U}}(x)}$ have *equal status* as universal complexity measures, since

$$K(x) - c' \le \log \frac{1}{P_{\mathcal{U}}(x)} \le K(x). \qquad (7.87)$$

Recall that the complexity defined with respect to two different computers $K_{\mathcal{U}}$ and $K_{\mathcal{U}'}$ are essentially equivalent complexity measures if $|K_{\mathcal{U}}(x) - K_{\mathcal{U}'}(x)|$ is bounded. Theorem 7.11.1 shows that $K_{\mathcal{U}}(x)$ and $\log \frac{1}{P_{\mathcal{U}}(x)}$ are essentially equivalent complexity measures.

Notice the striking similarity between the relationship of $K(x)$ and $\log \frac{1}{P_{\mathcal{U}}(x)}$ in Kolmogorov complexity and the relationship of $H(X)$ and $\log \frac{1}{p(x)}$ in information theory. The Shannon code length assignment $l(x) = \lceil \log \frac{1}{p(x)} \rceil$ achieves an *average* description length $H(X)$, while in Kolmogorov complexity theory, $\log \frac{1}{P_{\mathcal{U}}(x)}$ is almost *equal* to $K(x)$. Thus $\log \frac{1}{p(x)}$ is the natural notion of descriptive complexity of x in algorithmic as well as probabilistic settings.

The upper bound in (7.87) is obvious from the definitions, but the lower bound is more difficult to prove. The result is very surprising, since there are an infinite number of programs that print x. From any program, it is possible to produce longer programs by padding the program with irrelevant instructions. The theorem proves that although there are an infinite number of such programs, the universal probability is essentially determined by the largest term, which is $2^{-K(x)}$. If $P_{\mathcal{U}}(x)$ is large, then $K(x)$ is small, and vice versa.

However, there is another way to look at the upper bound that makes it less surprising. Consider any computable probability mass function on strings $p(x)$. Using this mass function, we can construct a Shannon-Fano code (Section 5.9) for the source, and then describe each string by the corresponding codeword, which will have length $\log \frac{1}{p(x)}$. Hence for any computable distribution, we can construct a description of a string using not more than $\log \frac{1}{p(x)} + c$ bits, which is an upper bound on the Kolmogorov complexity $K(x)$. Even though $P_{\mathcal{U}}(x)$ is not a computable probability mass function, we are able to finesse the problem using the rather involved tree construction procedure described below.

Proof (*of Theorem 7.11.1*): The first inequality is simple. Let p^* be the shortest program for x. Then

$$P_{\mathcal{U}}(x) = \sum_{p:\mathcal{U}(p)=x} 2^{-l(p)} \geq 2^{-l(p^*)} = 2^{-K(x)}, \qquad (7.88)$$

as we wished to show.

We can rewrite the second inequality as

$$K(x) \leq \log \frac{1}{P_{\mathcal{U}}(x)} + c. \qquad (7.89)$$

Our objective in the proof is to find a short program to describe the strings that have high $P_{\mathcal{U}}(x)$.

An obvious idea is some kind of Huffman coding based on $P_{\mathcal{U}}(x)$, but $P_{\mathcal{U}}(x)$ cannot be effectively calculated, and hence a procedure using Huffman coding is not implementable on a computer. Similarly the process using the Shannon-Fano code also cannot be implemented. However, if we have the Shannon-Fano code tree, we can reconstruct the string by looking for the corresponding node in the tree. This is the basis for the following tree construction procedure.

To overcome the problem of non-computability of $P_{\mathcal{U}}(x)$, we use a modified approach, trying to construct a code tree directly. Unlike Huffman coding, this approach is not optimal in terms of minimum expected codeword length. However, it is good enough for us to derive a code for which each codeword for x has a length that is within a constant of $\log \frac{1}{P_{\mathcal{U}}(x)}$.

Before we get into the details of the proof, let us outline our approach. We want to construct a code tree in such a way that strings with high probability have low depth. Since we cannot calculate the probability of a string, we do not know *a priori* the depth of the string on the tree. Instead, we successively assign x to the nodes of the tree, assigning x to nodes closer and closer to the root as our estimate of $P_{\mathcal{U}}(x)$ improves. We want the computer to be able to recreate the tree and use the lowest depth node corresponding to the string x to reconstruct the string.

We now consider the set of programs and their corresponding outputs $\{(p, x)\}$. We try to assign these pairs to the tree. But we immediately come across a problem—there are an infinite number of programs for a given string, and we do not have enough nodes of low depth. However, as we shall show, if we trim the list of program-output pairs, we will be able to define a more manageable list that can be assigned to the tree.

We now demonstrate the existence of programs for x of length $\log \frac{1}{P_{\mathcal{U}}(x)}$.

Tree construction procedure. For the universal computer $\mathcal{U}$, we simulate all programs using the technique explained in Section 7.8. We list all binary programs:

$$\Lambda, 0, 1, 00, 01, 10, 11, 000, 001, 010, 011, \ldots \qquad (7.90)$$

Then let the computer execute one clock cycle of Λ for the first stage. In the next stage, let the computer execute two clock cycles of Λ and two clock cycles of the program 0. In the third stage, let the computer execute three clock cycles of each of the first three programs, and so on. In this way, the computer will eventually run all possible programs and run them for longer and longer times, so that if any program halts, it will be discovered to halt eventually. We use this method to produce a list of all programs that halt in the order in which they halt together with their associated outputs. For each program and its corresponding output, (p_k, x_k), we calculate n_k, which is chosen so that it corresponds to the current estimate of $P_{\mathcal{U}}(x)$. Specifically,

$$n_k = \left\lceil \log \frac{1}{\hat{P}_{\mathcal{U}}(x_k)} \right\rceil, \qquad (7.91)$$

where

$$\hat{P}_{\mathcal{U}}(x_k) = \sum_{(p_i, x_i): x_i = x_k, \, i \leq k} 2^{-l(p_i)}. \qquad (7.92)$$

Note that $\hat{P}_{\mathcal{U}}(x_k) \uparrow P_{\mathcal{U}}(x)$ on the subsequence of times k such that $x_k = x$. We are now ready to construct a tree. As we add to the list of triplets, (p_k, x_k, n_k), of programs that halt, we map some of them onto nodes of a binary tree. For the purposes of the construction, we must ensure that all the n_i's corresponding to a particular x_k are distinct. To ensure this, we remove from the list all triplets that have the same x and n as some previous triplet. This will ensure that there is at most one node at each level of the tree that corresponds to a given x.

Let $\{(p_i', x_i', n_i'): i = 1, 2, 3, \ldots\}$ denote the new list. On the winnowed list, we assign the triplet (p_k', x_k', n_k') to the first available node at level $n_k' + 1$. As soon as a node is assigned, all of its descendants become unavailable for assignment. (This keeps the assignment prefix-free.)

We illustrate this by means of an example:

$(p_1, x_1, n_1) = (10111, 1110, 5),$ $\quad n_1 = 5$ because $\hat{P}_{\mathcal{U}}(x_1) \geq 2^{-l(p_1)} = 2^{-5}$

$(p_2, x_2, n_2) = (11, 10, 2),$ $\quad n_2 = 2$ because $\hat{P}_{\mathcal{U}}(x_2) \geq 2^{-l(p_2)} = 2^{-2}$

$(p_3, x_3, n_3) = (0, 1110, 1),$ $\quad n_3 = 1$ because $\hat{P}_{\mathcal{U}}(x_3) \geq 2^{-l(p_3)} + 2^{-l(p_1)} = 2^{-5} + 2^{-1}$
$\qquad \qquad \qquad \qquad \qquad \qquad \qquad \qquad \geq 2^{-1}$

$(p_4, x_4, n_4) = (1010, 1111, 4),$ $\quad n_4 = 4$ because $\hat{P}_{\mathcal{U}}(x_4) \geq 2^{-l(p_4)} = 2^{-4}$

$(p_5, x_5, n_5) = (101101, 1110, 1),$ $\quad n_5 = 1$ because $\hat{P}_{\mathcal{U}}(x_5) \geq 2^{-1} + 2^{-5} + 2^{-5}$
$\qquad \qquad \qquad \qquad \qquad \qquad \qquad \qquad \geq 2^{-1}$

$(p_6, x_6, n_6) = (100, 1, 3),$ $\quad n_6 = 3$ because $\hat{P}_{\mathcal{U}}(x_6) \geq 2^{-l(p_6)} = 2^{-3}$

$\vdots$

$$(7.93)$$

We note that the string $x = (1110)$ appears in positions 1, 3 and 5 in the list, but $n_3 = n_5$. The estimate of the probability $\hat{P}_\mathcal{U}(1110)$ has not jumped sufficiently for (p_5, x_5, n_5) to survive the cut. Thus the winnowed list becomes

$$
\begin{aligned}
(p_1', x_1', n_1') &= (10111, 1110, 5), \\
(p_2', x_2', n_2') &= (11, 10, 2), \\
(p_3', x_3', n_3') &= (0, 1110, 1), \\
(p_4', x_4', n_4') &= (1010, 1111, 4), \\
(p_5', x_5', n_5') &= (100, 1, 3), \\
&\vdots
\end{aligned}
\tag{7.94}
$$

The assignment of the winnowed list to nodes of the tree is illustrated in Figure 7.3. In the example, we are able to find nodes at level $n_k + 1$ to which we can assign the triplets. Now we shall prove that there are always enough nodes so that the assignment can be completed. We can perform the assignment of triplets to nodes if and only if the Kraft inequality is satisfied.

We now drop the primes and deal only with the winnowed list illustrated in (7.94). We start with the infinite sum in the Kraft inequality corresponding to (7.94) and split it according to the output strings:

$$
\sum_{k=1}^{\infty} 2^{-(n_k+1)} = \sum_{x \subset \{0,1\}^*} \sum_{h : x_k = x} 2^{-(n_k+1)}.
\tag{7.95}
$$

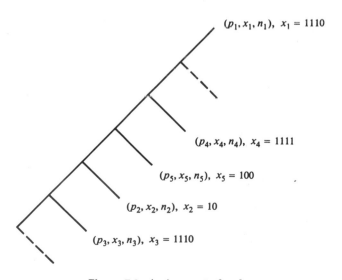

Figure 7.3. Assignment of nodes.

We then write the inner sum as

$$\sum_{k\,:\,x_k=x} 2^{-(n_k+1)} = 2^{-1} \sum_{k\,:\,x_k=x} 2^{-n_k} \tag{7.96}$$

$$\leq 2^{-1}(2^{\lfloor \log P_{\mathcal{U}}(x)\rfloor} + 2^{\lfloor \log P_{\mathcal{U}}(x)\rfloor-1} + 2^{\lfloor \log P_{\mathcal{U}}(x)\rfloor-2} + \cdots) \tag{7.97}$$

$$= 2^{-1} 2^{\lfloor \log P_{\mathcal{U}}(x)\rfloor}\left(1 + \frac{1}{2} + \frac{1}{4} + \cdots\right) \tag{7.98}$$

$$= 2^{-1} 2^{\lfloor \log P_{\mathcal{U}}(x)\rfloor} 2 \tag{7.99}$$

$$\leq P_{\mathcal{U}}(x), \tag{7.100}$$

where (7.97) is true because there is at most one node at each level that prints out a particular x. More precisely, the n_k's on the winnowed list for a particular output string x are all different integers. Hence

$$\sum_k 2^{-(n_k+1)} \leq \sum_x \sum_{k\,:\,x_k=x} 2^{-(n_k+1)} \leq \sum_x P_{\mathcal{U}}(x) \leq 1, \tag{7.101}$$

and we can construct a tree with the nodes labeled by the triplets.

If we are given the tree constructed above, then it is easy to identify a given x by the path to the lowest depth node that prints x. Call this node $\tilde{p}$. (By construction, $l(\tilde{p}) \leq \log \frac{1}{P_{\mathcal{U}}(x)} + 2$.) To use this tree in a program to print x, we specify $\tilde{p}$ and ask the computer to execute the above simulation of all programs. Then the computer will construct the tree as described above, and wait for the particular node $\tilde{p}$ to be assigned. Since the computer executes the same construction as the sender, eventually the node $\tilde{p}$ will be assigned. At this point, the computer will halt and print out the x assigned to that node.

This is an effective (finite, mechanical) procedure for the computer to reconstruct x. However, there is no effective procedure to find the lowest depth node corresponding to x. All that we have proved is that there is an (infinite) tree with a node corresponding to x at level $\lceil \log \frac{1}{P_{\mathcal{U}}(x)}\rceil + 1$. But this accomplishes our purpose.

With reference to the example, the description of $x = 1110$ is the path to the node (p_3, x_3, n_3), i.e., 01, and the description of $x = 1111$ is the path 00001. If we wish to describe the string 1110, we ask the computer to perform the (simulation) tree construction until node 01 is assigned. Then we ask the computer to execute the program corresponding to node 01, i.e., p_3. The output of this program is the desired string, $x = 1110$.

The length of the program to reconstruct x is essentially the length of the description of the position of the lowest depth node $\tilde{p}$ corresponding to x in the tree. The length of this program for x is $l(\tilde{p}) + c$, where

$$l(\tilde{p}) \le \left\lceil \log \frac{1}{P_{\mathcal{U}}(x)} \right\rceil + 1 , \qquad (7.102)$$

and hence the complexity of x satisfies

$$K(x) \le \left\lceil \log \frac{1}{P_{\mathcal{U}}(x)} \right\rceil + c . \qquad (7.103)$$

Thus we have proved the theorem. $\square$

7.12   THE KOLMOGOROV SUFFICIENT STATISTIC

Suppose we are given a sample sequence from a Bernoulli(θ) process. What are the regularities or deviations from randomness in this sequence? One way to address the question is to find the Kolmogorov complexity $K(x^n|n)$, which we discover to be roughly $nH_0(\theta) + \log n + c$. Since, for $\theta \ne \frac{1}{2}$, this is much less than n, we conclude that x^n has structure and is not randomly drawn Bernoulli($\frac{1}{2}$). But what is the structure? The first attempt to find the structure is to investigate the shortest program p^* for x^n. But the shortest description of p^* is about as long as p^* itself; otherwise, we could further compress the description of x^n, contradicting the minimality of p^*. So this attempt is fruitless.

A hint at a good approach comes from examination of the way in which p^* describes x^n. The program "The sequence has k 1's; of such sequences, it is the ith" is optimal to first order for Bernoulli(θ) sequences. We note that it is a two-stage description, and all of the structure of the sequence is captured in the first stage. Moreover, x^n is maximally complex given the first stage of the description. The first stage, the description of k, requires $\log(n + 1)$ bits and defines a set $S = \{x \in \{0, 1\}^n : \Sigma\, x_i = k\}$. The second stage requires $\log |S| = \log(\binom{n}{k}) \approx nH_0(\bar{x}_n) \approx nH_0(\theta)$ bits and reveals nothing extraordinary about x^n.

We mimic this process for general sequences by looking for a simple set S that contains x^n. We then follow it with a brute force description of x^n in S using $\log|S|$ bits.

We begin with a definition of the smallest set containing x^n that is describable in no more than k bits.

Definition: The *Kolmogorov structure function* $K_k(x^n|n)$ of a binary string $x \in \{0, 1\}^n$ is defined as

$$K_k(x^n|n) = \min_{\substack{p\,:\,l(p)\le k \\ \mathcal{U}(p,\, n)=S \\ x^n \in S \subseteq \{0,1\}^n}} \log|S| \qquad (7.104)$$

The set S is the smallest set which can be described with no more than k bits and which includes x^n. By $\mathcal{U}(p, n) = S$, we mean that running the program p with data n on the universal computer $\mathcal{U}$ will print out the indicator function of the set S.

Definition: For a given small constant c, let k^* be the least k such that

$$K_k(x^n|n) + k \leq K(x^n|n) + c . \tag{7.105}$$

Let S^{**} be the corresponding set and let p^{**} be the program that prints out the indicator function of S^{**}. Then we shall say that p^{**} is a *Kolmogorov minimal sufficient statistic* for x^n.

Consider the programs p^* describing sets S^* such that

$$K_k(x^n|n) + k = K(x^n|n) . \tag{7.106}$$

All the programs p^* are "sufficient statistics" in that the complexity of x^n given S^* is maximal. But the minimal sufficient statistic is the shortest "sufficient statistic."

The equality in the above definition is up to a large constant depending on the computer U. Then k^* corresponds to the least k for which the two-stage description of x^n is as good as the best single stage description of x^n. The second stage of the description merely provides the index of x^n within the set S^{**}; this takes $K_k(x^n|n)$ bits if x^n is conditionally maximally complex given the set S^{**}. Hence the set S^{**} captures all the structure within x^n. The remaining description of x^n within S^{**} is essentially the description of the randomness within the string. Hence S^{**} or p^{**} is called the Kolmogorov sufficient statistic for x^n.

This is parallel to the definition of a sufficient statistic in mathematical statistics. A statistic T is said to be sufficient for a parameter θ if the distribution of the sample given the sufficient statistic is independent of the parameter, i.e.,

$$\theta \to T(X) \to X \tag{7.107}$$

forms a Markov chain in that order. For the Kolmogorov sufficient statistic, the program p^{**} is sufficient for the "structure" of the string x^n; the remainder of the description of x^n is essentially independent of the "structure" of x^n. In particular, x^n is maximally complex given S^{**}.

A typical graph of the structure function is illustrated in Figure 7.4. When $k = 0$, the only set that can be described is the entire set $\{0, 1\}^n$, so that the corresponding log set size is n. As we increase k, the size of the set drops rapidly until

$$k + K_k(x^n|n) \approx K(x^n|n) . \tag{7.108}$$

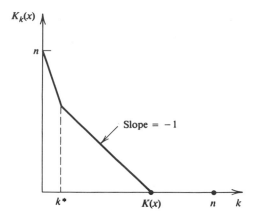

Figure 7.4. Kolmogorov sufficient statistic.

After this, each additional bit of k reduces the set by half, and we proceed along the line of slope -1 until $k = K(x^n|n)$. For $k \geq K(x^n|n)$, the smallest set that can be described that includes x^n is the singleton $\{x^n\}$, and hence $K_k(x^n|n) = 0$.

We will now illustrate the concept with a few examples.

1. *Bernoulli(θ) sequence.* Consider a sample of length n from a Bernoulli sequence with an unknown parameter θ. In this case, the best two-stage description consists of giving the number of 1's in the sequence first and then giving the index of the given sequence in the set of all sequences having the same number of 1's. This two-stage description clearly corresponds to p^{**} and the corresponding $k^{**} \approx \log n$. (See Figure 7.5.) Note, however, if θ is a special number like $\frac{1}{3}$ or e/π^2, then p^{**} is a description of θ, and $k^{**} = c$.

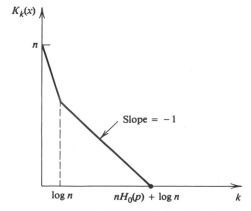

Figure 7.5. Kolmogorov sufficient statistic for a Bernoulli sequence.

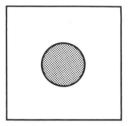

Figure 7.6. Mona Lisa.

2. *Sample from a Markov chain.* In the same vein as the preceding example, consider a sample from a first-order binary Markov chain. In this case again, p^{**} will correspond to describing the Markov type of the sequence (the number of occurrences of 00's, 01's, 10's and 11's in the sequence); this conveys all the structure in the sequence. The remainder of the description will be the index of the sequence in the set of all sequences of this Markov type. Hence in this case, $k^* \approx 2 \log n$, corresponding to describing two elements of the conditional joint type. (The other elements of the conditional joint type can be determined from these two.)

3. *Mona Lisa.* Consider an image which consists of a gray circle on a white background. The circle is not uniformly gray but Bernoulli with parameter θ. This is illustrated in Figure 7.6.

   In this case, the best two-stage description is to first describe the size and position of the circle and its average gray level and then to describe the index of the circle among all the circles with the same gray level. In this case, p^{**} corresponds to a program that gives the position and size of the circle and the average gray level, requiring about $\log n$ bits for each quantity. Hence $k^* \approx 3 \log n$ in this case.

SUMMARY OF CHAPTER 7

Definition: The *Kolmogorov complexity* $K(x)$ of a string x is

$$K(x) = \min_{p \,:\, \mathcal{U}(p)=x} l(p), \tag{7.109}$$

$$K(x|l(x)) = \min_{p \,:\, \mathcal{U}(p,\,l(x))=x} l(p). \tag{7.110}$$

Universality of Kolmogorov complexity: There exists a universal computer $\mathcal{U}$, such that for any other computer $\mathcal{A}$,

$$K_{\mathcal{U}}(x) \le K_{\mathcal{A}}(x) + c_{\mathcal{A}}, \tag{7.111}$$

for any string x, where the constant $c_{\mathscr{A}}$ does not depend on x. If $\mathscr{U}$ and $\mathscr{A}$ are universal, $|K_{\mathscr{U}}(x) - K_{\mathscr{A}}(x)| \le c$ for all x.

Upper bound on Kolmogorov complexity:

$$K(x|l(x)) \le l(x) + c. \tag{7.112}$$

$$K(x) \le K(x|l(x)) + 2\log l(x) + c \tag{7.113}$$

Kolmogorov complexity and entropy: If $X_1, X_2, \ldots$ are i.i.d. integer valued random variables with entropy H, then there exists a constant c, such that for all n,

$$H \le \frac{1}{n}EK(X^n|n) \le H + |\mathscr{X}|\frac{\log n}{n} + \frac{c}{n}. \tag{7.114}$$

Lower bound on Kolmogorov complexity: There are no more than 2^k strings x with complexity $K(x) < k$. If $X_1, X_2, \ldots, X_n$ are drawn according to a Bernoulli($\frac{1}{2}$) process, then

$$\Pr(K(X_1 X_2 \ldots X_n|n) \le n - k) \le 2^{-k}. \tag{7.115}$$

Definition: A sequence $x_1, x_2, \ldots, x_n$ is said to be *incompressible* if $K(x_1, x_2, \ldots, x_n|n)/n \to 1$.

Strong law of large numbers for incompressible sequences:

$$\frac{K(x_1, x_2, \ldots, x_n)}{n} \to 1 \Rightarrow \frac{1}{n}\sum_{i=1}^{n} x_i \to \frac{1}{2}. \tag{7.116}$$

Definition: The *universal probability* of a string x is

$$P_{\mathscr{U}}(x) = \sum_{p:\,\mathscr{U}(p)=x} 2^{-l(p)} = \Pr(\mathscr{U}(p) = x). \tag{7.117}$$

Universality of $P_{\mathscr{U}}(x)$: For every computer $\mathscr{A}$,

$$P_{\mathscr{U}}(x) \ge c_{\mathscr{A}} P_{\mathscr{A}}(x) \tag{7.118}$$

for every string $x \in \{0, 1\}^*$, where the constant $c_{\mathscr{A}}'$ depends only on $\mathscr{U}$ and $\mathscr{A}$.

Definition: $\Omega = \Sigma_{p:\,\mathscr{U}(p)\,\text{halts}}\, 2^{-l(p)} = \Pr(\mathscr{U}(p)\,\text{halts})$ is the probability that the computer halts when the input p to the computer is a binary string drawn according to a Bernoulli($\frac{1}{2}$) process.

Properties of Ω:

1. Ω *is not computable.*
2. Ω *is a "Philosopher's Stone".*
3. Ω *is algorithmically random (incompressible).*

Equivalence of $K(x)$ and $\log \frac{1}{P_{\mathcal{U}}(x)}$: There exists a constant c, independent of x, such that

$$\left| \log \frac{1}{P_{\mathcal{U}}(x)} - K(x) \right| \leq c , \tag{7.119}$$

for all strings x. Thus the universal probability of a string x is essentially determined by its Kolmogorov complexity.

Definition: The *Kolmogorov structure function* $K_k(x^n|n)$ of a binary string $x \in \{0,1\}^n$ is defined as

$$K_k(x^n|n) = \min_{\substack{p\,:\,l(p)\leq k \\ \mathcal{U}(p,\,n)=S \\ x\in S}} \log|S| \tag{7.120}$$

Definition: Let k^* be the least k such that

$$K_{k^*}(x^n|n) + k^* = K(x^n|n) . \tag{7.121}$$

Let S^{**} be the corresponding set and let p^{**} be the program that prints out the indicator function of S^{**}. Then p^{**} is the *Kolmogorov minimal sufficient statistic* for x.

PROBLEMS FOR CHAPTER 7

1. *Kolmogorov complexity of two sequences.* Let $x, y \in \{0,1\}^*$. Argue that $K(x, y) \leq K(x) + K(y) + c$.

2. *Complexity of the sum.*
   (a) Argue that $K(n) \leq \log n + 2 \log \log n + c$.
   (b) Argue that $K(n_1 + n_2) \leq K(n_1) + K(n_2) + c$.
   (c) Give an example in which n_1 and n_2 are complex but the sum is relatively simple.

3. *Images.* Consider an $n \times n$ array x of 0's and 1's . Thus x has n^2 bits.

   Find the Kolmogorov complexity $K(x|n)$ (to first order) if
   (a) x is a horizontal line.
   (b) x is a square.
   (c) x is the union of two lines, each line being vertical or horizontal.

4. *Monkeys on a computer.* Suppose a random program is typed into a computer. Give a rough estimate of the probability that the computer prints the following sequence:

    (a) 0^n followed by any arbitrary sequence.

    (b) $\pi_1 \pi_2 \ldots \pi_n$ followed by any arbitrary sequence, where π_i is the ith bit in the expansion of π.

    (c) $0^n 1$ followed by any arbitrary sequence.

    (d) $\omega_1 \omega_2 \ldots \omega_n$ followed by any arbitrary sequence.

    (e) (Optional) A proof of the 4-color theorem.

5. *Kolmogorov complexity and ternary programs.* Suppose that the input programs for a universal computer $\mathcal{U}$ are sequences in $\{0,1,2\}^*$ (ternary inputs). Also, suppose $\mathcal{U}$ prints ternary outputs. Let $K(x|l(x)) = \min_{\mathcal{U}(p,\, l(x))=x} l(p)$. Show that

    (a) $K(x^n|n) \le n + c$.

    (b) $\#\{x^n \in \{0,1\}^* : K(x^n|n) < k\} < 3^k$.

6. *Do computers reduce entropy?* Let $X = \mathcal{U}(P)$, where P is a Bernoulli $(1/2)$ sequence. Here the binary sequence X is either undefined or is in $\{0,1\}^*$. Let $H(X)$ be the Shannon entropy of X. Argue that $H(X) = \infty$. Thus although the computer turns nonsense into sense, the output entropy is still infinite.

7. *A law of large numbers.* Using ternary inputs and outputs as in Problem 5, outline an argument demonstrating that if a sequence x is algorithmically random, i.e., if $K(x|l(x)) \approx l(x)$, then the proportion of 0's, 1's, and 2's in x must each be near $1/3$. You may wish to use Stirling's approximation $n! \approx (n/e)^n$.

8. *Image complexity.* Consider two binary subsets A and B (of an $n \times n$ grid). For example,

    Find general upper and lower bounds, in terms of $K(A|n)$ and $K(B|n)$, for

    (a) $K(A^c|n)$.

    (b) $K(A \cup B|n)$.

    (c) $K(A \cap B|n)$.

9. *Random program.* Suppose that a random program (symbols i.i.d. uniform over the symbol set) is fed into the nearest available computer.

    To our surprise the first n bits of the binary expansion of $1/\sqrt{2}$ are printed out. Roughly what would you say the probability is that the next output bit will agree with the corresponding bit in the expansion of $1/\sqrt{2}$?

10. *The face vase illusion.*

(a) What is an upper bound on the complexity of a pattern on an $m \times m$ grid that has mirror image symmetry about a vertical axis through the center of the grid *and* consists of horizontal line segments?

(b) What is the complexity K if the image differs in one cell from the pattern described above?

HISTORICAL NOTES

The original ideas of Kolmogorov complexity were put forth independently and almost simultaneously by Kolmogorov [159, 158], Solomonoff [256] and Chaitin [50]. These ideas were developed further by students of Kolmogorov like Martin-Löf [187], who defined the notion of algorithmically random sequences and algorithmic tests for randomness, and by Gacs and Levin [177], who explored the ideas of universal probability and its relationship to complexity. A series of papers by Chaitin [53, 51, 52] develop the relationship between Kolmogorov complexity and mathematical proofs. C. P. Schnorr studied the universal notion of randomness in [234, 235, 236].

The concept of the Kolmogorov structure function was defined by Kolmogorov at a talk at the Tallin conference in 1973, but these results were not published. V'yugin [267] has shown that there are some very strange sequences x^n that reveal their structure arbitrarily slowly in the sense that $K_k(x^n|n) = n - k$, $k < K(x^n|n)$. Zurek [293, 292, 294] addresses the fundamental questions of Maxwell's demon and the second law of thermodynamics by establishing the physical consequences of Kolmogorov complexity.

Rissanen's minimum description length (MDL) principle is very close in spirit to the Kolmogorov sufficient statistic. Rissanen [221, 222] finds a low complexity model that yields a high likelihood of the data.

A non-technical introduction to the different measures of complexity can be found in the thought-provoking book by Pagels [206]. Additional references to work in the area can be found in the paper by Cover, Gács and Gray [70] on Kolmogorov's contributions to information theory and algorithmic complexity.

Chapter 8

Channel Capacity

What do we mean when we say that A communicates with B? We mean that the physical acts of A have induced a desired physical state in B. This transfer of information is a physical process and therefore is subject to the uncontrollable ambient noise and imperfections of the physical signalling process itself. The communication is successful if the receiver B and the transmitter A agree on what was sent.

In this chapter we find the maximum number of distinguishable signals for n uses of a communication channel. This number grows exponentially with n, and the exponent is known as the channel capacity. The channel capacity theorem is the central and most famous success of information theory.

The mathematical analog of a physical signalling system is shown in Fig. 8.1. Source symbols from some finite alphabet are mapped into some sequence of channel symbols, which then produces the output sequence of the channel. The output sequence is random but has a distribution that depends on the input sequence. From the output sequence, we attempt to recover the transmitted message.

Each of the possible input sequences induces a probability distribution on the output sequences. Since two different input sequences may give rise to the same output sequence, the inputs are confusable. In the next few sections, we will show that we can choose a "non-confusable" subset of input sequences so that with high probability, there is only one highly likely input that could have caused the particular output. We can then reconstruct the input sequences at the output with negligible probability of error. By mapping the source into the appropriate "widely spaced" input sequences to the channel, we can transmit a message with very low probability of error and

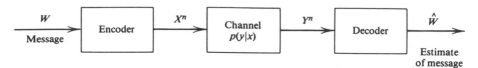

Figure 8.1. A communication system.

reconstruct the source message at the output. The maximum rate at which this can be done is called the capacity of the channel.

Definition: We define a *discrete channel* to be a system consisting of an input alphabet $\mathcal{X}$ and output alphabet $\mathcal{Y}$ and a probability transition matrix $p(y|x)$ that expresses the probability of observing the output symbol y given that we send the symbol x. The channel is said to be *memoryless* if the probability distribution of the output depends only on the input at that time and is conditionally independent of previous channel inputs or outputs.

Definition: We define the *"information" channel capacity* of a discrete memoryless channel as

$$C = \max_{p(x)} I(X; Y),\qquad(8.1)$$

where the maximum is taken over all possible input distributions $p(x)$.

We shall soon give an operational definition of channel capacity as the highest rate in bits per channel use at which information can be sent with arbitrarily low probability of error. Shannon's second theorem establishes that the "information" channel capacity is equal to the "operational" channel capacity. Thus we drop the word "information" in most discussions of channel capacity.

There is a duality between the problems of data compression and data transmission. During compression, we remove all the redundancy in the data to form the most compressed version possible, whereas during data transmission, we add redundancy in a controlled fashion to combat errors in the channel. In the last section of this chapter, we show that a general communication system can be broken into two parts and that the problems of data compression and data transmission can be considered separately.

8.1 EXAMPLES OF CHANNEL CAPACITY

8.1.1 Noiseless Binary Channel

Suppose we have a channel whose the binary input is reproduced exactly at the output. This channel is illustrated in Figure 8.2. In this

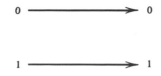

Figure 8.2. Noiseless binary channel.

case, any transmitted bit is received without error. Hence, 1 error-free bit can be transmitted per use of the channel, and the capacity is 1 bit. We can also calculate the information capacity $C = \max I(X; Y) = 1$ bit, which is achieved by using $p(x) = (\frac{1}{2}, \frac{1}{2})$.

8.1.2 Noisy Channel with Nonoverlapping Outputs

This channel has two possible outputs corresponding to each of the two inputs, as illustrated in Figure 8.3. The channel appears to be noisy, but really is not.

Even though the output of the channel is a random consequence of the input, the input can be determined from the output, and hence every transmitted bit can be recovered without error. The capacity of this channel is also 1 bit per transmission. We can also calculate the information capacity $C = \max I(X; Y) = 1$ bit, which is achieved by using $p(x) = (\frac{1}{2}, \frac{1}{2})$.

8.1.3 Noisy Typewriter

In this case, the channel input is either received unchanged at the output with probability $\frac{1}{2}$ or is transformed into the next letter with probability $\frac{1}{2}$ (Figure 8.4). If the input has 26 symbols and we use every alternate input symbol, then we can transmit 13 symbols without error with each transmission. Hence the capacity of this channel is $\log 13$ bits per transmission. We can also calculate the information capacity $C =$

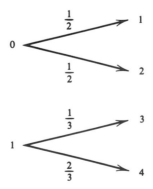

Figure 8.3. Noisy channel with nonoverlapping outputs.

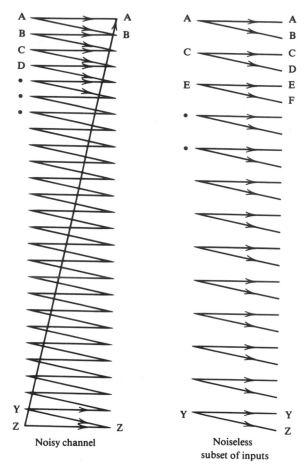

Figure 8.4. Noisy typewriter.

$$\max I(X; Y) = \max[H(Y) - H(Y|X)] = \max H(Y) - 1 = \log 26 - 1 = \log 13,$$
achieved by using $p(x)$ uniformly distributed over all the inputs.

8.1.4 Binary Symmetric Channel

Consider the binary symmetric channel (BSC), which is shown in Figure 8.5. This is a binary channel in which the input symbols are complemented with probability p. This is the simplest model of a channel with errors; yet it captures most of the complexity of the general problem.

When an error occurs, a 0 is received as a 1 and vice versa. The received bits do not reveal where the errors have occurred. In a sense, all the received bits are unreliable. Later we show that we can still use such a communication channel to send information at a non-zero rate with an arbitrarily small probability of error.

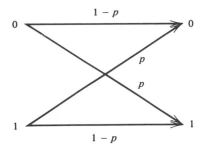

Figure 8.5. Binary symmetric channel.

We bound the mutual information by

$$I(X; Y) = H(Y) - H(Y|X) \tag{8.2}$$

$$= H(Y) - \sum p(x)H(Y|X = x) \tag{8.3}$$

$$= H(Y) - \sum p(x)H(p) \tag{8.4}$$

$$= H(Y) - H(p) \tag{8.5}$$

$$\leq 1 - H(p), \tag{8.6}$$

where the last inequality follows because Y is a binary random variable. Equality is achieved when the input distribution is uniform. Hence the information capacity of a binary symmetric channel with parameter p is

$$C = 1 - H(p) \text{ bits}. \tag{8.7}$$

8.1.5 Binary Erasure Channel

The analog of the binary symmetric channel in which some bits are lost (rather than corrupted) is called the binary erasure channel. In the binary erasure channel, a fraction α of the bits are erased. The receiver knows which bits have been erased. The binary erasure channel has two inputs and three outputs as shown in Figure 8.6.

We calculate the capacity of the binary erasure channel as follows:

$$C = \max_{p(x)} I(X; Y) \tag{8.8}$$

$$= \max_{p(x)} (H(Y) - H(Y|X)) \tag{8.9}$$

$$= \max_{p(x)} H(Y) - H(\alpha). \tag{8.10}$$

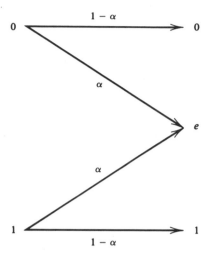

Figure 8.6. Binary erasure channel.

The first guess for the maximum of $H(Y)$ would be $\log 3$, but we cannot achieve this by any choice of input distribution $p(x)$. Letting E be the event $\{Y = e\}$, using the expansion

$$H(Y) = H(Y, E) = H(E) + H(Y|E), \qquad (8.11)$$

and letting $\Pr(X = 1) = \pi$, we have

$$H(Y) = H((1 - \pi)(1 - \alpha), \alpha, \pi(1 - \alpha)) = H(\alpha) + (1 - \alpha)H(\pi).$$

$$(8.12)$$

Hence

$$C = \max_{p(x)} H(Y) - H(\alpha) \qquad (8.13)$$

$$= \max_{\pi}(1 - \alpha)H(\pi) + H(\alpha) - H(\alpha) \qquad (8.14)$$

$$= \max_{\pi}(1 - \alpha)H(\pi) \qquad (8.15)$$

$$= 1 - \alpha, \qquad (8.16)$$

where capacity is achieved by $\pi = \frac{1}{2}$.

The expression for the capacity has some intuitive meaning: since a proportion α of the bits are lost in the channel, we can recover (at most) a proportion $1 - \alpha$ of the bits. Hence the capacity is at most $1 - \alpha$. It is not immediately obvious that it is possible to achieve this rate. This will follow from Shannon's second theorem.

In many practical channels, the sender receives some feedback from the receiver. If feedback is available for the binary erasure channel, it is very clear what to do: if a bit is lost, retransmit it until it gets through. Since the bits get through with probability $1 - \alpha$, the effective rate of transmission is $1 - \alpha$. In this way we are easily able to achieve a capacity of $1 - \alpha$ with feedback.

Later in the chapter, we will prove that the rate $1 - \alpha$ is the best that can be achieved both with and without feedback. This is one of the consequences of the surprising fact that feedback does not increase the capacity of discrete memoryless channels.

8.2 SYMMETRIC CHANNELS

The capacity of the binary symmetric channel is $C = 1 - H(p)$ bits per transmission and the capacity of the binary erasure channel is $C = 1 - \alpha$ bits per transmission.

Now consider the channel with transmission matrix:

$$p(y|x) = \begin{bmatrix} 0.3 & 0.2 & 0.5 \\ 0.5 & 0.3 & 0.2 \\ 0.2 & 0.5 & 0.3 \end{bmatrix}. \tag{8.17}$$

Here the entry in the xth row and the yth column denotes the conditional probability $p(y|x)$ that y is received when x is sent. In this channel, all the rows of the probability transition matrix are permutations of each other and so are the columns. Such a channel is said to be *symmetric*. Another example of a symmetric channel is one of the form

$$Y = X + Z \pmod{c}, \tag{8.18}$$

where Z has some distribution on the integers $\{0, 1, 2, \ldots, c - 1\}$, and X has the same alphabet as Z, and Z is independent of X.

In both these cases, we can easily find an explicit expression for the capacity of the channel. Letting $\mathbf{r}$ be a row of the transition matrix, we have

$$I(X; Y) = H(Y) - H(Y|X) \tag{8.19}$$

$$= H(Y) - H(\mathbf{r}) \tag{8.20}$$

$$\leq \log|\mathcal{Y}| - H(\mathbf{r}) \tag{8.21}$$

with equality if the output distribution is uniform. But $p(x) = 1/|\mathcal{X}|$ achieves a uniform distribution on Y, as seen from

$$p(y) = \sum_{x \in \mathcal{X}} p(y|x)p(x) = \frac{1}{|\mathcal{X}|} \sum p(y|x) = c \frac{1}{|\mathcal{X}|} = \frac{1}{|\mathcal{Y}|}, \quad (8.22)$$

where c is the sum of the entries in one column of the probability transition matrix.

Thus the channel in (8.17) has capacity

$$C = \max_{p(x)} I(X; Y) = \log 3 - H(0.5, 0.3, 0.2), \quad (8.23)$$

and C is achieved by a uniform distribution on the input.

The transition matrix of the symmetric channel defined above is doubly stochastic. In the computation of the capacity, we used the facts that the rows were permutations of one another and that all the column sums were equal.

Considering these properties, we can define a generalization of the concept of a symmetric channel as follows:

Definition: A channel is said to be *symmetric* if the rows of the channel transition matrix $p(y|x)$ are permutations of each other, and the columns are permutations of each other. A channel is said to be *weakly symmetric* if every row of the transition matrix $p(\cdot|x)$ is a permutation of every other row, and all the column sums $\sum_x p(y|x)$ are equal.

For example, the channel with transition matrix

$$p(y|x) = \begin{pmatrix} \frac{1}{3} & \frac{1}{6} & \frac{1}{2} \\ \frac{1}{3} & \frac{1}{2} & \frac{1}{6} \end{pmatrix} \quad (8.24)$$

is weakly symmetric but not symmetric.

The above derivation for symmetric channels carries over to weakly symmetric channels as well. We have the following theorem for weakly symmetric channels:

Theorem 8.2.1: *For a weakly symmetric channel,*

$$C = \log|\mathcal{Y}| - H(\text{row of transition matrix}), \quad (8.25)$$

and this is achieved by a uniform distribution on the input alphabet.

8.3 PROPERTIES OF CHANNEL CAPACITY

1. $C \geq 0$, since $I(X; Y) \geq 0$.
2. $C \leq \log|\mathcal{X}|$ since $C = \max I(X; Y) \leq \max H(X) = \log|\mathcal{X}|$.

3. $C \le \log|\mathcal{Y}|$ for the same reason.
4. $I(X; Y)$ is a continuous function of $p(x)$.
5. $I(X; Y)$ is a concave function of $p(x)$ (Theorem 2.7.4).

Since $I(X; Y)$ is a concave function over a closed convex set, a local maximum is a global maximum. From properties (2) and (3), the maximum is finite, and we are justified in using the term maximum, rather than supremum in the definition of capacity.

The maximum can then be found by standard nonlinear optimization techniques like gradient search. Some of the methods that can be used include the following:

- Constrained maximization using calculus and the Kuhn-Tucker conditions.
- The Frank-Wolfe gradient search algorithm.
- An iterative algorithm developed by Arimoto [11] and Blahut [37]. We will describe the algorithm in Section 13.8.

In general, there is no closed form solution for the capacity. But for many simple channels it is possible to calculate the capacity using properties like symmetry. Some of the examples considered earlier are of this form.

8.4 PREVIEW OF THE CHANNEL CODING THEOREM

So far, we have defined the information capacity of a discrete memoryless channel. In the next section, we prove Shannon's second theorem, which gives an operational meaning to the definition of capacity as the number of bits we can transmit reliably over the channel.

But first we will try to give an intuitive idea as to why we can transmit C bits of information over a channel. The basic idea is that, for large block lengths, every channel looks like the noisy typewriter channel (Figure 8.4) and the channel has a subset of inputs that produce essentially disjoint sequences at the output.

For each (typical) input n-sequence, there are approximately $2^{nH(Y|X)}$ possible Y sequences, all of them equally likely (Figure 8.7). We wish to ensure that no two X sequences produce the same Y output sequence. Otherwise, we will not be able to decide which X sequence was sent.

The total number of possible (typical) Y sequences is $\approx 2^{nH(Y)}$. This set has to be divided into sets of size $2^{nH(Y|X)}$ corresponding to the different input X sequences. The total number of disjoint sets is less than or equal to $2^{n(H(Y)-H(Y|X))} = 2^{nI(X; Y)}$. Hence we can send at most $\approx 2^{nI(X; Y)}$ distinguishable sequences of length n.

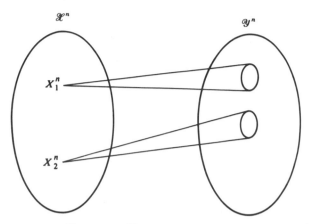

Figure 8.7. Channels after n uses.

Although the above derivation outlines an upper bound on the capacity, a stronger version of the above argument will be used in the next section to prove that this rate I is achievable, with an arbitrarily low probability of error.

Before we proceed to the proof of Shannon's second theorem, we need a few definitions.

8.5 DEFINITIONS

We analyze a communication system as shown in Figure 8.8.

A message W, drawn from the index set $\{1, 2, \ldots, M\}$, results in the signal $X^n(W)$, which is received as a random sequence $Y^n \sim p(y^n|x^n)$ by the receiver. The receiver then guesses the index W by an appropriate decoding rule $\hat{W} = g(Y^n)$. The receiver makes an error if $\hat{W}$ is not the same as the index W that was transmitted.

We now define these ideas formally.

Definition: A *discrete channel*, denoted by $(\mathscr{X}, p(y|x), \mathscr{Y})$, consists of two finite sets $\mathscr{X}$ and $\mathscr{Y}$ and a collection of probability mass functions $p(y|x)$, one for each $x \in \mathscr{X}$, such that for every x and y, $p(y|x) \geq 0$, and for every x, $\Sigma_y\, p(y|x) = 1$, with the interpretation that X is the input and Y is the output of the channel.

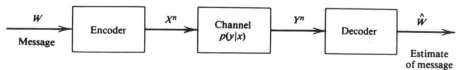

Figure 8.8. A communication channel.

Definition: The *nth extension of the discrete memoryless channel* (DMC) is the channel $(\mathscr{X}^n, p(y^n|x^n), \mathscr{Y}^n)$, where

$$p(y_k|x^k, y^{k-1}) = p(y_k|x_k), \qquad k = 1, 2, \ldots, n\,. \qquad (8.26)$$

Remark: If the channel is used *without feedback*, i.e., if the input symbols do not depend on the past output symbols, namely, $p(x_k|x^{k-1}, y^{k-1}) = p(x_k|x^{k-1})$, then the channel transition function for the n-th extension of the discrete memoryless channel reduces to

$$p(y^n|x^n) = \prod_{i=1}^{n} p(y_i|x_i)\,. \qquad (8.27)$$

When we refer to the discrete memoryless channel, we shall mean the discrete memoryless channel without feedback, unless we explicitly state otherwise.

Definition: An (M, n) *code* for the channel $(\mathscr{X}, p(y|x), \mathscr{Y})$ consists of the following:

1. An index set $\{1, 2, \ldots, M\}$.
2. An encoding function $X^n : \{1, 2, \ldots, M\} \to \mathscr{X}^n$, yielding codewords $X^n(1), X^n(2), \ldots, X^n(M)$. The set of codewords is called the codebook.
3. A decoding function

$$g : \mathscr{Y}^n \to \{1, 2, \ldots, M\}\,, \qquad (8.28)$$

which is a deterministic rule which assigns a guess to each possible received vector.

Definition (*Probability of error*): Let

$$\lambda_i = \Pr(g(Y^n) \neq i | X^n = X^n(i)) = \sum_{y^n} p(y^n|x^n(i)) I(g(y^n) \neq i) \quad (8.29)$$

be the conditional probability of error given that index i was sent, where $I(\cdot)$ is the indicator function.

Definition: The *maximal probability of error* $\lambda^{(n)}$ for an (M, n) code is defined as

$$\lambda^{(n)} = \max_{i \in \{1, 2, \ldots, M\}} \lambda_i\,. \qquad (8.30)$$

Definition: The (arithmetic) *average probability of error* $P_e^{(n)}$ for an (M, n) code is defined as

$$P_e^{(n)} = \frac{1}{M} \sum_{i=1}^{M} \lambda_i . \qquad (8.31)$$

Note that

$$P_e^{(n)} = \Pr(I \neq g(Y^n)) \qquad (8.32)$$

if the index I is chosen uniformly on the set $\{1, 2, \ldots, M\}$. Also obviously

$$P_e^{(n)} \leq \lambda^{(n)} . \qquad (8.33)$$

One would expect the maximal probability of error to behave quite differently from the average probability. But in the next section, we will prove that a small average probability of error implies a small maximal probability of error at essentially the same rate.

Definition: The *rate* R of an (M, n) code is

$$R = \frac{\log M}{n} \text{ bits per transmission}. \qquad (8.34)$$

Definition: A rate R is said to be *achievable* if there exists a sequence of $(\lceil 2^{nR} \rceil, n)$ codes such that the maximal probability of error $\lambda^{(n)}$ tends to 0 as $n \to \infty$.

Later, we will write $(2^{nR}, n)$ codes to mean $(\lceil 2^{nR} \rceil, n)$ codes. This will simplify the notation.

Definition: The *capacity* of a discrete memoryless channel is the supremum of all achievable rates.

Thus rates less than capacity yield arbitrarily small probability of error for sufficiently large block lengths.

8.6   JOINTLY TYPICAL SEQUENCES

Roughly speaking, we will decode a channel output Y^n as the ith index if the codeword $X^n(i)$ is "jointly typical" with the received signal Y^n. We now define the important idea of joint typicality and find the probability of joint typicality when $X^n(i)$ is the true cause of Y^n and when it is not.

Definition: The set $A_\epsilon^{(n)}$ of *jointly typical* sequences $\{(x^n, y^n)\}$ with respect to the distribution $p(x, y)$ is the set of n-sequences with empirical entropies ϵ-close to the true entropies, i.e.,

$$A_\epsilon^{(n)} = \left\{(x^n, y^n) \in \mathcal{X}^n \times \mathcal{Y}^n : \right. \tag{8.35}$$

$$\left| -\frac{1}{n} \log p(x^n) - H(X) \right| < \epsilon, \tag{8.36}$$

$$\left| -\frac{1}{n} \log p(y^n) - H(Y) \right| < \epsilon, \tag{8.37}$$

$$\left. \left| -\frac{1}{n} \log p(x^n, y^n) - H(X, Y) \right| < \epsilon \right\}, \tag{8.38}$$

where

$$p(x^n, y^n) = \prod_{i=1}^n p(x_i, y_i). \tag{8.39}$$

Theorem 8.6.1 (*Joint AEP*): *Let* (X^n, Y^n) *be sequences of length* n *drawn i.i.d. according to* $p(x^n, y^n) = \prod_{i=1}^n p(x_i, y_i)$. *Then*

1. $\Pr((X^n, Y^n) \in A_\epsilon^{(n)}) \to 1$ *as* $n \to \infty$.
2. $|A_\epsilon^{(n)}| \le 2^{n(H(X, Y) + \epsilon)}$.
3. *If* $(\tilde{X}^n, \tilde{Y}^n) \sim p(x^n)p(y^n)$, *i.e.*, $\tilde{X}^n$ *and* $\tilde{Y}^n$ *are independent with the same marginals as* $p(x^n, y^n)$, *then*

$$\Pr((\tilde{X}^n, \tilde{Y}^n) \in A_\epsilon^{(n)}) \le 2^{-n(I(X; Y) - 3\epsilon)}. \tag{8.40}$$

Also, for sufficiently large n,

$$\Pr((\tilde{X}^n, \tilde{Y}^n) \in A_\epsilon^{(n)}) \ge (1 - \epsilon)2^{-n(I(X; Y) + 3\epsilon)}. \tag{8.41}$$

Proof: By the weak law of large numbers,

$$-\frac{1}{n} \log p(X^n) \to -E[\log p(X)] = H(X) \quad \text{in probability}. \tag{8.42}$$

Hence, given $\epsilon > 0$, there exists n_1, such that for all $n > n_1$,

$$\Pr\left(\left| -\frac{1}{n} \log p(X^n) - H(X) \right| > \epsilon \right) < \frac{\epsilon}{3}. \tag{8.43}$$

Similarly, by the weak law,

$$-\frac{1}{n} \log p(Y^n) \to -E[\log p(Y)] = H(Y) \quad \text{in probability}, \tag{8.44}$$

and

$$-\frac{1}{n}\log p(X^n, Y^n) \rightarrow -E[\log p(X, Y)] = H(X, Y) \quad \text{in probability},$$

(8.45)

and there exist n_2 and n_3 such that for all $n \geq n_2$,

$$\Pr\left(\left|-\frac{1}{n}\log p(Y^n) - H(Y)\right| > \epsilon\right) < \frac{\epsilon}{3}$$

(8.46)

and for all $n \geq n_3$,

$$\Pr\left(\left|-\frac{1}{n}\log p(X^n, Y^n) - H(X, Y)\right| > \epsilon\right) < \frac{\epsilon}{3}.$$

(8.47)

Choosing $n > \max\{n_1, n_2, n_3\}$, the probability of the union of the sets in (8.43), (8.46) and (8.47) must be less than ϵ. Hence for n sufficiently large, the probability of the set $A_\epsilon^{(n)}$ is greater than $1 - \epsilon$, establishing the first part of the theorem.

To prove the second part of the theorem, we have

$$1 = \sum p(x^n, y^n)$$

(8.48)

$$\geq \sum_{A_\epsilon^{(n)}} p(x^n, y^n)$$

(8.49)

$$\geq |A_\epsilon^{(n)}| 2^{-n(H(X, Y)+\epsilon)},$$

(8.50)

and hence

$$|A_\epsilon^{(n)}| \leq 2^{n(H(X, Y)+\epsilon)}.$$

(8.51)

For sufficiently large n, $\Pr(A_\epsilon^{(n)}) \geq 1 - \epsilon$, and therefore

$$1 - \epsilon \leq \sum_{(x^n, y^n) \in A_\epsilon^{(n)}} p(x^n, y^n)$$

(8.52)

$$\leq |A_\epsilon^{(n)}| 2^{-n(H(X, Y)-\epsilon)},$$

(8.53)

and

$$|A_\epsilon^{(n)}| \geq (1 - \epsilon) 2^{n(H(X, Y)-\epsilon)}.$$

(8.54)

Now if $\tilde{X}^n$ and $\tilde{Y}^n$ are independent but have the same marginals as X^n and Y^n, then

$$\Pr((\tilde{X}^n, \tilde{Y}^n) \in A_\epsilon^{(n)}) = \sum_{(x^n, y^n) \in A_\epsilon^{(n)}} p(x^n)p(y^n) \tag{8.55}$$

$$\leq 2^{n(H(X,Y)+\epsilon)} 2^{-n(H(X)-\epsilon)} 2^{-n(H(Y)-\epsilon)} \tag{8.56}$$

$$= 2^{-n(I(X;Y)-3\epsilon)}. \tag{8.57}$$

By similar arguments, we can also show that

$$\Pr((\tilde{X}^n, \tilde{Y}^n) \in A_\epsilon^{(n)}) = \sum_{A_\epsilon^{(n)}} p(x^n)p(y^n) \tag{8.58}$$

$$\geq (1-\epsilon) 2^{n(H(X,Y)-\epsilon)} 2^{-n(H(X)+\epsilon)} 2^{-n(H(Y)+\epsilon)} \tag{8.59}$$

$$= (1-\epsilon) 2^{-n(I(X;Y)+3\epsilon)}. \tag{8.60}$$

This completes the proof of the theorem. □

The jointly typical set is illustrated in Figure 8.9. There are about $2^{nH(X)}$ typical X sequences, and about $2^{nH(Y)}$ typical Y sequences. However, since there are only $2^{nH(X,Y)}$ jointly typical sequences, not all pairs of typical X^n and typical Y^n are also jointly typical. The probability that any randomly chosen pair is jointly typical is about $2^{-nI(X;Y)}$. Hence, for a fixed Y^n, we can consider about $2^{nI(X;Y)}$ such pairs before we are likely to come across a jointly typical pair. This suggests that there are about $2^{nI(X;Y)}$ distinguishable signals X^n.

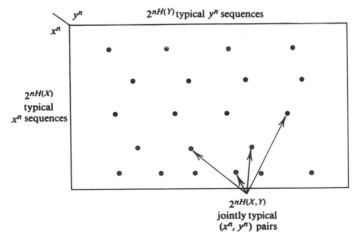

Figure 8.9. Jointly typical sequences.

8.7   THE CHANNEL CODING THEOREM

We now prove what is perhaps the basic theorem of information theory, the achievability of channel capacity. The basic argument was first stated by Shannon in his original 1948 paper. The result is rather counterintuitive; if the channel introduces errors, how can one correct them all? Any correction process is also subject to error, ad infinitum.

Shannon used a number of new ideas in order to prove that information can be sent reliably over a channel at all rates up to the channel capacity. These ideas include

- Allowing an arbitrarily small but non-zero probability of error,
- Using the channel many times in succession, so that the law of large numbers comes into effect, and
- Calculating the average of the probability of error over a random choice of codebooks, which symmetrizes the probability, and which can then be used to show the existence of at least one good code.

Shannon's outline of the proof was based on the idea of typical sequences, but the proof was not made rigorous until much later. The proof given below makes use of the properties of typical sequences and is probably the simplest of the proofs developed so far. As in all the proofs, we use the same essential ideas—random code selection, calculation of the average probability of error for a random choice of codewords, etc. The main difference is in the decoding rule. In the proof, we decode by joint typicality; we look for a codeword that is jointly typical with the received sequence. If we find a unique codeword satisfying this property, we declare that word to be the transmitted codeword. By the properties of joint typicality stated previously, with high probability the transmitted codeword and the received sequence are jointly typical, since they are probabilistically related. Also, the probability that any other codeword looks jointly typical with the received sequence is 2^{-nI}. Hence, if we have fewer then 2^{nI} codewords, then with high probability, there will be no other codewords that can be confused with the transmitted codeword, and the probability of error is small.

Although jointly typical decoding is suboptimal, it is simple to analyze and still achieves all rates below capacity.

We shall now give the complete statement and proof of Shannon's second theorem:

Theorem 8.7.1 (*The channel coding theorem*): *All rates below capacity C are achievable. Specifically, for every rate $R < C$, there exists a sequence of $(2^{nR}, n)$ codes with maximum probability of error $\lambda^{(n)} \to 0$.*

Conversely, any sequence of $(2^{nR}, n)$ codes with $\lambda^{(n)} \to 0$ must have $R \le C$.

Proof: We prove that rates $R < C$ are achievable and postpone the proof of the converse to Section 8.9.

Achievability: Fix $p(x)$. Generate a $(2^{nR}, n)$ code at random according to the distribution $p(x)$. Specifically, we independently generate 2^{nR} codewords according to the distribution,

$$p(x^n) = \prod_{i=1}^{n} p(x_i). \tag{8.61}$$

We exhibit the 2^{nR} codewords as the rows of a matrix:

$$\mathcal{C} = \begin{bmatrix} x_1(1) & x_2(1) & \cdots & x_n(1) \\ \vdots & \vdots & \ddots & \vdots \\ x_1(2^{nR}) & x_2(2^{nR}) & \cdots & x_n(2^{nR}) \end{bmatrix}. \tag{8.62}$$

Each entry in this matrix is generated i.i.d. according to $p(x)$. Thus the probability that we generate a particular code $\mathcal{C}$ is

$$\Pr(\mathcal{C}) = \prod_{w=1}^{2^{nR}} \prod_{i=1}^{n} p(x_i(w)). \tag{8.63}$$

Consider the following sequence of events:

1. A random code $\mathcal{C}$ is generated as described in (8.63) according to $p(x)$.
2. The code $\mathcal{C}$ is then revealed to both sender and receiver. Both sender and receiver are also assumed to know the channel transition matrix $p(y|x)$ for the channel.
3. A message W is chosen according to a uniform distribution

$$\Pr(W = w) = 2^{-nR}, \qquad w = 1, 2, \ldots, 2^{nR}. \tag{8.64}$$

4. The wth codeword $X^n(w)$, corresponding to the wth row of $\mathcal{C}$, is sent over the channel.
5. The receiver receives a sequence Y^n according to the distribution:

$$P(y^n|x^n(w)) = \prod_{i=1}^{n} p(y_i|x_i(w)). \tag{8.65}$$

6. The receiver guesses which message was sent. (The optimum procedure to minimize probability of error is maximum likelihood decoding, i.e., the receiver should choose the *a posteriori* most likely message. But this procedure is difficult to analyze. Instead, we will use *typical set decoding*, which is described below. Typical

set decoding is easier to analyze and is asymptotically optimal.)
The receiver declares that the index $\hat{W}$ was sent if the following
conditions are satisfied:

- $(X^n(\hat{W}), Y^n)$ is jointly typical.
- There is no other index k, such that $(X^n(k), Y^n) \in A_\epsilon^{(n)}$.

If no such $\hat{W}$ exists or if there is more than one such, then an error
is declared. (We may assume that the receiver outputs a dummy
index such as 0 in this case.)

7. There is a decoding error if $\hat{W} \neq W$. Let $\mathcal{E}$ be the event $\{\hat{W} \neq W\}$.

Analysis of the probability of error

Outline: We first outline the analysis.

Instead of calculating the probability of error for a single code, we
calculate the average over all codes generated at random according to
the distribution (8.63). By the symmetry of the code construction, the
average probability of error does not depend on the particular index that
was sent. For a typical codeword, there are two different sources of error
when we use typical set decoding: either the output Y^n is not jointly
typical with the transmitted codeword or there is some other codeword
that is jointly typical with Y^n. The probability that the transmitted
codeword and the received sequence are jointly typical goes to one as
shown by the joint AEP. For any rival codeword, the probability that it
is jointly typical with the received sequence is approximately 2^{-nI}, and
hence we can use about 2^{nI} codewords and still have low probability of
error. We will later extend the argument to find a code with low
maximal probability of error.

Detailed calculation of the probability of error: We will calculate the
average probability of error, averaged over all codewords in the
codebook, and averaged over all codebooks, i.e., we calculate

$$\Pr(\mathcal{E}) = \sum_{\mathcal{C}} P(\mathcal{C}) P_e^{(n)}(\mathcal{C}) \tag{8.66}$$

$$= \sum_{\mathcal{C}} P(\mathcal{C}) \frac{1}{2^{nR}} \sum_{w=1}^{2^{nR}} \lambda_w(\mathcal{C}) \tag{8.67}$$

$$= \frac{1}{2^{nR}} \sum_{w=1}^{2^{nR}} \sum_{\mathcal{C}} P(\mathcal{C}) \lambda_w(\mathcal{C}), \tag{8.68}$$

where $P_e^{(n)}(\mathcal{C})$ is defined for typical set decoding.

By the symmetry of the code construction, the average probability of error averaged over all codes does not depend on the particular index that was sent, i.e., $\sum_{\mathscr{C}} P(\mathscr{C})\lambda_w(\mathscr{C})$ does not depend on w. Thus we can assume without loss of generality that the message $W = 1$ was sent, since

$$\Pr(\mathscr{E}) = \frac{1}{2^{nR}} \sum_{w=1}^{2^{nR}} \sum_{\mathscr{C}} P(\mathscr{C})\lambda_w(\mathscr{C}) \qquad (8.69)$$

$$= \sum_{\mathscr{C}} P(\mathscr{C})\lambda_1(\mathscr{C}) \qquad (8.70)$$

$$= \Pr(\mathscr{E}|W = 1). \qquad (8.71)$$

Define the following events:

$$E_i = \{(X^n(i), Y^n) \text{ is in } A_\epsilon^{(n)}\}, \quad i \in \{1, 2, \ldots, 2^{nR}\}, \qquad (8.72)$$

where E_i is the event that the ith codeword and Y^n are jointly typical. Recall that Y^n is the result of sending the first codeword $X^n(1)$ over the channel.

Then an error occurs in the decoding scheme if either E_1^c occurs (when the transmitted codeword and the received sequence are not jointly typical) or $E_2 \cup E_3 \cup \cdots \cup E_{2^{nR}}$ occurs (when a wrong codeword is jointly typical with the received sequence). Hence, letting $P(\mathscr{E})$ denote $\Pr\{\mathscr{E}|W = 1\}$, we have

$$\Pr(\mathscr{E}|W = 1) = P(E_1^c \cup E_2 \cup E_3 \cup \cdots \cup E_{2^{nR}}) \qquad (8.73)$$

$$\leq P(E_1^c) + \sum_{i=2}^{2^{nR}} P(E_i), \qquad (8.74)$$

by the union of events bound for probabilities. Now, by the joint AEP, $P(E_1^c) \to 0$, and hence

$$P(E_1^c) \leq \epsilon, \quad \text{for } n \text{ sufficiently large}. \qquad (8.75)$$

Since by the code generation process, $X^n(1)$ and $X^n(i)$ are independent, so are Y^n and $X^n(i)$, $i \neq 1$. Hence, the probability that $X^n(i)$ and Y^n are jointly typical is $\leq 2^{-n(I(X;Y)-3\epsilon)}$ by the joint AEP. Consequently,

$$P(\mathscr{E}) = P(\mathscr{E}|W = 1) \leq P(E_1^c) + \sum_{i=2}^{2^{nR}} P(E_i) \qquad (8.76)$$

$$\leq \epsilon + \sum_{i=2}^{2^{nR}} 2^{-n(I(X;Y)-3\epsilon)} \qquad (8.77)$$

$$= \epsilon + (2^{nR} - 1)2^{-n(I(X;Y)-3\epsilon)} \qquad (8.78)$$

$$\leq \epsilon + 2^{3n\epsilon}2^{-n(I(X;Y)-R)} \qquad (8.79)$$

$$\leq 2\epsilon \qquad (8.80)$$

if n is sufficiently large and $R < I(X;Y) - 3\epsilon$.

Hence, if $R < I(X;Y)$, we can choose ϵ and n so that the average probability of error, averaged over codebooks and codewords, is less than 2ϵ.

To finish the proof, we will strengthen this conclusion by a series of code selections.

1. Choose $p(x)$ in the proof to be $p^*(x)$, the distribution on X that achieves capacity. Then the condition $R < I(X;Y)$ can be replaced by the achievability condition $R < C$.

2. Get rid of the average over codebooks. Since the average probability of error over codebooks is small ($\leq 2\epsilon$), there exists at least one codebook $\mathscr{C}^*$ with a small average probability of error. Thus $P_e^n(\mathscr{C}^*) \leq 2\epsilon$. Determination of $\mathscr{C}^*$ can be achieved by an exhaustive search over all $(2^{nR}, n)$ codes.

3. Throw away the worst half of the codewords in the best codebook $\mathscr{C}^*$. Since the average probability of error for this code is less then 2ϵ, we have

$$2\epsilon \geq \frac{1}{2^{nR}} \sum \lambda_i(\mathscr{C}^*), \qquad (8.81)$$

   which implies that at least half the indices i and their associated codewords $X^n(i)$ must have conditional probability of error λ_i less than 4ϵ (otherwise, these codewords themselves would contribute more than 2ϵ to the sum). Hence the best half of the codewords have a maximal probability of error less than 4ϵ. If we reindex these codewords, we have 2^{nR-1} codewords. Throwing out half the codewords has changed the rate from R to $R - \frac{1}{n}$, which is negligible for large n.

Combining all these improvements, we have constructed a code of rate $R' = R - \frac{1}{n}$, with maximal probability of error $\lambda^{(n)} \leq 4\epsilon$. This proves the achievability of any rate below capacity. $\square$

Random coding is the method of proof for the above theorem, not the method of signalling. Codes are selected at random in the proof merely to symmetrize the mathematics and to show the existence of a good deterministic code. We proved that the average over all codes of block length n has small probability of error. We can find the best code within this set by an exhaustive search. Incidentally, this shows that the Kolmogorov complexity of the best code is a small constant. This means that the revelation (in step 2) to the sender and receiver of the best code $\mathscr{C}^*$ requires no channel. The sender and receiver merely agree to use the best $(2^{nR}, n)$ code for the channel.

Although the theorem shows that there exist good codes with exponentially small probability of error for long block lengths, it does not provide a way of constructing the best codes. If we used the scheme suggested by the proof and generate a code at random with the appropriate distribution, the code constructed is likely to be good for long block lengths. However, without some structure in the code, it is very difficult to decode (the simple scheme of table lookup requires an exponentially large table). Hence the theorem does not provide a practical coding scheme. Ever since Shannon's original paper on information theory, researchers have tried to develop structured codes that are easy to encode and decode. So far, they have developed many codes with interesting and useful structures, but the asymptotic rates of these codes are not yet near capacity.

8.8   ZERO-ERROR CODES

The outline of the proof of the converse is most clearly motivated by going through the argument when absolutely no errors are allowed. We will now prove that $P_e^{(n)} = 0$ implies $R \le C$.

Assume that we have a $(2^{nR}, n)$ code with zero probability of error, i.e., the decoder output $g(Y^n)$ is equal to the input index W with probability 1. Then the input index W is determined by the output sequence, i.e., $H(W|Y^n) = 0$. Now, to obtain a strong bound, we arbitrarily assume that W is uniformly distributed over $\{1, 2, \ldots, 2^{nR}\}$. Thus $H(W) = nR$. We can now write the string of inequalities:

$$nR = H(W) = \underbrace{H(W|Y^n)}_{=0} + I(W; Y^n) \tag{8.82}$$

$$= I(W; Y^n) \tag{8.83}$$

$$\overset{(a)}{\le} I(X^n; Y^n) \tag{8.84}$$

$$\overset{(b)}{\le} \sum_{i=1}^{n} I(X_i; Y_i) \tag{8.85}$$

$$\overset{(c)}{\le} nC, \tag{8.86}$$

where (a) follows from the data processing inequality (since $W \rightarrow X^n(W) \rightarrow Y^n$ forms a Markov chain), (b) will be proved in Lemma 8.9.2 using the discrete memoryless assumption, and (c) follows from the definition of (information) capacity.

Hence, for any zero-error $(2^{nR}, n)$ code, for all n,

$$R \leq C. \tag{8.87}$$

8.9   FANO'S INEQUALITY AND THE CONVERSE TO THE CODING THEOREM

We now extend the proof that was derived for zero-error codes to the case of codes with very small probabilities of error. The new ingredient will be Fano's inequality, which gives a lower bound on the probability of error in terms of the conditional entropy. Recall the proof of Fano's inequality, which is repeated here in a new context for reference.

Let us define the setup under consideration. The index W is uniformly distributed on the set $\mathcal{W} = \{1, 2, \ldots, 2^{nR}\}$, and the sequence Y^n is probabilistically related to W. From Y^n, we estimate the index W that was sent. Let the estimate be $\hat{W} = g(Y^n)$. Define the probability of error

$$P_e^{(n)} = \Pr(\hat{W} \neq W). \tag{8.88}$$

Define

$$E = \begin{cases} 1, & \text{if } \hat{W} \neq W, \\ 0, & \text{if } \hat{W} = W. \end{cases} \tag{8.89}$$

Then using the chain rule for entropies to expand $H(E, W|Y^n)$ in two different ways, we have

$$H(E, W|Y^n) = H(W|Y^n) + H(E|W, Y^n) \tag{8.90}$$

$$= H(E|Y^n) + H(W|E, Y^n). \tag{8.91}$$

Now since E is a function of W and $g(Y^n)$, it follows that $H(E|W, Y^n) = 0$. Also, $H(E) \leq 1$, since E is a binary valued random variable. The remaining term, $H(W|E, Y^n)$, can be bounded as follows:

$$H(W|E, Y^n) = P(E = 0)H(W|Y^n, E = 0) + P(E = 1)H(W|Y^n, E = 1) \tag{8.92}$$

$$\leq (1 - P_e^{(n)})0 + P_e^{(n)} \log(|\mathcal{W}| - 1) \tag{8.93}$$

$$\leq P_e^{(n)} nR, \tag{8.94}$$

since given $E = 0$, $W = g(Y^n)$, and when $E = 1$, we can upper bound the conditional entropy by the logarithm of the number of outcomes. Combining these results, we obtain Fano's inequality:

$$H(W|Y^n) \le 1 + P_e^{(n)} nR . \tag{8.95}$$

Since for a fixed code $X^n(W)$ is a function of W,

$$H(X^n(W)|Y^n) \le H(W|Y^n) . \tag{8.96}$$

Then we have the following lemma.

Lemma 8.9.1 (*Fano's inequality*): *For a discrete memoryless channel with a codebook $\mathscr{C}$ and the input messages uniformly distributed, let $P_e^{(n)} = \Pr(W \neq g(Y^n))$. Then*

$$H(X^n|Y^n) \le 1 + P_e^{(n)} nR . \tag{8.97}$$

We will now prove a lemma which shows that the capacity per transmission is not increased if we use a discrete memoryless channel many times.

Lemma 8.9.2: *Let Y^n be the result of passing X^n through a discrete memoryless channel. Then*

$$I(X^n; Y^n) \le nC, \qquad \text{for all } p(x^n) . \tag{8.98}$$

Proof:

$$I(X^n; Y^n) = H(Y^n) - H(Y^n|X^n) \tag{8.99}$$

$$= H(Y^n) - \sum_{i=1}^{n} H(Y_i|Y_1, \ldots, Y_{i-1}, X^n) \tag{8.100}$$

$$= H(Y^n) - \sum_{i=1}^{n} H(Y_i|X_i) , \tag{8.101}$$

since by the definition of a discrete memoryless channel, Y_i depends only on X_i and is conditionally independent of everything else. Continuing the series of inequalities, we have

$$I(X^n; Y^n) = H(Y^n) - \sum_{i=1}^{n} H(Y_i|X_i) \tag{8.102}$$

$$\le \sum_{i=1}^{n} H(Y_i) - \sum_{i=1}^{n} H(Y_i|X_i) \tag{8.103}$$

$$= \sum_{i=1}^{n} I(X_i; Y_i) \tag{8.104}$$

$$\leq nC, \tag{8.105}$$

where (8.103) follows from the fact that the entropy of a collection of random variables is less than the sum of their individual entropies, and (8.105) follows from the definition of capacity. Thus we have proved that using the channel many times does not increase the information capacity in bits per transmission. □

We are now in a position to prove the converse to the channel coding theorem.

Proof: *Converse to Theorem 8.7.1, (the channel coding theorem)*: We have to show that any sequence of $(2^{nR}, n)$ codes with $\lambda^{(n)} \to 0$ must have $R \leq C$.

If the maximal probability of error tends to zero, then the average probability of error for the sequence of codes also goes to zero, i.e., $\lambda^{(n)} \to 0$ implies $P_e^{(n)} \to 0$, where $P_e^{(n)}$ is defined in (8.31). For each n, let W be drawn according to a uniform distribution over $\{1, 2, \ldots, 2^{nR}\}$. Since W has a uniform distribution, $P_e^{(n)} = \Pr(\hat{W} \neq W)$. Hence

$$nR = H(W) = H(W|Y^n) + I(W; Y^n) \tag{8.106}$$

$$\leq H(W|Y^n) + I(X^n(W); Y^n) \tag{8.107}$$

$$\leq 1 + P_e^{(n)} nR + I(X^n(W); Y^n) \tag{8.108}$$

$$\leq 1 + P_e^{(n)} nR + nC \tag{8.109}$$

by Lemma 8.9.1 and Lemma 8.9.2. Dividing by n, we obtain

$$R \leq P_e^{(n)} R + \frac{1}{n} + C. \tag{8.110}$$

Now letting $n \to \infty$, we see that the first two terms on the right hand side tend to 0, and hence

$$R \leq C. \tag{8.111}$$

We can rewrite (8.110) as

$$P_e^{(n)} \geq 1 - \frac{C}{R} - \frac{1}{nR}. \tag{8.112}$$

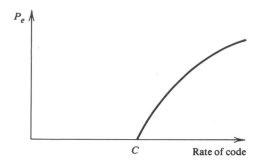

Figure 8.10. Lower bound on the probability of error.

This equation shows that if $R > C$, the probability of error is bounded away from 0 for sufficiently large n (and hence for all n, since if $P_e^{(n)} = 0$ for small n, we can construct codes for large n with $P_e^{(n)} = 0$ by concatenating these codes). Hence we cannot achieve an arbitrarily low probability of error at rates above capacity. This inequality is illustrated graphically in Figure 8.10.   □

This converse is sometimes called the weak converse to the channel coding theorem. It is also possible to prove a strong converse, which states that for rates above capacity, the probability of error goes exponentially to 1. Hence, the capacity is a very clear dividing point—at rates below capacity, $P_e^{(n)} \to 0$ exponentially, and at rates above capacity, $P_e^{(n)} \to 1$ exponentially.

8.10   EQUALITY IN THE CONVERSE TO THE CHANNEL CODING THEOREM

We have proved the channel coding theorem and its converse. In essence, these theorems state that when $R < C$, it is possible to send information with an arbitrarily low probability of error, and when $R > C$, the probability of error is bounded away from zero.

It is interesting and rewarding to examine the consequences of equality in the converse; hopefully, it will give some ideas as to the kind of codes that achieve capacity. Repeating the steps of the converse in the case when $P_e = 0$, we have

$$nR = H(W) \tag{8.113}$$

$$\overset{(a)}{=} H(X^n(W)) \tag{8.114}$$

$$= \underbrace{H(X^n | Y^n)}_{=0, \text{ since } P_e = 0} + I(X^n; Y^n) \tag{8.115}$$

$$= I(X^n; Y^n) \tag{8.116}$$

$$= H(Y^n) - H(Y^n | X^n) \tag{8.117}$$

$$= H(Y^n) - \sum_{i=1}^{n} H(Y_i | X_i) \quad \text{(since channel is a DMC)} \tag{8.118}$$

$$\overset{(b)}{\leq} \sum_{i=1}^{n} H(Y_i) - \sum_{i=1}^{n} H(Y_i | X_i) \tag{8.119}$$

$$= \sum_{i=1}^{n} I(X_i; Y_i) \tag{8.120}$$

$$\overset{(c)}{\leq} nC. \tag{8.121}$$

We have equality in (a) only if all the codewords are distinct. We have equality in (b) only if the Y_i's are independent, and equality in (c) only if the distribution of X_i is $p^*(x)$, the distribution on X that achieves capacity. We have equality in the converse only if these conditions are satisfied. This indicates that for an efficient code that achieves capacity, the codewords are distinct and the distribution of the Y_i's looks i.i.d. according to

$$p^*(y) = \sum_{x} p^*(x) p(y|x), \tag{8.122}$$

the distribution on Y induced by the optimum distribution on X. The distribution referred to in the converse is the empirical distribution on X and Y induced by a uniform distribution over codewords, i.e.,

$$p(x_i, y_i) = \frac{1}{2^{nR}} \sum_{w=1}^{2^{nR}} I(X_i(w) = x_i) p(y_i | x_i). \tag{8.123}$$

We can check this result in examples of codes which achieve capacity:

1. *Noisy typewriter.* In this case, we have an input alphabet of 26 letters, and each letter is either printed out correctly or changed to the next letter with probability $\frac{1}{2}$. A simple code that achieves capacity (log 13) for this channel is to use every alternate input letter so that no two letters can be confused. In this case, there are 13 codewords of blocklength 1. If we choose the codewords i.i.d. according to a uniform distribution on $\{1, 3, 5, 7, \ldots, 25\}$, then the output of the channel is also i.i.d. and uniformly distributed on $\{1, 2, \ldots, 26\}$, as expected.

2. *Binary symmetric channel.* Since given any input sequence, every possible output sequence has some positive probability, it will not be possible to distinguish even two codewords with zero probability of error. Hence the zero-error capacity of the BSC is zero.

However, even in this case, we can draw some useful conclusions. The efficient codes will still induce a distribution on Y that looks i.i.d. $\sim$ Bernoulli($\frac{1}{2}$). Also, from the arguments that lead up to the converse, we can see that at rates close to capacity, we have almost entirely covered the set of possible output sequences with decoding sets corresponding to the codewords. At rates above capacity, the decoding sets begin to overlap, and the probability of error can no longer be made arbitrarily small.

8.11   HAMMING CODES

The channel coding theorem promises the existence of block codes that will allow us to transmit information at rates below capacity with an arbitrarily small probability of error if the block length is large enough. Ever since the appearance of Shannon's original paper, people have searched for such codes. In addition to achieving low probabilities of error, useful codes should be "simple" so that they can be encoded and decoded efficiently.

The search for simple good codes has come a long way since the publication of Shannon's original paper in 1948. The entire field of coding theory has been developed during this search. We will not be able to describe the many elegant and intricate coding schemes that have been developed since 1948. We will only describe the simplest such scheme developed by Hamming [129]. It illustrates some of the basic ideas underlying most codes.

The object of coding is to introduce redundancy so that even if some of the information is lost or corrupted, it will still be possible to recover the message at the receiver. The most obvious coding scheme is to repeat information. For example, to send a 1, we send 11111, and to send a 0, we send 00000. This scheme uses 5 symbols to sent 1 bit, and therefore has a *rate* of $\frac{1}{5}$ bits per symbol. If this code is used on a binary symmetric channel, the optimum decoding scheme is to take the majority vote of each block of 5 received bits. If 3 or more bits are 1, we decode the block as a 1, otherwise we decode it as 0. An error occurs if and only if more than 3 of the bits are changed. By using longer repetition codes, we can achieve an arbitrarily low probability of error. But the rate of the code also goes to zero with block length, and so even though the code is "simple," it is really not a very useful code.

Instead of simply repeating the bits, we can combine the bits in some intelligent fashion so that each extra bit checks whether there is an error in some subset of the information bits. A simple example of this is a parity check code. Starting with a block of $n - 1$ information bits, we choose the n-th bit so that the parity of the entire block is 0 (the number of 1's in the block is even). Then if there is an odd number of errors during the transmission, the receiver will notice that the parity has changed and detect the error. This is the simplest example of an *error detecting code*. The code does not detect an even number of errors and does not give any information about how to correct the errors that occur.

We can extend the idea of parity checks to allow for more than one parity check bit and to allow the parity checks to depend on various subsets of the information bits. The Hamming code that we describe below is an example of a parity check code. We describe it using some simple ideas from linear algebra.

To illustrate the principles of Hamming codes, we consider a binary code of block length 7. All operations will be done modulo 2. Consider the set of all non-zero binary vectors of length 3. Arrange them in columns to form a matrix,

$$H = \begin{bmatrix} 0 & 0 & 0 & 1 & 1 & 1 & 1 \\ 0 & 1 & 1 & 0 & 0 & 1 & 1 \\ 1 & 0 & 1 & 0 & 1 & 0 & 1 \end{bmatrix}. \tag{8.124}$$

Consider the set of vectors of length 7 in the null space of H (the vectors which when multiplied by H give 000). From the theory of linear spaces, since H has rank 3, we expect the null space of H to have dimension 4. We list these 2^4 codewords in Table 8.1.

Since the set of codewords is the null-space of a matrix, it is *linear* in the sense that the sum of any two codewords is also a codeword. The set of codewords therefore forms a linear subspace of dimension 4 in the vector space of dimension 7.

Looking at the codewords, we notice that other than the all 0 codeword, the minimum number of 1's in any codeword is 3. This is called the *minimum weight* of the code. We can see that the minimum weight of a code has to be at least 3 since all the columns of H are different and so no two columns can add to 000. The fact that the minimum distance is exactly 3 can be seen from the fact that the sum of any two columns must be one of the columns of the matrix.

Table 8.1. The Hamming (7,4) Code

0000000	0100101	1000011	1100110
0001111	0101010	1001100	1101001
0010110	0110011	1010101	1110000
0011001	0111100	1011010	1111111

Since the code is linear, the difference between any two codewords is also a codeword, and hence any two codewords differ in at least 3 places. The minimum number of places in which two codewords differ is called the *minimum distance* of the code. The minimum distance of the code is a measure of how far apart the codewords are and will determine how distinguishable the codewords will be at the output of the channel. The minimum distance is equal to the minimum weight for a linear code. We aim to develop codes that have a large minimum distance.

For the code described above, the minimum distance is 3. Hence if a codeword c is corrupted in only one place, it will differ from any other codeword in at least two places, and therefore be closer to c than to any other codeword. But can we discover which is the closest codeword without searching over all the codewords?

The answer is yes. We can use the structure of the matrix H for decoding. The matrix H is called the *parity check matrix* and has the property that for every codeword c, $Hc = 0$. Let e_i be a vector with a 1 in the ith position and 0's elsewhere. If the codeword is corrupted at position i, then the received vector $r = c + e_i$. If we multiply this received vector by the matrix H, we obtain

$$Hr = H(c + e_i) = Hc + He_i = He_i , \qquad (8.125)$$

which is the vector corresponding to the ith column of H. Hence looking at Hr, we can find which position of the received vector was corrupted. Reversing this bit will give us a codeword.

This yields a simple procedure for correcting one error in the received sequence. We have constructed a codebook with 16 codewords of block length 7, which can correct up to one error. This code is called a *Hamming code*.

We have not yet identified a simple encoding procedure; we could use any mapping from a set of 16 messages into the codewords. But if we examine the first 4 bits of the codewords in the table, we observe that they cycle through all 2^4 combinations of 4 bits. Thus we could use these 4 bits to be the 4 bits of the message we want to send; the other 3 bits are then determined by the code. In general, it is possible to modify a linear code so that the mapping is explicit, so that the first k bits in each codeword represent the message, and the last $n - k$ bits are parity check bits. Such a code is called a *systematic code*. The code is often identified by its block length n, the number of information bits k and the minimum distance d. For example, the above code is called a $(7, 4, 3)$ Hamming code, i.e., $n = 7$, $k = 4$ and $d = 3$.

We can easily generalize this procedure to construct larger matrices H. In general, if we use l rows in H, then the code that we obtain will have block length $n = 2^l - 1$, $k = 2^l - l - 1$, and minimum distance 3. All these codes are called Hamming codes and can correct one error.

Hamming codes are the simplest examples of linear parity check codes. They demonstrate the principle that underlies the construction of other linear codes. But with large block lengths it is likely that there will be more than one error in the block. In the early 1950's, Reed and Solomon found a class of multiple error correcting codes for non-binary channels. In the late 1950's, Bose and Chaudhuri [42] and Hocquenghem [134] generalized the ideas of Hamming codes using Galois field theory to construct t-error correcting codes (called BCH codes) for any t. Since then various authors have developed other codes and also developed efficient decoding algorithms for these codes. With the advent of integrated circuits, it has become feasible to implement fairly complex codes in hardware and realize some of the error correcting performance promised by Shannon's channel capacity theorem. For example, all compact disc players include error correction circuitry based on two interleaved $(32, 28, 5)$ and $(28, 24, 5)$ Reed-Solomon codes that allow the decoder to correct bursts of up to 4000 errors.

All the codes described above are block codes—they map a block of information bits onto a channel codeword and there is no dependence on past information bits. It is also possible to design codes where each output block depends not only on the current input block, but also on some of the past inputs as well. A highly structured form of such a code is called a *convolutional code*. The theory of convolutional codes has developed considerably over the last 25 years. We will not go into the details, but refer the interested reader to textbooks on coding theory [41], [179].

Although there has been much progress in the design of good codes for the binary symmetric channel, it is still not possible to design codes that meet the bounds suggested by Shannon's channel capacity theorem. For a binary symmetric channel with crossover probability p, we would need a code that could correct up to np errors in a block of length n and have $n(1 - H(p))$ information bits. None of the codes known so far achieve this performance. For example, the repetition code suggested earlier corrects up to $n/2$ errors in a block of length n, but its rate goes to 0 with n. Until 1972, all known codes that could correct $n\alpha$ errors for block length n had asymptotic rate 0. In 1972, Justesen [147] described a class of codes with positive asymptotic rate and positive asymptotic minimum distance as a fraction of the block length. However, these codes are good only for long block lengths.

8.12   FEEDBACK CAPACITY

The channel with feedback is illustrated in Figure 8.11. We assume that all the received symbols are sent back immediately and noiselessly to the transmitter, which can then use them to decide which symbol to send next.

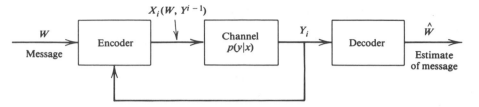

Figure 8.11. Discrete memoryless channel with feedback.

Can we do better with feedback? The surprising answer is no, which we shall now prove. We define a $(2^{nR}, n)$ *feedback code* as a sequence of mappings $x_i(W, Y^{i-1})$, where each x_i is a function only of W and the previous received values, $Y_1, Y_2, \ldots, Y_{i-1}$, and a sequence of decoding functions $g: \mathcal{Y}^n \rightarrow \{1, 2, \ldots, 2^{nR}\}$. Thus

$$P_e^{(n)} = \Pr\{g(Y^n) \neq W\}, \tag{8.126}$$

when W is uniformly distributed over $\{1, 2, \ldots, 2^{nR}\}$.

Definition: The *capacity with feedback*, C_{FB}, of a discrete memoryless channel is the supremum of all rates achievable by feedback codes.

Theorem 8.12.1 (*Feedback capacity*):

$$C_{FB} = C = \max_{p(x)} I(X; Y). \tag{8.127}$$

Proof: Since a non-feedback code is a special case of a feedback code, any rate that can be achieved without feedback can be achieved with feedback, and hence

$$C_{FB} \geq C. \tag{8.128}$$

Proving the inequality the other way is slightly more tricky. We cannot use the same proof that we used for the converse to the coding theorem without feedback. Lemma 8.9.2 is no longer true, since X_i depends on the past received symbols, and it is no longer true that Y_i depends only on X_i and is conditionally independent of the future X's in (8.101).

There is a simple change that will make the method work; instead of using X^n, we will use the index W and prove a similar series of inequalities. Let W be uniformly distributed over $\{1, 2, \ldots, 2^{nR}\}$. Then

$$nR = H(W) = H(W|Y^n) + I(W; Y^n) \tag{8.129}$$

$$\leq 1 + P_e^{(n)} nR + I(W; Y^n) \tag{8.130}$$

by Fano's inequality.

Now we can bound $I(W; Y^n)$ as follows:

$$I(W; Y^n) = H(Y^n) - H(Y^n|W) \tag{8.131}$$

$$= H(Y^n) - \sum_{i=1}^{n} H(Y_i|Y_1, Y_2, \ldots, Y_{i-1}, W) \tag{8.132}$$

$$= H(Y^n) - \sum_{i=1}^{n} H(Y_i|Y_1, Y_2, \ldots, Y_{i-1}, W, X_i) \tag{8.133}$$

$$= H(Y^n) - \sum_{i=1}^{n} H(Y_i|X_i) \tag{8.134}$$

since X_i is a function of $Y_1, \ldots, Y_{i-1}$ and W; and conditional on X_i, Y_i is independent of W and past samples of Y. Then using the entropy bound, we have

$$I(W; Y^n) = H(Y^n) - \sum_{i=1}^{n} H(Y_i|X_i) \tag{8.135}$$

$$\leq \sum_{i=1}^{n} H(Y_i) - \sum_{i=1}^{n} H(Y_i|X_i) \tag{8.136}$$

$$= \sum_{i=1}^{n} I(X_i; Y_i) \tag{8.137}$$

$$\leq nC \tag{8.138}$$

from the definition of capacity for a discrete memoryless channel.

Putting these together, we obtain

$$nR \leq P_e^{(n)} nR + 1 + nC, \tag{8.139}$$

and dividing by n and letting $n \to \infty$, we conclude

$$R \leq C. \tag{8.140}$$

Thus we cannot achieve any higher rates with feedback than we can without feedback, and

$$C_{FB} = C. \quad \square \tag{8.141}$$

As we have seen in the example of the binary erasure channel, feedback can help enormously in simplifying encoding and decoding. However, it cannot increase the capacity of the channel.

8.13 THE JOINT SOURCE CHANNEL CODING THEOREM

It is now time to combine the two main results that we have proved so far: data compression ($R > H$: Theorem 5.4.2) and data transmission ($R < C$: Theorem 8.7.1). Is the condition $H < C$ necessary and sufficient for sending a source over a channel?

For example, consider sending digitized speech or music over a discrete memoryless channel. We could design a code to map the sequence of speech samples directly into the input of the channel, or we could compress the speech into its most efficient representation, then use the appropriate channel code to send it over the channel. It is not immediately clear that we are not losing something by using the two-stage method, since the data compression does not depend on the channel and the channel coding does not depend on the source distribution.

We will prove in this section that the two-stage method is as good as any other method of transmitting information over a noisy channel. This result has some important practical implications. It implies that we can consider the design of a communication system as a combination of two parts, source coding and channel coding. We can design source codes for the most efficient representation of the data. We can separately and independently design channel codes appropriate for the channel. The combination will be as efficient as anything we could design by considering both problems together.

The common representation for random data uses a binary alphabet. Most modern communication systems are digital, and data is reduced to a binary representation for transmission over the common channel. This offers an enormous reduction in complexity. A system like ISDN (Integrated Services Digital Network) uses the common binary representation to allow speech and digital data to use the same communication channel.

The result that a two-stage process is as good as any one stage process seems so obvious that it may be appropriate to point out that it is not always true. There are examples of multiuser channels where the decomposition breaks down.

We will also consider two simple situations where the theorem appears to be misleading. A simple example is that of sending English text over an erasure channel. We can look for the most efficient binary representation of the text and send it over the channel. But the errors will be very difficult to decode. If however we send the English text directly over the channel, we can lose up to about half the letters and yet be able to make sense out of the message. Similarly, the human ear has some unusual properties that enable it to distinguish speech under very high noise levels if the noise is white. In such cases, it may be appropriate to send the uncompressed speech over the noisy channel rather than the compressed version. Apparently the redundancy in the source is suited to the channel.

Let us define the setup under consideration. We have a source V, that generates symbols from an alphabet $\mathcal{V}$. We will not make any assumptions about the kind of stochastic process produced by V other than that it is from a finite alphabet and satisfies the AEP. Examples of such processes include a sequence of i.i.d. random variables and the sequence of states of a stationary irreducible Markov chain. Any stationary ergodic source satisfies the AEP, as will be shown in Section 15.7.

We want to send the sequence of symbols $V^n = V_1, V_2, \ldots, V_n$ over the channel so that the receiver can reconstruct the sequence. To do this, we map the sequence onto a codeword $X^n(V^n)$ and send the codeword over the channel. The receiver looks at his received sequence Y^n and makes an estimate $\hat{V}^n$ of the sequence V^n that was sent. The receiver makes an error if $V^n \neq \hat{V}^n$. We define the probability of error $P_e^{(n)}$ as

$$P_e^{(n)} = \Pr(V^n \neq \hat{V}^n) = \sum_{y^n} \sum_{v^n} p(v^n) p(y^n | x^n(v^n)) I(g(y^n) \neq v^n),$$

$$(8.142)$$

where I is the indicator function and $g(y^n)$ is the decoding function. The system is illustrated in Figure 8.12.

We can now state the joint source channel coding theorem:

Theorem 8.13.1 (*Source-channel coding theorem*): *If $V_1, V_2, \ldots, V_n$ is a finite alphabet stochastic process that satisfies the AEP, then there exists a source channel code with $P_e^{(n)} \to 0$ if $H(\mathcal{V}) < C$.*

Conversely, for any stationary stochastic process, if $H(\mathcal{V}) > C$, the probability of error is bounded away from zero, and it is not possible to send the process over the channel with arbitrarily low probability of error.

Proof:

Achievability: The essence of the forward part of the proof is the two-stage encoding described earlier. Since we have assumed that the stochastic process satisfies the AEP, it implies that there exists a typical set $A_\epsilon^{(n)}$ of size $\leq 2^{n(H(\mathcal{V}) + \epsilon)}$ which contains most of the probability. We

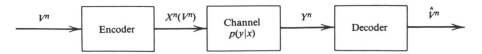

Figure 8.12. Joint source and channel coding.

will encode only the source sequences belonging to the typical set; all other sequences will result in an error. This will contribute at most ϵ to the probability of error.

We index all the sequences belonging to $A_\epsilon^{(n)}$. Since there are at most $2^{n(H+\epsilon)}$ such sequences, $n(H+\epsilon)$ bits suffice to index them. We can transmit the desired index to the receiver with probability of error less than ϵ if

$$H(\mathcal{V}) + \epsilon = R < C . \tag{8.143}$$

The receiver can reconstruct V^n by enumerating the typical set $A_\epsilon^{(n)}$ and choosing the sequence corresponding to the estimated index. This sequence will agree with the transmitted sequence with high probability. To be precise,

$$P_e^{(n)} = P(V^n \neq \hat{V}^n) \tag{8.144}$$

$$\leq P(V^n \notin A_\epsilon^{(n)}) + P(g(Y^n) \neq V^n | V^n \in A_\epsilon^{(n)}) \tag{8.145}$$

$$\leq \epsilon + \epsilon = 2\epsilon \tag{8.146}$$

for n sufficiently large. Hence, we can reconstruct the sequence with low probability of error for n sufficiently large if

$$H(\mathcal{V}) < C . \tag{8.147}$$

Converse: We wish to show that $P_e^{(n)} \to 0$ implies that $H(\mathcal{V}) \leq C$ for any sequence of source-channel codes

$$X^n(V^n): \mathcal{V}^n \to \mathcal{X}^n , \tag{8.148}$$

$$g_n(Y^n): \mathcal{Y}^n \to \mathcal{V}^n . \tag{8.149}$$

By Fano's inequality, we must have

$$H(V^n | \hat{V}^n) \leq 1 + P_e^{(n)} \log|\mathcal{V}^n| = 1 + P_e^{(n)} n \log|\mathcal{V}| . \tag{8.150}$$

Hence for the code,

$$H(\mathcal{V}) \overset{(a)}{\leq} \frac{H(V_1, V_2, \ldots, V_n)}{n} \tag{8.151}$$

$$= \frac{H(V^n)}{n} \tag{8.152}$$

$$= \frac{1}{n} H(V^n | \hat{V}^n) + \frac{1}{n} I(V^n; \hat{V}^n) \tag{8.153}$$

$$\overset{(b)}{\le} \frac{1}{n}\left(1 + P_e^{(n)}n\log|\mathcal{V}|\right) + \frac{1}{n}I(V^n; \hat{V}^n) \qquad (8.154)$$

$$\overset{(c)}{\le} \frac{1}{n}\left(1 + P_e^{(n)}n\log|\mathcal{V}|\right) + \frac{1}{n}I(X^n; Y^n) \qquad (8.155)$$

$$\overset{(d)}{\le} \frac{1}{n} + P_e^{(n)}\log|\mathcal{V}| + C, \qquad (8.156)$$

where (a) follows from the definition of entropy rate of a stationary process, (b) follows from Fano's inequality, (c) from the data processing inequality (since $V^n \to X^n \to Y^n \to \hat{V}^n$ forms a Markov chain) and (d) from the memorylessness of the channel. Now letting $n \to \infty$, we have $P_e^{(n)} \to 0$ and hence

$$H(\mathcal{V}) \le C. \quad \Box \qquad (8.157)$$

Hence we can transmit a stationary ergodic source over a channel if and only if its entropy rate is less than the capacity of the channel.

With this result, we have tied together the two basic theorems of information theory: data compression and data transmission. We will try to summarize the proofs of the two results in a few words. The data compression theorem is a consequence of the AEP, which shows that there exists a "small" subset (of size 2^{nH}) of all possible source sequences that contain most of the probability and that we can therefore represent the source with a small probability of error using H bits per symbol. The data transmission theorem is based on the joint AEP; it uses the fact that for long block lengths, the output sequence of the channel is very likely to be jointly typical with the input codeword, while any other codeword is jointly typical with probability $\approx 2^{-nI}$. Hence we can use about 2^{nI} codewords and still have negligible probability of error. The source channel separation theorem shows that we can design the source code and the channel code separately and combine the results to achieve optimal performance.

SUMMARY OF CHAPTER 8

Information capacity: $C = \max_{p(x)} I(X; Y)$.

Examples:

- Binary symmetric channel: $C = 1 - H(p)$.
- Binary erasure channel: $C = 1 - \alpha$.
- Symmetric channel: $C = \log|\mathcal{Y}| - H(\text{row of transition matrix})$.

Properties of C:
1. $0 \le C \le \min\{\log|\mathcal{X}|, \log|\mathcal{Y}|\}$.
2. $I(X; Y)$ is a continuous concave function of $p(x)$.

Definition: The set $A_\epsilon^{(n)}$ of *jointly typical* sequences $\{(x^n, y^n)\}$ with respect to the distribution $p(x, y)$ is given by

$$A_\epsilon^{(n)} = \left\{(x^n, y^n) \in \mathcal{X}^n \times \mathcal{Y}^n: \right. \tag{8.158}$$

$$\left| -\frac{1}{n} \log p(x^n) - H(X) \right| < \epsilon, \tag{8.159}$$

$$\left| -\frac{1}{n} \log p(y^n) - H(Y) \right| < \epsilon, \tag{8.160}$$

$$\left. \left| -\frac{1}{n} \log p(x^n, y^n) - H(X, Y) \right| < \epsilon \right\}, \tag{8.161}$$

where $p(x^n, y^n) = \prod_{i=1}^n p(x_i, y_i)$.

Joint AEP: Let (X^n, Y^n) be sequences of length n drawn i.i.d. according to $p(x^n, y^n) = \prod_{i=1}^n p(x_i, y_i)$. Then

1. $\Pr((X^n, Y^n) \in A_\epsilon^{(n)}) \to 1$ as $n \to \infty$.
2. $|A_\epsilon^{(n)}| \le 2^{n(H(X, Y) + \epsilon)}$.
3. If $(\tilde{X}^n, \tilde{Y}^n) \sim p(x^n)p(y^n)$, then $\Pr((\tilde{X}^n, \tilde{Y}^n) \in A_\epsilon^{(n)}) \le 2^{-n(I(X; Y) - 3\epsilon)}$.

The channel coding theorem: All rates below capacity C are achievable, that is, for every $\epsilon > 0$ and rate $R < C$, there exists a sequence of $(2^{nR}, n)$ codes with maximum probability of error

$$\lambda^{(n)} \le \epsilon, \tag{8.162}$$

for n sufficiently large. Conversely, if $\lambda^{(n)} \to 0$, then $R \le C$.

Feedback capacity: Feedback does not increase capacity for discrete memoryless channels, i.e., $C_{FB} = C$.

Source channel theorem: A stochastic process with entropy rate $H(\mathcal{V})$ cannot be sent reliably over a discrete memoryless channel if $H(\mathcal{V}) > C$. Conversely, if the process satisfies the AEP, then the source can be transmitted reliably if $H(\mathcal{V}) < C$.

PROBLEMS FOR CHAPTER 8

1. *Preprocessing the output.* One is given a communication channel with transition probabilities $p(y|x)$ and channel capacity $C = \max_{p(x)} I(X; Y)$. A helpful statistician preprocesses the output by forming $\tilde{Y} = g(Y)$. He claims that this will strictly improve the capacity.
    (a) Show that he is wrong.
    (b) Under what conditions does he not strictly decrease the capacity?

2. *Maximum likelihood decoding.* A source produces independent, equally probable symbols from an alphabet (a_1, a_2) at a rate of one symbol every 3 seconds. These symbols are transmitted over a binary symmetric channel which is used once each second by encoding the source symbol a_1 as 000 and the source symbol a_2 as 111. If in the corresponding 3 second interval of the channel output, any of the sequences 000,001,010,100 is received, a_1 is decoded; otherwise, a_2 is decoded. Let $\epsilon < \frac{1}{2}$ be the channel crossover probability.
    (a) For each possible received 3-bit sequence in the interval corresponding to a given source letter, find the probability that a_1 came out of the source given that received sequence.
    (b) Using part (a), show that the above decoding rule minimizes the probability of an incorrect decision.
    (c) Find the probability of an incorrect decision (using part (a) is not the easy way here).
    (d) If the source is slowed down to produce one letter every $2n + 1$ seconds, a_1 being encoded by $2n + 1$ 0's and a_2 being encoded by $2n + 1$ 1's. What decision rule minimizes the probability of error at the decoder? Find the probability of error as $n \to \infty$.

3. *An additive noise channel.* Find the channel capacity of the following discrete memoryless channel:

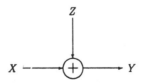

    where $\Pr\{Z = 0\} = \Pr\{Z = a\} = \frac{1}{2}$. The alphabet for x is $\mathcal{X} = \{0, 1\}$. Assume that Z is independent of X.
    Observe that the channel capacity depends on the value of a.

4. *Channels with memory have higher capacity.* Consider a binary symmetric channel with $Y_i = X_i \oplus Z_i$, where $\oplus$ is mod 2 addition, and $X_i, Y_i \in \{0, 1\}$.
    Suppose that $\{Z_i\}$ has constant marginal probabilities $\Pr\{Z_i = 1\} = p = 1 - \Pr\{Z_i = 0\}$, but that $Z_1, Z_2, \ldots, Z_n$ are not necessarily in-

dependent. Assume that Z^n is independent of the input X^n. Let $C = 1 - H(p, 1 - p)$. Show that $\max_{p(x_1, x_2, \ldots, x_n)} I(X_1, X_2, \ldots, X_n; Y_1, Y_2, \ldots, Y_n) \geq nC$.

5. *Channel capacity.* Consider the discrete memoryless channel $Y = X + Z \pmod{11}$, where

$$Z = \begin{pmatrix} 1, & 2, & 3 \\ 1/3, & 1/3, & 1/3 \end{pmatrix}$$

and $X \in \{0, 1, \ldots, 10\}$. Assume that Z is independent of X.
(a) Find the capacity.
(b) What is the maximizing $p^*(x)$?

6. *Using two channels at once.* Consider two discrete memoryless channels $(\mathcal{X}_1, p(y_1|x_1), \mathcal{Y}_1)$ and $(\mathcal{X}_2, p(y_2|x_2), \mathcal{Y}_2)$ with capacities C_1 and C_2 respectively. A new channel $(\mathcal{X}_1 \times \mathcal{X}_2, p(y_1|x_1) \times p(y_2|x_2), \mathcal{Y}_1 \times \mathcal{Y}_2)$ is formed in which $x_1 \in \mathcal{X}_1$ and $x_2 \in \mathcal{X}_2$, are simultaneously sent, resulting in y_1, y_2. Find the capacity of this channel.

7. *Noisy typewriter.* Consider a 26-key typewriter.
(a) If pushing a key results in printing the associated letter, what is the capacity C in bits?
(b) Now suppose that pushing a key results in printing that letter or the next (with equal probability). Thus $A \rightarrow A$ or $B, \ldots, Z \rightarrow Z$ or A. What is the capacity?
(c) What is the highest rate code with block length one that you can find that achieves zero probability of error for the channel in part (b).

8. *Cascade of binary symmetric channels.* Show that a cascade of n identical binary symmetric channels,

$$X_0 \rightarrow \boxed{\text{BSC}\#1} \rightarrow X_1 \rightarrow \cdots \rightarrow X_{n-1} \rightarrow \boxed{\text{BSC}\#n} \rightarrow X_n$$

each with raw error probability p, is equivalent to a single BSC with error probability $\frac{1}{2}(1 - (1 - 2p)^n)$ and hence that $\lim_{n \rightarrow \infty} I(X_0; X_n) = 0$ if $p \neq 0, 1$. No encoding or decoding takes place at the intermediate terminals $X_1, \ldots, X_{n-1}$. Thus the capacity of the cascade tends to zero.

9. *The Z channel.* The Z channel has binary input and output alphabets and transition probabilities $p(y|x)$ given by the following matrix:

$$Q = \begin{bmatrix} 1 & 0 \\ 1/2 & 1/2 \end{bmatrix} \qquad x, y \in \{0, 1\}$$

Find the capacity of the Z channel and the maximizing input probability distribution.

10. *Suboptimal codes.* For the Z channel of the previous problem, assume that we choose a $(2^{nR}, n)$ code at random, where each codeword is a

sequence of *fair* coin tosses. This will not achieve capacity. Find the maximum rate R such that the probability of error $P_e^{(n)}$, averaged over the randomly generated codes, tends to zero as the block length n tends to infinity.

11. *Zero-error capacity.* A channel with alphabet $\{0, 1, 2, 3, 4\}$ has transition probabilities of the form

$$p(y|x) = \begin{cases} 1/2 & \text{if } y = x \pm 1 \bmod 5 \\ 0 & \text{otherwise} . \end{cases}$$

(a) Compute the capacity of this channel in bits.

(b) The zero-error capacity of a channel is the number of bits per channel use that can be transmitted with zero probability of error. Clearly, the zero-error capacity of this pentagonal channel is at least 1 bit (transmit 0 or 1 with probability 1/2). Find a block code that shows that the zero-error capacity is greater than 1 bit. Can you estimate the exact value of the zero-error capacity?

(*Hint*: Consider codes of length 2 for this channel.)

The zero-error capacity of this channel was found by Lovasz [182].

12. *Time-varying channels.* Consider a time-varying discrete *memoryless* channel. Let $Y_1, Y_2, \ldots, Y_n$ be conditionally independent given $X_1, X_2, \ldots, X_n$, with conditional distribution given by $p(y|x) = \prod_{i=1}^{n} p_i(y_i|x_i)$.

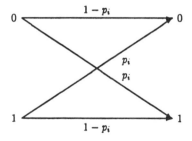

Let $\mathbf{X} = (X_1, X_2, \ldots, X_n)$, $\mathbf{Y} = (Y_1, Y_2, \ldots, Y_n)$. Find $\max_{p(\mathbf{x})} I(\mathbf{X}; \mathbf{Y})$.

HISTORICAL NOTES

The idea of mutual information and its relationship to channel capacity was first developed by Shannon in his original paper [238]. In this paper, he stated the channel capacity theorem and outlined the proof using typical sequences in an argument similar to the one described here. The first rigorous proof was due to Feinstein [107], who used a painstaking "cookie-cutting" argument to find the number of codewords that can be sent with a low probability of error. A simpler proof using a random coding exponent was developed by Gallager [118]. Our proof is based on Cover [62] and on Forney's unpublished course notes [115].

The converse was proved by Fano [105], who used the inequality bearing his name. The strong converse was first proved by Wolfowitz [276], using techniques that are closely related to typical sequences. An iterative algorithm to calculate the channel capacity was developed independently by Arimoto [11] and Blahut [37].

The idea of the zero-error capacity was developed by Shannon [239]; in the same paper, he also proved that feedback does not increase the capacity of a discrete memoryless channel. The problem of finding the zero-error capacity is essentially combinatorial; the first important result in this area is due to Lovasz [182].

Chapter 9

Differential Entropy

We now introduce the concept of *differential entropy*, which is the entropy of a continuous random variable. Differential entropy is also related to the shortest description length, and is similar in many ways to the entropy of a discrete random variable. But there are some important differences, and there is need for some care in using the concept.

9.1 DEFINITIONS

Definition: Let X be a random variable with cumulative distribution function $F(x) = \Pr(X \le x)$. If $F(x)$ is continuous, the random variable is said to be continuous. Let $f(x) = F'(x)$ when the derivative is defined. If $\int_{-\infty}^{\infty} f(x) = 1$, then $f(x)$ is called the *probability density function* for X. The set where $f(x) > 0$ is called the *support set* of X.

Definition: The *differential entropy* $h(X)$ of a continuous random variable X with a density $f(x)$ is defined as

$$h(X) = -\int_S f(x) \log f(x) \, dx , \tag{9.1}$$

where S is the support set of the random variable.

As in the discrete case, the differential entropy depends only on the probability density of the random variable, and hence the differential entropy is sometimes written as $h(f)$ rather than $h(X)$.

Remark: As in every example involving an integral, or even a density, we should include the statement *if it exists*. It is easy to construct examples of random variables for which a density function does not exist or for which the above integral does not exist.

Example 9.1.1 (*Uniform distribution*): Consider a random variable distributed uniformly from 0 to a, so that its density is $1/a$ from 0 to a and 0 elsewhere. Then its differential entropy is

$$h(X) = -\int_0^a \frac{1}{a} \log \frac{1}{a} \, dx = \log a \,. \tag{9.2}$$

Note: For $a < 1$, $\log a < 0$, and the differential entropy is negative. Hence, unlike discrete entropy, differential entropy can be negative. However, $2^{h(X)} = 2^{\log a} = a$ is the volume of the support set, which is always non-negative, as we expect.

Example 9.1.2 (*Normal distribution*): Let $X \sim \phi(x) = (1/\sqrt{2\pi\sigma^2}) \times e^{-x^2/2\sigma^2}$. Then calculating the differential entropy in nats, we obtain

$$h(\phi) = -\int \phi \ln \phi \tag{9.3}$$

$$= -\int \phi(x) \left[-\frac{x^2}{2\sigma^2} - \ln \sqrt{2\pi\sigma^2} \right] \tag{9.4}$$

$$= \frac{EX^2}{2\sigma^2} + \frac{1}{2} \ln 2\pi\sigma^2 \tag{9.5}$$

$$= \frac{1}{2} + \frac{1}{2} \ln 2\pi\sigma^2 \tag{9.6}$$

$$= \frac{1}{2} \ln e + \frac{1}{2} \ln 2\pi\sigma^2 \tag{9.7}$$

$$= \frac{1}{2} \ln 2\pi e\sigma^2 \text{ nats} \,. \tag{9.8}$$

Changing the base of the logarithm, we have

$$h(\phi) = \frac{1}{2} \log 2\pi e\sigma^2 \text{ bits} \,. \tag{9.9}$$

9.2   THE AEP FOR CONTINUOUS RANDOM VARIABLES

One of the important roles of the entropy for discrete random variables is in the AEP, which states that for a sequence of i.i.d. random variables, $p(X_1, X_2, \ldots, X_n)$ is close to $2^{-nH(X)}$ with high probability. This enables us to define the typical set and characterize the behavior of typical sequences.

We can do the same for a continuous random variable.

Theorem 9.2.1: *Let* $X_1, X_2, \ldots, X_n$ *be a sequence of random variables drawn i.i.d. according to the density* $f(x)$. *Then*

$$-\frac{1}{n} \log f(X_1, X_2, \ldots, X_n) \to E[-\log f(X)] = h(X) \quad \text{in probability}.$$

(9.10)

Proof: The proof follows directly from the weak law of large numbers. □

This leads to the following definition of the typical set.

Definition: For $\epsilon > 0$ and any n, we define the *typical set* $A_\epsilon^{(n)}$ with respect to $f(x)$ as follows:

$$A_\epsilon^{(n)} = \left\{ (x_1, x_2, \ldots, x_n) \in S^n : \left| -\frac{1}{n} \log f(x_1, x_2, \ldots, x_n) - h(X) \right| \leq \epsilon \right\},$$

(9.11)

where $f(x_1, x_2, \ldots, x_n) = \prod_{i=1}^{n} f(x_i)$.

The properties of the typical set for continuous random variables parallel those for discrete random variables. The analog of the cardinality of the typical set for the discrete case is the volume of the typical set in the continuous case.

Definition: The *volume* Vol(A) of a set $A \in \mathcal{R}^n$ is defined as

$$\text{Vol}(A) = \int_A dx_1 \, dx_2 \cdots dx_n .$$

(9.12)

Theorem 9.2.2: *The typical set* $A_\epsilon^{(n)}$ *has the following properties:*

1. $\Pr(A_\epsilon^{(n)}) > 1 - \epsilon$ *for* n *sufficiently large.*
2. $\text{Vol}(A_\epsilon^{(n)}) \leq 2^{n(h(X)+\epsilon)}$ *for all* n.
3. $\text{Vol}(A_\epsilon^{(n)}) \geq (1 - \epsilon) 2^{n(h(X)-\epsilon)}$ *for* n *sufficiently large.*

Proof: By the AEP, $-\frac{1}{n} \log f(x_1, x_2, \ldots, x_n) = -\frac{1}{n} \sum \log f(x_i) \to h(X)$ in probability, establishing property 1.

Also,

$$1 = \int_{S^n} f(x_1, x_2, \ldots, x_n)\, dx_1\, dx_2 \ldots dx_n \qquad (9.13)$$

$$\geq \int_{A_\epsilon^{(n)}} f(x_1, x_2, \ldots, x_n)\, dx_1\, dx_2 \ldots dx_n \qquad (9.14)$$

$$\geq \int_{A_\epsilon^{(n)}} 2^{-n(h(X)+\epsilon)}\, dx_1\, dx_2 \ldots dx_n \qquad (9.15)$$

$$= 2^{-n(h(X)+\epsilon)} \int_{A_\epsilon^{(n)}} dx_1\, dx_2 \ldots dx_n \qquad (9.16)$$

$$= 2^{-n(h(X)+\epsilon)}\, \mathrm{Vol}(A_\epsilon^{(n)}). \qquad (9.17)$$

Hence we have property 2.

We argue further that the volume of the typical set is at least this large. If n is sufficiently large so that property 1 is satisfied, then

$$1 - \epsilon \leq \int_{A_\epsilon^{(n)}} f(x_1, x_2, \ldots, x_n)\, dx_1\, dx_2 \ldots dx_n \qquad (9.18)$$

$$\leq \int_{A_\epsilon^{(n)}} 2^{-n(h(X)-\epsilon)}\, dx_1\, dx_2 \ldots dx_n \qquad (9.19)$$

$$= 2^{-n(h(X)-\epsilon)} \int_{A_\epsilon^{(n)}} dx_1\, dx_2 \ldots dx_n \qquad (9.20)$$

$$- 2^{-n(h(X)-\epsilon)}\, \mathrm{Vol}(A_\epsilon^{(n)}), \qquad (9.21)$$

establishing property 3. Thus for n sufficiently large, we have

$$(1 - \epsilon)2^{n(h(X)-\epsilon)} \leq \mathrm{Vol}(A_\epsilon^{(n)}) \leq 2^{n(h(X)+\epsilon)}. \qquad \square \qquad (9.22)$$

Theorem 9.2.3: *The set $A_\epsilon^{(n)}$ is the smallest volume set with probability $\geq 1 - \epsilon$, to first order in the exponent.*

Proof: Same as in the discrete case. $\square$

This theorem indicates that the volume of the smallest set that contains most of the probability is approximately 2^{nh}. This is an n-dimensional volume, so the corresponding side length is $(2^{nh})^{1/n} = 2^h$. This provides an interpretation of the differential entropy: it is the logarithm of the equivalent side length of the smallest set that contains most of the probability. Hence low entropy implies that the random variable is confined to a small effective volume and high entropy indicates that the random variable is widely dispersed.

Note: Just as the entropy is related to the volume of the typical set, there is a quantity called Fisher information which is related to the surface area of the typical set. We will say more about this in Section 16.7.

9.3   RELATION OF DIFFERENTIAL ENTROPY TO DISCRETE ENTROPY

Consider a random variable X with density $f(x)$ illustrated in Figure 9.1.

Suppose we divide the range of X into bins of length Δ. Let us assume that the density is continuous within the bins. Then by the mean value theorem, there exists a value x_i within each bin such that

$$f(x_i)\Delta = \int_{i\Delta}^{(i+1)\Delta} f(x)\,dx .$$

(9.23)

Consider the quantized random variable X^Δ, which is defined by

$$X^\Delta = x_i , \quad \text{if} \quad i\Delta \le X < (i+1)\Delta$$

(9.24)

Then the probability that $X^\Delta = x_i$ is

$$p_i = \int_{i\Delta}^{(i+1)\Delta} f(x)\,dx = f(x_i)\Delta .$$

(9.25)

The entropy of the quantized version is

$$H(X^\Delta) = -\sum_{-\infty}^{\infty} p_i \log p_i$$

(9.26)

$$= -\sum_{-\infty}^{\infty} f(x_i)\Delta \log(f(x_i)\Delta)$$

(9.27)

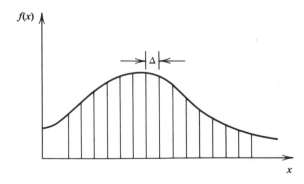

Figure 9.1. Quantization of a continuous random variable.

$$= -\sum \Delta f(x_i) \log f(x_i) - \sum f(x_i) \Delta \log \Delta \qquad (9.28)$$

$$= -\sum \Delta f(x_i) \log f(x_i) - \log \Delta, \qquad (9.29)$$

since $\sum f(x_i)\Delta = \int f(x) = 1$. If $f(x) \log f(x)$ is Riemann integrable (a condition to ensure the limit is well defined [272]), then the first term approaches the integral of $-f(x) \log f(x)$ by definition of Riemann integrability. This proves the following.

Theorem 9.3.1: *If the density $f(x)$ of the random variable X is Riemann integrable, then*

$$H(X^\Delta) + \log \Delta \to h(f) = h(X), \quad as \ \Delta \to 0. \qquad (9.30)$$

Thus the entropy of an n-bit quantization of a continuous random variable X is approximately $h(X) + n$.

Examples:

1. If X has a uniform distribution on $[0, 1]$, and we let $\Delta = 2^{-n}$, then $h = 0$, $H(X^\Delta) = n$ and n bits suffice to describe X to n bit accuracy.
2. If X is uniformly distributed on $[0, \frac{1}{8}]$, then the first 3 bits to the right of the decimal point must be 0. To describe X to n bit accuracy requires only $n - 3$ bits, which agrees with $h(X) = -3$.

In the above two examples, every value of X requires the same number of bits to describe. In general, however $h(X) + n$ is the number of bits *on the average* required to describe X to n bit accuracy.

The differential entropy of a discrete random variable can be considered to be $-\infty$. Note that $2^{-\infty} = 0$, agreeing with the idea that the volume of the support set of a discrete random variable is zero.

9.4   JOINT AND CONDITIONAL DIFFERENTIAL ENTROPY

As in the discrete case, we can extend the definition of differential entropy of a single random variable to several random variables.

Definition: The *differential entropy* of a set $X_1, X_2, \ldots, X_n$ of random variables with density $f(x_1, x_2, \ldots, x_n)$ is defined as

$$h(X_1, X_2, \ldots, X_n)$$

$$= -\int f(x_1, x_2, \ldots, x_n) \log f(x_1, x_2, \ldots, x_n) \, dx_1 \, dx_2 \ldots dx_n. \qquad (9.31)$$

Definition: If X, Y have a joint density function $f(x, y)$, we can define the conditional differential entropy $h(X|Y)$ as

$$h(X|Y) = -\int f(x, y) \log f(x|y) \, dx \, dy . \qquad (9.32)$$

Since in general $f(x|y) = f(x, y)/f(y)$, we can also write

$$h(X|Y) = h(X, Y) - h(Y) . \qquad (9.33)$$

But we must be careful if any of the differential entropies are infinite. The next entropy evaluation is frequently used in the text.

Theorem 9.4.1 (*Entropy of a multivariate normal distribution*): *Let $X_1, X_2, \ldots, X_n$ have a multivariate normal distribution with mean μ and covariance matrix K. (We use $\mathcal{N}_n(\mu, K)$ or $\mathcal{N}(\mu, K)$ to denote this distribution.) Then*

$$h(X_1, X_2, \ldots, X_n) = h(\mathcal{N}_n(\mu, K)) = \frac{1}{2} \log(2\pi e)^n |K| \text{ bits} , \qquad (9.34)$$

where $|K|$ denotes the determinant of K.

Proof: The probability density function of $X_1, X_2, \ldots, X_n$ is

$$f(\mathbf{x}) = \frac{1}{(\sqrt{2\pi})^n |K|^{1/2}} \, e^{-\frac{1}{2}(x-\mu)^T K^{-1}(x-\mu)} . \qquad (9.35)$$

Then

$$h(f) = -\int f(\mathbf{x}) \left[-\frac{1}{2}(\mathbf{x} - \mu)^T K^{-1}(\mathbf{x} - \mu) - \ln(\sqrt{2\pi})^n |K|^{1/2} \right] d\mathbf{x} \qquad (9.36)$$

$$= \frac{1}{2} E\left[\sum_{i,j} (x_i - \mu_i)(K^{-1})_{ij}(x_j - \mu_j) \right] + \frac{1}{2} \ln(2\pi)^n |K| \qquad (9.37)$$

$$= \frac{1}{2} E\left[\sum_{i,j} (x_i - \mu_i)(x_j - \mu_j)(K^{-1})_{ij} \right] + \frac{1}{2} \ln(2\pi)^n |K| \qquad (9.38)$$

$$= \frac{1}{2} \sum_{i,j} E[(x_j - \mu_j)(x_i - \mu_i)](K^{-1})_{ij} + \frac{1}{2} \ln(2\pi)^n |K| \qquad (9.39)$$

$$= \frac{1}{2} \sum_j \sum_i K_{ji}(K^{-1})_{ij} + \frac{1}{2} \ln(2\pi)^n |K| \qquad (9.40)$$

$$= \frac{1}{2} \sum_j (KK^{-1})_{jj} + \frac{1}{2} \ln(2\pi)^n |K| \qquad (9.41)$$

$$= \frac{1}{2} \sum_j I_{jj} + \frac{1}{2} \ln(2\pi)^n |K| \qquad (9.42)$$

$$= \frac{n}{2} + \frac{1}{2} \ln(2\pi)^n |K| \tag{9.43}$$

$$= \frac{1}{2} \ln(2\pi e)^n |K| \text{ nats} \tag{9.44}$$

$$= \frac{1}{2} \log(2\pi e)^n |K| \text{ bits} . \quad \square \tag{9.45}$$

9.5   RELATIVE ENTROPY AND MUTUAL INFORMATION

We now extend the definition of two familiar quantities, $D(f\|g)$ and $I(X; Y)$, to probability densities.

Definition: The *relative entropy* (or *Kullback Leibler distance*) $D(f\|g)$ between two densities f and g is defined by

$$D(f\|g) = \int f \log \frac{f}{g} . \tag{9.46}$$

Note that $D(f\|g)$ is finite only if the support set of f is contained in the support set of g. (Motivated by continuity, we set $0 \log \frac{0}{0} = 0$.)

Definition: The *mutual information* $I(X; Y)$ between two random variables with joint density $f(x, y)$ is defined as

$$I(X; Y) = \int f(x, y) \log \frac{f(x, y)}{f(x)f(y)} \, dx \, dy . \tag{9.47}$$

From the definition it is clear that

$$I(X; Y) = h(X) - h(X|Y) = h(Y) - h(Y|X) \tag{9.48}$$

and

$$I(X; Y) = D(f(x, y)\| f(x)f(y)) . \tag{9.49}$$

The properties of $D(f\|g)$ and $I(X; Y)$ are the same as in the discrete case. In particular, the mutual information between two random variables is the limit of the mutual information between their quantized versions, since

$$I(X^\Delta; Y^\Delta) = H(X^\Delta) - H(X^\Delta|Y^\Delta) \tag{9.50}$$

$$\approx h(X) - \log \Delta - (h(X|Y) - \log \Delta) \tag{9.51}$$

$$= I(X; Y) . \tag{9.52}$$

Certain authors (e.g., Gallager [120]) prefer to define the mutual information between two continuous random variables directly as the above limit, and not consider differential entropies at all.

9.6 PROPERTIES OF DIFFERENTIAL ENTROPY, RELATIVE ENTROPY AND MUTUAL INFORMATION

Theorem 9.6.1:

$$D(f\|g) \geq 0 . \tag{9.53}$$

with equality iff $f = g$ almost everywhere (a.e.).

Proof: Let S be the support set of f. Then

$$-D(f\|g) = \int_S f \log \frac{g}{f} \tag{9.54}$$

$$\leq \log \int_S f \frac{g}{f} \quad \text{(by Jensen's inequality)} \tag{9.55}$$

$$= \log \int_S g \tag{9.56}$$

$$\leq \log 1 = 0 . \tag{9.57}$$

We have equality iff we have equality in Jensen's inequality, which occurs iff $f = g$ a.e. $\square$

Corollary: $I(X; Y) \geq 0$ *with equality iff X and Y are independent.*

Corollary: $h(X|Y) \leq h(X)$ *with equality iff X and Y are independent.*

Theorem 9.6.2: *Chain rule for differential entropy:*

$$h(X_1, X_2, \ldots, X_n) = \sum_{i=1}^{n} h(X_i|X_1, X_2, \ldots, X_{i-1}) \tag{9.58}$$

Proof: Follows directly from the definitions. $\square$

Corollary:

$$h(X_1, X_2, \ldots, X_n) \leq \sum h(X_i) , \tag{9.59}$$

with equality iff $X_1, X_2, \ldots, X_n$ are independent.

Proof: Follows directly from Theorem 9.6.2 and the corollary to Theorem 9.6.1. ☐

Application (Hadamard's inequality): If we let $\mathbf{X} \sim \mathcal{N}(0, K)$ be a multivariate normal random variable, then substituting the definitions of entropy in the above inequality gives us

$$|K| \leq \prod_{i=1}^{n} K_{ii} , \qquad (9.60)$$

which is Hadamard's inequality. A number of determinant inequalities can be derived from information theoretic inequalities in this fashion (Chapter 16).

Theorem 9.6.3:

$$h(X + c) = h(X) . \qquad (9.61)$$

Translation does not change the differential entropy.

Proof: Follows directly from the definition of differential entropy. ☐

Theorem 9.6.4:

$$h(aX) = h(X) + \log|a| . \qquad (9.62)$$

Proof: Let $Y = aX$. Then $f_Y(y) = \frac{1}{|a|} f_X(\frac{y}{a})$, and

$$h(aX) = -\int f_Y(y) \log f_Y(y) \, dy \qquad (9.63)$$

$$= -\int \frac{1}{|a|} f_X\left(\frac{y}{a}\right) \log \left(\frac{1}{|a|} f_X\left(\frac{y}{a}\right)\right) dy \qquad (9.64)$$

$$= -\int f_X(x) \log f_X(x) + \log|a| \qquad (9.65)$$

$$= h(X) + \log|a| , \qquad (9.66)$$

after a change of variables in the integral. ☐

Similarly we can prove the following corollary for vector-valued random variables:

Corollary:

$$h(A\mathbf{X}) = h(\mathbf{X}) + \log|A|,\qquad(9.67)$$

where $|A|$ is the absolute value of the determinant.

We will now show that the multivariate normal distribution maximizes the entropy over all distributions with the same covariance.

Theorem 9.6.5: *Let the random vector $\mathbf{X} \in \mathbf{R}^n$ have zero mean and covariance $K = E\mathbf{X}\mathbf{X}^t$, i.e., $K_{ij} = EX_iX_j$, $1 \le i,\ j \le n$. Then $h(\mathbf{X}) \le \frac{1}{2}\log(2\pi e)^n|K|$, with equality iff $\mathbf{X} \sim \mathcal{N}(0, K)$.*

Proof: Let $g(\mathbf{X})$ be any density satisfying $\int g(\mathbf{x})x_ix_j\,d\mathbf{x} = K_{ij}$, for all i, j. Let ϕ_K be the density of a $\mathcal{N}(0, K)$ vector as given in 9.35, where we set $\mu = 0$. Note that $\log \phi_K(\mathbf{x})$ is a quadratic form and $\int x_ix_j\phi_K(\mathbf{x})\,d\mathbf{x} = K_{ij}$. Then

$$0 \le D(g\|\phi_K)\qquad(9.68)$$

$$= \int g\,\log(g/\phi_K)\qquad(9.69)$$

$$= -h(g) - \int g\,\log\phi_K\qquad(9.70)$$

$$= -h(g) - \int \phi_K\,\log\phi_K\qquad(9.71)$$

$$= -h(g) + h(\phi_K),\qquad(9.72)$$

where the substitution $\int g\,\log\phi_K = \int \phi_K\,\log\phi_K$ follows from the fact that g and ϕ_K yield the same moments of the quadratic form $\log\phi_K(\mathbf{x})$. $\square$

9.7 DIFFERENTIAL ENTROPY BOUND ON DISCRETE ENTROPY

Of all distributions with the same variance, the normal maximizes the entropy. So the entropy of the normal gives a good bound on the differential entropy in terms of the variance of the random variable. We will use this bound to give a bound on the discrete entropy of a random variable. It will not be in terms of the variance of the random variable itself, since a discrete random variable can have arbitrarily small variance and still have high discrete entropy. Instead, the bound is in terms of an integer-valued random variable with the same probabilities (and hence the same entropy).

Let X be a discrete random variable on the set $\mathcal{X} = \{a_1, a_2, \dots\}$ with

$$\Pr(X = a_i) = p_i \,. \tag{9.73}$$

Theorem 9.7.1:

$$H(p_1, p_2, \dots) \le \frac{1}{2} \log(2\pi e)\left(\sum_{i=1}^{\infty} p_i i^2 - \left(\sum_{i=1}^{\infty} ip_i\right)^2 + \frac{1}{12}\right). \tag{9.74}$$

Moreover, for every permutation σ,

$$H(p_1, p_2, \dots) \le \frac{1}{2} \log(2\pi e)\left(\sum_{i-1}^{\infty} p_{\sigma(i)} i^2 - \left(\sum_{i-1}^{\infty} ip_{\sigma(i)}\right)^2 + \frac{1}{12}\right). \tag{9.75}$$

Proof: Define two new random variables. The first, X_0, is an integer-valued discrete random variable with the distribution

$$\Pr(X_0 = i) = p_i \,. \tag{9.76}$$

Let U be a random variable uniformly distributed on the range $[0, 1]$, independent of X_0. Define the continuous random variable $\tilde{X}$ by

$$\tilde{X} = X_0 + U \,. \tag{9.77}$$

The distribution of the r.v. $\tilde{X}$ is shown in Figure 9.2.

It is clear that $H(X) = H(X_0)$, since discrete entropy depends only on the probabilities and not on the values of the outcomes. Now

$$H(X_0) = -\sum_{i=1}^{\infty} p_i \log p_i \tag{9.78}$$

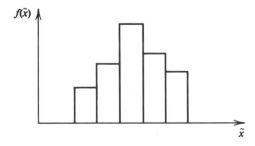

Figure 9.2. Distribution of $\tilde{X}$.

$$= -\sum_{i=1}^{\infty} \left(\int_{i}^{i+1} f_{\tilde{X}}(x)\, dx \right) \log \left(\int_{i}^{i+1} f_{\tilde{X}}(x)\, dx \right) \qquad (9.79)$$

$$= -\sum_{i=1}^{\infty} \int_{i}^{i+1} f_{\tilde{X}}(x) \log f_{\tilde{X}}(x)\, dx \qquad (9.80)$$

$$= -\int_{1}^{\infty} f_{\tilde{X}}(x) \log f_{\tilde{X}}(x)\, dx \qquad (9.81)$$

$$= h(\tilde{X}), \qquad (9.82)$$

since $f_{\tilde{X}}(x) = p_i$ for $i \le x < i+1$.

Hence we have the following chain of inequalities:

$$H(X) = H(X_0) \qquad (9.83)$$

$$= h(\tilde{X}) \qquad (9.84)$$

$$\le \frac{1}{2} \log(2\pi e) \operatorname{Var}(\tilde{X}) \qquad (9.85)$$

$$= \frac{1}{2} \log(2\pi e)(\operatorname{Var}(X_0) + \operatorname{Var}(U)) \qquad (9.86)$$

$$= \frac{1}{2} \log(2\pi e)\left(\sum_{i=1}^{\infty} p_i i^2 - \left(\sum_{i=1}^{\infty} i p_i \right)^2 + \frac{1}{12} \right). \quad \square \qquad (9.87)$$

Since entropy is invariant with respect to permutation of $p_1, p_2, \ldots,$ we can also obtain a bound by a permutation of the p_i's. We conjecture that a good bound on the variance will be achieved when the high probabilities are close together, i.e, by the assignment $\ldots, p_5,$ $p_3, p_1, p_2, p_4, \ldots$ for $p_1 \ge p_2 \ge \cdots$.

How good is this bound? Let X be a Bernoulli random variable with parameter $\frac{1}{2}$, which implies that $H(X) = 1$. The corresponding random variable X_0 has variance $\frac{1}{4}$, so the bound is

$$H(X) \le \frac{1}{2} \log(2\pi e)\left(\frac{1}{4} + \frac{1}{12} \right) = 1.255 \text{ bits}. \qquad (9.88)$$

SUMMARY OF CHAPTER 9

$$h(X) = h(f) = -\int_{S} f(x) \log f(x)\, dx. \qquad (9.89)$$

$$f(X^n) \doteq 2^{-nh(X)}, \text{ a.e.} \qquad (9.90)$$

$$\operatorname{Vol}(A_{\epsilon}^{(n)}) \doteq 2^{nh(X)}. \qquad (9.91)$$

$$H([X]_{2^{-n}}) \approx h(X) + n \,. \tag{9.92}$$

$$h(\mathcal{N}(0, \sigma^2)) = \frac{1}{2} \log 2\pi e \sigma^2 \,. \tag{9.93}$$

$$h(\mathcal{N}_n(\mu, K)) = \frac{1}{2} \log(2\pi e)^n |K| \,. \tag{9.94}$$

$$D(f\|g) = \int f \log \frac{f}{g} \ge 0 \,. \tag{9.95}$$

$$h(X_1, X_2, \ldots, X_n) = \sum_{i=1}^{n} h(X_i | X_1, X_2, \ldots, X_{i-1}) \,. \tag{9.96}$$

$$h(X|Y) \le h(X) \,. \tag{9.97}$$

$$h(aX) = h(X) + \log|a| \,. \tag{9.98}$$

$$I(X; Y) = \int f(x, y) \log \frac{f(x, y)}{f(x)f(y)} \ge 0 \,. \tag{9.99}$$

$$\max_{EXX^t = K} h(\mathbf{X}) = \frac{1}{2} \log(2\pi e)^n |K| \,. \tag{9.100}$$

$2^{H(X)}$ is the effective alphabet size for a discrete random variable.
$2^{h(X)}$ is the effective support set size for a continuous random variable.
2^C is the effective alphabet size of a channel of capacity C.

PROBLEMS FOR CHAPTER 9

1. *Differential entropy.* Evaluate the differential entropy $h(X) = -\int f \ln f$ for the following:
   (a) The exponential density, $f(x) = \lambda e^{-\lambda x}$, $x \ge 0$.
   (b) The Laplace density, $f(x) = \frac{1}{2} \lambda e^{-\lambda|x|}$.
   (c) The sum of X_1 and X_2, where X_1 and X_2 are independent normal random variables with means μ_i and variances σ_i^2, $i = 1, 2$.

2. *Concavity of determinants.* Let K_1 and K_2 be two symmetric nonnegative definite $n \times n$ matrices. Prove the result of Ky Fan [103]:

$$|\lambda K_1 + \bar{\lambda} K_2| \ge |K_1|^\lambda |K_2|^{\bar{\lambda}}, \quad \text{for } 0 \le \lambda \le 1, \ \bar{\lambda} = 1 - \lambda \,,$$

   where $|K|$ denotes the determinant of K.
   Hint: Let $\mathbf{Z} = \mathbf{X}_\theta$, where $\mathbf{X}_1 \sim N(0, K_1)$, $\mathbf{X}_2 \sim N(0, K_2)$ and $\theta =$ Bernoulli(λ). Then use $H(\mathbf{Z}|\theta) \le H(\mathbf{Z})$.

3. *Mutual information for correlated normals.* Find the mutual information $I(X; Y)$, where

$$\begin{pmatrix} X \\ Y \end{pmatrix} \sim N_2 \left(0, \begin{bmatrix} \sigma^2 & \rho\sigma^2 \\ \rho\sigma^2 & \sigma^2 \end{bmatrix} \right).$$

Evaluate $I(X; Y)$ for $\rho = 1$, $\rho = 0$, and $\rho = -1$, and comment.

4. *Uniformly distributed noise.* Let the input random variable X for a channel be uniformly distributed over the interval $-1/2 \leq x \leq +1/2$. Let the output of the channel be $Y = X + Z$, where the noise random variable is uniformly distributed over the interval $-a/2 \leq z \leq +a/2$.

(a) Find $I(X; Y)$ as a function of a.

(b) For $a = 1$ find the capacity of the channel when the input X is peak-limited; that is, the range of X is limited to $-1/2 \leq x \leq +1/2$. What probability distribution on X maximizes the mutual information $I(X; Y)$?

(c) (Optional) Find the capacity of the channel for all values of a, again assuming that the range of X is limited to $-1/2 \leq x \leq +1/2$.

5. *Quantized random variables.* Roughly how many bits are required on the average to describe to 3 digit accuracy the decay time (in years) of a radium atom if the half-life of radium is 80 years? Note that half-life is the median of the distribution.

6. *Scaling.* Let $h(\mathbf{X}) = -\int f(\mathbf{x}) \log f(\mathbf{x}) \, d\mathbf{x}$. Show $h(A\mathbf{X}) = \log|\det(A)| + h(\mathbf{X})$.

HISTORICAL NOTES

Differential entropy and discrete entropy were introduced in Shannon's original paper [238]. The general rigorous definition of relative entropy and mutual information for arbitrary random variables was developed by Kolmogorov [156] and Pinsker [212], who defined mutual information as $\sup_{P, Q} I([X]_P; [Y]_Q)$, where the supremum is over all finite partitions P and Q. The differential entropy bound on discrete entropy was developed independently by J. Massey (unpublished) and by F. Willems (unpublished).

Chapter 10

The Gaussian Channel

The most important continuous alphabet channel is the Gaussian channel depicted in Figure 10.1. This is a time discrete channel with output Y_i at time i, where Y_i is the sum of the input X_i and the noise Z_i. The noise Z_i is drawn i.i.d. from a Gaussian distribution with variance N. Thus

$$Y_i = X_i + Z_i, \qquad Z_i \sim \mathcal{N}(0, N). \tag{10.1}$$

The noise Z_i is assumed to be independent of the signal X_i. This channel is a good model for some common communication channels. Without further conditions, the capacity of this channel may be infinite. If the noise variance is zero, then the receiver receives the transmitted symbol perfectly. Since X can take on any real value, the channel can transmit an arbitrary real number with no error.

If the noise variance is non-zero and there is no constraint on the input, we can choose an infinite subset of inputs arbitrarily far apart, so that they are distinguishable at the output with arbitrarily small probability of error. Such a scheme has an infinite capacity as well. Thus if the noise variance is zero or the input is unconstrained, the capacity of the channel is infinite.

The most common limitation on the input is an energy or power constraint. We assume an average power constraint. For any codeword $(x_1, x_2, \ldots, x_n)$ transmitted over the channel, we require

$$\frac{1}{n} \sum_{i=1}^{n} x_i^2 \le P. \tag{10.2}$$

This communication channel models many practical channels, including

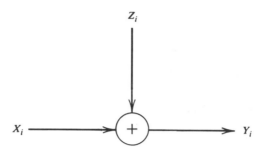

Figure 10.1. The Gaussian channel.

radio and satellite links. The additive noise in such channels may be due to a variety of causes. However, by the central limit theorem, the cumulative effect of a large number of small random effects will be approximately normal, so the Gaussian assumption is valid in a large number of situations.

We first analyze a simple suboptimal way to use this channel. Assume that we want to send 1 bit over the channel in 1 use of the channel. Given the power constraint, the best that we can do is to send one of two levels $+\sqrt{P}$ or $-\sqrt{P}$. The receiver looks at the corresponding received Y and tries to decide which of the two levels was sent. Assuming both levels are equally likely (this would be the case if we wish to send exactly 1 bit of information), the optimum decoding rule is to decide that $+\sqrt{P}$ was sent if $Y > 0$ and decide $-\sqrt{P}$ was sent if $Y < 0$. The probability of error with such a decoding scheme is

$$P_e = \frac{1}{2} \Pr(Y < 0 | X = +\sqrt{P}) + \frac{1}{2} \Pr(Y > 0 | X = -\sqrt{P}) \tag{10.3}$$

$$= \frac{1}{2} \Pr(Z < -\sqrt{P} | X = +\sqrt{P}) + \frac{1}{2} \Pr(Z > \sqrt{P} | X = -\sqrt{P}) \tag{10.4}$$

$$= \Pr(Z > \sqrt{P}) \tag{10.5}$$

$$= 1 - \Phi\left(\sqrt{\frac{P}{N}}\right), \tag{10.6}$$

where $\Phi(x)$ is the cumulative normal function

$$\Phi(x) = \int_{-\infty}^{x} \frac{1}{\sqrt{2\pi}} e^{-\frac{t^2}{2}} \, dt . \tag{10.7}$$

Using such a scheme, we have converted the Gaussian channel into a discrete binary symmetric channel with crossover probability P_e. Similarly, by using a four level input signal, we can convert the Gaussian channel into a discrete four input channel. In some practical modulation schemes, similar ideas are used to convert the continuous channel into a discrete channel. The main advantage of a discrete channel is ease of processing of the output signal for error correction, but some information is lost in the quantization.

10.1   THE GAUSSIAN CHANNEL: DEFINITIONS

We now define the (information) capacity of the channel as the maximum of the mutual information between the input and output over all distributions on the input that satisfy the power constraint.

Definition: The *information capacity* of the Gaussian channel with power constraint P is

$$C = \max_{p(x):EX^2 \le P} I(X; Y). \qquad (10.8)$$

We can calculate the information capacity as follows: Expanding $I(X; Y)$, we have

$$I(X; Y) = h(Y) - h(Y|X) \qquad (10.9)$$

$$= h(Y) - h(X + Z|X) \qquad (10.10)$$

$$= h(Y) - h(Z|X) \qquad (10.11)$$

$$= h(Y) - h(Z), \qquad (10.12)$$

since Z is independent of X. Now, $h(Z) = \frac{1}{2} \log 2\pi e N$. Also,

$$EY^2 = E(X + Z)^2 = EX^2 + 2EXEZ + EZ^2 = P + N, \qquad (10.13)$$

since X and Z are independent and $EZ = 0$. Given $EY^2 = P + N$, the entropy of Y is bounded by $\frac{1}{2} \log 2\pi e(P + N)$ by Theorem 9.6.5 (the normal maximizes the entropy for a given variance).

Applying this result to bound the mutual information, we obtain

$$I(X; Y) = h(Y) - h(Z) \qquad (10.14)$$

$$\le \frac{1}{2} \log 2\pi e(P + N) - \frac{1}{2} \log 2\pi e N \qquad (10.15)$$

$$= \frac{1}{2} \log\left(1 + \frac{P}{N}\right). \qquad (10.16)$$

Hence the information capacity of the Gaussian channel is

$$C = \max_{EX^2 \leq P} I(X; Y) = \frac{1}{2} \log\left(1 + \frac{P}{N}\right), \qquad (10.17)$$

and the maximum is attained when $X \sim \mathcal{N}(0, P)$.

We will now show that this capacity is also the supremum of the achievable rates for the channel. The arguments are similar to the arguments for a discrete channel. We will begin with the corresponding definitions.

Definition: A (M, n) code for the Gaussian channel with power constraint P consists of the following:

1. An index set $\{1, 2, \ldots, M\}$.
2. An encoding function $x : \{1, 2, \ldots, M\} \to \mathcal{X}^n$, yielding codewords $x^n(1), x^n(2), \ldots, x^n(M)$, satisfying the power constraint P, i.e., for every codeword

$$\sum_{i=1}^{n} x_i^2(w) \leq nP, \qquad w = 1, 2, \ldots, M. \qquad (10.18)$$

3. A decoding function

$$g : \mathcal{Y}^n \to \{1, 2, \ldots, M\}. \qquad (10.19)$$

The rate and probability of error of the code are defined as in Chapter 8 for the discrete case.

Definition: A rate R is said to be *achievable* for a Gaussian channel with a power constraint P if there exists a sequence of $(2^{nR}, n)$ codes with codewords satisfying the power constraint such that the maximal probability of error $\lambda^{(n)}$ tends to zero. The capacity of the channel is the supremum of the achievable rates.

Theorem 10.1.1: *The capacity of a Gaussian channel with power constraint P and noise variance N is*

$$C = \frac{1}{2} \log\left(1 + \frac{P}{N}\right) \text{ bits per transmission.} \qquad (10.20)$$

Remark: We will first present a plausibility argument as to why we may be able to construct $(2^{nC}, n)$ codes with low probability of error. Consider any codeword of length n. The received vector is normally distributed with mean equal to the true codeword and variance equal to the noise variance. With high probability, the received vector is contained in a sphere of radius $\sqrt{n(N + \epsilon)}$ around the true codeword. If we assign everything within this sphere to the given codeword, then when this codeword is sent, there will be an error only if the received vector falls outside the sphere, which has low probability.

Similarly we can choose other codewords and their corresponding decoding spheres. How many such codewords can we choose? The volume of an n-dimensional sphere is of the form $A_n r^n$ where r is the radius of the sphere. In this case, each of the decoding spheres has radius $\sqrt{nN}$. These spheres are scattered throughout the space of received vectors. The received vectors have energy no greater than $n(P + N)$ so they lie in a sphere of radius $\sqrt{n(P + N)}$. The maximum number of non-intersecting decoding spheres in this volume is no more than

$$\frac{A_n(n(P + N))^{\frac{n}{2}}}{A_n(nN)^{\frac{n}{2}}} = 2^{\frac{n}{2} \log\left(1 + \frac{P}{N}\right)} \tag{10.21}$$

and the rate of the code is $\frac{1}{2} \log\left(1 + \frac{P}{N}\right)$. This idea is illustrated in Figure 10.2.

This sphere packing argument indicates that we cannot hope to send at rates greater than C with low probability of error. However, we can actually do almost as well as this, as is proved next.

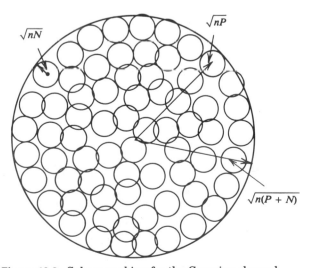

Figure 10.2. Sphere packing for the Gaussian channel.

Proof (*Achievability*): We will use the same ideas as in the proof of the channel coding theorem in the case of discrete channels, namely, random codes and joint typicality decoding. However, we must make some modifications to take into account the power constraint and the fact that the variables are continuous and not discrete.

1. *Generation of the codebook.* We wish to generate a codebook in which all the codewords satisfy the power constraint. To ensure this, we generate the codewords with each element i.i.d. according to a normal distribution with variance $P - \epsilon$. Since for large n, $\frac{1}{n} \sum X_i^2 \to P - \epsilon$, the probability that a codeword does not satisfy the power constraint will be small. However, we do not delete the bad codewords, as this will disturb the symmetry of later arguments.

   Let $X_i(w)$, $i = 1, 2, \ldots, n$, $w = 1, 2, \ldots, 2^{nR}$ be i.i.d. $\sim \mathcal{N}(0, P - \epsilon)$, forming codewords $X^n(1), X^n(2), \ldots, X^n(2^{nR}) \in \mathscr{R}^n$.

2. *Encoding.* After the generation of the codebook, the codebook is revealed to both the sender and the receiver. To send the message index w, the transmitter sends the wth codeword $X^n(w)$ in the codebook.

3. *Decoding.* The receiver looks down the list of codewords $\{X^n(w)\}$ and searches for one that is jointly typical with the received vector. If there is one and only one such codeword, the receiver declares it to be the transmitted codeword. Otherwise the receiver declares an error. The receiver also declares an error if the chosen codeword does not satisfy the power constraint.

4. *Probability of error.* Without loss of generality, assume that codeword 1 was sent. Thus $Y^n = X^n(1) + Z^n$.

Define the following events:

$$E_0 = \left\{ \frac{1}{n} \sum_{i=1}^{n} X_i^2(1) > P \right\} \tag{10.22}$$

and

$$E_i = \{(X^n(i), Y^n) \text{ is in } A_\epsilon^{(n)}\} . \tag{10.23}$$

Then an error occurs if E_0 occurs (the power constraint is violated) or E_1^c occurs (the transmitted codeword and the received sequence are not jointly typical) or $E_2 \cup E_3 \cup \ldots \cup E_{2^{nR}}$ occurs (some wrong codeword is jointly typical with the received sequence). Let $\mathscr{E}$ denote the event $\hat{W} \neq W$ and let P denote the conditional probability given $W = 1$. Hence

$$\Pr(\mathscr{E}|W = 1) = P(\mathscr{E}) = P(E_0 \cup E_1^c \cup E_2 \cup E_3 \cup \cdots \cup E_{2^{nR}}) \tag{10.24}$$

$$\leq P(E_0) + P(E_1^c) + \sum_{i=2}^{2^{nR}} P(E_i), \qquad (10.25)$$

by the union of events bound for probabilities. By the law of large numbers, $P(E_0) \to 0$ as $n \to \infty$. Now, by the joint AEP (which can be proved using the same argument used in the discrete case), $P(E_1^c) \to 0$, and hence

$$P(E_1^c) \leq \epsilon \quad \text{for } n \text{ sufficiently large}. \qquad (10.26)$$

Since by the code generation process, $X^n(1)$ and $X^n(i)$ are independent, so are Y^n and $X^n(i)$. Hence, the probability that $X^n(i)$ and Y^n will be jointly typical is $\leq 2^{-n(I(X;Y)-3\epsilon)}$ by the joint AEP. Hence

$$P_e^{(n)} = \Pr(\mathcal{E}) = \Pr(\mathcal{E}|W=1) = P(\mathcal{E}) \qquad (10.27)$$

$$\leq P(E_0) + P(E_1^c) + \sum_{i=2}^{2^{nR}} P(E_i) \qquad (10.28)$$

$$\leq \epsilon + \epsilon + \sum_{i=2}^{2^{nR}} 2^{-n(I(X;Y)-3\epsilon)} \qquad (10.29)$$

$$= 2\epsilon + (2^{nR} - 1)2^{-n(I(X;Y)-3\epsilon)} \qquad (10.30)$$

$$\leq 2\epsilon + 2^{3n\epsilon}2^{-n(I(X;Y)-R)} \qquad (10.31)$$

$$\leq 3\epsilon \qquad (10.32)$$

for n sufficiently large and $R < I(X;Y) - 3\epsilon$.

This proves the existence of a good $(2^{nR}, n)$ code.

Now choosing a good codebook and deleting the worst half of the codewords, we obtain a code with low maximal probability of error. In particular, the power constraint is satisfied by each of the remaining codewords (since the codewords that do not satisfy the power constraint have probability of error 1 and must belong to the worst half of the codewords).

Hence we have constructed a code which achieves a rate arbitrarily close to capacity. The forward part of the theorem is proved. In the next section, we show that the rate cannot exceed the capacity. $\square$

10.2 CONVERSE TO THE CODING THEOREM FOR GAUSSIAN CHANNELS

In this section, we complete the proof that the capacity of a Gaussian channel is $C = \frac{1}{2} \log(1 + \frac{P}{N})$ by proving that rates $R > C$ are not achievable. The proof parallels the proof for the discrete channel. The main new ingredient is the power constraint.

Proof (*Converse to Theorem 10.1.1*): We must show that if $P_e^{(n)} \to 0$ for a sequence of $(2^{nR}, n)$ codes for a Gaussian channel with power constraint P, then

$$R \le C = \frac{1}{2} \log\left(1 + \frac{P}{N}\right). \tag{10.33}$$

Consider any $(2^{nR}, n)$ code that satisfies the power constraint, i.e.,

$$\frac{1}{n} \sum_{i=1}^{n} x_i^2(w) \le P, \tag{10.34}$$

for $w = 1, 2, \ldots, 2^{nR}$. Proceeding as in the converse for the discrete case, the uniform distribution over the index set $w \in \{1, 2, \ldots, 2^{nR}\}$ induces a distribution on the input codewords, which in turn induces a distribution over the input alphabet. Since we can decode the index W from the output vector Y^n with low probability of error, we can apply Fano's inequality to obtain

$$H(W|Y^n) \le 1 + nRP_e^{(n)} = n\epsilon_n, \tag{10.35}$$

where $\epsilon_n \to 0$ as $P_e^{(n)} \to 0$. Hence

$$nR = H(W) = I(W; Y^n) + H(W|Y^n) \tag{10.36}$$

$$\le I(W; Y^n) + n\epsilon_n \tag{10.37}$$

$$\le I(X^n; Y^n) + n\epsilon_n \tag{10.38}$$

$$= h(Y^n) - h(Y^n|X^n) + n\epsilon_n \tag{10.39}$$

$$= h(Y^n) - h(Z^n) + n\epsilon_n \tag{10.40}$$

$$\le \sum_{i=1}^{n} h(Y_i) - h(Z^n) + n\epsilon_n \tag{10.41}$$

$$= \sum_{i=1}^{n} h(Y_i) - \sum_{i=1}^{n} h(Z_i) + n\epsilon_n \tag{10.42}$$

$$= \sum_{i=1}^{n} I(X_i; Y_i) + n\epsilon_n. \tag{10.43}$$

Here $X_i = X_i(W)$, where W is drawn according to the uniform distribution on $\{1, 2, \ldots, 2^{nR}\}$. Now let P_i be the average power of the ith column of the codebook, i.e.,

$$P_i = \frac{1}{2^{nR}} \sum_w x_i^2(w).$$
(10.44)

Then, since $Y_i = X_i + Z_i$ and since X_i and Z_i are independent, the average power of Y_i is $P_i + N$. Hence, since entropy is maximized by the normal distribution,

$$h(Y_i) \le \frac{1}{2} \log 2\pi e(P_i + N).$$
(10.45)

Continuing with the inequalities of the converse, we obtain

$$nR \le \sum (h(Y_i) - h(Z_i)) + n\epsilon_n$$
(10.46)

$$\le \sum \left(\frac{1}{2} \log(2\pi e(P_i + N)) - \frac{1}{2} \log 2\pi eN \right) + n\epsilon_n$$
(10.47)

$$= \sum \frac{1}{2} \log \left(1 + \frac{P_i}{N} \right) + n\epsilon_n.$$
(10.48)

Since each of the codewords satisfies the power constraint, so does their average, and hence

$$\frac{1}{n} \sum_i P_i \le P.$$
(10.49)

Since $f(x) = \frac{1}{2} \log(1 + x)$ is a concave function of x, we can apply Jensen's inequality to obtain

$$\frac{1}{n} \sum_{i=1}^{n} \frac{1}{2} \log \left(1 + \frac{P_i}{N} \right) \le \frac{1}{2} \log \left(1 + \frac{1}{n} \sum_{i=1}^{n} \frac{P_i}{N} \right)$$
(10.50)

$$\le \frac{1}{2} \log \left(1 + \frac{P}{N} \right).$$
(10.51)

Thus $R \le \frac{1}{2} \log(1 + \frac{P}{N}) + \epsilon_n$, $\epsilon_n \to 0$, and we have the required converse. $\square$

Note that the power constraint enters the standard proof in (10.44).

10.3   BAND-LIMITED CHANNELS

A common model for communication over a radio network or a telephone line is a band-limited channel with white noise. This is a continuous time channel. The output of such a channel can be described as

$$Y(t) = (X(t) + Z(t)) * h(t),$$
(10.52)

where $X(t)$ is the signal waveform, $Z(t)$ is the waveform of the white Gaussian noise, and $h(t)$ is the impulse response of an ideal bandpass filter, which cuts out all frequencies greater than W. In this section, we give simplified arguments to calculate the capacity of such a channel.

We begin with a representation theorem due to Nyquist [199] and Shannon [240], which shows that sampling a band-limited signal at a sampling rate $\frac{1}{2W}$ is sufficient to reconstruct the signal from the samples. Intuitively, this is due to the fact that if a signal is band-limited to W, then it cannot change by a substantial amount in a time less than half a cycle of the maximum frequency in the signal, that is, the signal cannot change very much in time intervals less than $\frac{1}{2W}$ seconds.

Theorem 10.3.1: *Suppose a function $f(t)$ is band-limited to W, namely, the spectrum of the function is 0 for all frequencies greater than W. Then the function is completely determined by samples of the function spaced $\frac{1}{2W}$ seconds apart.*

Proof: Let $F(\omega)$ be the frequency spectrum of $f(t)$. Then

$$f(t) = \frac{1}{2\pi} \int_{-\infty}^{\infty} F(\omega)e^{i\omega t} \, d\omega \tag{10.53}$$

$$= \frac{1}{2\pi} \int_{-2\pi W}^{2\pi W} F(\omega)e^{i\omega t} \, d\omega , \tag{10.54}$$

since $F(\omega)$ is 0 outside the band $-2\pi W \le \omega \le 2\pi W$. If we consider samples spaced $\frac{1}{2W}$ seconds apart, the value of the signal at the sample points can be written

$$f\left(\frac{n}{2W}\right) = \frac{1}{2\pi} \int_{-2\pi W}^{2\pi W} F(\omega)e^{i\omega \frac{n}{2W}} \, d\omega . \tag{10.55}$$

The right hand side of this equation is also the definition of the coefficients of the Fourier series expansion of the periodic extension of the function $F(\omega)$, taking the interval $-2\pi W$ to $2\pi W$ as the fundamental period. Thus the sample values $f(\frac{n}{2W})$ determine the Fourier coefficients and, by extension, they determine the value of $F(\omega)$ in the interval $(-2\pi W, 2\pi W)$. Since a function is uniquely specified by its Fourier transform, and since $F(\omega)$ is 0 outside the band W, we can determine the function uniquely from the samples.

Consider the function

$$\text{sinc}(t) = \frac{\sin(2\pi Wt)}{2\pi Wt} . \tag{10.56}$$

This function is 1 at $t = 0$ and is 0 for $t = n/2W$, $n \ne 0$. The spectrum of this function is constant in the band $(-W, W)$ and is zero outside this band. Now define

$$g(t) = \sum_{n=-\infty}^{\infty} f\left(\frac{n}{2W}\right) \text{sinc}\left(t - \frac{n}{2W}\right). \qquad (10.57)$$

From the properties of the sinc function, it follows that $g(t)$ is band-limited to W and is equal to $f(n/2W)$ at $t = n/2W$. Since there is only one function satisfying these constraints, we must have $g(t) = f(t)$. This provides an explicit representation of $f(t)$ in terms of its samples. □

A general function has an infinite number of degrees of freedom—the value of the function at every point can be chosen independently. The Nyquist-Shannon sampling theorem shows that a band-limited function has only $2W$ degrees of freedom per second. The values of the function at the sample points can be chosen independently, and this specifies the entire function.

If a function is band-limited, it cannot be limited in time. But we can consider functions that have most of their energy in bandwidth W and have most of their energy in a finite time interval, say $(0, T)$. We can describe these functions using a basis of *prolate spheroidal functions*. We do not go into the details of this theory here; it suffices to say that there are about $2TW$ orthonormal basis functions for the set of almost time-limited, almost band-limited functions, and we can describe any function within the set by its coordinates in this basis. The details can be found in a series of papers by Slepian, Landau and Pollak [169], [168], [253]. Moreover, the projection of white noise on these basis vectors forms an i.i.d. Gaussian process. The above arguments enable us to view the band-limited, time-limited functions as vectors in a vector space of $2TW$ dimensions.

Now we return to the problem of communication over a band-limited channel. Assuming that the channel has bandwidth W, we can represent both the input and the output by samples taken $1/2W$ seconds apart. Each of the input samples is corrupted by noise to produce the corresponding output sample. Since the noise is white and Gaussian, it can be shown that each of the noise samples is an independent, identically distributed Gaussian random variable. If the noise has power spectral density $N_0/2$ and bandwidth W, then the noise has power $\frac{N_0}{2} 2W = N_0 W$ and each of the $2WT$ noise samples in time T has variance $N_0 WT/ 2WT = N_0/2$. Looking at the input as a vector in the $2TW$ dimensional space, we see that the received signal is spherically normally distributed about this point with covariance $\frac{N_0}{2} I$.

Now we can use the theory derived earlier for discrete time Gaussian channels, where it was shown that the capacity of such a channel is

$$C = \frac{1}{2} \log\left(1 + \frac{P}{N}\right) \text{ bits per transmission}. \qquad (10.58)$$

Let the channel be used over the time interval $[0, T]$. In this case, the power per sample is $PT/2WT = P/2W$, the noise variance per sample is $\frac{N_0}{2} 2W \frac{T}{2WT} = N_0/2$, and hence the capacity per sample is

$$C = \frac{1}{2} \log\left(1 + \frac{\frac{P}{2W}}{\frac{N_0}{2}}\right) = \frac{1}{2} \log\left(1 + \frac{P}{N_0 W}\right) \text{ bits per sample}.$$

(10.59)

Since there are $2W$ samples each second, the capacity of the channel can be rewritten as

$$C = W \log\left(1 + \frac{P}{N_0 W}\right) \text{ bits per second}. \qquad (10.60)$$

This equation is one of the most famous formulae of information theory. It gives the capacity of a band-limited Gaussian channel with noise spectral density $N_0/2$ watts/Hz and power P watts.

If we let $W \to \infty$ in (10.60), we obtain

$$C = \frac{P}{N_0} \log_2 e \text{ bits per second}, \qquad (10.61)$$

as the capacity of a channel with an infinite bandwidth, power P and noise spectral density $N_0/2$. Thus for infinite bandwidth channels, the capacity grows linearly with the power.

Example 10.3.1 (*Telephone line*): To allow multiplexing of many channels, telephone signals are band-limited to 3300 Hz. Using a bandwidth of 3300 Hz and a SNR (signal to noise ratio) of 20 dB (i.e., $P/N_0 W = 100$), in (10.60), we find the capacity of the telephone channel to be about 22,000 bits per second. Practical modems achieve transmission rates up to 19,200 bits per second. In real telephone channels, there are other factors such as crosstalk, interference, echoes, non-flat channels, etc. which must be compensated for to achieve this capacity.

10.4   PARALLEL GAUSSIAN CHANNELS

In this section, we consider k independent Gaussian channels in parallel with a common power constraint. The objective is to distribute the total power among the channels so as to maximize the capacity. This channel models a non-white additive Gaussian noise channel where each parallel component represents a different frequency.

Assume that we have a set of Gaussian channels in parallel as illustrated in Figure 10.3. The output of each channel is the sum of the input and Gaussian noise. For channel j,

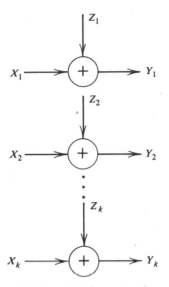

Figure 10.3. Parallel Gaussian channels.

$$Y_j = X_j + Z_j, \quad j = 1, 2, \ldots, k , \tag{10.62}$$

with

$$Z_j \sim \mathcal{N}(0, N_j) , \tag{10.63}$$

and the noise is assumed to be independent from channel to channel. We assume that there is a common power constraint on the total power used, i.e.,

$$E \sum_{j=1}^{k} X_j^2 \leq P . \tag{10.64}$$

We wish to distribute the power among the various channels so as to maximize the total capacity.

The information capacity of the channel C is

$$C = \max_{f(x_1, x_2, \ldots, x_k) : \Sigma\, EX_i^2 \leq P} I(X_1, X_2, \ldots, X_k; Y_1, Y_2, \ldots, Y_k) . \tag{10.65}$$

We calculate the distribution that achieves the information capacity for this channel. The fact that the information capacity is the supremum of achievable rates can be proved by methods identical to those in the proof of the capacity theorem for single Gaussian channels and will be omitted.

Since $Z_1, Z_2, \ldots, Z_k$ are independent,

$$I(X_1, X_2, \ldots, X_k; Y_1, Y_2, \ldots, Y_k)$$
$$= h(Y_1, Y_2, \ldots, Y_k) - h(Y_1, Y_2, \ldots, Y_k | X_1, X_2, \ldots, X_k)$$
$$= h(Y_1, Y_2, \ldots, Y_k) - h(Z_1, Z_2, \ldots, Z_k | X_1, X_2, \ldots, X_k)$$

$$= h(Y_1, Y_2, \ldots, Y_k) - h(Z_1, Z_2, \ldots, Z_k) \tag{10.66}$$

$$= h(Y_1, Y_2, \ldots, Y_k) - \sum_i h(Z_i) \tag{10.67}$$

$$\leq \sum_i h(Y_i) - h(Z_i) \tag{10.68}$$

$$\leq \sum_i \frac{1}{2} \log\left(1 + \frac{P_i}{N_i}\right), \tag{10.69}$$

where $P_i = EX_i^2$, and $\Sigma P_i = P$. Equality is achieved by

$$(X_1, X_2, \ldots, X_k) \sim \mathcal{N}\left(0, \begin{bmatrix} P_1 & 0 & \cdots & 0 \\ 0 & P_2 & \cdots & 0 \\ \vdots & \vdots & \ddots & \vdots \\ 0 & 0 & \cdots & P_k \end{bmatrix}\right). \tag{10.70}$$

So the problem is reduced to finding the power allotment that maximizes the capacity subject to the constraint that $\Sigma P_i = P$. This is a standard optimization problem and can be solved using Lagrange multipliers. Writing the functional as

$$J(P_1, \ldots, P_k) = \sum \frac{1}{2} \log\left(1 + \frac{P_i}{N_i}\right) + \lambda\left(\sum P_i\right) \tag{10.71}$$

and differentiating with respect to P_i, we have

$$\frac{1}{2} \frac{1}{P_i + N_i} + \lambda = 0, \tag{10.72}$$

or

$$P_i = \nu - N_i. \tag{10.73}$$

However since the P_i's must be non-negative, it may not always be possible to find a solution of this form. In this case, we use the Kuhn-Tucker conditions to verify that the solution

$$P_i = (\nu - N_i)^+ \tag{10.74}$$

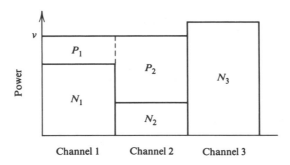

Figure 10.4. Water-filling for parallel channels.

is the assignment that maximizes capacity, where ν is chosen so that

$$\sum (\nu - N_i)^+ = P. \qquad (10.75)$$

Here $(x)^+$ denotes the positive part of x, i.e.,

$$(x)^+ = \begin{cases} x & \text{if } x \geq 0, \\ 0 & \text{if } x < 0. \end{cases} \qquad (10.76)$$

This solution is illustrated graphically in Figure 10.4. The vertical levels indicate the noise levels in the various channels. As signal power is increased from zero, we allot the power to the channels with the lowest noise. When the available power is increased still further, some of the power is put into noisier channels. The process by which the power is distributed among the various bins is identical to the way in which water distributes itself in a vessel. Hence this process is sometimes referred to as "water-filling."

10.5   CHANNELS WITH COLORED GAUSSIAN NOISE

In the previous section, we considered the case of a set of parallel independent Gaussian channels in which the noise samples from different channels were independent. Now we will consider the case when the noise is dependent. This represents not only the case of parallel channels, but also the case when the channel has Gaussian noise with memory. For channels with memory, we can consider a block of n consecutive uses of the channel as n channels in parallel with dependent noise. As in the previous section, we will only calculate the information capacity for this channel.

Let K_Z be the covariance matrix of the noise, and let K_X be the input covariance matrix. The power constraint on the input can then be written as

$$\frac{1}{n} \sum_i EX_i^2 \le P, \tag{10.77}$$

or equivalently,

$$\frac{1}{n} \operatorname{tr}(K_X) \le P. \tag{10.78}$$

Unlike the previous section, the power constraint here depends on n; the capacity will have to be calculated for each n.

Just as in the case of independent channels, we can write

$$I(X_1, X_2, \ldots, X_n; Y_1, Y_2, \ldots, Y_n)$$
$$= h(Y_1, Y_2, \ldots, Y_n) - h(Z_1, Z_2, \ldots, Z_n). \tag{10.79}$$

Here $h(Z_1, Z_2, \ldots, Z_n)$ is determined only by the distribution of the noise and is not dependent on the choice of input distribution. So finding the capacity amounts to maximizing $h(Y_1, Y_2, \ldots, Y_n)$. The entropy of the output is maximized when Y is normal, which is achieved when the input is normal. Since the input and the noise are independent, the covariance of the output Y is $K_Y = K_X + K_Z$ and the entropy is

$$h(Y_1, Y_2, \ldots, Y_n) = \frac{1}{2} \log((2\pi e)^n |K_X + K_Z|). \tag{10.80}$$

Now the problem is reduced to choosing K_X so as to maximize $|K_X + K_Z|$, subject to a trace constraint on K_X. To do this, we decompose K_Z into its diagonal form,

$$K_Z = Q\Lambda Q^t, \quad \text{where } QQ^t = I. \tag{10.81}$$

Then

$$|K_X + K_Z| = |K_X + Q\Lambda Q^t| \tag{10.82}$$

$$= |Q||Q^t K_X Q + \Lambda||Q^t| \tag{10.83}$$

$$= |Q^t K_X Q + \Lambda| \tag{10.84}$$

$$= |A + \Lambda|, \tag{10.85}$$

where $A = Q^t K_X Q$. Since for any matrices B and C,

$$\operatorname{tr}(BC) = \operatorname{tr}(CB), \tag{10.86}$$

we have

$$\text{tr}(A) = \text{tr}(Q'K_X Q) \tag{10.87}$$

$$= \text{tr}(QQ'K_X) \tag{10.88}$$

$$= \text{tr}(K_X) . \tag{10.89}$$

Now the problem is reduced to maximizing $|A + \Lambda|$ subject to a trace constraint $\text{tr}(A) \leq nP$.

Now we apply Hadamard's inequality, mentioned in Chapter 9. Hadamard's inequality states that the determinant of any positive definite matrix K is less than the product of its diagonal elements, i.e.,

$$|K| \leq \prod_i K_{ii} \tag{10.90}$$

with equality iff the matrix is diagonal. Thus

$$|A + \Lambda| \leq \prod_i (A_{ii} + \lambda_i) \tag{10.91}$$

with equality iff A is diagonal. Since A is subject to a trace constraint,

$$\frac{1}{n} \sum_i A_{ii} \leq P , \tag{10.92}$$

and $A_{ii} \geq 0$, the maximum value of $\prod_i (A_{ii} + \lambda_i)$ is attained when

$$A_{ii} + \lambda_i = \nu . \tag{10.93}$$

However, given the constraints, it may not be always possible to satisfy this equation with positive A_{ii}. In such cases, we can show by standard Kuhn-Tucker conditions that the optimum solution corresponds to setting

$$A_{ii} = (\nu - \lambda_i)^+ , \tag{10.94}$$

where ν is chosen so that $\sum A_{ii} = nP$. This value of A maximizes the entropy of Y and hence the mutual information. We can use Figure 10.4 to see the connection between the methods described above and "water-filling".

Consider a channel in which the additive Gaussian noise forms a stochastic process with finite dimensional covariance matrix $K_Z^{(n)}$. If the process is stationary, then the covariance matrix is Toeplitz and the eigenvalues tend to a limit as $n \to \infty$. The density of eigenvalues on the real line tends to the power spectrum of the stochastic process [126]. In this case, the above "water-filling" argument translates to water-filling in the spectral domain.

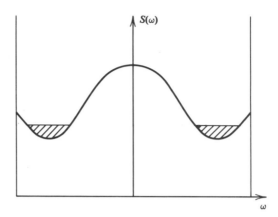

Figure 10.5. Water-filling in the spectral domain.

Hence for channels in which the noise forms a stationary stochastic process, the input signal should be chosen to be a Gaussian process with a spectrum which is large at frequencies where the noise spectrum is small. This is illustrated in Figure 10.5. The capacity of an additive Gaussian noise channel with noise power spectrum $N(f)$ can be shown to be [120]

$$C = \int \frac{1}{2} \log\left(1 + \frac{(\nu - N(f))^+}{N(f)}\right) df,   \tag{10.95}$$

where ν is chosen so that $\int (\nu - N(f))^+ df = P$.

10.6 GAUSSIAN CHANNELS WITH FEEDBACK

In Chapter 8, we proved that feedback does not increase the capacity for discrete memoryless channels. It can greatly help in reducing the complexity of encoding or decoding. The same is true of an additive noise channel with white noise. As in the discrete case, feedback does not increase capacity for memoryless Gaussian channels. However, for channels with memory, where the noise is correlated from time instant to time instant, feedback does increase capacity. The capacity without feedback can be calculated using water-filling, but we do not have a simple explicit characterization of the capacity with feedback. In this section, we describe an expression for the capacity in terms of the covariance matrix of the noise Z. We prove a converse for this expression for capacity. We then derive a simple bound on the increase in capacity due to feedback.

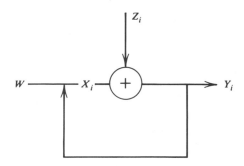

Figure 10.6. Gaussian channel with feedback.

The Gaussian channel with feedback is illustrated in Figure 10.6. The output of the channel Y_i is

$$Y_i = X_i + Z_i, \quad Z_i \sim \mathcal{N}(0, K_Z^{(n)}). \tag{10.96}$$

The feedback allows the input of the channel to depend on the past values of the output.

A $(2^{nR}, n)$ code for the Gaussian channel with feedback consists of a sequence of mappings $x_i(W, Y^{i-1})$, where $W \in \{1, 2, \ldots, 2^{nR}\}$ is the input message and Y^{i-1} is the sequence of past values of the output. Thus $x(W, \cdot)$ is a code function rather than a codeword. In addition, we require that the code satisfy a power constraint,

$$E\left[\frac{1}{n} \sum_{i=1}^{n} x_i^2(w, Y^{i-1})\right] \le P, \quad w \subset \{1, 2, \ldots, 2^{nR}\}, \tag{10.97}$$

where the expectation is over all possible noise sequences.

We will characterize the capacity of the Gaussian channel is terms of the covariance matrices of the input X and the noise Z. Because of the feedback, X^n and Z^n are not independent; X_i depends causally on the past values of Z. In the next section, we prove a converse for the Gaussian channel with feedback and show that we achieve capacity if we take X to be Gaussian.

We now state an informal characterization of the capacity of the channel with and without feedback.

1. *With feedback.* The capacity $C_{n, FB}$ in bits per transmission of the time-varying Gaussian channel with feedback is

$$C_{n, FB} = \max_{\frac{1}{n} \mathrm{tr}(K_X^{(n)}) \le P} \frac{1}{2n} \log \frac{|K_{X+Z}^{(n)}|}{|K_Z^{(n)}|} \tag{10.98}$$

where the maximization is taken over all X^n of the form

$$X_i = \sum_{j=1}^{i-1} b_{ij} Z_j + V_i, \quad i = 1, 2, \ldots, n, \qquad (10.99)$$

and V^n is independent of Z^n.

To verify that the maximization over (10.99) involves no loss of generality, note that the distribution on $X^n + Z^n$ achieving the maximum entropy is Gaussian. Since Z^n is also Gaussian, it can be verified that a jointly Gaussian distribution on $(X^n, Z^n, X^n + Z^n)$ achieves the maximization in (10.98). But since $Z^n = Y^n - X^n$, the most general jointly normal causal dependence of X^n on Y^n is of the form (10.99), where V^n plays the role of the innovations process. Recasting (10.98) and (10.99) using $X = BZ + V$ and $Y = X + Z$, we can write

$$C_{n,FB} = \max \frac{1}{2n} \log \frac{|(B+I)K_Z^{(n)}(B+I)^t + K_V|}{|K_Z^{(n)}|} \qquad (10.100)$$

where the maximum is taken over all nonnegative definite K_V and strictly lower triangular B such that

$$\text{tr}(BK_Z^{(n)}B^t + K_V) \le nP. \qquad (10.101)$$

(Without feedback, B is necessarily 0.)

2. *Without feedback.* The capacity C_n of the time-varying Gaussian channel without feedback is given by

$$C_n = \max_{\frac{1}{n} \text{tr}(K_X^{(n)}) \le P} \frac{1}{2n} \log \frac{|K_X^{(n)} + K_Z^{(n)}|}{|K_Z^{(n)}|}. \qquad (10.102)$$

This reduces to water-filling on the eigenvalues $\{\lambda_i^{(n)}\}$ of $K_Z^{(n)}$. Thus

$$C_n = \frac{1}{2n} \sum_{i=1}^{n} \log\left(1 + \frac{(\lambda - \lambda_i^{(n)})^+}{\lambda_i^{(n)}}\right), \qquad (10.103)$$

where $(y)^+ = \max\{y, 0\}$ and where λ is chosen so that

$$\sum_{i=1}^{n} (\lambda - \lambda_i^{(n)})^+ = nP. \qquad (10.104)$$

We now prove an upper bound for the capacity of the Gaussian channel with feedback. This bound is actually achievable, and is therefore the capacity, but we do not prove this here.

Theorem 10.6.1: *The rate R_n for any $(2^{nR_n}, n)$ code with $P_e^{(n)} \to 0$ for the Gaussian channel with feedback satisfies*

$$R_n \leq \frac{1}{n} \frac{1}{2} \log \frac{|K_Y^{(n)}|}{|K_Z^{(n)}|} + \epsilon_n , \qquad (10.105)$$

with $\epsilon_n \to 0$ as $n \to \infty$.

Proof: By Fano's inequality,

$$H(W|Y^n) \leq 1 + nR_n P_e^{(n)} = n\epsilon_n , \qquad (10.106)$$

where $\epsilon_n \to 0$ as $P_e^{(n)} \to 0$. We can then bound the rate as follows:

$$nR_n = H(W) \qquad (10.107)$$

$$= I(W; Y^n) + H(W|Y^n) \qquad (10.108)$$

$$\leq I(W; Y^n) + n\epsilon_n \qquad (10.109)$$

$$= \sum I(W; Y_i|Y^{i-1}) + n\epsilon_n \qquad (10.110)$$

$$\stackrel{(a)}{=} \sum [h(Y_i|Y^{i-1}) - h(Y_i|W, Y^{i-1}, X_i, X^{i-1}, Z^{i-1})] + n\epsilon_n \qquad (10.111)$$

$$\stackrel{(b)}{=} \sum [h(Y_i|Y^{i-1}) - h(Z_i|W, Y^{i-1}, X_i, X^{i-1}, Z^{i-1})] + n\epsilon_n \qquad (10.112)$$

$$\stackrel{(c)}{=} \sum [h(Y_i|Y^{i-1}) - h(Z_i|Z^{i-1})] + n\epsilon_n \qquad (10.113)$$

$$= h(Y^n) - h(Z^n) + n\epsilon_n , \qquad (10.114)$$

where (a) follows from the fact that X_i is a function of W and the past Y_i's, and Z^{i-1} is $Y^{i-1} - X^{i-1}$, (b) follows from $Y_i = X_i + Z_i$ and the fact that $h(X + Z|X) = h(Z|X)$, and (c) follows from the fact Z_i and (W, Y^{i-1}, X^i) are conditionally independent given Z^{i-1}. Continuing the chain of inequalities after dividing by n, we have

$$R_n \leq \frac{1}{n} [h(Y^n) - h(Z^n)] + \epsilon_n \leq \frac{1}{2n} \log \frac{|K_Y^{(n)}|}{|K_Z^{(n)}|} + \epsilon_n , \qquad (10.115)$$

by the entropy maximizing property of the normal. $\square$

We have proved an upper bound on the capacity of the Gaussian channel with feedback in terms of the covariance matrix $K_{X+Z}^{(n)}$. We now derive bounds on the capacity with feedback in terms of $K_X^{(n)}$ and $K_Z^{(n)}$, which will then be used to derive bounds in terms of the capacity without feedback. For simplicity of notation, we will drop the superscript n in the symbols for covariance matrices.

We first prove a series of lemmas about matrices and determinants.

Lemma 10.6.1: *Let X and Z be n-dimensional random vectors. Then*

$$K_{X+Z} + K_{X-Z} = 2K_X + 2K_Z \qquad (10.116)$$

Proof:

$$K_{X+Z} = E(X + Z)(X + Z)^t \qquad (10.117)$$

$$= EXX^t + EXZ^t + EZX^t + EZZ^t \qquad (10.118)$$

$$= K_X + K_{XZ} + K_{ZX} + K_Z. \qquad (10.119)$$

Similarly,

$$K_{X-Z} = K_X - K_{XZ} - K_{ZX} + K_Z. \qquad (10.120)$$

Adding these two equations completes the proof. $\square$

Lemma 10.6.2: *For two $n \times n$ positive definite matrices A and B, if $A - B$ is positive definite, then $|A| \geq |B|$.*

Proof: Let $C = A - B$. Since B and C are positive definite, we can consider them as covariance matrices. Consider two independent normal random vectors $\mathbf{X}_1 \sim \mathcal{N}(0, B)$ and $\mathbf{X}_2 \sim \mathcal{N}(0, C)$. Let $\mathbf{Y} = \mathbf{X}_1 + \mathbf{X}_2$. Then

$$h(\mathbf{Y}) \geq h(\mathbf{Y}|\mathbf{X}_2) \qquad (10.121)$$

$$= h(\mathbf{X}_1|\mathbf{X}_2) \qquad (10.122)$$

$$= h(\mathbf{X}_1), \qquad (10.123)$$

where the inequality follows from the fact that conditioning reduces differential entropy, and the final equality from the fact that $\mathbf{X}_1$ and $\mathbf{X}_2$ are independent. Substituting the expressions for the differential entropies of a normal random variable, we obtain

$$\frac{1}{2} \log(2\pi e)^n |A| > \frac{1}{2} \log(2\pi e)^n |B|, \qquad (10.124)$$

which is equivalent to the desired lemma.   □

Lemma 10.6.3: *For two n-dimensional random vectors X and Z,*

$$|K_{X+Z}| \le 2^n |K_X + K_Z|. \qquad (10.125)$$

Proof: From Lemma 10.6.1,

$$2(K_X + K_Z) - K_{X+Z} = K_{X-Z} \ge 0, \qquad (10.126)$$

where $A \ge 0$ means that A is non-negative definite. Hence, applying Lemma 10.6.2, we have

$$|K_{X+Z}| \le |2(K_X + K_Z)| = 2^n |K_X + K_Z|, \qquad (10.127)$$

which is the desired result.   □

We are now in a position to prove that feedback increases the capacity of a non-white Gaussian additive noise channel by at most half a bit.

Theorem: 10.6.2:

$$C_{n,FB} \le C_n + \frac{1}{2} \text{ bits per transmission} \qquad (10.128)$$

Proof: Combining all the lemmas, we obtain

$$C_{n,FB} \le \max_{\text{tr}(K_X) \le nP} \frac{1}{2n} \log \frac{|K_Y|}{|K_Z|} \qquad (10.129)$$

$$\le \max_{\text{tr}(K_X) \le nP} \frac{1}{2n} \log \frac{2^n |K_X + K_Z|}{|K_Z|} \qquad (10.130)$$

$$= \max_{\text{tr}(K_X) \le nP} \frac{1}{2n} \log \frac{|K_X + K_Z|}{|K_Z|} + \frac{1}{2} \qquad (10.131)$$

$$\le C_n + \frac{1}{2} \text{ bits per transmission}, \qquad (10.132)$$

where the inequalities follow from Theorem 10.6.1, Lemma 10.6.3 and the definition of capacity without feedback, respectively.   □

SUMMARY OF CHAPTER 10

Maximum entropy: $\max_{EX^2=\alpha} h(X) = \frac{1}{2} \log 2\pi e\alpha$.

The Gaussian channel: $Y_i = X_i + Z_i$, $Z_i \sim \mathcal{N}(0, N)$, power constraint $\frac{1}{n} \sum_{i=1}^{n} x_i^2 \leq P$,

$$C = \frac{1}{2} \log\left(1 + \frac{P}{N}\right) \text{ bits per transmission.} \tag{10.133}$$

Band-limited additive white Gaussian noise channel: Bandwidth W, two-sided power spectral density $N_0/2$, signal power P,

$$C = W \log\left(1 + \frac{P}{N_0 W}\right) \text{ bits per second.} \tag{10.134}$$

Water-filling (k parallel Gaussian channels): $Y_j = X_j + Z_j, j = 1, 2, \ldots, k$, $Z_j \sim \mathcal{N}(0, N_j)$, $\sum_{j=1}^{k} X_j^2 \leq P$,

$$C = \sum_{i=1}^{k} \frac{1}{2} \log\left(1 + \frac{(\nu - N_i)^+}{N_i}\right) \tag{10.135}$$

where ν is chosen so that $\Sigma(\nu - N_i)^+ = P$.

Additive non-white Gaussian noise channel: $Y_i = X_i + Z_i$, $Z^n \sim \mathcal{N}(0, K_Z)$

$$C = \frac{1}{n} \sum_{i=1}^{n} \frac{1}{2} \log\left(1 + \frac{(\nu - \lambda_i)^+}{\lambda_i}\right) \tag{10.136}$$

where $\lambda_1, \lambda_2, \ldots, \lambda_n$ are the eigenvalues of K_Z and ν is chosen so that $\Sigma_i (\nu - \lambda_i)^+ = nP$.

Capacity without feedback:

$$C_n = \max_{tr(K_X) \leq nP} \frac{1}{2n} \log \frac{|K_X + K_Z|}{|K_Z|}. \tag{10.137}$$

Capacity with feedback:

$$C_{n, FB} = \max_{tr(K_X) \leq nP} \frac{1}{2n} \log \frac{|K_{X+Z}|}{|K_Z|}. \tag{10.138}$$

Feedback bound:

$$C_{n, FB} \leq C_n + \frac{1}{2}. \tag{10.139}$$

PROBLEMS FOR CHAPTER 10

1. *A mutual information game.* Consider the following channel:

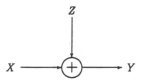

Throughout this problem we shall constrain the signal power

$$EX = 0, \qquad EX^2 = P, \qquad\qquad (10.140)$$

and the noise power

$$EZ = 0, \qquad EZ^2 = N, \qquad\qquad (10.141)$$

and assume that X and Z are independent. The channel capacity is given by $I(X; X + Z)$.

Now for the game. The noise player chooses a distribution on Z to minimize $I(X; X + Z)$, while the signal player chooses a distribution on X to maximize $I(X; X + Z)$.

Letting $X^* \sim \mathcal{N}(0, P)$, $Z^* \sim \mathcal{N}(0, N)$, show that X^* and Z^* satisfy the saddlepoint conditions

$$I(X; X + Z^*) \le I(X^*; X^* + Z^*) \le I(X^*; X^* + Z). \qquad (10.142)$$

Thus

$$\min_Z \max_X I(X; X + Z) = \max_X \min_Z I(X; X + Z) \qquad (10.143)$$

$$= \frac{1}{2} \log\left(1 + \frac{P}{N}\right), \qquad\qquad (10.144)$$

and the game has a value. In particular, a deviation from normal for either player worsens the mutual information from that player's standpoint. Can you discuss the implications of this?

Note: Part of the proof hinges on the entropy power inequality from Section 16.7, which states that if **X** and **Y** are independent random n-vectors with densities, then

$$e^{\frac{2}{n}h(\mathbf{X+Y})} \ge e^{\frac{2}{n}h(\mathbf{X})} + e^{\frac{2}{n}h(\mathbf{Y})}. \qquad (10.145)$$

2. *A channel with two independent looks at Y.* Let Y_1 and Y_2 be conditionally independent and conditionally identically distributed given X.
    (a) Show $I(X; Y_1, Y_2) = 2I(X; Y_1) - I(Y_1; Y_2)$.
    (b) Conclude that the capacity of the channel

$$X \rightarrow \boxed{} \rightarrow (Y_1, Y_2)$$

is less than twice the capacity of the channel

$$X \rightarrow \boxed{} \rightarrow Y_1$$

3. *The two-look Gaussian channel.*

$$X \rightarrow \boxed{} \rightarrow (Y_1, Y_2)$$

Consider the ordinary Shannon Gaussian channel with two correlated looks at X, i.e., $Y = (Y_1, Y_2)$, where

$$Y_1 = X + Z_1 \tag{10.146}$$

$$Y_2 = X + Z_2 \tag{10.147}$$

with a power constraint P on X, and $(Z_1, Z_2) \sim \mathcal{N}_2(0, K)$, where

$$K = \begin{bmatrix} N & N\rho \\ N\rho & N \end{bmatrix}. \tag{10.148}$$

Find the capacity C for
(a) $\rho = 1$
(b) $\rho = 0$
(c) $\rho = -1$

4. *Parallel channels and waterfilling.* Consider a pair of parallel Gaussian channels, i.e.,

$$\begin{pmatrix} Y_1 \\ Y_2 \end{pmatrix} = \begin{pmatrix} X_1 \\ X_2 \end{pmatrix} + \begin{pmatrix} Z_1 \\ Z_2 \end{pmatrix}, \tag{10.149}$$

where

$$\begin{pmatrix} Z_1 \\ Z_2 \end{pmatrix} \sim \mathcal{N}\left(0, \begin{bmatrix} \sigma_1^2 & 0 \\ 0 & \sigma_2^2 \end{bmatrix}\right), \tag{10.150}$$

and there is a power constraint $E(X_1^2 + X_2^2) \leq 2P$. Assume that $\sigma_1^2 > \sigma_2^2$. At what power does the channel stop behaving like a single channel with noise variance σ_2^2, and begin behaving like a pair of channels?

HISTORICAL NOTES

The Gaussian channel was first analyzed by Shannon in his original paper [238]. The water-filling solution to the capacity of the colored noise Gaussian channel was developed by Holsinger [135]. Pinsker [210] and Ebert [94] showed that feedback at most doubles the capacity of a non-white Gaussian channel; a simple proof can be found in Cover and Pombra [76]. Cover and Pombra also show that feedback increases the capacity of the non-white Gaussian channel by at most half a bit.

Chapter 11

Maximum Entropy and Spectral Estimation

The temperature of a gas corresponds to the average kinetic energy of the molecules in the gas. What can we say about the distribution of velocities in the gas at a given temperature? We know from physics that this distribution is the maximum entropy distribution under the temperature constraint, otherwise known as the Maxwell-Boltzmann distribution. The maximum entropy distribution corresponds to the macrostate (as indexed by the empirical distribution) that has the most microstates (the actual gas velocities). Implicit in the use of maximum entropy methods in physics is a sort of AEP that says that all microstates are equally probable.

11.1 MAXIMUM ENTROPY DISTRIBUTIONS

Consider the following problem:

Maximize the entropy $h(f)$ over all probability densities f satisfying

1. $f(x) \geq 0$, with equality outside the support set S,
2. $\int_S f(x) \, dx = 1$, $\qquad\qquad$ (11.1)
3. $\int_S f(x) r_i(x) \, dx = \alpha_i, \quad$ for $1 \leq i \leq m$.

Thus f is a density on support set S meeting certain moment constraints $\alpha_1, \alpha_2, \ldots, \alpha_m$.

Approach 1 (*Calculus*): The differential entropy $h(f)$ is a concave function over a convex set. We form the functional

$$J(f) = -\int f \ln f + \lambda_0 \int f + \sum_{i=1}^{m} \lambda_i \int f r_i \qquad (11.2)$$

and "differentiate" with respect to $f(x)$, the xth component of f to obtain

$$\frac{\partial J}{\partial f(x)} = -\ln f(x) - 1 + \lambda_0 + \sum_{i=1}^{m} \lambda_i r_i(x). \qquad (11.3)$$

Setting this equal to zero, we obtain the form of the maximizing density

$$f(x) = e^{\lambda_0 - 1 + \sum_{i=1}^{m} \lambda_i r_i(x)}, \quad x \in S, \qquad (11.4)$$

where $\lambda_0, \lambda_1, \ldots, \lambda_m$ are chosen so that f satisfies the constraints.

The approach using calculus only suggests the form of the density that maximizes the entropy. To prove that this is indeed the maximum, we can take the second variation. It is simpler to use the information inequality $D(g \| f) \geq 0$.

Approach 2 (*Information inequality*): If g satisfies (11.1) and if f^* is of the form (11.4), then $0 \leq D(g \| f^*) = -h(g) + h(f^*)$. Thus $h(g) \leq h(f^*)$ for all g satisfying the constraints. We prove this in the following theorem.

Theorem 11.1.1 (*Maximum entropy distribution*): Let $f^*(x) = f_\lambda(x) = e^{\lambda_0 + \sum_{i=1}^{m} \lambda_i r_i(x)}$, $x \in S$, where $\lambda_0, \ldots, \lambda_m$ are chosen so that f^* satisfies (11.1). Then f^* uniquely maximizes $h(f)$ over all probability densities f satisfying constraints (11.1).

Proof: Let g satisfy the constraints (11.1). Then

$$h(g) = -\int_S g \ln g \qquad (11.5)$$

$$= -\int_S g \ln \frac{g}{f^*} f^* \qquad (11.6)$$

$$= -D(g \| f^*) - \int_S g \ln f^* \qquad (11.7)$$

$$\overset{(a)}{\leq} -\int_S g \ln f^* \qquad (11.8)$$

$$\overset{(b)}{=} -\int_S g \left(\lambda_0 + \sum \lambda_i r_i \right) \qquad (11.9)$$

$$\overset{(c)}{=} -\int_S f^* \left(\lambda_0 + \sum \lambda_i r_i \right) \qquad (11.10)$$

$$= -\int_S f^* \ln f^* \tag{11.11}$$

$$= h(f^*), \tag{11.12}$$

where (a) follows from the non-negativity of relative entropy, (b) from the definition of f^* and (c) from the fact that both f^* and g satisfy the constraints. Note that equality holds in (a) if and only if $g(x) = f^*(x)$ for all x, except for a set of measure 0, thus proving uniqueness. $\square$

The same approach holds for discrete entropies and for multivariate distributions.

11.2   EXAMPLES

Example 11.2.1 (*One dimensional gas with a temperature constraint*): Let the constraints be $EX = 0$, and $EX^2 = \sigma^2$. Then the form of the maximizing distribution is

$$f(x) = e^{\lambda_0 + \lambda_1 x + \lambda_2 x^2}. \tag{11.13}$$

To find the appropriate constants, we first recognize that this distribution has the same form as a normal distribution. Hence the density that satisfies the constraints and also maximizes the entropy is the $\mathcal{N}(0, \sigma^2)$ distribution.

Example 11.2.2 (*Dice, no constraints*): Let $S = \{1, 2, 3, 4, 5, 6\}$. The distribution that maximizes the entropy is the uniform distribution, $p(x) = \frac{1}{6}$ for $x \in S$.

Example 11.2.3 (*Dice, with $EX = \Sigma\, ip_i = \alpha$*): This important example was used by Boltzmann. Suppose n dice are thrown on the table and we are told that the total number of spots showing is $n\alpha$. What proportion of the dice are showing face i, $i = 1, 2, \ldots, 6$?

One way of going about this is to count the number of ways that n dice can fall so that n_i dice show face i. There are $\binom{n}{n_1, n_2, \ldots, n_6}$ such ways. This is a macrostate indexed by $(n_1, n_2, \ldots, n_6)$ corresponding to $\binom{n}{n_1, n_2, \ldots, n_6}$ microstates, each having probability $\frac{1}{6^n}$. To find the most probable macrostate, we wish to maximize $\binom{n}{n_1, n_2, \ldots, n_6}$ under the observed constraint on the total number of spots,

$$\sum_{i=1}^{6} in_i = n\alpha. \tag{11.14}$$

Using a crude Stirling's approximation, $n! \approx (\frac{n}{e})^n$, we find

$$\binom{n}{n_1, n_2, \ldots, n_6} \approx \frac{\left(\frac{n}{e}\right)^n}{\prod_{i=1}^{6} \left(\frac{n_i}{e}\right)^{n_i}} \qquad (11.15)$$

$$= \prod_{i=1}^{6} \left(\frac{n}{n_i}\right)^{n_i} \qquad (11.16)$$

$$= e^{nH\left(\frac{n_1}{n}, \frac{n_2}{n}, \ldots, \frac{n_6}{n}\right)}. \qquad (11.17)$$

Thus maximizing $\binom{n}{n_1, n_2, \ldots, n_6}$ under the constraint (11.14) is almost equivalent to maximizing $H(p_1, p_2, \ldots, p_6)$ under the constraint $\Sigma\, ip_i = \alpha$. Using Theorem 11.1.1 under this constraint, we find the maximum entropy probability mass function to be

$$p_i^* = \frac{e^{\lambda i}}{\Sigma_{i=1}^{6} e^{\lambda i}}, \qquad (11.18)$$

where λ is chosen so that $\Sigma\, ip_i^* = \alpha$. Thus the most probable macrostate is $(np_1^*, np_2^*, \ldots, np_6^*)$, and we expect to find $n_i^* = np_i^*$ dice showing face i.

In Chapter 12, we shall show that the reasoning and the approximations are essentially correct. In fact, we shall show that not only is the maximum entropy macrostate the most likely, but it also contains almost all of the probability. Specifically, for rational α,

$$\Pr\left\{\left|\frac{N_i}{n} - p_i^*\right| < \epsilon, i = 1, 2, \ldots, 6 \,\Big|\, \sum_{i=1}^{n} X_i = n\alpha\right\} \to 1\,, \qquad (11.19)$$

as $n \to \infty$ along the subsequence such that $n\alpha$ is an integer.

Example 11.2.4: Let $S = [a, b]$, with no other constraints. Then the maximum entropy distribution is the uniform distribution over this range.

Example 11.2.5: $S = [0, \infty)$ and $EX = \mu$. Then the entropy maximizing distribution is

$$f(x) = \frac{1}{\mu} e^{-\frac{x}{\mu}}, \quad x \geq 0. \qquad (11.20)$$

This problem has a physical interpretation. Consider the distribution of the height X of molecules in the atmosphere. The average potential energy of the molecules is fixed, and the gas tends to the distribution that has the maximum entropy subject to the constraint that $E[mgX]$ is fixed. This is the exponential distribution with density $f(x) = \lambda e^{-\lambda x}, x \geq 0$. The density of the atmosphere does indeed have this distribution.

Example 11.2.6: $S = (-\infty, \infty)$, and $EX = \mu$. Here the maximum entropy is infinite, and there is no maximum entropy distribution. (Consider normal distributions with larger and larger variances.)

Example 11.2.7: $S = (-\infty, \infty)$, $EX = \alpha_1$ and $EX^2 = \alpha_2$. The maximum entropy distribution is $\mathcal{N}(\alpha_1, \alpha_2 - \alpha_1^2)$.

Example 11.2.8: $S = \mathcal{R}^n$, $EX_iX_j = K_{ij}$, $1 \leq i, j \leq n$. This is a multivariate example, but the same analysis holds and the maximum entropy density is of the form

$$f(\mathbf{x}) = e^{\lambda_0 + \Sigma_{i, j} \lambda_{ij} x_i x_j} . \tag{11.21}$$

Since the exponent is a quadratic form, it is clear by inspection that the density is a multivariate normal with zero mean. Since we have to satisfy the second moment constraints, we must have a multivariate normal with covariance K_{ij}, and hence the density is

$$f(\mathbf{x}) = \frac{1}{(\sqrt{2\pi})^n |K|^{\frac{1}{2}}} e^{-\frac{1}{2}\mathbf{x}^T K^{-1}\mathbf{x}} , \tag{11.22}$$

which has an entropy

$$h(\mathcal{N}_n(0, K)) = \frac{1}{2} \log(2\pi e)^n |K| , \tag{11.23}$$

as derived in Chapter 9.

11.3   AN ANOMALOUS MAXIMUM ENTROPY PROBLEM

We have proved that the maximum entropy distribution subject to the constraints

$$\int_S h_i(x)f(x) \, dx = \alpha_i \tag{11.24}$$

is of the form

$$f(x) = e^{\lambda_0 + \Sigma \, \lambda_i h_i(x)} \tag{11.25}$$

if $\lambda_0, \lambda_1, \ldots, \lambda_p$ satisfying the constraints (11.24) exist.

We now consider a tricky problem in which the λ_i cannot be chosen to satisfy the constraints. Nonetheless, the "maximum" entropy can be found. We consider the following problem: maximize the entropy subject to the constraints

$$\int_{-\infty}^{\infty} f(x) \, dx = 1 \,, \tag{11.26}$$

$$\int_{-\infty}^{\infty} x f(x) \, dx = \alpha_1 \,, \tag{11.27}$$

$$\int_{-\infty}^{\infty} x^2 f(x) \, dx = \alpha_2 \,, \tag{11.28}$$

$$\int_{-\infty}^{\infty} x^3 f(x) \, dx = \alpha_3 \,. \tag{11.29}$$

In this case, the maximum entropy distribution, if it exists, must be of the form

$$f(x) = e^{\lambda_0 + \lambda_1 x + \lambda_2 x^2 + \lambda_3 x^3} \,. \tag{11.30}$$

But if λ_3 is non-zero, then $\int_{-\infty}^{\infty} f = \infty$ and the density cannot be normalized. So λ_3 must be 0. But then we have four equations and only three variables, so that in general it is not possible to choose the appropriate constants. The method seems to have failed in this case.

The reason for the apparent failure is simple: the entropy has an upper bound under these constraints, but it is not possible to attain it. Consider the corresponding problem with only first and second moment constraints. In this case, the results of Example 11.2.1 show that the entropy maximizing distribution is the normal with the appropriate moments. With the additional third moment constraint, the maximum entropy cannot be higher. Is it possible to achieve this value?

We cannot achieve it, but we can come arbitrarily close. Consider a normal distribution with a small "wiggle" at a very high value of x. The moments of the new distribution are almost the same as the old one, with the biggest change being in the third moment. We can bring the first and second moments back to their original values by adding new wiggles to balance out the changes caused by the first. By choosing the position of the wiggles, we can get any value of the third moment without significantly reducing the entropy below that of the associated normal. Using this method, we can come arbitrarily close to the upper bound for the maximum entropy distribution. We conclude that

$$\sup h(f) = h(\mathcal{N}(0, \alpha_2 - \alpha_1^2)) = \frac{1}{2} \ln 2\pi e(\alpha_2 - \alpha_1^2). \qquad (11.31)$$

This example shows that the maximum entropy may only be ϵ-achievable.

11.4 SPECTRUM ESTIMATION

Given a stationary zero mean stochastic process $\{X_i\}$, we define the autocorrelation function as

$$R(k) = EX_i X_{i+k}. \qquad (11.32)$$

The Fourier transform of the autocorrelation function for a zero mean process is the power spectral density $S(\lambda)$, i.e.,

$$S(\lambda) = \sum_{m=-\infty}^{\infty} R(m)e^{-im\lambda}, \quad -\pi < \lambda \le \pi. \qquad (11.33)$$

Since the power spectral density is indicative of the structure of the process, it is useful to form an estimate from a sample of the process.

There are many methods to estimate the power spectrum. The simplest way is to estimate the autocorrelation function by taking sample averages for a sample of length n,

$$\hat{R}(k) = \frac{1}{n-k} \sum_{i=1}^{n-k} X_i X_{i+k}. \qquad (11.34)$$

If we use all the values of the sample correlation function $\hat{R}(\cdot)$ to calculate the spectrum, the estimate that we obtain from (11.33) does not converge to the true power spectrum for large n. Hence this method, called the periodogram method, is rarely used.

One of the reasons for the problem with the periodogram method is that the estimates of the autocorrelation function from the data have different accuracies. The estimates for low values of k (called the lags) are based on a large number of samples and those for high k on very few samples. So the estimates are more accurate at low k. The method can be modified so that it depends only on the autocorrelations at low k by setting the higher lag autocorrelations to 0. However this introduces some artifacts because of the sudden transition to zero autocorrelation. Various windowing schemes have been suggested to smooth out the transition. However, windowing reduces spectral resolution and can give rise to negative power spectral estimates.

In the late 1960s, while working on the problem of spectral estimation for geophysical applications, Burg suggested an alternative method. Instead of setting the autocorrelations at high lags to zero, he set them to values that make the fewest assumptions about the data, i.e., values that maximize the entropy rate of the process. This is consistent with the maximum entropy principle as articulated by Jaynes [143]. Burg assumed the process to be stationary and Gaussian and found that the process which maximizes the entropy subject to the correlation constraints is an autoregressive Gaussian process of the appropriate order. In some applications where we can assume an underlying autoregressive model for the data, this method has proved useful in determining the parameters of the model (e.g., linear predictive coding for speech). This method (known as the maximum entropy method or Burg's method) is a popular method for estimation of spectral densities. We prove Burg's theorem in Section 11.6.

11.5 ENTROPY RATES OF A GAUSSIAN PROCESS

In Chapter 9, we defined the differential entropy of a continuous random variable. We can now extend the definition of entropy rates to real-valued stochastic processes.

Definition: The *differential entropy rate* of a stochastic process $\{X_i\}, X_i \in \mathcal{R}$, is defined to be

$$h(\mathcal{X}) = \lim_{n \to \infty} \frac{h(X_1, X_2, \ldots, X_n)}{n} \qquad (11.35)$$

if the limit exists.

Just as in the discrete case, we can show that the limit exists for stationary processes and that the limit is given by the two expressions

$$h(\mathcal{X}) = \lim_{n \to \infty} \frac{h(X_1, X_2, \ldots, X_n)}{n} \qquad (11.36)$$

$$= \lim_{n \to \infty} h(X_n | X_{n-1}, \ldots, X_1). \qquad (11.37)$$

For any sample of a stationary Gaussian stochastic process, we have

$$h(X_1, X_2, \ldots, X_n) = \frac{1}{2} \log(2\pi e)^n |K^{(n)}|, \qquad (11.38)$$

where the covariance matrix $K^{(n)}$ is Toeplitz with entries $R(0)$, $R(1), \ldots, R(n-1)$ along the top row. Thus $K_{ij}^{(n)} = R(|i-j|) = E(X_i - EX_i)(X_j - EX_j)$. As $n \to \infty$, the density of the eigenvalues of the covariance matrix tends to a limit, which is the spectrum of the stochastic process. Indeed, Kolmogorov showed that the entropy rate of a stationary Gaussian stochastic process can be expressed as

$$h(\mathcal{X}) = \frac{1}{2} \log 2\pi e + \frac{1}{4\pi} \int_{-\pi}^{\pi} \log S(\lambda) \, d\lambda \, . \qquad (11.39)$$

The entropy rate is also $\lim_{n \to \infty} h(X_n | X^{n-1})$. Since the stochastic process is Gaussian, the conditional distribution is also Gaussian and hence the conditional entropy is $\frac{1}{2} \log 2\pi e \sigma_\infty^2$, where σ_∞^2 is the variance of the error in the best estimate of X_n given the infinite past. Thus

$$\sigma_\infty^2 = \frac{1}{2\pi e} 2^{2h(\mathcal{X})} \, , \qquad (11.40)$$

where $h(\mathcal{X})$ is given by (11.39). Hence the entropy rate corresponds to the minimum mean squared error of the best estimator of a sample of the process given the infinite past.

11.6 BURG'S MAXIMUM ENTROPY THEOREM

Theorem 11.6.1: *The maximum entropy rate stochastic process $\{X_i\}$ satisfying the constraints*

$$EX_i X_{i+k} = \alpha_k, \quad k = 0, 1, \ldots, p, \quad \text{for all } i \, , \qquad (11.41)$$

is the pth order Gauss-Markov process of the form

$$X_i = -\sum_{k=1}^{p} a_k X_{i-k} + Z_i \, , \qquad (11.42)$$

where the Z_i are i.i.d. $\sim \mathcal{N}(0, \sigma^2)$ and $a_1, a_2, \ldots, a_p, \sigma^2$ are chosen to satisfy (11.41).

Remark: We do not assume that $\{X_i\}$ is (a) zero mean, (b) Gaussian, or (c) wide-sense stationary.

Proof: Let $X_1, X_2, \ldots, X_n$ be any stochastic process that satisfies the constraints (11.41). Let $Z_1, Z_2, \ldots, Z_n$ be a Gaussian process with the same covariance matrix as $X_1, X_2, \ldots, X_n$. Then since the multivariate normal distribution maximizes the entropy over all vector-valued random variables under a covariance constraint, we have

$$h(X_1, X_2, \ldots, X_n) \le h(Z_1, Z_2, \ldots, Z_n) \tag{11.43}$$

$$= h(Z_1, \ldots, Z_p) + \sum_{i=p+1}^{n} h(Z_i | Z_{i-1}, Z_{i-2}, \ldots, Z_1) \tag{11.44}$$

$$\le h(Z_1, \ldots, Z_p) + \sum_{i=p+1}^{n} h(Z_i | Z_{i-1}, Z_{i-2}, \ldots, Z_{i-p}) \tag{11.45}$$

by the chain rule and the fact that conditioning reduces entropy. Now define $Z_1', Z_2', \ldots, Z_n'$ as a pth order Gauss-Markov process with the same distribution as $Z_1, Z_2, \ldots, Z_n$ for all orders up to p. (Existence of such a process will be verified using the Yule-Walker equations immediately after the proof.) Then since $h(Z_i | Z_{i-1}, \ldots, Z_{i-p})$ depends only on the pth order distribution, $h(Z_i | Z_{i-1}, \ldots, Z_{i-p}) = h(Z_i' | Z'_{i-1}, \ldots, Z'_{i-p})$, and continuing the chain of inequalities, we obtain

$$h(X_1, X_2, \ldots, X_n) \le h(Z_1, \ldots, Z_p) + \sum_{i=p+1}^{n} h(Z_i | Z_{i-1}, Z_{i-2}, \ldots, Z_{i-p}) \tag{11.46}$$

$$= h(Z_1', \ldots, Z_p') + \sum_{i=p+1}^{n} h(Z_i' | Z'_{i-1}, Z'_{i-2}, \ldots, Z'_{i-p}) \tag{11.47}$$

$$= h(Z_1', Z_2', \ldots, Z_n'), \tag{11.48}$$

where the last equality follows from the pth order Markovity of the $\{Z_i'\}$. Dividing by n and taking the limit, we obtain

$$\overline{\lim} \frac{1}{n} h(X_1, X_2, \ldots, X_n) \le \lim \frac{1}{n} h(Z_1', Z_2', \ldots, Z_n') = h^*, \tag{11.49}$$

where

$$h^* = \frac{1}{2} \log 2\pi e \sigma^2, \tag{11.50}$$

which is the entropy rate of the Gauss-Markov process. Hence, the maximum entropy rate stochastic process satisfying the constraints is the pth order Gauss-Markov process satisfying the constraints. $\square$

A bare bones summary of the proof is that the entropy of a finite segment of a stochastic process is bounded above by the entropy of a segment of a Gaussian random process with the same covariance structure. This entropy is in turn bounded above by the entropy of the minimal order Gauss-Markov process satisfying the given covariance constraints. Such a process exists and has a convenient characterization by means of the Yule-Walker equations given below.

Note on the choice of $a_1, \ldots, a_p$ *and* σ^2: Given a sequence of covariances $R(0), R(1), \ldots, R(p)$, does there exist a pth order Gauss-Markov process with these covariances? Given a process of the form (11.42), can we choose the a_k's to satisfy the constraints? Multiplying (11.42) by X_{i-l} and taking expectations, and noting that $R(k) = R(-k)$, we get

$$R(0) = -\sum_{k=1}^{p} a_k R(-k) + \sigma^2 \qquad (11.51)$$

and

$$R(l) = -\sum_{k=1}^{p} a_k R(l-k), \quad l = 1, 2, \ldots . \qquad (11.52)$$

These equations are called the *Yule-Walker* equations. There are $p + 1$ equations in the $p + 1$ unknowns $a_1, a_2, \ldots, a_p, \sigma^2$. Therefore, we can solve for the parameters of the process from the covariances.

Fast algorithms such as the Levinson algorithm and the Durbin algorithm [213] have been devised to use the special structure of these equations to efficiently calculate the coefficients $a_1, a_2, \ldots, a_p$ from the covariances. (We set $a_0 = 1$ for a consistent notation.) Not only do the Yule-Walker equations provide a convenient set of linear equations for calculating the a_k's and σ^2 from the $R(k)$'s, they also indicate how the autocorrelations behave for lags greater than p. The autocorrelations for high lags are an extension of the values for lags less than p. These values are called the Yule-Walker extension of the autocorrelations. The spectrum of the maximum entropy process is seen to be

$$S(l) = \frac{\sigma^2}{\left|1 + \Sigma_{k=1}^{p} a_k e^{-ikl}\right|^2} . \qquad (11.53)$$

This is the maximum entropy spectral density subject to the constraints $R(0), R(1), \ldots, R(p)$.

In a practical problem, we are generally given a sample sequence $X_1, X_2, \ldots, X_n$, from which we calculate the autocorrelations. An important question is how many autocorrelation lags we should consider, i.e., what is the optimum value of p? A logically sound method is to choose the value of p that minimizes the total description length in a two stage description of the data. This method has been proposed by Rissanen [218, 223] and Barron [17] and is closely related to the idea of Kolmogorov complexity.

SUMMARY OF CHAPTER 11

Maximum entropy distribution: Let f be a probability density satisfying the constraints

$$\int_S f(x)r_i(x) = \alpha_i, \quad \text{for } 1 \leq i \leq m. \tag{11.54}$$

Let $f^*(x) = f_\lambda(x) = e^{\lambda_0 + \sum_{i=1}^m \lambda_i r_i(x)}$, $x \in S$, and let $\lambda_0, \ldots, \lambda_m$ be chosen so that f^* satisfies (11.54). Then f^* uniquely maximizes $h(f)$ over all f satisfying these constraints.

Maximum entropy spectral density estimation: The entropy rate of a stochastic process subject to autocorrelation constraints $R_0, R_1, \ldots, R_p$ is maximized by the pth order zero-mean Gauss-Markov process satisfying these constraints. The maximum entropy spectrum is

$$S(l) = \frac{\sigma^2}{|1 + \sum_{k=1}^p a_k e^{-ikl}|^2}. \tag{11.55}$$

PROBLEMS FOR CHAPTER 11

1. *Maximum entropy.* Find the maximum entropy density f defined for $x \geq 0$ satisfying $EX - \alpha_1, E \ln X = \alpha_2$. That is, maximize $-\int f \ln f$ subject to $\int x f(x)\, dx = \alpha_1$, $\int (\ln x) f(x)\, dx = \alpha_2$, where the integrals are over $0 \leq x < \infty$. What family of densities is this?

2. *Min $D(P\|Q)$ under constraints on P.* We wish to find the (parametric form) of the probability mass function $P(x), x \in \{1, 2, \ldots\}$ that minimizes the relative entropy $D(P\|Q)$ over all P such that $\sum P(x)g_i(x) = \alpha_i, i = 1, 2, \ldots$.
   (a) Use Lagrange multipliers to guess that

$$P^*(x) = Q(x)e^{\sum_{i=1}^\infty \lambda_i g_i(x) + \lambda_0} \tag{11.56}$$

   achieves this minimum if there exist λ_i's satisfying the α_i constraints. This generalizes the theorem on maximum entropy distributions subject to constraints.
   (b) Verify that P^* minimizes $D(P\|Q)$.

3. *Maximum entropy processes.* Find the maximum entropy rate stochastic process $\{X_i\}_{-\infty}^\infty$ subject to the constraints:
   (a) $EX_i^2 = 1$, $i = 1, 2, \ldots$,
   (b) $EX_i^2 = 1$, $EX_i X_{i+1} = \frac{1}{2}, i = 1, 2, \ldots$.

4. Find the maximum entropy spectrum for the processes in parts (a) and (b) of Problem 3.

5. *Maximum entropy with marginals.* What is the maximum entropy distribution $p(x, y)$ that has the following marginals? Hint: You may wish to guess and verify a more general result.

x \ y	1	2	3	
1	p_{11}	p_{12}	p_{13}	1/2
2	p_{21}	p_{22}	p_{23}	1/4
3	p_{31}	p_{32}	p_{33}	1/4
	2/3	1/6	1/6	

6. *Processes with fixed marginals.* Consider the set of all densities with fixed pairwise marginals $f_{X_1, X_2}(x_1, x_2)$, $f_{X_2, X_3}(x_2, x_3)$, ..., $f_{X_{n-1}, X_n}(x_{n-1}, x_n)$. Show that the maximum entropy process with these marginals is the first-order (possibly time-varying) Markov process with these marginals. Identify the maximizing $f^*(x_1, x_2, \ldots, x_n)$.

7. *Every density is a maximum entropy density.* Let $f_0(x)$ be a given density. Given $r(x)$, consider the parametric family of densities $g_\alpha(x)$ maximizing $h(X)$ over all f satisfying $\int f(x)r(x)\, dx = \alpha$. Now let $r(x) = \ln f_0(x)$. Show that $g_\alpha(x) = f_0(x)$ for an appropriate choice $\alpha = \alpha_0$. Thus $f_0(x)$ is a maximum entropy density under the constraint $\int f \ln f_0 = \alpha_0$.

HISTORICAL NOTES

The maximum entropy principle arose in statistical mechanics in the nineteenth century and has been advocated for use in a broader context by Jaynes [143]. It was applied to spectral estimation by Burg [47]. The information theoretic proof of Burg's theorem is from Choi and Cover [56].

Chapter 12

Information Theory and Statistics

We now explore the relationship between information theory and statistics. We begin by describing the method of types, which is a powerful technique in large deviation theory. We use the method of types to calculate the probability of rare events and to show the existence of universal source codes. We also consider the problem of testing hypotheses and derive the best possible error exponents for such tests (Stein's lemma). Finally, we treat the estimation of the parameters of a distribution and describe the role of Fisher information.

12.1 THE METHOD OF TYPES

The AEP for discrete random variables (Chapter 3) focuses our attention on a small subset of typical sequences. The method of types is an even more powerful procedure in which we consider the sequences that have the same empirical distribution. With this restriction, we can derive strong bounds on the number of sequences of a particular empirical distribution and the probability of each sequence in this set. It is then possible to derive strong error bounds for the channel coding theorem and prove a variety of rate-distortion results. The method of types was fully developed by Csiszár and Körner [83], who obtained most of their results from this point of view.

Let $X_1, X_2, \ldots, X_n$ be a sequence of n symbols from an alphabet $\mathcal{X} = \{a_1, a_2, \ldots, a_{|\mathcal{X}|}\}$. We will use the notation x^n and $\mathbf{x}$ interchangeably to denote a sequence $x_1, x_2, \ldots, x_n$.

Definition: The *type* $P_{\mathbf{x}}$ (or empirical probability distribution) of a sequence $x_1, x_2, \ldots, x_n$ is the relative proportion of occurrences of each symbol of $\mathscr{X}$, i.e., $P_{\mathbf{x}}(a) = N(a|\mathbf{x})/n$ for all $a \in \mathscr{X}$, where $N(a|\mathbf{x})$ is the number of times the symbol a occurs in the sequence $\mathbf{x} \in \mathscr{X}^n$.

The type of a sequence $\mathbf{x}$ is denoted as $P_{\mathbf{x}}$. It is a probability mass function on $\mathscr{X}$. (Note that in this chapter, we will use capital letters to denote types and distributions. We will also loosely use the word "distribution" to mean a probability mass function.)

Definition: Let $\mathscr{P}_n$ denote the *set of types with denominator n*.

For example, if $\mathscr{X} = \{0, 1\}$, then the set of possible types with denominator n is

$$\mathscr{P}_n = \left\{ (P(0), P(1)) : \left(\frac{0}{n}, \frac{n}{n}\right), \left(\frac{1}{n}, \frac{n-1}{n}\right), \ldots, \left(\frac{n}{n}, \frac{0}{n}\right) \right\}. \qquad (12.1)$$

Definition: If $P \in \mathscr{P}_n$, then the set of sequences of length n and type P is called the *type class* of P, denoted $T(P)$, i.e.,

$$T(P) = \{\mathbf{x} \in \mathscr{X}^n : P_{\mathbf{x}} = P\}. \qquad (12.2)$$

The type class is sometimes called the composition class of P.

Example 12.1.1: Let $\mathscr{X} = \{1, 2, 3\}$, a ternary alphabet. Let $\mathbf{x} = 11321$. Then the type $P_{\mathbf{x}}$ is

$$P_{\mathbf{x}}(1) = \frac{3}{5}, \quad P_{\mathbf{x}}(2) = \frac{1}{5}, \quad P_{\mathbf{x}}(3) = \frac{1}{5}. \qquad (12.3)$$

The type class of $P_{\mathbf{x}}$ is the set of all sequences of length 5 with three 1's, one 2 and one 3. There are 20 such sequences, and

$$T(P_{\mathbf{x}}) = \{11123, 11132, 11213, \ldots, 32111\}. \qquad (12.4)$$

The number of elements in $T(P)$ is

$$|T(P)| = \binom{5}{3, 1, 1} = \frac{5!}{3!1!1!} = 20. \qquad (12.5)$$

The essential power of the method of types arises from the following theorem, which shows that the number of types is at most polynomial in n.

Theorem 12.1.1:

$$|\mathscr{P}_n| \leq (n+1)^{|\mathscr{X}|}. \qquad (12.6)$$

Proof: There are $|\mathcal{X}|$ components in the vector that specifies $P_{\mathbf{x}}$. The numerator in each component can take on only $n+1$ values. So there are at most $(n+1)^{|\mathcal{X}|}$ choices for the type vector. Of course, these choices are not independent (for example, the last choice is fixed by the others). But this is a sufficiently good upper bound for our needs. $\square$

The crucial point here is that there are only a polynomial number of types of length n. Since the number of sequences is exponential in n, it follows that at least one type has exponentially many sequences in its type class. In fact, the largest type class has essentially the same number of elements as the entire set of sequences, to first order in the exponent.

Now, we will assume that the sequence $X_1, X_2, \ldots, X_n$ is drawn i.i.d. according to a distribution $Q(x)$. All sequences with the same type will have the same probability, as shown in the following theorem. Let $Q^n(x^n) = \prod_{i=1}^n Q(x_i)$ denote the product distribution associated with Q.

Theorem 12.1.2: *If $X_1, X_2, \ldots, X_n$ are drawn i.i.d. according to $Q(x)$, then the probability of $\mathbf{x}$ depends only on its type and is given by*

$$Q^n(\mathbf{x}) = 2^{-n(H(P_{\mathbf{x}})+D(P_{\mathbf{x}}\|Q))} . \tag{12.7}$$

Proof:

$$Q^n(\mathbf{x}) = \prod_{i=1}^n Q(x_i) \tag{12.8}$$

$$= \prod_{a \in \mathcal{X}} Q(a)^{N(a|\mathbf{x})} \tag{12.9}$$

$$= \prod_{a \in \mathcal{X}} Q(a)^{nP_{\mathbf{x}}(a)} \tag{12.10}$$

$$= \prod_{a \in \mathcal{X}} 2^{nP_{\mathbf{x}}(a) \log Q(a)} \tag{12.11}$$

$$= \prod_{a \in \mathcal{X}} 2^{n(P_{\mathbf{x}}(a) \log Q(a) - P_{\mathbf{x}}(a) \log P_{\mathbf{x}}(a) + P_{\mathbf{x}}(a) \log P_{\mathbf{x}}(a))} \tag{12.12}$$

$$= 2^{n \sum_{a \in \mathcal{X}} (-P_{\mathbf{x}}(a) \log \frac{P_{\mathbf{x}}(a)}{Q(a)} + P_{\mathbf{x}}(a) \log P_{\mathbf{x}}(a))} \tag{12.13}$$

$$= 2^{n(-D(P_{\mathbf{x}}\|Q) - H(P_{\mathbf{x}}))} . \quad \square \tag{12.14}$$

Corollary: *If $\mathbf{x}$ is in the type class of Q, then*

$$Q^n(\mathbf{x}) = 2^{-nH(Q)} . \tag{12.15}$$

Proof: If $\mathbf{x} \in T(Q)$, then $P_{\mathbf{x}} = Q$, which can be substituted into (12.14). $\square$

Example 12.1.2: The probability that a fair die produces a particular sequence of length n with precisely $n/6$ occurrences of each face (n is a multiple of 6) is $2^{-nH(\frac{1}{6}, \frac{1}{6}, \cdots, \frac{1}{6})} = 6^{-n}$. This is obvious. However, if the die has a probability mass function $(\frac{1}{3}, \frac{1}{3}, \frac{1}{6}, \frac{1}{12}, \frac{1}{12}, 0)$, the probability of observing a particular sequence with precisely these frequencies is precisely $2^{-nH(\frac{1}{3}, \frac{1}{3}, \frac{1}{6}, \frac{1}{12}, \frac{1}{12}, 0)}$ for n a multiple of 12. This is more interesting.

We now give an estimate of the size of a type class $T(P)$.

Theorem 12.1.3 (*Size of a type class $T(P)$*): *For any type $P \in \mathscr{P}_n$,*

$$\frac{1}{(n+1)^{|\mathscr{X}|}} 2^{nH(P)} \leq |T(P)| \leq 2^{nH(P)} . \tag{12.16}$$

Proof: The exact size of $T(P)$ is easy to calculate. It is a simple combinatorial problem—the number of ways of arranging $nP(a_1)$, $nP(a_2), \ldots, nP(a_{|\mathscr{X}|})$ objects in a sequence, which is

$$|T(P)| = \binom{n}{nP(a_1), nP(a_2), \ldots, nP(a_{|\mathscr{X}|})} . \tag{12.17}$$

This value is hard to manipulate, so we derive simple exponential bounds on its value.

We suggest two alternative proofs for the exponential bounds.

The first proof uses Stirling's formula [110] to bound the factorial function, and after some algebra, we can obtain the bounds of the theorem.

We give an alternative proof. We first prove the upper bound. Since a type class must have probability ≤ 1, we have

$$1 \geq P^n(T(P)) \tag{12.18}$$

$$= \sum_{\mathbf{x} \in T(P)} P^n(\mathbf{x}) \tag{12.19}$$

$$= \sum_{\mathbf{x} \in T(P)} 2^{-nH(P)} \tag{12.20}$$

$$= |T(P)| 2^{-nH(P)} , \tag{12.21}$$

using Theorem 12.1.2. Thus

$$|T(P)| \leq 2^{nH(P)} . \tag{12.22}$$

Now for the lower bound. We first prove that the type class $T(P)$ has the highest probability among all type classes under the probability distribution P, i.e.,

$$P^n(T(P)) \geq P^n(T(\hat{P})), \quad \text{for all } \hat{P} \in \mathscr{P}_n . \tag{12.23}$$

We lower bound the ratio of probabilities,

$$\frac{P^n(T(P))}{P^n(T(\hat{P}))} = \frac{|T(P)| \Pi_{a \in \mathscr{X}} P(a)^{nP(a)}}{|T(\hat{P})| \Pi_{a \in \mathscr{X}} P(a)^{n\hat{P}(a)}} \tag{12.24}$$

$$= \frac{\binom{n}{nP(a_1), nP(a_2), \ldots, nP(a_{|\mathscr{X}|})} \Pi_{a \in \mathscr{X}} P(a)^{nP(a)}}{\binom{n}{n\hat{P}(a_1), n\hat{P}(a_2), \ldots, n\hat{P}(a_{|\mathscr{X}|})} \Pi_{a \in \mathscr{X}} P(a)^{n\hat{P}(a)}} \tag{12.25}$$

$$= \prod_{a \in \mathscr{X}} \frac{(n\hat{P}(a))!}{(nP(a))!} P(a)^{n(P(a) - \hat{P}(a))} . \tag{12.26}$$

Now using the simple bound (easy to prove by separately considering the cases $m \geq n$ and $m < n$)

$$\frac{m!}{n!} \geq n^{m-n} , \tag{12.27}$$

we obtain

$$\frac{P^n(T(P))}{P^n(T(\hat{P}))} \geq \prod_{a \in \mathscr{X}} (nP(a))^{n\hat{P}(a) - nP(a)} P(a)^{n(P(a) - \hat{P}(a))} \tag{12.28}$$

$$= \prod_{a \in \mathscr{X}} n^{n(\hat{P}(a) - P(a))} \tag{12.29}$$

$$= n^{n(\Sigma_{a \in \mathscr{X}} \hat{P}(a) - \Sigma_{a \in \mathscr{X}} P(a))} \tag{12.30}$$

$$= n^{n(1-1)} \tag{12.31}$$

$$= 1 . \tag{12.32}$$

Hence $P^n(T(P)) \geq P^n(T(\hat{P}))$. The lower bound now follows easily from this result, since

$$1 = \sum_{Q \in \mathscr{P}_n} P^n(T(Q)) \tag{12.33}$$

$$\leq \sum_{Q \in \mathscr{P}_n} \max_Q P^n(T(Q)) \tag{12.34}$$

$$= \sum_{Q \in \mathscr{P}_n} P^n(T(P)) \tag{12.35}$$

$$\leq (n+1)^{|\mathscr{X}|} P^n(T(P)) \tag{12.36}$$

$$= (n+1)^{|\mathscr{X}|} \sum_{\mathbf{x} \in T(P)} P^n(\mathbf{x}) \tag{12.37}$$

$$= (n+1)^{|\mathscr{X}|} \sum_{\mathbf{x} \in T(P)} 2^{-nH(P)} \tag{12.38}$$

$$= (n+1)^{|\mathscr{X}|} |T(P)| 2^{-nH(P)}, \tag{12.39}$$

where (12.36) follows from Theorem 12.1.1 and (12.38) follows from Theorem 12.1.2. $\square$

We give a slightly better approximation for the binary case.

Example 12.1.3 (*Binary alphabet*): In this case, the type is defined by the number of 1's in the sequence, and the size of the type class is therefore $\binom{n}{k}$. We show that

$$\frac{1}{n+1} 2^{nH(\frac{k}{n})} \leq \binom{n}{k} \leq 2^{nH(\frac{k}{n})} . \tag{12.40}$$

These bounds can be proved using Stirling's approximation for the factorial function. But we provide a more intuitive proof below.

We first prove the upper bound. From the binomial formula, for any p,

$$\sum_{k=0}^{n} \binom{n}{k} p^k (1-p)^{n-k} = 1 . \tag{12.41}$$

Since all the terms of the sum are positive for $0 \leq p \leq 1$, each of the terms is less than 1. Setting $p = \frac{k}{n}$ and taking the kth term, we get

$$1 \geq \binom{n}{k} \left(\frac{k}{n}\right)^k \left(1 - \frac{k}{n}\right)^{n-k} \tag{12.42}$$

$$= \binom{n}{k} 2^{k \log \frac{k}{n} + (n-k) \log \frac{n-k}{n}} \tag{12.43}$$

$$= \binom{n}{k} 2^{n(\frac{k}{n} \log \frac{k}{n} + \frac{n-k}{n} \log \frac{n-k}{n})} \tag{12.44}$$

$$= \binom{n}{k} 2^{-nH(\frac{k}{n})} . \tag{12.45}$$

Hence

$$\binom{n}{k} \leq 2^{nH(\frac{k}{n})} . \tag{12.46}$$

For the lower bound, let S be a random variable with a binomial distribution with parameters n and p. The most likely value of S is $S = \langle np \rangle$. This can be easily verified from the fact that

$$\frac{P(S = i + 1)}{P(S = i)} = \frac{n - i}{i + 1} \frac{p}{1 - p} \tag{12.47}$$

and considering the cases when $i < np$ and when $i > np$. Then, since there are $n + 1$ terms in the binomial sum,

$$1 = \sum_{k=0}^{n} \binom{n}{k} p^k (1 - p)^{n-k} \le (n + 1) \max_k \binom{n}{k} p^k (1 - p)^{n-k} \tag{12.48}$$

$$= (n + 1) \binom{n}{\langle np \rangle} p^{\langle np \rangle} (1 - p)^{n - \langle np \rangle}. \tag{12.49}$$

Now let $p = \frac{k}{n}$. Then we have

$$1 \le (n + 1) \binom{n}{k} \left(\frac{k}{n}\right)^k \left(1 - \frac{k}{n}\right)^{n-k}, \tag{12.50}$$

which by the arguments in (12.45) is equivalent to

$$\frac{1}{n + 1} \le \binom{n}{k} 2^{-nH(\frac{k}{n})}, \tag{12.51}$$

or

$$\binom{n}{k} \ge \frac{2^{nH(\frac{k}{n})}}{n + 1}. \tag{12.52}$$

Combining the two results, we see that

$$\binom{n}{k} \doteq 2^{nH\left(\frac{k}{n}\right)}. \tag{12.53}$$

Theorem 12.1.4 (*Probability of type class*): *For any $P \in \mathcal{P}_n$ and any distribution Q, the probability of the type class $T(P)$ under Q^n is $2^{-nD(P\|Q)}$ to first order in the exponent. More precisely,*

$$\frac{1}{(n + 1)^{|\mathcal{X}|}} 2^{-nD(P\|Q)} \le Q^n(T(P)) \le 2^{-nD(P\|Q)}. \tag{12.54}$$

Proof: We have

$$Q^n(T(P)) = \sum_{\mathbf{x} \in T(P)} Q^n(\mathbf{x}) \tag{12.55}$$

$$= \sum_{\mathbf{x} \in T(P)} 2^{-n(D(P\|Q)+H(P))} \tag{12.56}$$

$$= |T(P)| 2^{-n(D(P\|Q)+H(P))} , \tag{12.57}$$

by Theorem 12.1.2. Using the bounds on $|T(P)|$ derived in Theorem 12.1.3, we have

$$\frac{1}{(n+1)^{|\mathscr{X}|}} 2^{-nD(P\|Q)} \le Q^n(T(P)) \le 2^{-nD(P\|Q)} . \quad \Box \tag{12.58}$$

We can summarize the basic theorems concerning types in four equations:

$$|\mathscr{P}_n| \le (n+1)^{|\mathscr{X}|} , \tag{12.59}$$

$$Q^n(\mathbf{x}) = 2^{-n(D(P_\mathbf{x}\|Q)+H(P_\mathbf{x}))} , \tag{12.60}$$

$$|T(P)| \doteq 2^{nH(P)} , \tag{12.61}$$

$$Q^n(T(P)) \doteq 2^{-nD(P\|Q)} . \tag{12.62}$$

These equations state that there are only a polynomial number of types and that there are an exponential number of sequences of each type. We also have an exact formula for the probability of any sequence of type P under distribution Q and an approximate formula for the probability of a type class.

These equations allow us to calculate the behavior of long sequences based on the properties of the type of the sequence. For example, for long sequences drawn i.i.d. according to some distribution, the type of the sequence is close to the distribution generating the sequence, and we can use the properties of this distribution to estimate the properties of the sequence. Some of the applications that will be dealt with in the next few sections are as follows:

- The law of large numbers.
- Universal source coding.
- Sanov's theorem.
- Stein's lemma and hypothesis testing.
- Conditional probability and limit theorems.

12.2 THE LAW OF LARGE NUMBERS

The concept of type and type classes enables us to give an alternative interpretation to the law of large numbers. In fact, it can be used as a proof of a version of the weak law in the discrete case.

The most important property of types is that there are only a polynomial number of types, and an exponential number of sequences of each type. Since the probability of each type class depends exponentially on the relative entropy distance between the type P and the distribution Q, type classes that are far from the true distribution have exponentially smaller probability.

Given an $\epsilon > 0$, we can define a typical set T_Q^ϵ of sequences for the distribution Q^n as

$$T_Q^\epsilon = \{x^n : D(P_{x^n} \| Q) \le \epsilon\} \,. \tag{12.63}$$

Then the probability that x^n is not typical is

$$1 - Q^n(T_Q^\epsilon) = \sum_{P : D(P \| Q) > \epsilon} Q^n(T(P)) \tag{12.64}$$

$$\le \sum_{P : D(P \| Q) > \epsilon} 2^{-nD(P \| Q)} \quad \text{(Theorem 12.1.4)} \tag{12.65}$$

$$\le \sum_{P : D(P \| Q) > \epsilon} 2^{-n\epsilon} \tag{12.66}$$

$$\le (n + 1)^{|\mathcal{X}|} 2^{-n\epsilon} \quad \text{(Theorem 12.1.1)} \tag{12.67}$$

$$= 2^{-n\left(\epsilon - |\mathcal{X}| \frac{\log(n+1)}{n}\right)}, \tag{12.68}$$

which goes to 0 as $n \to \infty$. Hence, the probability of the typical set goes to 1 as $n \to \infty$. This is similar to the AEP proved in Chapter 3, which is a form of the weak law of large numbers.

Theorem 12.2.1: *Let $X_1, X_2, \ldots, X_n$ be i.i.d. $\sim P(x)$. Then*

$$\Pr\{D(P_{x^n} \| P) > \epsilon\} < 2^{-n\left(\epsilon - |\mathcal{X}| \frac{\log(n+1)}{n}\right)}, \tag{12.69}$$

and consequently, $D(P_{x^n} \| P) \to 0$ with probability 1.

Proof: The inequality (12.69) was proved in (12.68). Summing over n, we find

$$\sum_{n=1}^{\infty} \Pr\{D(P_{x^n} \| P) > \epsilon\} < \infty \,. \tag{12.70}$$

Thus the expected number of occurrences of the event $\{D(P_{x^n} \| P) > \epsilon\}$ for all n is finite, which implies that the actual number of such occurrences is also finite with probability 1 (Borel-Cantelli lemma). Hence $D(P_{x^n} \| P) \to 0$ with probability 1. $\square$

We now define a stronger version of typicality.

Definition: We will define the *strongly typical set* $A_\epsilon^{(n)}$ to be the set of sequences in $\mathscr{X}^n$ for which the sample frequencies are close to the true values, i.e.,

$$A_\epsilon^{(n)} = \left\{ \mathbf{x} \in \mathscr{X}^n : \left| \frac{1}{n} N(a|\mathbf{x}) - P(a) \right| < \frac{\epsilon}{|\mathscr{X}|}, \text{ for all } a \in \mathscr{X} \right\}$$

(12.71)

Hence the typical set consists of sequences whose type does not differ from the true probabilities by more than $\epsilon/|\mathscr{X}|$ in any component.

By the strong law of large numbers, it follows that the probability of the strongly typical set goes to 1 as $n \to \infty$.

The additional power afforded by strong typicality is useful in proving stronger results, particularly in universal coding, rate distortion theory and large deviation theory.

12.3 UNIVERSAL SOURCE CODING

Huffman coding compresses an i.i.d. source with a known distribution $p(x)$ to its entropy limit $H(X)$. However, if the code is designed for some incorrect distribution $q(x)$, a penalty of $D(p\|q)$ is incurred. Thus Huffman coding is sensitive to the assumed distribution.

What compression can be achieved if the true distribution $p(x)$ is unknown? Is there a universal code of rate R, say, that suffices to describe every i.i.d. source with entropy $H(X) < R$? The surprising answer is yes.

The idea is based on the method of types. There are $2^{nH(P)}$ sequences of type P. Since there are only a polynomial number of types with denominator n, an enumeration of all sequences x^n with type P_{x^n} such that $H(P_{x^n}) < R$ will require roughly nR bits. Thus, by describing all such sequences, we are prepared to describe any sequence that is likely to arise from any distribution Q with $H(Q) < R$. We begin with a definition.

Definition: A *fixed rate block code* of rate R for a source $X_1, X_2, \ldots, X_n$ which has an unknown distribution Q consists of two mappings, the encoder,

$$f_n : \mathscr{X}^n \to \{1, 2, \ldots, 2^{nR}\},$$

(12.72)

and the decoder,

$$\phi_n : \{1, 2, \ldots, 2^{nR}\} \to \mathscr{X}^n.$$

(12.73)

Here R is called the rate of the code. The probability of error for the code with respect to the distribution Q is

$$P_e^{(n)} = Q^n(X_1, X_2, \ldots, X_n : \phi_n(f_n(X_1, X_2, \ldots, X_n)) \neq (X_1, X_2, \ldots, X_n)) .$$
(12.74)

Definition: A rate R block code for a source will be called *universal* if the functions f_n and ϕ_n do not depend on the distribution Q and if $P_e^{(n)} \to 0$ as $n \to \infty$ if $R > H(Q)$.

We now describe one such universal encoding scheme, due to Csiszár and Körner [83], that is based on the fact that the number of sequences of the type P increases exponentially with the entropy and the fact that there are only a polynomial number of types.

Theorem 12.3.1: *There exists a sequence of $(2^{nR}, n)$ universal source codes such that $P_e^{(n)} \to 0$ for every source Q such that $H(Q) < R$.*

Proof: Fix the rate R for the code. Let

$$R_n = R - |\mathcal{X}| \frac{\log(n + 1)}{n} .$$
(12.75)

Consider the set of sequences

$$A = \{\mathbf{x} \in \mathcal{X}^n : H(P_\mathbf{x}) \le R_n\} .$$
(12.76)

Then

$$|A| = \sum_{P \in \mathcal{P}_n : H(P) \le R_n} |T(P)|$$
(12.77)

$$\le \sum_{P \in \mathcal{P}_n : H(P) \le R_n} 2^{nH(P)}$$
(12.78)

$$\le \sum_{P \in \mathcal{P}_n : H(P) \le R_n} 2^{nR_n}$$
(12.79)

$$\le (n + 1)^{|\mathcal{X}|} 2^{nR_n}$$
(12.80)

$$= 2^{n\left(R_n + |\mathcal{X}| \frac{\log(n+1)}{n}\right)}$$
(12.81)

$$= 2^{nR} .$$
(12.82)

By indexing the elements of A, we define the encoding f_n as

$$f_n(\mathbf{x}) = \begin{cases} \text{index of } \mathbf{x} \text{ in } A & \text{if } x \in A, \\ 0 & \text{otherwise}. \end{cases} \qquad (12.83)$$

The decoding function maps each index onto the corresponding element of A. Hence all the elements of A are encoded correctly, and all the remaining sequences result in an error. The set of sequences that are encoded correctly is illustrated in Figure 12.1.

We will now show that this encoding scheme is universal. Assume that the distribution of $X_1, X_2, \ldots, X_n$ is Q and $H(Q) < R$. Then the probability of decoding error is given by

$$P_e^{(n)} = 1 - Q^n(A) \qquad (12.84)$$

$$= \sum_{P : H(P) > R_n} Q^n(T(P)) \qquad (12.85)$$

$$\leq (n+1)^{|\mathcal{X}|} \max_{P : H(P) > R_n} Q^n(T(P)) \qquad (12.86)$$

$$\leq (n+1)^{|\mathcal{X}|} 2^{-n \min_{P : H(P) > R_n} D(P\|Q)} \qquad (12.87)$$

Since $R_n \uparrow R$ and $H(Q) < R$, there exists n_0 such that for all $n \geq n_0$, $R_n > H(Q)$. Then for $n \geq n_0$, $\min_{P : H(P) > R_n} D(P\|Q)$ must be greater than 0, and the probability of error $P_e^{(n)}$ converges to 0 exponentially fast as $n \to \infty$.

On the other hand, if the distribution Q is such that the entropy $H(Q)$ is greater than the rate R, then with high probability, the sequence will have a type outside the set A. Hence, in such cases the probability of error is close to 1.

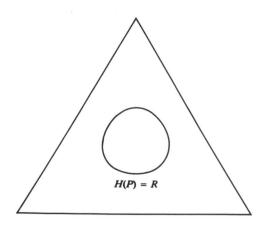

Figure 12.1. Universal code and the probability simplex.

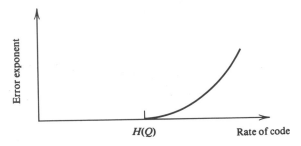

Figure 12.2. Error exponent for the universal code.

The exponent in the probability of error is

$$D_{R,Q}^* = \min_{P\,:\,H(P)>R} D(P\|Q)\,, \tag{12.88}$$

which is illustrated in Figure 12.2.   □

The universal coding scheme described here is only one of many such schemes. It is universal over the set of i.i.d. distributions. There are other schemes like the Lempel-Ziv algorithm, which is a variable rate universal code for all ergodic sources. The Lempel-Ziv algorithm, discussed in Section 12.10, is often used in practice to compress data which cannot be modeled simply, such as English text or computer source code.

One may wonder why it is ever necessary to use Huffman codes, which are specific to a probability distribution. What do we lose in using a universal code?

Universal codes need a longer block length to obtain the same performance as a code designed specifically for the probability distribution. We pay the penalty for this increase in block length by the increased complexity of the encoder and decoder. Hence a distribution specific code is best if one knows the distribution of the source.

12.4   LARGE DEVIATION THEORY

The subject of large deviation theory can be illustrated by an example. What is the probability that $\frac{1}{n}\sum X_i$ is near $1/3$, if $X_1, X_2, \ldots, X_n$ are drawn i.i.d. Bernoulli($1/3$)? This is a small deviation (from the expected outcome) and the probability is near 1. Now what is the probability that $\frac{1}{n}\sum X_i$ is greater than $3/4$ given that $X_1, X_2, \ldots, X_n$ are Bernoulli($1/3$)? This is a large deviation, and the probability is exponentially small. We might estimate the exponent using the central limit theorem, but this is a poor approximation for more than a few standard deviations. We note that $\frac{1}{n}\sum X_i = 3/4$ is equivalent to $P_{\mathbf{x}} = (1/4, 3/4)$. Thus the probability that $\bar{X}_n$ is near $3/4$ is the probability of the corresponding type. The probability of this large deviation will turn out to be $\approx 2^{-nD((\frac{3}{4}, \frac{1}{4})\|(\frac{1}{3}, \frac{2}{3}))}$. In this section, we estimate the probability of a set of non-typical types.

Let E be a subset of the set of probability mass functions. For example, E may be the set of probability mass functions with mean μ. With a slight abuse of notation, we write

$$Q^n(E) = Q^n(E \cap \mathscr{P}_n) = \sum_{\mathbf{x}: P_{\mathbf{x}} \in E \cap \mathscr{P}_n} Q^n(\mathbf{x}). \qquad (12.89)$$

If E contains a relative entropy neighborhood of Q, then by the weak law of large numbers (Theorem 12.2.1), $Q^n(E) \to 1$. On the other hand, if E does not contain Q or a neighborhood of Q, then by the weak law of large numbers, $Q^n(E) \to 0$ exponentially fast. We will use the method of types to calculate the exponent.

Let us first give some examples of the kind of sets E that we are considering. For example, assume that by observation we find that the sample average of $g(X)$ is greater than or equal to α, i.e., $\frac{1}{n} \sum_i g(X_i) \geq \alpha$. This event is equivalent to the event $P_{\mathbf{x}} \in E \cap \mathscr{P}_n$, where

$$E = \left\{ P : \sum_{a \in \mathscr{X}} g(a)P(a) \geq \alpha \right\}, \qquad (12.90)$$

because

$$\frac{1}{n} \sum_{i=1}^{n} g(X_i) \geq \alpha \Leftrightarrow \sum_{a \in \mathscr{X}} P_{\mathbf{x}}(a)g(a) \geq \alpha \qquad (12.91)$$

$$\Leftrightarrow P_{\mathbf{x}} \in E \cap \mathscr{P}_n. \qquad (12.92)$$

Thus

$$\Pr\left(\frac{1}{n} \sum_{i=1}^{n} g(X_i) \geq \alpha\right) = Q^n(E \cap \mathscr{P}_n) = Q^n(E). \qquad (12.93)$$

Here E is a half space in the space of probability vectors, as illustrated in Figure 12.3.

Theorem 12.4.1 (*Sanov's theorem*): *Let* $X_1, X_2, \ldots, X_n$ *be i.i.d.* $\sim Q(x)$. *Let* $E \subseteq \mathscr{P}$ *be a set of probability distributions. Then*

$$Q^n(E) = Q^n(E \cap \mathscr{P}_n) \leq (n+1)^{|\mathscr{X}|} 2^{-nD(P^*\|Q)}, \qquad (12.94)$$

where

$$P^* = \arg \min_{P \in E} D(P\|Q), \qquad (12.95)$$

is the distribution in E *that is closest to* Q *in relative entropy.*

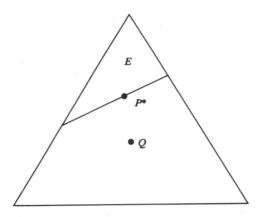

Figure 12.3. The probability simplex and Sanov's theorem.

If, in addition, the set E is the closure of its interior, then

$$\frac{1}{n} \log Q^n(E) \to -D(P^* \| Q) .$$

(12.96)

Proof: We first prove the upper bound:

$$Q^n(E) = \sum_{P \in E \cap \mathscr{P}_n} Q^n(T(P))$$

(12.97)

$$\le \sum_{P \in E \cap \mathscr{P}_n} 2^{-nD(P\|Q)}$$

(12.98)

$$\le \sum_{P \in E \cap \mathscr{P}_n} \max_{P \in E \cap \mathscr{P}_n} 2^{-nD(P\|Q)}$$

(12.99)

$$= \sum_{P \in E \cap \mathscr{P}_n} 2^{-n \min_{P \in E \cap \mathscr{P}_n} D(P\|Q)}$$

(12.100)

$$\le \sum_{P \in E \cap \mathscr{P}_n} 2^{-n \min_{P \in E} D(P\|Q)}$$

(12.101)

$$= \sum_{P \in E \cap \mathscr{P}_n} 2^{-nD(P^*\|Q)}$$

(12.102)

$$\le (n+1)^{|\mathscr{X}|} 2^{-nD(P^*\|Q)}$$

(12.103)

where the last inequality follows from Theorem 12.1.1.

Note that P^* need not be a member of $\mathscr{P}_n$. We now come to the lower bound, for which we need a "nice" set E, so that for all large n, we can find a distribution in $E \cap \mathscr{P}_n$ which is close to P^*. If we now assume that E is the closure of its interior (thus the interior must be non-empty), then since $\bigcup_n \mathscr{P}_n$ is dense in the set of all distributions, it follows that $E \cap \mathscr{P}_n$ is non-empty for all $n \geq n_0$ for some n_0. We can then find a sequence of distributions P_n such that $P_n \in E \cap \mathscr{P}_n$ and $D(P_n \| Q) \to D(P^* \| Q)$. For each $n \geq n_0$,

$$Q^n(E) = \sum_{P \in E \cap \mathscr{P}_n} Q^n(T(P)) \tag{12.104}$$

$$\geq Q^n(T(P_n)) \tag{12.105}$$

$$\geq \frac{1}{(n+1)^{|\mathscr{X}|}} 2^{-nD(P_n \| Q)} . \tag{12.106}$$

Consequently,

$$\liminf \frac{1}{n} \log Q^n(E) \geq \liminf \left(-\frac{|\mathscr{X}| \log(n+1)}{n} - D(P_n \| Q) \right)$$

$$= -D(P^* \| Q) . \tag{12.107}$$

Combining this with the upper bound establishes the theorem. $\quad\square$

This argument can also be extended to continuous distributions using quantization.

12.5   EXAMPLES OF SANOV'S THEOREM

Suppose we wish to find $\Pr\{\frac{1}{n} \sum_{i=1}^n g_j(X_i) \geq \alpha_j, j = 1, 2, \ldots, k\}$. Then the set E is defined as

$$E = \left\{ P : \sum_a P(a) g_j(a) \geq \alpha_j, j = 1, 2, \ldots, k \right\} . \tag{12.108}$$

To find the closest distribution in E to Q, we minimize $D(P \| Q)$ subject to the constraints in (12.108). Using Lagrange multipliers, we construct the functional

$$J(P) = \sum_x P(x) \log \frac{P(x)}{Q(x)} + \sum_i \lambda_i \sum_x P(x) g_i(x) + \nu \sum_x P(x) . \tag{12.109}$$

We then differentiate and calculate the closest distribution to Q to be of the form

$$P^*(x) = \frac{Q(x) e^{\sum_i \lambda_i g_i(x)}}{\sum_{a \in \mathscr{X}} Q(a) e^{\sum_i \lambda_i g_i(a)}} , \tag{12.110}$$

where the constants λ_i are chosen to satisfy the constraints. Note that if Q is uniform, then P^* is the maximum entropy distribution. Verification that P^* is indeed the minimum follows from the same kind of arguments as given in Chapter 11.

Let us consider some specific examples:

Example 12.5.1 *(Dice)*: Suppose we toss a fair die n times; what is the probability that the average of the throws is greater than or equal to 4? From Sanov's theorem, it follows that

$$Q^n(E) \doteq 2^{-nD(P^* \| Q)} , \qquad (12.111)$$

where P^* minimizes $D(P \| Q)$ over all distributions P that satisfy

$$\sum_{i=1}^{6} iP(i) \geq 4 . \qquad (12.112)$$

From (12.110), it follows that P^* has the form

$$P^*(x) = \frac{2^{\lambda x}}{\sum_{i=1}^{6} 2^{\lambda i}} , \qquad (12.113)$$

with λ chosen so that $\sum iP^*(i) = 4$. Solving numerically, we obtain $\lambda = 0.2519$, and $P^* = (0.1031, 0.1227, 0.1461, 0.1740, 0.2072, 0.2468)$, and therefore $D(P^* \| Q) = 0.0624$ bits. Thus, the probability that the average of 10000 throws is greater than or equal to 4 is $\approx 2^{-624}$.

Example 12.5.2 *(Coins)*: Suppose we have a fair coin, and want to estimate the probability of observing more than 700 heads in a series of 1000 tosses. The problem is like the previous example. The probability is

$$P(\bar{X}_n \geq 0.7) \doteq 2^{-nD(P^* \| Q)} \qquad (12.114)$$

where P^* is the $(0.7, 0.3)$ distribution and Q is the $(0.5, 0.5)$ distribution. In this case, $D(P^* \| Q) = 1 - H(P^*) = 1 - H(0.7) = 0.119$. Thus the probability of 700 or more heads in 1000 trials is approximately 2^{-119}.

Example 12.5.3 *(Mutual dependence)*: Let $Q(x, y)$ be a given joint distribution and let $Q_0(x, y) = Q(x)Q(y)$ be the associated product distribution formed from the marginals of Q. We wish to know the likelihood that a sample drawn according to Q_0 will "appear" to be jointly distributed according to Q. Accordingly, let (X_i, Y_i) be i.i.d. $\sim Q_0(x, y) = Q(x)Q(y)$. We define joint typicality as we did in Section 8.6, i.e., (x^n, y^n) is jointly typical with respect to a joint distribution $Q(x, y)$ iff the sample entropies are close to their true values, i.e.,

$$\left| -\frac{1}{n} \log Q(x^n) - H(X) \right| \le \epsilon, \qquad (12.115)$$

$$\left| -\frac{1}{n} \log Q(y^n) - H(Y) \right| \le \epsilon, \qquad (12.116)$$

and

$$\left| -\frac{1}{n} \log Q(x^n, y^n) - H(X, Y) \right| \le \epsilon. \qquad (12.117)$$

We wish to calculate the probability (under the product distribution) of seeing a pair (x^n, y^n) that looks jointly typical of Q, i.e., (x^n, y^n) satisfies (12.115)–(12.117). Thus (x^n, y^n) are jointly typical with respect to $Q(x, y)$ if $P_{x^n, y^n} \in E \cap \mathcal{P}_n(X, Y)$, where

$$E = \left\{ P(x, y) : \left| -\sum_{x, y} P(x, y) \log Q(x) - H(X) \right| \le \epsilon, \right.$$

$$\left| -\sum_{x, y} P(x, y) \log Q(y) - H(Y) \right| \le \epsilon,$$

$$\left. \left| -\sum_{x, y} P(x, y) \log Q(x, y) - H(X, Y) \right| \le \epsilon \right\}. \quad (12.118)$$

Using Sanov's theorem, the probability is

$$Q_0^n(E) \doteq 2^{-nD(P^* \| Q_0)}, \qquad (12.119)$$

where P^* is the distribution satisfying the constraints that is closest to Q_0 in relative entropy. In this case, as $\epsilon \to 0$, it can be verified (Problem 10) that P^* is the joint distribution Q, and Q_0 is the product distribution, so that the probability is $2^{-nD(Q(x, y) \| Q(x)Q(y))} = 2^{-nI(X; Y)}$, which is the same as the result derived in Chapter 8 for the joint AEP.

In the next section, we consider the empirical distribution of the sequence of outcomes given that the type is in a particular set of distributions E. We will show that not only is the probability of the set E essentially determined by $D(P^* \| Q)$, the distance of the closest element of E to Q, but also that the conditional type is essentially P^*, so that given that we are in set E, the type is very likely to be close to P^*.

12.6   THE CONDITIONAL LIMIT THEOREM

It has been shown that the probability of a set of types under a distribution Q is essentially determined by the probability of the closest element of the set to Q; the probability is 2^{-nD^*} to first order in the exponent, where

$$D^* = \min_{P \in E} D(P\|Q). \tag{12.120}$$

This follows because the probability of the set of types is the sum of the probabilities of each type, which is bounded by the largest term times the number of terms. Since the number of terms is polynomial in the length of the sequences, the sum is equal to the largest term to first order in the exponent.

We now strengthen the argument to show that not only is the probability of the set E essentially the same as the probability of the closest type P^* but also that the total probability of other types that are far away from P^* is negligible. This implies that with very high probability, the observed type is close to P^*. We call this a conditional limit theorem.

Before we prove this result, we prove a "Pythagorean" theorem, which gives some insight into the geometry of $D(P\|Q)$. Since $D(P\|Q)$ is not a metric, many of the intuitive properties of distance are not valid for $D(P\|Q)$. The next theorem shows a sense in which $D(P\|Q)$ behaves like the square of the Euclidean metric (Figure 12.4).

Theorem 12.6.1: *For a closed convex set $E \subset \mathscr{P}$ and distribution $Q \not\in E$, let $P^* \in E$ be the distribution that achieves the minimum distance to Q, i.e.,*

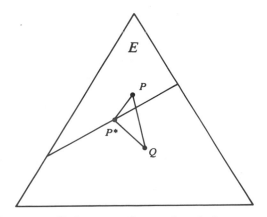

Figure 12.4. Pythagorean theorem for relative entropy.

$$D(P^*\|Q) = \min_{P \in E} D(P\|Q) .$$

(12.121)

Then

$$D(P\|Q) \ge D(P\|P^*) + D(P^*\|Q)$$

(12.122)

for all $P \in E$.

Note: The main use of this theorem is as follows: suppose we have a sequence $P_n \in E$ that yields $D(P_n\|Q) \to D(P^*\|Q)$. Then from the Pythagorean theorem, $D(P_n\|P^*) \to 0$ as well.

Proof: Consider any $P \in E$. Let

$$P_\lambda = \lambda P + (1 - \lambda)P^* .$$

(12.123)

Then $P_\lambda \to P^*$ as $\lambda \to 0$. Also since E is convex, $P_\lambda \in E$ for $0 \le \lambda \le 1$. Since $D(P^*\|Q)$ is the minimum of $D(P_\lambda\|Q)$ along the path $P^* \to P$, the derivative of $D(P_\lambda\|Q)$ as a function of λ is non-negative at $\lambda = 0$. Now

$$D_\lambda = D(P_\lambda\|Q) = \sum P_\lambda(x) \log \frac{P_\lambda(x)}{Q(x)} ,$$

(12.124)

and

$$\frac{dD_\lambda}{d\lambda} = \sum \left((P(x) - P^*(x)) \log \frac{P_\lambda(x)}{Q(x)} + (P(x) - P^*(x)) \right) .$$

(12.125)

Setting $\lambda = 0$, so that $P_\lambda = P^*$ and using the fact that $\sum P(x) = \sum P^*(x) = 1$, we have

$$0 \le \left(\frac{dD_\lambda}{d\lambda} \right)_{\lambda=0}$$

(12.126)

$$= \sum (P(x) - P^*(x)) \log \frac{P^*(x)}{Q(x)}$$

(12.127)

$$= \sum P(x) \log \frac{P^*(x)}{Q(x)} - \sum P^*(x) \log \frac{P^*(x)}{Q(x)}$$

(12.128)

$$= \sum P(x) \log \frac{P(x)}{Q(x)} \frac{P^*(x)}{P(x)} - \sum P^*(x) \log \frac{P^*(x)}{Q(x)}$$

(12.129)

$$= D(P\|Q) - D(P\|P^*) - D(P^*\|Q) ,$$

(12.130)

which proves the theorem. $\square$

Note that the relative entropy $D(P\|Q)$ behaves like the square of the Euclidean distance. Suppose we have a convex set E in $\mathscr{R}^n$. Let A be a point outside the set, B the point in the set closest to A, and C any other point in the set. Then the angle between the lines BA and BC must be obtuse, which implies that $l^2_{AC} \geq l^2_{AB} + l^2_{BC}$, which is of the same form as the above theorem. This is illustrated in Figure 12.5.

We now prove a useful lemma which shows that convergence in relative entropy implies convergence in the $\mathscr{L}_1$ norm.

Definition: The $\mathscr{L}_1$ distance between any two distributions is defined as

$$\|P_1 - P_2\|_1 = \sum_{a \in \mathscr{X}} |P_1(a) - P_2(a)| . \qquad (12.131)$$

Let A be the set on which $P_1(x) > P_2(x)$. Then

$$\|P_1 - P_2\|_1 = \sum_{x \in \mathscr{X}} |P_1(x) - P_2(x)| \qquad (12.132)$$

$$= \sum_{x \in A} (P_1(x) - P_2(x)) + \sum_{x \in A^c} (P_2(x) - P_1(x)) \qquad (12.133)$$

$$= P_1(A) - P_2(A) + P_2(A^c) - P_1(A^c) \qquad (12.134)$$

$$= P_1(A) - P_2(A) + 1 - P_2(A) - 1 + P_1(A) \qquad (12.135)$$

$$= 2(P_1(A) - P_2(A)) . \qquad (12.136)$$

Also note that

$$\max_{B \subseteq \mathscr{X}}(P_1(B) - P_2(B)) = P_1(A) - P_2(A) = \frac{\|P_1 - P_2\|_1}{2} . \qquad (12.137)$$

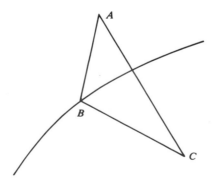

Figure 12.5. Triangle inequality for distance squared.

The left hand side of (12.137) is called the *variational distance* between P_1 and P_2.

Lemma 12.6.1:

$$D(P_1 \| P_2) \geq \frac{1}{2 \ln 2} \| P_1 - P_2 \|_1^2 \qquad (12.138)$$

Proof: We first prove it for the binary case. Consider two binary distributions with parameters p and q with $p \geq q$. We will show that

$$p \log \frac{p}{q} + (1 - p) \log \frac{1 - p}{1 - q} \geq \frac{4}{2 \ln 2} (p - q)^2 . \qquad (12.139)$$

The difference $g(p, q)$ between the two sides is

$$g(p, q) = p \log \frac{p}{q} + (1 - p) \log \frac{1 - p}{1 - q} - \frac{4}{2 \ln 2} (p - q)^2 . \qquad (12.140)$$

Then

$$\frac{dg(p, q)}{dq} = -\frac{p}{q \ln 2} + \frac{1 - p}{(1 - q) \ln 2} - \frac{4}{2 \ln 2} 2(q - p) \qquad (12.141)$$

$$= \frac{q - p}{q(1 - q) \ln 2} - \frac{4}{\ln 2} (q - p) \qquad (12.142)$$

$$\leq 0 , \qquad (12.143)$$

since $q(1 - q) \leq \frac{1}{4}$ and $q \leq p$. For $q = p$, $g(p, q) = 0$, and hence $g(p, q) \geq 0$ for $q \leq p$, which proves the lemma for the binary case.

For the general case, for any two distributions P_1 and P_2, let

$$A = \{x : P_1(x) > P_2(x)\} . \qquad (12.144)$$

Define a new binary random variable $Y = \phi(X)$, the indicator of the set A, and let $\hat{P}_1$ and $\hat{P}_2$ be the distributions of Y. Thus $\hat{P}_1$ and $\hat{P}_2$ correspond to the quantized versions of P_1 and P_2. Then by the data processing inequality applied to relative entropies (which is proved in the same way as the data processing inequality for mutual information), we have

$$D(P_1 \| P_2) \geq D(\hat{P}_1 \| \hat{P}_2) \qquad (12.145)$$

$$\geq \frac{4}{2 \ln 2} (P_1(A) - P_2(A))^2 \qquad (12.146)$$

$$= \frac{1}{2 \ln 2} \|P_1 - P_2\|_1^2 \qquad (12.147)$$

by (12.137), and the lemma is proved.   □

We can now begin the proof of the conditional limit theorem. We first outline the method used. As stated at the beginning of the chapter, the essential idea is that the probability of a type under Q depends exponentially on the distance of the type from Q, and hence types that are further away are exponentially less likely to occur. We divide the set of types in E into two categories: those at about the same distance from Q as P^* and those a distance 2δ farther away. The second set has exponentially less probability than the first, and hence the first set has a conditional probability tending to 1. We then use the Pythagorean theorem to establish that all the elements in the first set are close to P^*, which will establish the theorem.

The following theorem is an important strengthening of the maximum entropy principle.

Theorem 12.6.2 (*Conditional limit theorem*): *Let E be a closed convex subset of $\mathscr{P}$ and let Q be a distribution not in E. Let $X_1, X_2, \ldots, X_n$ be discrete random variables drawn i.i.d. $\sim Q$. Let P^* achieve $\min_{P \in E} D(P\|Q)$. Then*

$$\Pr(X_1 = a | P_{X^n} \in E) \to P^*(a) \qquad (12.148)$$

in probability as $n \to \infty$, i.e., the conditional distribution of X_1, given that the type of the sequence is in E, is close to P^* for large n.

Example 12.6.1: If X_i i.i.d. $\sim Q$, then

$$\Pr\left\{X_1 = a \middle| \frac{1}{n} \sum X_i^2 \geq \alpha\right\} \to P^*(a), \qquad (12.149)$$

where $P^*(a)$ minimizes $D(P\|Q)$ over P satisfying $\sum P(a)a^2 \geq \alpha$. This minimization results in

$$P^*(a) = Q(a) \frac{e^{\lambda a^2}}{\sum_a Q(a) e^{\lambda a^2}}, \qquad (12.150)$$

where λ is chosen to satisfy $\sum P^*(a)a^2 = \alpha$. Thus the conditional distribution on X_1 given a constraint on the sum of the squares is a (normalized) product of the original probability mass function and the maximum entropy probability mass function (which in this case is Gaussian).

Proof of Theorem: Define the sets

$$S_t = \{P \in \mathcal{P} : D(P\|Q) \le t\} \ . \tag{12.151}$$

The sets S_t are convex since $D(P\|Q)$ is a convex function of P. Let

$$D^* = D(P^*\|Q) = \min_{P \in E} D(P\|Q) \ . \tag{12.152}$$

Then P^* is unique, since $D(P\|Q)$ is strictly convex in P.
Now define the set

$$A = S_{D^*+2\delta} \cap E \tag{12.153}$$

and

$$B = E - S_{D^*+2\delta} \cap E \ . \tag{12.154}$$

Thus $A \cup B = E$. These sets are illustrated in Figure 12.6. Then

$$Q^n(B) = \sum_{P \in E \cap \mathcal{P}_n : D(P\|Q) > D^*+2\delta} Q^n(T(P)) \tag{12.155}$$

$$\le \sum_{P \in E \cap \mathcal{P}_n : D(P\|Q) > D^*+2\delta} 2^{-nD(P\|Q)} \tag{12.156}$$

$$\le \sum_{P \in E \cap \mathcal{P}_n : D(P\|Q) > D^*+2\delta} 2^{-n(D^*+2\delta)} \tag{12.157}$$

$$\le (n+1)^{|\mathcal{X}|} 2^{-n(D^*+2\delta)} \ , \tag{12.158}$$

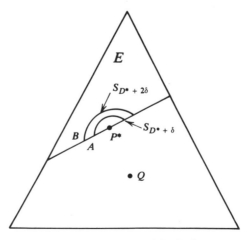

Figure 12.6. The conditional limit theorem.

since there are only a polynomial number of types. On the other hand,

$$Q^n(A) \geq Q^n(S_{D*+\delta} \cap E) \tag{12.159}$$

$$= \sum_{P \in E \cap \mathscr{P}_n : D(P\|Q) \leq D*+\delta} Q^n(T(P)) \tag{12.160}$$

$$\geq \sum_{P \in E \cap \mathscr{P}_n : D(P\|Q) \leq D*+\delta} \frac{1}{(n+1)^{|\mathscr{X}|}} 2^{-nD(P\|Q)} \tag{12.161}$$

$$\geq \frac{1}{(n+1)^{|\mathscr{X}|}} 2^{-n(D*+\delta)}, \qquad \text{for } n \text{ sufficiently large}, \tag{12.162}$$

since the sum is greater than one of the terms, and for sufficiently large n, there exists at least one type in $S_{D*+\delta} \cap E \cap \mathscr{P}_n$. Then for n sufficiently large

$$\Pr(P_{X^n} \in B | P_{X^n} \in E) = \frac{Q^n(B \cap E)}{Q^n(E)} \tag{12.163}$$

$$\leq \frac{Q^n(B)}{Q^n(A)} \tag{12.164}$$

$$\leq \frac{(n+1)^{|\mathscr{X}|} 2^{-n(D*+2\delta)}}{\frac{1}{(n+1)^{|\mathscr{X}|}} 2^{-n(D*+\delta)}} \tag{12.165}$$

$$= (n+1)^{2|\mathscr{X}|} 2^{-n\delta}, \tag{12.166}$$

which goes to 0 as $n \to \infty$. Hence the conditional probability of B goes to 0 as $n \to \infty$, which implies that the conditional probability of A goes to 1.

We now show that all the members of A are close to $P*$ in relative entropy. For all members of A,

$$D(P\|Q) \leq D* + 2\delta. \tag{12.167}$$

Hence by the "Pythagorean" theorem (Theorem 12.6.1),

$$D(P\|P*) + D(P*\|Q) \leq D(P\|Q) \leq D* + 2\delta, \tag{12.168}$$

which in turn implies that

$$D(P\|P*) \leq 2\delta, \tag{12.169}$$

since $D(P*\|Q) = D*$. Thus $P_\mathbf{x} \in A$ implies that $D(P_\mathbf{x}\|Q) \leq D* + 2\delta$, and therefore that $D(P_\mathbf{x}\|P*) \leq 2\delta$. Consequently, since $\Pr\{P_{X^n} \in A | P_{X^n} \in E\} \to 1$, it follows that

$$\Pr(D(P_{X^n}\|P^*)\leq 2\delta|P_{X^n}\in E)\rightarrow 1 \qquad (12.170)$$

as $n\rightarrow\infty$.

By Lemma 12.6.1, the fact that the relative entropy is small implies that the $\mathscr{L}_1$ distance is small, which in turn implies that $\max_{a\in\mathscr{X}}|P_{X^n}(a)-P^*(a)|$ is small. Thus $\Pr(|P_{X^n}(a)-P^*(a)|\geq\epsilon|P_{X^n}\in E)\rightarrow 0$ as $n\rightarrow\infty$. Alternatively, this can be written as

$$\Pr(X_1=a|P_{X^n}\in E)\rightarrow P^*(a)\quad\text{in probability}. \qquad (12.171)$$

In this theorem, we have only proved that the marginal distribution goes to P^* as $n\rightarrow\infty$. Using a similar argument, we can prove a stronger version of this theorem, i.e.,

$$\Pr(X_1=a_1,X_2=a_2,\ldots,X_m=a_m|P_{X^n}\in E)\rightarrow\prod_{i=1}^m P^*(a_i)\quad\text{in probability}.$$

$$(12.172)$$

This holds for fixed m as $n\rightarrow\infty$. The result is not true for $m=n$, since there are end effects; given that the type of the sequence is in E, the last elements of the sequence can be determined from the remaining elements, and the elements are no longer independent. The conditional limit theorem states that the first few elements are asymptotically independent with common distribution P^*.

Example 12.6.2: As an example of the conditional limit theorem, let us consider the case when n fair dice are rolled. Suppose that the sum of the outcomes exceeds $4n$. Then by the conditional limit theorem, the probability that the first die shows a number $a\in\{1,2,\ldots,6\}$ is approximately $P^*(a)$, where $P^*(a)$ is the distribution in E that is closest to the uniform distribution, where $E=\{P:\Sigma P(a)a\geq 4\}$. This is the maximum entropy distribution given by

$$P^*(x)=\frac{2^{\lambda x}}{\Sigma_{i=1}^6 2^{\lambda i}}, \qquad (12.173)$$

with λ chosen so that $\Sigma iP^*(i)=4$ (see Chapter 11). Here P^* is the conditional distribution on the first (or any other) die. Apparently the first few dice inspected will behave as if they are independently drawn according to an exponential distribution.

12.7 HYPOTHESIS TESTING

One of the standard problems in statistics is to decide between two alternative explanations for the observed data. For example, in medical testing, one may wish to test whether a new drug is effective or not. Similarly, a sequence of coin tosses may reveal whether the coin is biased or not.

These problems are examples of the general hypothesis testing problem. In the simplest case, we have to decide between two i.i.d. distributions. The general problem can be stated as follows:

Problem: Let $X_1, X_2, \ldots, X_n$ be i.i.d. $\sim Q(x)$. We consider two hypotheses:

- $H_1: Q = P_1$.
- $H_2: Q = P_2$.

Consider the general decision function $g(x_1, x_2, \ldots, x_n)$, where $g(x_1, x_2, \ldots, x_n) = 1$ implies that H_1 is accepted and $g(x_1, x_2, \ldots, x_n) = 2$ implies that H_2 is accepted. Since the function takes on only two values, the test can also be specified by specifying the set A over which $g(x_1, x_2, \ldots, x_n)$ is 1; the complement of this set is the set where $g(x_1, x_2, \ldots, x_n)$ has the value 2. We define the two probabilities of error:

$$\alpha = \Pr(g(X_1, X_2, \ldots, X_n) = 2 | H_1 \text{ true}) = P_1^n(A^c) \qquad (12.174)$$

and

$$\beta = \Pr(g(X_1, X_2, \ldots, X_n) = 1 | H_2 \text{ true}) = P_2^n(A). \qquad (12.175)$$

In general, we wish to minimize both probabilities, but there is a trade-off. Thus we minimize one of the probabilities of error subject to a constraint on the other probability of error. The best achievable error exponent in the probability of error for this problem is given by Stein's lemma.

We first prove the Neyman-Pearson lemma, which derives the form of the optimum test between two hypotheses. We derive the result for discrete distributions; the same results can be derived for continuous distributions as well.

Theorem 12.7.1 (*Neyman-Pearson lemma*): *Let* $X_1, X_2, \ldots, X_n$ *be drawn i.i.d. according to probability mass function P. Consider the decision problem corresponding to hypotheses* $Q = P_1$ *vs.* $Q = P_2$. *For* $T \geq 0$, *define a region*

$$A_n(T) = \left\{ \frac{P_1(x_1, x_2, \ldots, x_n)}{P_2(x_1, x_2, \ldots, x_n)} > T \right\}. \qquad (12.176)$$

Let

$$\alpha^* = P_1^n(A_n^c(T)), \qquad \beta^* = P_2^n(A_n(T)), \qquad (12.177)$$

*be the corresponding probabilities of error corresponding to decision
region A_n. Let B_n be any other decision region with associated probabilities of error α and β. If $\alpha \le \alpha^*$, then $\beta \ge \beta^*$.*

Proof: Let $A = A_n(T)$ be the region defined in (12.176) and let $B \in \mathcal{X}^n$ be any other acceptance region. Let ϕ_A and ϕ_B be the indicator functions of the decision regions A and B respectively. Then for all $\mathbf{x} = (x_1, x_2, \ldots, x_n) \in \mathcal{X}^n$,

$$[\phi_A(\mathbf{x}) - \phi_B(\mathbf{x})][P_1(\mathbf{x}) - TP_2(\mathbf{x})] \ge 0 . \tag{12.178}$$

This can be seen by considering separately the cases $\mathbf{x} \in A$ and $\mathbf{x} \notin A$. Multiplying out and integrating this over the entire space, we obtain

$$0 \le \sum (\phi_A P_1 - T\phi_A P_2 - P_1 \phi_B + TP_2 \phi_B) \tag{12.179}$$

$$= \sum_A (P_1 - TP_2) - \sum_B (P_1 - TP_2) \tag{12.180}$$

$$= (1 - \alpha^*) - T\beta^* - (1 - \alpha) + T\beta \tag{12.181}$$

$$= T(\beta - \beta^*) - (\alpha^* - \alpha) . \tag{12.182}$$

Since $T \ge 0$, we have proved the theorem. $\square$

The Neyman-Pearson lemma indicates that the optimum test for two hypotheses is of the form

$$\frac{P_1(X_1, X_2, \ldots, X_n)}{P_2(X_1, X_2, \ldots, X_n)} > T . \tag{12.183}$$

This is the likelihood ratio test and the quantity $\frac{P_1(X_1, X_2, \ldots, X_n)}{P_2(X_1, X_2, \ldots, X_n)}$ is called the *likelihood ratio*.

For example, in a test between two Gaussian distributions, i.e., between $f_1 = \mathcal{N}(1, \sigma^2)$ and $f_2 = \mathcal{N}(-1, \sigma^2)$, the likelihood ratio becomes

$$\frac{f_1(X_1, X_2, \ldots, X_n)}{f_2(X_1, X_2, \ldots, X_n)} = \frac{\prod_{i=1}^n \frac{1}{\sqrt{2\pi\sigma^2}} e^{-\frac{(X_i-1)^2}{2\sigma^2}}}{\prod_{i=1}^n \frac{1}{\sqrt{2\pi\sigma^2}} e^{-\frac{(X_i+1)^2}{2\sigma^2}}} \tag{12.184}$$

$$= e^{+\frac{2\sum_{i=1}^n X_i}{\sigma^2}} \tag{12.185}$$

$$= e^{+\frac{2n\bar{X}_n}{\sigma^2}} . \tag{12.186}$$

Hence the likelihood ratio test consists of comparing the sample mean

$\bar{X}_n$ with a threshold. If we want the two probabilities of error to be equal, we should set $T = 1$. This is illustrated in Figure 12.7.

In the above theorem, we have shown that the optimum test is a likelihood ratio test. We can rewrite the log-likelihood ratio as

$$L(X_1, X_2, \ldots, X_n) = \log \frac{P_1(X_1, X_2, \ldots, X_n)}{P_2(X_1, X_2, \ldots, X_n)} \tag{12.187}$$

$$= \sum_{i=1}^{n} \log \frac{P_1(X_i)}{P_2(X_i)} \tag{12.188}$$

$$= \sum_{a \in \mathcal{X}} n P_{X^n}(a) \log \frac{P_1(a)}{P_2(a)} \tag{12.189}$$

$$= \sum_{a \in \mathcal{X}} n P_{X^n}(a) \log \frac{P_1(a)}{P_2(a)} \frac{P_{X^n}(a)}{P_{X^n}(a)} \tag{12.190}$$

$$= \sum_{a \in \mathcal{X}} n P_{X^n}(a) \log \frac{P_{X^n}(a)}{P_2(a)} - \sum_{a \in \mathcal{X}} n P_{X^n}(a) \log \frac{P_{X^n}(a)}{P_1(a)} \tag{12.191}$$

$$= n D(P_{X^n} \| P_2) - n D(P_{X^n} \| P_1), \tag{12.192}$$

the difference between the relative entropy distances of the sample type to each of the two distributions. Hence the likelihood ratio test

$$\frac{P_1(X_1, X_2, \ldots, X_n)}{P_2(X_1, X_2, \ldots, X_n)} > T \tag{12.193}$$

is equivalent to

$$D(P_{X^n} \| P_2) - D(P_{X^n} \| P_1) > \frac{1}{n} \log T . \tag{12.194}$$

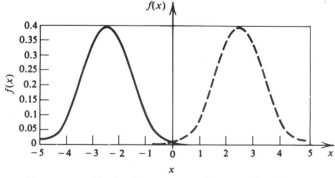

Figure 12.7. Testing between two Gaussian distributions.

We can consider the test to be equivalent to specifying a region of the simplex of types which corresponds to choosing hypothesis 1. The optimum region is of the form (12.194), for which the boundary of the region is the set of types for which the difference between the distances is a constant. This boundary is the analog of the perpendicular bisector in Euclidean geometry. The test is illustrated in Figure 12.8.

We now offer some informal arguments based on Sanov's theorem to show how to choose the threshold to obtain different probabilities of error. Let B denote the set on which hypothesis 1 is accepted. The probability of error of the first kind is

$$\alpha_n = P_1^n(P_{X^n} \in B^c) . \tag{12.195}$$

Since the set B^c is convex, we can use Sanov's theorem to show that the probability of error is essentially determined by the relative entropy of the closest member of B^c to P_1. Therefore,

$$\alpha_n \doteq 2^{-nD(P_1^*\|P_1)} , \tag{12.196}$$

where P_1^* is the closest element of B^c to distribution P_1. Similarly,

$$\beta_n \doteq 2^{-nD(P_2^*\|P_2)} , \tag{12.197}$$

where P_2^* is the closest element in B to the distribution P_2.

Now minimizing $D(P\|P_2)$ subject to the constraint $D(P\|P_2) - D(P\|P_1) \ge \frac{1}{n} \log T$ will yield the type in B that is closest to P_2. Setting up the minimization of $D(P\|P_2)$ subject to $D(P\|P_2) - D(P\|P_1) = \frac{1}{n} \log T$ using Lagrange multipliers, we have

$$J(P) = \sum P(x) \log \frac{P(x)}{P_2(x)} + \lambda \sum P(x) \log \frac{P_1(x)}{P_2(x)} + \nu \sum P(x) . \tag{12.198}$$

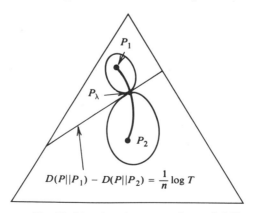

Figure 12.8. The likelihood ratio test on the probability simplex.

Differentiating with respect to $P(x)$ and setting to 0, we have

$$\log \frac{P(x)}{P_2(x)} + 1 + \lambda \log \frac{P_1(x)}{P_2(x)} + \nu = 0 . \tag{12.199}$$

Solving this set of equations, we obtain the minimizing P of the form

$$P_2^* = P_{\lambda*} = \frac{P_1^\lambda(x) P_2^{1-\lambda}(x)}{\sum_{a \in \mathscr{X}} P_1^\lambda(a) P_2^{1-\lambda}(a)} , \tag{12.200}$$

where λ is chosen so that $D(P_{\lambda*} \| P_1) - D(P_{\lambda*} \| P_2) = \frac{\log T}{n}$.

From the symmetry of expression (12.200), it is clear that $P_1^* - P_2^*$ and that the probabilities of error behave exponentially with exponents given by the relative entropies $D(P^* \| P_1)$ and $D(P^* \| P_2)$. Also note from the equation that as $\lambda \to 1$, $P_\lambda \to P_1$ and as $\lambda \to 0$, $P_\lambda \to P_2$. The line that P_λ traces out as λ varies is a geodesic in the simplex. Here P_λ is a normalized convex combination, where the combination is in the exponent (Figure 12.8).

In the next section, we calculate the best error exponent when one of the two types of error goes to zero arbitrarily slowly (Stein's lemma). We will also minimize the weighted sum of the two probabilities of error and obtain the Chernoff bound.

12.8   STEIN'S LEMMA

We now consider the case when one of the probabilities of error is fixed and we wish to minimize the other probability of error. The best error exponent in this case is given by Stein's lemma.

Theorem 12.8.1 (*Stein's lemma*): *Let* $X_1, X_2, \ldots, X_n$ *be i.i.d.* $\sim Q$. *Consider the hypothesis test between two alternatives,* $Q = P_1$ *and* $Q = P_2$, *where* $D(P_1 \| P_2) < \infty$. *Let* $A_n \subseteq \mathscr{X}^n$ *be an acceptance region for hypothesis 1. Let the probabilities of error be*

$$\alpha_n = P_1^n(A_n^c) , \qquad \beta_n = P_2^n(A_n) . \tag{12.201}$$

and for $0 < \epsilon < \frac{1}{2}$, *define*

$$\beta_n^\epsilon = \min_{\substack{A_n \subseteq \mathscr{X}^n \\ \alpha_n < \epsilon}} \beta_n . \tag{12.202}$$

Then

$$\lim_{\epsilon \to 0} \lim_{n \to \infty} \frac{1}{n} \log \beta_n^\epsilon = -D(P_1 \| P_2) . \tag{12.203}$$

Proof: To prove the theorem, we construct a sequence of acceptance regions $A_n \subseteq \mathscr{X}^n$ such that $\alpha_n < \epsilon$ and $\beta_n \doteq 2^{-nD(P_1\|P_2)}$. We then show that no other sequence of tests has an asymptotically better exponent.

First, we define

$$A_n = \left\{ \mathbf{x} \in \mathscr{X}^n : 2^{+n(D(P_1\|P_2)-\delta)} \le \frac{P_1(\mathbf{x})}{P_2(\mathbf{x})} \le 2^{+n(D(P_1\|P_2)+\delta)} \right\}. \quad (12.204)$$

Then we have the following properties:

1. $P_1^n(A_n) \to 1$. This follows from

$$P_1^n(A_n) = P_1^n\left(\frac{1}{n} \sum_{i=1}^n \log \frac{P_1(X_i)}{P_2(X_i)} \in (D(P_1\|P_2) - \delta, D(P_1\|P_2) + \delta) \right)$$

$$(12.205)$$

$$\to 1 \quad (12.206)$$

by the strong law of large numbers, since $D(P_1\|P_2) = E_{P_1}\left(\log \frac{P_1(X)}{P_2(X)} \right)$. Hence for sufficiently large n, $\alpha_n < \epsilon$.

2. $P_2^n(A_n) \le 2^{-n(D(P_1\|P_2)-\delta)}$. Using the definition of A_n, we have

$$P_2^n(A_n) = \sum_{A_n} P_2(\mathbf{x}) \quad (12.207)$$

$$\le \sum_{A_n} P_1(\mathbf{x}) 2^{-n(D(P_1\|P_2)-\delta)} \quad (12.208)$$

$$= 2^{-n(D(P_1\|P_2)-\delta)} \sum_{A_n} P_1(\mathbf{x}) \quad (12.209)$$

$$= 2^{-n(D(P_1\|P_2)-\delta)}(1 - \alpha_n). \quad (12.210)$$

Similarly, we can show that

$$P_2^n(A_n) \ge 2^{-n(D(P_1\|P_2)+\delta)}(1 - \alpha_n). \quad (12.211)$$

Hence

$$\frac{1}{n} \log \beta_n \le -D(P_1\|P_2) + \delta + \frac{\log(1 - \alpha_n)}{n}, \quad (12.212)$$

and

$$\frac{1}{n} \log \beta_n \ge -D(P_1\|P_2) - \delta + \frac{\log(1 - \alpha_n)}{n}. \quad (12.213)$$

Hence

$$\lim_{n \to \infty} \lim \frac{1}{n} \log \beta_n = -D(P_1 \| P_2). \tag{12.214}$$

3. We now prove that no other sequence of acceptance regions does better. Let $B_n \subseteq \mathcal{X}^n$ be any other sequence of acceptance regions with $\alpha_{n, B_n} = P_1^n(B_n^c) < \epsilon$. Let $\beta_{n, B_n} = P_2^n(B_n)$. We will show that $\beta_{n, B_n} \geq 2^{-n(D(P_1 \| P_2) - \epsilon)}$.

Here

$$\beta_{n, B_n} = P_2^n(B_n) \geq P_2^n(A_n \cap B_n) \tag{12.215}$$

$$= \sum_{A_n \cap B_n} P_2(\mathbf{x}) \tag{12.216}$$

$$\geq \sum_{A_n \cap B_n} P_1(\mathbf{x}) 2^{-n(D(P_1 \| P_2) + \delta)} \tag{12.217}$$

$$= 2^{-n(D(P_1 \| P_2) + \delta)} \sum_{A_n \cap B_n} P_1(\mathbf{x}) \tag{12.218}$$

$$\geq (1 - \alpha_n - \alpha_{n, B_n}) 2^{-n(D(P_1 \| P_2) + \delta)}, \tag{12.219}$$

where the last inequality follows from the union of events bound as follows:

$$\sum_{A_n \cap B_n} P_1(\mathbf{x}) = P_1(A_n \cap B_n) \tag{12.220}$$

$$= 1 - P_1(A_n^c \cup B_n^c) \tag{12.221}$$

$$\geq 1 - P_1(A_n^c) - P_1(B_n^c) \tag{12.222}$$

$$= 1 - \alpha_n - \alpha_{n, B_n}. \tag{12.223}$$

Hence

$$\frac{1}{n} \log \beta_{n, B_n} \geq -D(P_1 \| P_2) - \delta - \frac{\log(1 - \alpha_n - \alpha_{n, B_n})}{n}, \tag{12.224}$$

and since $\delta > 0$ is arbitrary,

$$\lim_{n \to \infty} \lim \frac{1}{n} \log \beta_{n, B_n} \geq -D(P_1 \| P_2). \tag{12.225}$$

Thus no sequence of sets B_n has an exponent better than $D(P_1 \| P_2)$. But the sequence A_n achieves the exponent $D(P_1 \| P_2)$. Thus A_n is asymptotically optimal, and the best error exponent is $D(P_1 \| P_2)$. $\square$

12.9   CHERNOFF BOUND

We have considered the problem of hypothesis testing in the classical setting, in which we treat the two probabilities of error separately. In the derivation of Stein's lemma, we set $\alpha_n \le \epsilon$ and achieved $\beta_n \doteq 2^{-nD}$. But this approach lacks symmetry. Instead, we can follow a Bayesian approach, in which we assign prior probabilities to both the hypotheses. In this case, we wish to minimize the overall probability of error given by the weighted sum of the individual probabilities of error. The resulting error exponent is the Chernoff information.

The setup is as follows: $X_1, X_2, \ldots, X_n$ i.i.d. $\sim Q$. We have two hypotheses: $Q = P_1$ with prior probability π_1 and $Q = P_2$ with prior probability π_2. The overall probability of error is

$$P_e^{(n)} = \pi_1 \alpha_n + \pi_2 \beta_n . \tag{12.226}$$

Let

$$D^* = \lim_{n \to \infty} \min_{A_n \subseteq \mathscr{X}^n} - \frac{1}{n} \log P_e^{(n)} . \tag{12.227}$$

Theorem 12.9.1 (*Chernoff*): *The best achievable exponent in the Bayesian probability of error is D^*, where*

$$D^* = D(P_{\lambda*} \| P_1) = D(P_{\lambda*} \| P_2) , \tag{12.228}$$

with

$$P_\lambda = \frac{P_1^\lambda(x) P_2^{1-\lambda}(x)}{\sum_{a \in \mathscr{X}} P_1^\lambda(a) P_2^{1-\lambda}(a)} \tag{12.229}$$

and λ^* the value of λ such that

$$D(P_{\lambda*} \| P_1) = D(P_{\lambda*} \| P_2) . \tag{12.230}$$

Proof: The basic details of the proof were given in the previous section. We have shown that the optimum test is a likelihood ratio test, which can be considered to be of the form

$$D(P_{X^n} \| P_2) - D(P_{X^n} \| P_1) > T . \tag{12.231}$$

The test divides the probability simplex into regions corresponding to hypothesis 1 and hypothesis 2, respectively. This is illustrated in Figure 12.9.

Let A be the set of types associated with hypothesis 1. From the

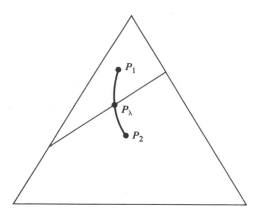

Figure 12.9. The probability simplex and Chernoff's bound.

discussion preceding (12.200), it follows that the closest point in the set A^c to P_1 is on the boundary of A, and is of the form given by (12.229). Then from the discussion in the last section, it is clear that P_λ is the distribution in A that is closest to P_2; it is also the distribution in A^c that is closest to P_1. By Sanov's theorem, we can calculate the associated probabilities of error

$$\alpha_n = P_1^n(A^c) \doteq 2^{-nD(P_{\lambda*}\|P_1)} \tag{12.232}$$

and

$$\beta_n = P_2^n(A) \doteq 2^{-nD(P_{\lambda*}\|P_2)} . \tag{12.233}$$

In the Bayesian case, the overall probability of error is the weighted sum of the two probabilities of error,

$$P_e \doteq \pi_1 2^{-nD(P_\lambda\|P_1)} + \pi_2 2^{-nD(P_\lambda\|P_2)} \doteq 2^{-n \min\{D(P_\lambda\|P_1), D(P_\lambda\|P_2)\}} , \tag{12.234}$$

since the exponential rate is determined by the worst exponent. Since $D(P_\lambda\|P_1)$ increases with λ and $D(P_\lambda\|P_2)$ decreases with λ, the maximum value of the minimum of $\{D(P_\lambda\|P_1), D(P_\lambda\|P_2)\}$ is attained when they are equal. This is illustrated in Figure 12.10.

Hence, we choose λ so that

$$D(P_\lambda\|P_1) = D(P_\lambda\|P_2) \overset{\triangle}{=} C(P_1, P_2) . \tag{12.235}$$

Thus $C(P_1, P_2)$ is the highest achievable exponent for the probability of error and is called the Chernoff information. $\square$

The above definition is equivalent to the standard definition of *Chernoff information*,

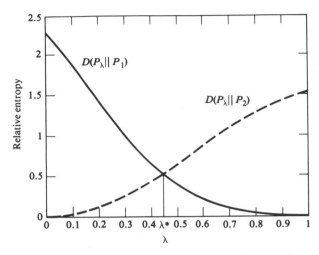

Figure 12.10. Relative entropy $D(P_\lambda\|P_1)$ and $D(P_\lambda\|P_2)$ as a function of λ.

$$C(P_1, P_2) = -\min_{0\le\lambda\le1} \log\left(\sum_x P_1^\lambda(x)P_2^{1-\lambda}(x)\right). \qquad (12.236)$$

It is left as an exercise to the reader to show (algebraically) the equivalence of (12.235) and (12.236). We will briefly outline the usual derivation of the Chernoff bound. The maximum *a posteriori* probability decision rule minimizes the Bayesian probability of error. The decision region A for hypothesis 1 for the maximum *a posteriori* rule is

$$A = \left\{\mathbf{x}: \frac{\pi_1 P_1(\mathbf{x})}{\pi_2 P_2(\mathbf{x})} > 1\right\}, \qquad (12.237)$$

the set of outcomes where the *a posteriori* probability of hypothesis 1 is greater than the *a posteriori* probability of hypothesis 2. The probability of error for this rule is

$$P_e = \pi_1 \alpha_n + \pi_2 \beta_n \qquad (12.238)$$

$$= \sum_{A^c} \pi_1 P_1 + \sum_A \pi_2 P_2 \qquad (12.239)$$

$$= \sum \min\{\pi_1 P_1, \pi_2 P_2\}. \qquad (12.240)$$

Now for any two positive numbers a and b, we have

$$\min\{a, b\} \le a^\lambda b^{1-\lambda}, \quad \text{for all } 0\le\lambda\le1. \qquad (12.241)$$

Using this to continue the chain, we have

$$P_e = \sum \min\{\pi_1 P_1, \pi_2 P_2\} \qquad (12.242)$$

$$\leq \sum (\pi_1 P_1)^\lambda (\pi_2 P_2)^{1-\lambda} \qquad (12.243)$$

$$\leq \sum P_1^\lambda P_2^{1-\lambda} . \qquad (12.244)$$

For a sequence of i.i.d. observations, $P_k(\mathbf{x}) = \prod_{i=1}^n P_k(x_i)$, and

$$P_e^{(n)} \leq \sum \pi_1^\lambda \pi_2^{1-\lambda} \prod_i P_1^\lambda(x_i) P_2^{1-\lambda}(x_i) \qquad (12.245)$$

$$= \pi_1^\lambda \pi_2^{1-\lambda} \prod_i \sum P_1^\lambda(x_i) P_2^{1-\lambda}(x_i) \qquad (12.246)$$

$$\overset{(a)}{\leq} \prod_i \sum P_1^\lambda P_2^{1-\lambda} \qquad (12.247)$$

$$= \left(\sum P_1^\lambda P_2^{1-\lambda} \right)^n , \qquad (12.248)$$

where (a) follows since $\pi_1 \leq 1$, $\pi_2 \leq 1$. Hence, we have

$$\frac{1}{n} \log P_e^{(n)} \leq \log \sum P_1^\lambda(x) P_2^{1-\lambda}(x) \qquad (12.249)$$

Since this is true for all λ, we can take the minimum over $0 \leq \lambda \leq 1$, resulting in the Chernoff bound. This proves that the exponent is no better than $C(P_1, P_2)$. Achievability follows from Theorem 12.9.1.

Note that the Bayesian error exponent does not depend on the actual value of π_1 and π_2, as long as they are non-zero. Essentially, the effect of the prior is washed out for large sample sizes. The optimum decision rule is to choose the hypothesis with the maximum *a posteriori* probability, which corresponds to the test

$$\frac{\pi_1 P_1(X_1, X_2, \ldots, X_n)}{\pi_2 P_2(X_1, X_2, \ldots, X_n)} \gtrless 1 . \qquad (12.250)$$

Taking the log and dividing by n, this test can be rewritten as

$$\frac{1}{n} \log \frac{\pi_1}{\pi_2} + \frac{1}{n} \sum_i \log \frac{P_1(X_i)}{P_2(X_i)} \lessgtr 0 , \qquad (12.251)$$

where the second term tends to $D(P_1 \| P_2)$ or $- D(P_2 \| P_1)$ accordingly as P_1 or P_2 is the true distribution. The first term tends to 0, and the effect of the prior distribution washes out.

Finally, to round off our discussion of large deviation theory and hypothesis testing, we consider an example of the conditional limit theorem.

Example 12.9.1: Suppose major league baseball players have a batting average of 260 with a standard deviation of 15 and suppose that minor league ballplayers have a batting average of 240 with a standard deviation of 15. A group of 100 ballplayers from one of the leagues (the league is chosen at random) is found to have a group batting average greater than 250, and is therefore judged to be major leaguers. We are now told that we are mistaken; these players are minor leaguers. What can we say about the distribution of batting averages among these 100 players? It will turn out that the distribution of batting averages among these players will have a mean of 250 and a standard deviation of 15. This follows from the conditional limit theorem. To see this, we abstract the problem as follows.

Let us consider an example of testing between two Gaussian distributions, $f_1 = \mathcal{N}(1, \sigma^2)$ and $f_2 = \mathcal{N}(-1, \sigma^2)$, with different means and the same variance. As discussed in the last section, the likelihood ratio test in this case is equivalent to comparing the sample mean with a threshold. The Bayes test is "Accept the hypothesis $f = f_1$ if $\frac{1}{n} \sum_{i=1}^{n} X_i > 0$."

Now assume that we make an error of the first kind (we say $f = f_1$ when indeed $f = f_2$) in this test. What is the conditional distribution of the samples given that we have made an error?

We might guess at various possibilities:

- The sample will look like a $(\frac{1}{2}, \frac{1}{2})$ mix of the two normal distributions. Plausible as this is, it is incorrect.
- $X_i \approx 0$ for all i. This is quite clearly very very unlikely, although it is conditionally likely that $\bar{X}_n$ is close to 0.
- The correct answer is given by the conditional limit theorem. If the true distribution is f_2 and the sample type is in the set A, the conditional distribution is close to f^*, the distribution in A that is closest to f_2. By symmetry, this corresponds to $\lambda = \frac{1}{2}$ in (12.229). Calculating the distribution, we get

$$f^*(x) = \frac{\left(\frac{1}{\sqrt{2\pi\sigma^2}} e^{-\frac{(x-1)^2}{2\sigma^2}}\right)^{1/2} \left(\frac{1}{\sqrt{2\pi\sigma^2}} e^{-\frac{(x+1)^2}{2\sigma^2}}\right)^{1/2}}{\int \left(\frac{1}{\sqrt{2\pi\sigma^2}} e^{-\frac{(x-1)^2}{2\sigma^2}}\right)^{1/2} \left(\frac{1}{\sqrt{2\pi\sigma^2}} e^{-\frac{(x+1)^2}{2\sigma^2}}\right)^{1/2} dx} \qquad (12.252)$$

$$= \frac{\frac{1}{\sqrt{2\pi\sigma^2}} e^{-\frac{(x^2+1)}{2\sigma^2}}}{\int \frac{1}{\sqrt{2\pi\sigma^2}} e^{-\frac{(x^2+1)}{2\sigma^2}} dx} \qquad (12.253)$$

$$= \frac{1}{\sqrt{2\pi\sigma^2}} \, e^{-\frac{x^2}{2\sigma^2}} \tag{12.254}$$

$$= \mathcal{N}(0, \sigma^2). \tag{12.255}$$

It is interesting to note that the conditional distribution is normal with mean 0 and with the same variance as the original distributions. This is strange but true; if we mistake a normal population for another, the "shape" of this population still looks normal with the same variance and a different mean. Apparently, this rare event does not result from bizarre looking data.

Example 12.9.2 (*Large deviation theory and football*): Consider a very simple version of football in which the score is directly related to the number of yards gained. Assume that the coach has a choice between two strategies: running or passing. Associated with each strategy is a distribution on the number of yards gained. For example, in general, running results in a gain of a few yards with very high probability, while passing results in huge gains with low probability. Examples of the distributions are illustrated in Figure 12.11.

At the beginning of the game, the coach uses the strategy that promises the greatest expected gain. Now assume that we are in the closing minutes of the game and one of the teams is leading by a large margin. (Let us ignore first downs and adaptable defenses.) So the trailing team will win only if it is very lucky. If luck is required to win, then we might as well assume that we will be lucky and play accordingly. What is the appropriate strategy?

Assume that the team has only n plays left and it must gain l yards, where l is much larger than n times the expected gain under each play. The probability that the team succeeds in achieving l yards is exponentially small; hence, we can use the large deviation results and Sanov's theorem to calculate the probability of this event.

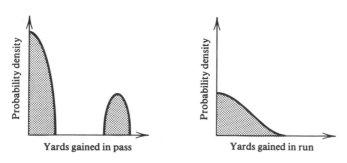

Figure 12.11. Distribution of yards gained in a run or a pass play.

To be precise, we wish to calculate the probability that $\Sigma_{i=1}^{n} Z_i \geq n\alpha$, where Z_i are independent random variables, and Z_i has a distribution corresponding to the strategy chosen.

The situation is illustrated in Figure 12.12. Let E be the set of types corresponding to the constraint,

$$E = \left\{ P: \sum_{a \in \mathcal{X}} P(a)a \geq \alpha \right\}. \tag{12.256}$$

If P_1 is the distribution corresponding to passing all the time, then the probability of winning is the probability that the sample type is in E, which by Sanov's theorem is $2^{-nD(P_1^*\|P_1)}$, where P_1^* is the distribution in E that is closest to P_1. Similarly, if the coach uses the running game all the time, the probability of winning is $2^{-nD(P_2^*\|P_2)}$. What if he uses a mixture of strategies? Is it possible that $2^{-nD(P_\lambda^*\|P_\lambda)}$, the probability of winning with a mixed strategy, $P_\lambda = \lambda P_1 + (1-\lambda)P_2$, is better than the probability of winning with either pure passing or pure running?

The somewhat surprising answer is yes, as can be shown by example. This provides a reason to use a mixed strategy other than the fact that it confuses the defense.

We end this section with another inequality due to Chernoff, which is a special version of Markov's inequality. This inequality is called the Chernoff bound.

Lemma 12.9.1: *Let Y be any random variable and let $\psi(s)$ be the moment generating function of Y,*

$$\psi(s) = Ee^{sY}. \tag{12.257}$$

Then for all $s \geq 0$,

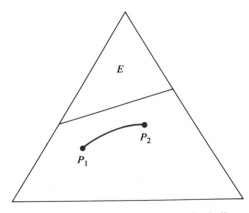

Figure 12.12. Probability simplex for a football game.

$$\Pr(Y \geq a) \leq e^{-sa} \psi(s) . \qquad (12.258)$$

Proof: Apply Markov's inequality to the non-negative random variable e^{sY}. $\square$

12.10   LEMPEL-ZIV CODING

We now describe a scheme for universal data compression due to Ziv and Lempel [291], which is simple to implement and has an asymptotic rate approaching the entropy of the source. The algorithm is particularly simple and has become popular as the standard algorithm for file compression on computers because of its speed and efficiency.

We will consider a binary source throughout this section. The results generalize easily to any finite alphabet.

Algorithm: The source sequence is sequentially parsed into strings that have not appeared so far. For example, if the string is 1011010100010..., we parse it as 1,0,11,01,010,00,10,.... After every comma, we look along the input sequence until we come to the shortest string that has not been marked off before. Since this is the shortest such string, all its prefixes must have occurred earlier. In particular, the string consisting of all but the last bit of this string must have occurred earlier. We code this phrase by giving the location of the prefix and the value of the last bit.

Let $c(n)$ be the number of phrases in the parsing of the input n-sequence. We need $\log c(n)$ bits to describe the location of the prefix to the phrase and 1 bit to describe the last bit. For example, the code for the above sequence is (000,1)(000,0)(001,1)(010,1)(100,0)(010,0)(001,0), where the first number of each pair gives the index of the prefix and the second number gives the last bit of the phrase. Decoding the coded sequence is straightforward and we can recover the source sequence without error.

The above algorithm requires two passes over the string—in the first pass, we parse the string and calculate $c(n)$, the number of phrases in the parsed string. We then use that to decide how many bits ($\log c(n)$) to allot to the pointers in the algorithm. In the second pass, we calculate the pointers and produce the coded string as indicated above. The algorithm described above allots an equal number of bits to all the pointers. This is not necessary, since the range of the pointers is smaller at the initial portion of the string. The algorithm can be modified so that it requires only one pass over the string and uses fewer bits for the initial pointers. These modifications do not affect the asymptotic efficiency of the algorithm. Some of the implementation details are discussed by Welch [269] and Bell, Cleary and Witten [22].

In the example, we have not compressed the string; instead, we have expanded the number of bits by more than a factor of 2. But for long strings the phrases will get longer, and describing the phrases by describing the location of the prefix will be more efficient. We will show that this algorithm asymptotically achieves the entropy rate for the unknown ergodic source.

Without loss of generality, we will assume that the source alphabet is binary. Thus $\mathscr{X} = \{0, 1\}$ throughout this section. We first define a parsing of the string to be a decomposition into phrases.

Definition: A *parsing* S of a binary string $x_1 x_2 \ldots x_n$ is a division of the string into phrases, separated by commas. A *distinct parsing* is a parsing such that no two phrases are identical.

For example, 0,111,1 is a distinct parsing of 01111, but 0,11,11 is a parsing which is not distinct.

The Lempel-Ziv algorithm described above gives a distinct parsing of the source sequence. Let $c(n)$ denote the number of phrases in the Lempel-Ziv parsing of a sequence of length n. Of course, $c(n)$ depends on the sequence X^n. The compressed sequence (after applying the Lempel-Ziv algorithm) consists of a list of $c(n)$ pairs of numbers, each pair consisting of a pointer to the previous occurrence of the prefix of the phrase and the last bit of the phrase. Each pointer requires $\log c(n)$ bits, and hence the total length of the compressed sequence is $c(n)(\log c(n) + 1)$ bits. We will now show that $\frac{c(n)(\log c(n) + 1)}{n} \to H(\mathscr{X})$ for a stationary ergodic sequence $X_1, X_2, \ldots, X_n$. Our proof is based on the simple proof of asymptotic optimality of Lempel-Ziv coding due to Wyner and Ziv [285].

We first prove a few lemmas that we need for the proof of the theorem. The first is a bound on the number of phrases possible in a distinct parsing of a binary sequence of length n.

Lemma 12.10.1 (*Lempel and Ziv*): *The number of phrases $c(n)$ in a distinct parsing of a binary sequence $X_1, X_2, \ldots, X_n$ satisfies*

$$c(n) \leq \frac{n}{(1 - \epsilon_n) \log n} \tag{12.259}$$

where $\epsilon_n \to 0$ as $n \to \infty$.

Proof: Let

$$n_k = \sum_{j=1}^{k} j 2^j = (k - 1) 2^{k+1} + 2 \tag{12.260}$$

be the sum of the lengths of all distinct strings of length less than or equal to k. The number of phrases c in a distinct parsing of a sequence of length n is maximized when all the phrases are as short as possible. If $n = n_k$, this occurs when all the phrases are of length $\leq k$, and thus

$$c(n_k) \leq \sum_{j=1}^{k} 2^j = 2^{k+1} - 2 < 2^{k+1} \leq \frac{n_k}{k-1} . \qquad (12.261)$$

If $n_k \leq n < n_{k+1}$, we write $n = n_k + \Delta$, where $\Delta < (k+1)2^{k+1}$. Then the parsing into shortest phrases has each of the phrases of length $\leq k$ and $\Delta/(k+1)$ phrases of length $k+1$. Thus

$$c(n) \leq \frac{n_k}{k-1} + \frac{\Delta}{k+1} \leq \frac{n_k + \Delta}{k-1} = \frac{n}{k-1} . \qquad (12.262)$$

We now bound the size of k for a given n. Let $n_k \leq n < n_{k+1}$. Then

$$n \geq n_k = (k-1)2^{k+1} + 2 \geq 2^k , \qquad (12.263)$$

and therefore

$$k \leq \log n . \qquad (12.264)$$

Moreover,

$$n \leq n_{k+1} = k2^{k+2} + 2 \leq (k+2)2^{k+2} \leq (\log n + 2)2^{k+2} \qquad (12.265)$$

by (12.264), and therefore

$$k + 2 \geq \log \frac{n}{\log n + 2} , \qquad (12.266)$$

or, for all $n \geq 4$,

$$k - 1 \geq \log n - \log(\log n + 2) - 3 \qquad (12.267)$$

$$= \left(1 - \frac{\log(\log n + 2) + 3}{\log n} \right) \log n \qquad (12.268)$$

$$\geq \left(1 - \frac{\log(2 \log n) + 3}{\log n} \right) \log n \qquad (12.269)$$

$$= \left(1 - \frac{\log(\log n) + 4}{\log n} \right) \log n \qquad (12.270)$$

$$= (1 - \epsilon_n) \log n . \qquad (12.271)$$

Note that $\epsilon_n = \min\{1, \frac{\log(\log n) + 4}{\log n}\}$. Combining (12.271) with (12.262), we obtain the lemma. $\square$

We will need a simple result on maximum entropy in the proof of the main theorem.

Lemma 12.10.2: *Let Z be a positive integer valued random variable with mean μ. Then the entropy $H(Z)$ is bounded by*

$$H(Z) \le (\mu + 1) \log(\mu + 1) - \mu \log \mu . \qquad (12.272)$$

Proof: The lemma follows directly from the results of Chapter 11, which show that the probability mass function that maximizes entropy subject to a constraint on the mean is the geometric distribution, for which we can compute the entropy. The details are left as an exercise for the reader. $\square$

Let $\{X_i\}_{i=-\infty}^{\infty}$ be a stationary ergodic process with probability mass function $P(x_1, x_2, \ldots, x_n)$. (Ergodic processes are discussed in greater detail in Section 15.7.) For a fixed integer k, define the kth order Markov approximation to P as

$$Q_k(x_{-(k-1)}, \ldots, x_0, x_1, \ldots, x_n) \triangleq P(x^0_{-(k-1)}) \prod_{j=1}^{n} P(x_j | x_{j-k}^{j-1}), \quad (12.273)$$

where $x_i^j \triangleq (x_i, x_{i+1}, \ldots, x_j)$, $i \le j$, and the initial state $x^0_{-(k-1)}$ will be part of the specification of Q_k. Since $P(X_n | X_{n-k}^{n-1})$ is itself an ergodic process, we have

$$-\frac{1}{n} \log Q_k(X_1, X_2, \ldots, X_n | X^0_{-(k-1)}) = -\frac{1}{n} \sum_{j=1}^{n} \log P(X_j | X_{j-k}^{j-1}) \quad (12.274)$$

$$\to -E \log P(X_j | X_{j-k}^{j-1}) \qquad (12.275)$$

$$= H(X_j | X_{j-k}^{j-1}) . \qquad (12.276)$$

We will bound the rate of the Lempel-Ziv code by the entropy rate of the kth order Markov approximation for all k. The entropy rate of the Markov approximation $H(X_j | X_{j-k}^{j-1})$ converges to the entropy rate of the process as $k \to \infty$ and this will prove the result.

Suppose $X^n_{-(k-1)} = x^n_{-(k-1)}$, and suppose that x_1^n is parsed into c distinct phrases, $y_1, y_2, \ldots, y_c$. Let ν_i be the index of the start of the ith phrase, i.e., $y_i = x_{\nu_i}^{\nu_{i+1}-1}$. For each $i = 1, 2, \ldots, c$, define $s_i = x_{\nu_i - k}^{\nu_i - 1}$. Thus s_i is the k bits of x preceding y_i. Of course, $s_1 = x^0_{-(k-1)}$.

Let c_{ls} be the number of phrases y_i with length l and preceding state $s_i = s$ for $l = 1, 2, \ldots$ and $s \in \mathcal{X}^k$. We then have

$$\sum_{l, s} c_{ls} = c \qquad (12.277)$$

and
$$\sum_{l,\,s} lc_{ls} = n . \tag{12.278}$$

We now prove a surprising upper bound on the probability of a string based on the parsing of the string.

Lemma 12.10.3 (*Ziv's inequality*): *For any distinct parsing (in particular, the Lempel-Ziv parsing) of the string $x_1 x_2 \ldots x_n$, we have*

$$\log Q_k(x_1, x_2, \ldots, x_n | s_1) \le -\sum_{l,\,s} c_{ls} \log c_{ls} . \tag{12.279}$$

Note that the right hand side does not depend on Q_k.

Proof: We write

$$Q_k(x_1, x_2, \ldots, x_n | s_1) = Q(y_1, y_2, \ldots, y_c | s_1) \tag{12.280}$$

$$= \prod_{i=1}^{c} P(y_i | s_i) , \tag{12.281}$$

or

$$\log Q_k(x_1, x_2, \ldots, x_n | s_1) = \sum_{i=1}^{c} \log P(y_i | s_i) \tag{12.282}$$

$$= \sum_{l,\,s} \sum_{i\,:\,|y_i|=l,\,s_i=s} \log P(y_i | s_i) \tag{12.283}$$

$$= \sum_{l,\,s} c_{ls} \sum_{i\,:\,|y_i|=l,\,s_i=s} \frac{1}{c_{ls}} \log P(y_i | s_i) \tag{12.284}$$

$$\le \sum_{l,\,s} c_{ls} \log \left(\sum_{i\,:\,|y_i|=l,\,s_i=s} \frac{1}{c_{ls}} P(y_i | s_i) \right) , \tag{12.285}$$

where the inequality follows from Jensen's inequality and the concavity of the logarithm.

Now since the y_i are distinct, we have $\sum_{i\,:\,|y_i|=l,\,s_i=s} P(y_i | s_i) \le 1$. Thus

$$\log Q_k(x_1, x_2, \ldots, x_n | s_1) \le \sum_{l,\,s} c_{ls} \log \frac{1}{c_{ls}} , \tag{12.286}$$

proving the lemma. $\square$

We can now prove the main theorem:

Theorem 12.10.1: *Let $\{X_n\}$ be a stationary ergodic process with entropy rate $H(\mathcal{X})$, and let $c(n)$ be the number of phrases in a distinct parsing of a sample of length n from this process. Then*

$$\limsup_{n \to \infty} \frac{c(n) \log c(n)}{n} \le H(\mathcal{X}) \qquad (12.287)$$

with probability 1.

Proof: We will begin with Ziv's inequality, which we rewrite as

$$\log Q_k(x_1, x_2, \dots, x_n | s_1) \le -\sum_{l, s} c_{ls} \log \frac{c_{ls} c}{c} \qquad (12.288)$$

$$= -c \log c - c \sum_{ls} \frac{c_{ls}}{c} \log \frac{c_{ls}}{c}. \qquad (12.289)$$

Writing $\pi_{ls} = \frac{c_{ls}}{c}$, we have

$$\sum_{l, s} \pi_{ls} = 1, \qquad \sum_{l, s} l\pi_{ls} = \frac{n}{c}, \qquad (12.290)$$

from (12.227) and (12.278). We now define random variables U, V, such that

$$\Pr(U = l, V = s) = \pi_{ls}. \qquad (12.291)$$

Thus $EU = \frac{n}{c}$ and

$$\log Q_k(x_1, x_2, \dots, x_n | s_1) \le cH(U, V) - c \log c \qquad (12.292)$$

or

$$-\frac{1}{n} \log Q_k(x_1, x_2, \dots, x_n | s_1) \ge \frac{c}{n} \log c - \frac{c}{n} H(U, V). \qquad (12.293)$$

Now

$$H(U, V) \le H(U) + H(V), \qquad (12.294)$$

and $H(V) \le \log|\mathcal{X}|^k = k$. By Lemma 12.10.2, we have

$$H(U) \le (EU + 1) \log(EU + 1) - EU \log EU \qquad (12.295)$$

$$= \left(\frac{n}{c} + 1\right) \log\left(\frac{n}{c} + 1\right) - \frac{n}{c} \log \frac{n}{c} \qquad (12.296)$$

$$= \log \frac{n}{c} + \left(\frac{n}{c} + 1\right) \log\left(\frac{c}{n} + 1\right). \qquad (12.297)$$

Thus

$$\frac{c}{n} H(U, V) \le \frac{c}{n} k + \frac{c}{n} \log \frac{n}{c} + o(1) . \qquad (12.298)$$

For a given n, the maximum of $\frac{c}{n} \log \frac{n}{c}$ is attained for the maximum value of c (for $\frac{c}{n} \le \frac{1}{e}$). But from Lemma 12.10.1, $c \le \frac{n}{\log n}(1 + o(1))$. Thus

$$\frac{c}{n} \log \frac{n}{c} \le O\left(\frac{\log \log n}{\log n}\right) \qquad (12.299)$$

and therefore $\frac{c}{n} H(U, V) \to 0$ as $n \to \infty$.

Therefore

$$\frac{c(n) \log c(n)}{n} \le -\frac{1}{n} \log Q_k(x_1, x_2, \ldots, x_n | s_1) + \epsilon_k(n) \qquad (12.300)$$

where $\epsilon_k(n) \to 0$ as $n \to \infty$. Hence, with probability 1,

$$\limsup_{n \to \infty} \frac{c(n) \log c(n)}{n} \le \lim_{n \to \infty} -\frac{1}{n} \log Q_k(X_1, X_2, \ldots, X_n | X^0_{-(k-1)})$$

$$(12.301)$$

$$= H(X_0 | X_{-1}, \ldots, X_{-k}) \qquad (12.302)$$

$$\to H(\mathscr{X}) \qquad \text{as } k \to \infty . \quad \square \qquad (12.303)$$

We now prove that Lempel-Ziv coding is asymptotically optimal.

Theorem 12.10.2: *Let* $\{X_i\}^{\infty}_{-\infty}$ *be a stationary ergodic stochastic process. Let* $l(X_1, X_2, \ldots, X_n)$ *be the Lempel-Ziv codeword length associated with* $X_1, X_2, \ldots, X_n$. *Then*

$$\limsup_{n \to \infty} \frac{1}{n} l(X_1, X_2, \ldots, X_n) \le H(\mathscr{X}) \quad \text{with probability 1}$$

$$(12.304)$$

where $H(\mathscr{X})$ *is the entropy rate of the process.*

Proof: We have shown that $l(X_1, X_2, \ldots, X_n) = c(n)(\log c(n) + 1)$, where $c(n)$ is the number of phrases in the Lempel-Ziv parsing of the string $X_1, X_2, \ldots, X_n$. By Lemma 12.10.1, $\limsup c(n)/n = 0$, and thus Theorem 12.10.1 establishes that

$$\limsup \frac{l(X_1, X_2, \ldots, X_n)}{n} = \limsup \left(\frac{c(n) \log c(n)}{n} + \frac{c(n)}{n}\right) \le H(\mathscr{X})$$

$$\text{with probability 1} . \quad \square \qquad (12.305)$$

Thus the length per source symbol of the Lempel-Ziv encoding of an ergodic source is asymptotically no greater than the entropy rate of the source. The Lempel-Ziv code is a simple example of a universal code, i.e., a code that does not depend on the distribution of the source. This code can be used without knowledge of the source distribution and yet will achieve an asymptotic compression equal to the entropy rate of the source.

The Lempel-Ziv algorithm is now the standard algorithm for compression of files—it is implemented in the *compress* program in UNIX and in the *arc* program for PC's. The algorithm typically compresses ASCII text files by about a factor of 2. It has also been implemented in hardware and is used to effectively double the capacity of communication links for text files by compressing the file at one end and decompressing it at the other end.

12.11 FISHER INFORMATION AND THE CRAMÉR-RAO INEQUALITY

A standard problem in statistical estimation is to determine the parameters of a distribution from a sample of data drawn from that distribution. For example, let $X_1, X_2, \ldots, X_n$ be drawn i.i.d. $\sim \mathcal{N}(\theta, 1)$. Suppose we wish to estimate θ from a sample of size n. There are a number of functions of the data that we can use to estimate θ. For example, we can use the first sample X_1. Although the expected value of X_1 is θ, it is clear that we can do better by using more of the data. We guess that the best estimate of θ is the sample mean $\bar{X}_n = \frac{1}{n} \Sigma X_i$. Indeed, it can be shown that $\bar{X}_n$ is the minimum mean squared error unbiased estimator.

We begin with a few definitions. Let $\{f(x; \theta)\}, \theta \in \Theta$, denote an indexed family of densities, $f(x; \theta) \geq 0$, $\int f(x; \theta) \, dx = 1$ for all $\theta \in \Theta$. Here Θ is called the *parameter set*.

Definition: An *estimator* for θ for sample size n is a function $T : \mathcal{X}^n \to \Theta$.

An estimator is meant to approximate the value of the parameter. It is therefore desirable to have some idea of the goodness of the approximation. We will call the difference $T - \theta$ the *error* of the estimator. The error is a random variable.

Definition: The *bias* of an estimator $T(X_1, X_2, \ldots, X_n)$ for the parameter θ is the expected value of the error of the estimator, i.e., the bias is $E_\theta T(X_1, X_2, \ldots, X_n) - \theta$. The subscript θ means that the expectation is with respect to the density $f(\cdot \, ; \theta)$. The estimator is said to be *unbiased* if the bias is zero, i.e., the expected value of the estimator is equal to the parameter.

Example 12.11.1: Let $X_1, X_2, \ldots, X_n$ drawn i.i.d. $\sim f(x) = (1/\lambda) \, e^{-x/\lambda}$, $x \geq 0$ be a sequence of exponentially distributed random variables. Estimators of λ include X_1 and $\bar{X}_n$. Both estimators are unbiased.

The bias is the expected value of the error, and the fact that it is zero does not guarantee that the error is low with high probability. We need to look at some loss function of the error; the most commonly chosen loss function is the expected square of the error. A good estimator should have a low expected squared error and should have an error that approaches 0 as the sample size goes to infinity. This motivates the following definition:

Definition: An estimator $T(X_1, X_2, \ldots, X_n)$ for θ is said to be *consistent in probability* if $T(X_1, X_2, \ldots, X_n) \to \theta$ in probability as $n \to \infty$.

Consistency is a desirable asymptotic property, but we are interested in the behavior for small sample sizes as well. We can then rank estimators on the basis of their mean squared error.

Definition: An estimator $T_1(X_1, X_2, \ldots, X_n)$ is said to *dominate* another estimator $T_2(X_1, X_2, \ldots, X_n)$ if, for all θ,

$$E_\theta(T_1(X_1, X_2, \ldots, X_n) - \theta)^2 \leq E_\theta(T_2(X_1, X_2, \ldots, X_n) - \theta)^2 , \quad (12.306)$$

This definition raises a natural question: what is the minimum variance unbiased estimator of θ? To answer this question, we derive the Cramér-Rao lower bound on the mean squared error of any estimator. We first define the score function of the distribution $f(x; \theta)$. We then use the Cauchy-Schwarz inequality to prove the Cramér-Rao lower bound on the variance of all unbiased estimators.

Definition: The *score* V is a random variable defined by

$$V = \frac{\partial}{\partial \theta} \ln f(X; \theta) = \frac{\frac{\partial}{\partial \theta} f(X; \theta)}{f(X; \theta)} , \quad (12.307)$$

where $X \sim f(x; \theta)$.

The mean value of the score is

$$EV = \int \frac{\frac{\partial}{\partial \theta} f(x; \theta)}{f(x; \theta)} \, f(x; \theta) \, dx \quad (12.308)$$

$$= \int \frac{\partial}{\partial \theta} f(x; \theta) \, dx \tag{12.309}$$

$$= \frac{\partial}{\partial \theta} \int f(x; \theta) \, dx \tag{12.310}$$

$$= \frac{\partial}{\partial \theta} 1 \tag{12.311}$$

$$= 0, \tag{12.312}$$

and therefore $EV^2 = \text{var}(V)$. The variance of the score has a special significance.

Definition: The *Fisher information* $J(\theta)$ is the variance of the score, i.e.,

$$J(\theta) = E_\theta \left[\frac{\partial}{\partial \theta} \ln f(x; \theta) \right]^2 . \tag{12.313}$$

If we consider a sample of n random variables $X_1, X_2, \ldots, X_n$ drawn i.i.d. $\sim f(x; \theta)$, we have

$$f(x_1, x_2, \ldots, x_n; \theta) = \prod_{i=1}^{n} f(x_i; \theta), \tag{12.314}$$

and the score function is the sum of the individual score functions,

$$V(X_1, X_2, \ldots, X_n) = \frac{\partial}{\partial \theta} \ln f(X_1, X_2, \ldots, X_n; \theta) \tag{12.315}$$

$$= \sum_{i=1}^{n} \frac{\partial}{\partial \theta} \ln f(X_i; \theta) \tag{12.316}$$

$$= \sum_{i=1}^{n} V(X_i), \tag{12.317}$$

where the $V(X_i)$ are independent, identically distributed with zero mean. Hence the Fisher information is

$$J_n(\theta) = E_\theta \left[\frac{\partial}{\partial \theta} \ln f(x_1, x_2, \ldots, x_n; \theta) \right]^2 \tag{12.318}$$

$$= E_\theta V^2(X_1, X_2, \ldots, X_n) \tag{12.319}$$

$$= E_\theta \left(\sum_{i=1}^{n} V(X_i) \right)^2 \tag{12.320}$$

$$= \sum_{i=1}^{n} E_\theta V^2(X_i) \tag{12.321}$$

$$= nJ(\theta). \tag{12.322}$$

Consequently, the Fisher information for n i.i.d. samples is n times the individual Fisher information. The significance of the Fisher information is shown in the following theorem:

Theorem: 12.11.1 (*Cramér-Rao inequality*): *The mean squared error of any unbiased estimator $T(X)$ of the parameter θ is lower bounded by the reciprocal of the Fisher information, i.e.,*

$$\operatorname{var}(T) \geq \frac{1}{J(\theta)} \, . \tag{12.323}$$

Proof: Let V be the score function and T be the estimator. By the Cauchy-Schwarz inequality, we have

$$(E_\theta[(V - E_\theta V)(T - E_\theta T)])^2 \leq E_\theta(V - E_\theta V)^2 E_\theta(T - E_\theta T)^2 \, . \tag{12.324}$$

By (12.312), $E_\theta V = 0$ and hence $E_\theta(V - E_\theta V)(T - E_\theta T) = E_\theta(VT)$. Also, by definition, $\operatorname{var}(V) = J(\theta)$. Substituting these conditions in (12.324), we have

$$[E_\theta(VT)]^2 \leq J(\theta) \operatorname{var}(T) \, . \tag{12.325}$$

Now,

$$E_\theta(VT) - \int \frac{\frac{\partial}{\partial \theta} f(x; \theta)}{f(x; \theta)} \, T(x) f(x; \theta) \, dx \tag{12.326}$$

$$= \int \frac{\partial}{\partial \theta} f(x; \theta) T(x) \, dx \tag{12.327}$$

$$= \frac{\partial}{\partial \theta} \int f(x; \theta) T(x) \, dx \tag{12.328}$$

$$= \frac{\partial}{\partial \theta} E_\theta T \tag{12.329}$$

$$= \frac{\partial}{\partial \theta} \theta \tag{12.330}$$

$$= 1 \, . \tag{12.331}$$

where the interchange of differentiation and integration in (12.328) can be justified using the bounded convergence theorem for appropriately well behaved $f(x; \theta)$ and (12.330) follows from the fact that the estimator T is unbiased. Substituting this in (12.325), we obtain

$$\text{var}(T) \geq \frac{1}{J(\theta)}, \tag{12.332}$$

which is the Cramér-Rao inequality for unbiased estimators. □

By essentially the same arguments, we can show that for any estimator

$$E_\theta(T - \theta)^2 \geq \frac{[1 + b_T'(\theta)]^2}{J(\theta)} + b_T^2(\theta), \tag{12.333}$$

where $b_T(\theta) = E_\theta T - \theta$ and $b_T'(\theta)$ is the derivative of $b_T(\theta)$ with respect to θ. The proof of this is left as an exercise at the end of the chapter.

Example 12.11.2: Let $X_1, X_2, \ldots, X_n$ be i.i.d. $\sim \mathcal{N}(\theta, \sigma^2)$, σ^2 known. Here $J(\theta) = \frac{n}{\sigma^2}$. Let $T(X_1, X_2, \ldots, X_n) = \bar{X}_n = \frac{1}{n} \Sigma X_i$. Then $E_\theta(\bar{X}_n - \theta)^2 = \frac{\sigma^2}{n} = \frac{1}{J(\theta)}$. Thus $\bar{X}_n$ is the minimum variance unbiased estimator of θ, since it achieves the Cramér-Rao lower bound.

The Cramér-Rao inequality gives us the lowest possible variance for all unbiased estimators. We now use it to define the most efficient estimator.

Definition: An unbiased estimator T is said to be *efficient* if it meets the Cramér-Rao bound with equality, i.e., if $\text{var}(T) = \frac{1}{J(\theta)}$.

The Fisher information is therefore a measure of the amount of "information" about θ that is present in the data. It gives a lower bound on the error in estimating θ from the data. However, it is possible that there does not exist an estimator meeting this lower bound.
We can generalize the concept of Fisher information to the multi-parameter case, in which case we define the Fisher information matrix $J(\theta)$ with elements

$$J_{ij}(\theta) = \int f(x; \theta) \frac{\partial}{\partial \theta_i} \ln f(x; \theta) \frac{\partial}{\partial \theta_j} \ln f(x; \theta) \, dx. \tag{12.334}$$

The Cramér-Rao inequality becomes the matrix inequality

$$\Sigma \geq J^{-1}(\theta), \tag{12.335}$$

where Σ is the covariance matrix of a set of unbiased estimators for the parameters θ and $\Sigma \geq J^{-1}(\theta)$ in the sense that the difference $\Sigma - J^{-1}$ is a non-negative definite matrix. We will not go into the details of the proof for multiple parameters; the basic ideas are similar.

Is there a relationship between the Fisher information $J(\theta)$ and quantities like entropy defined earlier? Note that Fisher information is defined with respect to a family of parametric distributions, unlike entropy, which is defined for all distributions. But we can parametrize any distribution, $f(x)$, by a location parameter θ and define Fisher information with respect to the family of densities $\{f(x - \theta)\}$ under translation. We will explore the relationship in greater detail in Section 16.7, where we show that while entropy is related to the volume of the typical set, the Fisher information is related to the surface area of the typical set. Further relationships of Fisher information to relative entropy are developed in the exercises.

SUMMARY OF CHAPTER 12

Basic identities:

$$Q^n(\mathbf{x}) = 2^{-n(D(P_\mathbf{x}\|Q) + H(P_\mathbf{x}))} \,, \tag{12.336}$$

$$|\mathscr{P}_n| \le (n+1)^{|\mathscr{X}|} \,, \tag{12.337}$$

$$|T(P)| \doteq 2^{nH(P)} \,, \tag{12.338}$$

$$Q^n(T(P)) \doteq 2^{-nD(P\|Q)} \,. \tag{12.339}$$

Universal data compression:

$$P_e^{(n)} \le 2^{-nD(\Gamma_R^*\|Q)}, \quad \text{for all } Q \,, \tag{12.340}$$

where

$$D(P_R^*\|Q) = \min_{P \,:\, H(P) \ge R} D(P\|Q) \tag{12.341}$$

Large deviations (Sanov's theorem):

$$Q^n(E) = Q^n(E \cap \mathscr{P}_n) \le (n+1)^{|\mathscr{X}|} 2^{-nD(P^*\|Q)} \,, \tag{12.342}$$

$$D(P^*\|Q) = \min_{P \in E} D(P\|Q) \,, \tag{12.343}$$

If E is the closure of its interior, then

$$Q^n(E) \doteq 2^{-nD(P^*\|Q)} \,. \tag{12.344}$$

$\mathscr{L}_1$ bound on relative entropy:

$$D(P_1\|P_2) \ge \frac{1}{2\ln 2} \|P_1 - P_2\|_1^2 \tag{12.345}$$

Pythagorean theorem: If E is a convex set of types, distribution $Q \notin E$, and P^* achieves $D(P^* \| Q) = \min_{P \in E} D(P \| Q)$, we have

$$D(P \| Q) \geq D(P \| P^*) + D(P^* \| Q) \tag{12.346}$$

for all $P \in E$.

Conditional limit theorem: If $X_1, X_2, \ldots, X_n$ i.i.d. $\sim Q$, then

$$\Pr(X_1 = a | P_{X^n} \in E) \to P^*(a) \quad \text{in probability}, \tag{12.347}$$

where P^* minimizes $D(P \| Q)$ over $P \in E$. In particular,

$$\Pr\left\{X_1 = a \,\middle|\, \frac{1}{n} \sum_{i=1}^{n} X_i \geq \alpha\right\} \to \frac{Q(a)e^{\lambda a}}{\sum_x Q(x)e^{\lambda x}}. \tag{12.348}$$

Neyman-Pearson lemma: The optimum test between two densities P_1 and P_2 has a decision region of the form "Accept $P = P_1$ if $\frac{P_1(x_1, x_2, \ldots, x_n)}{P_2(x_1, x_2, \ldots, x_n)} > T$."

Stein's lemma: The best achievable error exponent β_n^ϵ if $\alpha_n \leq \epsilon$:

$$\beta_n^\epsilon = \min_{\substack{A_n \subseteq \mathcal{X}^n \\ \alpha_n < \epsilon}} \beta_n. \tag{12.349}$$

$$\lim_{\epsilon \to 0} \lim_{n \to \infty} \frac{1}{n} \log \beta_n^\epsilon = -D(P_1 \| P_2). \tag{12.350}$$

Chernoff information: The best achievable exponent for a Bayesian probability of error is

$$D^* = D(P_{\lambda^*} \| P_1) = D(P_{\lambda^*} \| P_2), \tag{12.351}$$

where

$$P_\lambda = \frac{P_1^\lambda(x) P_2^{1-\lambda}(x)}{\sum_{a \in \mathcal{X}} P_1^\lambda(a) P_2^{1-\lambda}(a)} \tag{12.352}$$

with $\lambda = \lambda^*$ chosen so that

$$D(P_\lambda \| P_1) = D(P_\lambda \| P_2). \tag{12.353}$$

Lempel-Ziv: Universal data compression. For a stationary ergodic source,

$$\limsup \frac{l(X_1, X_2, \ldots, X_n)}{n} = \limsup \frac{c(n) \log c(n)}{n} \leq H(\mathcal{X}). \tag{12.354}$$

Fisher information:

$$J(\theta) = E_\theta \left[\frac{\partial}{\partial \theta} \ln f(x; \theta) \right]^2. \tag{12.355}$$

Cramér-Rao inequality: For any unbiased estimator T of θ,

$$E_\theta (T(X) - \theta)^2 = \text{var}(T) \geq \frac{1}{J(\theta)}. \tag{12.356}$$

PROBLEMS FOR CHAPTER 12

1. *Stein's lemma.* Consider the two hypothesis test

$$H_1 : f = f_1 \quad \text{vs.} \quad H_2 : f = f_2$$

Find $D(f_1 \| f_2)$ if
   (a) $f_i(x) = N(0, \sigma_i^2)$, $i = 1, 2$
   (b) $f_i(x) = \lambda_i e^{-\lambda_i x}$, $x \ge 0$, $i = 1, 2$
   (c) $f_1(x)$ is the uniform density over the interval $[0, 1]$ and $f_2(x)$ is the uniform density over $[a, a + 1]$. Assume $0 < a < 1$.
   (d) f_1 corresponds to a fair coin and f_2 corresponds to a two-headed coin.

2. *A relation between $D(P\|Q)$ and chi-square.* Show that the χ^2 statistic

$$\chi^2 = \sum_x \frac{(P(x) - Q(x))^2}{Q(x)}$$

   is (twice) the first term in the Taylor series expansion of $D(P\|Q)$ about Q. Thus $D(P\|Q) = \frac{1}{2}\chi^2 + \cdots$.
   Hint: Write $\frac{P}{Q} = 1 + \frac{P-Q}{Q}$ and expand the log.

3. *Error exponent for universal codes.* A universal source code of rate R achieves a probability of error $P_e^{(n)} \doteq e^{-nD(P^*\|Q)}$, where Q is the true distribution and P^* achieves min $D(P\|Q)$ over all P such that $H(P) \ge R$.
   (a) Find P^* in terms of Q and R.
   (b) Now let X be binary. Find the region of source probabilities $Q(x)$, $x \in \{0, 1\}$, for which rate R is sufficient for the universal source code to achieve $P_e^{(n)} \to 0$.

4. *Sequential projection.* We wish to show that projecting Q onto P_1 and then projecting the projection $\hat{Q}$ onto $P_1 \cap P_2$ is the same as projecting Q directly onto $P_1 \cap P_2$. Let $\mathscr{P}_1$ be the set of probability mass functions on $\mathscr{X}$ satisfying

$$\sum_x p(x) = 1, \tag{12.357}$$

$$\sum_x p(x) h_i(x) \ge \alpha_i, \quad i = 1, 2, \ldots, r. \tag{12.358}$$

Let $\mathscr{P}_2$ be the set of probability mass functions on $\mathscr{X}$ satisfying

$$\sum_x p(x) = 1, \tag{12.359}$$

$$\sum_x p(x) g_j(x) \ge \beta_j, \quad j = 1, 2, \ldots, s. \tag{12.360}$$

Suppose $Q \not\subset P_1 \cup P_2$. Let P^* minimize $D(P\|Q)$ over all $P \in \mathscr{P}_1$. Let R^* minimize $D(R\|Q)$ over all $R \in \mathscr{P}_1 \cap \mathscr{P}_2$. Argue that R^* minimizes $D(R\|P^*)$ over all $R \in P_1 \cap P_2$.

5. *Counting.* Let $\mathscr{X} = \{1, 2, \ldots, m\}$. Show that the number of sequences $x^n \in \mathscr{X}^n$ satisfying $\frac{1}{n} \sum_{i=1}^{n} g(x_i) \geq \alpha$ is approximately equal to 2^{nH^*}, to first order in the exponent, for n sufficiently large, where

$$H^* = \max_{P : \Sigma_{i=1}^{m} P(i)g(i) \geq \alpha} H(P). \qquad (12.361)$$

6. *Biased estimates may be better.* Consider the problem of estimating μ and σ^2 from n samples of data drawn i.i.d. from a $\mathcal{N}(\mu, \sigma^2)$ distribution.

    (a) Show that $\bar{X}$ is an unbiased estimator of μ.

    (b) Show that the estimator

$$S_n^2 = \frac{1}{n} \sum_{i=1}^{n} (X_i - \bar{X}_n)^2 \qquad (12.362)$$

    is biased and the estimator

$$S_{n-1}^2 = \frac{1}{n-1} \sum_{i=1}^{n} (X_i - \bar{X}_n)^2 \qquad (12.363)$$

    is unbiased.

    (c) Show that S_n^2 has a lower mean squared error than S_{n-1}^2. This illustrates the idea that a biased estimator may be "better" than an unbiased estimator.

7. *Fisher information and relative entropy.* Show for a parametric family $\{p_\theta(x)\}$ that

$$\lim_{\theta' \to \theta} \frac{1}{(\theta - \theta')^2} D(p_\theta \| p_{\theta'}) = \frac{1}{\ln 4} J(\theta). \qquad (12.364)$$

8. *Examples of Fisher information.* The Fisher information $J(\theta)$ for the family $f_\theta(x), \theta \in \mathbf{R}$ is defined by

$$J(\theta) = E_\theta \left(\frac{\partial f_\theta(X)/\partial \theta}{f_\theta(X)} \right)^2 = \int \frac{(f_\theta')^2}{f_\theta}.$$

    Find the Fisher information for the following families:

    (a) $f_\theta(x) = N(0, \theta) = \frac{1}{\sqrt{2\pi\theta}} e^{-\frac{x^2}{2\theta}}$

    (b) $f_\theta(x) = \theta e^{-\theta x}, x \geq 0$

    (c) What is the Cramér-Rao lower bound on $E_\theta(\hat{\theta}(X) - \theta)^2$, where $\hat{\theta}(X)$ is an unbiased estimator of θ for (a) and (b)?

9. *Two conditionally independent looks double the Fisher information.* Let $g_\theta(x_1, x_2) = f_\theta(x_1) f_\theta(x_2)$. Show $J_g(\theta) = 2J_f(\theta)$.

10. *Joint distributions and product distributions.* Consider a joint distribution $Q(x, y)$ with marginals $Q(x)$ and $Q(y)$. Let E be the set of types that look jointly typical with respect to Q, i.e.,

$$E = \{P(x, y): -\sum_{x, y} P(x, y) \log Q(x) - H(X) = 0,$$

$$-\sum_{x, y} P(x, y) \log Q(y) - H(Y) = 0,$$

$$-\sum_{x, y} P(x, y) \log Q(x, y) - H(X, Y) = 0\}. \qquad (12.365)$$

(a) Let $Q_0(x, y)$ be another distribution on $\mathcal{X} \times \mathcal{Y}$. Argue that the distribution P^* in E that is closest to Q_0 is of the form

$$P^*(x, y) = Q_0(x, y)e^{\lambda_0 + \lambda_1 \log Q(x) + \lambda_2 \log Q(y) + \lambda_3 \log Q(x, y)},$$

$$(12.366)$$

where $\lambda_0, \lambda_1, \lambda_2$ and λ_3 are chosen to satisfy the constraints. Argue that this distribution is unique.

(b) Now let $Q_0(x, y) = Q(x)Q(y)$. Verify that $Q(x, y)$ is of the form (12.366) and satisfies the constraints. Thus $P^*(x, y) = Q(x, y)$, i.e., the distribution in E closest to the product distribution is the joint distribution.

11. *Cramér-Rao inequality with a bias term.* Let $X \sim f(x; \theta)$ and let $T(X)$ be an estimator for θ. Let $b_T(\theta) = E_\theta T - \theta$ be the bias of the estimator. Show that

$$E_\theta(T \quad \theta)^2 \geq \frac{[1 + b_T'(\theta)]^2}{J(\theta)} + b_T^2(\theta). \qquad (12.367)$$

12. *Lempel-Ziv.* Give the Lempel-Ziv parsing and encoding of 000000110-10100000110101.

HISTORICAL NOTES

The method of types evolved from notions of weak typicality and strong typicality; some of the ideas were used by Wolfowitz [277] to prove channel capacity theorems. The method was fully developed by Csiszár and Körner [83], who derived the main theorems of information theory from this viewpoint. The method of types described in Section 12.1 follows the development in Csiszár and Körner. The $\mathcal{L}_1$ lower bound on relative entropy is due to Csiszár [78], Kullback [151] and Kemperman [227]. Sanov's theorem [175] was generalized by Csiszár [289] using the method of types.

The parsing algorithm for Lempel-Ziv encoding was introduced by Lempel and Ziv [175] and was proved to achieve the entropy rate by Ziv [289]. The algorithm described in the text was first described in Ziv and Lempel [289]. A more transparent proof was provided by Wyner and Ziv [285], which we have used to prove the results in Section 12.10. A number of different variations of the basic Lempel-Ziv algorithm are described in the book by Bell, Cleary and Witten [22].

Chapter 13

Rate Distortion Theory

The description of an arbitrary real number requires an infinite number of bits, so a finite representation of a continuous random variable can never be perfect. How well can we do? To frame the question appropriately, it is necessary to define the "goodness" of a representation of a source. This is accomplished by defining a distortion measure which is a measure of distance between the random variable and its representation. The basic problem in rate distortion theory can then be stated as follows: given a source distribution and a distortion measure, what is the minimum expected distortion achievable at a particular rate? Or, equivalently, what is the minimum rate description required to achieve a particular distortion?

One of the most intriguing aspects of this theory is that joint descriptions are more efficient than individual descriptions. It is simpler to describe an elephant and a chicken with one description than to describe each alone. This is true even for independent random variables. It is simpler to describe X_1 and X_2 together (at a given distortion for each) than to describe each by itself. Why don't independent problems have independent solutions? The answer is found in the geometry. Apparently rectangular grid points (arising from independent descriptions) do not fill up the space efficiently.

Rate distortion theory can be applied to both discrete and continuous random variables. The zero-error data compression theory of Chapter 5 is an important special case of rate distortion theory applied to a discrete source with zero distortion.

We will begin by considering the simple problem of representing a single continuous random variable by a finite number of bits.

13.1   QUANTIZATION

This section on quantization motivates the elegant theory of rate distortion by showing how complicated it is to solve the quantization problem exactly for a single random variable.

Since a continuous random source requires infinite precision to represent exactly, we cannot reproduce it exactly using a finite rate code. The question is then to find the best possible representation for any given data rate.

We first consider the problem of representing a single sample from the source. Let the random variable to be represented be X and let the representation of X be denoted as $\hat{X}(X)$. If we are given R bits to represent X, then the function $\hat{X}$ can take on 2^R values. The problem is to find the optimum set of values for $\hat{X}$ (called the reproduction points or codepoints) and the regions that are associated with each value $\hat{X}$.

For example, let $X \sim \mathcal{N}(0, \sigma^2)$, and assume a squared error distortion measure. In this case, we wish to find the function $\hat{X}(X)$ such that $\hat{X}$ takes on at most 2^R values and minimizes $E(X - \hat{X}(X))^2$. If we are given 1 bit to represent X, it is clear that the bit should distinguish whether $X > 0$ or not. To minimize squared error, each reproduced symbol should be at the conditional mean of its region. This is illustrated in Figure 13.1. Thus

$$\hat{X}(x) = \begin{cases} \sqrt{\dfrac{2}{\pi}}\sigma, & \text{if } x \geq 0, \\[2mm] -\sqrt{\dfrac{2}{\pi}}\sigma, & \text{if } x < 0. \end{cases} \qquad (13.1)$$

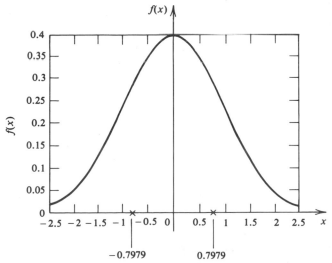

Figure 13.1. One bit quantization of a Gaussian random variable.

If we are given 2 bits to represent the sample, the situation is not as simple. Clearly, we want to divide the real line into four regions and use a point within each region to represent the sample. But it is no longer immediately obvious what the representation regions and the reconstruction points should be.

We can however state two simple properties of optimal regions and reconstruction points for the quantization of a single random variable:

- Given a set of reconstruction points, the distortion is minimized by mapping a source random variable X to the representation $\hat{X}(w)$ that is closest to it. The set of regions of $\mathcal{X}$ defined by this mapping is called a Voronoi or Dirichlet partition defined by the reconstruction points.

- The reconstruction points should minimize the conditional expected distortion over their respective assignment regions.

These two properties enable us to construct a simple algorithm to find a "good" quantizer: we start with a set of reconstruction points, find the optimal set of reconstruction regions (which are the nearest neighbor regions with respect to the distortion measure), then find the optimal reconstruction points for these regions (the centroids of these regions if the distortion is squared error), and then repeat the iteration for this new set of reconstruction points. The expected distortion is decreased at each stage in the algorithm, so the algorithm will converge to a local minimum of the distortion. This algorithm is called the *Lloyd algorithm* [181] (for real-valued random variables) or the *generalized Lloyd algorithm* [80] (for vector-valued random variables) and is frequently used to design quantization systems.

Instead of quantizing a single random variable, let us assume that we are given a set of n i.i.d. random variables drawn according to a Gaussian distribution. These random variables are to be represented using nR bits. Since the source is i.i.d., the symbols are independent, and it may appear that the representation of each element is an independent problem to be treated separately. But this is not true, as the results on rate distortion theory will show. We will represent the entire sequence by a single index taking 2^{nR} values. This treatment of entire sequences at once achieves a lower distortion for the same rate than independent quantization of the individual samples.

13.2 DEFINITIONS

Assume that we have a source that produces a sequence $X_1, X_2, \ldots, X_n$ i.i.d. $\sim p(x), x \in \mathcal{X}$. We will assume that the alphabet is finite for the proofs in this chapter; but most of the proofs can be extended to continuous random variables.

The encoder describes the source sequence X^n by an index $f_n(X^n) \in \{1, 2, \ldots, 2^{nR}\}$. The decoder represents X^n by an estimate $\hat{X}^n \in \hat{\mathscr{X}}^n$, as illustrated in Figure 13.2.

Definition: A *distortion function* or *distortion measure* is a mapping

$$d: \mathscr{X} \times \hat{\mathscr{X}} \to R^+ \tag{13.2}$$

from the set of source alphabet-reproduction alphabet pairs into the set of non-negative real numbers. The distortion $d(x, \hat{x})$ is a measure of the cost of representing the symbol x by the symbol $\hat{x}$.

Definition: A distortion measure is said to be *bounded* if the maximum value of the distortion is finite, i.e.,

$$d_{\max} \overset{\text{def}}{=} \max_{x \in \mathscr{X}, \hat{x} \in \hat{X}} d(x, \hat{x}) < \infty . \tag{13.3}$$

In most cases, the reproduction alphabet $\hat{\mathscr{X}}$ is the same as the source alphabet $\mathscr{X}$. Examples of common distortion functions are

- *Hamming (probability of error) distortion.* The Hamming distortion is given by

$$d(x, \hat{x}) = \begin{cases} 0 & \text{if } x = \hat{x} \\ 1 & \text{if } x \neq \hat{x} \end{cases}, \tag{13.4}$$

which results in a probability of error distortion, since $Ed(X, \hat{X}) = \Pr(X \neq \hat{X})$.

- *Squared error distortion.* The squared error distortion,

$$d(x, \hat{x}) = (x - \hat{x})^2 , \tag{13.5}$$

is the most popular distortion measure used for continuous alphabets. Its advantages are its simplicity and its relationship to least squares prediction. But in applications such as image and

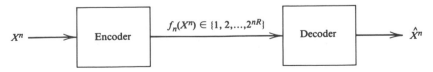

Figure 13.2. Rate distortion encoder and decoder.

speech coding, various authors have pointed out that the mean squared error is not an appropriate measure of distortion as observed by a human observer. For example, there is a large squared error distortion between a speech waveform and another version of the same waveform slightly shifted in time, even though both would sound very similar to a human observer.

Many alternatives have been proposed; a popular measure of distortion in speech coding is the Itakura-Saito distance, which is the relative entropy between multivariate normal processes. In image coding, however, there is at present no real alternative to using the mean squared error as the distortion measure.

The distortion measure is defined on a symbol-by-symbol basis. We extend the definition to sequences by using the following definition:

Definition: The *distortion between sequences* x^n and $\hat{x}^n$ is defined by

$$d(x^n, \hat{x}^n) = \frac{1}{n} \sum_{i=1}^{n} d(x_i, \hat{x}_i).$$ (13.6)

So the distortion for a sequence is the average of the per symbol distortion of the elements of the sequence. This is not the only reasonable definition. For example, one may want to measure distortion between two sequences by the maximum of the per symbol distortions. The theory derived below does not apply directly to this case.

Definition: A $(2^{nR}, n)$ *rate distortion code* consists of an encoding function,

$$f_n : \mathscr{X}^n \to \{1, 2, \ldots, 2^{nR}\},$$ (13.7)

and a decoding (reproduction) function,

$$g_n : \{1, 2, \ldots, 2^{nR}\} \to \hat{\mathscr{X}}^n.$$ (13.8)

The distortion associated with the $(2^{nR}, n)$ code is defined as

$$D = Ed(X^n, g_n(f_n(X^n))),$$ (13.9)

where the expectation is with respect to the probability distribution on X, i.e.,

$$D = \sum_{x^n} p(x^n)\, d(x^n, g_n(f_n(x^n))).$$ (13.10)

The set of n-tuples $g_n(1), g_n(2), \ldots, g_n(2^{nR})$, denoted by $\hat{X}^n(1), \ldots,$ $\hat{X}^n(2^{nR})$, constitutes the *codebook*, and $f_n^{-1}(1), \ldots, f_n^{-1}(2^{nR})$ are the associated *assignment regions*.

Many terms are used to describe the replacement of X^n by its quantized version $\hat{X}^n(w)$. It is common to refer to $\hat{X}^n$ as the *vector quantization, reproduction, reconstruction, representation, source code,* or *estimate* of X^n.

Definition: A rate distortion pair (R, D) is said to be *achievable* if there exists a sequence of $(2^{nR}, n)$ rate distortion codes (f_n, g_n) with $\lim_{n \to \infty} Ed(X^n, g_n(f_n(X^n))) \le D$.

Definition: The *rate distortion region* for a source is the closure of the set of achievable rate distortion pairs (R, D).

Definition: The *rate distortion function* $R(D)$ is the infimum of rates R such that (R, D) is in the rate distortion region of the source for a given distortion D.

Definition: The *distortion rate function* $D(R)$ is the infimum of all distortions D such that (R, D) is in the rate distortion region of the source for a given rate R.

The distortion rate function defines another way of looking at the boundary of the rate distortion region, which is the set of achievable rate distortion pairs. We will in general use the rate distortion function rather than the distortion rate function to describe this boundary, though the two approaches are equivalent.

We now define a mathematical function of the source, which we call the information rate distortion function. The main result of this chapter is the proof that the information rate distortion function is equal to the rate distortion function defined above, i.e., it is the infimum of rates that achieve a particular distortion.

Definition: The *information rate distortion function* $R^{(I)}(D)$ for a source X with distortion measure $d(x, \hat{x})$ is defined as

$$R^{(I)}(D) = \min_{p(\hat{x}|x) \,:\, \Sigma_{(x, \hat{x})} \, p(x)p(\hat{x}|x)d(x, \hat{x}) \le D} I(X; \hat{X}) \qquad (13.11)$$

where the minimization is over all conditional distributions $p(\hat{x}|x)$ for which the joint distribution $p(x, \hat{x}) = p(x)p(\hat{x}|x)$ satisfies the expected distortion constraint.

Paralleling the discussion of channel capacity in Chapter 8, we initially consider the properties of the information rate distortion function and calculate it for some simple sources and distortion measures. Later we prove that we can actually achieve this function, i.e., there exist codes with rate $R^{(I)}(D)$ with distortion D. We also prove a converse establishing that $R \geq R^{(I)}(D)$ for any code that achieves distortion D.

The main theorem of rate distortion theory can now be stated as follows:

Theorem 13.2.1: *The rate distortion function for an i.i.d. source X with distribution $p(x)$ and bounded distortion function $d(x, \hat{x})$ is equal to the associated information rate distortion function. Thus*

$$R(D) = R^{(I)}(D) = \min_{p(\hat{x}|x) : \sum_{(x, \hat{x})} p(x)p(\hat{x}|x)d(x, \hat{x}) \leq D} I(X; \hat{X}) \qquad (13.12)$$

is the minimum achievable rate at distortion D.

This theorem shows that the operational definition of the rate distortion function is equal to the information definition. Hence we will use $R(D)$ from now on to denote both definitions of the rate distortion function. Before coming to the proof of the theorem, we calculate the information rate distortion function for some simple sources and distortions.

13.3   CALCULATION OF THE RATE DISTORTION FUNCTION

13.3.1 Binary Source

We now find the description rate $R(D)$ required to describe a Bernoulli(p) source with an expected proportion of errors less than or equal to D.

Theorem 13.3.1: *The rate distortion function for a Bernoulli(p) source with Hamming distortion is given by*

$$R(D) = \begin{cases} H(p) - H(D), & 0 \leq D \leq \min\{p, 1-p\}, \\ 0, & D > \min\{p, 1-p\}. \end{cases} \qquad (13.13)$$

Proof: Consider a binary source $X \sim$ Bernoulli(p) with a Hamming distortion measure. Without loss of generality, we may assume that $p < \frac{1}{2}$. We wish to calculate the rate distortion function,

$$R(D) = \min_{p(\hat{x}|x) : \sum_{(x, \hat{x})} p(x)p(\hat{x}|x)d(x, \hat{x}) \leq D} I(X; \hat{X}). \qquad (13.14)$$

Let $\oplus$ denote modulo 2 addition. Thus $X \oplus \hat{X} = 1$ is equivalent to $X \neq \hat{X}$.

We cannot minimize $I(X; \hat{X})$ directly; instead, we find a lower bound and then show that this lower bound is achievable. For any joint distribution satisfying the distortion constraint, we have

$$I(X; \hat{X}) = H(X) - H(X|\hat{X}) \tag{13.15}$$

$$= H(p) - H(X \oplus \hat{X}|\hat{X}) \tag{13.16}$$

$$\geq H(p) - H(X \oplus \hat{X}) \tag{13.17}$$

$$\geq H(p) - H(D), \tag{13.18}$$

since $\Pr(X \neq \hat{X}) \leq D$ and $H(D)$ increases with D for $D \leq \frac{1}{2}$. Thus

$$R(D) \geq H(p) - H(D). \tag{13.19}$$

We will now show that the lower bound is actually the rate distortion function by finding a joint distribution that meets the distortion constraint and has $I(X; \hat{X}) = R(D)$. For $0 \leq D \leq p$, we can achieve the value of the rate distortion function in (13.19) by choosing $(X, \hat{X})$ to have the joint distribution given by the binary symmetric channel shown in Figure 13.3.

We choose the distribution of $\hat{X}$ at the input of the channel so that the output distribution of X is the specified distribution. Let $r = \Pr(\hat{X} = 1)$. Then choose r so that

$$r(1 - D) + (1 - r)D = p, \tag{13.20}$$

or

$$r = \frac{p - D}{1 - 2D}. \tag{13.21}$$

If $D \leq p \leq \frac{1}{2}$, then $\Pr(\hat{X} = 1) \geq 0$ and $\Pr(\hat{X} = 0) \geq 0$. We then have

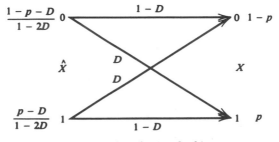

Figure 13.3. Joint distribution for binary source.

$$I(X; \hat{X}) = H(X) - H(X|\hat{X}) = H(p) - H(D), \quad (13.22)$$

and the expected distortion is $P(X \neq \hat{X}) = D$.

If $D \geq p$, then we can achieve $R(D) = 0$ by letting $\hat{X} = 0$ with probability 1. In this case, $I(X; \hat{X}) = 0$ and $D = p$. Similarly, if $D \geq 1 - p$, we can achieve $R(D) = 0$ by setting $\hat{X} = 1$ with probability 1.

Hence the rate distortion function for a binary source is

$$R(D) = \begin{cases} H(p) - H(D), & 0 \leq D \leq \min\{p, 1-p\}, \\ 0, & D > \min\{p, 1-p\}. \end{cases} \quad (13.23)$$

This function is illustrated in Figure 13.4. □

The above calculations may seem entirely unmotivated. Why should minimizing mutual information have anything to do with quantization? The answer to this question must wait until we prove Theorem 13.2.1.

13.3.2 Gaussian Source

Although Theorem 13.2.1 is proved only for discrete sources with a bounded distortion measure, it can also be proved for well-behaved continuous sources and unbounded distortion measures. Assuming this general theorem, we calculate the rate distortion function for a Gaussian source with squared error distortion:

Theorem 13.3.2: *The rate distortion function for a $\mathcal{N}(0, \sigma^2)$ source with squared error distortion is*

$$R(D) = \begin{cases} \dfrac{1}{2} \log \dfrac{\sigma^2}{D}, & 0 \leq D \leq \sigma^2, \\ 0, & D > \sigma^2. \end{cases} \quad (13.24)$$

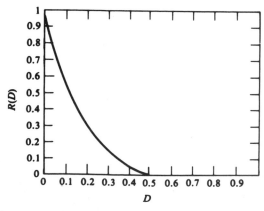

Figure 13.4. Rate distortion function for a binary source.

Proof: Let X be $\sim \mathcal{N}(0, \sigma^2)$. By the rate distortion theorem, we have

$$R(D) = \min_{f(\hat{x}|x)\,:\,E(\hat{X}-X)^2 \leq D} I(X; \hat{X}). \qquad (13.25)$$

As in the previous example, we first find a lower bound for the rate distortion function and then prove that this is achievable. Since $E(X - \hat{X})^2 \leq D$, we observe

$$I(X; \hat{X}) = h(X) - h(X|\hat{X}) \qquad (13.26)$$

$$= \frac{1}{2} \log(2\pi e)\sigma^2 - h(X - \hat{X}|\hat{X}) \qquad (13.27)$$

$$\geq \frac{1}{2} \log(2\pi e)\sigma^2 - h(X - \hat{X}) \qquad (13.28)$$

$$\geq \frac{1}{2} \log(2\pi e)\sigma^2 - h(\mathcal{N}(0, E(X - \hat{X})^2)) \qquad (13.29)$$

$$= \frac{1}{2} \log(2\pi e)\sigma^2 - \frac{1}{2} \log(2\pi e)E(X - \hat{X})^2 \qquad (13.30)$$

$$\geq \frac{1}{2} \log(2\pi e)\sigma^2 - \frac{1}{2} \log(2\pi e)D \qquad (13.31)$$

$$= \frac{1}{2} \log \frac{\sigma^2}{D}, \qquad (13.32)$$

where (13.28) follows from the fact that conditioning reduces entropy and (13.29) follows from the fact that the normal distribution maximizes the entropy for a given second moment (Theorem 9.6.5). Hence

$$R(D) \geq \frac{1}{2} \log \frac{\sigma^2}{D}. \qquad (13.33)$$

To find the conditional density $f(\hat{x}|x)$ that achieves this lower bound, it is usually more convenient to look at the conditional density $f(x|\hat{x})$, which is sometimes called the *test channel* (thus emphasizing the duality of rate distortion with channel capacity). As in the binary case, we construct $f(x|\hat{x})$ to achieve equality in the bound. We choose the joint distribution as shown in Figure 13.5. If $D \leq \sigma^2$, we choose

$$X = \hat{X} + Z, \quad \hat{X} \sim \mathcal{N}(0, \sigma^2 - D), \quad Z \sim \mathcal{N}(0, D), \qquad (13.34)$$

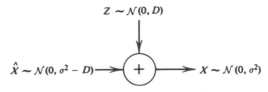

Figure 13.5. Joint distribution for Gaussian source.

where $\hat{X}$ and Z are independent. For this joint distribution, we calculate

$$I(X; \hat{X}) = \frac{1}{2} \log \frac{\sigma^2}{D} , \qquad (13.35)$$

and $E(X - \hat{X})^2 = D$, thus achieving the bound in (13.33). If $D > \sigma^2$, we choose $\hat{X} = 0$ with probability 1, achieving $R(D) = 0$.

Hence the rate distortion function for the Gaussian source with squared error distortion is

$$R(D) = \begin{cases} \dfrac{1}{2} \log \dfrac{\sigma^2}{D} , & 0 \le D \le \sigma^2 , \\ 0, & D > \sigma^2 , \end{cases} \qquad (13.36)$$

as illustrated in Figure 13.6. □

We can rewrite (13.36) to express the distortion in terms of the rate,

$$D(R) = \sigma^2 2^{-2R} . \qquad (13.37)$$

Each bit of description reduces the expected distortion by a factor of 4. With a 1 bit description, the best expected square error is $\sigma^2/4$. We can compare this with the result of simple 1 bit quantization of a $\mathcal{N}(0, \sigma^2)$ random variable as described in Section 13.1. In this case, using the two regions corresponding to the positive and negative real lines and reproduction points as the centroids of the respective regions, the expected distortion is $\frac{\pi - 2}{\pi} \sigma^2 = 0.3633\sigma^2$. (See Problem 1.) As we prove later, the rate distortion limit $R(D)$ is achieved by considering long block lengths. This example shows that we can achieve a lower distortion by considering several distortion problems in succession (long block lengths) than can be achieved by considering each problem separately. This is somewhat surprising because we are quantizing independent random variables.

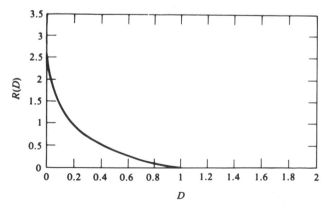

Figure 13.6. Rate distortion function for a Gaussian source.

13.3.3 Simultaneous Description of Independent Gaussian Random Variables

Consider the case of representing m independent (but not identically distributed) normal random sources $X_1, \ldots, X_m$, where X_i are $\sim \mathcal{N}(0, \sigma_i^2)$, with squared error distortion. Assume that we are given R bits with which to represent this random vector. The question naturally arises as to how we should allot these bits to the different components to minimize the total distortion. Extending the definition of the information rate distortion function to the vector case, we have

$$R(D) = \min_{f(\hat{x}^m | x^m) : Ed(X^m, \hat{X}^m) \leq D} I(X^m; \hat{X}^m), \tag{13.38}$$

where $d(x^m, \hat{x}^m) = \sum_{i=1}^{m} (x_i - \hat{x}_i)^2$. Now using the arguments in the previous example, we have

$$I(X^m; \hat{X}^m) = h(X^m) - h(X^m | \hat{X}^m) \tag{13.39}$$

$$- \sum_{i=1}^{m} h(X_i) \quad \sum_{i=1}^{m} h(X_i | X^{i-1}, \hat{X}^m) \tag{13.40}$$

$$\geq \sum_{i=1}^{m} h(X_i) - \sum_{i=1}^{m} h(X_i | \hat{X}_i) \tag{13.41}$$

$$= \sum_{i=1}^{m} I(X_i; \hat{X}_i) \tag{13.42}$$

$$\geq \sum_{i=1}^{m} R(D_i) \tag{13.43}$$

$$= \sum_{i=1}^{m} \left(\frac{1}{2} \log \frac{\sigma_i^2}{D_i} \right)^{+}, \tag{13.44}$$

where $D_i = E(X_i - \hat{X}_i)^2$ and (13.41) follows from the fact that conditioning reduces entropy. We can achieve equality in (13.41) by choosing $f(x^m | \hat{x}^m) = \prod_{i=1}^{m} f(x_i | \hat{x}_i)$ and in (13.43) by choosing the distribution of each $\hat{X}_i \sim \mathcal{N}(0, \sigma_i^2 - D_i)$, as in the previous example. Hence the problem of finding the rate distortion function can be reduced to the following optimization (using nats for convenience):

$$R(D) = \min_{\Sigma D_i = D} \sum_{i=1}^{m} \max \left\{ \frac{1}{2} \ln \frac{\sigma_i^2}{D_i}, 0 \right\}. \tag{13.45}$$

Using Lagrange multipliers, we construct the functional

$$J(D) = \sum_{i=1}^{m} \frac{1}{2} \ln \frac{\sigma_i^2}{D_i} + \lambda \sum_{i=1}^{m} D_i, \tag{13.46}$$

and differentiating with respect to D_i and setting equal to 0, we have

$$\frac{\partial J}{\partial D_i} = -\frac{1}{2}\frac{1}{D_i} + \lambda = 0,$$ (13.47)

or

$$D_i = \lambda'.$$ (13.48)

Hence the optimum allotment of the bits to the various descriptions results in an equal distortion for each random variable. This is possible if the constant λ' in (13.48) is less than σ_i^2 for all i. As the total allowable distortion D is increased, the constant λ' increases until it exceeds σ_i^2 for some i. At this point the solution (13.48) is on the boundary of the allowable region of distortions. If we increase the total distortion, we must use the Kuhn-Tucker conditions to find the minimum in (13.46). In this case the Kuhn-Tucker conditions yield

$$\frac{\partial J}{\partial D_i} = -\frac{1}{2}\frac{1}{D_i} + \lambda,$$ (13.49)

where λ is chosen so that

$$\frac{\partial J}{\partial D_i} \begin{cases} = 0, & \text{if } D_i < \sigma_i^2, \\ \leq 0, & \text{if } D_i \geq \sigma_i^2. \end{cases}$$ (13.50)

It is easy to check that the solution to the Kuhn-Tucker equations is given by the following theorem:

Theorem 13.3.3 (*Rate distortion for a parallel Gaussian source*): *Let* $X_i \sim \mathcal{N}(0, \sigma_i^2)$, $i = 1, 2, \ldots, m$ *be independent Gaussian random variables and let the distortion measure be* $d(x^m, \hat{x}^m) = \sum_{i=1}^{m} (x_i - \hat{x}_i)^2$. *Then the rate distortion function is given by*

$$R(D) = \sum_{i=1}^{m} \frac{1}{2} \log \frac{\sigma_i^2}{D_i},$$ (13.51)

where

$$D_i = \begin{cases} \lambda, & \text{if } \lambda < \sigma_i^2, \\ \sigma_i^2, & \text{if } \lambda \geq \sigma_i^2, \end{cases}$$ (13.52)

where λ *is chosen so that* $\sum_{i=1}^{m} D_i = D$.

This gives rise to a kind of reverse "water-filling" as illustrated in Figure 13.7. We choose a constant λ and only describe those random

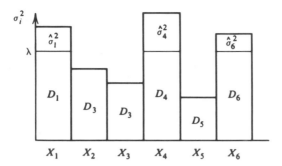

Figure 13.7. Reverse water-filling for independent Gaussian random variables.

variables with variances greater than λ. No bits are used to describe random variables with variance less than λ.

More generally, the rate distortion function for a multivariate normal vector can be obtained by reverse water-filling on the eigenvalues. We can also apply the same arguments to a Gaussian stochastic process. By the spectral representation theorem, a Gaussian stochastic process can be represented as an integral of independent Gaussian processes in the different frequency bands. Reverse water-filling on the spectrum yields the rate distortion function.

13.4 CONVERSE TO THE RATE DISTORTION THEOREM

In this section, we prove the converse to Theorem 13.2.1 by showing that we cannot achieve a distortion less than D if we describe X at a rate less than $R(D)$, where

$$R(D) = \min_{\substack{p(\hat{x}|x):\ \sum_{(x,\hat{x})} p(x)p(\hat{x}|x)d(x,\hat{x}) \le D}} I(X; \hat{X}). \qquad (13.53)$$

The minimization is over all conditional distributions $p(\hat{x}|x)$ for which the joint distribution $p(x, \hat{x}) = p(x)p(\hat{x}|x)$ satisfies the expected distortion constraint. Before proving the converse, we establish some simple properties of the information rate distortion function.

Lemma 13.4.1 (*Convexity of $R(D)$*): *The rate distortion function $R(D)$ given in (13.53) is a non-increasing convex function of D.*

Proof: $R(D)$ is the minimum of the mutual information over increasingly larger sets as D increases. Thus $R(D)$ is non-increasing in D.

To prove that $R(D)$ is convex, consider two rate distortion pairs (R_1, D_1) and (R_2, D_2) which lie on the rate-distortion curve. Let the joint distributions that achieve these pairs be $p_1(x, \hat{x}) = p(x)p_1(\hat{x}|x)$ and $p_2(x, \hat{x}) = p(x)p_2(\hat{x}|x)$. Consider the distribution $p_\lambda = \lambda p_1 + (1 - \lambda)p_2$. Since the distortion is a linear function of the distribution, we have $D(p_\lambda) = \lambda D_1 + (1 - \lambda)D_2$. Mutual information, on the other hand, is a convex function of the conditional distribution (Theorem 2.7.4) and hence

$$I_{p_\lambda}(X; \hat{X}) \le \lambda I_{p_1}(X; \hat{X}) + (1 - \lambda)I_{p_2}(X; \hat{X}) . \tag{13.54}$$

Hence by the definition of the rate distortion function,

$$R(D_\lambda) \le I_{p_\lambda}(X; \hat{X}) \tag{13.55}$$

$$\le \lambda I_{p_1}(X; \hat{X}) + (1 - \lambda)I_{p_2}(X; \hat{X}) \tag{13.56}$$

$$= \lambda R(D_1) + (1 - \lambda)R(D_2) , \tag{13.57}$$

which proves that $R(D)$ is a convex function of D. $\square$

The converse can now be proved.

Proof: (*Converse in Theorem 13.2.1*): We must show, for any source X drawn i.i.d. $\sim p(x)$ with distortion measure $d(x, \hat{x})$, and any $(2^{nR}, n)$ rate distortion code with distortion $\le D$, that the rate R of the code satisfies $R \ge R(D)$.

Consider any $(2^{nR}, n)$ rate distortion code defined by functions f_n and g_n. Let $\hat{X}^n = \hat{X}^n(X^n) = g_n(f_n(X^n))$ be the reproduced sequence corresponding to X^n. Then we have the following chain of inequalities:

$$nR \overset{(a)}{\ge} H(\hat{X}^n) \tag{13.58}$$

$$\overset{(b)}{\ge} H(\hat{X}^n) - H(\hat{X}^n|X^n) \tag{13.59}$$

$$\overset{(c)}{=} I(\hat{X}^n; X^n) \tag{13.60}$$

$$= H(X^n) - H(X^n|\hat{X}^n) \tag{13.61}$$

$$\overset{(d)}{=} \sum_{i=1}^{n} H(X_i) - H(X^n|\hat{X}^n) \tag{13.62}$$

$$\overset{(e)}{=} \sum_{i=1}^{n} H(X_i) - \sum_{i=1}^{n} H(X_i|\hat{X}^n, X_{i-1}, \ldots, X_1) \tag{13.63}$$

$$\overset{(f)}{\ge} \sum_{i=1}^{n} H(X_i) - \sum_{i=1}^{n} H(X_i|\hat{X}_i) \tag{13.64}$$

$$= \sum_{i=1}^{n} I(X_i; \hat{X}_i) \tag{13.65}$$

$$\overset{(g)}{\geq} \sum_{i=1}^{n} R(Ed(X_i, \hat{X}_i)) \tag{13.66}$$

$$= n \sum_{i=1}^{n} \frac{1}{n} R(Ed(X_i, \hat{X}_i)) \tag{13.67}$$

$$\overset{(h)}{\geq} nR\left(\frac{1}{n} \sum_{i=1}^{n} Ed(X_i, \hat{X}_i)\right) \tag{13.68}$$

$$\overset{(i)}{=} nR(Ed(X^n, \hat{X}^n)) \tag{13.69}$$

$$- nR(D), \tag{13.70}$$

where

(a) follows from the fact that there are at most 2^{nR} $\hat{X}^n$'s in the range of the encoding function,

(b) from the fact that $\hat{X}^n$ is a function of X^n and thus $H(\hat{X}^n|X^n) = 0$,

(c) from the definition of mutual information,

(d) from the fact that the X_i are independent,

(e) from the chain rule for entropy,

(f) from the fact that conditioning reduces entropy,

(g) from the definition of the rate distortion function,

(h) from the convexity of the rate distortion function (Lemma 13.4.1) and Jensen's inequality, and

(i) from the definition of distortion for blocks of length n.

This shows that the rate R of any rate distortion code exceeds the rate distortion function $R(D)$ evaluated at the distortion level $D = Ed(X^n, \hat{X}^n)$ achieved by that code.   □

13.5   ACHIEVABILITY OF THE RATE DISTORTION FUNCTION

We now prove the achievability of the rate distortion function. We begin with a modified version of the joint AEP in which we add the condition that the pair of sequences be typical with respect to the distortion measure.

Definition: Let $p(x, \hat{x})$ be a joint probability distribution on $\mathscr{X} \times \hat{\mathscr{X}}$ and let $d(x, \hat{x})$ be a distortion measure on $\mathscr{X} \times \hat{\mathscr{X}}$. For any $\epsilon > 0$, a pair of sequences $(x^n, \hat{x}^n)$ is said to be *distortion ϵ-typical* or simply distortion typical if

$$\left| -\frac{1}{n} \log p(x^n) - H(X) \right| < \epsilon \tag{13.71}$$

$$\left| -\frac{1}{n} \log p(\hat{x}^n) - H(\hat{X}) \right| < \epsilon \tag{13.72}$$

$$\left| -\frac{1}{n} \log p(x^n, \hat{x}^n) - H(X, \hat{X}) \right| < \epsilon \tag{13.73}$$

$$\left| d(x^n, \hat{x}^n) - Ed(X, \hat{X}) \right| < \epsilon \tag{13.74}$$

The set of distortion typical sequences is called the *distortion typical set* and is denoted $A_{d, \epsilon}^{(n)}$.

Note that this is the definition of the jointly typical set (Section 8.6) with the additional constraint that the distortion be close to the expected value. Hence, the distortion typical set is a subset of the jointly typical set, i.e., $A_{d, \epsilon}^{(n)} \subset A_{\epsilon}^{(n)}$. If $(X_i, \hat{X}_i)$ are drawn i.i.d $\sim p(x, \hat{x})$, then the distortion between two random sequences

$$d(X^n, \hat{X}^n) = \frac{1}{n} \sum_{i=1}^{n} d(X_i, \hat{X}_i) \tag{13.75}$$

is an average of i.i.d. random variables, and the law of large numbers implies that it is close to its expected value with high probability. Hence we have the following lemma.

Lemma 13.5.1: *Let $(X_i, \hat{X}_i)$ be drawn i.i.d. $\sim p(x, \hat{x})$. Then $\Pr(A_{d, \epsilon}^{(n)}) \to 1$ as $n \to \infty$.*

Proof: The sums in the four conditions in the definition of $A_{d, \epsilon}^{(n)}$ are all normalized sums of i.i.d random variables and hence, by the law of large numbers, tend to their respective expected values with probability 1. Hence the set of sequences satisfying all four conditions has probability tending to 1 as $n \to \infty$. $\square$

The following lemma is a direct consequence of the definition of the distortion typical set.

Lemma 13.5.2: *For all $(x^n, \hat{x}^n) \in A_{d, \epsilon}^{(n)}$,*

$$p(\hat{x}^n) \geq p(\hat{x}^n | x^n) 2^{-n(I(X; \hat{X}) + 3\epsilon)}. \tag{13.76}$$

Proof: Using the definition of $A_{d, \epsilon}^{(n)}$, we can bound the probabilities $p(x^n)$, $p(\hat{x}^n)$ and $p(x^n, \hat{x}^n)$ for all $(x^n, \hat{x}^n) \in A_{d, \epsilon}^{(n)}$, and hence

$$p(\hat{x}^n | x^n) = \frac{p(x^n, \hat{x}^n)}{p(x^n)} \tag{13.77}$$

$$= p(\hat{x}^n) \frac{p(x^n, \hat{x}^n)}{p(x^n) p(\hat{x}^n)} \tag{13.78}$$

$$\leq p(\hat{x}^n) \frac{2^{-n(H(X, \hat{X}) - \epsilon)}}{2^{-n(H(X) + \epsilon)} 2^{-n(H(\hat{X}) + \epsilon)}} \tag{13.79}$$

$$= p(\hat{x}^n) 2^{n(I(X; \hat{X}) + 3\epsilon)}, \tag{13.80}$$

and the lemma follows immediately. $\square$

We also need the following interesting inequality.

Lemma 13.5.3: *For* $0 \leq x, y \leq 1$, $n > 0$,

$$(1 - xy)^n \leq 1 - x + e^{-yn}. \tag{13.81}$$

Proof: Let $f(y) = e^{-y} - 1 + y$. Then $f(0) = 0$ and $f'(y) = -e^{-y} + 1 > 0$ for $y > 0$, and hence $f(y) > 0$ for $y > 0$. Hence for $0 \leq y \leq 1$, we have $1 - y \leq e^{-y}$, and raising this to the nth power, we obtain

$$(1 - y)^n \leq e^{-yn}. \tag{13.82}$$

Thus the lemma is satisfied for $x = 1$. By examination, it is clear that the inequality is also satisfied for $x = 0$. By differentiation, it is easy to see that $g_y(x) = (1 - xy)^n$ is a convex function of x and hence for $0 \leq x \leq 1$, we have

$$(1 - xy)^n = g_y(x) \tag{13.83}$$

$$\leq (1 - x) g_y(0) + x g_y(1) \tag{13.84}$$

$$= (1 - x)1 + x(1 - y)^n \tag{13.85}$$

$$\leq 1 - x + xe^{-yn} \tag{13.86}$$

$$\leq 1 - x + e^{-yn}. \square \tag{13.87}$$

We use this to prove the achievability of Theorem 13.2.1.

Proof (*Achievability in Theorem 13.2.1*): Let $X_1, X_2, \ldots, X_n$ be drawn i.i.d. $\sim p(x)$ and let $d(x, \hat{x})$ be a bounded distortion measure for this source. Let the rate distortion function for this source be $R(D)$.

Then for any D, and any $R > R(D)$, we will show that the rate distortion pair (R, D) is achievable, by proving the existence a sequence of rate distortion codes with rate R and asymptotic distortion D.

Fix $p(\hat{x}|x)$, where $p(\hat{x}|x)$ achieves equality in (13.53). Thus $I(X; \hat{X}) = R(D)$. Calculate $p(\hat{x}) = \Sigma_x p(x)p(\hat{x}|x)$. Choose $\delta > 0$. We will prove the existence of a rate distortion code with rate R and distortion less than or equal to $D + \delta$.

> *Generation of codebook.* Randomly generate a rate distortion codebook $\mathscr{C}$ consisting of 2^{nR} sequences $\hat{X}^n$ drawn i.i.d. $\sim \Pi_{i=1}^n p(\hat{x}_i)$. Index these codewords by $w \in \{1, 2, \ldots, 2^{nR}\}$. Reveal this codebook to the encoder and decoder.
>
> *Encoding.* Encode X^n by w if there exists a w such that $(X^n, \hat{X}^n(w)) \in A_{d, \epsilon}^{(n)}$, the distortion typical set. If there is more than one such w, send the least. If there is no such w, let $w = 1$. Thus nR bits suffice to describe the index w of the jointly typical codeword.
>
> *Decoding.* The reproduced sequence is $\hat{X}^n(w)$.
>
> *Calculation of distortion.* As in the case of the channel coding theorem, we calculate the expected distortion over the random choice of codebooks $\mathscr{C}$ as
>
> $$\bar{D} = E_{X^n, \mathscr{C}} d(X^n, \hat{X}^n) \qquad (13.88)$$
>
> where the expectation is over the random choice of codebooks and over X^n.

For a fixed codebook $\mathscr{C}$ and choice of $\epsilon > 0$, we divide the sequences $x^n \in \mathscr{X}^n$ into two categories:

- Sequences x^n such that there exists a codeword $\hat{X}^n(w)$ that is distortion typical with x^n, i.e., $d(x^n, \hat{x}^n(w)) < D + \epsilon$. Since the total probability of these sequences is at most 1, these sequences contribute at most $D + \epsilon$ to the expected distortion.

- Sequences x^n such that there does not exist a codeword $\hat{X}^n(w)$ that is distortion typical with x^n. Let P_e be the total probability of these sequences. Since the distortion for any individual sequence is bounded by $d_{\max}$, these sequences contribute at most $P_e d_{\max}$ to the expected distortion.

Hence we can bound the total distortion by

$$Ed(X^n, \hat{X}^n(X^n)) \le D + \epsilon + P_e d_{\max}, \qquad (13.89)$$

which can be made less than $D + \delta$ for an appropriate choice of ϵ if P_e is small enough. Hence, if we show that P_e is small, then the expected distortion is close to D and the theorem is proved.

Calculation of P_e. We must bound the probability that, for a random choice of codebook $\mathscr{C}$ and a randomly chosen source sequence, there is no codeword that is distortion typical with the source sequence. Let $J(\mathscr{C})$ denote the set of source sequences x^n such that at least one codeword in $\mathscr{C}$ is distortion typical with x^n.

Then

$$P_e = \sum_{\mathscr{C}} P(\mathscr{C}) \sum_{x^n : x^n \notin J(\mathscr{C})} p(x^n). \qquad (13.90)$$

This is the probability of all sequences not well represented by a code, averaged over the randomly chosen code. By changing the order of summation, we can also interpret this as the probability of choosing a codebook that does not well represent sequence x^n, averaged with respect to $p(x^n)$. Thus

$$P_e = \sum_{x^n} p(x^n) \sum_{\mathscr{C} : x^n \notin J(\mathscr{C})} p(\mathscr{C}). \qquad (13.91)$$

Let us define

$$K(x^n, \hat{x}^n) = \begin{cases} 1 & \text{if } (x^n, \hat{x}^n) \in A_{d, \epsilon}^{(n)}, \\ 0 & \text{if } (x^n, \hat{x}^n) \notin A_{d, \epsilon}^{(n)}. \end{cases} \qquad (13.92)$$

The probability that a single randomly chosen codeword X^n does not well represent a fixed x^n is

$$\Pr((x^n, \hat{X}^n) \notin A_{d, \epsilon}^{(n)}) = \Pr(K(x^n, \hat{X}^n) = 0) = 1 - \sum_{\hat{x}^n} p(\hat{x}^n) K(x^n, \hat{x}^n), \quad (13.93)$$

and therefore the probability that 2^{nR} independently chosen codewords do not represent x^n, averaged over $p(x^n)$, is

$$P_e = \sum_{x^n} p(x^n) \sum_{\mathscr{C} : x^n \notin J(\mathscr{C})} p(\mathscr{C}) \qquad (13.94)$$

$$= \sum_{x^n} p(x^n) \left[1 - \sum_{\hat{x}^n} p(\hat{x}^n) K(x^n, \hat{x}^n) \right]^{2^{nR}}. \qquad (13.95)$$

We now use Lemma 13.5.2 to bound the sum within the brackets. From Lemma 13.5.2, it follows that

$$\sum_{\hat{x}^n} p(\hat{x}^n) K(x^n, \hat{x}^n) \geq \sum_{\hat{x}^n} p(\hat{x}^n | x^n) 2^{-n(I(X; \hat{X}) + 3\epsilon)} K(x^n, \hat{x}^n), \qquad (13.96)$$

and hence

$$P_e \le \sum_{x^n} p(x^n) \left(1 - 2^{-n(I(X; \hat{X}) + 3\epsilon)} \sum_{\hat{x}^n} p(\hat{x}^n | x^n) K(x^n, \hat{x}^n) \right)^{2^{nR}}. \quad (13.97)$$

We now use Lemma 13.5.3 to bound the term on the right hand side of (13.97) and obtain

$$\left(1 - 2^{-n(I(X; \hat{X}) + 3\epsilon)} \sum_{\hat{x}^n} p(\hat{x}^n | x^n) K(x^n, \hat{x}^n) \right)^{2^{nR}}$$

$$\le 1 - \sum_{\hat{x}^n} p(\hat{x}^n | x^n) K(x^n, \hat{x}^n) + e^{-(2^{-n(I(X; \hat{X}) + 3\epsilon)} 2^{nR})}. \quad (13.98)$$

Substituting this inequality in (13.97), we obtain

$$P_e \le 1 - \sum_{x^n} p(x^n) p(\hat{x}^n | x^n) K(x^n, \hat{x}^n) + e^{-2^{-n(I(X; \hat{X}) + 3\epsilon)} 2^{nR}}. \quad (13.99)$$

The last term in the bound is equal to

$$e^{-2^{n(R - I(X; \hat{X}) - 3\epsilon)}}, \quad (13.100)$$

which goes to zero exponentially fast with n if $R > I(X; \hat{X}) + 3\epsilon$. Hence if we choose $p(\hat{x} | x)$ to be the conditional distribution that achieves the minimum in the rate distortion function, then $R > R(D)$ implies $R > I(X; \hat{X})$ and we can choose ϵ small enough so that the last term in (13.99) goes to 0.

The first two terms in (13.99) give the probability under the joint distribution $p(x^n, \hat{x}^n)$ that the pair of sequences is not distortion typical. Hence using Lemma 13.5.1,

$$1 - \sum_{x^n} \sum_{\hat{x}^n} p(x^n, \hat{x}^n) K(x^n, \hat{x}^n) = \Pr((X^n, \hat{X}^n) \notin A_{d, \epsilon}^{(n)}) \quad (13.101)$$

$$< \epsilon \quad (13.102)$$

for n sufficiently large. Therefore, by an appropriate choice of ϵ and n, we can make P_e as small as we like.

So for any choice of $\delta > 0$ there exists an ϵ and n such that over all randomly chosen rate R codes of block length n, the expected distortion is less than $D + \delta$. Hence there must exist at least one code $\mathscr{C}^*$ with this rate and block length with average distortion less than $D + \delta$. Since δ was arbitrary, we have shown that (R, D) is achievable if $R > R(D)$. $\square$

We have proved the existence of a rate distortion code with an expected distortion close to D and a rate close to $R(D)$. The similarities between the random coding proof of the rate distortion theorem and the random coding proof of the channel coding theorem are now evident. We will explore the parallels further by considering the Gaussian example, which provides some geometric insight into the problem. It turns out that channel coding is sphere packing and rate distortion coding is sphere covering.

Channel coding for the Gaussian channel. Consider a Gaussian channel, $Y_i = X_i + Z_i$, where the Z_i are i.i.d. $\sim \mathcal{N}(0, N)$ and there is a power constraint P on the power per symbol of the transmitted codeword. Consider a sequence of n transmissions. The power constraint implies that the transmitted sequence lies within a sphere of radius $\sqrt{nP}$ in $\mathcal{R}^n$. The coding problem is equivalent to finding a set of 2^{nR} sequences within this sphere such that the probability of any of them being mistaken for any other is small— the spheres of radius $\sqrt{nN}$ around each of them are almost disjoint. This corresponds to filling a sphere of radius $\sqrt{n(P + N)}$ with spheres of radius $\sqrt{nN}$. One would expect that the largest number of spheres that could be fit would be the ratio of their volumes, or, equivalently, the nth power of the ratio of their radii. Thus if M is the number of codewords that can be transmitted efficiently, we have

$$M \leq \frac{(\sqrt{n(P + N)})^n}{(\sqrt{nN})^n} = \left(\frac{P + N}{N}\right)^{n/2}. \tag{13.103}$$

The results of the channel coding theorem show that it is possible to do this efficiently for large n; it is possible to find approximately

$$2^{nC} = \left(\frac{P + N}{N}\right)^{n/2} \tag{13.104}$$

codewords such that the noise spheres around them are almost disjoint (the total volume of their intersection is arbitrarily small).

Rate distortion for the Gaussian source. Consider a Gaussian source of variance σ^2. A $(2^{nR}, n)$ rate distortion code for this source with distortion D is a set of 2^{nR} sequences in $\mathcal{R}^n$ such that most source sequences of length n (all those that lie within a sphere of radius $\sqrt{n\sigma^2}$) are within a distance $\sqrt{nD}$ of some codeword. Again, by the sphere packing argument, it is clear that the minimum number of codewords required is

$$2^{nR(D)} = \left(\frac{\sigma^2}{D}\right)^{n/2}. \tag{13.105}$$

The rate distortion theorem shows that this minimum rate is asymptotically achievable, i.e., that there exists a collection of spheres of radius $\sqrt{nD}$ that cover the space except for a set of arbitrarily small probability.

The above geometric arguments also enable us to transform a good code for channel transmission into a good code for rate distortion. In both cases, the essential idea is to fill the space of source sequences: in channel transmission, we want to find the largest set of codewords which have a large minimum distance between codewords, while in rate distortion, we wish to find the smallest set of codewords that covers the entire space. If we have any set that meets the sphere packing bound for one, it will meet the sphere packing bound for the other. In the Gaussian case, choosing the codewords to be Gaussian with the appropriate variance is asymptotically optimal for both rate distortion and channel coding.

13.6 STRONGLY TYPICAL SEQUENCES AND RATE DISTORTION

In the last section, we proved the existence of a rate distortion code of rate $R(D)$ with average distortion close to D. But a stronger statement is true—not only is the average distortion close to D, but the total probability that the distortion is greater than $D + \delta$ is close to 0. The proof of this stronger result is more involved; we will only give an outline of the proof. The method of proof is similar to the proof in the previous section; the main difference is that we will use strongly typical sequences rather than weakly typical sequences. This will enable us to give a lower bound to the probability that a typical source sequence is not well represented by a randomly chosen codeword in (13.93). This will give a more intuitive proof of the rate distortion theorem.

We will begin by defining strong typicality and quoting a basic theorem bounding the probability that two sequences are jointly typical. The properties of strong typicality were introduced by Berger [28] and were explored in detail in the book by Csiszár and Körner [83]. We will define strong typicality (as in Chapter 12) and state a fundamental lemma. The proof of the lemma will be left as a problem at the end of the chapter.

Definition: A sequence $x^n \in \mathcal{X}^n$ is said to be ϵ-*strongly typical* with respect to a distribution $p(x)$ on $\mathcal{X}$ if

1. For all $a \in \mathcal{X}$ with $p(a) > 0$, we have

$$\left| \frac{1}{n} N(a|x^n) - p(a) \right| < \frac{\epsilon}{|\mathcal{X}|} , \tag{13.106}$$

2. For all $a \in \mathcal{X}$ with $p(a) = 0$, $N(a|x^n) = 0$.

$N(a|x^n)$ is the number of occurrences of the symbol a in the sequence x^n.

The set of sequences $x^n \in \mathcal{X}^n$ such that x^n is strongly typical is called the *strongly typical* set and is denoted $A_{\epsilon}^{*(n)}(X)$ or $A_{\epsilon}^{*(n)}$ when the random variable is understood from the context.

Definition: A pair of sequences $(x^n, y^n) \in \mathcal{X}^n \times \mathcal{Y}^n$ is said to be ϵ-*strongly typical* with respect to a distribution $p(x, y)$ on $\mathcal{X} \times \mathcal{Y}$ if

1. For all $(a, b) \in \mathcal{X} \times \mathcal{Y}$ with $p(a, b) > 0$, we have

$$\left| \frac{1}{n} N(a, b|x^n, y^n) - p(a, b) \right| < \frac{\epsilon}{|\mathcal{X}||\mathcal{Y}|}, \qquad (13.107)$$

2. For all $(a, b) \in \mathcal{X} \times \mathcal{Y}$ with $p(a, b) = 0$, $N(a, b|x^n, y^n) = 0$.

$N(a, b|x^n, y^n)$ is the number of occurrences of the pair (a, b) in the pair of sequences (x^n, y^n).

The set of sequences $(x^n, y^n) \in \mathcal{X}^n \times \mathcal{Y}^n$ such that (x^n, y^n) is strongly typical is called the *strongly typical* set and is denoted $A_{\epsilon}^{*(n)}(X, Y)$ or $A_{\epsilon}^{*(n)}$.

From the definition, it follows that if $(x^n, y^n) \in A_{\epsilon}^{*(n)}(X, Y)$, then $x^n \in A_{\epsilon}^{*(n)}(X)$.

From the strong law of large numbers, the following lemma is immediate.

Lemma 13.6.1: *Let (X_i, Y_i) be drawn i.i.d. $\sim p(x, y)$. Then $\Pr(A_{\epsilon}^{*(n)}) \to 1$ as $n \to \infty$.*

We will use one basic result, which bounds the probability that an independently drawn sequence will be seen as jointly strongly typical with a given sequence. Theorem 8.6.1 shows that if we choose X^n and Y^n independently, the probability that they will be weakly jointly typical is $\approx 2^{-nI(X; Y)}$. The following lemma extends the result to strongly typical sequences. This is stronger than the earlier result in that it gives a lower bound on the probability that a randomly chosen sequence is jointly typical with a fixed typical x^n.

Lemma 13.6.2: *Let $Y_1, Y_2, \ldots, Y_n$ be drawn i.i.d. $\sim \Pi\, p(y)$. For $x^n \in A_{\epsilon}^{*(n)}$, the probability that $(x^n, Y^n) \in A_{\epsilon}^{*(n)}$ is bounded by*

$$2^{-n(I(X; Y)+\epsilon_1)} \le \Pr((x^n, Y^n) \in A_{\epsilon}^{*(n)}) \le 2^{-n(I(X; Y)-\epsilon_1)}, \qquad (13.108)$$

where ϵ_1 goes to 0 as $\epsilon \to 0$ and $n \to \infty$.

Proof: We will not prove this lemma, but instead outline the proof in a problem at the end of the chapter. In essence, the proof involves finding a lower bound on the size of the conditionally typical set. $\square$

We will proceed directly to the achievability of the rate distortion function. We will only give an outline to illustrate the main ideas. The construction of the codebook and the encoding and decoding are similar to the proof in the last section.

Proof: Fix $p(\hat{x}|x)$. Calculate $p(\hat{x}) = \Sigma_x \, p(x)p(\hat{x}|x)$. Fix $\epsilon > 0$. Later we will choose ϵ appropriately to achieve an expected distortion less than $D + \delta$.

Generation of codebook. Generate a rate distortion codebook $\mathscr{C}$ consisting of 2^{nR} sequences $\hat{X}^n$ drawn i.i.d. $\sim\Pi_i p(\hat{x}_i)$. Denote the sequences $\hat{X}^n(1), \ldots, \hat{X}^n(2^{nR})$.

Encoding. Given a sequence X^n, index it by w if there exists a w such that $(X^n, \hat{X}^n(w)) \in A_\epsilon^{*(n)}$, the strongly jointly typical set. If there is more than one such w, send the first in lexicographic order. If there is no such w, let $w = 1$.

Decoding. Let the reproduced sequence be $\hat{X}^n(w)$.

Calculation of distortion. As in the case of the proof in the last section, we calculate the expected distortion over the random choice of codebook as

$$D = E_{X^n, \, \mathscr{C}} d(X^n, \hat{X}^n) \tag{13.109}$$

$$= E_{\mathscr{C}} \sum_{x^n} p(x^n) d(x^n, \hat{X}^n(x^n)) \tag{13.110}$$

$$= \sum_{x^n} p(x^n) E_{\mathscr{C}} d(x^n, \hat{X}^n), \tag{13.111}$$

where the expectation is over the random choice of codebook.

For a fixed codebook $\mathscr{C}$, we divide the sequences $x^n \in \mathscr{X}^n$ into three categories as shown in Figure 13.8.

- *The non-typical sequences* $x^n \notin A_\epsilon^{*(n)}$. The total probability of these sequences can be made less than ϵ by choosing n large enough. Since the individual distortion between any two sequences is bounded by $d_{\max}$, the non-typical sequences can contribute at most $\epsilon d_{\max}$ to the expected distortion.
- *Typical sequences* $x^n \in A_\epsilon^{*(n)}$ *such that there exists a codeword* $\hat{X}^n$ *that is jointly typical with* x^n. In this case, since the source sequence and the codeword are strongly jointly typical, the continuity of the

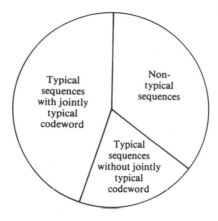

Figure 13.8. Classes of source sequences in rate distortion theorem.

distortion as a function of the joint distribution ensures that they are also distortion typical. Hence the distortion between these x^n and their codewords is bounded by $D + \epsilon d_{max}$, and since the total probability of these sequences is at most 1, these sequences contribute at most $D + \epsilon d_{max}$ to the expected distortion.

- *Typical sequences $x^n \in A_\epsilon^{*(n)}$ such that there does not exist a codeword $\hat{X}^n$ that is jointly typical with x^n.* Let P_e be the total probability of these sequences. Since the distortion for any individual sequence is bounded by d_{max}, these sequences contribute at most $P_e d_{max}$ to the expected distortion.

The sequences in the first and third categories are the sequences that may not be well represented by this rate distortion code. The probability of the first category of sequences is less than ϵ for sufficiently large n. The probability of the last category is P_e, which we will show can be made small. This will prove the theorem that the total probability of sequences that are not well represented is small. In turn, we use this to show that the average distortion is close to D.

  Calculation of P_e. We must bound the probability that there is no codeword that is jointly typical with the given sequence X^n. From the joint AEP, we know that the probability that X^n and any $\hat{X}^n$ are jointly typical is $\doteq 2^{-nI(X;\hat{X})}$. Hence the expected number of jointly typical $\hat{X}^n(w)$ is $2^{nR}2^{-nI(X;\hat{X})}$, which is exponentially large if $R > I(X;\hat{X})$.

But this is not sufficient to show that $P_e \to 0$. We must show that the probability that there is no codeword that is jointly typical with X^n goes to zero. The fact that the expected number of jointly typical codewords is exponentially large does not ensure that there will at least one with high probability.

Just as in (13.93), we can expand the probability of error as

$$P_e = \sum_{x^n \in A_\epsilon^{*(n)}} p(x^n)[1 - \Pr((x^n, \hat{X}^n) \in A_\epsilon^{*(n)})]^{2^{nR}}. \qquad (13.112)$$

From Lemma 13.6.2, we have

$$\Pr((x^n, \hat{X}^n) \in A_\epsilon^{*(n)}) \geq 2^{-n(I(X; \hat{X}) + \epsilon_1)}. \qquad (13.113)$$

Substituting this in (13.112) and using the inequality $(1 - x)^n \leq e^{-nx}$, we have

$$P_e \leq e^{-(2^{nR} 2^{-n(I(X; \hat{X}) + \epsilon_1)})} \qquad (13.114)$$

which goes to 0 as $n \to \infty$ if $R > I(X; \hat{X}) + \epsilon_1$. Hence for an appropriate choice of ϵ and n, we can get the total probability of all badly represented sequences to be as small as we want. Not only is the expected distortion close to D, but with probability going to 1, we will find a codeword whose distortion with respect to the given sequence is less than $D + \delta$. $\square$

13.7 CHARACTERIZATION OF THE RATE DISTORTION FUNCTION

We have defined the information rate distortion function as

$$R(D) = \min_{q(\hat{x}|x) : \sum_{(x, \hat{x})} p(x)q(\hat{x}|x)d(x, \hat{x}) \leq D} I(X; \hat{X}), \qquad (13.115)$$

where the minimization is over all conditional distributions $q(\hat{x}|x)$ for which the joint distribution $p(x)q(\hat{x}|x)$ satisfies the expected distortion constraint. This is a standard minimization problem of a convex function over the convex set of all $q(\hat{x}|x) \geq 0$ satisfying $\sum_{\hat{x}} q(\hat{x}|x) = 1$ for all x and $\sum q(\hat{x}|x)p(x)d(x, \hat{x}) \leq D$.

We can use the method of Lagrange multipliers to find the solution. We set up the functional

$$J(q) = \sum_x \sum_{\hat{x}} p(x)q(\hat{x}|x) \log \frac{q(\hat{x}|x)}{\sum_x p(x)q(\hat{x}|x)} + \lambda \sum_x \sum_{\hat{x}} p(x)q(\hat{x}|x)d(x, \hat{x}) \qquad (13.116)$$

$$+ \sum_x \nu(x) \sum_{\hat{x}} q(\hat{x}|x), \qquad (13.117)$$

where the last term corresponds to the constraint that $q(\hat{x}|x)$ is a conditional probability mass function. If we let $q(\hat{x}) = \Sigma_x \, p(x)q(\hat{x}|x)$ be the distribution on $\hat{X}$ induced by $q(\hat{x}|x)$, we can rewrite $J(q)$ as

$$J(q) = \sum_x \sum_{\hat{x}} p(x)q(\hat{x}|x) \log \frac{q(\hat{x}|x)}{q(\hat{x})} + \lambda \sum_x \sum_{\hat{x}} p(x)q(\hat{x}|x)d(x, \hat{x}) \quad (13.118)$$

$$+ \sum_x \nu(x) \sum_{\hat{x}} q(\hat{x}|x) . \quad (13.119)$$

Differentiating with respect to $q(\hat{x}|x)$, we have

$$\frac{\partial J}{\partial q(\hat{x}|x)} = p(x) \log \frac{q(\hat{x}|x)}{q(\hat{x})} + p(x) - \sum_{x'} p(x')q(\hat{x}|x')\frac{1}{q(\hat{x})}p(x) + \lambda p(x)d(x, \hat{x})$$

$$+ \nu(x) = 0 . \quad (13.120)$$

Setting $\log \mu(x) = \nu(x)/p(x)$, we obtain

$$p(x)\left[\log \frac{q(\hat{x}|x)}{q(\hat{x})} + \lambda d(x, \hat{x}) + \log \mu(x) \right] = 0 \quad (13.121)$$

or

$$q(\hat{x}|x) = \frac{q(\hat{x})e^{-\lambda d(x, \hat{x})}}{\mu(x)} . \quad (13.122)$$

Since $\Sigma_{\hat{x}} \, q(\hat{x}|x) = 1$, we must have

$$\mu(x) = \sum_{\hat{x}} q(\hat{x})e^{-\lambda d(x, \hat{x})} \quad (13.123)$$

or

$$q(\hat{x}|x) = \frac{q(\hat{x})e^{-\lambda d(x, \hat{x})}}{\Sigma_{\hat{x}} \, q(\hat{x})e^{-\lambda d(x, \hat{x})}} . \quad (13.124)$$

Multiplying this by $p(x)$ and summing over all x, we obtain

$$q(\hat{x}) = q(\hat{x}) \sum_x \frac{p(x)e^{-\lambda d(x, \hat{x})}}{\Sigma_{\hat{x}'} \, q(\hat{x}')e^{-\lambda d(x, \hat{x}')}} . \quad (13.125)$$

If $q(\hat{x}) > 0$, we can divide both sides by $q(\hat{x})$ and obtain

$$\sum_x \frac{p(x)e^{-\lambda d(x, \hat{x})}}{\Sigma_{\hat{x}'} \, q(\hat{x}')e^{-\lambda d(x, \hat{x}')}} = 1 \quad (13.126)$$

for all $\hat{x} \in \hat{\mathcal{X}}$. We can combine these $|\hat{\mathcal{X}}|$ equations with the equation defining the distortion and calculate λ and the $|\hat{\mathcal{X}}|$ unknowns $q(\hat{x})$. We can use this and (13.124) to find the optimum conditional distribution.

The above analysis is valid if all the output symbols are active, i.e., $q(\hat{x}) > 0$ for all $\hat{x}$. But this is not necessarily the case. We would then have to apply the Kuhn-Tucker conditions to characterize the minimum. The inequality condition $q(\hat{x}) > 0$ is covered by the Kuhn-Tucker conditions, which reduce to

$$\frac{\partial J}{\partial q(\hat{x}|x)} \begin{cases} = 0 & \text{if } q(\hat{x}|x) > 0, \\ \geq 0 & \text{if } q(\hat{x}|x) = 0. \end{cases} \tag{13.127}$$

Substituting the value of the derivative, we obtain the conditions for the minimum as

$$\sum_x \frac{p(x)e^{-\lambda d(x,\hat{x})}}{\sum_{\hat{x}'} q(\hat{x}')e^{-\lambda d(x,\hat{x}')}} = 1 \quad \text{if } q(\hat{x}) > 0, \tag{13.128}$$

$$\sum_x \frac{p(x)e^{-\lambda d(x,\hat{x})}}{\sum_{\hat{x}'} q(\hat{x}')e^{-\lambda d(x,\hat{x}')}} \leq 1 \quad \text{if } q(\hat{x}) = 0. \tag{13.129}$$

This characterization will enable us to check if a given $q(\hat{x})$ is a solution to the minimization problem. However, it is not easy to solve for the optimum output distribution from these equations. In the next section, we provide an iterative algorithm for computing the rate distortion function. This algorithm is a special case of a general algorithm for finding the minimum relative entropy distance between two convex sets of probability densities.

13.8 COMPUTATION OF CHANNEL CAPACITY AND THE RATE DISTORTION FUNCTION

Consider the following problem: Given two convex sets A and B in $\mathcal{R}^n$ as shown in Figure 13.9, we would like to the find the minimum distance between them

$$d_{\min} = \min_{a \in A, b \in B} d(a, b), \tag{13.130}$$

where $d(a, b)$ is the Euclidean distance between a and b. An intuitively obvious algorithm to do this would be to take any point $x \in A$, and find the $y \in B$ that is closest to it. Then fix this y and find the closest point in A. Repeating this process, it is clear that the distance decreases at each stage. Does it converge to the minimum distance between the two sets? Csiszár and Tusnády [85] have shown that if the sets are convex and if the distance satisfies certain conditions, then this alternating minimiza-

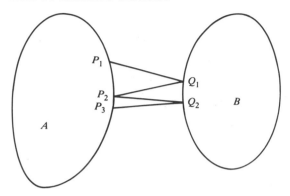

Figure 13.9. Distance between convex sets.

tion algorithm will indeed converge to the minimum. In particular, if the sets are sets of probability distributions and the distance measure is the relative entropy, then the algorithm does converge to the the minimum relative entropy between the two sets of distributions.

To apply this algorithm to rate distortion, we have to rewrite the rate distortion function as a minimum of the relative entropy between two sets. We begin with a simple lemma:

Lemma 13.8.1: *Let $p(x)p(y|x)$ be a given joint distribution. Then the distribution $r(y)$ that minimizes the relative entropy $D(p(x)p(y|x)\| p(x) r(y))$ is the marginal distribution $r^*(y)$ corresponding to $p(y|x)$, i.e.,*

$$D(p(x)p(y|x)\| p(x)r^*(y)) = \min_{r(y)} D(p(x)p(y|x)\| p(x)r(y)),$$

$$(13.131)$$

where $r^*(y) = \Sigma_x p(x)p(y|x)$. Also

$$\max_{r(x|y)} \sum_{x, y} p(x)p(y|x) \log \frac{r(x|y)}{p(x)} = \sum_{x, y} p(x)p(y|x) \log \frac{r^*(x|y)}{p(x)}, \quad (13.132)$$

where

$$r^*(x|y) = \frac{p(x)p(y|x)}{\Sigma_x p(x)p(y|x)}.$$

$$(13.133)$$

Proof:

$$D(p(x)p(y|x)\| p(x)r(y)) - D(p(x)p(y|x)\| p(x)r^*(y))$$

$$= \sum_{x, y} p(x)p(y|x) \log \frac{p(x)p(y|x)}{p(x)r(y)} \quad (13.134)$$

$$-\sum_{x, y} p(x)p(y|x) \log \frac{p(x)p(y|x)}{p(x)r^*(y)} \qquad (13.135)$$

$$= \sum_{x, y} p(x)p(y|x) \log \frac{r^*(y)}{r(y)} \qquad (13.136)$$

$$= \sum_{y} r^*(y) \log \frac{r^*(y)}{r(y)} \qquad (13.137)$$

$$= D(r^*\|r) \qquad (13.138)$$

$$\geq 0 . \qquad (13.139)$$

The proof of the second part of the lemma is left as an exercise. □

We can use this lemma to rewrite the minimization in the definition of the rate distortion function as a double minimization,

$$R(D) = \min_{r(\hat{x})} \quad \min_{q(\hat{x}|x) : \Sigma\ p(x)q(\hat{x}|x)d(x,\,\hat{x}) \leq D} \sum_{x} \sum_{\hat{x}} p(x)q(\hat{x}|x) \log \frac{q(\hat{x}|x)}{r(\hat{x})} .$$

$$(13.140)$$

If A is the set of all joint distributions with marginal $p(x)$ that satisfy the distortion constraints and if B the set of product distributions $p(x)r(\hat{x})$ with arbitrary $r(\hat{x})$, then we can write

$$R(D) = \min_{q \in B} \min_{p \in A} D(p\|q) . \qquad (13.141)$$

We now apply the process of alternating minimization, which is called the Blahut-Arimoto algorithm in this case. We begin with a choice of λ and an initial output distribution $r(\hat{x})$ and calculate the $q(\hat{x}|x)$ that minimizes the mutual information subject to a distortion constraint. We can use the method of Lagrange multipliers for this minimization to obtain

$$q(\hat{x}|x) = \frac{r(\hat{x})e^{-\lambda d(x,\,\hat{x})}}{\Sigma_{\hat{x}}\ r(\hat{x})e^{-\lambda d(x,\,\hat{x})}} . \qquad (13.142)$$

For this conditional distribution $q(\hat{x}|x)$, we calculate the output distribution $r(\hat{x})$ that minimizes the mutual information, which by Lemma 13.8.1 is

$$r(\hat{x}) = \sum_{x} p(x)q(\hat{x}|x) . \qquad (13.143)$$

We use this output distribution as the starting point of the next iteration. Each step in the iteration, minimizing over $q(\cdot\,|\,\cdot)$ and then minimizing over $r(\cdot)$ reduces the right hand side of (13.140). Thus there is a limit, and the limit has been shown to be $R(D)$ by Csiszár [79], where the value of D and $R(D)$ depends on λ. Thus choosing λ appropriately sweeps out the $R(D)$ curve.

A similar procedure can be applied to the calculation of channel capacity. Again we rewrite the definition of channel capacity,

$$C = \max_{r(x)} I(X; Y) = \max_{r(x)} \sum_x \sum_y r(x)p(y|x) \log \frac{r(x)p(y|x)}{r(x)\sum_{x'} r(x')p(y|x')}$$

$$(13.144)$$

as a double maximization using Lemma 13.8.1,

$$C - \max_{q(x|y)} \max_{r(x)} \sum_x \sum_y r(x)p(y|x) \log \frac{q(x|y)}{r(x)}.$$ (13.145)

In this case, the Csiszár-Tusnady algorithm becomes one of alternating maximization—we start with a guess of the maximizing distribution $r(x)$ and find the best conditional distribution, which is, by Lemma 13.8.1,

$$q(x|y) = \frac{r(x)p(y|x)}{\sum_x r(x)p(y|x)}.$$ (13.146)

For this conditional distribution, we find the best input distribution $r(x)$ by solving the constrained maximization problem with Lagrange multipliers. The optimum input distribution is

$$r(x) = \frac{\Pi_y(q(x|y))^{p(y|x)}}{\sum_x \Pi_y(q(x|y))^{p(y|x)}},$$ (13.147)

which we can use as the basis for the next iteration.

These algorithms for the computation of the channel capacity and the rate distortion function were established by Blahut [37] and Arimoto [11] and the convergence for the rate distortion computation was proved by Csiszár [79]. The alternating minimization procedure of Csiszár and Tusnady can be specialized to many other situations as well, including the EM algorithm [88], and the algorithm for finding the log-optimal portfolio for a stock market [64].

SUMMARY OF CHAPTER 13

Rate distortion: The rate distortion function for a source $X \sim p(x)$ and distortion measure $d(x, \hat{x})$ is

$$R(D) = \min_{p(\hat{x}|x) : \sum_{(x, \hat{x})} p(x)p(\hat{x}|x)d(x, \hat{x}) \leq D} I(X; \hat{X}),$$ (13.148)

where the minimization is over all conditional distributions $p(\hat{x}|x)$ for which the joint distribution $p(x, \hat{x}) = p(x)p(\hat{x}|x)$ satisfies the expected distortion constraint.

Rate distortion theorem: If $R > R(D)$, there exists a sequence of codes $\hat{X}^n(X^n)$ with number of codewords $|\hat{X}^n(\cdot)| \leq 2^{nR}$ with $Ed(X^n, \hat{X}^n(X^n)) \to D$. If $R < R(D)$, no such codes exist.

Bernoulli source: For a Bernoulli source with Hamming distortion,

$$R(D) = H(p) - H(D). \tag{13.149}$$

Gaussian source: For a Gaussian source with squared error distortion,

$$R(D) = \frac{1}{2} \log \frac{\sigma^2}{D}. \tag{13.150}$$

Multivariate Gaussian source: The rate distortion function for a multivariate normal vector with Euclidean mean squared error distortion is given by reverse water-filling on the eigenvalues.

PROBLEMS FOR CHAPTER 13

1. *One bit quantization of a single Gaussian random variable.* Let $X \sim \mathcal{N}(0, \sigma^2)$ and let the distortion measure be squared error. Here we do not allow block descriptions. Show that the optimum reproduction points for 1 bit quantization are $\pm \sqrt{\frac{2}{\pi}} \sigma$, and that the expected distortion for 1 bit quantization is $\frac{\pi - 2}{\pi} \sigma^2$.
   Compare this with the distortion rate bound $D = \sigma^2 2^{-2R}$ for $R = 1$.

2. *Rate distortion function with infinite distortion.* Find the rate distortion function $R(D) = \min I(X; \hat{X})$ for $X \sim$ Bernoulli $(\frac{1}{2})$ and distortion

$$d(x, \hat{x}) = \begin{cases} 0, & x = \hat{x}, \\ 1, & x = 1, \hat{x} = 0, \\ \infty, & x = 0, \hat{x} = 1. \end{cases}$$

3. *Rate distortion for binary source with asymmetric distortion.* Fix $p(x|\hat{x})$ and evaluate $I(X; \hat{X})$ and D for

$$X \sim \text{Bern}(1/2),$$

$$d(x, \hat{x}) = \begin{bmatrix} 0 & a \\ b & 0 \end{bmatrix}.$$

   ($R(D)$ cannot be expressed in closed form.)

4. *Properties of $R(D)$.* Consider a discrete source $X \in \mathcal{X} = \{1, 2, \ldots, m\}$ with distribution $p_1, p_2, \ldots, p_m$ and a distortion measure $d(i, j)$. Let $R(D)$ be the rate distortion function for this source and distortion measure. Let $d'(i, j) = d(i, j) - w_i$ be a new distortion measure and

let $R'(D)$ be the corresponding rate distortion function. Show that $R'(D) = R(D + \bar{w})$, where $\bar{w} = \Sigma\, p_i w_i$, and use this to show that there is no essential loss of generality in assuming that $\min_{\hat{x}} d(i, \hat{x}) = 0$, i.e., for each $x \in \mathscr{X}$, there is one symbol $\hat{x}$ which reproduces the source with zero distortion.

This result is due to Pinkston [209].

5. *Rate distortion for uniform source with Hamming distortion.* Consider a source X uniformly distributed on the set $\{1, 2, \ldots, m\}$. Find the rate distortion function for this source with Hamming distortion, i.e.,

$$d(x, \hat{x}) = \begin{cases} 0 & \text{if } x = \hat{x}, \\ 1 & \text{if } x \neq \hat{x}. \end{cases}$$

6. *Shannon lower bound for the rate distortion function.* Consider a source X with a distortion measure $d(x, \hat{x})$ that satisfies the following property: all columns of the distortion matrix are permutations of the set $\{d_1, d_2, \ldots, d_m\}$. Define the function

$$\phi(D) = \max_{\mathbf{p}\,:\,\sum_{i=1}^{m} p_i d_i \leq D} H(\mathbf{p}). \tag{13.151}$$

The Shannon lower bound on the rate distortion function [245] is proved by the following steps:

(a) Show that $\phi(D)$ is a concave function of D.

(b) Justify the following series of inequalities for $I(X; \hat{X})$ if $Ed(X, \hat{X}) \leq D$,

$$I(X; \hat{X}) = H(X) - H(X|\hat{X}) \tag{13.152}$$

$$= H(X) - \sum_{\hat{x}} p(\hat{x}) H(X|\hat{X} = \hat{x}) \tag{13.153}$$

$$\geq H(X) - \sum_{\hat{x}} p(\hat{x}) \phi(D_{\hat{x}}) \tag{13.154}$$

$$\geq H(X) - \phi\!\left(\sum_{\hat{x}} p(\hat{x}) D_{\hat{x}} \right) \tag{13.155}$$

$$\geq H(X) - \phi(D), \tag{13.156}$$

where $D_{\hat{x}} = \Sigma_x\, p(x|\hat{x}) d(x, \hat{x})$.

(c) Argue that

$$R(D) \geq H(X) - \phi(D), \tag{13.157}$$

which is the Shannon lower bound on the rate distortion function.

(d) If in addition, we assume that the source has a uniform distribution and that the rows of the distortion matrix are permutations of each other, then $R(D) = H(X) - \phi(D)$, i.e., the lower bound is tight.

7. *Erasure distortion.* Consider $X \sim$ Bernoulli($\frac{1}{2}$), and let the distortion measure be given by the matrix

$$d(x, \hat{x}) = \begin{bmatrix} 0 & 1 & \infty \\ \infty & 1 & 0 \end{bmatrix}. \qquad (13.158)$$

Calculate the rate distortion function for this source. Can you suggest a simple scheme to achieve any value of the rate distortion function for this source?

8. *Bounds on the rate distortion function for squared error distortion.* For the case of a continuous random variable X with mean zero and variance σ^2 and squared error distortion, show that

$$h(X) - \frac{1}{2} \log(2\pi e)D \le R(D) \le \frac{1}{2} \log \frac{\sigma^2}{D}. \qquad (13.159)$$

For the upper bound, consider the joint distribution shown in Figure 13.10. Are Gaussian random variables harder or easier to describe than other random variables with the same variance?

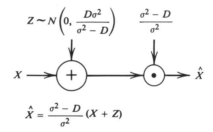

$$\hat{X} = \frac{\sigma^2 - D}{\sigma^2} (X + Z)$$

Figure 13.10. Joint distribution for upper bound on rate distortion function.

9. *Properties of optimal rate distortion code.* A good (R, D) rate distortion code with $R \approx R(D)$ puts severe constraints on the relationship of the source X^n and the representations $\hat{X}^n$. Examine the chain of inequalities (13.58–13.70) considering the conditions for equality and interpret as properties of a good code. For example, equality in (13.59) implies that $\hat{X}^n$ is a deterministic function of X^n.

10. *Probability of conditionally typical sequences.* In Chapter 8, we calculated the probability that two independently drawn sequences X^n and Y^n will be weakly jointly typical. To prove the rate distortion theorem, however, we need to calculate this probability when one of the sequences is fixed and the other is random.

    The techniques of weak typicality allow us only to calculate the average set size of the conditionally typical set. Using the ideas of strong typicality on the other hand provides us with stronger bounds which work for all typical x^n sequences. We will outline the proof that $\Pr\{(x^n, Y^n) \in A_\epsilon^{*(n)}\} \approx 2^{-nI(X;Y)}$ for all typical x^n. This approach was introduced by Berger [28] and is fully developed in the book by Csiszár and Körner [83].

Let (X_i, Y_i) be drawn i.i.d. $\sim p(x, y)$. Let the marginals of X and Y be $p(x)$ and $p(y)$ respectively.

(a) Let $A_\epsilon^{*(n)}$ be the strongly typical set for X. Show that

$$|A_\epsilon^{*(n)}| \doteq 2^{nH(X)} \qquad (13.160)$$

Hint: Theorem 12.1.1 and 12.1.3.

(b) The *joint type* of a pair of sequences (x^n, y^n) is the proportion of times $(x_i, y_i) = (a, b)$ in the pair of sequences, i.e.,

$$P_{x^n, y^n}(a, b) = \frac{1}{n} N(a, b | x^n, y^n) = \frac{1}{n} \sum_{i-1}^{n} I(x_i = a, y_i = b). \quad (13.161)$$

The *conditional type* of a sequence y^n given x^n is a stochastic matrix that gives the proportion of times a particular element of $\mathcal{Y}$ occurred with each element of $\mathcal{X}$ in the pair of sequences. Specifically, the conditional type $V_{y^n|x^n}(b|a)$ is defined as

$$V_{y^n|x^n}(b|a) = \frac{N(a, b | x^n, y^n)}{N(a | x^n)}. \qquad (13.162)$$

Show that the number of conditional types is bounded by $(n + 1)^{|\mathcal{X}||\mathcal{Y}|}$.

(c) The set of sequences $y^n \in \mathcal{Y}^n$ with conditional type V with respect to a sequence x^n is called the conditional type class $T_V(x^n)$. Show that

$$\frac{1}{(n+1)^{|\mathcal{X}||\mathcal{Y}|}} 2^{nH(Y|X)} \leq |T_V(x^n)| < 2^{nH(Y|X)}. \qquad (13.163)$$

(d) The sequence $y^n \in \mathcal{Y}^n$ is said to be ϵ-*strongly conditionally typical* with the sequence x^n with respect to the conditional distribution $V(\cdot|\cdot)$ if the conditional type is close to V. The conditional type should satisfy the following two conditions:

i. For all $(a, b) \in \mathcal{X} \times \mathcal{Y}$ with $V(b|a) > 0$,

$$\frac{1}{n}\left| N(a, b | x^n, y^n) - V(b|a)N(a|x^n) \right| \leq \frac{\epsilon}{|\mathcal{Y}| + 1}. \qquad (13.164)$$

ii. $N(a, b | x^n, y^n) = 0$ for all (a, b) such that $V(b|a) = 0$.

The set of such sequences is called the conditionally typical set and is denoted $A_\epsilon^{*(n)}(Y|x^n)$. Show that the number of sequences y^n that are conditionally typical with a given $x^n \in \mathcal{X}^n$ is bounded by

$$\frac{1}{(n+1)^{|\mathcal{X}||\mathcal{Y}|}} 2^{n(H(Y|X)-\epsilon_1)} \leq |A_\epsilon^{*(n)}(Y|x^n)| \leq (n+1)^{|\mathcal{X}||\mathcal{Y}|} 2^{n(H(Y|X)+\epsilon_1)},$$

$$(13.165)$$

where $\epsilon_1 \to 0$ as $\epsilon \to 0$.

(e) For a pair of random variables (X, Y) with joint distribution $p(x, y)$, the ϵ-*strongly typical* set $A_{\epsilon}^{*(n)}$ is the set of sequences $(x^n, y^n) \in \mathcal{X}^n \times \mathcal{Y}^n$ satisfying

i.

$$\left| \frac{1}{n} N(a, b | x^n, y^n) - p(a, b) \right| < \frac{\epsilon}{|\mathcal{X}||\mathcal{Y}|} \qquad (13.166)$$

for every pair $(a, b) \in \mathcal{X} \times \mathcal{Y}$ with $p(a, b) > 0$.

ii. $N(a, b | x^n, y^n) = 0$ for all $(a, b) \in \mathcal{X} \times \mathcal{Y}$ with $p(a, b) = 0$.

The set of ϵ-strongly jointly typical sequences is called the ϵ-strongly jointly typical set and is denoted $A_{\epsilon}^{*(n)}(X, Y)$.

Let (X, Y) be drawn i.i.d. $\sim p(x, y)$. For any x^n such that there exists at least one pair $(x^n, y^n) \in A_{\epsilon}^{*(n)}(X, Y)$, the set of sequences y^n such that $(x^n, y^n) \in A_{\epsilon}^{*(n)}$ satisfies

$$\frac{1}{(n + 1)^{|\mathcal{X}||\mathcal{Y}|}} 2^{n(H(Y|X) - \delta(\epsilon))} \leq |\{y^n : (x^n, y^n) \in A_{\epsilon}^{*(n)}\}|$$

$$\leq (n + 1)^{|\mathcal{X}||\mathcal{Y}|} 2^{n(H(Y|X) + \delta(\epsilon))},$$

$$(13.167)$$

where $\delta(\epsilon) \to 0$ as $\epsilon \to 0$. In particular, we can write

$$2^{n(H(Y|X) - \epsilon_2)} \leq |\{y^n : (x^n, y^n) \in A_{\epsilon}^{*(n)}\}| \leq 2^{n(H(Y|X) + \epsilon_2)},$$

$$(13.168)$$

where we can make ϵ_2 arbitrarily small with an appropriate choice of ϵ and n.

(f) Let $Y_1, Y_2, \ldots, Y_n$ be drawn i.i.d. $\sim \prod p(y_i)$. For $x^n \in A_{\epsilon}^{*(n)}$, the probability that $(x^n, Y^n) \in A_{\epsilon}^{*(n)}$ is bounded by

$$2^{-n(I(X; Y) + \epsilon_3)} \leq \Pr((x^n, Y^n) \in A_{\epsilon}^{*(n)}) \leq 2^{-n(I(X; Y) - \epsilon_3)}, \quad (13.169)$$

where ϵ_3 goes to 0 as $\epsilon \to 0$ and $n \to \infty$.

HISTORICAL NOTES

The idea of rate distortion was introduced by Shannon in his original paper [238]. He returned to it and dealt with it exhaustively in his 1959 paper [245], which proved the first rate distortion theorem. Meanwhile, Kolmogorov and his school in the Soviet Union began to develop rate distortion theory in 1956. Stronger versions of the rate-distortion theorem have been proved for more general sources in the comprehensive book by Berger [27].

The inverse water-filling solution for the rate-distortion function for parallel Gaussian sources was established by McDonald and Schultheiss [190]. An iterative algorithm for the calculation of the rate distortion function for a general i.i.d. source and arbitrary distortion measure was described by Blahut [37] and Arimoto [11] and Csiszár [79]. This algorithm is a special case of general alternating minimization algorithm due to Csiszár and Tusnady [85].

Chapter 14

Network Information Theory

A system with many senders and receivers contains many new elements in the communication problem: interference, cooperation and feedback. These are the issues that are the domain of network information theory. The general problem is easy to state. Given many senders and receivers and a channel transition matrix which describes the effects of the interference and the noise in the network, decide whether or not the sources can be transmitted over the channel. This problem involves distributed source coding (data compression) as well as distributed communication (finding the capacity region of the network). This general problem has not yet been solved, so we consider various special cases in this chapter.

Examples of large communication networks include computer networks, satellite networks and the phone system. Even within a single computer, there are various components that talk to each other. A complete theory of network information would have wide implications for the design of communication and computer networks.

Suppose that m stations wish to communicate with a common satellite over a common channel, as shown in Figure 14.1. This is known as a multiple access channel. How do the various senders cooperate with each other to send information to the receiver? What rates of communication are simultaneously achievable? What limitations does interference among the senders put on the total rate of communication? This is the best understood multi-user channel, and the above questions have satisfying answers.

In contrast, we can reverse the network and consider one TV station sending information to m TV receivers, as in Figure 14.2. How does the sender encode information meant for different receivers in a common

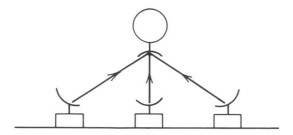

Figure 14.1. A multiple access channel.

signal? What are the rates at which information can be sent to the different receivers? For this channel, the answers are known only in special cases.

There are other channels such as the relay channel (where there is one source and one destination, but one or more intermediate sender-receiver pairs that act as relays to facilitate the communication between the source and the destination), the interference channel (two senders and two receivers with crosstalk) or the two-way channel (two sender-receiver pairs sending information to each other). For all these channels, we only have some of the answers to questions about achievable communication rates and the appropriate coding strategies.

All these channels can be considered special cases of a general communication network that consists of m nodes trying to communicate with each other, as shown in Figure 14.3. At each instant of time, the ith node sends a symbol x_i that depends on the messages that it wants to send and on past received symbols at the node. The simultaneous transmission of the symbols $(x_1, x_2, \ldots, x_m)$ results in random received symbols $(Y_1, Y_2, \ldots, Y_m)$ drawn according to the conditional probability distribution $p(y^{(1)}, y^{(2)}, \ldots, y^{(m)} | x^{(1)}, x^{(2)}, \ldots, x^{(m)})$. Here $p(\cdot | \cdot)$ expresses the effects of the noise and interference present in the network. If $p(\cdot | \cdot)$ takes on only the values 0 and 1, the network is deterministic.

Associated with some of the nodes in the network are stochastic data sources, which are to be communicated to some of the other nodes in the network. If the sources are independent, the messages sent by the nodes

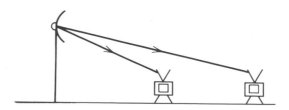

Figure 14.2. A broadcast channel.

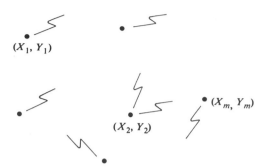

(X_1, Y_1)

(X_2, Y_2)

(X_m, Y_m)

Figure 14.3. A communication network.

are also independent. However, for full generality, we must allow the sources to be dependent. How does one take advantage of the dependence to reduce the amount of information transmitted? Given the probability distribution of the sources and the channel transition function, can one transmit these sources over the channel and recover the sources at the destinations with the appropriate distortion?

We consider various special cases of network communication. We consider the problem of source coding when the channels are noiseless and without interference. In such cases, the problem reduces to finding the set of rates associated with each source such that the required sources can be decoded at the destination with low probability of error (or appropriate distortion). The simplest case for distributed source coding is the Slepian-Wolf source coding problem, where we have two sources which must be encoded separately, but decoded together at a common node. We consider extensions to this theory when only one of the two sources needs to be recovered at the destination.

The theory of flow in networks has satisfying answers in domains like circuit theory and the flow of water in pipes. For example, for the single-source single-sink network of pipes shown in Figure 14.4, the maximum flow from A to B can be easily computed from the Ford-Fulkerson theorem. Assume that the edges have capacities C_i as shown. Clearly, the maximum flow across any cut-set cannot be greater than

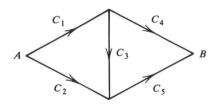

$$C = \min\{C_1 + C_2, C_2 + C_3 + C_4, C_4 + C_5, C_1 + C_3 + C_5\}$$

Figure 14.4. Network of water pipes.

the sum of the capacities of the cut edges. Thus minimizing the maximum flow across cut-sets yields an upper bound on the capacity of the network. The Ford-Fulkerson [113] theorem shows that this capacity can be achieved.

The theory of information flow in networks does not have the same simple answers as the theory of flow of water in pipes. Although we prove an upper bound on the rate of information flow across any cut-set, these bounds are not achievable in general. However, it is gratifying that some problems like the relay channel and the cascade channel admit a simple max flow min cut interpretation. Another subtle problem in the search for a general theory is the absence of a source-channel separation theorem, which we will touch on briefly in the last section of this chapter. A complete theory combining distributed source coding and network channel coding is still a distant goal.

In the next section, we consider Gaussian examples of some of the basic channels of network information theory. The physically motivated Gaussian channel lends itself to concrete and easily interpreted answers. Later we prove some of the basic results about joint typicality that we use to prove the theorems of multiuser information theory. We then consider various problems in detail—the multiple access channel, the coding of correlated sources (Slepian-Wolf data compression), the broadcast channel, the relay channel, the coding of a random variable with side information and the rate distortion problem with side information. We end with an introduction to the general theory of information flow in networks. There are a number of open problems in the area, and there does not yet exist a comprehensive theory of information networks. Even if such a theory is found, it may be too complex for easy implementation. But the theory will be able to tell communication designers how close they are to optimality and perhaps suggest some means of improving the communication rates.

14.1   GAUSSIAN MULTIPLE USER CHANNELS

Gaussian multiple user channels illustrate some of the important features of network information theory. The intuition gained in Chapter 10 on the Gaussian channel should make this section a useful introduction. Here the key ideas for establishing the capacity regions of the Gaussian multiple access, broadcast, relay and two-way channels will be given without proof. The proofs of the coding theorems for the discrete memoryless counterparts to these theorems will be given in later sections of this chapter.

The basic discrete time additive white Gaussian noise channel with input power P and noise variance N is modeled by

$$Y_i = X_i + Z_i, \qquad i = 1, 2, \ldots \tag{14.1}$$

where the Z_i are i.i.d. Gaussian random variables with mean 0 and variance N. The signal $\mathbf{X} = (X_1, X_2, \ldots, X_n)$ has a power constraint

$$\frac{1}{n} \sum_{i=1}^{n} X_i^2 \le P. \tag{14.2}$$

The Shannon capacity C is obtained by maximizing $I(X; Y)$ over all random variables X such that $EX^2 \le P$, and is given (Chapter 10) by

$$C = \frac{1}{2} \log\left(1 + \frac{P}{N}\right) \text{ bits per transmission} . \tag{14.3}$$

In this chapter we will restrict our attention to discrete-time memoryless channels; the results can be extended to continuous time Gaussian channels.

14.1.1 Single User Gaussian Channel

We first review the single user Gaussian channel studied in Chapter 10. Here $Y = X + Z$. Choose a rate $R < \frac{1}{2} \log(1 + \frac{P}{N})$. Fix a good $(2^{nR}, n)$ codebook of power P. Choose an index i in the set 2^{nR}. Send the ith codeword $\mathbf{X}(i)$ from the codebook generated above. The receiver observes $\mathbf{Y} = \mathbf{X}(i) + \mathbf{Z}$ and then finds the index $\hat{i}$ of the closest codeword to $\mathbf{Y}$. If n is sufficiently large, the probability of error $\Pr(i \ne \hat{i})$ will be arbitrarily small. As can be seen from the definition of joint typicality, this minimum distance decoding scheme is essentially equivalent to finding the codeword in the codebook that is jointly typical with the received vector $\mathbf{Y}$.

14.1.2 The Gaussian Multiple Access Channel with m Users

We consider m transmitters, each with a power P. Let

$$Y = \sum_{i=1}^{m} X_i + Z . \tag{14.4}$$

Let

$$C\left(\frac{P}{N}\right) = \frac{1}{2} \log\left(1 + \frac{P}{N}\right) \tag{14.5}$$

denote the capacity of a single user Gaussian channel with signal to noise ratio P/N. The achievable rate region for the Gaussian channel takes on the simple form given in the following equations:

$$R_i < C\left(\frac{P}{N}\right) \tag{14.6}$$

$$R_i + R_j < C\left(\frac{2P}{N}\right) \tag{14.7}$$

$$R_i + R_j + R_k < C\left(\frac{3P}{N}\right) \tag{14.8}$$

$$\vdots \tag{14.9}$$

$$\sum_{i=1}^{m} R_i < C\left(\frac{mP}{N}\right). \tag{14.10}$$

Note that when all the rates are the same, the last inequality dominates the others.

Here we need m codebooks, the ith codebook having 2^{nR_i} codewords of power P. Transmission is simple. Each of the independent transmitters chooses an arbitrary codeword from its own codebook. The users simultaneously send these vectors. The receiver sees these codewords added together with the Gaussian noise $\mathbf{Z}$.

Optimal decoding consists of looking for the m codewords, one from each codebook, such that the vector sum is closest to $\mathbf{Y}$ in Euclidean distance. If $(R_1, R_2, \ldots, R_m)$ is in the capacity region given above, then the probability of error goes to 0 as n tends to infinity.

Remarks: It is exciting to see in this problem that the sum of the rates of the users $C(mP/N)$ goes to infinity with m. Thus in a cocktail party with m celebrants of power P in the presence of ambient noise N, the intended listener receives an unbounded amount of information as the number of people grows to infinity. A similar conclusion holds, of course, for ground communications to a satellite.

It is also interesting to note that the optimal transmission scheme here does not involve time division multiplexing. In fact, each of the transmitters uses all of the bandwidth all of the time.

14.1.3 The Gaussian Broadcast Channel

Here we assume that we have a sender of power P and two distant receivers, one with Gaussian noise power N_1 and the other with Gaussian noise power N_2. Without loss of generality, assume $N_1 < N_2$. Thus receiver Y_1 is less noisy than receiver Y_2. The model for the channel is $Y_1 = X + Z_1$ and $Y_2 = X + Z_2$, where Z_1 and Z_2 are arbitrarily correlated Gaussian random variables with variances N_1 and N_2, respectively. The sender wishes to send independent messages at rates R_1 and R_2 to receivers Y_1 and Y_2, respectively.

Fortunately, all Gaussian broadcast channels belong to the class of degraded broadcast channels discussed in Section 14.6.2. Specializing that work, we find that the capacity region of the Gaussian broadcast channel is

$$R_1 < C\left(\frac{\alpha P}{N_1}\right) \tag{14.11}$$

$$R_2 < C\left(\frac{(1-\alpha)P}{\alpha P + N_2}\right) \tag{14.12}$$

where α may be arbitrarily chosen $(0 \leq \alpha \leq 1)$ to trade off rate R_1 for rate R_2 as the transmitter wishes.

To encode the messages, the transmitter generates two codebooks, one with power αP at rate R_1, and another codebook with power $\bar{\alpha}P$ at rate R_2, where R_1 and R_2 lie in the capacity region above. Then to send an index $i \in \{1, 2, \ldots, 2^{nR_1}\}$ and $j \in \{1, 2, \ldots, 2^{nR_2}\}$ to Y_1 and Y_2, respectively, the transmitter takes the codeword $\mathbf{X}(i)$ from the first codebook and codeword $\mathbf{X}(j)$ from the second codebook and computes the sum. He sends the sum over the channel.

The receivers must now decode their messages. First consider the bad receiver Y_2. He merely looks through the second codebook to find the closest codeword to the received vector $\mathbf{Y}_2$. His effective signal to noise ratio is $\bar{\alpha}P/(\alpha P + N_2)$, since Y_1's message acts as noise to Y_2. (This can be proved.)

The good receiver Y_1 first decodes Y_2's codeword, which he can accomplish because of his lower noise N_1. He subtracts this codeword $\hat{\mathbf{X}}_2$ from $\mathbf{Y}_1$. He then looks for the codeword in the first codebook closest to $\mathbf{Y}_1 - \hat{\mathbf{X}}_2$. The resulting probability of error can be made as low as desired.

A nice dividend of optimal encoding for degraded broadcast channels is that the better receiver Y_1 always knows the message intended for receiver Y_2 in addition to the message intended for himself.

14.1.4 The Gaussian Relay Channel

For the relay channel, we have a sender X and an ultimate intended receiver Y. Also present is the relay channel intended solely to help the receiver. The Gaussian relay channel (Figure 14.30) is given by

$$Y_1 = X + Z_1, \tag{14.13}$$

$$Y = X + Z_1 + X_1 + Z_2, \tag{14.14}$$

where Z_1 and Z_2 are independent zero mean Gaussian random variables with variance N_1 and N_2, respectively. The allowed encoding by the relay is the causal sequence

$$X_{1i} = f_i(Y_{11}, Y_{12}, \ldots, Y_{1i-1}). \tag{14.15}$$

The sender X has power P and sender X_1 has power P_1. The capacity is

$$C = \max_{0 \le \alpha \le 1} \min\left\{ C\left(\frac{P + P_1 + 2\sqrt{\bar{\alpha} P P_1}}{N_1 + N_2}\right), C\left(\frac{\alpha P}{N_1}\right)\right\}, \quad (14.16)$$

where $\bar{\alpha} = 1 - \alpha$. Note that if

$$\frac{P_1}{N_2} \ge \frac{P}{N_1}, \quad (14.17)$$

it can be seen that $C = C(P/N_1)$, which is achieved by $\alpha = 1$. The channel appears to be noise-free after the relay, and the capacity $C(P/N_1)$ from X to the relay can be achieved. Thus the rate $C(P/(N_1 + N_2))$ without the relay is increased by the presence of the relay to $C(P/N_1)$. For large N_2, and for $P_1/N_2 \ge P/N_1$, we see that the increment in rate is from $C(P/(N_1 + N_2)) \approx 0$ to $C(P/N_1)$.

Let $R_1 < C(\alpha P/N_1)$. Two codebooks are needed. The first codebook has 2^{nR_1} words of power αP. The second has 2^{nR_0} codewords of power $\bar{\alpha} P$. We shall use codewords from these codebooks successively in order to create the opportunity for cooperation by the relay. We start by sending a codeword from the first codebook. The relay now knows the index of this codeword since $R_1 < C(\alpha P/N_1)$, but the intended receiver has a list of possible codewords of size $2^{n(R_1 - C(\alpha P/(N_1+N_2)))}$. This list calculation involves a result on list codes.

In the next block, the transmitter and the relay wish to cooperate to resolve the receiver's uncertainty about the previously sent codeword on the receiver's list. Unfortunately, they cannot be sure what this list is because they do not know the received signal Y. Thus they randomly partition the first codebook into 2^{nR_0} cells with an equal number of codewords in each cell. The relay, the receiver, and the transmitter agree on this partition. The relay and the transmitter find the cell of the partition in which the codeword from the first codebook lies and cooperatively send the codeword from the second codebook with that index. That is, both X and X_1 send the same designated codeword. The relay, of course, must scale this codeword so that it meets his power constraint P_1. They now simultaneously transmit their codewords. An important point to note here is that the cooperative information sent by the relay and the transmitter is sent coherently. So the power of the sum as seen by the receiver Y is $(\sqrt{\bar{\alpha} P} + \sqrt{P_1})^2$.

However, this does not exhaust what the transmitter does in the second block. He also chooses a fresh codeword from the first codebook, adds it "on paper" to the cooperative codeword from the second codebook, and sends the sum over the channel.

The reception by the ultimate receiver Y in the second block involves first finding the cooperative index from the second codebook by looking for the closest codeword in the second codebook. He subtracts the codeword from the received sequence, and then calculates a list of indices of size 2^{nR_0} corresponding to all codewords of the first codebook that might have been sent in the second block.

Now it is time for the intended receiver to complete computing the codeword from the first codebook sent in the first block. He takes his list of possible codewords that might have been sent in the first block and intersects it with the cell of the partition that he has learned from the cooperative relay transmission in the second block. The rates and powers have been chosen so that it is highly probable that there is only one codeword in the intersection. This is Y's guess about the information sent in the first block.

We are now in steady state. In each new block, the transmitter and the relay cooperate to resolve the list uncertainty from the previous block. In addition, the transmitter superimposes some fresh information from his first codebook to this transmission from the second codebook and transmits the sum.

The receiver is always one block behind, but for sufficiently many blocks, this does not affect his overall rate of reception.

14.1.5 The Gaussian Interference Channel

The interference channel has two senders and two receivers. Sender 1 wishes to send information to receiver 1. He does not care what receiver 2 receives or understands. Similarly with sender 2 and receiver 2. Each channel interferes with the other. This channel is illustrated in Figure 14.5. It is not quite a broadcast channel since there is only one intended receiver for each sender, nor is it a multiple access channel because each receiver is only interested in what is being sent by the corresponding transmitter. For symmetric interference, we have

$$Y_1 = X_1 + aX_2 + Z_1 \tag{14.18}$$

$$Y_2 = X_2 + aX_1 + Z_2 , \tag{14.19}$$

where Z_1, Z_2 are independent $\mathcal{N}(0, N)$ random variables. This channel

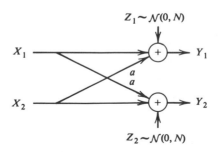

Figure 14.5. The Gaussian interference channel.

has not been solved in general even in the Gaussian case. But remarkably, in the case of high interference, it can be shown that the capacity region of this channel is the same as if there were no interference whatsoever.

To achieve this, generate two codebooks, each with power P and rate $C(P/N)$. Each sender independently chooses a word from his book and sends it. Now, if the interference a satisfies $C(a^2P/(P+N)) > C(P/N)$, the first transmitter perfectly understands the index of the second transmitter. He finds it by the usual technique of looking for the closest codeword to his received signal. Once he finds this signal, he subtracts it from his received waveform. Now there is a clean channel between him and his sender. He then searches the sender's codebook to find the closest codeword and declares that codeword to be the one sent.

14.1.6. The Gaussian Two-Way Channel

The two-way channel is very similar to the interference channel, with the additional provision that sender 1 is attached to receiver 2 and sender 2 is attached to receiver 1 as shown in Figure 14.6. Hence, sender 1 can use information from previous received symbols of receiver 2 to decide what to send next. This channel introduces another fundamental aspect of network information theory, namely, feedback. Feedback enables the senders to use the partial information that each has about the other's message to cooperate with each other.

The capacity region of the two-way channel is not known in general. This channel was first considered by Shannon [246], who derived upper and lower bounds on the region. (See Problem 15 at the end of this chapter.) For Gaussian channels, these two bounds coincide and the capacity region is known; in fact, the Gaussian two-way channel decomposes into two independent channels.

Let P_1 and P_2 be the powers of transmitters 1 and 2 respectively and let N_1 and N_2 be the noise variances of the two channels. Then the rates $R_1 < C(P_1/N_1)$ and $R_2 < C(P_2/N_2)$ can be achieved by the techniques described for the interference channel. In this case, we generate two codebooks of rates R_1 and R_2. Sender 1 sends a codeword from the first codebook. Receiver 2 receives the sum of the codewords sent by the two senders plus some noise. He simply subtracts out the codeword of sender

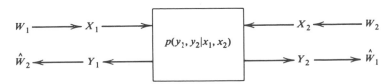

Figure 14.6. The two-way channel.

2 and he has a clean channel from sender 1 (with only the noise of variance N_1). Hence the two-way Gaussian channel decomposes into two independent Gaussian channels. But this is not the case for the general two-way channel; in general there is a trade-off between the two senders so that both of them cannot send at the optimal rate at the same time.

14.2 JOINTLY TYPICAL SEQUENCES

We have previewed the capacity results for networks by considering multi-user Gaussian channels. We will begin a more detailed analysis in this section, where we extend the joint AEP proved in Chapter 8 to a form that we will use to prove the theorems of network information theory. The joint AEP will enable us to calculate the probability of error for jointly typical decoding for the various coding schemes considered in this chapter.

Let $(X_1, X_2, \ldots, X_k)$ denote a finite collection of discrete random variables with some fixed joint distribution, $p(x_1, x_2, \ldots, x_k)$, $(x_1, x_2, \ldots, x_k) \in \mathscr{X}_1 \times \mathscr{X}_2 \times \cdots \times \mathscr{X}_k$. Let S denote an ordered subset of these random variables and consider n independent copies of S. Thus

$$\Pr\{S = s\} = \prod_{i=1}^{n} \Pr\{S_i = s_i\}, \qquad s \in \mathscr{S}^n. \tag{14.20}$$

For example, if $S = (X_j, X_l)$, then

$$\Pr\{S = s\} = \Pr\{(\mathbf{X}_j, \mathbf{X}_l) = (\mathbf{x}_j, \mathbf{x}_l)\} \tag{14.21}$$

$$= \prod_{i=1}^{n} p(x_{ji}, x_{li}). \tag{14.22}$$

To be explicit, we will sometimes use $X(S)$ for S. By the law of large numbers, for any subset S of random variables,

$$-\frac{1}{n} \log p(S_1, S_2, \ldots, S_n) = -\frac{1}{n} \sum_{i=1}^{n} \log p(S_i) \to H(S), \tag{14.23}$$

where the convergence takes place simultaneously with probability 1 for all 2^k subsets, $S \subseteq \{X_1, X_2, \ldots, X_k\}$.

Definition: The set $A_\epsilon^{(n)}$ of ϵ-typical n-sequences $(\mathbf{x}_1, \mathbf{x}_2, \ldots, \mathbf{x}_k)$ is defined by

$$A_\epsilon^{(n)}(X_1, X_2, \ldots, X_k)$$

$$= A_\epsilon^{(n)}$$

$$= \left\{ (\mathbf{x}_1, \mathbf{x}_2, \ldots, \mathbf{x}_k): \right.$$

$$\left. \left| -\frac{1}{n} \log p(\mathbf{s}) - H(S) \right| < \epsilon, \quad \forall S \subseteq \{X_1, X_2, \ldots, X_k\} \right\}. \tag{14.24}$$

Let $A_\epsilon^{(n)}(S)$ denote the restriction of $A_\epsilon^{(n)}$ to the coordinates of S. Thus if $S = (X_1, X_2)$, we have

$$A_\epsilon^{(n)}(X_1, X_2) = \left\{ (\mathbf{x}_1, \mathbf{x}_2): \right.$$

$$\left| -\frac{1}{n} \log p(\mathbf{x}_1, \mathbf{x}_2) - H(X_1, X_2) \right| < \epsilon,$$

$$\left| -\frac{1}{n} \log p(\mathbf{x}_1) - H(X_1) \right| < \epsilon,$$

$$\left. \left| -\frac{1}{n} \log p(\mathbf{x}_2) - H(X_2) \right| < \epsilon \right\}. \tag{14.25}$$

Definition: We will use the notation $a_n \doteq 2^{n(b \pm \epsilon)}$ to mean

$$\left| \frac{1}{n} \log a_n - b \right| < \epsilon \tag{14.26}$$

for n sufficiently large.

Theorem 14.2.1: *For any $\epsilon > 0$, for sufficiently large n,*

1. $$P(A_\epsilon^{(n)}(S)) \geq 1 - \epsilon, \quad \forall S \subseteq \{X_1, X_2, \ldots, X_k\}. \tag{14.27}$$

2. $$\mathbf{s} \in A_\epsilon^{(n)}(S) \Rightarrow p(\mathbf{s}) \doteq 2^{-n(H(S) \pm \epsilon)}. \tag{14.28}$$

3. $$|A_\epsilon^{(n)}(S)| \doteq 2^{n(H(S) \pm 2\epsilon)}. \tag{14.29}$$

4. *Let $S_1, S_2 \subseteq \{X_1, X_2, \ldots, X_k\}$. If $(\mathbf{s}_1, \mathbf{s}_2) \in A_\epsilon^{(n)}(S_1, S_2)$, then*

$$p(\mathbf{s}_1 | \mathbf{s}_2) \doteq 2^{-n(H(S_1 | S_2) \pm 2\epsilon)}. \tag{14.30}$$

Proof:

1. This follows from the law of large numbers for the random variables in the definition of $A_\epsilon^{(n)}(S)$.

2. This follows directly from the definition of $A_\epsilon^{(n)}(S)$.

3. This follows from

$$1 \geq \sum_{\mathbf{s} \in A_\epsilon^{(n)}(S)} p(\mathbf{s}) \tag{14.31}$$

$$\geq \sum_{\mathbf{s} \in A_\epsilon^{(n)}(S)} 2^{-n(H(S)+\epsilon)} \tag{14.32}$$

$$= |A_\epsilon^{(n)}(S)| 2^{-n(H(S)+\epsilon)} . \tag{14.33}$$

If n is sufficiently large, we can argue that

$$1 - \epsilon \leq \sum_{\mathbf{s} \in A_\epsilon^{(n)}(S)} p(\mathbf{s}) \tag{14.34}$$

$$\leq \sum_{\mathbf{s} \in A_\epsilon^{(n)}(S)} 2^{-n(H(S)-\epsilon)} \tag{14.35}$$

$$= |A_\epsilon^{(n)}(S)| 2^{-n(H(S)-\epsilon)} . \tag{14.36}$$

Combining (14.33) and (14.36), we have $|A_\epsilon^{(n)}(S)| \doteq 2^{n(H(S) \pm 2\epsilon)}$ for sufficiently large n.

4. For $(\mathbf{s}_1, \mathbf{s}_2) \in A_\epsilon^{(n)}(S_1, S_2)$, we have $p(\mathbf{s}_1) \doteq 2^{-n(H(S_1) \pm \epsilon)}$ and $p(\mathbf{s}_1, \mathbf{s}_2) \doteq 2^{-n(H(S_1, S_2) \pm \epsilon)}$. Hence

$$p(\mathbf{s}_2|\mathbf{s}_1) = \frac{p(\mathbf{s}_1, \mathbf{s}_2)}{p(\mathbf{s}_1)} \doteq 2^{-n(H(S_2|S_1) \pm 2\epsilon)} . \quad \square \tag{14.37}$$

The next theorem bounds the number of conditionally typical sequences for a given typical sequence.

Theorem 14.2.2: *Let S_1, S_2 be two subsets of $X_1, X_2, \ldots, X_k$. For any $\epsilon > 0$, define $A_\epsilon^{(n)}(S_1|\mathbf{s}_2)$ to be the set of $\mathbf{s}_1$ sequences that are jointly ϵ-typical with a particular $\mathbf{s}_2$ sequence. If $\mathbf{s}_2 \in A_\epsilon^{(n)}(S_2)$, then for sufficiently large n, we have*

$$|A_\epsilon^{(n)}(S_1|\mathbf{s}_2)| \leq 2^{n(H(S_1|S_2)+2\epsilon)} , \tag{14.38}$$

and

$$(1 - \epsilon)2^{n(H(S_1|S_2)-2\epsilon)} \leq \sum_{\mathbf{s}_2} p(\mathbf{s}_2)|A_\epsilon^{(n)}(S_1|\mathbf{s}_2)| . \tag{14.39}$$

Proof: As in part 3 of the previous theorem, we have

$$1 \geq \sum_{\mathbf{s}_1 \in A_\epsilon^{(n)}(S_1|\mathbf{s}_2)} p(\mathbf{s}_1|\mathbf{s}_2) \tag{14.40}$$

$$\geq \sum_{\mathbf{s}_1 \in A_\epsilon^{(n)}(S_1|\mathbf{s}_2)} 2^{-n(H(S_1|S_2)+2\epsilon)} \tag{14.41}$$

$$= |A_\epsilon^{(n)}(S_1|\mathbf{s}_2)| 2^{-n(H(S_1|S_2)+2\epsilon)}. \tag{14.42}$$

If n is sufficiently large, then we can argue from (14.27) that

$$1 - \epsilon \leq \sum_{\mathbf{s}_2} p(\mathbf{s}_2) \sum_{\mathbf{s}_1 \in A_\epsilon^{(n)}(S_1|\mathbf{s}_2)} p(\mathbf{s}_1|\mathbf{s}_2) \tag{14.43}$$

$$\leq \sum_{\mathbf{s}_2} p(\mathbf{s}_2) \sum_{\mathbf{s}_1 \in A_\epsilon^{(n)}(S_1|\mathbf{s}_2)} 2^{-n(H(S_1|S_2)-2\epsilon)} \tag{14.44}$$

$$= \sum_{\mathbf{s}_2} p(\mathbf{s}_2) |A_\epsilon^{(n)}(S_1|\mathbf{s}_2)| 2^{-n(H(S_1|S_2)-2\epsilon)}. \quad \square \tag{14.45}$$

To calculate the probability of decoding error, we need to know the probability that conditionally independent sequences are jointly typical. Let S_1, S_2 and S_3 be three subsets of $\{X_1, X_2, \ldots, X_k\}$. If S_1' and S_2' are conditionally independent given S_3' but otherwise share the same pairwise marginals of (S_1, S_2, S_3), we have the following probability of joint typicality.

Theorem 14.2.3: *Let $A_\epsilon^{(n)}$ denote the typical set for the probability mass function $p(s_1, s_2, s_3)$, and let*

$$P(\mathbf{S}_1' = \mathbf{s}_1, \mathbf{S}_2' = \mathbf{s}_2, \mathbf{S}_3' = \mathbf{s}_3) = \prod_{i-1}^{n} p(s_{1i}|s_{3i})p(s_{2i}|s_{3i})p(s_{3i}). \tag{14.46}$$

Then

$$P\{(\mathbf{S}_1', \mathbf{S}_2', \mathbf{S}_3') \in A_\epsilon^{(n)}\} \doteq 2^{n(I(S_1; S_2|S_3)\pm 6\epsilon)}. \tag{14.47}$$

Proof: We use the $\doteq$ notation from (14.26) to avoid calculating the upper and lower bounds separately. We have

$$P\{(\mathbf{S}_1', \mathbf{S}_2', \mathbf{S}_3') \in A_\epsilon^{(n)}\}$$

$$= \sum_{(\mathbf{s}_1, \mathbf{s}_2, \mathbf{s}_3) \in A_\epsilon^{(n)}} p(\mathbf{s}_3)p(\mathbf{s}_1|\mathbf{s}_3)p(\mathbf{s}_2|\mathbf{s}_3) \tag{14.48}$$

$$\doteq |A_\epsilon^{(n)}(S_1, S_2, S_3)| 2^{-n(H(S_3)\pm\epsilon)}2^{-n(H(S_1|S_3)\pm 2\epsilon)}2^{-n(H(S_2|S_3)\pm 2\epsilon)} \tag{14.49}$$

$$\doteq 2^{n(H(S_1, S_2, S_3)\pm\epsilon)}2^{-n(H(S_3)\pm\epsilon)}2^{-n(H(S_1|S_3)\pm2\epsilon)}2^{-n(H(S_2|S_3)\pm2\epsilon)} \qquad (14.50)$$

$$\doteq 2^{-n(I(S_1; S_2|S_3)\pm6\epsilon)} . \quad \square \qquad\qquad\qquad\qquad (14.51)$$

We will specialize this theorem to particular choices of S_1, S_2 and S_3 for the various achievability proofs in this chapter.

14.3   THE MULTIPLE ACCESS CHANNEL

The first channel that we examine in detail is the multiple access channel, in which two (or more) senders send information to a common receiver. The channel is illustrated in Figure 14.7.

A common example of this channel is a satellite receiver with many independent ground stations. We see that the senders must contend not only with the receiver noise but with interference from each other as well.

Definition: A *discrete memoryless multiple access channel* consists of three alphabets, $\mathcal{X}_1$, $\mathcal{X}_2$ and $\mathcal{Y}$, and a probability transition matrix $p(y|x_1, x_2)$.

Definition: A $((2^{nR_1}, 2^{nR_2}), n)$ code for the multiple access channel consists of two sets of integers $\mathcal{W}_1 = \{1, 2, \ldots, 2^{nR_1}\}$ and $\mathcal{W}_2 = \{1, 2, \ldots, 2^{nR_2}\}$ called the *message sets*, two *encoding functions*,

$$X_1 : \mathcal{W}_1 \to \mathcal{X}_1^n , \qquad\qquad\qquad\qquad (14.52)$$

$$X_2 : \mathcal{W}_2 \to \mathcal{X}_2^n \qquad\qquad\qquad\qquad (14.53)$$

and a *decoding function*

$$g : \mathcal{Y}^n \to \mathcal{W}_1 \times \mathcal{W}_2 . \qquad\qquad\qquad (14.54)$$

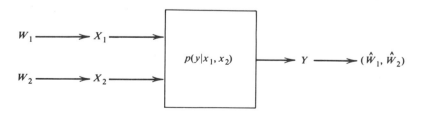

Figure 14.7. The multiple access channel.

There are two senders and one receiver for this channel. Sender 1 chooses an index W_1 uniformly from the set $\{1, 2, \ldots, 2^{nR_1}\}$ and sends the corresponding codeword over the channel. Sender 2 does likewise. Assuming that the distribution of messages over the product set $\mathcal{W}_1 \times \mathcal{W}_2$ is uniform, i.e., the messages are independent and equally likely, we define the *average probability of error* for the $((2^{nR_1}, 2^{nR_2}), n)$ code as follows:

$$P_e^{(n)} = \frac{1}{2^{n(R_1+R_2)}} \sum_{(w_1, w_2) \in \mathcal{W}_1 \times \mathcal{W}_2} \Pr\{g(Y^n) \neq (w_1, w_2) | (w_1, w_2) \text{ sent}\}.$$

$$(14.55)$$

Definition: A rate pair (R_1, R_2) is said to be *achievable* for the multiple access channel if there exists a sequence of $((2^{nR_1}, 2^{nR_2}), n)$ codes with $P_e^{(n)} \to 0$.

Definition: The *capacity region* of the multiple access channel is the closure of the set of achievable (R_1, R_2) rate pairs.

An example of the capacity region for a multiple access channel is illustrated in Figure 14.8.

We first state the capacity region in the form of a theorem.

Theorem 14.3.1 (*Multiple access channel capacity*): *The capacity of a multiple access channel* $(\mathcal{X}_1 \times \mathcal{X}_2, p(y|x_1, x_2), \mathcal{Y})$ *is the closure of the convex hull of all* (R_1, R_2) *satisfying*

$$R_1 < I(X_1; Y | X_2), \tag{14.56}$$

$$R_2 < I(X_2; Y | X_1), \tag{14.57}$$

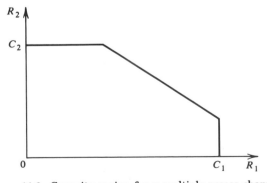

Figure 14.8. Capacity region for a multiple access channel.

$$R_1 + R_2 < I(X_1, X_2; Y) \tag{14.58}$$

for some product distribution $p_1(x_1)p_2(x_2)$ on $\mathcal{X}_1 \times \mathcal{X}_2$.

Before we prove that this is the capacity region of the multiple access channel, let us consider a few examples of multiple access channels:

Example 14.3.1 (*Independent binary symmetric channels*): Assume that we have two independent binary symmetric channels, one from sender 1 and the other from sender 2, as shown in Figure 14.9.

In this case, it is obvious from the results of Chapter 8 that we can send at rate $1 - H(p_1)$ over the first channel and at rate $1 - H(p_2)$ over the second channel. Since the channels are independent, there is no interference between the senders. The capacity region in this case is shown in Figure 14.10.

Example 14.3.2 (*Binary multiplier channel*): Consider a multiple access channel with binary inputs and output

$$Y = X_1 X_2 . \tag{14.59}$$

Such a channel is called a binary multiplier channel. It is easy to see that by setting $X_2 = 1$, we can send at a rate of 1 bit per transmission from sender 1 to the receiver. Similarly, setting $X_1 = 1$, we can achieve $R_2 = 1$. Clearly, since the output is binary, the combined rates $R_1 + R_2$ of

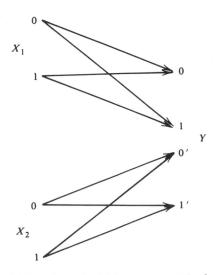

Figure 14.9. Independent binary symmetric channels.

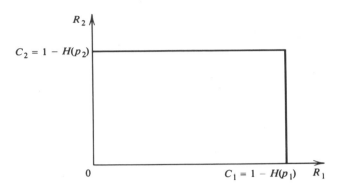

Figure 14.10. Capacity region for independent BSC's.

sender 1 and sender 2 cannot be more than 1 bit. By timesharing, we can achieve any combination of rates such that $R_1 + R_2 = 1$. Hence the capacity region is as shown in Figure 14.11.

Example 14.3.3 (*Binary erasure multiple access channel*): This multiple access channel has binary inputs, $\mathcal{X}_1 = \mathcal{X}_2 = \{0, 1\}$ and a ternary output $Y = X_1 + X_2$. There is no ambiguity in (X_1, X_2) if $Y = 0$ or $Y = 2$ is received; but $Y = 1$ can result from either $(0, 1)$ or $(1, 0)$.

We now examine the achievable rates on the axes. Setting $X_2 = 0$, we can send at a rate of 1 bit per transmission from sender 1. Similarly, setting $X_1 = 0$, we can send at a rate $R_2 = 1$. This gives us two extreme points of the capacity region.

Can we do better? Let us assume that $R_1 = 1$, so that the codewords of X_1 must include all possible binary sequences; X_1 would look like a

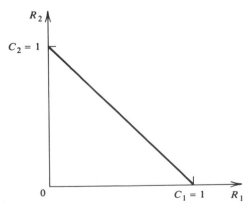

Figure 14.11. Capacity region for binary multiplier channel.

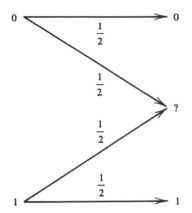

Figure 14.12. Equivalent single user channel for user 2 of a binary erasure multiple access channel.

Bernoulli($\frac{1}{2}$) process. This acts like noise for the transmission from X_2. For X_2, the channel looks like the channel in Figure 14.12.

This is the binary erasure channel of Chapter 8. Recalling the results, the capacity of this channel is $\frac{1}{2}$ bit per transmission.

Hence when sending at maximum rate 1 for sender 1, we can send an additional $\frac{1}{2}$ bit from sender 2. Later on, after deriving the capacity region, we can verify that these rates are the best that can be achieved.

The capacity region for a binary erasure channel is illustrated in Figure 14.13.

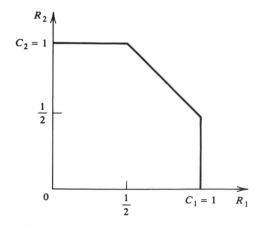

Figure 14.13. Capacity region for binary erasure multiple access channel.

14.3.1 Achievability of the Capacity Region for the Multiple Access Channel

We now prove the achievability of the rate region in Theorem 14.3.1; the proof of the converse will be left until the next section. The proof of achievability is very similar to the proof for the single user channel. We will therefore only emphasize the points at which the proof differs from the single user case. We will begin by proving the achievability of rate pairs that satisfy (14.58) for some fixed product distribution $p(x_1)p(x_2)$. In Section 14.3.3, we will extend this to prove that all points in the convex hull of (14.58) are achievable.

Proof *(Achievability in Theorem 14.3.1)*: Fix $p(x_1, x_2) = p_1(x_1)p_2(x_2)$.

Codebook generation. Generate 2^{nR_1} independent codewords $\mathbf{X}_1(i)$, $i \in \{1, 2, \ldots, 2^{nR_1}\}$, of length n, generating each element i.i.d. $\sim \Pi_{i=1}^{n} p_1(x_{1i})$. Similarly, generate 2^{nR_2} independent codewords $\mathbf{X}_2(j)$, $j \in \{1, 2, \ldots, 2^{nR_2}\}$, generating each element i.i.d. $\sim \Pi_{i=1}^{n} p_2(x_{2i})$. These codewords form the codebook, which is revealed to the senders and the receiver.

Encoding. To send index i, sender 1 sends the codeword $\mathbf{X}_1(i)$. Similarly, to send j, sender 2 sends $\mathbf{X}_2(j)$.

Decoding. Let $A_\epsilon^{(n)}$ denote the set of typical $(\mathbf{x}_1, \mathbf{x}_2, \mathbf{y})$ sequences. The receiver Y^n chooses the pair (i, j) such that

$$(\mathbf{x}_1(i), \mathbf{x}_2(j), \mathbf{y}) \in A_\epsilon^{(n)} \tag{14.60}$$

if such a pair (i, j) exists and is unique; otherwise, an error is declared.

Analysis of the probability of error. By the symmetry of the random code construction, the conditional probability of error does not depend on which pair of indices is sent. Thus the conditional probability of error is the same as the unconditional probability of error. So, without loss of generality, we can assume that $(i, j) = (1, 1)$ was sent.

We have an error if either the correct codewords are not typical with the received sequence or there is a pair of incorrect codewords that are typical with the received sequence. Define the events

$$E_{ij} = \{(\mathbf{X}_1(i), \mathbf{X}_2(j), \mathbf{Y}) \in A_\epsilon^{(n)}\} . \tag{14.61}$$

Then by the union of events bound,

$$P_e^{(n)} = P(E_{11}^c \cup \cup_{(i,j)\neq(1,1)} E_{ij}) \tag{14.62}$$

$$\leq P(E_{11}^c) + \sum_{i\neq1,j=1} P(E_{i1}) + \sum_{i=1,j\neq1} P(E_{1j}) + \sum_{i\neq1,j\neq1} P(E_{ij}), \tag{14.63}$$

where P is the conditional probability given that $(1,1)$ was sent. From the AEP, $P(E_{11}^c) \to 0$.

By Theorem 14.2.1 and Theorem 14.2.3, for $i \neq 1$, we have

$$P(E_{i1}) = P((\mathbf{X}_1(i), \mathbf{X}_2(1), \mathbf{Y}) \in A_\epsilon^{(n)}) \tag{14.64}$$

$$= \sum_{(\mathbf{x}_1,\mathbf{x}_2,\mathbf{y})\in A_\epsilon^{(n)}} p(\mathbf{x}_1)p(\mathbf{x}_2,\mathbf{y}) \tag{14.65}$$

$$\leq |A_\epsilon^{(n)}| 2^{-n(H(X_1)-\epsilon)} 2^{-n(H(X_2,Y)-\epsilon)} \tag{14.66}$$

$$\leq 2^{-n(H(X_1)+H(X_2,Y)-H(X_1,X_2,Y)-3\epsilon)} \tag{14.67}$$

$$= 2^{-n(I(X_1;X_2,Y)-3\epsilon)} \tag{14.68}$$

$$= 2^{-n(I(X_1;Y|X_2)-3\epsilon)}, \tag{14.69}$$

since X_1 and X_2 are independent, and therefore $I(X_1;X_2,Y) = I(X_1;X_2) + I(X_1;Y|X_2) = I(X_1;Y|X_2)$.

Similarly, for $j \neq 1$,

$$P(E_{1j}) \leq 2^{-n(I(X_2;Y|X_1)-3\epsilon)}, \tag{14.70}$$

and for $i \neq 1, j \neq 1$,

$$P(E_{ij}) \leq 2^{-n(I(X_1,X_2;Y)-4\epsilon)}. \tag{14.71}$$

It follows that

$$P_e^{(n)} \leq P(E_{11}^c) + 2^{nR_1} 2^{-n(I(X_1;Y|X_2)-3\epsilon)} + 2^{nR_2} 2^{-n(I(X_2;Y|X_1)-3\epsilon)}$$

$$+ 2^{n(R_1+R_2)} 2^{-n(I(X_1,X_2;Y)-4\epsilon)}. \tag{14.72}$$

Since $\epsilon > 0$ is arbitrary, the conditions of the theorem imply that each term tends to 0 as $n \to \infty$.

The above bound shows that the average probability of error, averaged over all choices of codebooks in the random code construction, is arbitrarily small. Hence there exists at least one code $\mathscr{C}^*$ with arbitrarily small probability of error.

This completes the proof of achievability of the region in (14.58) for a fixed input distribution. Later, in Section 14.3.3, we will show that timesharing allows any (R_1, R_2) in the convex hull to be achieved, completing the proof of the forward part of the theorem.   □

14.3.2 Comments on the Capacity Region for the Multiple Access Channel

We have now proved the achievability of the capacity region of the multiple access channel, which is the closure of the convex hull of the set of points (R_1, R_2) satisfying

$$R_1 < I(X_1; Y|X_2), \tag{14.73}$$

$$R_2 < I(X_2; Y|X_1), \tag{14.74}$$

$$R_1 + R_2 < I(X_1, X_2; Y) \tag{14.75}$$

for some distribution $p_1(x_1)p_2(x_2)$ on $\mathcal{X}_1 \times \mathcal{X}_2$.

For a particular $p_1(x_1)p_2(x_2)$, the region is illustrated in Figure 14.14.

Let us now interpret the corner points in the region. The point A corresponds to the maximum rate achievable from sender 1 to the receiver when sender 2 is not sending any information. This is

$$\max R_1 = \max_{p_1(x_1)p_2(x_2)} I(X_1; Y|X_2). \tag{14.76}$$

Now for any distribution $p_1(x_1)p_2(x_2)$,

$$I(X_1; Y|X_2) = \sum_{x_2} p_2(x_2)I(X_1; Y|X_2 = x_2) \tag{14.77}$$

$$\leq \max_{x_2} I(X_1; Y|X_2 = x_2), \tag{14.78}$$

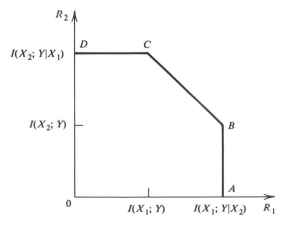

Figure 14.14. Achievable region of multiple access channel for a fixed input distribution.

since the average is less than the maximum. Therefore, the maximum in (14.76) is attained when we set $X_2 = x_2$, where x_2 is the value that maximizes the conditional mutual information between X_1 and Y. The distribution of X_1 is chosen to maximize this mutual information. Thus X_2 must facilitate the transmission of X_1 by setting $X_2 = x_2$.

The point B corresponds to the maximum rate at which sender 2 can send as long as sender 1 sends at his maximum rate. This is the rate that is obtained if X_1 is considered as noise for the channel from X_2 to Y. In this case, using the results from single user channels, X_2 can send at a rate $I(X_2; Y)$. The receiver now knows which X_2 codeword was used and can "subtract" its effect from the channel. We can consider the channel now to be an indexed set of single user channels, where the index is the X_2 symbol used. The X_1 rate achieved in this case is the average mutual information, where the average is over these channels, and each channel occurs as many times as the corresponding X_2 symbol appears in the codewords. Hence the rate achieved is

$$\sum_{x_2} p(x_2) I(X_1; Y | X_2 = x_2) = I(X_1; Y | X_2) \, . \tag{14.79}$$

The points C and D correspond to B and A respectively with the roles of the senders reversed.

The non-corner points can be achieved by timesharing. Thus, we have given a single user interpretation and justification for the capacity region of a multiple access channel.

The idea of considering other signals as part of the noise, decoding one signal and then "subtracting" it from the received signal is a very useful one. We will come across the same concept again in the capacity calculations for the degraded broadcast channel.

14.3.3 Convexity of the Capacity Region of the Multiple Access Channel

We now recast the capacity region of the multiple access channel in order to take into account the operation of taking the convex hull by introducing a new random variable. We begin by proving that the capacity region is convex.

Theorem 14.3.2: *The capacity region $\mathscr{C}$ of a multiple access channel is convex, i.e., if $(R_1, R_2) \in \mathscr{C}$ and $(R_1', R_2') \in \mathscr{C}$, then $(\lambda R_1 + (1 - \lambda)R_1', \lambda R_2 + (1 - \lambda)R_2') \in \mathscr{C}$ for $0 \le \lambda \le 1$.*

Proof: The idea is timesharing. Given two sequences of codes at different rates $\mathbf{R} = (R_1, R_2)$ and $\mathbf{R}' = (R_1', R_2')$, we can construct a third codebook at a rate $\lambda \mathbf{R} + (1 - \lambda)\mathbf{R}'$ by using the first codebook for the first λn symbols and using the second codebook for the last $(1 - \lambda)n$ symbols. The number of X_1 codewords in the new code is

$$2^{n\lambda R_1}2^{n(1-\lambda)R_1'} = 2^{n(\lambda R_1 + (1-\lambda)R_1')} \tag{14.80}$$

and hence the rate of the new code is $\lambda \mathbf{R} + (1 - \lambda)\mathbf{R}'$. Since the overall probability of error is less than the sum of the probabilities of error for each of the segments, the probability of error of the new code goes to 0 and the rate is achievable. $\square$

We will now recast the statement of the capacity region for the multiple access channel using a timesharing random variable Q.

Theorem 14.3.3: *The set of achievable rates of a discrete memoryless multiple access channel is given by the closure of the set of all (R_1, R_2) pairs satisfying*

$$R_1 < I(X_1; Y|X_2, Q),$$

$$R_2 < I(X_2; Y|X_1, Q),$$

$$R_1 + R_2 < I(X_1, X_2; Y|Q) \tag{14.81}$$

for some choice of the joint distribution $p(q)p(x_1|q)p(x_2|q)p(y|x_1, x_2)$ with $|\mathcal{Q}| \leq 4$.

Proof: We will show that every rate pair lying in the region in the theorem is achievable, i.e., it lies in the convex closure of the rate pairs satisfying Theorem 14.3.1. We will also show that every point in the convex closure of the region in Theorem 14.3.1 is also in the region defined in (14.81).

Consider a rate point $\mathbf{R}$ satisfying the inequalities (14.81) of the theorem. We can rewrite the right hand side of the first inequality as

$$I(X_1; Y|X_2, Q) = \sum_{k=1}^{m} p(q)I(X_1; Y|X_2, Q = q) \tag{14.82}$$

$$= \sum_{k=1}^{m} p(q)I(X_1; Y|X_2)_{p_{1q}, p_{2q}}, \tag{14.83}$$

where m is the cardinality of the support set of Q. We can similarly expand the other mutual informations in the same way.

For simplicity in notation, we will consider a rate pair as a vector and denote a pair satisfying the inequalities in (14.58) for a specific input product distribution $p_{1q}(x_1)p_{2q}(x_2)$ as $\mathbf{R}_q$. Specifically, let $\mathbf{R}_q = (R_{1q}, R_{2q})$ be a rate pair satisfying

$$R_{1q} < I(X_1; Y|X_2)_{p_{1q}(x_1)p_{2q}(x_2)}, \tag{14.84}$$

$$R_{2q} < I(X_2; Y|X_1)_{p_{1q}(x_1)p_{2q}(x_2)}, \tag{14.85}$$

$$R_{1q} + R_{2q} < I(X_1, X_2; Y)_{p_{1q}(x_1)p_{2q}(x_2)} .$$ (14.86)

Then by Theorem 14.3.1, $\mathbf{R}_q = (R_{1q}, R_{2q})$ is achievable.

Then since $\mathbf{R}$ satisfies (14.81), and we can expand the right hand sides as in (14.83), there exists a set of pairs $\mathbf{R}_q$ satisfying (14.86) such that

$$\mathbf{R} = \sum_{q=1}^{m} p(q)\mathbf{R}_q .$$ (14.87)

Since a convex combination of achievable rates is achievable, so is $\mathbf{R}$. Hence we have proved the achievability of the region in the theorem. The same argument can be used to show that every point in the convex closure of the region in (14.58) can be written as the mixture of points satisfying (14.86) and hence can be written in the form (14.81).

The converse will be proved in the next section. The converse shows that all achievable rate pairs are of the form (14.81), and hence establishes that this is the capacity region of the multiple access channel.

The cardinality bound on the time-sharing random variable Q is a consequence of Carathéodory's theorem on convex sets. See the discussion below. $\square$

The proof of the convexity of the capacity region shows that any convex combination of achievable rate pairs is also achievable. We can continue this process, taking convex combinations of more points. Do we need to use an arbitrary number of points ? Will the capacity region be increased? The following theorem says no.

Theorem 14.3.4 (*Carathéodory*): *Any point in the convex closure of a connected compact set A in a d dimensional Euclidean space can be represented as a convex combination of d + 1 or fewer points in the original set A.*

Proof: The proof can be found in Eggleston [95] and Grünbaum [127], and is omitted here. $\square$

This theorem allows us to restrict attention to a certain finite convex combination when calculating the capacity region. This is an important property because without it we would not be able to compute the capacity region in (14.81), since we would never know whether using a larger alphabet $\mathcal{Q}$ would increase the region.

In the multiple access channel, the bounds define a connected compact set in three dimensions. Therefore all points in its closure can be defined as the convex combination of four points. Hence, we can restrict the cardinality of Q to at most 4 in the above definition of the capacity region.

14.3.4 Converse for the Multiple Access Channel

We have so far proved the achievability of the capacity region. In this section, we will prove the converse.

Proof (*Converse to Theorem 14.3.1 and Theorem 14.3.3*): We must show that given any sequence of $((2^{nR_1}, 2^{nR_2}), n)$ codes with $P_e^{(n)} \to 0$, that the rates must satisfy

$$R_1 \leq I(X_1; Y|X_2, Q),$$

$$R_2 \leq I(X_2; Y|X_1, Q),$$

$$R_1 + R_2 \leq I(X_1, X_2; Y|Q) \tag{14.88}$$

for some choice of random variable Q defined on $\{1, 2, 3, 4\}$ and joint distribution $p(q)p(x_1|q)p(x_2|q)p(y|x_1, x_2)$.

Fix n. Consider the given code of block length n. The joint distribution on $\mathcal{W}_1 \times \mathcal{W}_2 \times \mathcal{X}_1^n \times \mathcal{X}_2^n \times \mathcal{Y}^n$ is well defined. The only randomness is due to the random uniform choice of indices W_1 and W_2 and the randomness induced by the channel. The joint distribution is

$$p(w_1, w_2, x_1^n, x_2^n, y^n) = \frac{1}{2^{nR_1}} \frac{1}{2^{nR_2}} p(x_1^n|w_1)p(x_2^n|w_2) \prod_{i=1}^{n} p(y_i|x_{1i}, x_{2i}),$$

$$\tag{14.89}$$

where $p(x_1^n|w_1)$ is either 1 or 0 depending on whether $x_1^n = \mathbf{x}_1(w_1)$, the codeword corresponding to w_1, or not, and similarly, $p(x_2^n|w_2) = 1$ or 0 according to whether $x_2^n = \mathbf{x}_2(w_2)$ or not. The mutual informations that follow are calculated with respect to this distribution.

By the code construction, it is possible to estimate (W_1, W_2) from the received sequence Y^n with a low probability of error. Hence the conditional entropy of (W_1, W_2) given Y^n must be small. By Fano's inequality,

$$H(W_1, W_2|Y^n) \leq n(R_1 + R_2)P_e^{(n)} + H(P_e^{(n)}) \triangleq n\epsilon_n. \tag{14.90}$$

It is clear that $\epsilon_n \to 0$ as $P_e^{(n)} \to 0$.

Then we have

$$H(W_1|Y^n) \leq H(W_1, W_2|Y^n) \leq n\epsilon_n, \tag{14.91}$$

$$H(W_2|Y^n) \le H(W_1, W_2|Y^n) \le n\epsilon_n . \tag{14.92}$$

We can now bound the rate R_1 as

$$nR_1 = H(W_1) \tag{14.93}$$

$$= I(W_1; Y^n) + H(W_1|Y^n) \tag{14.94}$$

$$\overset{(a)}{\le} I(W_1; Y^n) + n\epsilon_n \tag{14.95}$$

$$\overset{(b)}{\le} I(X_1^n(W_1); Y^n) + n\epsilon_n \tag{14.96}$$

$$= H(X_1^n(W_1)) - H(X_1^n(W_1)|Y^n) + n\epsilon_n \tag{14.97}$$

$$\overset{(c)}{\le} H(X_1^n(W_1)|X_2^n(W_2)) - H(X_1^n(W_1)|Y^n, X_2^n(W_2)) + n\epsilon_n \tag{14.98}$$

$$= I(X_1^n(W_1); Y^n|X_2^n(W_2)) + n\epsilon_n \tag{14.99}$$

$$= H(Y^n|X_2^n(W_2)) - H(Y^n|X_1^n(W_1), X_2^n(W_2)) + n\epsilon_n \tag{14.100}$$

$$\overset{(d)}{=} H(Y^n|X_2^n(W_2)) - \sum_{i=1}^{n} H(Y_i|Y^{i-1}, X_1^n(W_1), X_2^n(W_2)) + n\epsilon_n \tag{14.101}$$

$$\overset{(e)}{=} H(Y^n|X_2^n(W_2)) - \sum_{i=1}^{n} H(Y_i|X_{1i}, X_{2i}) + n\epsilon_n \tag{14.102}$$

$$\overset{(f)}{\le} \sum_{i=1}^{n} H(Y_i|X_2^n(W_2)) - \sum_{i=1}^{n} H(Y_i|X_{1i}, X_{2i}) + n\epsilon_n \tag{14.103}$$

$$\overset{(g)}{\le} \sum_{i=1}^{n} H(Y_i|X_{2i}) - \sum_{i=1}^{n} H(Y_i|X_{1i}, X_{2i}) + n\epsilon_n \tag{14.104}$$

$$= \sum_{i=1}^{n} I(X_{1i}; Y_i|X_{2i}) + n\epsilon_n , \tag{14.105}$$

where

(a) follows from Fano's inequality,

(b) from the data processing inequality,

(c) from the fact that since W_1 and W_2 are independent, so are $X_1^n(W_1)$ and $X_2^n(W_2)$, and hence $H(X_1^n(W_1)|X_2^n(W_2)) = H(X_1^n(W_1))$, and $H(X_1^n(W_1)|Y^n, X_2^n(W_2)) \le H(X_1^n(W_1)|Y^n)$ by conditioning,

(d) follows from the chain rule,

(e) from the fact that Y_i depends only on X_{1i} and X_{2i} by the memoryless property of the channel,

(f) from the chain rule and removing conditioning, and

(g) follows from removing conditioning.

Hence, we have

$$R_1 \le \frac{1}{n} \sum_{i=1}^{n} I(X_{1i}; Y_i | X_{2i}) + \epsilon_n .$$
(14.106)

Similarly, we have

$$R_2 \le \frac{1}{n} \sum_{i=1}^{n} I(X_{2i}; Y_i | X_{1i}) + \epsilon_n .$$
(14.107)

To bound the sum of the rates, we have

$$n(R_1 + R_2) = H(W_1, W_2)$$
(14.108)

$$= I(W_1, W_2; Y^n) + H(W_1, W_2 | Y^n)$$
(14.109)

$$\overset{(a)}{\le} I(W_1, W_2; Y^n) + n\epsilon_n$$
(14.110)

$$\overset{(b)}{\le} I(X_1^n(W_1), X_2^n(W_2); Y^n) + n\epsilon_n$$
(14.111)

$$= H(Y^n) - H(Y^n | X_1^n(W_1), X_2^n(W_2)) + n\epsilon_n$$
(14.112)

$$\overset{(c)}{=} H(Y^n) - \sum_{i=1}^{n} H(Y_i | Y^{i-1}, X_1^n(W_1), X_2^n(W_2)) + n\epsilon_n$$
(14.113)

$$\overset{(d)}{=} H(Y^n) - \sum_{i=1}^{n} H(Y_i | X_{1i}, X_{2i}) + n\epsilon_n$$
(14.114)

$$\overset{(e)}{\le} \sum_{i=1}^{n} H(Y_i) - \sum_{i=1}^{n} H(Y_i | X_{1i}, X_{2i}) + n\epsilon_n$$
(14.115)

$$= \sum_{i=1}^{n} I(X_{1i}, X_{2i}; Y_i) + n\epsilon_n ,$$
(14.116)

where

- (a) follows from Fano's inequality,
- (b) from the data processing inequality,
- (c) from the chain rule,
- (d) from the fact that Y_i depends only on X_{1i} and X_{2i} and is conditionally independent of everything else, and
- (e) follows from the chain rule and removing conditioning.

Hence we have

$$R_1 + R_2 \le \frac{1}{n} \sum_{i=1}^{n} I(X_{1i}, X_{2i}; Y_i) + \epsilon_n .$$
(14.117)

The expressions in (14.106), (14.107) and (14.117) are the averages of the mutual informations calculated at the empirical distributions in column i of the codebook. We can rewrite these equations with the new variable Q, where $Q = i \in \{1, 2, \ldots, n\}$ with probability $\frac{1}{n}$. The equations become

$$R_1 \le \frac{1}{n} \sum_{i=1}^{n} I(X_{1i}; Y_i | X_{2i}) + \epsilon_n \tag{14.118}$$

$$= \frac{1}{n} \sum_{i=1}^{n} I(X_{1q}; Y_q | X_{2q}, Q = i) + \epsilon_n \tag{14.119}$$

$$= I(X_{1Q}; Y_Q | X_{2Q}, Q) + \epsilon_n \tag{14.120}$$

$$= I(X_1; Y | X_2, Q) + \epsilon_n , \tag{14.121}$$

where $X_1 \overset{\triangle}{=} X_{1Q}$, $X_2 \overset{\triangle}{=} X_{2Q}$ and $Y \overset{\triangle}{=} Y_Q$ are new random variables whose distributions depend on Q in the same way as the distributions of X_{1i}, X_{2i} and Y_i depend on i. Since W_1 and W_2 are independent, so are $X_{1i}(W_1)$ and $X_{2i}(W_2)$, and hence

$$\Pr(X_{1i}(W_1) = x_1, X_{2i}(W_2) = x_2)$$

$$\overset{\triangle}{=} \Pr\{X_{1Q} = x_1 | Q = i\} \Pr\{X_{2Q} = x_2 | Q = i\} . \tag{14.122}$$

Hence, taking the limit as $n \to \infty$, $P_e^{(n)} \to 0$, we have the following converse:

$$R_1 \le I(X_1; Y | X_2, Q),$$

$$R_2 \le I(X_2; Y | X_1, Q),$$

$$R_1 + R_2 \le I(X_1, X_2; Y | Q) \tag{14.123}$$

for some choice of joint distribution $p(q)p(x_1|q)p(x_2|q)p(y|x_1, x_2)$.

As in the previous section, the region is unchanged if we limit the cardinality of $\mathcal{Q}$ to 4.

This completes the proof of the converse. $\square$

Thus the achievability of the region of Theorem 14.3.1 was proved in Section 14.3.1. In Section 14.3.3, we showed that every point in the region defined by (14.88) was also achievable. In the converse, we showed that the region in (14.88) was the best we can do, establishing that this is indeed the capacity region of the channel. Thus the region in

(14.58) cannot be any larger than the region in (14.88), and this is the capacity region of the multiple access channel.

14.3.5 *m*-User Multiple Access Channels

We will now generalize the result derived for two senders to m senders, $m \geq 2$. The multiple access channel in this case is shown in Figure 14.15.

We send independent indices $w_1, w_2, \ldots, w_m$ over the channel from the senders $1, 2, \ldots, m$ respectively. The codes, rates and achievability are all defined in exactly the same way as the two sender case.

Let $S \subseteq \{1, 2, \ldots, m\}$. Let S^c denote the complement of S. Let $R(S) = \sum_{i \in S} R_i$, and let $X(S) = \{X_i : i \in S\}$. Then we have the following theorem.

Theorem 14.3.5: *The capacity region of the m-user multiple access channel is the closure of the convex hull of the rate vectors satisfying*

$$R(S) \leq I(X(S); Y|X(S^c)) \quad \textit{for all } S \subseteq \{1, 2, \ldots, m\} \quad (14.124)$$

for some product distribution $p_1(x_1)p_2(x_2) \ldots p_m(x_m)$.

Proof: The proof contains no new ideas. There are now $2^m - 1$ terms in the probability of error in the achievability proof and an equal number of inequalities in the proof of the converse. Details are left to the reader.   □

In general, the region in (14.124) is a beveled box.

14.3.6 Gaussian Multiple Access Channels

We now discuss the Gaussian multiple access channel of Section 14.1.2 in somewhat more detail.

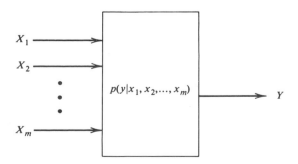

Figure 14.15. *m*-user multiple access channel.

There are two senders, X_1 and X_2, sending to the single receiver Y. The received signal at time i is

$$Y_i = X_{1i} + X_{2i} + Z_i, \qquad (14.125)$$

where $\{Z_i\}$ is a sequence of independent, identically distributed, zero mean Gaussian random variables with variance N (Figure 14.16). We will assume that there is a power constraint P_j on sender j, i.e., for each sender, for all messages, we must have

$$\frac{1}{n} \sum_{i=1}^{n} x_{ji}^2(w_j) \le P_j, \quad w_j \in \{1, 2, \dots, 2^{nR_j}\}, j = 1, 2. \qquad (14.126)$$

Just as the proof of achievability of channel capacity for the discrete case (Chapter 8) was extended to the Gaussian channel (Chapter 10), we can extend the proof the discrete multiple access channel to the Gaussian multiple access channel. The converse can also be extended similarly, so we expect the capacity region to be the convex hull of the set of rate pairs satisfying

$$R_1 \le I(X_1; Y|X_2), \qquad (14.127)$$

$$R_2 \le I(X_2; Y|X_1), \qquad (14.128)$$

$$R_1 + R_2 \le I(X_1, X_2; Y) \qquad (14.129)$$

for some input distribution $f_1(x_1)f_2(x_2)$ satisfying $EX_1^2 \le P_1$ and $EX_2^2 \le P_2$.

Now, we can expand the mutual information in terms of relative entropy, and thus

$$I(X_1; Y|X_2) = h(Y|X_2) - h(Y|X_1, X_2) \qquad (14.130)$$

$$= h(X_1 + X_2 + Z|X_2) - h(X_1 + X_2 + Z|X_1, X_2) \qquad (14.131)$$

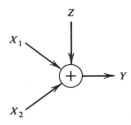

Figure 14.16. Gaussian multiple access channel.

$$= h(X_1 + Z|X_2) - h(Z|X_1, X_2) \tag{14.132}$$

$$= h(X_1 + Z|X_2) - h(Z) \tag{14.133}$$

$$= h(X_1 + Z) - h(Z) \tag{14.134}$$

$$= h(X_1 + Z) - \frac{1}{2} \log(2\pi e)N \tag{14.135}$$

$$\leq \frac{1}{2} \log(2\pi e)(P_1 + N) - \frac{1}{2} \log(2\pi e)N \tag{14.136}$$

$$= \frac{1}{2} \log\left(1 + \frac{P_1}{N}\right), \tag{14.137}$$

where (14.133) follows from the fact that Z is independent of X_1 and X_2, (14.134) from the independence of X_1 and X_2, and (14.136) from the fact that the normal maximizes entropy for a given second moment. Thus the maximizing distribution is $X_1 \sim \mathcal{N}(0, P_1)$ and $X_2 \sim \mathcal{N}(0, P_2)$ with X_1 and X_2 independent. This distribution simultaneously maximizes the mutual information bounds in (14.127)–(14.129).

Definition: We define the channel capacity function

$$C(x) \overset{\triangle}{=} \frac{1}{2} \log(1 + x), \tag{14.138}$$

corresponding to the channel capacity of a Gaussian white noise channel with signal to noise ratio x.

Then we write the bound on R_1 as

$$R_1 \leq C\left(\frac{P_1}{N}\right). \tag{14.139}$$

Similarly,

$$R_2 \leq C\left(\frac{P_2}{N}\right), \tag{14.140}$$

and

$$R_1 + R_2 \leq C\left(\frac{P_1 + P_2}{N}\right). \tag{14.141}$$

These upper bounds are achieved when $X_1 \sim \mathcal{N}(0, P_1)$ and $X_2 = \mathcal{N}(0, P_2)$ and define the capacity region.

The surprising fact about these inequalities is that the sum of the rates can be as large as $C(\frac{P_1 + P_2}{N})$, which is that rate achieved by a single transmitter sending with a power equal to the sum of the powers.

The interpretation of the corner points is very similar to the interpretation of the achievable rate pairs for a discrete multiple access channel for a fixed input distribution. In the case of the Gaussian channel, we can consider decoding as a two-stage process: in the first stage, the receiver decodes the second sender, considering the first sender as part of the noise. This decoding will have low probability of error if $R_2 < C(\frac{P_2}{P_1 + N})$. After the second sender has been successfully decoded, it can be subtracted out and the first sender can be decoded correctly if $R_1 < C(\frac{P_1}{N})$. Hence, this argument shows that we can achieve the rate pairs at the corner points of the capacity region.

If we generalize this to m senders with equal power, the total rate is $C(\frac{mP}{N})$, which goes to ∞ as $m \to \infty$. The average rate per sender, $\frac{1}{m} C(\frac{mP}{N})$ goes to 0. Thus when the total number of senders is very large, so that there is a lot of interference, we can still send a total amount of information which is arbitrarily large even though the rate per individual sender goes to 0.

The capacity region described above corresponds to Code Division Multiple Access (CDMA), where orthogonal codes are used for the different senders, and the receiver decodes them one by one. In many practical situations, though, simpler schemes like time division multiplexing or frequency division multiplexing are used.

With frequency division multiplexing, the rates depend on the bandwidth allotted to each sender. Consider the case of two senders with powers P_1 and P_2 and using bandwidths non-intersecting frequency bands W_1 and W_2, where $W_1 + W_2 = W$ (the total bandwidth). Using the formula for the capacity of a single user bandlimited channel, the following rate pair is achievable:

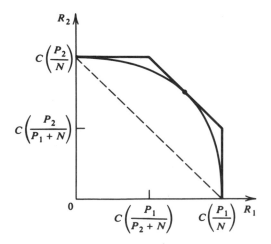

Figure 14.17. Gaussian multiple access channel capacity.

$$R_1 = \frac{W_1}{2} \log\left(1 + \frac{P_1}{NW_1}\right),$$ (14.142)

$$R_2 = \frac{W_2}{2} \log\left(1 + \frac{P_2}{NW_2}\right).$$ (14.143)

As we vary W_1 and W_2, we trace out the curve as shown in Figure 14.17. This curve touches the boundary of the capacity region at one point, which corresponds to allotting bandwidth to each channel proportional to the power in that channel. We conclude that no allocation of frequency bands to radio stations can be optimal unless the allocated powers are proportional to the bandwidths.

As Figure 14.17 illustrates, in general the capacity region is larger than that achieved by time division or frequency division multiplexing. But note that the multiple access capacity region derived above is achieved by use of a common decoder for all the senders. However in many practical systems, simplicity of design is an important consideration, and the improvement in capacity due to the multiple access ideas presented earlier may not be sufficient to warrant the increased complexity.

For a Gaussian multiple access system with m sources with powers $P_1, P_2, \ldots, P_m$ and ambient noise of power N, we can state the equivalent of Gauss's law for any set S in the form

$$\sum_{i \in S} R_i = \text{Total rate of information flow across boundary of } S \quad (14.144)$$

$$\leq C\left(\frac{\sum_{i \in S} P_i}{N}\right).$$ (14.145)

14.4   ENCODING OF CORRELATED SOURCES

We now turn to distributed data compression. This problem is in many ways the data compression dual to the multiple access channel problem.

We know how to encode a source X. A rate $R > H(X)$ is sufficient. Now suppose that there are two sources $(X, Y) \sim p(x, y)$. A rate $H(X, Y)$ is sufficient if we are encoding them together. But what if the X-source and the Y-source must be separately described for some user who wishes to reconstruct both X and Y? Clearly, by separate encoding X and Y, it is seen that a rate $R = R_x + R_y > H(X) + H(Y)$ is sufficient. However, in a surprising and fundamental paper by Slepian and Wolf [255], it is shown that a total rate $R = H(X, Y)$ is sufficient even for separate encoding of correlated sources.

Let $(X_1, Y_1), (X_2, Y_2), \ldots$ be a sequence of jointly distributed random variables i.i.d. $\sim p(x, y)$. Assume that the X sequence is available at a location A and the Y sequence is available at a location B. The situation is illustrated in Figure 14.18.

Before we proceed to the proof of this result, we will give a few definitions.

Definition: A $((2^{nR_1}, 2^{nR_2}), n)$ *distributed source code* for the joint source (X, Y) consists of two encoder maps,

$$f_1 : \mathscr{X}^n \to \{1, 2, \ldots, 2^{nR_1}\}, \tag{14.146}$$

$$f_2 : \mathscr{Y}^n \to \{1, 2, \ldots, 2^{nR_2}\} \tag{14.147}$$

and a decoder map,

$$g : \{1, 2, \ldots, 2^{nR_1}\} \times \{1, 2, \ldots, 2^{nR_2}\} \to \mathscr{X}^n \times \mathscr{Y}^n. \tag{14.148}$$

Here $f_1(X^n)$ is the index corresponding to X^n, $f_2(Y^n)$ is the index corresponding to Y^n and (R_1, R_2) is the rate pair of the code.

Definition: The *probability of error* for a distributed source code is defined as

$$P_e^{(n)} = P(g(f_1(X^n), f_2(Y^n)) \neq (X^n, Y^n)). \tag{14.149}$$

Definition: A rate pair (R_1, R_2) is said to be *achievable* for a distributed source if there exists a sequence of $((2^{nR_1}, 2^{nR_2}), n)$ distributed source codes with probability of error $P_e^{(n)} \to 0$. The *achievable rate region* is the closure of the set of achievable rates.

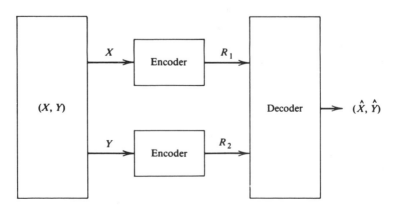

Figure 14.18. Slepian-Wolf coding.

Theorem 14.4.1 (*Slepian-Wolf*): *For the distributed source coding problem for the source (X, Y) drawn i.i.d $\sim p(x, y)$, the achievable rate region is given by*

$$R_1 \geq H(X|Y), \qquad (14.150)$$

$$R_2 \geq H(Y|X), \qquad (14.151)$$

$$R_1 + R_2 \geq H(X, Y). \qquad (14.152)$$

Let us illustrate the result with some examples.

Example 14.4.1: Consider the weather in Gotham and Metropolis. For the purposes of our example, we will assume that Gotham is sunny with probability 0.5 and that the weather in Metropolis is the same as in Gotham with probability 0.89. The joint distribution of the weather is given as follows:

	Metropolis	
$p(x, y)$	Rain	Shine
Gotham Rain	0.445	0.055
Shine	0.055	0.445

Assume that we wish to transmit 100 days of weather information to the National Weather Service Headquarters in Washington. We could send all the 100 bits of the weather in both places, making 200 bits in all. If we decided to compress the information independently, then we would still need $100H(0.5) = 100$ bits of information from each place for a total of 200 bits.

If instead we use Slepian-Wolf encoding, we need only $H(X) + H(Y|X) = 100H(0.5) + 100H(0.89) = 100 + 50 = 150$ bits total.

Example 14.4.2: Consider the following joint distribution:

$p(u, v)$	0	1
0	1/3	1/3
1	0	1/3

In this case, the total rate required for the transmission of this source is $H(U) + H(V|U) = \log 3 = 1.58$ bits, rather than the 2 bits which would be needed if the sources were transmitted independently without Slepian-Wolf encoding.

14.4.1 Achievability of the Slepian-Wolf Theorem

We now prove the achievability of the rates in the Slepian-Wolf theorem. Before we proceed to the proof, we will first introduce a new coding procedure using random bins.

The essential idea of random bins is very similar to hash functions: we choose a large random index for each source sequence. If the set of typical source sequences is small enough (or equivalently, the range of the hash function is large enough), then with high probability, different source sequences have different indices, and we can recover the source sequence from the index.

Let us consider the application of this idea to the encoding of a single source. In Chapter 3, the method that we considered was to index all elements of the typical set and not bother about elements outside the typical set. We will now describe the random binning procedure, which indexes all sequences, but rejects untypical sequences at a later stage.

Consider the following procedure: For each sequence X^n, draw an index at random from $\{1, 2, \ldots, 2^{nR}\}$. The set of sequences X^n which have the same index are said to form a bin, since this can be viewed as first laying down a row of bins and then throwing the X^n's at random into the bins. For decoding the source from the bin index, we look for a typical X^n sequence in the bin. If there is one and only one typical X^n sequence in the bin, we declare it to be the estimate $\hat{X}^n$ of the source sequence; otherwise, an error is declared.

The above procedure defines a source code. To analyze the probability of error for this code, we will now divide the X^n sequences into two types, the typical sequences and the non-typical sequences.

If the source sequence is typical, then the bin corresponding to this source sequence will contain at least one typical sequence (the source sequence itself). Hence there will be an error only if there is more than one typical sequence in this bin. If the source sequence is non-typical, then there will always be an error. But if the number of bins is much larger than the number of typical sequences, the probability that there is more than one typical sequence in a bin is very small, and hence the probability that a typical sequence will result in an error is very small.

Formally, let $f(X^n)$ be the bin index corresponding to X^n. Call the decoding function g. The probability of error (averaged over the random choice of codes f) is

$$P(g(f(\mathbf{X})) \neq \mathbf{X}) \leq P(\mathbf{X} \notin A_\epsilon^{(n)}) + \sum_{\mathbf{x}} P(\exists \mathbf{x}' \neq \mathbf{x} : \mathbf{x}' \in A_\epsilon^{(n)}, f(\mathbf{x}') = f(\mathbf{x}))p(\mathbf{x})$$

$$\leq \epsilon + \sum_{\mathbf{x}} \sum_{\substack{\mathbf{x}' \in A_\epsilon^{(n)} \\ \mathbf{x}' \neq \mathbf{x}}} P(f(\mathbf{x}') = f(\mathbf{x}))p(\mathbf{x}) \qquad (14.153)$$

$$\le \epsilon + \sum_{\mathbf{x}} \sum_{\mathbf{x}' \in A_\epsilon^{(n)}} 2^{-nR} p(\mathbf{x}) \tag{14.154}$$

$$= \epsilon + \sum_{\mathbf{x}' \in A_\epsilon^{(n)}} 2^{-nR} \sum_{\mathbf{x}} p(\mathbf{x}) \tag{14.155}$$

$$\le \epsilon + \sum_{\mathbf{x}' \in A_\epsilon^{(n)}} 2^{-nR} \tag{14.156}$$

$$\le \epsilon + 2^{n(H(X)+\epsilon)} 2^{-nR} \tag{14.157}$$

$$\le 2\epsilon \tag{14.158}$$

if $R > H(X) + \epsilon$ and n is sufficiently large. Hence if the rate of the code is greater than the entropy, the probability of error is arbitrarily small and the code achieves the same results as the code described in Chapter 3.

The above example illustrates the fact that there are many ways to construct codes with low probabilities of error at rates above the entropy of the source; the universal source code is another example of such a code. Note that the binning scheme does not require an explicit characterization of the typical set at the encoder; it is only needed at the decoder. It is this property that enables this code to continue to work in the case of a distributed source, as will be illustrated in the proof of the theorem.

We now return to the consideration of the distributed source coding and prove the achievability of the rate region in the Slepian-Wolf theorem.

Proof (*Achievability in Theorem 14.4.1*): The basic idea of the proof is to partition the space of $\mathcal{X}^n$ into 2^{nR_1} bins and the space of $\mathcal{Y}^n$ into 2^{nR_2} bins.

Random code generation. Independently assign every $\mathbf{x} \in \mathcal{X}^n$ to one of 2^{nR_1} bins according to a uniform distribution on $\{1, 2, \ldots, 2^{nR_1}\}$. Similarly, randomly assign every $\mathbf{y} \in \mathcal{Y}^n$ to one of 2^{nR_2} bins. Reveal the assignments f_1 and f_2 to both the encoder and decoder.

Encoding. Sender 1 sends the index of the bin to which $\mathbf{X}$ belongs. Sender 2 sends the index of the bin to which $\mathbf{Y}$ belongs.

Decoding. Given the received index pair (i_0, j_0), declare $(\hat{\mathbf{x}}, \hat{\mathbf{y}}) = (\mathbf{x}, \mathbf{y})$, if there is one and only one pair of sequences $(\mathbf{x}, \mathbf{y})$ such that $f_1(\mathbf{x}) = i_0$, $f_2(\mathbf{y}) = j_0$ and $(\mathbf{x}, \mathbf{y}) \in A_\epsilon^{(n)}$. Otherwise declare an error. The scheme is illustrated in Figure 14.19. The set of X sequences and the set of Y sequences are divided into bins in such a way that the pair of indices specifies a product bin.

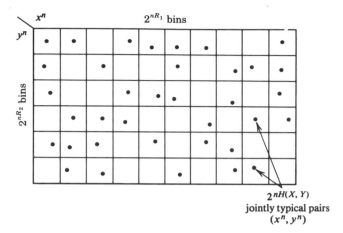

Figure 14.19. Slepian-Wolf encoding: the jointly typical pairs are isolated by the product bins.

Probability of error. Let $(X_i, Y_i) \sim p(x, y)$. Define the events

$$E_0 = \{(\mathbf{X}, \mathbf{Y}) \notin A_\epsilon^{(n)}\},\qquad(14.159)$$

$$E_1 = \{\exists \mathbf{x}' \neq \mathbf{X} : f_1(\mathbf{x}') = f_1(\mathbf{X}) \text{ and } (\mathbf{x}', \mathbf{Y}) \in A_\epsilon^{(n)}\},\quad(14.160)$$

$$E_2 = \{\exists \mathbf{y}' \neq \mathbf{Y} : f_2(\mathbf{y}') = f_2(\mathbf{Y}) \text{ and } (\mathbf{X}, \mathbf{y}') \in A_\epsilon^{(n)}\},\quad(14.161)$$

and

$$E_{12} = \{\exists (\mathbf{x}', \mathbf{y}') : \mathbf{x}' \neq \mathbf{X}, \mathbf{y}' \neq \mathbf{Y}, f_1(\mathbf{x}') = f_1(\mathbf{X}), f_2(\mathbf{y}') \neq f_2(\mathbf{Y})$$
$$\text{and } (\mathbf{x}', \mathbf{y}') \in A_\epsilon^{(n)}\}.\quad(14.162)$$

Here $\mathbf{X}, \mathbf{Y}, f_1$ and f_2 are random. We have an error if $(\mathbf{X}, \mathbf{Y})$ is not in $A_\epsilon^{(n)}$ or if there is another typical pair in the same bin. Hence by the union of events bound,

$$P_e^{(n)} = P(E_0 \cup E_1 \cup E_2 \cup E_{12})\qquad(14.163)$$

$$\leq P(E_0) + P(E_1) + P(E_2) + P(E_{12}).\qquad(14.164)$$

First consider E_0. By the AEP, $P(E_0) \to 0$ and hence for n sufficiently large, $P(E_0) < \epsilon$.

To bound $P(E_1)$, we have

$$P(E_1) = P\{\exists \mathbf{x}' \neq \mathbf{X} : f_1(\mathbf{x}') = f_1(\mathbf{X}), \text{ and } (\mathbf{x}', \mathbf{Y}) \in A_\epsilon^{(n)}\}\quad(14.165)$$

$$= \sum_{(\mathbf{x}, \mathbf{y})} p(\mathbf{x}, \mathbf{y}) P\{\exists \mathbf{x}' \neq \mathbf{x} : f_1(\mathbf{x}') = f_1(\mathbf{x}), (\mathbf{x}', \mathbf{y}) \in A_\epsilon^{(n)}\} \quad (14.166)$$

$$\leq \sum_{(\mathbf{x}, \mathbf{y})} p(\mathbf{x}, \mathbf{y}) \sum_{\substack{\mathbf{x}' \neq \mathbf{x} \\ (\mathbf{x}', \mathbf{y}) \in A_\epsilon^{(n)}}} P(f_1(\mathbf{x}') = f_1(\mathbf{x})) \quad (14.167)$$

$$= \sum_{(\mathbf{x}, \mathbf{y})} p(\mathbf{x}, \mathbf{y}) 2^{-nR_1} |A_\epsilon(X|\mathbf{y})| \quad (14.168)$$

$$\leq 2^{-nR_1} 2^{n(H(X|Y)+\epsilon)} \text{ (by Theorem 14.2.2)}, \quad (14.169)$$

which goes to 0 if $R_1 > H(X|Y)$. Hence for sufficiently large n, $P(E_1) < \epsilon$. Similarly, for sufficiently large n, $P(E_2) < \epsilon$ if $R_2 > H(Y|X)$ and $P(E_{12}) < \epsilon$ if $R_1 + R_2 > H(X, Y)$.

Since the average probability of error is $< 4\epsilon$, there exists at least one code (f_1^*, f_2^*, g^*) with probability of error $< 4\epsilon$. Thus, we can construct a sequence of codes with $P_e^{(n)} \to 0$ and the proof of achievability is complete. $\square$

14.4.2   Converse for the Slepian-Wolf Theorem

The converse for the Slepian-Wolf theorem follows obviously from from the results for single source, but we will provide it for completeness.

Proof (*Converse to Theorem 14.4.1*): As usual, we begin with Fano's inequality. Let f_1, f_2, g be fixed. Let $I_0 = f_1(X^n)$ and $J_0 = f_2(Y^n)$. Then

$$H(X^n, Y^n|I_0, J_0) \leq P_e^{(n)} n(\log|\mathcal{X}| + \log|\mathcal{Y}|) + 1 = n\epsilon_n, \quad (14.170)$$

where $\epsilon_n > 0$ as $n \to \infty$. Now adding conditioning, we also have

$$H(X^n|Y^n, I_0, J_0) \leq P_e^{(n)} n\epsilon_n, \quad (14.171)$$

and

$$H(Y^n|X^n, I_0, J_0) \leq P_e^{(n)} n\epsilon_n. \quad (14.172)$$

We can write a chain of inequalities

$$n(R_1 + R_2) \overset{(a)}{\geq} H(I_0, J_0) \quad (14.173)$$

$$= I(X^n, Y^n; I_0, J_0) + H(I_0, J_0|X^n, Y^n) \quad (14.174)$$

$$\overset{(b)}{=} I(X^n, Y^n; I_0, J_0) \quad (14.175)$$

$$= H(X^n, Y^n) - H(X^n, Y^n | I_0, J_0) \qquad (14.176)$$

$$\overset{(c)}{\geq} H(X^n, Y^n) - n\epsilon_n \qquad (14.177)$$

$$\overset{(d)}{=} nH(X, Y) - n\epsilon_n, \qquad (14.178)$$

where

(a) follows from the fact that $I_0 \in \{1, 2, \ldots, 2^{nR_1}\}$ and $J_0 \in \{1, 2, \ldots, 2^{nR_2}\}$,

(b) from the fact the I_0 is a function of X^n and J_0 is a function of Y^n,

(c) from Fano's inequality (14.170), and

(d) from the chain rule and the fact that (X_i, Y_i) are i.i.d.

Similarly, using (14.171), we have

$$nR_1 \overset{(a)}{\geq} H(I_0) \qquad (14.179)$$

$$\geq H(I_0 | Y^n) \qquad (14.180)$$

$$= I(X^n; I_0 | Y^n) + H(I_0 | X^n, Y^n) \qquad (14.181)$$

$$\overset{(b)}{=} I(X^n; I_0 | Y^n) \qquad (14.182)$$

$$= H(X^n | Y^n) - H(X^n | I_0, J_0, Y^n) \qquad (14.183)$$

$$\overset{(c)}{\geq} H(X^n | Y^n) - n\epsilon_n \qquad (14.184)$$

$$\overset{(d)}{=} nH(X | Y) - n\epsilon_n, \qquad (14.185)$$

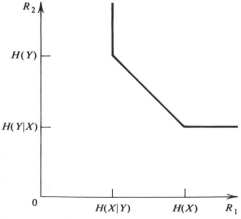

Figure 14.20. Rate region for Slepian-Wolf encoding.

where the reasons are the same as for the equations above. Similarly, we can show that

$$nR_2 \geq nH(Y|X) - n\epsilon_n . \qquad (14.186)$$

Dividing these inequalities by n and taking the limit as $n \to \infty$, we have the desired converse. $\square$

The region described in the Slepian-Wolf theorem is illustrated in Figure 14.20.

14.4.3 Slepian-Wolf Theorem for Many Sources

The results of the previous section can easily be generalized to many sources. The proof follows exactly the same lines.

Theorem 14.4.2: Let $(X_{1i}, X_{2i}, \ldots, X_{mi})$ be i.i.d. $\sim p(x_1, x_2, \ldots, x_m)$. Then the set of rate vectors achievable for distributed source coding with separate encoders and a common decoder is defined by

$$R(S) > H(X(S)|X(S^c)) \qquad (14.187)$$

for all $S \subseteq \{1, 2, \ldots, m\}$ where

$$R(S) = \sum_{i \in S} R_i , \qquad (14.188)$$

and $X(S) = \{X_j : j \in S\}$.

Proof: The proof is identical to the case of two variables and is omitted. $\square$

The achievability of Slepian-Wolf encoding has been proved for an i.i.d. correlated source, but the proof can easily be extended to the case of an arbitrary joint source that satisfies the AEP; in particular, it can be extended to the case of any jointly ergodic source [63]. In these cases the entropies in the definition of the rate region are replaced by the corresponding entropy rates.

14.4.4 Interpretation of Slepian-Wolf Coding

We will consider an interpretation of the corner points of the rate region in Slepian-Wolf encoding in terms of graph coloring. Consider the point with rate $R_1 = H(X), R_2 = H(Y|X)$. Using $nH(X)$ bits, we can encode X^n efficiently, so that the decoder can reconstruct X^n with arbitrarily low probability of error. But how do we code Y^n with $nH(Y|X)$ bits?

Looking at the picture in terms of typical sets, we see that associated with every X^n is a typical "fan" of Y^n sequences that are jointly typical with the given X^n as shown in Figure 14.21.

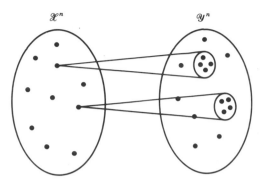

Figure 14.21. Jointly typical fans.

If the Y encoder knows X^n, the encoder can send the index of the Y^n within this typical fan. The decoder, also knowing X^n, can then construct this typical fan and hence reconstruct Y^n. But the Y encoder does not know X^n. So instead of trying to determine the typical fan, he randomly colors all Y^n sequences with 2^{nR_2} colors. If the number of colors is high enough, then with high probability, all the colors in a particular fan will be different and the color of the Y^n sequence will uniquely define the Y^n sequence within the X^n fan. If the rate $R_2 > H(Y|X)$, the number of colors is exponentially larger than the number of elements in the fan and we can show that the scheme will have exponentially small probability of error.

14.5 DUALITY BETWEEN SLEPIAN-WOLF ENCODING AND MULTIPLE ACCESS CHANNELS

With multiple access channels, we considered the problem of sending independent messages over a channel with two inputs and only one output. With Slepian-Wolf encoding, we considered the problem of sending a correlated source over a noiseless channel, with a common decoder for recovery of both sources. In this section, we will explore the duality between the two systems.

In Figure 14.22, two independent messages are to be sent over the channel as X_1^n and X_2^n sequences. The receiver estimates the messages from the received sequence. In Figure 14.23, the correlated sources are encoded as "independent" messages i and j. The receiver tries to estimate the source sequences from knowledge of i and j.

In the proof of the achievability of the capacity region for the multiple access channel, we used a random map from the set of messages to the sequences X_1^n and X_2^n. In the proof for Slepian-Wolf coding, we used a random map from the set of sequences X^n and Y^n to a set of messages.

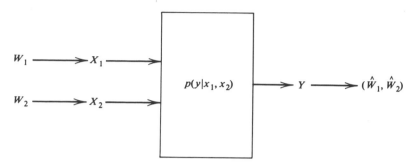

Figure 14.22. Multiple access channels.

In the proof of the coding theorem for the multiple access channel, the probability of error was bounded by

$$P_e^{(n)} \le \epsilon + \sum_{\text{codewords}} \text{Pr(codeword jointly typical with received sequence)}$$
$$(14.189)$$

$$= \epsilon + \sum_{2^{nR_1} \text{ terms}} 2^{-nI_1} + \sum_{2^{nR_2} \text{ terms}} 2^{-nI_2} + \sum_{2^{n(R_1 + R_2)} \text{ terms}} 2^{-nI_3}, \quad (14.190)$$

where ϵ is the probability the sequences are not typical, R_i are the rates corresponding to the number of codewords that can contribute to the probability of error, and I_i is the corresponding mutual information that corresponds to the probability that the codeword is jointly typical with the received sequence.

In the case of Slepian-Wolf encoding, the corresponding expression for the probability of error is

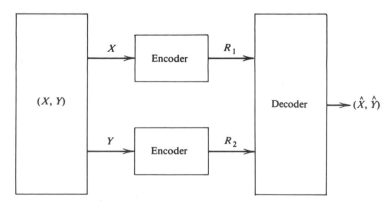

Figure 14.23. Correlated source encoding.

$$P_e^{(n)} \le \epsilon + \sum_{\substack{\text{Jointly typical sequences}}} \text{Pr(have same codeword)} \qquad (14.191)$$

$$= \epsilon + \sum_{2^{nH_1} \text{ terms}} 2^{-nR_1} + \sum_{2^{nH_2} \text{ terms}} 2^{-nR_2} + \sum_{2^{nH_3} \text{ terms}} 2^{-n(R_1+R_2)}$$

$$(14.192)$$

where again the probability that the constraints of the AEP are not satisfied is bounded by ϵ, and the other terms refer to the various ways in which another pair of sequences could be jointly typical and in the same bin as the given source pair.

The duality of the multiple access channel and correlated source encoding is now obvious. It is rather surprising that these two systems are duals of each other; one would have expected a duality between the broadcast channel and the multiple access channel.

14.6   THE BROADCAST CHANNEL

The broadcast channel is a communication channel in which there is one sender and two or more receivers. It is illustrated in Figure 14.24. The basic problem is to find the set of simultaneously achievable rates for communication in a broadcast channel.

Before we begin the analysis, let us consider some examples:

Example 14.6.1 (*TV station*): The simplest example of the broadcast channel is a radio or TV station. But this example is slightly degenerate in the sense that normally the station wants to send the same information to everybody who is tuned in; the capacity is essentially $\max_{p(x)} \min_i I(X; Y_i)$, which may be less than the capacity of the worst receiver.

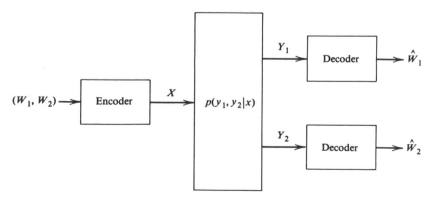

Figure 14.24. Broadcast channel.

But we may wish to arrange the information in such a way that the better receivers receive extra information, which produces a better picture or sound, while the worst receivers continue to receive more basic information. As TV stations introduce High Definition TV (HDTV), it may be necessary to encode the information so that bad receivers will receive the regular TV signal, while good receivers will receive the extra information for the high definition signal. The methods to accomplish this will be explained in the discussion of the broadcast channel.

Example 14.6.2 (*Lecturer in classroom*): A lecturer in a classroom is communicating information to the students in the class. Due to differences among the students, they receive various amounts of information. Some of the students receive most of the information; others receive only a little. In the ideal situation, the lecturer would be able to tailor his or her lecture in such a way that the good students receive more information and the poor students receive at least the minimum amount of information. However, a poorly prepared lecture proceeds at the pace of the weakest student. This situation is another example of a broadcast channel.

Example 14.6.3 (*Orthogonal broadcast channels*): The simplest broadcast channel consists of two independent channels to the two receivers. Here we can send independent information over both channels, and we can achieve rate R_1 to receiver 1 and rate R_2 to receiver 2, if $R_1 < C_1$ and $R_2 < C_2$. The capacity region is the rectangle shown in Figure 14.25.

Example 14.6.4 (*Spanish and Dutch speaker*): To illustrate the idea of superposition, we will consider a simplified example of a speaker who can speak both Spanish and Dutch. There are two listeners: one understands only Spanish and the other understands only Dutch. Assume for simplicity that the vocabulary of each language is 2^{20} words

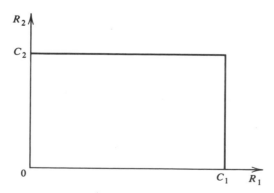

Figure 14.25. Capacity region for two orthogonal broadcast channels.

and that the speaker speaks at the rate of 1 word per second in either language. Then he can transmit 20 bits of information per second to receiver 1 by speaking to him all the time; in this case, he sends no information to receiver 2. Similarly, he can send 20 bits per second to receiver 2 without sending any information to receiver 1. Thus he can achieve any rate pair with $R_1 + R_2 = 20$ by simple timesharing. But can he do better?

Recall that the Dutch listener, even though he does not understand Spanish, can recognize when the word is Spanish. Similarly, the Spanish listener can recognize when Dutch occurs. The speaker can use this to convey information; for example, if the proportion of time he uses each language is 50%, then of a sequence of 100 words, about 50 will be Dutch and about 50 will be Spanish. But there are many ways to order the Spanish and Dutch words; in fact, there are about $\binom{100}{50} \approx 2^{100H(\frac{1}{2})}$ ways to order the words. Choosing one of these orderings conveys information to both listeners. This method enables the speaker to send information at a rate of 10 bits per second to the Dutch receiver, 10 bits per second to the Spanish receiver, and 1 bit per second of common information to both receivers, for a total rate of 21 bits per second, which is more than that achievable by simple time sharing. This is an example of superposition of information.

The results of the broadcast channel can also be applied to the case of a single user channel with an unknown distribution. In this case, the objective is to get at least the minimum information through when the channel is bad and to get some extra information through when the channel is good. We can use the same superposition arguments as in the case of the broadcast channel to find the rates at which we can send information.

14.6.1 Definitions for a Broadcast Channel

Definition: A *broadcast channel* consists of an input alphabet $\mathcal{X}$ and two output alphabets $\mathcal{Y}_1$ and $\mathcal{Y}_2$ and a probability transition function $p(y_1, y_2 | x)$. The broadcast channel will be said to be *memoryless* if $p(y_1^n, y_2^n | x^n) = \prod_{i=1}^n p(y_{1i}, y_{2i} | x_i)$.

We define codes, probability of error, achievability and capacity regions for the broadcast channel as we did for the multiple access channel.

A $((2^{nR_1}, 2^{nR_2}), n)$ code for a broadcast channel with independent information consists of an encoder,

$$X : (\{1, 2, \ldots, 2^{nR_1}\} \times \{1, 2, \ldots, 2^{nR_2}\}) \rightarrow \mathcal{X}^n, \qquad (14.193)$$

and two decoders,

$$g_1 : \mathcal{Y}_1^n \to \{1, 2, \ldots, 2^{nR_1}\} \tag{14.194}$$

and

$$g_2 : \mathcal{Y}_2^n \to \{1, 2, \ldots, 2^{nR_2}\} . \tag{14.195}$$

We define the average probability of error as the probability the decoded message is not equal to the transmitted message, i.e.,

$$P_e^{(n)} = P(g_1(Y_1^n) \neq W_1 \text{ or } g_2(Y_2^n) \neq W_2), \tag{14.196}$$

where (W_1, W_2) are assumed to be uniformly distributed over $2^{nR_1} \times 2^{nR_2}$.

Definition: A rate pair (R_1, R_2) is said to be *achievable* for the broadcast channel if there exists a sequence of $((2^{nR_1}, 2^{nR_2}), n)$ codes with $P_e^{(n)} \to 0$.

We will now define the rates for the case where we have common information to be sent to both receivers.

A $((2^{nR_0}, 2^{nR_1}, 2^{nR_2}), n)$ code for a broadcast channel with common information consists of an encoder,

$$X : (\{1, 2, \ldots, 2^{nR_0}\} \times \{1, 2, \ldots, 2^{nR_1}\} \times \{1, 2, \ldots, 2^{nR_2}\})) \to \mathcal{X}^n ,$$
$$\tag{14.197}$$

and two decoders,

$$g_1 : \mathcal{Y}_1^n \to \{1, 2, \ldots, 2^{nR_0}\} \times \{1, 2, \ldots, 2^{nR_1}\} \tag{14.198}$$

and

$$g_2 : \mathcal{Y}_2^n \to \{1, 2, \ldots, 2^{nR_0}\} \times \{1, 2, \ldots, 2^{nR_2}\} . \tag{14.199}$$

Assuming that the distribution on (W_0, W_1, W_2) is uniform, we can define the probability of error as the probability the decoded message is not equal to the transmitted message, i.e.,

$$P_e^{(n)} = P(g_1(Y_1^n) \neq (W_0, W_1) \text{ or } g_2(Z^n) \neq (W_0, W_2)) . \tag{14.200}$$

Definition: A rate triple (R_0, R_1, R_2) is said to be *achievable* for the broadcast channel with common information if there exists a sequence of $((2^{nR_0}, 2^{nR_1}, 2^{nR_2}), n)$ codes with $P_e^{(n)} \to 0$.

Definition: The *capacity region* of the broadcast channel is the closure of the set of achievable rates.

Theorem 14.6.1: *The capacity region of a broadcast channel depends only on the conditional marginal distributions $p(y_1|x)$ and $p(y_2|x)$.*

Proof: See exercises. □

14.6.2 Degraded Broadcast Channels

Definition: A broadcast channel is said to be *physically degraded* if $p(y_1, y_2|x) = p(y_1|x)p(y_2|y_1)$.

Definition: A broadcast channel is said to be *stochastically degraded* if its conditional marginal distributions are the same as that of a physically degraded broadcast channel, i.e., if there exists a distribution $p'(y_2|y_1)$ such that

$$p(y_2|x) = \sum_{y_1} p(y_1|x)p'(y_2|y_1). \qquad (14.201)$$

Note that since the capacity of a broadcast channel depends only on the conditional marginals, the capacity region of the stochastically degraded broadcast channel is the same as that of the corresponding physically degraded channel. In much of the following, we will therefore assume that the channel is physically degraded.

14.6.3 Capacity Region for the Degraded Broadcast Channel

We now consider sending independent information over a degraded broadcast channel at rate R_1 to Y_1 and rate R_2 to Y_2.

Theorem 14.6.2: *The capacity region for sending independent information over the degraded broadcast channel $X \rightarrow Y_1 \rightarrow Y_2$ is the convex hull of the closure of all (R_1, R_2) satisfying*

$$R_2 \leq I(U; Y_2), \qquad (14.202)$$

$$R_1 \leq I(X; Y_1|U) \qquad (14.203)$$

for some joint distribution $p(u)p(x|u)p(y, z|x)$, where the auxiliary random variable U has cardinality bounded by $|\mathcal{U}| \leq \min\{|\mathcal{X}|, |\mathcal{Y}_1|, |\mathcal{Y}_2|\}$.

Proof: The cardinality bounds for the auxiliary random variable U are derived using standard methods from convex set theory and will not be dealt with here.

We first give an outline of the basic idea of superposition coding for the broadcast channel. The auxiliary random variable U will serve as a cloud center that can be distinguished by both receivers Y_1 and Y_2. Each cloud consists of 2^{nR_1} codewords X^n distinguishable by the receiver Y_1. The worst receiver can only see the clouds, while the better receiver can see the individual codewords within the clouds.

The formal proof of the achievability of this region uses a random coding argument: Fix $p(u)$ and $p(x|u)$.

Random codebook generation. Generate 2^{nR_2} independent codewords of length n, $\mathbf{U}(w_2)$, $w_2 \in \{1, 2, \ldots, 2^{nR_2}\}$, according to $\prod_{i=1}^{n} p(u_i)$.

For each codeword $\mathbf{U}(w_2)$, generate 2^{nR_1} independent codewords $\mathbf{X}(w_1, w_2)$ according to $\prod_{i=1}^{n} p(x_i|u_i(w_2))$.

Here $\mathbf{u}(i)$ plays the role of the cloud center understandable to both Y_1 and Y_2, while $\mathbf{x}(i, j)$ is the jth satellite codeword in the ith cloud.

Encoding. To send the pair (W_1, W_2), send the corresponding codeword $\mathbf{X}(W_1, W_2)$.

Decoding. Receiver 2 determines the unique $\hat{W}_2$ such that $(\mathbf{U}(\hat{W}_2), \mathbf{Y}_2) \in A_\epsilon^{(n)}$. If there are none such or more than one such, an error is declared.

Receiver 1 looks for the unique $(\hat{W}_1, \hat{W}_2)$ such that $(\mathbf{U}(\hat{W}_2), \mathbf{X}(\hat{W}_1, \hat{W}_2), \mathbf{Y}_1) \in A_\epsilon^{(n)}$. If there are none such or more than one such, an error is declared.

Analysis of the probability of error. By the symmetry of the code generation, the probability of error does not depend on which codeword was sent. Hence, without loss of generality, we can assume that the message pair $(W_1, W_2) = (1, 1)$ was sent. Let $P(\cdot)$ denote the conditional probability of an event given that $(1, 1)$ was sent.

Since we have essentially a single user channel from U to Y_2, we will be able to decode the U codewords with low probability of error if $R_2 < I(U; Y_2)$. To prove this, we define the events

$$E_{Yi} = \{(\mathbf{U}(i), \mathbf{Y}_2) \in A_\epsilon^{(n)}\}. \tag{14.204}$$

Then the probability of error at receiver 2 is

$$P_e^{(n)}(2) = P(E_{Y1}^c \cup \bigcup_{i \neq 1} E_{Yi}) \tag{14.205}$$

$$\leq P(E_{Y1}^c) + \sum_{i \neq 1} P(E_{Yi}) \tag{14.206}$$

$$\leq \epsilon + 2^{nR_2} 2^{-n(I(U; Y_2) - 2\epsilon)} \tag{14.207}$$

$$\leq 2\epsilon \tag{14.208}$$

if n is large enough and $R_2 < I(U; Y_2)$, where (14.207) follows from the AEP.

Similarly, for decoding for receiver 1, we define the following events

$$\tilde{E}_{Yi} = \{(\mathbf{U}(i), \mathbf{Y}_1) \in A_\epsilon^{(n)}\}, \tag{14.209}$$

$$\tilde{E}_{Yij} = \{(\mathbf{U}(i), \mathbf{X}(i, j), \mathbf{Y}_1) \in A_\epsilon^{(n)}\}, \tag{14.210}$$

where the tilde refers to events defined at receiver 1. Then, we can bound the probability of error as

$$P_e^{(n)}(1) = P\left(\tilde{E}_{Y1}^c \cup \bigcup_{i \neq 1} \tilde{E}_{Yi} \cup \bigcup_{j \neq 1} \tilde{E}_{Y1j}\right) \tag{14.211}$$

$$\leq P(\tilde{E}_{Y1}^c) + \sum_{i \neq 1} P(\tilde{E}_{Yi}) + \sum_{j \neq 1} P(\tilde{E}_{Y1j}). \tag{14.212}$$

By the same arguments as for receiver 2, we can bound $P(\tilde{E}_{Yi}) \leq 2^{-n(I(U; Y_1) - 3\epsilon)}$. Hence the second term goes to 0 if $R_2 < I(U; Y_1)$. But by the data processing inequality and the degraded nature of the channel, $I(U; Y_1) \geq I(U; Y_2)$, and hence the conditions of the theorem imply that the second term goes to 0. We can also bound the third term in the probability of error as

$$P(\tilde{E}_{Y1j}) = P((\mathbf{U}(1), \mathbf{X}(1, j), \mathbf{Y}_1) \in A_\epsilon^{(n)}) \tag{14.213}$$

$$= \sum_{(\mathbf{U}, \mathbf{X}, \mathbf{Y}_1) \in A_\epsilon^{(n)}} P((\mathbf{U}(1), \mathbf{X}(1, j), \mathbf{Y}_1)) \tag{14.214}$$

$$= \sum_{(\mathbf{U}, \mathbf{X}, \mathbf{Y}_1) \in A_\epsilon^{(n)}} P(\mathbf{U}(1))P(\mathbf{X}(1, j)|\mathbf{U}(1))P(\mathbf{Y}_1|\mathbf{U}(1)) \tag{14.215}$$

$$\leq \sum_{(\mathbf{U}, \mathbf{X}, \mathbf{Y}_1) \in A_\epsilon^{(n)}} 2^{-n(H(U)-\epsilon)} 2^{-n(H(X|U)-\epsilon)} 2^{-n(H(Y_1|U)-\epsilon)} \tag{14.216}$$

$$\leq 2^{n(H(U, X, Y_1)+\epsilon)} 2^{-n(H(U)-\epsilon)} 2^{-n(H(X|U)-\epsilon)} 2^{-n(H(Y_1|U)-\epsilon)} \tag{14.217}$$

$$= 2^{-n(I(X; Y_1|U)-4\epsilon)}. \tag{14.218}$$

Hence, if $R_1 < I(X; Y_1|U)$, the third term in the probability of error goes to 0. Thus we can bound the probability of error

$$P_e^{(n)}(1) \leq \epsilon + 2^{nR_2} 2^{-n(I(U; Y_1)-3\epsilon)} + 2^{nR_1} 2^{-n(I(X; Y_1|U)-4\epsilon)} \tag{14.219}$$

$$\leq 3\epsilon \tag{14.220}$$

if n is large enough and $R_2 < I(U; Y_1)$ and $R_1 < I(X; Y_1|U)$. The above bounds show that we can decode the messages with total probability of error that goes to 0. Hence theres exists a sequence of good $((2^{nR_1}, 2^{nR_2}), n)$ codes $\mathscr{C}_n^*$ with probability of error going to 0.

With this, we complete the proof of the achievability of the capacity region for the degraded broadcast channel. The proof of the converse is outlined in the exercises. $\square$

So far we have considered sending independent information to both receivers. But in certain situations, we wish to send common information to both the receivers. Let the rate at which we send common information be R_0. Then we have the following obvious theorem:

Theorem 14.6.3: *If the rate pair (R_1, R_2) is achievable for a broadcast channel with independent information, then the rate triple $(R_0, R_1 - R_0, R_2 - R_0)$ with a common rate R_0 is achievable, provided that $R_0 \le \min(R_1, R_2)$.*

In the case of a degraded broadcast channel, we can do even better. Since by our coding scheme the better receiver always decodes all the information that is sent to the worst receiver, one need not reduce the amount of information sent to the better receiver when we have common information. Hence we have the following theorem:

Theorem 14.6.4: *If the rate pair (R_1, R_2) is achievable for a degraded broadcast channel, the rate triple $(R_0, R_1, R_2 - R_0)$ is achievable for the channel with common information, provided that $R_0 < R_2$.*

We will end this section by considering the example of the binary symmetric broadcast channel.

Example 14.6.5: Consider a pair of binary symmetric channels with parameters p_1 and p_2 that form a broadcast channel as shown in Figure 14.26.

Without loss of generality in the capacity calculation, we can recast this channel as a physically degraded channel. We will assume that $p_1 < p_2 < \frac{1}{2}$. Then we can express a binary symmetric channel with parameter p_2 as a cascade of a binary symmetric channel with parameter p_1 with another binary symmetric channel. Let the crossover probability of the new channel be α. Then we must have

$$p_1(1 - \alpha) + (1 - p_1)\alpha = p_2 , \tag{14.221}$$

or

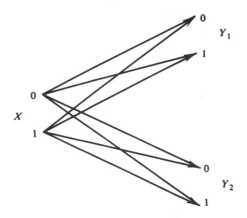

Figure 14.26. Binary symmetric broadcast channel.

$$\alpha = \frac{p_2 - p_1}{1 - 2p_1} . \qquad (14.222)$$

We now consider the auxiliary random variable in the definition of the capacity region. In this case, the cardinality of U is binary from the bound of the theorem. By symmetry, we connect U to X by another binary symmetric channel with parameter β, as illustrated in Figure 14.27.

We can now calculate the rates in the capacity region. It is clear by symmetry that the distribution on U that maximizes the rates is the uniform distribution on $\{0, 1\}$, so that

$$I(U; Y_2) = H(Y_2) - H(Y_2|U) \qquad (14.223)$$

$$= 1 - H(\beta * p_2), \qquad (14.224)$$

where

$$\beta * p_2 = \beta(1 - p_2) + (1 - \beta)p_2 . \qquad (14.225)$$

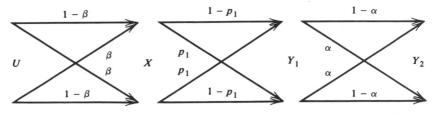

Figure 14.27. Physically degraded binary symmetric broadcast channel.

Similarly,

$$I(X; Y_1|U) = H(Y_1|U) - H(Y_1|X, U) \tag{14.226}$$

$$= H(Y_1|U) - H(Y_1|X) \tag{14.227}$$

$$= H(\beta * p_1) - H(p_1), \tag{14.228}$$

where

$$\beta * p_1 = \beta(1 - p_1) + (1 - \beta)p_1 . \tag{14.229}$$

Plotting these points as a function of β, we obtain the capacity region in Figure 14.28.

When $\beta = 0$, we have maximum information transfer to Y_2, i.e., $R_2 = 1 - H(p_2)$ and $R_1 = 0$. When $\beta = \frac{1}{2}$, we have maximum information transfer to Y_1, i.e., $R_1 = 1 - H(p_1)$, and no information transfer to Y_2. These values of β give us the corner points of the rate region.

Example 14.6.6 (*Gaussian broadcast channel*): The Gaussian broadcast channel is illustrated in Figure 14.29. We have shown it in the case where one output is a degraded version of the other output. Later, we will show that all Gaussian broadcast channels are equivalent to this type of degraded channel.

$$Y_1 = X + Z_1 , \tag{14.230}$$

$$Y_2 = X + Z_2 = Y_1 + Z_2' , \tag{14.231}$$

where $Z_1 \sim \mathcal{N}(0, N_1)$ and $Z_2' \sim \mathcal{N}(0, N_2 - N_1)$.

Extending the results of this section to the Gaussian case, we can show that the capacity region of this channel is given by

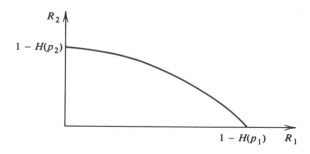

Figure 14.28. Capacity region of binary symmetric broadcast channel.

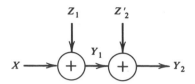

Figure 14.29. Gaussian broadcast channel.

$$R_1 < C\left(\frac{\alpha P}{N_1}\right) \qquad\qquad (14.232)$$

$$R_2 < C\left(\frac{(1-\alpha)P}{\alpha P + N_2}\right) \qquad\qquad (14.233)$$

where α may be arbitrarily chosen ($0 \le \alpha \le 1$). The coding scheme that achieves this capacity region is outlined in Section 14.1.3.

14.7 THE RELAY CHANNEL

The relay channel is a channel in which there is one sender and one receiver with a number of intermediate nodes which act as relays to help the communication from the sender to the receiver. The simplest relay channel has only one intermediate or relay node. In this case the channel consists of four finite sets $\mathcal{X}$, $\mathcal{X}_1$, $\mathcal{Y}$ and $\mathcal{Y}_1$ and a collection of probability mass functions $p(\cdot, \cdot | x, x_1)$ on $\mathcal{Y} \times \mathcal{Y}_1$, one for each $(x, x_1) \in \mathcal{X} \times \mathcal{X}_1$. The interpretation is that x is the input to the channel and y is the output of the channel, y_1 is the relay's observation and x_1 is the input symbol chosen by the relay, as shown in Figure 14.30. The problem is to find the capacity of the channel between the sender X and the receiver Y.

The relay channel combines a broadcast channel (X to Y and Y_1) and a multiple access channel (X and X_1 to Y). The capacity is known for the special case of the physically degraded relay channel. We will first prove an outer bound on the capacity of a general relay channel and later establish an achievable region for the degraded relay channel.

Definition: A $(2^{nR}, n)$ code for a relay channel consists of a set of integers $\mathcal{W} = \{1, 2, \ldots, 2^{nR}\}$, an encoding function

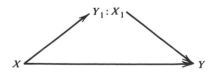

Figure 14.30. The relay channel.

$$X : \{1, 2, \ldots, 2^{nR}\} \to \mathscr{X}^n \,, \tag{14.234}$$

a set of relay functions $\{f_i\}_{i=1}^{n}$ such that

$$x_{1i} = f_i(Y_{11}, Y_{12}, \ldots, Y_{1i-1}), \qquad 1 \le i \le n \,, \tag{14.235}$$

and a decoding function,

$$g : \mathscr{Y}^n \to \{1, 2, \ldots, 2^{nR}\} \,. \tag{14.236}$$

Note that the definition of the encoding functions includes the non-anticipatory condition on the relay. The relay channel input is allowed to depend only on the past observations $y_{11}, y_{12}, \ldots, y_{1i-1}$. The channel is memoryless in the sense that (Y_i, Y_{1i}) depends on the past only through the current transmitted symbols (X_i, X_{1i}). Thus for any choice $p(w)$, $w \in \mathscr{W}$, and code choice $X : \{1, 2, \ldots, 2^{nR}\} \to \mathscr{X}_i^n$ and relay functions $\{f_i\}_{i=1}^{n}$, the joint probability mass function on $\mathscr{W} \times \mathscr{X}^n \times \mathscr{X}_1^n \times \mathscr{Y}^n \times \mathscr{Y}_1^n$ is given by

$$p(w, \mathbf{x}, \mathbf{x}_1, \mathbf{y}, \mathbf{y}_1)$$

$$= p(w) \prod_{i=1}^{n} p(x_i | w) p(x_{1i} | y_{11}, y_{12}, \ldots, y_{1i-1}) p(y_i, y_{1i} | x_i, x_{1i}) \,. \tag{14.237}$$

If the message $w \in [1, 2^{nR}]$ is sent, let

$$\lambda(w) = \Pr\{g(\mathbf{Y}) \ne w | w \text{ sent}\} \tag{14.238}$$

denote the conditional probability of error. We define the average probability of error of the code as

$$P_e^{(n)} = \frac{1}{2^{nR}} \sum_w \lambda(w) \,. \tag{14.239}$$

The probability of error is calculated under the uniform distribution over the codewords $w \in \{1, 2^{nR}\}$. The rate R is said to be achievable by the relay channel if there exists a sequence of $(2^{nR}, n)$ codes with $P_e^{(n)} \to 0$. The *capacity* C of a relay channel is the supremum of the set of achievable rates.

We first give an upper bound on the capacity of the relay channel.

Theorem 14.7.1: *For any relay channel* $(\mathscr{X} \times \mathscr{X}_1, p(y, y_1 | x, x_1), \mathscr{Y} \times \mathscr{Y}_1)$ *the capacity C is bounded above by*

$$C \le \sup_{p(x, x_1)} \min\{I(X, X_1; Y), I(X; Y, Y_1 | X_1)\} \,. \tag{14.240}$$

Proof: The proof is a direct consequence of a more general max flow min cut theorem to be given in Section 14.10. $\square$

This upper bound has a nice max flow min cut interpretation. The first term in (14.240) upper bounds the maximum rate of information transfer from senders X and X_1 to receiver Y. The second terms bound the rate from X to Y and Y_1.

We now consider a family of relay channels in which the relay receiver is better than the ultimate receiver Y in the sense defined below. Here the max flow min cut upper bound in the (14.240) is achieved.

Definition: The relay channel $(\mathcal{X} \times \mathcal{X}_1, p(y, y_1|x, x_1), \mathcal{Y} \times \mathcal{Y}_1)$ is said to be *physically degraded* if $p(y, y_1|x, x_1)$ can be written in the form

$$p(y, y_1|x, x_1) = p(y_1|x, x_1)p(y|y_1, x_1). \tag{14.241}$$

Thus Y is a random degradation of the relay signal Y_1.

For the physically degraded relay channel, the capacity is given by the following theorem.

Theorem 14.7.2: *The capacity C of a physically degraded relay channel is given by*

$$C = \sup_{p(x, x_1)} \min\{I(X, X_1; Y), I(X; Y_1|X_1)\}, \tag{14.242}$$

where the supremum is over all joint distributions on $\mathcal{X} \times \mathcal{X}_1$.

Proof (*Converse*): The proof follows from Theorem 14.7.1 and by degradedness, since for the degraded relay channel, $I(X; Y, Y_1|X_1) = I(X; Y_1|X_1)$.

Achievability. The proof of achievability involves a combination of the following basic techniques: (1) random coding, (2) list codes, (3) Slepian-Wolf partitioning, (4) coding for the cooperative multiple access channel, (5) superposition coding, and (6) block Markov encoding at the relay and transmitter.

We provide only an outline of the proof.

Outline of achievability. We consider B blocks of transmission, each of n symbols. A sequence of $B - 1$ indices, $w_i \in \{1, \ldots, 2^{nR}\}, i = 1, 2, \ldots, B - 1$ will be sent over the channel in nB transmissions. (Note that as $B \to \infty$, for a fixed n, the rate $R(B - 1)/B$ is arbitrarily close to R.)

We define a doubly-indexed set of codewords:

$$\mathscr{C} = \{\mathbf{x}(w|s), \mathbf{x}_1(s)\} : w \in \{1, 2^{nR}\}, s \in \{1, 2^{nR_0}\}, \mathbf{x} \in \mathscr{X}^n, \mathbf{x}_1 \in \mathscr{X}_1^n.$$
$$(14.243)$$

We will also need a partition

$$\mathscr{S} = \{S_1, S_2, \ldots, S_{2^{nR_0}}\} \text{ of } \mathcal{W} = \{1, 2, \ldots, 2^{nR}\} \quad (14.244)$$

into 2^{nR_0} cells, with $S_i \cap S_j = \phi, i \neq j$, and $\cup S_i = \mathcal{W}$. The partition will enable us to send side information to the receiver in the manner of Slepian and Wolf [255].

Generation of random code. Fix $p(x_1)p(x|x_1)$.

First generate at random 2^{nR_0} i.i.d. n-sequences in $\mathscr{X}_1^n$, each drawn according to $p(\mathbf{x}_1) = \prod_{i=1}^n p(x_{1i})$. Index them as $\mathbf{x}_1(s), s \in \{1, 2, \ldots, 2^{nR_0}\}$. For each $\mathbf{x}_1(s)$, generate 2^{nR} conditionally independent n-sequences $\mathbf{x}(w|s), w \in \{1, 2, \ldots, 2^{nR}\}$, drawn independently according to $p(\mathbf{x}|\mathbf{x}_1(s)) = \prod_{i=1}^n p(x_i|x_{1i}(s))$. This defines the random codebook $\mathscr{C} = \{\mathbf{x}(w|s), \mathbf{x}_1(s)\}$.

The random partition $\mathscr{S} = \{S_1, S_2, \ldots, S_{2^{nR_0}}\}$ of $\{1, 2, \ldots, 2^{nR}\}$ is defined as follows. Let each integer $w \in \{1, 2, \ldots, 2^{nR}\}$ be assigned independently, according to a uniform distribution over the indices $s = 1, 2, \ldots, 2^{nR_0}$, to cells S_s.

Encoding. Let $w_i \in \{1, 2, \ldots, 2^{nR}\}$ be the new index to be sent in block i, and let s_i be defined as the partition corresponding to w_{i-1}, i.e., $w_{i-1} \in S_{s_i}$. The encoder sends $\mathbf{x}(w_i|s_i)$. The relay has an estimate $\hat{w}_{i-1}$ of the previous index w_{i-1}. (This will be made precise in the decoding section.) Assume that $\hat{w}_{i-1} \in S_{\hat{s}_i}$. The relay encoder sends $\mathbf{x}_1(\hat{s}_i)$ in block i.

Decoding. We assume that at the end of block $i - 1$, the receiver knows $(w_1, w_2, \ldots, w_{i-2})$ and $(s_1, s_2, \ldots, s_{i-1})$ and the relay knows $(w_1, w_2, \ldots, w_{i-1})$ and consequently $(s_1, s_2, \ldots, s_i)$.

The decoding procedures at the end of block i are as follows:

1. Knowing s_i and upon receiving $\mathbf{y}_1(i)$, the *relay* receiver estimates the message of the transmitter $\hat{w}_i = w$ if and only if there exists a unique w such that $(\mathbf{x}(w|s_i), \mathbf{x}_1(s_i), \mathbf{y}_1(i))$ are jointly ϵ-typical. Using Theorem 14.2.3, it can be shown that $\hat{w}_i = w_i$ with an arbitrarily small probability of error if

$$R < I(X; Y_1|X_1) \quad (14.245)$$

and n is sufficiently large.

2. The *receiver* declares that $\hat{s}_i = s$ was sent iff there exists one and only one s such that $(\mathbf{x}_1(s), \mathbf{y}(i))$ are jointly ϵ-typical. From Theorem 14.2.1, we know that s_i can be decoded with arbitrarily small probability of error if

$$R_0 < I(X_1; Y) \qquad (14.246)$$

and n is sufficiently large.

3. Assuming that s_i is decoded correctly at the receiver, the receiver constructs a list $\mathcal{L}(\mathbf{y}(i-1))$ of indices that the receiver considers to be jointly typical with $\mathbf{y}(i-1)$ in the $(i-1)$th block. The receiver then declares $\hat{w}_{i-1} = w$ as the index sent in block $i-1$ if there is a unique w in $S_{s_i} \cap \mathcal{L}(\mathbf{y}(i-1))$. If n is sufficiently large and if

$$R < I(X; Y|X_1) + R_0, \qquad (14.247)$$

then $\hat{w}_{i-1} = w_{i-1}$ with arbitrarily small probability of error. Combining the two constraints (14.246) and (14.247), R_0 drops out, leaving

$$R < I(X; Y|X_1) + I(X_1; Y) = I(X, X_1; Y). \qquad (14.248)$$

For a detailed analysis of the probability of error, the reader is referred to Cover and El Gamal [67]. $\square$

Theorem 14.7.2 can also shown to be the capacity for the following classes of relay channels.

(i) Reversely degraded relay channel, i.e.,

$$p(y, y_1|x, x_1) = p(y|x, x_1)p(y_1|y, x_1). \qquad (14.249)$$

(ii) Relay channel with feedback.
(iii) Deterministic relay channel,

$$y_1 = f(x, x_1), \qquad y = g(x, x_1). \qquad (14.250)$$

14.8 SOURCE CODING WITH SIDE INFORMATION

We now consider the distributed source coding problem where two random variables X and Y are encoded separately but only X is to be recovered. We now ask how many bits R_1 are required to describe X if we are allowed R_2 bits to describe Y.

If $R_2 > H(Y)$, then Y can be described perfectly, and by the results of Slepian-Wolf coding, $R_1 = H(X|Y)$ bits suffice to describe X. At the other extreme, if $R_2 = 0$, we must describe X without any help, and $R_1 = H(X)$ bits are then necessary to describe X. In general, we will use $R_2 = I(Y; \hat{Y})$ bits to describe an approximate version of Y. This will allow us to describe X using $H(X|\hat{Y})$ bits in the presence of side information $\hat{Y}$. The following theorem is consistent with this intuition.

Theorem 14.8.1: *Let* $(X, Y) \sim p(x, y)$. *If* Y *is encoded at rate* R_2 *and* X *is encoded at rate* R_1, *we can recover* X *with an arbitrarily small probability of error if and only if*

$$R_1 \geq H(X|U), \tag{14.251}$$

$$R_2 \geq I(Y; U) \tag{14.252}$$

for some joint probability mass function $p(x, y)p(u|y)$, *where* $|\mathcal{U}| \leq |\mathcal{Y}| + 2$.

We prove this theorem in two parts. We begin with the converse, in which we show that for any encoding scheme that has a small probability of error, we can find a random variable U with a joint probability mass function as in the theorem.

Proof (*Converse*): Consider any source code for Figure 14.31. The source code consists of mappings $f_n(X^n)$ and $g_n(Y^n)$ such that the rates of f_n and g_n are less than R_1 and R_2, respectively, and a decoding mapping h_n such that

$$P_e^{(n)} = \Pr\{h_n(f_n(X^n), g_n(Y^n)) \neq X^n\} < \epsilon. \tag{14.253}$$

Define new random variables $S = f_n(X^n)$ and $T = g_n(Y^n)$. Then since we can recover X^n from S and T with low probability of error, we have, by Fano's inequality,

$$H(X^n|S, T) \leq n\epsilon_n. \tag{14.254}$$

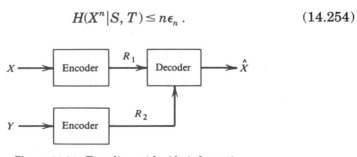

Figure 14.31. Encoding with side information.

Then

$$nR_2 \overset{(a)}{\geq} H(T) \tag{14.255}$$

$$\overset{(b)}{\geq} I(Y^n; T) \tag{14.256}$$

$$= \sum_{i=1}^{n} I(Y_i; T | Y_1, \ldots, Y_{i-1}) \tag{14.257}$$

$$\overset{(c)}{=} \sum_{i=1}^{n} I(Y_i; T, Y_1, \ldots, Y_{i-1}) \tag{14.258}$$

$$\overset{(d)}{=} \sum_{i=1}^{n} I(Y_i; U_i) \tag{14.259}$$

where

(a) follows from the fact that the range of g_n is $\{1, 2, \ldots, 2^{nR_2}\}$,
(b) follows from the properties of mutual information,
(c) follows from the chain rule and the fact that Y_i is independent of $Y_1, \ldots, Y_{i-1}$ and hence $I(Y_i; Y_1, \ldots, Y_{i-1}) = 0$, and
(d) follows if we define $U_i = (T, Y_1, \ldots, Y_{i-1})$.

We also have another chain for R_1,

$$nR_1 \overset{(a)}{\geq} H(S) \tag{14.260}$$

$$\overset{(b)}{\geq} H(S|T) \tag{14.261}$$

$$= H(S|T) + H(X^n|S, T) - H(X^n|S, T) \tag{14.262}$$

$$\overset{(c)}{\geq} H(X^n, S|T) - n\epsilon_n \tag{14.263}$$

$$\overset{(d)}{=} H(X^n|T) - n\epsilon_n \tag{14.264}$$

$$\overset{(e)}{=} \sum_{i=1}^{n} H(X_i|T, X_1, \ldots, X_{i-1}) - n\epsilon_n \tag{14.265}$$

$$\overset{(f)}{\geq} \sum_{i=1}^{n} H(X_i|T, X^{i-1}, Y^{i-1}) - n\epsilon_n \tag{14.266}$$

$$\overset{(g)}{=} \sum_{i=1}^{n} H(X_i | T, Y^{i-1}) - n\epsilon_n \qquad (14.267)$$

$$\overset{(h)}{=} \sum_{i=1}^{n} H(X_i | U_i) - n\epsilon_n \qquad (14.268)$$

where

(a) follows from the fact that the range of S is $\{1, 2, \ldots, 2^{nR_1}\}$,
(b) follows from the fact that conditioning reduces entropy,
(c) from Fano's inequality,
(d) from the chain rule and the fact that S is a function of X^n,
(e) from the chain rule for entropy,
(f) from the fact that conditioning reduces entropy,
(g) from the (subtle) fact that $X_i \rightarrow (T, Y^{i-1}) \rightarrow X^{i-1}$ forms a **Markov** chain since X_i does not contain any information about X^{i-1} that is not there in Y^{i-1} and T, and
(h) follows from the definition of U.

Also, since X_i contains no more information about U_i than is present in Y_i, it follows that $X_i \rightarrow Y_i \rightarrow U_i$ forms a Markov chain. Thus we have the following inequalities:

$$R_1 \geq \frac{1}{n} \sum_{i=1}^{n} H(X_i | U_i) \qquad (14.269)$$

$$R_2 \geq \frac{1}{n} \sum_{i=1}^{n} I(Y_i; U_i). \qquad (14.270)$$

We now introduce an timesharing random variable Q, so that we can rewrite these equations as

$$R_1 \geq \frac{1}{n} \sum_{i=1}^{n} H(X_i | U_i, Q = i) = H(X_Q | U_Q, Q) \qquad (14.271)$$

$$R_2 \geq \frac{1}{n} \sum_{i=1}^{n} I(Y_i; U_i | Q = i) = I(Y_Q; U_Q | Q) \qquad (14.272)$$

Now since Q is independent of Y_Q (the distribution of Y_i does not depend on i), we have

$$I(Y_Q; U_Q | Q) = I(Y_Q; U_Q, Q) - I(Y_Q; Q) = I(Y_Q; U_Q, Q). \qquad (14.273)$$

Now X_Q and Y_Q have the joint distribution $p(x, y)$ in the theorem.

Defining $U = (U_Q, Q)$, $X = X_Q$, and $Y = Y_Q$, we have shown the existence of a random variable U such that

$$R_1 \geq H(X|U), \qquad (14.274)$$

$$R_2 \geq I(Y; U) \qquad (14.275)$$

for any encoding scheme that has a low probability of error. Thus the converse is proved. □

Before we proceed to the proof of the achievability of this pair of rates, we will need a new lemma about strong typicality and Markov chains. Recall the definition of strong typicality for a triple of random variables X, Y and Z. A triplet of sequences x^n, y^n, z^n is said to be ϵ-strongly typical if

$$\left| \frac{1}{n} N(a, b, c|x^n, y^n, z^n) - p(a, b, c) \right| < \frac{\epsilon}{|\mathcal{X}||\mathcal{Y}||\mathcal{Z}|}. \qquad (14.276)$$

In particular, this implies that (x^n, y^n) are jointly strongly typical and that (y^n, z^n) are also jointly strongly typical. But the converse is not true: the fact that $(x^n, y^n) \in A_{\epsilon}^{*(n)}(X, Y)$ and $(y^n, z^n) \in A_{\epsilon}^{*(n)}(Y, Z)$ does not in general imply that $(x^n, y^n, z^n) \in A_{\epsilon}^{*(n)}(X, Y, Z)$. But if $X \to Y \to Z$ forms a Markov chain, this implication is true. We state this as a lemma without proof [28, 83].

Lemma 14.8.1: *Let (X, Y, Z) form a Markov chain $X \to Y \to Z$, i.e., $p(x, y, z) = p(x, y)p(z|y)$. If for a given $(y^n, z^n) \in A_{\epsilon}^{*(n)}(Y, Z)$, X^n is drawn $\sim \Pi_{i=1}^{n} p(x_i|y_i)$, then $\Pr\{(X^n, y^n, z^n) \in A_{\epsilon}^{*(n)}(X, Y, Z)\} > 1 - \epsilon$ for n sufficiently large.*

Remark: The theorem is true from the strong law of large numbers if $X^n \sim \Pi_{i=1}^{n} p(x_i|y_i, z_i)$. The Markovity of $X \to Y \to Z$ is used to show that $X^n \sim p(x_i|y_i)$ is sufficient for the same conclusion.

We now outline the proof of achievability in Theorem 14.8.1.

Proof (*Achievability in Theorem 14.8.1*): Fix $p(u|y)$. Calculate $p(u) = \Sigma_y p(y)p(u|y)$.

Generation of codebooks. Generate 2^{nR_2} independent codewords of length n, $\mathbf{U}(w_2)$, $w_2 \in \{1, 2, \ldots, 2^{nR_2}\}$ according to $\Pi_{i=1}^{n} p(u_i)$.
Randomly bin all the X^n sequences into 2^{nR_1} bins by independently generating an index b uniformly distributed on $\{1, 2, \ldots, 2^{nR_1}\}$ for each X^n. Let $B(i)$ denote the set of X^n sequences allotted to bin i.

Encoding. The X sender sends the index i of the bin in which X^n falls. The Y sender looks for an index s such that $(Y^n, U^n(s)) \in A_\epsilon^{*(n)}(Y, U)$. If there is more than one such s, it sends the least. If there is no such $U^n(s)$ in the codebook, it sends $s = 1$.

Decoding. The receiver looks for a unique $X^n \in B(i)$ such that $(X^n, U^n(s)) \in A_\epsilon^{*(n)}(X, U)$. If there is none or more than one, it declares an error.

Analysis of the probability of error. The various sources of error are as follows:

1. The pair (X^n, Y^n) generated by the source is not typical. The probability of this is small if n is large. Hence, without loss of generality, we can condition on the event that the source produces a particular typical sequence $(x^n, y^n) \in A_\epsilon^{*(n)}$.

2. The sequence Y^n is typical, but there does not exist a $U^n(s)$ in the codebook which is jointly typical with it. The probability of this is small from the arguments of Section 13.6, where we showed that if there are enough codewords, i.e., if

$$R_2 > I(Y; U), \tag{14.277}$$

then we are very likely to find a codeword that is jointly strongly typical with the given source sequence.

3. The codeword $U^n(s)$ is jointly typical with y^n but not with x^n. But by Lemma 14.8.1, the probability of this is small since $X \to Y \to U$ forms a Markov chain.

4. We also have an error if there exists another typical $X^n \in B(i)$ which is jointly typical with $U^n(s)$. The probability that any other X^n is jointly typical with $U^n(s)$ is less than $2^{-n(I(U; X) - 3\epsilon)}$, and therefore the probability of this kind of error is bounded above by

$$|B(i) \cap A_\epsilon^{*(n)}(X)| 2^{-n(I(X; U) - 3\epsilon)} \le 2^{n(H(X) + \epsilon)} 2^{-nR_1} 2^{-n(I(X; U) - 3\epsilon)},$$
$$\tag{14.278}$$

which goes to 0 if $R_1 > H(X|U)$.

Hence it is likely that the actual source sequence X^n is jointly typical with $U^n(s)$ and that no other typical source sequence in the same bin is also jointly typical with $U^n(s)$. We can achieve an arbitrarily low probability of error with an appropriate choice of n and ϵ, and this completes the proof of achievability. $\square$

14.9   RATE DISTORTION WITH SIDE INFORMATION

We know that $R(D)$ bits are sufficient to describe X within distortion D. We now ask how many bits are required given side information Y.

We will begin with a few definitions. Let (X_i, Y_i) be i.i.d. $\sim p(x, y)$ and encoded as shown in Figure 14.32.

Definition: The *rate distortion function with side information* $R_Y(D)$ is defined as the minimum rate required to achieve distortion D if the side information Y is available to the decoder. Precisely, $R_Y(D)$ is the infimum of rates R such that there exist maps $i_n : \mathscr{X}^n \to \{1, \dots, 2^{nR}\}$, $g_n : \mathscr{Y}^n \times \{1, \dots, 2^{nR}\} \to \hat{\mathscr{X}}^n$ such that

$$\limsup_{n \to \infty} Ed(X^n, g_n(Y^n, i_n(X^n))) \leq D . \tag{14.279}$$

Clearly, since the side information can only help, we have $R_Y(D) \leq R(D)$. For the case of zero distortion, this is the Slepian-Wolf problem and we will need $H(X|Y)$ bits. Hence $R_Y(0) = H(X|Y)$. We wish to determine the entire curve $R_Y(D)$. The result can be expressed in the following theorem:

Theorem 14.9.1 (*Rate distortion with side information*): *Let* (X, Y) *be drawn i.i.d.* $\sim p(x, y)$ *and let* $d(x^n, \hat{x}^n) = \frac{1}{n} \sum_{i=1}^{n} d(x_i, \hat{x}_i)$ *be given. The rate distortion function with side information is*

$$R_Y(D) = \min_{p(w|x)} \min_{f} (I(X; W) - I(Y; W)) \tag{14.280}$$

where the minimization is over all functions $f : \mathscr{Y} \times \mathscr{W} \to \hat{\mathscr{X}}$ *and conditional probability mass functions* $p(w|x)$, $|\mathscr{W}| \leq |\mathscr{X}| + 1$, *such that*

$$\sum_{x} \sum_{w} \sum_{y} p(x, y)p(w|x)\, d(x, f(y, w)) \leq D . \tag{14.281}$$

The function f in the theorem corresponds to the decoding map that maps the encoded version of the X symbols and the side information Y to

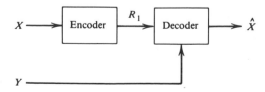

Figure 14.32. Rate distortion with side information.

the output alphabet. We minimize over all conditional distributions on W and functions f such that the expected distortion for the joint distribution is less than D.

We first prove the converse after considering some of the properties of the function $R_Y(D)$ defined in (14.280).

Lemma 14.9.1: *The rate distortion function with side information $R_Y(D)$ defined in (14.280) is a non-increasing convex function of D.*

Proof: The monotonicity of $R_Y(D)$ follows immediately from the fact that the domain of minimization in the definition of $R_Y(D)$ increases with D.

As in the case of rate distortion without side information, we expect $R_Y(D)$ to be convex. However, the proof of convexity is more involved because of the double rather than single minimization in the definition of $R_Y(D)$ in (14.280). We outline the proof here.

Let D_1 and D_2 be two values of the distortion and let W_1, f_1 and W_2, f_2 be the corresponding random variables and functions that achieve the minima in the definitions of $R_Y(D_1)$ and $R_Y(D_2)$, respectively. Let Q be a random variable independent of X, Y, W_1 and W_2 which takes on the value 1 with probability λ and the value 2 with probability $1 - \lambda$.

Define $W = (Q, W_Q)$ and let $f(W, Y) = f_Q(W_Q, Y)$. Specifically $f(W, Y) = f_1(W_1, Y)$ with probability λ and $f(W, Y) = f_2(W_2, Y)$ with probability $1 - \lambda$. Then the distortion becomes

$$D = Ed(X, \hat{X}) \tag{14.282}$$

$$= \lambda Ed(X, f_1(W_1, Y)) + (1 - \lambda)Ed(X, f_2(W_2, Y)) \tag{14.283}$$

$$= \lambda D_1 + (1 - \lambda)D_2, \tag{14.284}$$

and (14.280) becomes

$$I(W; X) - I(W; Y) = H(X) - H(X|W) - H(Y) + H(Y|W) \tag{14.285}$$

$$= H(X) - H(X|W_Q, Q) - H(Y) + H(Y|W_Q, Q) \tag{14.286}$$

$$= H(X) - \lambda H(X|W_1) - (1 - \lambda)H(X|W_2)$$
$$\quad - H(Y) + \lambda H(Y|W_1) + (1 - \lambda)H(Y|W_2) \tag{14.287}$$

$$= \lambda(I(W_1, X) - I(W_1; Y))$$
$$\quad + (1 - \lambda)\Big(I(W_2, X) - I(W_2; Y)\Big), \tag{14.288}$$

and hence

$$R_Y(D) = \min_{U\,:\,Ed \le D} (I(U;X) - I(U;Y)) \tag{14.289}$$

$$\le I(W;X) - I(W;Y) \tag{14.290}$$

$$= \lambda(I(W_1,X) - I(W_1;Y)) + (1-\lambda)(I(W_2,X) - I(W_2;Y))$$

$$= \lambda R_Y(D_1) + (1-\lambda)R_Y(D_2), \tag{14.291}$$

proving the convexity of $R_Y(D)$. $\square$

We are now in a position to prove the converse to the conditional rate distortion theorem.

Proof (*Converse to Theorem 14.9.1*): Consider any rate distortion code with side information. Let the encoding function be $f_n : \mathcal{X}^n \to \{1, 2, \ldots, 2^{nR}\}$. Let the decoding function be $g_n : \mathcal{Y}^n \times \{1, 2, \ldots, 2^{nR}\} \to \hat{\mathcal{X}}^n$ and let $g_{ni} : \mathcal{Y}^n \times \{1, 2, \ldots, 2^{nR}\} \to \hat{\mathcal{X}}$ denote the ith symbol produced by the decoding function. Let $T = f_n(X^n)$ denote the encoded version of X^n. We must show that if $Ed(X^n, g_n(Y^n, f_n(X^n))) \le D$, then $R \ge R_Y(D)$.
We have the following chain of inequalities:

$$nR \overset{(a)}{\ge} H(T) \tag{14.292}$$

$$\overset{(b)}{\ge} H(T|Y^n) \tag{14.293}$$

$$\ge I(X^n; T|Y^n) \tag{14.294}$$

$$\overset{(c)}{=} \sum_{i=1}^{n} I(X_i; T|Y^n, X^{i-1}) \tag{14.295}$$

$$= \sum_{i=1}^{n} H(X_i|Y^n, X^{i-1}) - H(X_i|T, Y^n, X^{i-1}) \tag{14.296}$$

$$\overset{(d)}{=} \sum_{i=1}^{n} H(X_i|Y_i) - H(X_i|T, Y^{i-1}, Y_i, Y^n_{i+1}, X^{i-1}) \tag{14.297}$$

$$\overset{(e)}{\ge} \sum_{i=1}^{n} H(X_i|Y_i) - H(X_i|T, Y^{i-1}, Y_i, Y^n_{i+1}) \tag{14.298}$$

$$\overset{(f)}{=} \sum_{i=1}^{n} H(X_i|Y_i) - H(X_i|W_i, Y_i) \tag{14.299}$$

$$\overset{(g)}{=} \sum_{i=1}^{n} I(X_i; W_i|Y_i) \tag{14.300}$$

$$= \sum_{i=1}^{n} H(W_i|Y_i) - H(W_i|X_i, Y_i) \tag{14.301}$$

$$\stackrel{(h)}{=} \sum_{i=1}^{n} H(W_i|Y_i) - H(W_i|X_i) \tag{14.302}$$

$$= \sum_{i=1}^{n} H(W_i) - H(W_i|X_i) - H(W_i) + H(W_i|Y_i) \tag{14.303}$$

$$= \sum_{i=1}^{n} I(W_i; X_i) - I(W_i; Y_i) \tag{14.304}$$

$$\stackrel{(i)}{\geq} \sum_{i=1}^{n} R_Y(Ed(X_i, g'_{ni}(W_i, Y_i))) \tag{14.305}$$

$$= n \frac{1}{n} \sum_{i=1}^{n} R_Y(Ed(X_i, g'_{ni}(W_i, Y_i))) \tag{14.306}$$

$$\stackrel{(j)}{\geq} nR_Y\!\left(E \frac{1}{n} \sum_{i=1}^{n} d(X_i, g'_{ni}(W_i, Y_i))\right) \tag{14.307}$$

$$\stackrel{(k)}{\geq} nR_Y(D), \tag{14.308}$$

where

(a) follows from the fact that the range of T is $\{1, 2, \ldots, 2^{nR}\}$,
(b) from the fact that conditioning reduces entropy,
(c) from the chain rule for mutual information,
(d) from the fact that X_i is independent of the past and future Y's and X's given Y_i,
(e) from the fact that conditioning reduces entropy,
(f) follows by defining $W_i = (T, Y^{i-1}, Y^n_{i+1})$,
(g) follows from the defintion of mutual information,
(h) follows from the fact that since Y_i depends only on X_i and is conditionally independent of T and the past and future Y's, and therefore $W_i \to X_i \to Y_i$ forms a Markov chain,
(i) follows from the definition of the (information) conditional rate distortion function, since $\hat{X}_i = g_{ni}(T, Y^n) \stackrel{\Delta}{=} g'_{ni}(W_i, Y_i)$, and hence $I(W_i; X_i) - I(W_i; Y_i) \geq \min_{W : Ed(X, \hat{X}) \leq D_i} I(W; X) - I(W; Y) = R_Y(D_i)$,
(j) follows from Jensen's inequality and the convexity of the conditional rate distortion function (Lemma 14.9.1), and
(k) follows from the definition of $D = E \frac{1}{n} \sum_{i=1}^{n} d(X_i, \hat{X}_i)$. $\square$

It is easy to see the parallels between this converse and the converse for rate distortion without side information (Section 13.4). The proof of achievability is also parallel to the proof of the rate distortion theorem using strong typicality. However, instead of sending the index of the codeword that is jointly typical with the source, we divide these codewords into bins and send the bin index instead. If the number of codewords in each bin is small enough, then the side information can be used to isolate the particular codeword in the bin at the receiver. Hence again we are combining random binning with rate distortion encoding to find a jointly typical reproduction codeword. We outline the details of the proof below.

Proof (*Achievability of Theorem 14.9.1*): Fix $p(w|x)$ and the function $f(w, y)$. Calculate $p(w) = \sum_x p(x)p(w|x)$.

Generation of codebook. Let $R_1 = I(X; W) + \epsilon$. Generate 2^{nR} i.i.d. codewords $W^n(s) \sim \prod_{i=1}^{n} p(w_i)$, and index them by $s \in \{1, 2, \ldots, 2^{nR_1}\}$.

Let $R_2 = I(X; W) - I(Y; W) + 5\epsilon$. Randomly assign the indices $s \in \{1, 2, \ldots, 2^{nR_1}\}$ to one of 2^{nR_2} bins using a uniform distribution over the bins. Let $B(i)$ denote the indices assigned to bin i. There are approximately $2^{n(R_1 - R_2)}$ indices in each bin.

Encoding. Given a source sequence X^n, the encoder looks for a codeword $W^n(s)$ such that $(X^n, W^n(s)) \in A_\epsilon^{*(n)}$. If there is no such W^n, the encoder sets $s = 1$. If there is more than one such s, the encoder uses the lowest s. The encoder sends the index of the bin in which s belongs.

Decoding. The decoder looks for a $W^n(s)$ such that $s \in B(i)$ and $(W^n(s), Y^n) \in A_\epsilon^{*(n)}$. If he finds a unique s, he then calculates $\hat{X}^n$, where $\hat{X}_i = f(W_i, Y_i)$. If he does not find any such s or more than one such s, he sets $\hat{X}^n = \hat{x}^n$, where $\hat{x}^n$ is an arbitrary sequence in $\hat{\mathcal{X}}^n$. It does not matter which default sequence is used; we will show that the probability of this event is small.

Analysis of the probability of error. As usual, we have various error events:

1. The pair $(X^n, Y^n) \notin A_\epsilon^{*(n)}$. The probability of this event is small for large enough n by the weak law of large numbers.
2. The sequence X^n is typical, but there does not exist an s such that $(X^n, W^n(s)) \in A_\epsilon^{*(n)}$. As in the proof of the rate distortion theorem, the probability of this event is small if

$$R_1 > I(W; X). \tag{14.309}$$

3. The pair of sequences $(X^n, W^n(s)) \in A_\epsilon^{*(n)}$ but $(W^n(s), Y^n) \notin A_\epsilon^{*(n)}$,

i.e., the codeword is not jointly typical with the Y^n sequence. By the Markov lemma (Lemma 14.8.1), the probability of this event is small if n is large enough.

4. There exists another s' with the same bin index such that $(W^n(s'), Y^n) \in A_\epsilon^{*(n)}$. Since the probability that a randomly chosen W^n is jointly typical with Y^n is $\approx 2^{-nI(Y;W)}$, the probability that there is another W^n in the same bin that is typical with Y^n is bounded by the number of codewords in the bin times the probability of joint typicality, i.e.,

$$\Pr(\exists s' \in B(i):(W^n(s'), Y^n) \in A_\epsilon^{*(n)}) \le 2^{n(R_1-R_2)}2^{-n(I(W;Y)-3\epsilon)},$$

(14.310)

which goes to zero since $R_1 - R_2 < I(Y;W) - 3\epsilon$.

5. If the index s is decoded correctly, then $(X^n, W^n(s)) \in A_\epsilon^{*(n)}$. By item 1, we can assume that $(X^n, Y^n) \in A_\epsilon^{*(n)}$. Thus by the Markov lemma, we have $(X^n, Y^n, W^n) \in A_\epsilon^{*(n)}$ and therefore the empirical joint distribution is close to the original distribution $p(x, y)p(w|x)$ that we started with, and hence $(X^n, \hat{X}^n)$ will have a joint distribution that is close to the distribution that achieves distortion D.

Hence with high probability, the decoder will produce $\hat{X}^n$ such that the distortion between X^n and $\hat{X}^n$ is close to nD. This completes the proof of the theorem. $\square$

The reader is referred to Wyner and Ziv [284] for the details of the proof.

After the discussion of the various situations of compressing distributed data, it might be expected that the problem is almost completely solved. But unfortunately this is not true. An immediate generalization

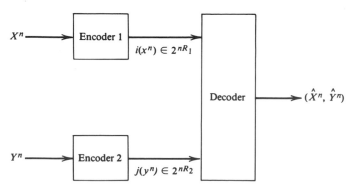

Figure 14.33. Rate distortion for two correlated sources.

of all the above problems is the rate distortion problem for correlated sources, illustrated in Figure 14.33. This is essentially the Slepian-Wolf problem with distortion in both X and Y. It is easy to see that the three distributed source coding problems considered above are all special cases of this setup. Unlike the earlier problems, though, this problem has not yet been solved and the general rate distortion region remains unknown.

14.10 GENERAL MULTITERMINAL NETWORKS

We conclude this chapter by considering a general multiterminal network of senders and receivers and deriving some bounds on the rates achievable for communication in such a network.

A general multiterminal network is illustrated in Figure 14.34. In this section, superscripts denote node indices and subscripts denote time indices. There are m nodes, and node i has an associated transmitted variable $X^{(i)}$ and a received variable $Y^{(i)}$. The node i sends information at rate $R^{(ij)}$ to node j. We assume that all the messages $W^{(ij)}$ being sent from node i to node j are independent and uniformly distributed over their respective ranges $\{1, 2, \ldots, 2^{nR^{(ij)}}\}$.

The channel is represented by the channel transition function $p(y^{(1)}, \ldots, y^{(m)} | x^{(1)}, \ldots, x^{(m)})$, which is the conditional probability mass function of the outputs given the inputs. This probability transition function captures the effects of the noise and the interference in the network. The channel is assumed to be memoryless, i.e., the outputs at any time instant depend only the current inputs and are conditionally independent of the past inputs.

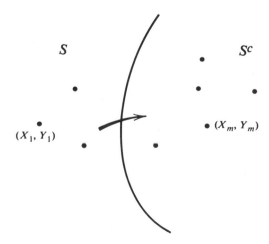

Figure 14.34. A general multiterminal network.

Corresponding to each transmitter-receiver node pair is a message $W^{(ij)} \in \{1, 2, \ldots, 2^{nR^{(ij)}}\}$. The input symbol $X^{(i)}$ at node i depends on $W^{(ij)}, j \in \{1, \ldots, m\}$, and also on the past values of the received symbol $Y^{(i)}$ at node i. Hence an encoding scheme of block length n consists of a set of encoding and decoding functions, one for each node:

- *Encoders.* $X_k^{(i)}(W^{(i1)}, W^{(i2)}, \ldots, W^{(im)}, Y_1^{(i)}, Y_2^{(i)}, \ldots, Y_{k-1}^{(i)})$, $k = 1, \ldots, n$. The encoder maps the messages and past received symbols into the symbol $X_k^{(i)}$ transmitted at time k.
- *Decoders.* $\hat{W}^{(ji)}(Y_1^{(i)}, \ldots, Y_n^{(i)}, W^{(i1)}, \ldots, W^{(im)})$, $j = 1, 2, \ldots, m$. The decoder j at node i maps the received symbols in each block and his own transmitted information to form estimates of the messages intended for him from node j, $j = 1, 2, \ldots, m$.

Associated with every pair of nodes is a rate and a corresponding probability of error that the message will not be decoded correctly,

$$P_e^{(n)(ij)} = \Pr(\hat{W}^{(ij)}(\mathbf{Y}^{(j)}, W^{(j1)}, \ldots, W^{(jm)}) \neq W^{(ij)}), \qquad (14.311)$$

where $P_e^{(n)(ij)}$ is defined under the assumption that all the messages are independent and uniformly distributed over their respective ranges.

A set of rates $\{R^{(ij)}\}$ is said to be achievable if there exist encoders and decoders with block length n with $P_e^{(n)(ij)} \to 0$ as $n \to \infty$ for all $i, j \in \{1, 2, \ldots, m\}$.

We use this formulation to derive an upper bound on the flow of information in any multiterminal network. We divide the nodes into two sets, S and the complement S^c. We now bound the rate of flow of information from nodes in S to nodes in S^c.

Theorem 14.10.1: *If the information rates $\{R^{(ij)}\}$ are achievable, then there exists some joint probability distribution $p(x^{(1)}, x^{(2)}, \ldots, x^{(m)})$, such that*

$$\sum_{i \in S, \, j \in S^c} R^{(ij)} \leq I(X^{(S)}; Y^{(S^c)} | X^{(S^c)}), \qquad (14.312)$$

for all $S \subset \{1, 2, \ldots, m\}$. Thus the total rate of flow of information across cut-sets is bounded by the conditional mutual information.

Proof: The proof follows the same lines as the proof of the converse for the multiple access channel. Let $T = \{(i, j) : i \in S, j \in S^c\}$ be the set of links that cross from S to S^c, and let T^c be all the other links in the network. Then

$$n \sum_{i \in S, j \in S^c} R^{(ij)} \tag{14.313}$$

$$\overset{(a)}{=} \sum_{i \in S, j \in S^c} H(W^{(ij)}) \tag{14.314}$$

$$\overset{(b)}{=} H(W^{(T)}) \tag{14.315}$$

$$\overset{(c)}{=} H(W^{(T)}|W^{(T^c)}) \tag{14.316}$$

$$= I(W^{(T)}; Y_1^{(S^c)}, \ldots, Y_n^{(S^c)}|W^{(T^c)}) \tag{14.317}$$

$$\quad + H(W^{(T)}|Y_1^{(S^c)}, \ldots, Y_n^{(S^c)}, W^{(T^c)}) \tag{14.318}$$

$$\overset{(d)}{\leq} I(W^{(T)}; Y_1^{(S^c)}, \ldots, Y_n^{(S^c)}|W^{(T^c)}) + n\epsilon_n \tag{14.319}$$

$$\overset{(e)}{=} \sum_{k=1}^{n} I(W^{(T)}; Y_k^{(S^c)}|Y_1^{(S^c)}, \ldots, Y_{k-1}^{(S^c)}, W^{(T^c)}) + n\epsilon_n \tag{14.320}$$

$$\overset{(f)}{=} \sum_{k=1}^{n} H(Y_k^{(S^c)}|Y_1^{(S^c)}, \ldots, Y_{k-1}^{(S^c)}, W^{(T^c)})$$
$$\quad - H(Y_k^{(S^c)}|Y_1^{(S^c)}, \ldots, Y_{k-1}^{(S^c)}, W^{(T^c)}, W^{(T)}) + n\epsilon_n \tag{14.321}$$

$$\overset{(g)}{\leq} \sum_{k=1}^{n} H(Y_k^{(S^c)}|Y_1^{(S^c)}, \ldots, Y_{k-1}^{(S^c)}, W^{(T^c)}, X_k^{(S^c)})$$
$$\quad - H(Y_k^{(S^c)}|Y_1^{(S^c)}, \ldots, Y_{k-1}^{(S^c)}, W^{(T^c)}, W^{(T)}, X_k^{(S)}, X_k^{(S^c)}) + n\epsilon_n \tag{14.322}$$

$$\overset{(h)}{\leq} \sum_{k=1}^{n} H(Y_k^{(S^c)}|X_k^{(S^c)}) - H(Y_k^{(S^c)}|X_k^{(S^c)}, X_k^{(S)}) + n\epsilon_n \tag{14.323}$$

$$= \sum_{k=1}^{n} I(X_k^{(S)}; Y_k^{(S^c)}|X_k^{(S^c)}) + n\epsilon_n \tag{14.324}$$

$$\overset{(i)}{=} n \frac{1}{n} \sum_{k=1}^{n} I(X_Q^{(S)}; Y_Q^{(S^c)}|X_Q^{(S^c)}, Q = k) + n\epsilon_n \tag{14.325}$$

$$\overset{(j)}{=} nI(X_Q^{(S)}; Y_Q^{(S^c)}|X_Q^{(S^c)}, Q) + n\epsilon_n \tag{14.326}$$

$$= n(H(Y_Q^{(S^c)}|X_Q^{(S^c)}, Q) - H(Y_Q^{(S^c)}|X_Q^{(S)}, X_Q^{(S^c)}, Q)) + n\epsilon_n \tag{14.327}$$

$$\overset{(k)}{\leq} n(H(Y_Q^{(S^c)}|X_Q^{(S^c)}) - H(Y_Q^{(S^c)}|X_Q^{(S)}, X_Q^{(S^c)}, Q)) + n\epsilon_n \tag{14.328}$$

$$\overset{(l)}{\leq} n(H(Y_Q^{(S^c)}|X_Q^{(S^c)}) - H(Y_Q^{(S^c)}|X_Q^{(S)}, X_Q^{(S^c)})) + n\epsilon_n \tag{14.329}$$

$$= nI(X_Q^{(S)}; Y_Q^{(S^c)}|X_Q^{(S^c)}) + n\epsilon_n , \tag{14.330}$$

where

(a) follows from the fact that the messages $W^{(ij)}$ are uniformly distributed over their respective ranges $\{1, 2, \ldots, 2^{nR^{(ij)}}\}$,

(b) follows from the definition of $W^{(T)} = \{W^{(ij)} : i \in S, j \in S^c\}$ and the fact that the messages are independent,

(c) follows from the independence of the messages for T and T^c,

(d) follows from Fano's inequality since the messages $W^{(T)}$ can be decoded from $Y^{(S)}$ and $W^{(T^c)}$,

(e) is the chain rule for mutual information,

(f) follows from the definition of mutual information,

(g) follows from the fact that $X_k^{(S^c)}$ is a function of the past received symbols $Y^{(S^c)}$ and the messages $W^{(T^c)}$ and the fact that adding conditioning reduces the second term,

(h) from the fact that $Y_k^{(S^c)}$ depends only on the current input symbols $X_k^{(S)}$ and $X_k^{(S^c)}$,

(i) follows after we introduce a new timesharing random variable Q uniformly distributed on $\{1, 2, \ldots, n\}$,

(j) follows from the definition of mutual information,

(k) follows from the fact that conditioning reduces entropy, and

(l) follows from the fact that $Y_Q^{(S^c)}$ depends only the inputs $X_Q^{(S)}$ and $X_Q^{(S^c)}$ and is conditionally independent of Q.

Thus there exist random variables $X^{(S)}$ and $X^{(S^c)}$ with some arbitrary joint distribution which satisfy the inequalities of the theorem. $\square$

The theorem has a simple max-flow-min-cut interpretation. The rate of flow of information across any boundary is less than the mutual information between the inputs on one side of the boundary and the outputs on the other side, conditioned on the inputs on the other side.

The problem of information flow in networks would be solved if the bounds of the theorem were achievable. But unfortunately these bounds are not achievable even for some simple channels. We now apply these bounds to a few of the channels that we have considered earlier.

- *Multiple access channel.* The multiple access channel is a network with many input nodes and one output node. For the case of a two-user multiple access channel, the bounds of Theorem 14.10.1 reduce to

$$R_1 \leq I(X_1; Y|X_2), \tag{14.331}$$

$$R_2 \leq I(X_2; Y|X_1), \tag{14.332}$$

$$R_1 + R_2 \leq I(X_1, X_2; Y) \tag{14.333}$$

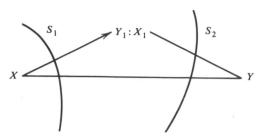

Figure 14.35. The relay channel.

for some joint distribution $p(x_1, x_2)p(y|x_1, x_2)$. These bounds coincide with the capacity region if we restrict the input distribution to be a product distribution and take the convex hull (Theorem 14.3.1).

- *Relay channel.* For the relay channel, these bounds give the upper bound of Theorem 14.7.1 with different choices of subsets as shown in Figure 14.35. Thus

$$C \leq \sup_{p(x, x_1)} \min\{I(X, X_1; Y), I(X; Y, Y_1|X_1)\} . \qquad (14.334)$$

This upper bound is the capacity of a physically degraded relay channel, and for the relay channel with feedback [67].

To complement our discussion of a general network, we should mention two features of single user channels that do not apply to a multi-user network.

- *The source channel separation theorem.* In Section 8.13, we discussed the source channel separation theorem, which proves that we can transmit the source noiselessly over the channel if and only if the entropy rate is less than the channel capacity. This allows us to characterize a source by a single number (the entropy rate) and the channel by a single number (the capacity).

    What about the multi-user case? We would expect that a distributed source could be transmitted over a channel if and only if the rate region for the noiseless coding of the source lay within the capacity region of the channel. To be specific, consider the transmission of a distributed source over a multiple access channel, as shown in Figure 14.36. Combining the results of Slepian-Wolf encoding with the capacity results for the multiple access channel, we can show that we can transmit the source over the channel and recover it with a low probability of error if

$$H(U|V) \leq I(X_1; Y|X_2, Q), \qquad (14.335)$$

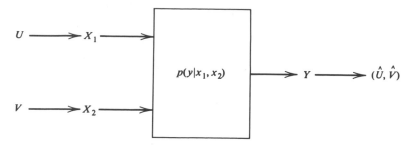

Figure 14.36. Transmission of correlated sources over a multiple access channel.

$$H(V|U) \leq I(X_2; Y|X_1, Q), \qquad (14.336)$$

$$H(U, V) \leq I(X_1, X_2; Y, Q) \qquad (14.337)$$

for some distribution $p(q)p(x_1|q)p(x_2|q)p(y|x_1, x_2)$. This condition is equivalent to saying that the Slepian-Wolf rate region of the source has a non-empty intersection with the capacity region of the multiple access channel.

But is this condition also necessary? No, as a simple example illustrates. Consider the transmission of the source of Example 14.4 over the binary erasure multiple access channel (Example 14.3). The Slepian-Wolf region does not intersect the capacity region, yet it is simple to devise a scheme that allows the source to be transmitted over the channel. We just let $X_1 = U$, and $X_2 = V$, and the value of Y will tell us the pair (U, V) with no error. Thus the conditions (14.337) are not necessary.

The reason for the failure of the source channel separation theorem lies in the fact that the capacity of the multiple access channel increases with the correlation between the inputs of the channel. Therefore, to maximize the capacity, one should preserve the correlation between the inputs of the channel. Slepian-Wolf encoding, on the other hand, gets rid of the correlation. Cover, El Gamal and Salehi [69] proposed an achievable region for transmission of a correlated source over a multiple access channel based on the idea of preserving the correlation. Han and Costa [131] have proposed a similar region for the transmission of a correlated source over a broadcast channel.

Capacity regions with feedback. Theorem 8.12.1 shows that feedback does not increase the capacity of a single user discrete memoryless channel. For channels with memory, on the other hand, feedback enables the sender to predict something about the noise and to combat it more effectively, thus increasing capacity.

What about multi-user channels? Rather surprisingly, feedback does increase the capacity region of multi-user channels, even when the channels are memoryless. This was first shown by Gaarder and Wolf [117], who showed how feedback helps increase the capacity of the binary erasure multiple access channel. In essence, feedback from the receiver to the two senders acts as a separate channel between the two senders. The senders can decode each other's transmissions before the receiver does. They then cooperate to resolve the uncertainty at the receiver, sending information at the higher cooperative capacity rather than the non-cooperative capacity. Using this scheme, Cover and Leung [73] established an achievable region for multiple access channel with feedback. Willems [273] showed that this region was the capacity for a class of multiple access channels that included the binary erasure multiple access channel. Ozarow [204] established the capacity region for the two user Gaussian multiple access channel. The problem of finding the capacity region for the multiple access channel with feedback is closely related to the capacity of a two-way channel with a common output.

There is as yet no unified theory of network information flow. But there can be no doubt that a complete theory of communication networks would have wide implications for the theory of communication and computation.

SUMMARY OF CHAPTER 14

Multiple access channel: The capacity of a multiple access channel ($\mathcal{X}_1 \times \mathcal{X}_2$, $p(y|x_1, x_2)$, $\mathcal{Y}$) is the closure of the convex hull of all (R_1, R_2) satisfying

$$R_1 < I(X_1; Y|X_2),\qquad\qquad (14.338)$$

$$R_2 < I(X_2; Y|X_1),\qquad\qquad (14.339)$$

$$R_1 + R_2 < I(X_1, X_2; Y)\qquad\qquad (14.340)$$

for some distribution $p_1(x_1)p_2(x_2)$ on $\mathcal{X}_1 \times \mathcal{X}_2$.

The capacity region of the m-user multiple access channel is the closure of the convex hull of the rate vectors satisfying

$$R(S) \leq I(X(S); Y|X(S^c))\quad \text{for all } S \subseteq \{1, 2, \ldots, m\}\qquad (14.341)$$

for some product distribution $p_1(x_1)p_2(x_2) \ldots p_m(x_m)$.

Gaussian multiple access channel: The capacity region of a two user Gaussian multiple access channel is

$$R_1 \le C\left(\frac{P_1}{N}\right),$$ (14.342)

$$R_2 \le C\left(\frac{P_2}{N}\right),$$ (14.343)

$$R_1 + R_2 \le C\left(\frac{P_1 + P_2}{N}\right),$$ (14.344)

where

$$C(x) = \frac{1}{2}\log(1 + x).$$ (14.345)

Slepian-Wolf coding: Correlated sources X and Y can be separately described at rates R_1 and R_2 and recovered with arbitrarily low probability of error by a common decoder if and only if

$$R_1 > H(X|Y),$$ (14.346)

$$R_2 > H(Y|X),$$ (14.347)

$$R_1 + R_2 > H(X, Y).$$ (14.348)

Broadcast channels: The capacity region of the degraded broadcast channel $X \to Y_1 \to Y_2$ is the convex hull of the closure of all (R_1, R_2) satisfying

$$R_2 \le I(U; Y_2),$$ (14.349)

$$R_1 \le I(X; Y_1|U)$$ (14.350)

for some joint distribution $p(u)p(x|u)p(y_1, y_2|x)$.

Relay channel: The capacity C of the physically degraded relay channel $p(y, y_1|x, x_1)$ is given by

$$C = \sup_{p(x, x_1)} \min\{I(X, X_1; Y), I(X; Y_1|X_1)\},$$ (14.351)

where the supremum is over all joint distributions on $\mathcal{X} \times \mathcal{X}_1$.

Source coding with side information: Let $(X, Y) \sim p(x, y)$. If Y is encoded at rate R_2 and X is encoded at rate R_1, we can recover X with an arbitrarily small probability of error iff

$$R_1 \ge H(X|U),$$ (14.352)

$$R_2 \geq I(Y; U) \tag{14.353}$$

for some distribution $p(y, u)$, such that $X \to Y \to U$.

Rate distortion with side information: Let $(X, Y) \sim p(x, y)$. The rate distortion function with side information is given by

$$R_Y(D) = \min_{p(w|x)} \min_{f: \mathcal{Y} \times \mathcal{W} \to \hat{\mathcal{X}}} I(X; W) - I(Y; W), \tag{14.354}$$

where the minimization is over all functions f and conditional distributions $p(w|x)$, $|\mathcal{W}| \leq |\mathcal{X}| + 1$, such that

$$\sum_x \sum_w \sum_y p(x, y) p(w|x) d(x, f(y, w)) \leq D. \tag{14.355}$$

PROBLEMS FOR CHAPTER 14

1. *The cooperative capacity of a multiple access channel.* (See Figure 14.37.)

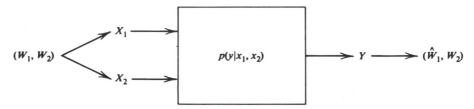

Figure 14.37. Multiple access channel with cooperating senders.

   (a) Suppose X_1 and X_2 have access to *both* indices $W_1 \in \{1, 2^{nR}\}$, $W_2 \in \{1, 2^{nR_2}\}$. Thus the codewords $\mathbf{X}_1(W_1, W_2), \mathbf{X}_2(W_1, W_2)$ depend on both indices. Find the capacity region.
   (b) Evaluate this region for the binary erasure multiple access channel $Y = X_1 + X_2, X_i \in \{0, 1\}$. Compare to the non-cooperative region.

2. *Capacity of multiple access channels.* Find the capacity region for each of the following multiple access channels:
   (a) Additive modulo 2 multiple access access channel. $X_1 \in \{0, 1\}$, $X_2 \in \{0, 1\}$, $Y = X_1 \oplus X_2$.
   (b) Multiplicative multiple access channel. $X_1 \in \{-1, 1\}, X_2 \in \{-1, 1\}$, $Y = X_1 \cdot X_2$.

3. *Cut-set interpretation of capacity region of multiple access channel.* For the multiple access channel we know that (R_1, R_2) is achievable if

$$R_1 < I(X_1; Y|X_2), \tag{14.356}$$

$$R_2 < I(X_2; Y|X_1), \tag{14.357}$$

$$R_1 + R_2 < I(X_1, X_2; Y), \qquad (14.358)$$

for X_1, X_2 independent. Show, for X_1, X_2 independent, that

$$I(X_1; Y | X_2) = I(X_1; Y, X_2).$$

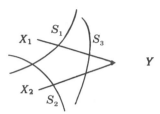

Interpret the information bounds as bounds on the rate of flow across cutsets S_1, S_2 and S_3.

4. *Gaussian multiple access channel capacity.* For the AWGN multiple access channel, prove, using typical sequences, the achievability of any rate pairs (R_1, R_2) satisfying

$$R_1 < \frac{1}{2} \log\left(1 + \frac{P_1}{N}\right), \qquad (14.359)$$

$$R_2 < \frac{1}{2} \log\left(1 + \frac{P_2}{N}\right), \qquad (14.360)$$

$$R_1 + R_2 < \frac{1}{2} \log\left(1 + \frac{P_1 + P_2}{N}\right). \qquad (14.361)$$

The proof extends the proof for the discrete multiple access channel in the same way as the proof for the single user Gaussian channel extends the proof for the discrete single user channel.

5. *Converse for the Gaussian multiple access channel.* Prove the converse for the Gaussian multiple access channel by extending the converse in the discrete case to take into account the power constraint on the codewords.

6. *Unusual multiple access channel.* Consider the following multiple access channel: $\mathscr{X}_1 = \mathscr{X}_2 = \mathscr{Y} = \{0, 1\}$. If $(X_1, X_2) = (0, 0)$, then $Y = 0$. If $(X_1, X_2) = (0, 1)$, then $Y = 1$. If $(X_1, X_2) = (1, 0)$, then $Y = 1$. If $(X_1, X_2) = (1, 1)$, then $Y = 0$ with probability $\frac{1}{2}$ and $Y = 1$ with probability $\frac{1}{2}$.

   (a) Show that the rate pairs $(1, 0)$ and $(0, 1)$ are achievable.
   (b) Show that for any non-degenerate distribution $p(x_1)p(x_2)$, we have $I(X_1, X_2; Y) < 1$.
   (c) Argue that there are points in the capacity region of this multiple access channel that can only be achieved by timesharing, i.e., there exist achievable rate pairs (R_1, R_2) which lie in the capacity region for the channel but not in the region defined by

$$R_1 \le I(X_1; Y | X_2), \qquad (14.362)$$

$$R_2 \leq I(X_2; Y|X_1), \tag{14.363}$$

$$R_1 + R_2 \leq I(X_1, X_2; Y) \tag{14.364}$$

for any product distribution $p(x_1)p(x_2)$. Hence the operation of convexification strictly enlarges the capacity region. This channel was introduced independently by Csiszár and Körner [83] and Bierbaum and Wallmeier [33].

7. *Convexity of capacity region of broadcast channel.* Let $\mathbf{C} \subseteq \mathbf{R}^2$ be the capacity region of all achievable rate pairs $\mathbf{R} = (R_1, R_2)$ for the broadcast channel. Show that $\mathbf{C}$ is a convex set by using a timesharing argument.

   Specifically, show that if $\mathbf{R}^{(1)}$ and $\mathbf{R}^{(2)}$ are achievable, then $\lambda \mathbf{R}^{(1)} + (1 - \lambda)\mathbf{R}^{(2)}$ is achievable for $0 \leq \lambda \leq 1$.

8. *Slepian-Wolf for deterministically related sources.* Find and sketch the Slepian-Wolf rate region for the simultaneous data compression of (X, Y), where $y = f(x)$ is some deterministic function of x.

9. *Slepian-Wolf.* Let X_i be i.i.d. Bernoulli(p). Let Z_i be i.i.d. $\sim$ Bernoulli(r), and let $\mathbf{Z}$ be independent of $\mathbf{X}$. Finally, let $\mathbf{Y} = \mathbf{X} \oplus \mathbf{Z}$ (mod 2 addition). Let $\mathbf{X}$ be described at rate R_1 and $\mathbf{Y}$ be described at rate R_2. What region of rates allows recovery of $\mathbf{X}, \mathbf{Y}$ with probability of error tending to zero?

10. *Broadcast capacity depends only on the conditional marginals.* Consider the general broadcast channel $(X, Y_1 \times Y_2, p(y_1, y_2|x))$. Show that the capacity region depends only on $p(y_1|x)$ and $p(y_2|x)$. To do this, for any given $((2^{nR_1}, 2^{nR_2}), n)$ code, let

$$P_1^{(n)} = P\{\hat{W}_1(\mathbf{Y}_1) \neq W_1\}, \tag{14.365}$$

$$P_2^{(n)} = P\{\hat{W}_2(\mathbf{Y}_2) \neq W_2\}, \tag{14.366}$$

$$P^{(n)} = P\{(\hat{W}_1, \hat{W}_2) \neq (W_1, W_2)\}. \tag{14.367}$$

Then show

$$\max\{P_1^{(n)}, P_2^{(n)}\} \leq P^{(n)} \leq P_1^{(n)} + P_2^{(n)}.$$

The result now follows by a simple argument.

   Remark: The probability of error $P^{(n)}$ *does* depend on the conditional joint distribution $p(y_1, y_2|x)$. But whether or not $P^{(n)}$ can be driven to zero (at rates (R_1, R_2)) *does not* (except through the conditional marginals $p(y_1|x)$, $p(y_2|x)$).

11. *Converse for the degraded broadcast channel.* The following chain of inequalities proves the converse for the degraded discrete memoryless broadcast channel. Provide reasons for each of the labeled inequalities.

Setup for converse for degraded broadcast channel capacity

$$(W_1, W_2)_{\text{indep.}} \to X^n(W_1, W_2) \to Y^n \to Z^n$$

Encoding

$$f_n : 2^{nR_1} \times 2^{nR_2} \to \mathscr{X}^n$$

Decoding

$$g_n : \mathscr{Y}^n \to 2^{nR_1}, \qquad h_n : \mathscr{Z}^n \to 2^{nR_2}$$

Let $U_i = (W_2, Y^{i-1})$. Then

$$nR_2 \stackrel{\cdot}{\le}_{Fano} I(W_2; Z^n) \tag{14.368}$$

$$\stackrel{(a)}{=} \sum_{i=1}^{n} I(W_2; Z_i | Z^{i-1}) \tag{14.369}$$

$$\stackrel{(b)}{=} \sum_i (H(Z_i | Z^{i-1}) - H(Z_i | W_2, Z^{i-1})) \tag{14.370}$$

$$\stackrel{(c)}{\le} \sum_i (H(Z_i) - H(Z_i | W_2, Z^{i-1}, Y^{i-1})) \tag{14.371}$$

$$\stackrel{(d)}{\le} \sum_i (H(Z_i) - H(Z_i | W_2, Y^{i-1})) \tag{14.372}$$

$$\stackrel{(e)}{=} \sum_{i=1}^{n} I(U_i; Z_i). \tag{14.373}$$

Continuation of converse. Give reasons for the labeled inequalities:

$$nR_1 \stackrel{\cdot}{\le}_{Fano} I(W_1; Y^n) \tag{14.374}$$

$$\stackrel{(f)}{\le} I(W_1; Y^n, W_2) \tag{14.375}$$

$$\stackrel{(g)}{\le} I(W_1; Y^n | W_2) \tag{14.376}$$

$$\stackrel{(h)}{=} \sum_{i-1}^{n} I(W_1; Y_i | Y^{i-1}, W_2) \tag{14.377}$$

$$\stackrel{(i)}{\le} \sum_{i=1}^{n} I(X_i; Y_i | U_i). \tag{14.378}$$

12. *Capacity points.*
    (a) For the degraded broadcast channel $X \to Y_1 \to Y_2$, find the points a and b where the capacity region hits the R_1 and R_2 axes (Figure 14.38).
    (b) Show that $b \le a$.

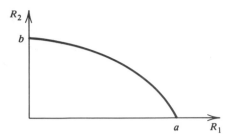

Figure 14.38. Capacity region of a broadcast channel.

13. *Degraded broadcast channel.* Find the capacity region for the degraded broadcast channel in Figure 14.39.

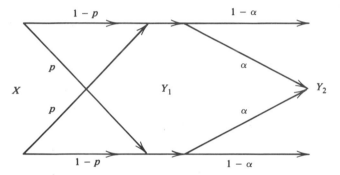

Figure 14.39. Broadcast channel–BSC and erasure channel.

14. *Channels with unknown parameters.* We are given a binary symmetric channel with parameter p. The capacity is $C = 1 - H(p)$.

Now we change the problem slightly. The receiver knows only that $p \in \{p_1, p_2\}$, i.e., $p = p_1$ or $p = p_2$, where p_1 and p_2 are given real numbers. The transmitter knows the actual value of p. Devise two codes for use by the transmitter, one to be used if $p = p_1$, the other to be used if $p = p_2$, such that transmission to the receiver can take place at rate $\approx C(p_1)$ if $p = p_1$ and at rate $\approx C(p_2)$ if $p = p_2$.

Hint: Devise a method for revealing p to the receiver without affecting the asymptotic rate. Prefixing the codeword by a sequence of 1's of appropriate length should work.

15. *Two-way channel.* Consider the two-way channel shown in Figure 14.6. The outputs Y_1 and Y_2 depend only on the current inputs X_1 and X_2.

(a) By using independently generated codes for the two senders, show that the following rate region is achievable:

$$R_1 < I(X_1; Y_2 | X_2), \tag{14.379}$$

$$R_2 < I(X_2; Y_1 | X_1) \tag{14.380}$$

for some product distribution $p(x_1)p(x_2)p(y_1, y_2 | x_1, x_2)$.

(b) Show that the rates for any code for a two-way channel with arbitrarily small probability of error must satisfy

$$R_1 \leq I(X_1; Y_2|X_2),\qquad (14.381)$$

$$R_2 \leq I(X_2; Y_1|X_1)\qquad (14.382)$$

for some joint distribution $p(x_1, x_2)p(y_1, y_2|x_1, x_2)$.

The inner and outer bounds on the capacity of the two-way channel are due to Shannon [246]. He also showed that the inner bound and the outer bound do not coincide in the case of the binary multiplying channel $\mathcal{X}_1 = \mathcal{X}_2 = \mathcal{Y}_1 - \mathcal{Y}_2 - \{0, 1\}$, $Y_1 = Y_2 = X_1 X_2$. The capacity of the two-way channel is still an open problem.

HISTORICAL NOTES

This chapter is based on the review in El Gamal and Cover [98]. The two-way channel was studied by Shannon [246] in 1961. He derived inner and outer bounds on the capacity region. Dueck [90] and Schalkwijk [232, 233] suggested coding schemes for two-way channels which achieve rates exceeding Shannon's inner bound; outer bounds for this channel were derived by Zhang, Berger and Schalkwijk [287] and Willems and Hekstra [274].

The multiple access channel capacity region was found by Ahlswede [3] and Liao [178] and was extended to the case of the multiple access channel with common information by Slepian and Wolf [254]. Gaarder and Wolf [117] were the first to show that feedback increases the capacity of a discrete memoryless multiple access channel. Cover and Leung [73] proposed an achievable region for the multiple access channel with feedback, which was shown to be optimal for a class of multiple access channels by Willems [273]. Ozarow [204] has determined the capacity region for a two user Gaussian multiple access channel with feedback. Cover, El Gamal and Salehi [69] and Ahlswede and Han [6] have considered the problem of transmission of a correlated source over a multiple access channel.

The Slepian-Wolf theorem was proved by Slepian and Wolf [255], and was extended to jointly ergodic sources by a binning argument in Cover [63].

Broadcast channels were studied by Cover in 1972 [60]; the capacity region for the degraded broadcast channel was determined by Bergmans [31] and Gallager [119]. The superposition codes used for the degraded broadcast channel are also optimal for the less noisy broadcast channel (Körner and Marton [160]) and the more capable broadcast channel (El Gamal [97]) and the broadcast channel with degraded message sets (Körner and Marton [161]). Van der Meulen [26] and Cover [62] proposed achievable regions for the general broadcast channel. The best known achievable region for broadcast channel is due to Marton [189]; a simpler proof of Marton's region was given by El Gamal and Van der Meulen [100]. The deterministic broadcast channel capacity was determined by Pinsker [211] and Marton [189]. El Gamal [96] showed that feedback does not increase the capacity of a physically degraded broadcast channel. Dueck [91] introduced an example to illustrate that feedback could increase the capacity of a memoryless broadcast channel; Ozarow and Leung [205] described a coding procedure for the Gaussian broadcast channel with feedback which increased the capacity region.

The relay channel was introduced by Van der Meulen [262]; the capacity region for the degraded relay channel was found by Cover and El Gamal [67]. The interference channel was introduced by Shannon [246]. It was studied by Ahlswede [4], who gave an example to show that the region conjectured by Shannon was not the capacity region of the interference channel. Carleial [49] introduced the Gaussian interference channel with power constraints, and showed that very strong interference is equivalent to no interference at all. Sato and Tanabe [231] extended the work of Carleial to discrete interference channels with strong interference. Sato [229] and Benzel [26] dealt with degraded interference channels. The best known achievable region for the general interference channel is due to Han and Kobayashi [132]. This region gives the capacity for Gaussian interference channels with interference parameters greater than 1, as was shown in Han and Kobayashi [132] and Sato [230]. Carleial [48] proved new bounds on the capacity region for interference channels.

The problem of coding with side information was introduced by Wyner and Ziv [283] and Wyner [280]; the achievable region for this problem was described in Ahlswede and Körner [7] and in a series of papers by Gray and Wyner [125] and Wyner [281, 282]. The problem of finding the rate distortion function with side information was solved by Wyner and Ziv [284]. The problem of multiple descriptions is treated in El Gamal and Cover [99].

The special problem of encoding a function of two random variables was discussed by Körner and Marton [162], who described a simple method to encode the modulo two sum of two binary random variables. A general framework for the description of source networks can be found in Csiszár and Körner [82], [83]. A common model which includes Slepian-Wolf encoding, coding with side information, and rate distortion with side information as special cases was described by Berger and Yeung [30].

Comprehensive surveys of network information theory can be found in El Gamal and Cover [98], Van der Meulen [262, 263, 264], Berger [28] and Csiszár and Körner [83].

Chapter 15

Information Theory and the Stock Market

The duality between the growth rate of wealth in the stock market and the entropy rate of the market is striking. We explore this duality in this chapter. In particular, we shall find the competitively optimal and growth rate optimal portfolio strategies. They are the same, just as the Shannon code is optimal both competitively and in expected value in data compression. We shall also find the asymptotic doubling rate for an ergodic stock market process.

15.1 THE STOCK MARKET: SOME DEFINITIONS

A stock market is represented as a vector of stocks $\mathbf{X} = (X_1, X_2, \ldots, X_m)$, $X_i \geq 0$, $i - 1, 2, \ldots, m$, where m is the number of stocks and the *price relative* X_i represents the ratio of the price at the end of the day to the price at the beginning of the day. So typically X_i is near 1. For example, $X_i = 1.03$ means that the ith stock went up 3% that day.

Let $\mathbf{X} \sim F(\mathbf{x})$, where $F(\mathbf{x})$ is the joint distribution of the vector of price relatives.

A *portfolio* $\mathbf{b} = (b_1, b_2, \ldots, b_m)$, $b_i \geq 0$, $\Sigma b_i = 1$, is an allocation of wealth across the stocks. Here b_i is the fraction of one's wealth invested in stock i.

If one uses a portfolio $\mathbf{b}$ and the stock vector is $\mathbf{X}$, the wealth relative (ratio of the wealth at the end of the day to the wealth at the beginning of the day) is $S = \mathbf{b}^t \mathbf{X}$.

We wish to maximize S in some sense. But S is a random variable, so there is controversy over the choice of the best distribution for S. The standard theory of stock market investment is based on the consideration of the first and second moments of S. The objective is to maximize the expected value of S, subject to a constraint on the variance. Since it is easy to calculate these moments, the theory is simpler than the theory that deals wth the entire distribution of S.

The mean-variance approach is the basis of the Sharpe-Markowitz theory of investment in the stock market and is used by business analysts and others. It is illustrated in Figure 15.1. The figure illustrates the set of achievable mean-variance pairs using various portfolios. The set of portfolios on the boundary of this region corresponds to the undominated portfolios: these are the portfolios which have the highest mean for a given variance. This boundary is called the efficient frontier, and if one is interested only in mean and variance, then one should operate along this boundary.

Normally the theory is simplified with the introduction of a *risk-free* asset, e.g., cash or Treasury bonds, which provide a fixed interest rate with variance 0. This stock corresponds to a point on the Y axis in the figure. By combining the risk-free asset with various stocks, one obtains all points below the tangent from the risk-free asset to the efficient frontier. This line now becomes part of the efficient frontier.

The concept of the efficient frontier also implies that there is a true value for a stock corresponding to its risk. This theory of stock prices is called the *Capital Assets Pricing Model* and is used to decide whether the market price for a stock is too high or too low.

Looking at the mean of a random variable gives information about the long term behavior of the sum of i.i.d. versions of the random variable. But in the stock market, one normally reinvests every day, so that the wealth at the end of n days is the product of factors, one for each day of the market. The behavior of the product is determined not by the expected value but by the expected logarithm. This leads us to define the doubling rate as follows:

Definition: The *doubling rate* of a stock market portfolio **b** is defined as

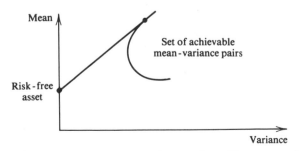

Figure 15.1. Sharpe-Markowitz theory: Set of achievable mean-variance pairs.

$$W(\mathbf{b}, F) = \int \log \mathbf{b}^t \mathbf{x} \, dF(\mathbf{x}) = E(\log \mathbf{b}^t \mathbf{X}) . \qquad (15.1)$$

Definition: The *optimal doubling rate* $W^*(F)$ is defined as

$$W^*(F) = \max_{\mathbf{b}} W(\mathbf{b}, F), \qquad (15.2)$$

where the maximum is over all possible portfolios $b_i \geq 0, \Sigma_i b_i = 1$.

Definition: A portfolio $\mathbf{b}^*$ that achieves the maximum of $W(\mathbf{b}, F)$ is called a *log-optimal portfolio*.

The definition of doubling rate is justified by the following theorem:

Theorem 15.1.1: *Let* $\mathbf{X}_1, \mathbf{X}_2, \ldots, \mathbf{X}_n$ *be i.i.d. according to* $F(\mathbf{x})$. *Let*

$$S_n^* = \prod_{i=1}^{n} \mathbf{b}^{*t} \mathbf{X}_i \qquad (15.3)$$

be the wealth after n days using the constant rebalanced portfolio $\mathbf{b}^*$. Then

$$\frac{1}{n} \log S_n^* \to W^* \quad \text{with probability 1}. \qquad (15.4)$$

Proof:

$$\frac{1}{n} \log S_n^* = \frac{1}{n} \sum_{i=1}^{n} \log \mathbf{b}^{*t} \mathbf{X}_i \qquad (15.5)$$

$$\to W^* \quad \text{with probability 1}, \qquad (15.6)$$

by the strong law of large numbers. Hence, $S_n^* \doteq 2^{nW^*}$. $\square$

We now consider some of the properties of the doubling rate.

Lemma 15.1.1: $W(\mathbf{b}, F)$ *is concave in $\mathbf{b}$ and linear in F. $W^*(F)$ is convex in F.*

Proof: The doubling rate is

$$W(\mathbf{b}, F) = \int \log \mathbf{b}^t \mathbf{x} \, dF(\mathbf{x}) . \qquad (15.7)$$

Since the integral is linear in F, so is $W(\mathbf{b}, F)$.
   Since

$$\log(\lambda \mathbf{b}_1 + (1 - \lambda)\mathbf{b}_2)^t \mathbf{X} \geq \lambda \log \mathbf{b}_1^t \mathbf{X} + (1 - \lambda) \log \mathbf{b}_2^t \mathbf{X}, \qquad (15.8)$$

by the concavity of the logarithm, it follows, by taking expectations, that $W(\mathbf{b}, F)$ is concave in $\mathbf{b}$.

Finally, to prove the convexity of $W^*(F)$ as a function of F, let F_1 and F_2 be two distributions on the stock market and let the corresponding optimal portfolios be $\mathbf{b}^*(F_1)$ and $\mathbf{b}^*(F_2)$ respectively. Let the log-optimal portfolio corresponding to $\lambda F_1 + (1 - \lambda)F_2$ be $\mathbf{b}^*(\lambda F_1 + (1 - \lambda)F_2)$. Then by linearity of $W(\mathbf{b}, F)$ with respect to F, we have

$$W^*(\lambda F_1 + (1 - \lambda)F_2) = W(\mathbf{b}^*(\lambda F_1 + (1 - \lambda)F_2), \lambda F_1 + (1 - \lambda)F_2) \qquad (15.9)$$

$$= \lambda W(\mathbf{b}^*(\lambda F_1 + (1 - \lambda)F_2), F_1) + (1 - \lambda)$$

$$\times W(\mathbf{b}^*(\lambda F_1 + (1 - \lambda)F_2), F_2)$$

$$\leq \lambda W(\mathbf{b}^*(F_1), F_1) + (1 - \lambda)W^*(\mathbf{b}^*(F_2), F_2), \qquad (15.10)$$

since $\mathbf{b}^*(F_1)$ maximizes $W(\mathbf{b}, F_1)$ and $\mathbf{b}^*(F_2)$ maximizes $W(\mathbf{b}, F_2)$. $\square$

Lemma 15.1.2: *The set of log-optimal portfolios forms a convex set.*

Proof: Let $\mathbf{b}_1^*$ and $\mathbf{b}_2^*$ be any two portfolios in the set of log-optimal portfolios. By the previous lemma, the convex combination of $\mathbf{b}_1^*$ and $\mathbf{b}_2^*$ has a doubling rate greater than or equal to the doubling rate of $\mathbf{b}_1^*$ or $\mathbf{b}_2^*$, and hence the convex combination also achieves the maximum doubling rate. Hence the set of portfolios that achieves the maximum is convex. $\square$

In the next section, we will use these properties to characterize the log-optimal portfolio.

15.2 KUHN-TUCKER CHARACTERIZATION OF THE LOG-OPTIMAL PORTFOLIO

The determination $\mathbf{b}^*$ that achieves $W^*(F)$ is a problem of maximization of a concave function $W(\mathbf{b}, F)$ over a convex set $\mathbf{b} \in B$. The maximum may lie on the boundary. We can use the standard Kuhn-Tucker conditions to characterize the maximum. Instead, we will derive these conditions from first principles.

Theorem 15.2.1: *The log-optimal portfolio $\mathbf{b}^*$ for a stock market $\mathbf{X}$, i.e., the portfolio that maximizes the doubling rate $W(\mathbf{b}, F)$, satisfies the following necessary and sufficient conditions:*

$$E\left(\frac{X_i}{\mathbf{b}^{*t}\mathbf{X}}\right) \begin{array}{ll} =1 & \text{if} \quad b_i^* > 0, \\ \leq 1 & \text{if} \quad b_i^* = 0. \end{array} \qquad (15.11)$$

Proof: The doubling rate $W(\mathbf{b}) = E(\log \mathbf{b}^t \mathbf{X})$ is concave in $\mathbf{b}$, where $\mathbf{b}$ ranges over the simplex of portfolios. It follows that $\mathbf{b}^*$ is log-optimum iff the directional derivative of $W(\cdot)$ in the direction from $\mathbf{b}^*$ to any alternative portfolio $\mathbf{b}$ is non-positive. Thus, letting $\mathbf{b}_\lambda = (1 - \lambda)\mathbf{b}^* + \lambda\mathbf{b}$ for $0 \leq \lambda \leq 1$, we have

$$\frac{d}{d\lambda} W(\mathbf{b}_\lambda)|_{\lambda=0+} \leq 0, \quad \mathbf{b} \in \mathcal{B}. \qquad (15.12)$$

These conditions reduce to (15.11) since the one-sided derivative at $\lambda = 0+$ of $W(\mathbf{b}_\lambda)$ is

$$\frac{d}{d\lambda} E(\log(\mathbf{b}_\lambda^t\mathbf{X}))\Big|_{\lambda=0+} = \lim_{\lambda\downarrow 0} \frac{1}{\lambda} E\left(\log\left(\frac{(1-\lambda)\mathbf{b}^{*t}\mathbf{X} + \lambda\mathbf{b}^t\mathbf{X}}{\mathbf{b}^{*t}\mathbf{X}}\right)\right) \qquad (15.13)$$

$$= E\left(\lim_{\lambda\downarrow 0} \frac{1}{\lambda} \log\left(1 + \lambda\left(\frac{\mathbf{b}^t\mathbf{X}}{\mathbf{b}^{*t}\mathbf{X}} - 1\right)\right)\right) \qquad (15.14)$$

$$= E\left(\frac{\mathbf{b}^t\mathbf{X}}{\mathbf{b}^{*t}\mathbf{X}}\right) - 1, \qquad (15.15)$$

where the interchange of limit and expectation can be justified using the dominated convergence theorem [20]. Thus (15.12) reduces to

$$E\left(\frac{\mathbf{b}^t\mathbf{X}}{\mathbf{b}^{*t}\mathbf{X}}\right) - 1 \leq 0 \qquad (15.16)$$

for all $\mathbf{b} \in \mathcal{B}$.

If the line segment from $\mathbf{b}$ to $\mathbf{b}^*$ can be extended beyond $\mathbf{b}^*$ in the simplex, then the two-sided derivative at $\lambda = 0$ of $W(\mathbf{b}_\lambda)$ vanishes and (15.16) holds with equality. If the line segment from $\mathbf{b}$ to $\mathbf{b}^*$ cannot be extended, then we have an inequality in (15.16).

The Kuhn-Tucker conditions will hold for all portfolios $\mathbf{b} \in \mathcal{B}$ if they hold for all extreme points of the simplex $\mathcal{B}$ since $E(\mathbf{b}^t\mathbf{X}/\mathbf{b}^{*t}\mathbf{X})$ is linear in $\mathbf{b}$. Furthermore, the line segment from the jth extreme point $(\mathbf{b}: b_j = 1, b_i = 0, i \neq j)$ to $\mathbf{b}^*$ can be extended beyond $\mathbf{b}^*$ in the simplex iff $b_j^* > 0$. Thus the Kuhn-Tucker conditions which characterize log-optimum $\mathbf{b}^*$ are equivalent to the following necessary and sufficient conditions:

$$E\left(\frac{X_i}{\mathbf{b}^{*t}\mathbf{X}}\right) \begin{array}{ll} =1 & \text{if} \quad b_i^* > 0, \\ \leq 1 & \text{if} \quad b_i^* = 0. \end{array} \quad \square \qquad (15.17)$$

This theorem has a few immediate consequences. One surprising result is expressed in the following theorem:

Theorem 15.2.2: *Let $S^* = \mathbf{b}^{*t}\mathbf{X}$ be the random wealth resulting from the log-optimal portfolio $\mathbf{b}^*$. Let $S = \mathbf{b}^t\mathbf{X}$ be the wealth resulting from any other portfolio $\mathbf{b}$. Then*

$$E\frac{S}{S^*} \le 1. \tag{15.18}$$

Conversely, if $E(S/S^*) \le 1$ for all portfolios $\mathbf{b}$, then $E \log S/S^* \le 0$ for all $\mathbf{b}$.

Remark: This theorem can be stated more symmetrically as

$$E \ln \frac{S}{S^*} \le 0, \text{ for all } S \quad \Leftrightarrow \quad E\frac{S}{S^*} \le 1, \text{ for all } S. \tag{15.19}$$

Proof: From the previous theorem, it follows that for a log-optimal portfolio $\mathbf{b}^*$,

$$E\left(\frac{X_i}{\mathbf{b}^{*t}\mathbf{X}}\right) \le 1 \tag{15.20}$$

for all i. Multiplying this equation by b_i and summing over i, we have

$$\sum_{i=1}^{m} b_i E\left(\frac{X_i}{\mathbf{b}^{*t}\mathbf{X}}\right) \le \sum_{i=1}^{m} b_i = 1, \tag{15.21}$$

which is equivalent to

$$E\frac{\mathbf{b}^t\mathbf{X}}{\mathbf{b}^{*t}\mathbf{X}} = E\frac{S}{S^*} \le 1. \tag{15.22}$$

The converse follows from Jensen's inequality, since

$$E \log \frac{S}{S^*} \le \log E\frac{S}{S^*} \le \log 1 = 0. \quad \Box \tag{15.23}$$

Thus expected log ratio optimality is equivalent to expected ratio optimality.

Maximizing the expected logarithm was motivated by the asymptotic growth rate. But we have just shown that the log-optimal portfolio, in addition to maximizing the asymptotic growth rate, also "maximizes" the wealth relative for one day. We shall say more about the short term optimality of the log-optimal portfolio when we consider the game theoretic optimality of this portfolio.

Another consequence of the Kuhn-Tucker characterization of the log-optimal portfolio is the fact that the expected proportion of wealth in each stock under the log-optimal portfolio is unchanged from day to day.

Consider the stocks at the end of the first day. The initial allocation of wealth is $\mathbf{b}^*$. The proportion of the wealth in stock i at the end of the day is $b_i^* X_i / \mathbf{b}^{*t} \mathbf{X}$, and the expected value of this proportion is

$$E \, \frac{b_i^* X_i}{\mathbf{b}^{*t} \mathbf{X}} = b_i^* E \, \frac{X_i}{\mathbf{b}^{*t} \mathbf{X}} = b_i^* 1 = b_i^* . \tag{15.24}$$

Hence the expected proportion of wealth in stock i at the end of the day is the same as the proportion invested in stock i at the beginning of the day.

15.3   ASYMPTOTIC OPTIMALITY OF THE LOG-OPTIMAL PORTFOLIO

In the previous section, we introduced the log-optimal portfolio and explained its motivation in terms of the long term behavior of a sequence of investments in a repeated independent versions of the stock market. In this section, we will expand on this idea and prove that with probability 1, the conditionally log-optimal investor will not do any worse than any other investor who uses a causal investment strategy.

We first consider an i.i.d. stock market, i.e., $\mathbf{X}_1, \mathbf{X}_2, \ldots, \mathbf{X}_n$ are i.i.d. according to $F(\mathbf{x})$. Let

$$S_n - \prod_{i=1}^{n} \mathbf{b}_i^t \mathbf{X}_i \tag{15.25}$$

be the wealth after n days for an investor who uses portfolio $\mathbf{b}_i$ on day i. Let

$$W^* = \max_{\mathbf{b}} W(\mathbf{b}, F) = \max_{\mathbf{b}} E \log \mathbf{b}^t \mathbf{X} \tag{15.26}$$

be the maximal doubling rate and let $\mathbf{b}^*$ be a portfolio that achieves the maximum doubling rate.

We only allow portfolios that depend causally on the past and are independent of the future values of the stock market.

From the definition of W^*, it immediately follows that the log-optimal portfolio maximizes the expected log of the final wealth. This is stated in the following lemma.

Lemma 15.3.1: *Let S_n^* be the wealth after n days for the investor using the log-optimal strategy on i.i.d. stocks, and let S_n be the wealth of any other investor using a causal portfolio strategy $\mathbf{b}_i$. Then*

$$E \log S_n^* = n W^* \geq E \log S_n . \tag{15.27}$$

Proof:

$$\max_{\mathbf{b}_1, \mathbf{b}_2, \ldots, \mathbf{b}_n} E \log S_n = \max_{\mathbf{b}_1, \mathbf{b}_2, \ldots, \mathbf{b}_n} E \sum_{i=1}^{n} \log \mathbf{b}_i^t \mathbf{X}_i \qquad (15.28)$$

$$= \sum_{i=1}^{n} \max_{\mathbf{b}_i(\mathbf{X}_1, \mathbf{X}_2, \ldots, \mathbf{X}_{i-1})} E \log \mathbf{b}_i^t (\mathbf{X}_1, \mathbf{X}_2, \ldots, \mathbf{X}_{i-1}) \mathbf{X}_i$$

$$(15.29)$$

$$= \sum_{i=1}^{n} E \log \mathbf{b}^{*t} \mathbf{X}_i \qquad (15.30)$$

$$= nW^*, \qquad (15.31)$$

and the maximum is achieved by a constant portfolio strategy $\mathbf{b}^*$. □

So far, we have proved two simple consequences of the definition of log optimal portfolios, i.e., that $\mathbf{b}^*$ (satisfying (15.11)) maximizes the expected log wealth and that the wealth S_n^* is equal to 2^{nW^*} to first order in the exponent, with high probability.

Now we will prove a much stronger result, which shows that S_n^* exceeds the wealth (to first order in the exponent) of any other investor for almost every sequence of outcomes from the stock market.

Theorem 15.3.1 (*Asymptotic optimality of the log-optimal portfolio*): *Let* $\mathbf{X}_1, \mathbf{X}_2, \ldots, \mathbf{X}_n$ *be a sequence of i.i.d. stock vectors drawn according to* $F(\mathbf{x})$. *Let* $S_n^* = \Pi \mathbf{b}^{*t} \mathbf{X}_i$, *where* $\mathbf{b}^*$ *is the log-optimal portfolio, and let* $S_n = \Pi \mathbf{b}_i^t \mathbf{X}_i$ *be the wealth resulting from any other causal portfolio. Then*

$$\limsup_{n \to \infty} \frac{1}{n} \log \frac{S_n}{S_n^*} \leq 0 \quad \text{with probability 1}. \qquad (15.32)$$

Proof: From the Kuhn-Tucker conditions, we have

$$E \frac{S_n}{S_n^*} \leq 1. \qquad (15.33)$$

Hence by Markov's inequality, we have

$$\Pr(S_n > t_n S_n^*) = \Pr\left(\frac{S_n}{S_n^*} > t_n\right) < \frac{1}{t_n}. \qquad (15.34)$$

Hence

$$\Pr\left(\frac{1}{n} \log \frac{S_n}{S_n^*} > \frac{1}{n} \log t_n\right) \leq \frac{1}{t_n}. \qquad (15.35)$$

Setting $t_n = n^2$ and summing over n, we have

$$\sum_{n=1}^{\infty} \Pr\left(\frac{1}{n} \log \frac{S_n}{S_n^*} > \frac{2 \log n}{n}\right) \le \sum_{n=1}^{\infty} \frac{1}{n^2} = \frac{\pi^2}{6} . \tag{15.36}$$

Then, by the Borel-Cantelli lemma,

$$\Pr\left(\frac{1}{n} \log \frac{S_n}{S_n^*} > \frac{2 \log n}{n}, \text{ infinitely often}\right) = 0 . \tag{15.37}$$

This implies that for almost every sequence from the stock market, there exists an N such that for all $n > N$, $\frac{1}{n} \log \frac{S_n}{S_n^*} < \frac{2 \log n}{n}$. Thus

$$\limsup \frac{1}{n} \log \frac{S_n}{S_n^*} \le 0 \quad \text{with probability 1} . \quad \Box \tag{15.38}$$

The theorem proves that the log-optimal portfolio will do as well or better than any other portfolio to first order in the exponent.

15.4   SIDE INFORMATION AND THE DOUBLING RATE

We showed in Chapter 6 that side information Y for the horse race X can be used to increase the doubling rate by $I(X; Y)$ in the case of uniform odds. We will now extend this result to the stock market. Here, $I(X; Y)$ will be a (possibly unachievable) upper bound on the increase in the doubling rate.

Theorem 15.4.1: *Let* $\mathbf{X}_1, \mathbf{X}_2, \ldots, \mathbf{X}_n$ *be drawn i.i.d.* $\sim f(\mathbf{x})$. *Let* $\mathbf{b}_f^*$ *be the log-optimal portfolio corresponding to* $f(\mathbf{x})$ *and let* $\mathbf{b}_g^*$ *be the log-optimal portfolio corresponding to some other density* $g(\mathbf{x})$. *Then the increase in doubling rate by using* $\mathbf{b}_f^*$ *instead of* $\mathbf{b}_g^*$ *is bounded by*

$$\Delta W = W(\mathbf{b}_f^*, F) - W(\mathbf{b}_g^*, F) \le D(f \| g) \tag{15.39}$$

Proof: We have

$$\Delta W = \int f(\mathbf{x}) \log \mathbf{b}_f^{*t} \mathbf{x} - \int f(\mathbf{x}) \log \mathbf{b}_g^{*t} \mathbf{x} \tag{15.40}$$

$$= \int f(\mathbf{x}) \log \frac{\mathbf{b}_f^{*t} \mathbf{x}}{\mathbf{b}_g^{*t} \mathbf{x}} \tag{15.41}$$

$$= \int f(\mathbf{x}) \log \frac{\mathbf{b}_f^{*t} \mathbf{x}}{\mathbf{b}_g^{*t} \mathbf{x}} \frac{g(\mathbf{x})}{f(\mathbf{x})} \frac{f(\mathbf{x})}{g(\mathbf{x})} \tag{15.42}$$

$$= \int f(\mathbf{x}) \log \frac{\mathbf{b}_f^{*t} \mathbf{x}}{\mathbf{b}_g^{*t} \mathbf{x}} \frac{g(\mathbf{x})}{f(\mathbf{x})} + D(f \| g) \tag{15.43}$$

$$\overset{(a)}{\leq} \log \int f(\mathbf{x}) \frac{\mathbf{b}_f^{*t} \mathbf{x}}{\mathbf{b}_g^{*t} \mathbf{x}} \frac{g(\mathbf{x})}{f(\mathbf{x})} + D(f \| g) \tag{15.44}$$

$$= \log \int g(\mathbf{x}) \frac{\mathbf{b}_f^{*t} \mathbf{x}}{\mathbf{b}_g^{*t} \mathbf{x}} + D(f \| g) \tag{15.45}$$

$$\overset{(b)}{\leq} \log 1 + D(f \| g) \tag{15.46}$$

$$= D(f \| g), \tag{15.47}$$

where (a) follows from Jensen's inequality and (b) follows from the Kuhn-Tucker conditions and the fact that $\mathbf{b}_g^*$ is log-optimal for g. $\square$

Theorem 15.4.2: *The increase ΔW in doubling rate due to side information Y is bounded by*

$$\Delta W \leq I(\mathbf{X}; Y). \tag{15.48}$$

Proof: Given side information $Y = y$, the log-optimal investor uses the conditional log-optimal portfolio for the conditional distribution $f(\mathbf{x}|Y = y)$. Hence, conditional on $Y = y$, we have, from Theorem 15.4.1,

$$\Delta W_{Y=y} \leq D(f(\mathbf{x}|Y = y) \| f(\mathbf{x})) = \int_{\mathbf{x}} f(\mathbf{x}|Y = y) \log \frac{f(\mathbf{x}|Y = y)}{f(\mathbf{x})} \, d\mathbf{x}. \tag{15.49}$$

Averaging this over possible values of Y, we have

$$\Delta W \leq \int_y f(y) \int_{\mathbf{x}} f(\mathbf{x}|Y = y) \log \frac{f(\mathbf{x}|Y = y)}{f(\mathbf{x})} \, d\mathbf{x} \, dy \tag{15.50}$$

$$= \int_y \int_{\mathbf{x}} f(y) f(\mathbf{x}|Y = y) \log \frac{f(\mathbf{x}|Y = y)}{f(\mathbf{x})} \frac{f(y)}{f(y)} \, d\mathbf{x} \, dy \tag{15.51}$$

$$= \int_y \int_{\mathbf{x}} f(\mathbf{x}, y) \log \frac{f(\mathbf{x}, y)}{f(\mathbf{x}) f(y)} \, d\mathbf{x} \, dy \tag{15.52}$$

$$= I(\mathbf{X}; Y). \tag{15.53}$$

Hence the increase in doubling rate is bounded above by the mutual information between the side information Y and the stock market $\mathbf{X}$. $\square$

15.5   INVESTMENT IN STATIONARY MARKETS

We now extend some of the results of the previous section from i.i.d. markets to time-dependent market processes.

Let $\mathbf{X}_1, \mathbf{X}_2, \ldots, \mathbf{X}_n, \ldots$ be a vector-valued stochastic process. We will consider investment strategies that depend on the past values of the market in a causal fashion, i.e., $\mathbf{b}_i$ may depend on $\mathbf{X}_1, \mathbf{X}_2, \ldots, \mathbf{X}_{i-1}$. Let

$$S_n = \prod_{i=1}^{n} \mathbf{b}_i^t(\mathbf{X}_1, \mathbf{X}_2, \ldots, \mathbf{X}_{i-1})\mathbf{X}_i . \tag{15.54}$$

Our objective is to maximize $E \log S_n$ over all such causal portfolio strategies $\{\mathbf{b}_i(\cdot)\}$. Now

$$\max_{\mathbf{b}_1, \mathbf{b}_2, \ldots, \mathbf{b}_n} E \log S_n = \sum_{i=1}^{n} \max_{\mathbf{b}_i^t(\mathbf{X}_1, \mathbf{X}_2, \ldots, \mathbf{X}_{i-1})} \log \mathbf{b}_i^t \mathbf{X}_i \tag{15.55}$$

$$= \sum_{i=1}^{n} \log \mathbf{b}_i^{*t} \mathbf{X}_i , \tag{15.56}$$

where $\mathbf{b}_i^*$ is the log-optimal portfolio for the conditional distribution of $\mathbf{X}_i$ given the past values of the stock market, i.e., $\mathbf{b}_i^*(\mathbf{x}_1, \mathbf{x}_2, \ldots, \mathbf{x}_{i-1})$ is the portfolio that achieves the conditional maximum, which is denoted by

$$\max_{\mathbf{b}} E[\log \mathbf{b}^t \mathbf{X}_i | (\mathbf{X}_1, \mathbf{X}_2, \ldots, \mathbf{X}_{i-1}) = (\mathbf{x}_1, \mathbf{x}_2, \ldots, \mathbf{x}_{i-1})]$$

$$= W^*(\mathbf{X}_i | \mathbf{x}_1, \mathbf{x}_2, \ldots, \mathbf{x}_{i-1}) \tag{15.57}$$

Taking the expectation over the past, we write

$$W^*(\mathbf{X}_i | \mathbf{X}_1, \mathbf{X}_2, \ldots, \mathbf{X}_{i-1}) = E \max_{\mathbf{b}} E[\log \mathbf{b}^{*t} \mathbf{X}_i | (\mathbf{X}_1, \mathbf{X}_2, \ldots, \mathbf{X}_{i-1})]$$

$$\tag{15.58}$$

as the conditional optimal doubling rate, where the maximum is over all portfolio-valued functions $\mathbf{b}$ defined on $\mathbf{X}_1, \ldots, \mathbf{X}_{i-1}$. Thus the highest expected log return is achieved by using the conditional log-optimal portfolio at each stage. Let

$$W^*(\mathbf{X}_1, \mathbf{X}_2, \ldots, \mathbf{X}_n) = \max_{\mathbf{b}_1, \mathbf{b}_2, \ldots, \mathbf{b}_n} E \log S_n \tag{15.59}$$

where the maximum is over all causal portfolio strategies. Then since $\log S_n^* = \sum_{i=1}^{m} \log \mathbf{b}_i^{*t} \mathbf{X}_i$, we have the following chain rule for W^*:

$$W^*(\mathbf{X}_1, \mathbf{X}_2, \ldots, \mathbf{X}_n) = \sum_{i=1}^{n} W^*(\mathbf{X}_i | \mathbf{X}_1, \mathbf{X}_2, \ldots, \mathbf{X}_{i-1}) . \tag{15.60}$$

This chain rule is formally the same as the chain rule for H. In some ways, W is the dual of H. In particular, conditioning reduces H but increases W.

Definition: The *doubling rate* W_∞^* is defined as

$$W_\infty^* = \lim_{n \to \infty} \frac{W^*(\mathbf{X}_1, \mathbf{X}_2, \ldots, \mathbf{X}_n)}{n} \qquad (15.61)$$

if the limit exists and is undefined otherwise.

Theorem 15.5.1: *For a stationary market, the doubling rate exists and is equal to*

$$W_\infty^* = \lim_{n \to \infty} W^*(\mathbf{X}_n | \mathbf{X}_1, \mathbf{X}_2, \ldots, \mathbf{X}_{n-1}) . \qquad (15.62)$$

Proof: By stationarity, $W^*(\mathbf{X}_n | \mathbf{X}_1, \mathbf{X}_2, \ldots, \mathbf{X}_{n-1})$ is non-decreasing in n. Hence it must have a limit, possibly ∞. Since

$$\frac{W^*(\mathbf{X}_1, \mathbf{X}_2, \ldots, \mathbf{X}_n)}{n} = \frac{1}{n} \sum_{i=1}^{n} W^*(\mathbf{X}_i | \mathbf{X}_1, \mathbf{X}_2, \ldots, \mathbf{X}_{i-1}), \qquad (15.63)$$

it follows by the theorem of the Cesáro mean that the left hand side has the same limit as the limit of the terms on the right hand side.

Hence W_∞^* exists and

$$W_\infty^* = \lim \frac{W^*(\mathbf{X}_1, \mathbf{X}_2, \ldots, \mathbf{X}_n)}{n} = \lim W^*(\mathbf{X}_n | \mathbf{X}_1, \mathbf{X}_2, \ldots, \mathbf{X}_{n-1}) . \quad \square$$

$$(15.64)$$

We can now extend the asymptotic optimality property to stationary markets. We have the following theorem.

Theorem 15.5.2: *Let S_n^* be the wealth resulting from a series of conditionally log-optimal investments in a stationary stock market $\{\mathbf{X}_i\}$. Let S_n be the wealth resulting from any other causal portfolio strategy. Then*

$$\limsup_{n \to \infty} \frac{1}{n} \log \frac{S_n}{S_n^*} \le 0 . \qquad (15.65)$$

Proof: From the Kuhn-Tucker conditions for the constrained maximization, we have

$$E \frac{S_n}{S_n^*} \le 1 , \qquad (15.66)$$

which follows from repeated application of the conditional version of the Kuhn-Tucker conditions, at each stage conditioning on all the previous outcomes. The rest of the proof is identical to the proof for the i.i.d. stock market and will not be repeated. □

For a stationary ergodic market, we can also extend the asymptotic equipartition property to prove the following theorem.

Theorem 15.5.3 (*AEP for the stock market*): *Let* $\mathbf{X}_1, \mathbf{X}_2, \ldots, \mathbf{X}_n$ *be a stationary ergodic vector-valued stochastic process. Let* S_n^* *be the wealth at time n for the conditionally log-optimal strategy, where*

$$S_n^* = \prod_{i=1}^{n} \mathbf{b}_i^{*t}(\mathbf{X}_1, \mathbf{X}_2, \ldots, \mathbf{X}_{i-1})\mathbf{X}_i \,. \tag{15.67}$$

Then

$$\frac{1}{n} \log S_n^* \to W^* \quad \text{with probability 1} \,. \tag{15.68}$$

Proof: The proof involves a modification of the sandwich argument that is used to prove the AEP in Section 15.7. The details of the proof are omitted. □

15.6 COMPETITIVE OPTIMALITY OF THE LOG-OPTIMAL PORTFOLIO

We now ask whether the log-optimal portfolio outperforms alternative portfolios at a given finite time n. As a direct consequence of the Kuhn-Tucker conditions, we have

$$E \frac{S_n}{S_n^*} \leq 1 \,, \tag{15.69}$$

and hence by Markov's inequality,

$$\Pr(S_n > tS_n^*) \leq \frac{1}{t} \,. \tag{15.70}$$

This result is similar to the result derived in Chapter 5 for the competitive optimality of Shannon codes.

By considering examples, it can be seen that it is not possible to get a better bound on the probability that $S_n > S_n^*$. Consider a stock market with two stocks and two possible outcomes,

$$(X_1, X_2) = \begin{cases} (1, 1 + \epsilon) & \text{with probability } 1 - \epsilon \,, \\ (1, 0) & \text{with probability } \epsilon \,. \end{cases} \qquad (15.71)$$

In this market, the log-optimal portfolio invests all the wealth in the first stock. (It is easy to verify $\mathbf{b} = (1, 0)$ satisfies the Kuhn-Tucker conditions.) However, an investor who puts all his wealth in the second stock earns more money with probability $1 - \epsilon$. Hence, we cannot prove that with high probability the log-optimal investor will do better than any other investor.

The problem with trying to prove that the log-optimal investor does best with a probability of at least one half is that there exist examples like the one above, where it is possible to beat the log optimal investor by a small amount most of the time. We can get around this by adding an additional fair randomization, which has the effect of reducing the effect of small differences in the wealth.

Theorem 15.6.1 (*Competitive optimality*): *Let S^* be the wealth at the end of one period of investment in a stock market $\mathbf{X}$ with the log-optimal portfolio, and let S be the wealth induced by any other portfolio. Let U^* be a random variable independent of $\mathbf{X}$ uniformly distributed on $[0, 2]$, and let V be any other random variable independent of $\mathbf{X}$ and U with $V \geq 0$ and $EV = 1$. Then*

$$\Pr(VS \geq U^*S^*) \leq \frac{1}{2} \,. \qquad (15.72)$$

Remark: Here U and V correspond to initial "fair" randomizations of the initial wealth. This exchange of initial wealth $S_0 = 1$ for "fair" wealth U can be achieved in practice by placing a fair bet.

Proof: We have

$$\Pr(VS \geq U^*S^*) = \Pr\left(\frac{VS}{S^*} \geq U^*\right) \qquad (15.73)$$

$$= \Pr(W \geq U^*) \,, \qquad (15.74)$$

where $W = \frac{VS}{S^*}$ is a non-negative valued random variable with mean

$$EW = E(V)E\left(\frac{S_n}{S_n^*}\right) \leq 1 \,, \qquad (15.75)$$

by the independence of V from $\mathbf{X}$ and the Kuhn-Tucker conditions.

Let F be the distribution function of W. Then since U^* is uniform on $[0, 2]$,

$$\Pr(W \geq U^*) = \int_0^2 \Pr(W > w) f_{U^*}(w) \, dw \qquad (15.76)$$

$$= \int_0^2 \Pr(W > w) \frac{1}{2} \, dw \qquad (15.77)$$

$$= \int_0^2 \frac{1 - F(w)}{2} \, dw \qquad (15.78)$$

$$\leq \int_0^\infty \frac{1 - F(w)}{2} \, dw \qquad (15.79)$$

$$= \frac{1}{2} EW \qquad (15.80)$$

$$\leq \frac{1}{2} , \qquad (15.81)$$

using the easily proved fact (by integrating by parts) that

$$EW = \int_0^\infty (1 - F(w)) \, dw \qquad (15.82)$$

for a positive random variable W. Hence we have

$$\Pr(VS \geq U^*S^*) = \Pr(W \geq U^*) \leq \frac{1}{2} . \quad \square \qquad (15.83)$$

This theorem provides a short term justification for the use of the log-optimal portfolio. If the investor's only objective is to be ahead of his opponent at the end of the day in the stock market, and if fair randomization is allowed, then the above theorem says that the investor should exchange his wealth for a uniform [0, 2] wealth and then invest using the log-optimal portfolio. This is the game theoretic solution to the problem of gambling competitively in the stock market.

Finally, to conclude our discussion of the stock market, we consider the example of the horse race once again. The horse race is a special case of the stock market, in which there are m stocks corresponding to the m horses in the race. At the end of the race, the value of the stock for horse i is either 0 or o_i, the value of the odds for horse i. Thus $\mathbf{X}$ is non-zero only in the component corresponding to the winning horse.

In this case, the log-optimal portfolio is proportional betting, i.e. $b_i^* = p_i$, and in the case of uniform fair odds

$$W^* = \log m - H(X) . \qquad (15.84)$$

When we have a sequence of correlated horse races, then the optimal portfolio is conditional proportional betting and the asymptotic doubling rate is

$$W^* = \log m - H(\mathscr{X}), \tag{15.85}$$

where $H(\mathscr{X}) = \lim \frac{1}{n} H(X_1, X_2, \ldots, X_n)$, if the limit exists. Then Theorem 15.5.3 asserts that

$$S_n^* \doteq 2^{nW^*}. \tag{15.86}$$

15.7 THE SHANNON-McMILLAN-BREIMAN THEOREM

The AEP for ergodic processes has come to be known as the Shannon-McMillan-Breiman theorem. In Chapter 3, we proved the AEP for i.i.d. sources. In this section, we offer a proof of the theorem for a general ergodic source. We avoid some of the technical details by using a "sandwich" argument, but this section is technically more involved than the rest of the book.

In a sense, an ergodic source is the most general dependent source for which the strong law of large numbers holds. The technical definition requires some ideas from probability theory. To be precise, an ergodic source is defined on a probability space $(\Omega, \mathscr{B}, P)$, where $\mathscr{B}$ is a sigma-algebra of subsets of Ω and P is a probability measure. A random variable X is defined as a function $X(\omega)$, $\omega \in \Omega$, on the probability space. We also have a transformation $T : \Omega \to \Omega$, which plays the role of a time shift. We will say that the transformation is *stationary* if $\mu(TA) = \mu(A)$, for all $A \in \mathscr{B}$. The transformation is called *ergodic* if every set A such that $TA = A$, a.e., satisfies $\mu(A) = 0$ or 1. If T is stationary and ergodic, we say that the process defined by $X_n(\omega) = X(T^n\omega)$ is stationary and ergodic. For a stationary ergodic source with a finite expected value, Birkhoff's ergodic theorem states that

$$\frac{1}{n} \sum_{i=1}^{n} X_i(\omega) \to EX = \int X \, dP \quad \text{with probability 1}. \tag{15.87}$$

Thus the law of large numbers holds for ergodic processes.

We wish to use the ergodic theorem to conclude that

$$-\frac{1}{n} \log p(X_0, X_1, \ldots, X_{n-1}) = -\frac{1}{n} \sum_{i=0}^{n-1} \log p(X_i | X_0^{i-1})$$

$$\to \lim_{n \to \infty} E[-\log p(X_n | X_0^{n-1})]. \tag{15.88}$$

But the stochastic sequence $p(X_i | X_0^{i-1})$ is not ergodic. However, the closely related quantities $p(X_i|X_{i-k}^{i-1})$ and $p(X_i|X_{-\infty}^{i-1})$ are ergodic and have expectations easily identified as entropy rates. We plan to sandwich $p(X_i|X_0^{i-1})$ between these two more tractable processes.

We define

$$H^k = E\{-\log p(X_k|X_{k-1}, X_{k-2}, \ldots, X_0)\} \qquad (15.89)$$

$$= E\{-\log p(X_0|X_{-1}, X_{-2}, \ldots, X_{-k})\}, \qquad (15.90)$$

where the last equation follows from stationarity. Recall that the entropy rate is given by

$$H = \lim_{k \to \infty} H^k \qquad (15.91)$$

$$= \lim_{n \to \infty} \frac{1}{n} \sum_{k=0}^{n-1} H^k . \qquad (15.92)$$

Of course, $H^k \searrow H$ by stationarity and the fact that conditioning does not increase entropy. It will be crucial that $H^k \searrow H = H^\infty$, where

$$H^\infty = E\{-\log p(X_0|X_{-1}, X_{-2}, \ldots)\} . \qquad (15.93)$$

The proof that $H^\infty = H$ involves exchanging expectation and limit.

The main idea in the proof goes back to the idea of (conditional) proportional gambling. A gambler with the knowledge of the k past will have a growth rate of wealth $1 - H^k$, while a gambler with a knowledge of the infinite past will have a growth rate of wealth of $1 - H^\infty$. We don't know the wealth growth rate of a gambler with growing knowledge of the past X_0^n, but it is certainly sandwiched between $1 - H^k$ and $1 - H^\infty$. But $H^k \searrow H = H^\infty$. Thus the sandwich closes and the growth rate must be $1 - H$.

We will prove the theorem based on lemmas that will follow the proof.

Theorem 15.7.1 (*AEP: The Shannon-McMillan-Breiman theorem*): *If H is the entropy rate of a finite-valued stationary ergodic process $\{X_n\}$, then*

$$-\frac{1}{n} \log p(X_0, \ldots, X_{n-1}) \to H, \quad \text{with probability 1} \qquad (15.94)$$

Proof: We argue that the sequence of random variables $-\frac{1}{n} \log p(X_0^{n-1})$ is asymptotically sandwiched between the upper bound H^k and the lower bound H^∞ for all $k \geq 0$. The AEP will follow since $H^k \to H^\infty$ and $H^\infty = H$.

The kth order Markov approximation to the probability is defined for $n \geq k$ as

$$p^k(X_0^{n-1}) = p(X_0^{k-1}) \prod_{i=k}^{n-1} p(X_i | X_{i-k}^{i-1}) \,. \tag{15.95}$$

From Lemma 15.7.3, we have

$$\limsup_{n \to \infty} \frac{1}{n} \log \frac{p^k(X_0^{n-1})}{p(X_0^{n-1})} \le 0 \,, \tag{15.96}$$

which we rewrite, taking the existence of the limit $\frac{1}{n} \log p^k(X_0^n)$ into account (Lemma 15.7.1), as

$$\limsup_{n \to \infty} \frac{1}{n} \log \frac{1}{p(X_0^{n-1})} \le \lim_{n \to \infty} \frac{1}{n} \log \frac{1}{p^k(X_0^{n-1})} = H^k \tag{15.97}$$

for $k = 1, 2, \dots$. Also, from Lemma 15.7.3, we have

$$\limsup_{n \to \infty} \frac{1}{n} \log \frac{p(X_0^{n-1})}{p(X_0^{n-1} | X_{-\infty}^{-1})} \le 0 \,, \tag{15.98}$$

which we rewrite as

$$\liminf \frac{1}{n} \log \frac{1}{p(X_0^{n-1})} \ge \lim \frac{1}{n} \log \frac{1}{p(X_0^{n-1} | X_{-\infty}^{-1})} = H^\infty \tag{15.99}$$

from the definition of H^∞ in Lemma 15.7.1.

Putting together (15.97) and (15.99), we have

$$H^\infty \le \liminf -\frac{1}{n} \log p(X_0^{n-1}) \le \limsup -\frac{1}{n} \log p(X_0^{n-1}) \le H^k \quad \text{for all } k \,. \tag{15.100}$$

But, by Lemma 15.7.2, $H^k \to H^\infty = H$. Consequently,

$$\lim -\frac{1}{n} \log p(X_0^n) = H \,. \quad \Box \tag{15.101}$$

We will now prove the lemmas that were used in the main proof. The first lemma uses the ergodic theorem.

Lemma 15.7.1 (*Markov approximations*): *For a stationary ergodic stochastic process* $\{X_n\}$,

$$-\frac{1}{n} \log p^k(X_0^{n-1}) \to H^k \qquad \text{with probability 1}, \tag{15.102}$$

$$-\frac{1}{n} \log p(X_0^{n-1} | X_{-\infty}^{-1}) \to H^\infty \quad \text{with probability 1}. \tag{15.103}$$

Proof: Functions $Y_n = f(X^n_{-\infty})$ of ergodic processes $\{X_i\}$ are ergodic processes. Thus $p(X_n|X^{n-1}_{n-k})$ and $\log p(X_n|X_{n-1}, X_{n-2}, \ldots,)$ are also ergodic processes, and

$$-\frac{1}{n} \log p^k(X^{n-1}_0) = -\frac{1}{n} \log p(X^{k-1}_0) - \frac{1}{n} \sum_{i=k}^{n-1} \log p(X_i|X^{i-1}_{i-k}) \quad (15.104)$$

$$\to 0 + H^k, \quad \text{with probability 1} \quad (15.105)$$

by the ergodic theorem. Similarly, by the ergodic theorem,

$$-\frac{1}{n} \log p(X^{n-1}_0|X_{-1}, X_{-2}, \ldots) - -\frac{1}{n} \sum_{i=k}^{n-1} \log p(X_i|X^{i-1}_{i-k}, X_{-1}, X_{-2}, \ldots) \quad (15.106)$$

$$\to H^\infty \quad \text{with probability 1.} \quad (15.107)$$

Lemma 15.7.2 (*No gap*): $H^k \searrow H^\infty$ and $H = H^\infty$.

Proof: We know that for stationary processes, $H^k \searrow H$, so it remains to show that $H^k \searrow H^\infty$, thus yielding $H = H^\infty$. Levy's martingale convergence theorem for conditional probabilities asserts that

$$p(x_0|X^{-1}_{-k}) \to p(x_0|X^{-1}_{-\infty}) \quad \text{with probability 1} \quad (15.108)$$

for all $x_0 \in \mathcal{X}$. Since $\mathcal{X}$ is finite and $p \log p$ is bounded and continuous in p for all $0 \le p \le 1$, the bounded convergence theorem allows interchange of expectation and limit, yielding

$$\lim_{k\to\infty} H^k = \lim_{k\to\infty} E\left\{ -\sum_{x_0 \in \mathcal{X}} p(x_0|X^{-1}_{-k}) \log p(x_0|X^{-1}_{-k}) \right\} \quad (15.109)$$

$$= E\left\{ -\sum_{x_0 \in \mathcal{X}} p(x_0|X^{-1}_{-\infty}) \log p(x_0|X^{-1}_{-\infty}) \right\} \quad (15.110)$$

$$= H^\infty. \quad (15.111)$$

Thus $H^k \searrow H = H^\infty$. $\square$

Lemma 15.7.3 (*Sandwich*):

$$\limsup_{n\to\infty} \frac{1}{n} \log \frac{p^k(X^{n-1}_0)}{p(X^{n-1}_0)} \le 0, \quad (15.112)$$

$$\limsup \frac{1}{n} \log \frac{p(X^{n-1}_0)}{p(X^{n-1}_0|X^{-1}_{-\infty})} \le 0. \quad (15.113)$$

Proof: Let A be the support set of $p(X_0^{n-1})$. Then

$$E\left\{\frac{p^k(X_0^{n-1})}{p(X_0^{n-1})}\right\} = \sum_{x_0^{n-1} \in A} p(x_0^{n-1}) \frac{p^k(x_0^{n-1})}{p(x_0^{n-1})} \tag{15.114}$$

$$= \sum_{x_0^{n-1} \in A} p^k(x_0^{n-1}) \tag{15.115}$$

$$= p^k(A) \tag{15.116}$$

$$\leq 1 . \tag{15.117}$$

Similarly, let $B(X_{-\infty}^{-1})$ denote the support set of $p(\cdot | X_{-\infty}^{-1})$. Then, we have

$$E\left\{\frac{p(X_0^{n-1})}{p(X_0^{n-1}|X_{-\infty}^{-1})}\right\} = E\left[E\left\{\frac{p(X_0^{n-1})}{p(X_0^{n-1}|X_{-\infty}^{-1})} \Big| X_{-\infty}^{-1}\right\}\right] \tag{15.118}$$

$$= E\left[\sum_{x^n \in B(X_{-\infty}^{-1})} \frac{p(x^n)}{p(x^n|X_{-\infty}^{-1})} p(x^n|X_{-\infty}^{-1})\right] \tag{15.119}$$

$$= E\left[\sum_{x^n \in B(X_{-\infty}^{-1})} p(x^n)\right] \tag{15.120}$$

$$\leq 1 . \tag{15.121}$$

By Markov's inequality and (15.117), we have

$$\Pr\left\{\frac{p^k(X_0^{n-1})}{p(X_0^{n-1})} \geq t_n\right\} \leq \frac{1}{t_n} \tag{15.122}$$

or

$$\Pr\left\{\frac{1}{n} \log \frac{p^k(X_0^{n-1})}{p(X_0^{n-1})} \geq \frac{1}{n} \log t_n\right\} \leq \frac{1}{t_n} . \tag{15.123}$$

Letting $t_n = n^2$ and noting that $\sum_{n=1}^{\infty} \frac{1}{n^2} < \infty$, we see by the Borel-Cantelli lemma that the event

$$\left\{\frac{1}{n} \log \frac{p^k(X_0^{n-1})}{p(X_0^{n-1})} \geq \frac{1}{n} \log t_n\right\} \tag{15.124}$$

occurs only finitely often with probability 1. Thus

$$\limsup \frac{1}{n} \log \frac{p^k(X_0^{n-1})}{p(X_0^{n-1})} \leq 0 \text{ with probability } 1 . \tag{15.125}$$

Applying the same arguments using Markov's inequality to (15.121), we obtain

$$\limsup \frac{1}{n} \log \frac{p(X_0^{n-1})}{p(X_0^{n-1}|X_{-\infty}^{-1})} \le 0 \quad \text{with probability } 1 ,$$

$$(15.126)$$

proving the lemma. $\square$

The arguments used in the proof can be extended to prove the AEP for the stock market (Theorem 15.5.3).

SUMMARY OF CHAPTER 15

Doubling rate: The *doubling rate* of a stock market portfolio **b** with respect to a distribution $F(\mathbf{x})$ is defined as

$$W(\mathbf{b}, F) = \int \log \mathbf{b}'\mathbf{x} \, dF(\mathbf{x}) = E(\log \mathbf{b}'\mathbf{X}) . \qquad (15.127)$$

Log-optimal portfolio: The *optimal doubling rate* is

$$W^*(F) = \max_{\mathbf{b}} W(\mathbf{b}, F) \qquad (15.128)$$

The portfolio **b*** that achieves the maximum of $W(\mathbf{b}, F)$ is called the *log-optimal portfolio*.

Concavity: $W(\mathbf{b}, F)$ is concave in **b** and linear in F. $W^*(F)$ is convex in F.

Optimality conditions: The portfolio **b*** is log-optimal if and only if

$$E\left(\frac{X_i}{\mathbf{b}^{*'}\mathbf{X}}\right) \begin{array}{l} = 1 \quad \text{if } b_i^* > 0 , \\ \le 1 \quad \text{if } b_i^* = 0 . \end{array} \qquad (15.129)$$

Expected ratio optimality: Letting $S_n^* = \prod_{i=1}^{n} \mathbf{b}^{*'}\mathbf{X}_i$, $S_n = \prod_{i=1}^{n} \mathbf{b}_i'\mathbf{X}_i$, we have

$$E \frac{S_n}{S_n^*} \le 1 . \qquad (15.130)$$

Growth rate (AEP):

$$\frac{1}{n} \log S_n^* \to W^*(F) \quad \text{with probability } 1 . \qquad (15.131)$$

Asymptotic optimality:

$$\limsup_{n \to \infty} \frac{1}{n} \log \frac{S_n}{S_n^*} \le 0 \quad \text{with probability } 1 . \qquad (15.132)$$

Wrong information: Believing g when f is true loses

$$\Delta W = W(\mathbf{b}_f^*, F) - W(\mathbf{b}_g^*, F) \le D(f \| g) . \tag{15.133}$$

Side information Y:

$$\Delta W \le I(\mathbf{X}; Y) . \tag{15.134}$$

Chain rule:

$$W^*(\mathbf{X}_i | \mathbf{X}_1, \mathbf{X}_2, \ldots, \mathbf{X}_{i-1}) = \max_{\mathbf{b}_i(\mathbf{x}_1, \mathbf{x}_2, \ldots, \mathbf{x}_{i-1})} E \log \mathbf{b}_i^t \mathbf{X}_i \tag{15.135}$$

$$W^*(\mathbf{X}_1, \mathbf{X}_2, \ldots, \mathbf{X}_n) = \sum_{i=1}^{n} W^*(\mathbf{X}_i | \mathbf{X}_1, \mathbf{X}_2, \ldots, \mathbf{X}_{i-1}) . \tag{15.136}$$

Doubling rate for a stationary market:

$$W_\infty^* = \lim \frac{W^*(\mathbf{X}_1, \mathbf{X}_2, \ldots, \mathbf{X}_n)}{n} \tag{15.137}$$

Competitive optimality of log-optimal portfolios:

$$\Pr(VS \ge U^*S^*) \le \frac{1}{2} . \tag{15.138}$$

AEP: If $\{X_i\}$ is stationary ergodic, then

$$-\frac{1}{n} \log p(X_1, X_2, \ldots, X_n) \to H(\mathcal{X}) \quad \text{with probability 1} . \tag{15.139}$$

PROBLEMS FOR CHAPTER 15

1. *Doubling rate.* Let

$$\mathbf{X} = \begin{cases} (1, a), & \text{with probability } 1/2 \\ (1, 1/a), & \text{with probability } 1/2 \end{cases},$$

where $a > 1$. This vector $\mathbf{X}$ represents a stock market vector of cash vs. a hot stock. Let

$$W(\mathbf{b}, F) = E \log \mathbf{b}^t \mathbf{X},$$

and

$$W^* = \max_{\mathbf{b}} W(\mathbf{b}, F)$$

be the doubling rate.
(a) Find the log optimal portfolio $\mathbf{b}^*$.
(b) Find the doubling rate W^*.

(c) Find the asymptotic behavior of

$$S_n = \prod_{i=1}^{n} \mathbf{b}^t \mathbf{X}_i$$

for all $\mathbf{b}$.

2. *Side information.* Suppose, in the previous problem, that

$$Y = \begin{cases} 1, & \text{if } (X_1, X_2) \geq (1, 1), \\ 0, & \text{if } (X_1, X_2) \leq (1, 1). \end{cases}$$

Let the portfolio $\mathbf{b}$ depend on Y. Find the new doubling rate W^{**} and verify that $\Delta W = W^{**} - W^*$ satisfies

$$\Delta W \leq I(X; Y).$$

3. *Stock market.* Consider a stock market vector

$$\mathbf{X} = (X_1, X_2).$$

Suppose $X_1 = 2$ with probability 1.

(a) Find necessary and sufficient conditions on the distribution of stock X_2 such that the log optimal portfolio $\mathbf{b}^*$ invests all the wealth in stock X_2, i.e., $\mathbf{b}^* = (0, 1)$.

(b) Argue that the doubling rate satisfies $W^* \geq 1$.

HISTORICAL NOTES

There is an extensive literature on the mean-variance approach to investment in the stock market. A good introduction is the book by Sharpe [250]. Log optimal portfolios were introduced by Kelly [150] and Latané [172] and generalized by Breiman [45]. See Samuelson [225, 226] for a criticism of log-optimal investment. An adaptive portfolio counterpart to universal data compression is given in Cover [66].

The proof of the competitive optimality of the log-optimal portfolio is due to Bell and Cover [20, 21]. The AEP for the stock market and the asymptotic optimality of log-optimal investment are given in Algoet and Cover [9]. The AEP for ergodic processes was proved in full generality by Barron [18] and Orey [202]. The sandwich proof for the AEP is based on Algoet and Cover [8].

Chapter 16

Inequalities in Information Theory

This chapter summarizes and reorganizes the inequalities found throughout this book. A number of new inequalities on the entropy rates of subsets and the relationship of entropy and $\mathcal{L}_p$ norms are also developed. The intimate relationship between Fisher information and entropy is explored, culminating in a common proof of the entropy power inequality and the Brunn-Minkowski inequality. We also explore the parallels between the inequalities in information theory and inequalities in other branches of mathematics such as matrix theory and probability theory.

16.1 BASIC INEQUALITIES OF INFORMATION THEORY

Many of the basic inequalities of information theory follow directly from convexity.

Definition: A function f is said to be convex if

$$f(\lambda x_1 + (1 - \lambda)x_2) \le \lambda f(x_1) + (1 - \lambda)f(x_2) \tag{16.1}$$

for all $0 \le \lambda \le 1$ and all x_1 and x_2 in the convex domain of f.

Theorem 16.1.1 (*Theorem 2.6.2: Jensen's inequality*): *If f is convex, then*

$$f(EX) \le Ef(X). \tag{16.2}$$

Lemma 16.1.1: *The function* $\log x$ *is a concave function and* $x \log x$ *is a convex function of* x, *for* $0 \leq x < \infty$.

Theorem 16.1.2 (*Theorem 2.7.1: Log sum inequality*): *For positive numbers,* $a_1, a_2, \ldots, a_n$ *and* $b_1, b_2, \ldots, b_n$,

$$\sum_{i=1}^{n} a_i \log \frac{a_i}{b_i} \geq \left(\sum_{i=1}^{n} a_i \right) \log \frac{(\sum_{i=1}^{n} a_i)}{(\sum_{i=1}^{n} b_i)} \tag{16.3}$$

with equality iff $\frac{a_i}{b_i} = constant$.

We have the following properties of entropy from Section 2.1.

Definition: The entropy $H(X)$ of a discrete random variable X is defined by

$$H(X) = - \sum_{x \in \mathcal{X}} p(x) \log p(x) . \tag{16.4}$$

Theorem 16.1.3 (*Lemma 2.1.1, Theorem 2.6.4: Entropy bound*):

$$0 \leq H(X) \leq \log|\mathcal{X}| \tag{16.5}$$

Theorem 16.1.4 (*Theorem 2.6.5: Conditioning reduces entropy*): *For any two random variables* X *and* Y,

$$H(X|Y) \leq H(X) , \tag{16.6}$$

with equality iff X *and* Y *are independent.*

Theorem 16.1.5 (*Theorem 2.5.1 with Theorem 2.6.6: Chain rule*):

$$H(X_1, X_2, \ldots, X_n) = \sum_{i=1}^{n} H(X_i|X_{i-1}, \ldots, X_1) \leq \sum_{i=1}^{n} H(X_i) , \tag{16.7}$$

with equality iff $X_1, X_2, \ldots, X_n$ *are independent.*

Theorem 16.1.6 (*Theorem 2.7.3*): $H(\mathbf{p})$ *is a concave function of* $\mathbf{p}$.

We now state some properties of relative entropy and mutual information (Section 2.3).

Definition: The *relative entropy* or *Kullback Leibler distance* between two probability mass functions $p(x)$ and $q(x)$ on the same set $\mathcal{X}$ is defined by

$$D(p\|q) = \sum_{x \in \mathcal{X}} p(x) \log \frac{p(x)}{q(x)} . \tag{16.8}$$

Definition: The mutual information between two random variables X and Y is defined by

$$I(X; Y) = \sum_{x \in \mathcal{X}} \sum_{y \in \mathcal{Y}} p(x, y) \log \frac{p(x, y)}{p(x)p(y)} = D(p(x, y)\|p(x)p(y)) . \tag{16.9}$$

The following basic information inequality can be used to prove many of the other inequalities in this chapter.

Theorem 16.1.7 (*Theorem 2.6.3: Information inequality*): *For any two probability mass functions* **p** *and* **q**,

$$D(\mathbf{p}\|\mathbf{q}) \geq 0 \tag{16.10}$$

with equality iff $p(x) = q(x)$ *for all* $x \in \mathcal{X}$.

Corollary: *For any two random variables, X and Y,*

$$I(X; Y) = D(p(x, y)\|p(x)p(y)) \geq 0 \tag{16.11}$$

with equality iff $p(x, y) = p(x)p(y)$, *i.e., X and Y are independent.*

Theorem 16.1.8 (*Theorem 2.7.2: Convexity of relative entropy*): $D(p\|q)$ *is convex in the pair* (p, q).

Theorem 16.1.9 (*Section 2.4*):

$$I(X; Y) = H(X) - H(X|Y) , \tag{16.12}$$

$$I(X; Y) = H(Y) - H(Y|X) , \tag{16.13}$$

$$I(X; Y) = H(X) + H(Y) - H(X, Y) , \tag{16.14}$$

$$I(X; X) = H(X) . \tag{16.15}$$

Theorem 16.1.10 (*Section 2.9*): *For a Markov chain:*

1. *Relative entropy* $D(\mu_n\|\mu_n')$ *decreases with time.*
2. *Relative entropy* $D(\mu_n\|\mu)$ *between a distribution and the stationary distribution decreases with time.*
3. *Entropy* $H(X_n)$ *increases if the stationary distribution is uniform.*

4. *The conditional entropy* $H(X_n|X_1)$ *increases with time for a stationary Markov chain.*

Theorem 16.1.11 (*Problem 34, Chapter 2*): *Let* $X_1, X_2, \ldots, X_n$ *be i.i.d.* $\sim p(x)$. *Let* $\hat{p}_n$ *be the empirical probability mass function of* $X_1, X_2, \ldots, X_n$. *Then*

$$ED(\hat{p}_n \| p) \le ED(\hat{p}_{n-1} \| p) . \tag{16.16}$$

16.2   DIFFERENTIAL ENTROPY

We now review some of the basic properties of differential entropy (Section 9.1).

Definition: The *differential entropy* $h(X_1, X_2, \ldots, X_n)$, sometimes written $h(f)$, is defined by

$$h(X_1, X_2, \ldots, X_n) = -\int f(\mathbf{x}) \log f(\mathbf{x}) \, d\mathbf{x} . \tag{16.17}$$

The differential entropy for many common densities is given in Table 16.1 (taken from Lazo and Rathie [265]).

Definition: The *relative entropy* between probability densities f and g is

$$D(f \| g) = \int f(\mathbf{x}) \log \left(f(\mathbf{x})/g(\mathbf{x}) \right) d\mathbf{x} . \tag{16.18}$$

The properties of the continuous version of relative entropy are identical to the discrete version. Differential entropy, on the other hand, has some properties that differ from those of discrete entropy. For example, differential entropy may be negative.

We now restate some of the theorems that continue to hold for differential entropy.

Theorem 16.2.1 (*Theorem 9.6.1: Conditioning reduces entropy*): $h(X|Y) \le h(X)$, *with equality iff* X *and* Y *are independent.*

Theorem 16.2.2 (*Theorem 9.6.2: Chain rule*):

$$h(X_1, X_2, \ldots, X_n) = \sum_{i=1}^{n} h(X_i|X_{i-1}, X_{i-2}, \ldots, X_1) \le \sum_{i=1}^{n} h(X_i) \tag{16.19}$$

with equality iff $X_1, X_2, \ldots, X_n$ *are independent.*

TABLE 16.1. Table of differential entropies. All entropies are in nats. $\Gamma(z) = \int_0^\infty e^{-t} t^{z-1}\, dt.$ $\psi(z) = \frac{d}{dz}\Gamma(z).$ $\gamma = $ **Euler's constant** $= 0.57721566\ldots.$ $B(p, q) = \Gamma(p)\Gamma(q)/\Gamma(p+q).$

Distribution		Entropy (in nats)
Name	Density	
Beta	$f(w) = \dfrac{x^{p-1}(1-x)^{q-1}}{B(p,q)},$ $0 \le x \le 1,\ p, q > 0$	$\ln B(p, q) - (p-1)$ $\times [\psi(p) - \psi(p+q)]$ $-(q-1)[\psi(q) - \psi(p+q)]$
Cauchy	$f(x) = \dfrac{\lambda}{\pi}\dfrac{1}{\lambda^2 + x^2},$ $-\infty < x < \infty,\ \lambda > 0$	$\ln(4\pi\lambda)$
Chi	$f(x) = \dfrac{2}{2^{n/2}\sigma^n\,\Gamma(n/2)}\, x^{n-1} e^{-\frac{x^2}{2\sigma^2}},$ $x > 0,\ n > 0$	$\ln \dfrac{\sigma\Gamma(n/2)}{\sqrt{2}} - \dfrac{n-1}{2}\,\psi\!\left(\dfrac{n}{2}\right) + \dfrac{n}{2}$
Chi-squared	$f(x) = \dfrac{1}{2^{n/2}\sigma^n\Gamma(n/2)}\, x^{\frac{n}{2}-1} e^{-\frac{x}{2\sigma^2}},$ $x > 0,\ n > 0$	$\ln 2\sigma^2\Gamma(n/2)$ $-\left(1 - \dfrac{n}{2}\right)\psi\!\left(\dfrac{n}{2}\right) + \dfrac{n}{2}$
Erlang	$f(x) = \dfrac{\beta^n}{(n-1)!}\, x^{n-1} e^{-\beta x},$ $x, \beta > 0,\ n > 0$	$(1-n)\psi(n) + \ln \dfrac{\Gamma(n)}{\beta} + n$
Exponential	$f(x) = \dfrac{1}{\lambda}\, e^{-\frac{x}{\lambda}},\quad x, \lambda > 0$	$1 + \ln \lambda$
F	$f(x) = \dfrac{n_1^{\frac{n_1}{2}} n_2^{\frac{n_2}{2}}}{B\!\left(\frac{n_1}{2}, \frac{n_2}{2}\right)}\, \dfrac{x^{\frac{n_1}{2}-1}}{(n_2 + n_1 x)^{\frac{n_1+n_2}{2}}},$	$\ln \dfrac{n_1}{n_2}\, B\!\left(\dfrac{n_1}{2}, \dfrac{n_2}{2}\right)$ $+ \left(1 - \dfrac{n_1}{2}\right)\psi\!\left(\dfrac{n_1}{2}\right)$ $- \left(1 + \dfrac{n_2}{2}\right)\psi\!\left(\dfrac{n_2}{2}\right)$ $+ \dfrac{n_1+n_2}{2}\,\psi\!\left(\dfrac{n_1+n_2}{2}\right)$
Gamma	$f(x) = \dfrac{x^{\alpha-1} e^{-\frac{x}{\beta}}}{\beta^\alpha \Gamma(\alpha)},$ $x, \alpha, \beta > 0$	$\ln(\beta\Gamma(\alpha)) + (1-\alpha)$ $\times \psi(\alpha) + \alpha$
Laplace	$f(x) = \dfrac{1}{2\lambda}\, e^{-\frac{|x-\theta|}{\lambda}},$ $-\infty < x, \theta < \infty,\ \lambda > 0$	$1 + \ln(2\lambda)$

TABLE 16.1. (*Continued*)

	Distribution		Entropy (in nats)
Name	Density		
Logistic	$f(x) = \dfrac{e^{-x}}{(1 + e^{-x})^2}$, $-\infty < x < \infty$		2
Lognormal	$f(x) = \dfrac{1}{\sigma x \sqrt{2\pi}} e^{-\frac{(\ln x - m)^2}{2\sigma^2}}$, $x > 0$, $-\infty < m < \infty$, $\sigma > 0$		$m + \frac{1}{2} \ln(2\pi e \sigma^2)$
Maxwell-Boltzmann	$f(x) = 4\pi^{-\frac{1}{2}} \beta^{\frac{3}{2}} x^2 e^{-\beta x^2}$, $x, \beta > 0$		$\frac{1}{2} \ln \frac{\pi}{\beta} + \gamma - \frac{1}{2}$
Normal	$f(x) = \dfrac{1}{\sqrt{2\pi\sigma^2}} e^{-\frac{(x-\mu)^2}{2\sigma^2}}$, $-\infty < x, \mu < \infty$, $\sigma > 0$		$\frac{1}{2} \ln(2\pi e \sigma^2)$
Generalized normal	$f(x) = \dfrac{2\beta^{\frac{\alpha}{2}}}{\Gamma(\frac{\alpha}{2})} x^{\alpha - 1} e^{-\beta x^2}$, $x, \alpha, \beta > 0$		$\ln \dfrac{\Gamma(\frac{\alpha}{2})}{2\beta^{\frac{1}{2}}} - \frac{\alpha - 1}{2} \psi(\frac{\alpha}{2}) + \frac{\alpha}{2}$
Pareto	$f(x) = \dfrac{ak^a}{x^{a+1}}$, $x \geq k > 0$, $a > 0$		$\ln \frac{k}{a} + 1 + \frac{1}{a}$
Rayleigh	$f(x) = \dfrac{x}{b^2} e^{-\frac{x^2}{2b^2}}$, $x, b > 0$		$1 + \ln \frac{b}{\sqrt{2}} + \frac{\gamma}{2}$
Student-t	$f(x) = \dfrac{(1 + x^2/n)^{-\frac{n+1}{2}}}{\sqrt{n}B(\frac{1}{2}, \frac{n}{2})}$, $-\infty < x < \infty$, $n > 0$		$\frac{n+1}{2} \psi(\frac{n+1}{2}) - \psi(\frac{n}{2})$ $+ \ln \sqrt{n} B(\frac{1}{2}, \frac{n}{2})$
Triangular	$f(x) = \begin{cases} \frac{2x}{a} & 0 \leq x \leq a \\ \frac{2(1-x)}{1-a} & a \leq x \leq 1 \end{cases}$		$\frac{1}{2} - \ln 2$
Uniform	$f(x) = \frac{1}{\beta - \alpha}$, $\alpha \leq x \leq \beta$		$\ln(\beta - \alpha)$
Weibull	$f(x) = \dfrac{c}{\alpha} x^{c-1} e^{-\frac{x^c}{\alpha}}$, $x, c, \alpha > 0$		$\frac{(c-1)\gamma}{c} + \ln \frac{\alpha^{1/c}}{c} + 1$

Lemma 16.2.1: *If X and Y are independent, then* $h(X + Y) \geq h(X)$.

Proof: $h(X + Y) \geq h(X + Y|Y) = h(X|Y) = h(X)$. □

Theorem 16.2.3 *(Theorem 9.6.5): Let the random vector* $\mathbf{X} \in \mathbf{R}^n$ *have zero mean and covariance* $K = \mathbf{EXX}^t$, *i.e.,* $K_{ij} = EX_iX_j$, $1 \leq i, j \leq n$. *Then*

$$h(\mathbf{X}) \leq \frac{1}{2} \log(2\pi e)^n |K|, \tag{16.20}$$

with equality iff $\mathbf{X} \sim \mathcal{N}(0, K)$.

16.3 BOUNDS ON ENTROPY AND RELATIVE ENTROPY

In this section, we revisit some of the bounds on the entropy function. The most useful is Fano's inequality, which is used to bound away from zero the probability of error of the best decoder for a communication channel at rates above capacity.

Theorem 16.3.1 *(Theorem 2.11.1: Fano's inequality): Given two random variables X and Y, let* P_e *be the probability of error in the best estimator of X given Y. Then*

$$H(P_e) + P_e \log(|\mathcal{X}| - 1) \geq H(X|Y). \tag{16.21}$$

Consequently, if $H(X|Y) > 0$, *then* $P_e > 0$.

Theorem 16.3.2 *(*$\mathcal{L}_1$ *bound on entropy): Let p and q be two probability mass functions on* $\mathcal{X}$ *such that*

$$\|p - q\|_1 = \sum_{x \in \mathcal{X}} |p(x) - q(x)| \leq \frac{1}{2}. \tag{16.22}$$

Then

$$|H(p) - H(q)| \leq -\|p - q\|_1 \log \frac{\|p - q\|_1}{|\mathcal{X}|}. \tag{16.23}$$

Proof: Consider the function $f(t) = -t \log t$ shown in Figure 16.1. It can be verified by differentiation that the function $f(\cdot)$ is concave. Also $f(0) = f(1) = 0$. Hence the function is positive between 0 and 1.

Consider the chord of the function from t to $t + \nu$ (where $\nu \leq \frac{1}{2}$). The maximum absolute slope of the chord is at either end (when $t = 0$ or $1 - \nu$). Hence for $0 \leq t \leq 1 - \nu$, we have

$$|f(t) - f(t + \nu)| \leq \max\{f(\nu), f(1 - \nu)\} = -\nu \log \nu. \tag{16.24}$$

Let $r(x) = |p(x) - q(x)|$. Then

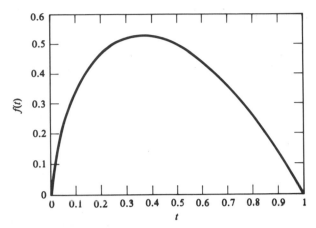

Figure 16.1. The function $f(t) = -t \log t$.

$$|H(p) - H(q)| = \left| \sum_{x \in \mathcal{X}} (-p(x) \log p(x) + q(x) \log q(x)) \right| \tag{16.25}$$

$$\leq \sum_{x \in \mathcal{X}} |(-p(x) \log p(x) + q(x) \log q(x))| \tag{16.26}$$

$$\leq \sum_{x \in \mathcal{X}} -r(x) \log r(x) \tag{16.27}$$

$$= \|p - q\|_1 \sum_{x \in \mathcal{X}} -\frac{r(x)}{\|p - q\|_1} \log \frac{r(x)}{\|p - q\|_1} \|p - q\|_1 \tag{16.28}$$

$$= -\|p - q\|_1 \log \|p - q\|_1 + \|p - q\|_1 H\left(\frac{r(x)}{\|p - q\|_1}\right) \tag{16.29}$$

$$\leq -\|p - q\|_1 \log \|p - q\|_1 + \|p - q\|_1 \log|\mathcal{X}|, \tag{16.30}$$

where (16.27) follows from (16.24).   □

We can use the concept of differential entropy to obtain a bound on the entropy of a distribution.

Theorem 16.3.3 (*Theorem 9.7.1*):

$$H(p_1, p_2, \dots) \leq \frac{1}{2} \log(2\pi e)\left(\sum_{i=1}^{\infty} p_i i^2 - \left(\sum_{i=1}^{\infty} ip_i\right)^2 + \frac{1}{12}\right). \tag{16.31}$$

Finally, relative entropy is stronger than the $\mathcal{L}_1$ norm in the following sense:

Lemma 16.3.1 (*Lemma 12.6.1*):

$$D(p_1 \| p_2) \geq \frac{1}{2 \ln 2} \|p_1 - p_2\|_1^2. \tag{16.32}$$

16.4 INEQUALITIES FOR TYPES

The method of types is a powerful tool for proving results in large deviation theory and error exponents. We repeat the basic theorems:

Theorem 16.4.1 (*Theorem 12.1.1*): *The number of types with denominator n is bounded by*

$$|\mathscr{P}_n| \leq (n+1)^{|\mathscr{X}|} . \tag{16.33}$$

Theorem 16.4.2 (*Theorem 12.1.2*): *If* $X_1, X_2, \ldots, X_n$ *are drawn i.i.d. according to* $Q(x)$, *then the probability of* x^n *depends only on its type and is given by*

$$Q^n(x^n) = 2^{-n(H(P_{x^n}) + D(P_{x^n} \| Q))} . \tag{16.34}$$

Theorem 16.4.3 (*Theorem 12.1.3: Size of a type class T(P)*): *For any type* $P \in \mathscr{P}_n$,

$$\frac{1}{(n+1)^{|\mathscr{X}|}} \, 2^{nH(P)} \leq |T(P)| \leq 2^{nH(P)} . \tag{16.35}$$

Theorem 16.4.4 (*Theorem 12.1.4*): *For any* $P \in \mathscr{P}_n$ *and any distribution* Q, *the probability of the type class* $T(P)$ *under* Q^n *is* $2^{-nD(P\|Q)}$ *to first order in the exponent. More precisely,*

$$\frac{1}{(n+1)^{|\mathscr{X}|}} \, 2^{-nD(P\|Q)} \leq Q^n(T(P)) \leq 2^{-nD(P\|Q)} . \tag{16.36}$$

16.5 ENTROPY RATES OF SUBSETS

We now generalize the chain rule for differential entropy. The chain rule provides a bound on the entropy rate of a collection of random variables in terms of the entropy of each random variable:

$$h(X_1, X_2, \ldots, X_n) \leq \sum_{i=1}^{n} h(X_i) . \tag{16.37}$$

We extend this to show that the entropy per element of a subset of a set of random variables decreases as the size of the set increases. This is not true for each subset but is true on the average over subsets, as expressed in the following theorem.

Definition: Let $(X_1, X_2, \ldots, X_n)$ have a density, and for every $S \subseteq \{1, 2, \ldots, n\}$, denote by $X(S)$ the subset $\{X_i : i \in S\}$. Let

$$h_k^{(n)} = \frac{1}{\binom{n}{k}} \sum_{S : |S|=k} \frac{h(X(S))}{k} . \tag{16.38}$$

Here $h_k^{(n)}$ is the average entropy in bits per symbol of a randomly drawn k-element subset of $\{X_1, X_2, \ldots, X_n\}$.

The following theorem by Han [130] says that the average entropy decreases monotonically in the size of the subset.

Theorem 16.5.1:

$$h_1^{(n)} \geq h_2^{(n)} \geq \cdots \geq h_n^{(n)} . \tag{16.39}$$

Proof: We first prove the last inequality, $h_n^{(n)} \leq h_{n-1}^{(n)}$. We write

$$h(X_1, X_2, \ldots, X_n) = h(X_1, X_2, \ldots, X_{n-1}) + h(X_n | X_1, X_2, \ldots, X_{n-1}),$$

$$h(X_1, X_2, \ldots, X_n) = h(X_1, X_2, \ldots, X_{n-2}, X_n)$$

$$+ h(X_{n-1} | X_1, X_2, \ldots, X_{n-2}, X_n)$$

$$\leq h(X_1, X_2, \ldots, X_{n-2}, X_n) + h(X_{n-1} | X_1, X_2, \ldots, X_{n-2}),$$

$$\vdots$$

$$h(X_1, X_2, \ldots, X_n) \leq h(X_2, X_3, \ldots, X_n) + h(X_1) .$$

Adding these n inequalities and using the chain rule, we obtain

$$nh(X_1, X_2, \ldots, X_n) \leq \sum_{i=1}^{n} h(X_1, X_2, \ldots, X_{i-1}, X_{i+1}, \ldots, X_n)$$

$$+ h(X_1, X_2, \ldots, X_n) \tag{16.40}$$

or

$$\frac{1}{n} h(X_1, X_2, \ldots, X_n) \leq \frac{1}{n} \sum_{i=1}^{n} \frac{h(X_1, X_2, \ldots, X_{i-1}, X_{i+1}, \ldots, X_n)}{n-1} , \tag{16.41}$$

which is the desired result $h_n^{(n)} \leq h_{n-1}^{(n)}$.

We now prove that $h_k^{(n)} \leq h_{k-1}^{(n)}$ for all $k \leq n$ by first conditioning on a k-element subset, and then taking a uniform choice over its $(k-1)$-element subsets. For each k-element subset, $h_k^{(k)} \leq h_{k-1}^{(k)}$, and hence the inequality remains true after taking the expectation over all k-element subsets chosen uniformly from the n elements. $\square$

Theorem 16.5.2: *Let $r > 0$, and define*

$$t_k^{(n)} = \frac{1}{\binom{n}{k}} \sum_{S\,:\,|S|=k} e^{\frac{rh(X(S))}{k}}.$$

(16.42)

Then

$$t_1^{(n)} \geq t_2^{(n)} \geq \cdots \geq t_n^{(n)}.$$

(16.43)

Proof: Starting from (16.41) in the previous theorem, we multiply both sides by r, exponentiate and then apply the arithmetic mean geometric mean inequality to obtain

$$e^{\frac{1}{n} rh(X_1, X_2, \ldots, X_n)} \leq e^{\frac{1}{n} \sum_{i=1}^{n} \frac{rh(X_1, X_2, \ldots, X_{i-1}, X_{i+1}, \ldots, X_n)}{n-1}}$$

(16.44)

$$\leq \frac{1}{n} \sum_{i=1}^{n} e^{\frac{rh(X_1, X_2, \ldots, X_{i-1}, X_{i+1}, \ldots, X_n)}{n-1}} \qquad \text{for all } r \geq 0,$$

(16.45)

which is equivalent to $t_n^{(n)} \leq t_{n-1}^{(n)}$. Now we use the same arguments as in the previous theorem, taking an average over all subsets to prove the result that for all $k \leq n$, $t_k^{(n)} \leq t_{k-1}^{(n)}$. $\quad\square$

Definition: The average *conditional entropy rate per element* for all subsets of size k is the average of the above quantities for k-element subsets of $\{1, 2, \ldots, n\}$, i.e.,

$$g_k^{(n)} = \frac{1}{\binom{n}{k}} \sum_{S\,:\,|S|=k} \frac{h(X(S)|X(S^c))}{k}.$$

(16.46)

Here $g_k(S)$ is the entropy per element of the set S conditional on the elements of the set S^c. When the size of the set S increases, one can expect a greater dependence among the elements of the set S, which explains Theorem 16.5.1.

In the case of the conditional entropy per element, as k increases, the size of the conditioning set S^c decreases and the entropy of the set S increases. The increase in entropy per element due to the decrease in conditioning dominates the decrease due to additional dependence among the elements, as can be seen from the following theorem due to Han [130]. Note that the conditional entropy ordering in the following theorem is the reverse of the unconditional entropy ordering in Theorem 16.5.1.

Theorem 16.5.3:

$$g_1^{(n)} \leq g_2^{(n)} \leq \cdots \leq g_n^{(n)}.$$

(16.47)

Proof: The proof proceeds on lines very similar to the proof of the theorem for the unconditional entropy per element for a random subset. We first prove that $g_n^{(n)} \geq g_{n-1}^{(n)}$ and then use this to prove the rest of the inequalities.

By the chain rule, the entropy of a collection of random variables is less than the sum of the entropies, i.e.,

$$h(X_1, X_2, \ldots, X_n) \leq \sum_{i=1}^{n} h(X_i). \tag{16.48}$$

Subtracting both sides of this inequality from $nh(X_1, X_2, \ldots, X_n)$, we have

$$(n-1)h(X_1, X_2, \ldots, X_n) \geq \sum_{i=1}^{n} (h(X_1, X_2, \ldots, X_n) - h(X_i)) \tag{16.49}$$

$$= \sum_{i=1}^{n} h(X_1, \ldots, X_{i-1}, X_{i+1}, \ldots, X_n | X_i). \tag{16.50}$$

Dividing this by $n(n-1)$, we obtain

$$\frac{h(X_1, X_2, \ldots, X_n)}{n} \geq \frac{1}{n} \sum_{i=1}^{n} \frac{h(X_1, X_2, \ldots, X_{i-1}, X_{i+1}, \ldots, X_n | X_i)}{n-1}, \tag{16.51}$$

which is equivalent to $g_n^{(n)} \geq g_{n-1}^{(n)}$.

We now prove that $g_k^{(n)} \geq g_{k-1}^{(n)}$ for all $k \leq n$ by first conditioning on a k-element subset, and then taking a uniform choice over its $(k-1)$-element subsets. For each k-element subset, $g_k^{(k)} \geq g_{k-1}^{(k)}$, and hence the inequality remains true after taking the expectation over all k-element subsets chosen uniformly from the n elements. $\square$

Theorem 16.5.4: *Let*

$$f_k^{(n)} = \frac{1}{\binom{n}{k}} \sum_{S : |S| = k} \frac{I(X(S); X(S^c))}{k}. \tag{16.52}$$

Then

$$f_1^{(n)} \geq f_2^{(n)} \geq \cdots \geq f_n^{(n)}. \tag{16.53}$$

Proof: The theorem follows from the identity $I(X(S); X(S^c)) = h(X(S)) - h(X(S)|X(S^c))$ and Theorems 16.5.1 and 16.5.3. $\square$

16.6 ENTROPY AND FISHER INFORMATION

The differential entropy of a random variable is a measure of its descriptive complexity. The Fisher information is a measure of the minimum error in estimating a parameter of a distribution. In this section, we will derive a relationship between these two fundamental quantities and use this to derive the entropy power inequality.

Let X be any random variable with density $f(x)$. We introduce a location parameter θ and write the density in a parametric form as $f(x - \theta)$. The Fisher information (Section 12.11) with respect to θ is given by

$$J(\theta) = \int_{-\infty}^{\infty} f(x - \theta)\left[\frac{\partial}{\partial \theta} \ln f(x - \theta)\right]^2 dx .\tag{16.54}$$

In this case, differentiation with respect to x is equivalent to differentiation with respect to θ. So we can write the Fisher information as

$$J(X) = \int_{-\infty}^{\infty} f(x - \theta)\left[\frac{\partial}{\partial x} \ln f(x - \theta)\right]^2 dx = \int_{-\infty}^{\infty} f(x)\left[\frac{\partial}{\partial x} \ln f(x)\right]^2 dx ,$$
$$\tag{16.55}$$

which we can rewrite as

$$J(X) = \int_{-\infty}^{\infty} f(x)\left[\frac{\frac{\partial}{\partial x} f(x)}{f(x)}\right]^2 dx .\tag{16.56}$$

We will call this the Fisher information of the distribution of X. Notice that, like entropy, it is a function of the density.

The importance of Fisher information is illustrated in the following theorem:

Theorem 16.6.1 (*Theorem 12.11.1: Cramér-Rao inequality*): *The mean squared error of any unbiased estimator $T(X)$ of the parameter θ is lower bounded by the reciprocal of the Fisher information, i.e.,*

$$\mathrm{var}(T) \geq \frac{1}{J(\theta)} .\tag{16.57}$$

We now prove a fundamental relationship between the differential entropy and the Fisher information:

Theorem 16.6.2 (*de Bruijn's identity: Entropy and Fisher information*): *Let X be any random variable with a finite variance with a* *density f(x). Let Z be an independent normally distributed random variable with zero mean and unit variance. Then*

$$\frac{\partial}{\partial t} h_e(X + \sqrt{t}Z) = \frac{1}{2} J(X + \sqrt{t}Z),\qquad(16.58)$$

where h_e is the differential entropy to base e. In particular, if the limit exists as $t \to 0$,

$$\frac{\partial}{\partial t} h_e(X + \sqrt{t}Z)\Big|_{t=0} = \frac{1}{2} J(X).\qquad(16.59)$$

Proof: Let $Y_t = X + \sqrt{t}Z$. Then the density of Y_t is

$$g_t(y) = \int_{-\infty}^{\infty} f(x) \frac{1}{\sqrt{2\pi t}} e^{-\frac{(y-x)^2}{2t}} dx .\qquad(16.60)$$

Then

$$\frac{\partial}{\partial t} g_t(y) = \int_{-\infty}^{\infty} f(x) \frac{\partial}{\partial t}\left[\frac{1}{\sqrt{2\pi t}} e^{-\frac{(y-x)^2}{2t}}\right] dx \qquad(16.61)$$

$$= \int_{-\infty}^{\infty} f(x)\left[-\frac{1}{2t}\frac{1}{\sqrt{2\pi t}} e^{-\frac{(y-x)^2}{2t}} + \frac{(y-x)^2}{2t^2}\frac{1}{\sqrt{2\pi t}} e^{-\frac{(y-x)^2}{2t}}\right] dx .$$
$$(16.62)$$

We also calculate

$$\frac{\partial}{\partial y} g_t(y) = \int_{-\infty}^{\infty} f(x) \frac{1}{\sqrt{2\pi t}} \frac{\partial}{\partial y}\left[e^{-\frac{(y-x)^2}{2t}}\right] dx \qquad(16.63)$$

$$= \int_{-\infty}^{\infty} f(x) \frac{1}{\sqrt{2\pi t}}\left[-\frac{y-x}{t} e^{-\frac{(y-x)^2}{2t}}\right] dx \qquad(16.64)$$

and

$$\frac{\partial^2}{\partial y^2} g_t(y) = \int_{-\infty}^{\infty} f(x) \frac{1}{\sqrt{2\pi t}} \frac{\partial}{\partial y}\left[-\frac{y-x}{t} e^{-\frac{(y-x)^2}{2t}}\right] dx \qquad(16.65)$$

$$= \int_{-\infty}^{\infty} f(x) \frac{1}{\sqrt{2\pi t}}\left[-\frac{1}{t} e^{-\frac{(y-x)^2}{2t}} + \frac{(y-x)^2}{t^2} e^{-\frac{(y-x)^2}{2t}}\right] dx. \qquad(16.66)$$

Thus

$$\frac{\partial}{\partial t} g_t(y) = \frac{1}{2} \frac{\partial^2}{\partial y^2} g_t(y).\qquad(16.67)$$

We will use this relationship to calculate the derivative of the entropy of Y_t, where the entropy is given by

$$h_e(Y_t) = -\int_{-\infty}^{\infty} g_t(y) \ln g_t(y)\, dy\,. \tag{16.68}$$

Differentiating, we obtain

$$\frac{\partial}{\partial t} h_e(Y_t) = -\int_{-\infty}^{\infty} \frac{\partial}{\partial t} g_t(y)\, dy - \int_{-\infty}^{\infty} \frac{\partial}{\partial t} g_t(y) \ln g_t(y)\, dy \tag{16.69}$$

$$= -\frac{\partial}{\partial t} \int_{-\infty}^{\infty} g_t(y)\, dy - \frac{1}{2}\int_{-\infty}^{\infty} \frac{\partial^2}{\partial y^2} g_t(y) \ln g_t(y)\, dy\,. \tag{16.70}$$

The first term is zero since $\int g_t(y)\, dy = 1$. The second term can be integrated by parts to obtain

$$\frac{\partial}{\partial t} h_e(Y_t) = -\frac{1}{2}\left[\frac{\partial g_t(y)}{\partial y} \ln g_t(y)\right]_{-\infty}^{\infty} + \frac{1}{2}\int_{-\infty}^{\infty}\left[\frac{\partial}{\partial y} g_t(y)\right]^2 \frac{1}{g_t(y)}\, dy\,. \tag{16.71}$$

The second term in (16.71) is $\frac{1}{2}J(Y_t)$. So the proof will be complete if we show that the first term in (16.71) is zero. We can rewrite the first term as

$$\frac{\partial g_t(y)}{\partial y} \ln g_t(y) = \left[\frac{\frac{\partial g_t(y)}{\partial y}}{\sqrt{g_t(y)}}\right][2\sqrt{g_t(y)} \ln \sqrt{g_t(y)}]\,. \tag{16.72}$$

The square of the first factor integrates to the Fisher information, and hence must be bounded as $y \to \pm\infty$. The second factor goes to zero since $x \ln x \to 0$ as $x \to 0$ and $g_t(y) \to 0$ as $y \to \pm\infty$. Hence the first term in (16.71) goes to 0 at both limits and the theorem is proved.

In the proof, we have exchanged integration and differentiation in (16.61), (16.63), (16.65) and (16.69). Strict justification of these exchanges requires the application of the bounded convergence and mean value theorems; the details can be found in Barron [15]. $\square$

This theorem can be used to prove the entropy power inequality, which gives a lower bound on the entropy of a sum of independent random variables.

Theorem 16.6.3: (*Entropy power inequality*): *If* **X** *and* **Y** *are independent random n-vectors with densities, then*

$$2^{\frac{2}{n}h(\mathbf{X}+\mathbf{Y})} \geq 2^{\frac{2}{n}h(\mathbf{X})} + 2^{\frac{2}{n}h(\mathbf{Y})}\,. \tag{16.73}$$

We outline the basic steps in the proof due to Stam [257] and Blachman [34]. The next section contains a different proof.

Stam's proof of the entropy power inequality is based on a perturbation argument. Let $X_t = X + \sqrt{f(t)}Z_1$, $Y_t = Y + \sqrt{g(t)}Z_2$, where Z_1 and Z_2 are independent $\mathcal{N}(0,1)$ random variables. Then the entropy power inequality reduces to showing that $s(0) \le 1$, where we define

$$s(t) = \frac{2^{2h(X_t)} + 2^{2h(Y_t)}}{2^{2h(X_t+Y_t)}} . \tag{16.74}$$

If $f(t) \to \infty$ and $g(t) \to \infty$ as $t \to \infty$, then it is easy to show that $s(\infty) = 1$. If, in addition, $s'(t) \ge 0$ for $t \ge 0$, this implies that $s(0) \le 1$. The proof of the fact that $s'(t) \ge 0$ involves a clever choice of the functions $f(t)$ and $g(t)$, an application of Theorem 16.6.2 and the use of a convolution inequality for Fisher information,

$$\frac{1}{J(X+Y)} \ge \frac{1}{J(X)} + \frac{1}{J(Y)} . \tag{16.75}$$

The entropy power inequality can be extended to the vector case by induction. The details can be found in papers by Stam [257] and Blachman [34].

16.7   THE ENTROPY POWER INEQUALITY AND THE BRUNN-MINKOWSKI INEQUALITY

The entropy power inequality provides a lower bound on the differential entropy of a sum of two independent random vectors in terms of their individual differential entropies. In this section, we restate and outline a new proof of the entropy power inequality. We also show how the entropy power inequality and the Brunn-Minkowski inequality are related by means of a common proof.

We can rewrite the entropy power inequality in a form that emphasizes its relationship to the normal distribution. Let X and Y be two independent random variables with densities, and let X' and Y' be independent normals with the same entropy as X and Y, respectively. Then $2^{2h(X)} = 2^{2h(X')} = (2\pi e)\sigma_{X'}^2$ and similarly $2^{2h(Y)} = (2\pi e)\sigma_{Y'}^2$. Hence the entropy power inequality can be rewritten as

$$2^{2h(X+Y)} \ge (2\pi e)(\sigma_{X'}^2 + \sigma_{Y'}^2) = 2^{2h(X'+Y')} , \tag{16.76}$$

since X' and Y' are independent. Thus we have a new statement of the entropy power inequality:

Theorem 16.7.1 (*Restatement of the entropy power inequality*): *For two independent random variables X and Y,*

$$h(X + Y) \geq h(X' + Y'), \qquad (16.77)$$

where X' and Y' are independent normal random variables with $h(X') = h(X)$ and $h(Y') = h(Y)$.

This form of the entropy power inequality bears a striking resemblance to the Brunn-Minkowski inequality, which bounds the volume of set sums.

Definition: The *set sum A + B* of two sets $A, B \subset \mathcal{R}^n$ is defined as the set $\{x + y : x \in A, y \in B\}$.

Example 16.7.1: The set sum of two spheres of radius 1 at the origin is a sphere of radius 2 at the origin.

Theorem 16.7.2 (*Brunn-Minkowski inequality*): *The volume of the set sum of two sets A and B is greater than the volume of the set sum of two spheres A' and B' with the same volumes as A and B, respectively, i.e.,*

$$V(A + B) \geq V(A' + B'), \qquad (16.78)$$

where A' and B' are spheres with $V(A') = V(A)$ and $V(B') = V(B)$.

The similarity between the two theorems was pointed out in [58]. A common proof was found by Dembo [87] and Lieb, starting from a strengthened version of Young's inequality. The same proof can be used to prove a range of inequalities which includes the entropy power inequality and the Brunn-Minkowski inequality as special cases. We will begin with a few definitions.

Definition: Let f and g be two densities over $\mathcal{R}^n$ and let $f * g$ denote the convolution of the two densities. Let the $\mathcal{L}_r$ norm of the density be defined by

$$\|f\|_r = \left(\int f^r(x) \, dx \right)^{1/r}. \qquad (16.79)$$

Lemma 16.7.1 (*Strengthened Young's inequality*): *For any two densities f and g,*

$$\|f * g\|_r \leq \left(\frac{C_p C_q}{C_r} \right)^{n/2} \|f\|_p \|g\|_q, \qquad (16.80)$$

where
$$\frac{1}{r} = \frac{1}{p} + \frac{1}{q} - 1 \tag{16.81}$$

and

$$C_p = \frac{p^{\frac{1}{p}}}{p'^{\frac{1}{p'}}}, \qquad \frac{1}{p} + \frac{1}{p'} = 1. \tag{16.82}$$

Proof: The proof of this inequality is rather involved; it can be found in [19] and [43]. □

We define a generalization of the entropy:

Definition: The *Renyi entropy* $h_r(X)$ of order r is defined as

$$h_r(X) = \frac{1}{1-r} \log\left[\int f^r(x)\, dx\right] \tag{16.83}$$

for $0 < r < \infty$, $r \neq 1$. If we take the limit as $r \to 1$, we obtain the Shannon entropy function

$$h(X) = h_1(X) = -\int f(x) \log f(x)\, dx. \tag{16.84}$$

If we take the limit as $r \to 0$, we obtain the logarithm of the volume of the support set,

$$h_0(X) = \log(\mu\{x : f(x) > 0\}). \tag{16.85}$$

Thus the zeroth order Renyi entropy gives the measure of the support set of the density f. We now define the equivalent of the entropy power for Renyi entropies.

Definition: The *Renyi entropy power* $V_r(X)$ of order r is defined as

$$V_r(X) = \begin{cases} [\int f^r(x)\, dx]^{-\frac{2}{n}\frac{r'}{r}}, & 0 < r \leq \infty, r \neq 1, \frac{1}{r} + \frac{1}{r'} = 1 \\ \exp[\frac{2}{n} h(X)], & r = 1 \\ \mu(\{x : f(x) > 0\})^{\frac{2}{n}}, & r = 0 \end{cases} \tag{16.86}$$

Theorem 16.7.3: *For two independent random variables X and Y and any $0 \leq r < \infty$ and any $0 \leq \lambda \leq 1$, we have*

$$\log V_r(X + Y) \geq \lambda \log V_p(X) + (1 - \lambda) \log V_q(Y) + H(\lambda)$$

$$+ \left(\frac{1+r}{1-r}\right)\left[H\left(\frac{r + \lambda(1-r)}{1+r}\right) - H\left(\frac{r}{1+r}\right)\right], \quad (16.87)$$

where $p = \frac{r}{r + \lambda(1-r)}$, $q = \frac{r}{r + (1-\lambda)(1-r)}$ *and* $H(\lambda) = -\lambda \log \lambda - (1 - \lambda) \log(1 - \lambda)$.

Proof: If we take the logarithm of Young's inequality (16.80), we obtain

$$\frac{1}{r'} \log V_r(X + Y) \geq \frac{1}{p'} \log V_p(X) + \frac{1}{q'} \log V_q(Y)$$

$$+ \log C_r - \log C_p - \log C_q . \quad (16.88)$$

Setting $\lambda = r'/p'$ and using (16.81), we have $1 - \lambda = r'/q'$, $p = \frac{r}{r + \lambda(1-r)}$ and $q = \frac{r}{r + (1 - \lambda)(1 - r)}$. Thus (16.88) becomes

$$\log V_r(X + Y) \geq \lambda \log V_p(X) + (1 - \lambda) \log V_q(Y) + \frac{r'}{r} \log r - \log r'$$

$$- \frac{r'}{p} \log p + \frac{r'}{p'} \log p' - \frac{r'}{q} \log q + \frac{r'}{q'} \log q' \quad (16.89)$$

$$= \lambda \log V_p(X) + (1 - \lambda) \log V_q(Y) + \frac{r'}{r} \log r - (\lambda + 1 - \lambda) \log r'$$

$$- \frac{r'}{p} \log p + \lambda \log p' - \frac{r'}{q} \log q + (1 - \lambda) \log q' \quad (16.90)$$

$$= \lambda \log V_p(X) + (1 - \lambda) \log V_q(Y) + \frac{1}{r - 1} \log r + H(\lambda)$$

$$- \frac{r + \lambda(1 - r)}{r - 1} \log \frac{r}{r + \lambda(1 - r)} \quad (16.91)$$

$$- \frac{r + (1 - \lambda)(1 - r)}{r - 1} \log \frac{r}{r + (1 - \lambda)(1 - r)} \quad (16.92)$$

$$= \lambda \log V_p(X) + (1 - \lambda) \log V_q(Y) + H(\lambda)$$

$$+ \left(\frac{1+r}{1-r}\right)\left[H\left(\frac{r + \lambda(1-r)}{1+r}\right) - H\left(\frac{r}{1+r}\right)\right], \quad (16.93)$$

where the details of the algebra for the last step are omitted. $\square$

The Brunn-Minkowski inequality and the entropy power inequality can then be obtained as special cases of this theorem.

- *The entropy power inequality.* Taking the limit of (16.87) as $r \to 1$ and setting

$$\lambda = \frac{V_1(X)}{V_1(X) + V_1(Y)}, \tag{16.94}$$

we obtain

$$V_1(X + Y) \geq V_1(X) + V_1(Y), \tag{16.95}$$

which is the entropy power inequality.

- *The Brunn-Minkowski inequality.* Similarly letting $r \to 0$ and choosing

$$\lambda = \frac{\sqrt{V_0(X)}}{\sqrt{V_0(X)} + \sqrt{V_0(Y)}}, \tag{16.96}$$

we obtain

$$\sqrt{V_0(X + Y)} \geq \sqrt{V_0(X)} + \sqrt{V_0(Y)}, \tag{16.97}$$

Now let A be the support set of X and B be the support set of Y. Then $A + B$ is the support set of $X + Y$, and (16.97) reduces to

$$[\mu(A + B)]^{1/n} \geq [\mu(A)]^{1/n} + [\mu(B)]^{1/n}, \tag{16.98}$$

which is the Brunn-Minkowski inequality.

The general theorem unifies the entropy power inequality and the Brunn-Minkowski inequality, and also introduces a continuum of new inequalities that lie between the entropy power inequality and the Brunn-Minkowski inequality. This furthers strengthens the analogy between entropy power and volume.

16.8   INEQUALITIES FOR DETERMINANTS

Throughout the remainder of this chapter, we will assume that K is a non-negative definite symmetric $n \times n$ matrix. Let $|K|$ denote the determinant of K.

We first prove a result due to Ky Fan [103].

Theorem 16.8.1: $\log|K|$ *is concave.*

Proof: Let X_1 and X_2 be normally distributed n-vectors, $\mathbf{X}_i \sim \mathcal{N}(0, K_i)$, $i = 1, 2$. Let the random variable θ have the distribution

$$\Pr\{\theta = 1\} = \lambda, \qquad (16.99)$$

$$\Pr\{\theta = 2\} = 1 - \lambda, \qquad (16.100)$$

for some $0 \le \lambda \le 1$. Let θ, $\mathbf{X}_1$ and $\mathbf{X}_2$ be independent and let $\mathbf{Z} = \mathbf{X}_\theta$. Then $\mathbf{Z}$ has covariance $K_Z = \lambda K_1 + (1 - \lambda)K_2$. However, $\mathbf{Z}$ will not be multivariate normal. By first using Theorem 16.2.3, followed by Theorem 16.2.1, we have

$$\frac{1}{2} \log(2\pi e)^n |\lambda K_1 + (1 - \lambda)K_2| \ge h(\mathbf{Z}) \qquad (16.101)$$

$$\ge h(\mathbf{Z}|\theta) \qquad (16.102)$$

$$= \lambda \tfrac{1}{2} \log(2\pi e)^n |K_1| + (1 - \lambda)\tfrac{1}{2} \log(2\pi e)^n |K_2|.$$

$$|\lambda K_1 + (1 - \lambda)K_2| \ge |K_1|^\lambda |K_2|^{1-\lambda}, \qquad (16.103)$$

as desired. $\square$

We now give Hadamard's inequality using an information theoretic proof [68].

Theorem 16.8.2 *(Hadamard):* $|K| \le \Pi K_{ii}$, *with equality iff* $K_{ij} = 0$, $i \ne j$.

Proof: Let $\mathbf{X} \sim \mathcal{N}(0, K)$. Then

$$\frac{1}{2} \log(2\pi e)^n |K| = h(X_1, X_2, \ldots, X_n) \le \sum h(X_i) = \sum_{i=1}^{n} \frac{1}{2} \log 2\pi e |K_{ii}|,$$

$$(16.104)$$

with equality iff $X_1, X_2, \ldots, X_n$ are independent, i.e., $K_{ij} = 0, i \ne j$. $\square$

We now prove a generalization of Hadamard's inequality due to Szasz [196]. Let $K(i_1, i_2, \ldots, i_k)$ be the $k \times k$ principal submatrix of K formed by the rows and columns with indices $i_1, i_2, \ldots, i_k$.

Theorem 16.8.3 *(Szasz): If K is a positive definite $n \times n$ matrix and P_k denotes the product of the determinants of all the principal k-rowed minors of K, i.e.,*

$$P_k = \prod_{1 \le i_1 < i_2 < \cdots < i_k \le n} |K(i_1, i_2, \ldots, i_k)|, \qquad (16.105)$$

then

$$P_1 \ge P_2^{1/\binom{n-1}{1}} \ge P_3^{1/\binom{n-1}{2}} \ge \cdots \ge P_n. \qquad (16.106)$$

Proof: Let $\mathbf{X} \sim \mathcal{N}(0, K)$. Then the theorem follows directly from Theorem 16.5.1, with the identification $h_k^{(n)} = \frac{1}{2n\binom{n-1}{k-1}} \log P_k + \frac{1}{2} \log 2\pi e$. $\square$

We can also prove a related theorem.

Theorem 16.8.4: *Let K be a positive definite $n \times n$ matrix and let*

$$S_k^{(n)} = \frac{1}{\binom{n}{k}} \sum_{1 \le i_1 < i_2 < \cdots < i_k \le n} |K(i_1, i_2, \ldots, i_k)|^{1/k}. \qquad (16.107)$$

Then

$$\frac{1}{n} \operatorname{tr}(K) = S_1^{(n)} \ge S_2^{(n)} \ge \cdots \ge S_n^{(n)} = |K|^{1/n}. \qquad (16.108)$$

Proof: This follows directly from the corollary to Theorem 16.5.1, with the identification $t_k^{(n)} = (2\pi e) S_k^{(n)}$ and $r = 2$. $\sqcap$

Theorem 16.8.5: *Let*

$$Q_k = \left(\prod_{S : |S| = k} \frac{|K|}{|K(S^c)|} \right)^{1/k\binom{n}{k}}. \qquad (16.109)$$

Then

$$\left(\prod_{i=1}^{n} \sigma_i^2 \right)^{1/n} = Q_1 \le Q_2 \le \cdots \le Q_{n-1} \le Q_n = |K|^{1/n}. \qquad (16.110)$$

Proof: The theorem follows immediately from Theorem 16.5.3 and the identification

$$h(X(S)|X(S^c)) = \frac{1}{2} \log(2\pi e)^k \frac{|K|}{|K(S^c)|}. \qquad \square \qquad (16.111)$$

The outermost inequality, $Q_1 \le Q_n$, can be rewritten as

$$|K| \ge \prod_{i=1}^{n} \sigma_i^2, \qquad (16.112)$$

where
$$\sigma_i^2 = \frac{|K|}{|K(1, 2 \ldots, i-1, i+1, \ldots, n)|} \qquad (16.113)$$

is the minimum mean squared error in the linear prediction of X_i from the remaining X's. Thus σ_i^2 is the conditional variance of X_i given the remaining X_j's if $X_1, X_2, \ldots, X_n$ are jointly normal. Combining this with Hadamard's inequality gives upper and lower bounds on the determinant of a positive definite matrix:

Corollary:

$$\prod_i K_{ii} \ge |K| \ge \prod_i \sigma_i^2. \qquad (16.114)$$

Hence the determinant of a covariance matrix lies between the product of the unconditional variances K_{ii} of the random variables X_i and the product of the conditional variances σ_i^2.

We now prove a property of Toeplitz matrices, which are important as the covariance matrices of stationary random processes. A Toeplitz matrix K is characterized by the property that $K_{ij} = K_{rs}$ if $|i - j| = |r - s|$. Let K_k denote the principal minor $K(1, 2, \ldots, k)$. For such a matrix, the following property can be proved easily from the properties of the entropy function.

Theorem 16.8.6: *If the positive definite $n \times n$ matrix K is Toeplitz, then*

$$|K_1| \ge |K_2|^{1/2} \ge 0 \cdots \ge |K_{n-1}|^{1/(n-1)} \ge |K_n|^{1/n} \qquad (16.115)$$

and $|K_k|/|K_{k-1}|$ is decreasing in k, and

$$\lim_{n \to \infty} |K_n|^{1/n} = \lim_{n \to \infty} \frac{|K_n|}{|K_{n-1}|}. \qquad (16.116)$$

Proof: Let $(X_1, X_2, \ldots, X_n) \sim \mathcal{N}(0, K_n)$. We observe that

$$h(X_k | X_{k-1}, \ldots, X_1) = h(X^k) - h(X^{k-1}) \qquad (16.117)$$

$$= \frac{1}{2} \log(2\pi e) \frac{|K_k|}{|K_{k-1}|}. \qquad (16.118)$$

Thus the monotonicity of $|K_k|/|K_{k-1}|$ follows from the monotonocity of $h(X_k | X_{k-1}, \ldots, X_1)$, which follows from

$$h(X_k | X_{k-1}, \ldots, X_1) = h(X_{k+1} | X_k, \ldots, X_2) \qquad (16.119)$$

$$\ge h(X_{k+1} | X_k, \ldots, X_2, X_1), \qquad (16.120)$$

where the equality follows from the Toeplitz assumption and the inequality from the fact that conditioning reduces entropy. Since $h(X_k|X_{k-1}, \ldots, X_1)$ is decreasing, it follows that the running averages

$$\frac{1}{k} h(X_1, \ldots, X_k) = \frac{1}{k} \sum_{i=1}^{k} h(X_i|X_{i-1}, \ldots, X_1) \qquad (16.121)$$

are decreasing in k. Then (16.115) follows from $h(X_1, X_2, \ldots, X_k) = \frac{1}{2} \log(2\pi e)^k |K_k|$. $\square$

Finally, since $h(X_n|X_{n-1}, \ldots, X_1)$ is a decreasing sequence, it has a limit. Hence by the Cesáro mean theorem,

$$\lim_{n \to \infty} \frac{h(X_1, X_2, \ldots, X_n)}{n} = \lim_{n \to \infty} \frac{1}{n} \sum_{k=1}^{n} h(X_k|X_{k-1}, \ldots, X_1)$$

$$= \lim_{n \to \infty} h(X_n|X_{n-1}, \ldots, X_1). \qquad (16.122)$$

Translating this to determinants, one obtains

$$\lim_{n \to \infty} |K_n|^{1/n} = \lim_{n \to \infty} \frac{|K_n|}{|K_{n-1}|} . \qquad (16.123)$$

Theorem 16.8.7 (*Minkowski inequality [195]*):

$$|K_1 + K_2|^{1/n} \geq |K_1|^{1/n} + |K_2|^{1/n} . \qquad (16.124)$$

Proof: Let $\mathbf{X}_1, \mathbf{X}_2$ be independent with $\mathbf{X}_i \sim \mathcal{N}(0, K_i)$. Noting that $\mathbf{X}_1 + \mathbf{X}_2 \sim \mathcal{N}(0, K_1 + K_2)$ and using the entropy power inequality (Theorem 16.6.3) yields

$$(2\pi e)|K_1 + K_2|^{1/n} = 2^{(2/n)h(\mathbf{X}_1 + \mathbf{X}_2)} \qquad (16.125)$$

$$\geq 2^{(2/n)h(\mathbf{X}_1)} + 2^{(2/n)h(\mathbf{X}_2)} \qquad (16.126)$$

$$= (2\pi e)|K_1|^{1/n} + (2\pi e)|K_2|^{1/n}. \quad \square \qquad (16.127)$$

16.9   INEQUALITIES FOR RATIOS OF DETERMINANTS

We now prove similar inequalities for ratios of determinants. Before developing the next theorem, we make an observation about minimum mean squared error linear prediction. If $(X_1, X_2, \ldots, X_n) \sim \mathcal{N}(0, K_n)$, we know that the conditional density of X_n given $(X_1, X_2, \ldots, X_{n-1})$ is univariate normal with mean linear in $X_1, X_2, \ldots, X_{n-1}$ and conditional variance σ_n^2. Here σ_n^2 is the minimum mean squared error $E(X_n - \hat{X}_n)^2$ over all linear estimators $\hat{X}_n$ based on $X_1, X_2, \ldots, X_{n-1}$.

Lemma 16.9.1: $\sigma_n^2 = |K_n|/|K_{n-1}|$.

Proof: Using the conditional normality of X_n, we have

$$\frac{1}{2} \log 2\pi e \sigma_n^2 = h(X_n | X_1, X_2, \ldots, X_{n-1}) \tag{16.128}$$

$$= h(X_1, X_2, \ldots, X_n) - h(X_1, X_2, \ldots, X_{n-1}) \tag{16.129}$$

$$= \frac{1}{2} \log(2\pi e)^n |K_n| - \frac{1}{2} \log(2\pi e)^{n-1} |K_{n-1}| \tag{16.130}$$

$$= \frac{1}{2} \log 2\pi e |K_n|/|K_{n-1}| . \quad \square \tag{16.131}$$

Minimization of σ_n^2 over a set of allowed covariance matrices $\{K_n\}$ is aided by the following theorem. Such problems arise in maximum entropy spectral density estimation.

Theorem 16.9.1 (*Bergstrøm [23]*): $\log(|K_n|/|K_{n-p}|)$ *is concave in* K_n.

Proof: We remark that Theorem 16.8.1 cannot be used because $\log(|K_n|/|K_{n-p}|)$ is the difference of two concave functions. Let $\mathbf{Z} = \mathbf{X}_\theta$, where $\mathbf{X}_1 \sim \mathcal{N}(0, S_n)$, $\mathbf{X}_2 \sim \mathcal{N}(0, T_n)$, $\Pr\{\theta = 1\} = \lambda = 1 - \Pr\{\theta = 2\}$ and let $\mathbf{X}_1, \mathbf{X}_2, \theta$ be independent. The covariance matrix K_n of $\mathbf{Z}$ is given by

$$K_n = \lambda S_n + (1 - \lambda) T_n . \tag{16.132}$$

The following chain of inequalities proves the theorem:

$$\lambda \frac{1}{2} \log(2\pi e)^p |S_n|/|S_{n-p}| + (1 - \lambda) \frac{1}{2} \log(2\pi e)^p |T_n|/|T_{n-p}|$$

$$\overset{(a)}{=} \lambda h(X_{1,n}, X_{1,n-1}, \ldots, X_{1,n-p+1} | X_{1,1}, \ldots, X_{1,n-p})$$

$$+ (1 - \lambda) h(X_{2,n}, X_{2,n-1}, \ldots, X_{2,n-p+1} | X_{2,1}, \ldots, X_{2,n-p}) \tag{16.133}$$

$$= h(Z_n, Z_{n-1}, \ldots, Z_{n-p+1} | Z_1, \ldots, Z_{n-p}, \theta) \tag{16.134}$$

$$\overset{(b)}{\leq} h(Z_n, Z_{n-1}, \ldots, Z_{n-p+1} | Z_1, \ldots, Z_{n-p}) \tag{16.135}$$

$$\overset{(c)}{\leq} \frac{1}{2} \log(2\pi e)^p \frac{|K_n|}{|K_{n-p}|} , \tag{16.136}$$

where(a) follows from $h(X_n, X_{n-1}, \ldots, X_{n-p+1}|X_1, \ldots, X_{n-p}) = h(X_1, \ldots, X_n) - h(X_1, \ldots, X_{n-p})$, (b) from the conditioning lemma, and (c) follows from a conditional version of Theorem 16.2.3. □

Theorem 16.9.2 *(Bergstrøm [23])*: $|K_n|/|K_{n-1}|$ *is concave in* K_n.

Proof: Again we use the properties of Gaussian random variables. Let us assume that we have two independent Gaussian random n-vectors, $\mathbf{X} \sim \mathcal{N}(0, A_n)$ and $\mathbf{Y} \sim \mathcal{N}(0, B_n)$. Let $\mathbf{Z} = \mathbf{X} + \mathbf{Y}$.
Then

$$\frac{1}{2} \log 2\pi e \frac{|A_n + B_n|}{|A_{n-1} + B_{n-1}|} \stackrel{(a)}{=} h(Z_n|Z_{n-1}, Z_{n-2}, \ldots, Z_1) \tag{16.137}$$

$$\stackrel{(b)}{\geq} h(Z_n|Z_{n-1}, Z_{n-2}, \ldots, Z_1, X_{n-1}, X_{n-2}, \ldots, X_1, Y_{n-1}, Y_{n-2}, \ldots, Y_1) \tag{16.138}$$

$$\stackrel{(c)}{=} h(X_n + Y_n|X_{n-1}, X_{n-2}, \ldots, X_1, Y_{n-1}, Y_{n-2}, \ldots, Y_1) \tag{16.139}$$

$$\stackrel{(d)}{=} E \frac{1}{2} \log[2\pi e \, \text{Var}(X_n + Y_n|X_{n-1}, X_{n-2}, \ldots, X_1, Y_{n-1}, Y_{n-2}, \ldots, Y_1)] \tag{16.140}$$

$$\stackrel{(e)}{=} E \frac{1}{2} \log[2\pi e (\text{Var}(X_n|X_{n-1}, X_{n-2}, \ldots, X_1) + \text{Var}(Y_n|Y_{n-1}, Y_{n-2}, \ldots, Y_1))] \tag{16.141}$$

$$\stackrel{(f)}{=} E \frac{1}{2} \log\left(2\pi e\left(\frac{|A_n|}{|A_{n-1}|} + \frac{|B_n|}{|B_{n-1}|}\right)\right) \tag{16.142}$$

$$= \frac{1}{2} \log\left(2\pi e\left(\frac{|A_n|}{|A_{n-1}|} + \frac{|B_n|}{|B_{n-1}|}\right)\right), \tag{16.143}$$

where

(a) follows from Lemma 16.9.1,

(b) from the fact the conditioning decreases entropy,

(c) from the fact that Z is a function of X and Y,

(d) since $X_n + Y_n$ is Gaussian conditioned on $X_1, X_2, \ldots, X_{n-1}$, $Y_1, Y_2, \ldots, Y_{n-1}$, and hence we can express its entropy in terms of its variance,

(e) from the independence of X_n and Y_n conditioned on the past $X_1, X_2, \ldots, X_{n-1}, Y_1, Y_2, \ldots, Y_{n-1}$, and

(f) follows from the fact that for a set of jointly Gaussian random variables, the conditional variance is constant, independent of the conditioning variables (Lemma 16.9.1).

Setting $A = \lambda S$ and $B = \bar{\lambda} T$, we obtain

$$\frac{|\lambda S_n + \bar{\lambda} T_n|}{|\lambda S_{n-1} + \bar{\lambda} T_{n-1}|} \geq \lambda \frac{|S_n|}{|S_{n-1}|} + \bar{\lambda} \frac{|T_n|}{|T_{n-1}|}, \qquad (16.144)$$

i.e., $|K_n|/|K_{n-1}|$ is concave. Simple examples show that $|K_n|/|K_{n-p}|$ is not necessarily concave for $p \geq 2$. $\square$

A number of other determinant inequalities can be proved by these techniques. A few of them are found in the exercises.

OVERALL SUMMARY

Entropy: $H(X) = -\Sigma\, p(x) \log p(x)$.

Relative entropy: $D(p\|q) = \Sigma\, p(x) \log \frac{p(x)}{q(x)}$.

Mutual information: $I(X; Y) = \Sigma\, p(x, y) \log \frac{p(x, y)}{p(x)p(y)}$.

Information inequality: $D(p\|q) \geq 0$.

Asymptotic equipartition property: $-\frac{1}{n} \log p(X_1, X_2, \ldots, X_n) \to H(X)$.

Data compression: $H(X) \leq L^* < H(X) + 1$.

Kolmogorov complexity: $K(x) = \min_{\mathcal{U}(p)=x} l(p)$.

Channel capacity: $C = \max_{p(x)} I(X; Y)$.

Data transmission:

- $R < C$: Asymptotically error-free communication possible
- $R > C$: Asymptotically error-free communication not possible

Capacity of a white Gaussian noise channel: $C = \frac{1}{2} \log(1 + \frac{P}{N})$.

Rate distortion: $R(D) = \min I(X; \hat{X})$
over all $p(\hat{x}|x)$ such that $E_{p(x)p(\hat{x}|x)} d(X, \hat{X}) \leq D$.

Doubling rate for stock market: $W^* = \max_{\mathbf{b}^*} E \log \mathbf{b}'\mathbf{X}$.

PROBLEMS FOR CHAPTER 16

1. *Sum of positive definite matrices.* For any two positive definite matrices, K_1 and K_2, show that $|K_1 + K_2| \geq |K_1|$.

2. *Ky Fan inequality [104] for ratios of determinants.* For all $1 \leq p \leq n$, for a positive definite K, show that

$$\frac{|K|}{|K(p+1, p+2, \ldots, n)|} \leq \prod_{i=1}^{p} \frac{|K(i, p+1, p+2, \ldots, n)|}{|K(p+1, p+2, \ldots, n)|} . \quad (16.145)$$

HISTORICAL NOTES

The entropy power inequality was stated by Shannon [238]; the first formal proofs are due to Stam [257] and Blachman [34]. The unified proof of the entropy power and Brunn-Minkowski inequalities is in Dembo [87].

Most of the matrix inequalities in this chapter were derived using information theoretic methods by Cover and Thomas [59]. Some of the subset inequalities for entropy rates can be found in Han [130].

Bibliography

[1]   N. M. Abramson. *Information Theory and Coding*. McGraw-Hill, New York, 1963.

[2]   R. L. Adler, D. Coppersmith, and M. Hassner. Algorithms for sliding block codes—an application of symbolic dynamics to information theory. *IEEE Trans. Inform. Theory*, IT-29: 5–22, 1983.

[3]   R. Ahlswede. Multi-way communication channels. In *Proc. 2nd. Int. Symp. Information Theory (Tsahkadsor, Armenian S.S.R.)*, pages 23–52, Prague, 1971. Publishing House of the Hungarian Academy of Sciences.

[4]   R. Ahlswede. The capacity region of a channel with two senders and two receivers. *Ann. Prob.*, 2: 805–814, 1974.

[5]   R. Ahlswede, Elimination of correlation in random codes for arbitrarily varying channels. *Zeitschrift für Wahrscheinlichkeitstheorie and verwandte Gebiete*, 33: 159–175, 1978.

[6]   R. Ahlswede and T. S. Han. On source coding with side information via a multiple access channel and related problems in multi-user information theory. *IEEE Trans. Inform. Theory*, IT-29: 396–412, 1983.

[7]   R. Ahlswede and J. Körner. Source coding with side information and a converse for the degraded broadcast channel. *IEEE Trans. Inform. Theory*, IT-21: 629–637, 1975.

[8]   P. Algoet and T. M. Cover. A sandwich proof of the Shannon-McMillan-Breiman theorem. *Annals of Probability*, 16: 899–909, 1988.

[9]   P. Algoet and T. M. Cover. Asymptotic optimality and asymptotic equipartition property of log-optimal investment. *Annals of Probability*, 16: 876–898, 1988.

[10] S. Amari. *Differential-Geometrical Methods in Statistics*. Springer-Verlag, New York, 1985.

[11] S. Arimoto. An algorithm for calculating the capacity of an arbitrary

discrete memoryless channel. *IEEE Trans. Inform. Theory*, IT-18: 14–20, 1972.

[12] S. Arimoto. On the converse to the coding theorem for discrete memoryless channels. *IEEE Trans. Inform. Theory*, IT-19: 357–359, 1973.

[13] R. B. Ash. *Information Theory*. Interscience, New York, 1965.

[14] J. Axzél and Z. Daróczy. *On Measures of Information and Their Characterization*. Academic Press, New York, 1975.

[15] A. Barron. Entropy and the Central Limit Theorem. *Annals of Probability*, 14: 336–342, April 1986.

[16] A. Barron and T. M. Cover. A bound on the financial value of information. *IEEE Trans. Inform. Theory*, IT-34: 1097–1100, 1988.

[17] A. R. Barron. Logically smooth density estimation. PhD Thesis, Department of Electrical Engineering, Stanford University, 1985.

[18] A. R. Barron. The strong ergodic theorem for densities: Generalized Shannon-McMillan-Breiman theorem. *Annals of Probability*, 13: 1292–1303, 1985.

[19] W. Beckner. Inequalities in Fourier Analysis. *Annals of Mathematics*, 102: 159–182, 1975.

[20] R. Bell and T. M. Cover. Competitive Optimality of Logarithmic Investment. *Mathematics of Operations Research*, 5: 161–166, 1980.

[21] R. Bell and T. M. Cover. Game-theoretic optimal portfolios. *Management Science*, 34: 724–733, 1988.

[22] T. C. Bell, J. G.Cleary, and I. H. Witten, *Text Compression*. Prentice-Hall, Englewood Cliffs, NJ, 1990.

[23] R. Bellman. Notes on Matrix Theory—IV: An inequality due to Bergstrøm. *Am. Math. Monthly*, 62: 172–173, 1955.

[24] C. H. Bennett. Demons, Engines and the Second Law. *Scientific American*, 259(5): 108–116, 1987.

[25] C. H. Bennett and R. Landauer. The fundamental physical limits of computation. *Scientific American*, 255: 48–56, 1985.

[26] R. Benzel. The capacity region of a class of discrete additive degraded interference channels. *IEEE Trans. Inform. Theory*, IT-25: 228–231, 1979.

[27] T. Berger. *Rate Distortion Theory: A Mathematical Basis for Data Compression*. Prentice-Hall, Englewood Cliffs, NJ, 1971.

[28] T. Berger. Multiterminal Source Coding. In G. Longo, editor, *The Information Theory Approach to Communications*. Springer-Verlag, New York, 1977.

[29] T. Berger. Multiterminal source coding. In *Lecture notes presented at the 1977 CISM Summer School, Udine, Italy*, pages 569–570, Prague, 1977. Princeton University Press, Princeton, NJ.

[30] T. Berger and R. W. Yeung. Multiterminal source encoding with one distortion criterion. *IEEE Trans. Inform. Theory*, IT-35: 228–236, 1989.

[31] P. Bergmans. Random coding theorem for broadcast channels with degraded components. *IEEE Trans. Inform. Theory*, IT-19: 197–207, 1973.

[32] E. R. Berlekamp. *Block Coding with Noiseless Feedback*. PhD Thesis, MIT, Cambridge, MA, 1964.

[33] M. Bierbaum and H. M. Wallmeier. A note on the capacity region of the multiple access channel. *IEEE Trans. Inform. Theory*, IT-25: 484, 1979.

[34] N. Blachman. The convolution inequality for entropy powers. *IEEE Trans. Inform. Theory*, IT-11: 267–271, 1965.

[35] D. Blackwell, L. Breiman, and A. J. Thomasian. The capacity of a class of channels. *Ann. Math. Stat.*, 30: 1229–1241, 1959.

[36] D. Blackwell, L. Breiman, and A. J. Thomasian. The capacities of certain channel classes under random coding. *Ann. Math. Stat.*, 31: 558–567, 1960.

[37] R. Blahut. Computation of Channel capacity and rate distortion functions. *IEEE Trans. Inform. Theory*, IT-18: 460–473, 1972.

[38] R. E. Blahut. Information bounds of the Fano-Kullback type. *IEEE Trans. Inform. Theory*, IT-22: 410–421, 1976.

[39] R. E. Blahut. *Principles and Practice of Information Theory*. Addison-Wesley, Reading, MA, 1987.

[40] R. E. Blahut. Hypothesis testing and Information theory. *IEEE Trans. Inform. Theory*, IT-20: 405–417, 1974.

[41] R. E. Blahut. *Theory and Practice of Error Control Codes*. Addison-Wesley, Reading, MA, 1983.

[42] R. C. Bose and D. K. Ray-Chaudhuri. On a class of error correcting binary group codes. *Inform. Contr.*, 3: 68–79, 1960.

[43] H. J. Brascamp and E. J. Lieb. Best constants in Young's inequality, its converse and its generalization to more than three functions. *Advances in Mathematics*, 20: 151–173, 1976.

[44] L. Breiman. The individual ergodic theorems of information theory. *Ann. Math. Stat.*, 28: 809–811, 1957.

[45] L. Breiman. Optimal Gambling systems for favourable games. In *Fourth Berkeley Symposium on Mathematical Statistics and Probability*, pages 65–78, Prague, 1961. University of California Press, Berkeley, CA.

[46] Leon. Brillouin. *Science and information theory*. Academic Press, New York, 1962.

[47] J. P. Burg. *Maximum entropy spectral analysis*. PhD Thesis, Department of Geophysics, Stanford University, Stanford, CA, 1975.

[48] A. Carleial. Outer bounds on the capacity of the interference channel. *IEEE Trans. Inform. Theory*, IT-29: 602–606, 1983.

[49] A. B. Carleial. A case where interference does not reduce capacity. *IEEE Trans. Inform. Theory*, IT-21: 569–570, 1975.

[50] G. J. Chaitin. On the length of programs for computing binary sequences. *J. Assoc. Comp. Mach.*, 13: 547–569, 1966.

[51] G. J. Chaitin. Information theoretical limitations of formal systems. *J. Assoc. Comp. Mach.*, 21: 403–424, 1974.

[52] G. J. Chaitin. Randomness and mathematical proof. *Scientific American*, 232: 47–52, 1975.

[53] G. J. Chaitin. Algorithmic information theory. *IBM Journal of Research and Development*, 21: 350–359, 1977.

[54] G. J. Chaitin. *Algorithmic Information Theory*. Cambridge University Press, Cambridge, 1987.

[55] H. Chernoff. A measure of the asymptotic efficiency of tests of a hypothesis based on a sum of observations. *Ann. Math. Stat.*, 23: 493–507, 1952.

[56] B. S. Choi and T. M. Cover. An information-theoretic proof of Burg's Maximum Entropy Spectrum. *Proc. IEEE*, 72: 1094–1095, 1984.

[57] K. L. Chung. A note on the ergodic theorem of information theory. *Ann. Math. Statist.*, 32: 612–614, 1961.

[58] M. Costa and T. M. Cover. On the similarity of the entropy power inequality and the Brunn-Minkowski inequality. *IEEE Trans. Inform. Theory*, IT-30: 837–839, 1984.

[59] T. M. Cover and J. A. Thomas. Determinant inequalities via information theory. *SIAM Journal of Matrix Analysis and its Applications*, 9: 384–392, 1988.

[60] T. M. Cover. Broadcast channels. *IEEE Trans. Inform. Theory*, IT-18: 2–14, 1972.

[61] T. M. Cover. Enumerative source encoding. *IEEE Trans. Inform. Theory*, IT-19: 73–77, 1973.

[62] T. M. Cover. An achievable rate region for the broadcast channel. *IEEE Trans. Inform. Theory*, IT-21: 399–404, 1975.

[63] T. M. Cover. A proof of the data compression theorem of Slepian and Wolf for ergodic sources. *IEEE Trans. Inform. Theory*, IT-22: 226–228, 1975.

[64] T. M. Cover. An algorithm for maximizing expected log investment return. *IEEE Trans. Inform. Theory*, IT-30: 369–373, 1984.

[65] T. M. Cover. Kolmogorov complexity, data compression and inference. In Skwirzynski, J., editor, *The Impact of Processing Techniques on Communications*. Martinus-Nijhoff Publishers, Dodrecht, 1985.

[66] T. M. Cover. Universal Portfolios. *Math. Finance*, 16: 876–898, 1991.

[67] T. M. Cover and A. El Gamal. Capacity theorems for the relay channel. *IEEE Trans. Inform. Theory*, IT-25: 572–584, 1979.

[68] T. M. Cover and A. El Gamal. An information theoretic proof of Hadamard's inequality. *IEEE Trans. Inform. Theory*, IT-29: 930–931, 1983.

[69] T. M. Cover, A. El Gamal, and M. Salehi. Multiple access channels with arbtirarily correlated sources. *IEEE Trans. Inform. Theory*, IT-26: 648–657, 1980.

[70] T. M. Cover, P. Gács, and R. M. Gray, Kolmogorov's contributions to information theory and algorithmic complexity. *Annals of Probability*, 17: 840–865, 1989.

[71] T. M. Cover and B. Gopinath. *Open Problems in Communication and Computation*. Springer-Verlag, New York, 1987.

[72] T. M. Cover and R. King. A convergent gambling estimate of the entropy of English. *IEEE Trans. Inform. Theory*, IT-24: 413–421, 1978.

[73] T. M. Cover and C. S. K. Leung. An achievable rate region for the multiple access channel with feedback. *IEEE Trans. Inform. Theory*, IT-27: 292–298, 1981.

[74] T. M. Cover and S. K. Leung. Some equivalences between Shannon entropy and Kolmogorov complexity. *IEEE Trans. Inform. Theory*, IT-24: 331–338, 1978.

[75] T. M. Cover, R. J. McEliece, and E. Posner. Asynchronous multiple access channel capacity. *IEEE Trans. Inform. Theory*, IT-27: 409–413, 1981.

[76] T. M. Cover and S. Pombra. Gaussian feedback capacity. *IEEE Trans. Inform. Theory*, IT-35: 37–43, 1989.

[77] H. Cramér. *Mathematical Methods of Statistics*. Princeton University Press, Princeton, NJ, 1946.

[78] I. Csiszár. Information type measures of difference of probability distributions and indirect observations. *Studia Sci. Math. Hungar.*, 2: 229–318, 1967.

[79] I. Csiszár. On the computation of rate distortion functions. *IEEE Trans. Inform. Theory*, IT-20: 122–124, 1974.

[80] I. Csiszár. Sanov property, generalized I-projection and a conditional limit theorem. *Annals of Probability*, 12: 768–793, 1984.

[81] I. Csiszár, T. M. Cover, and B. S. Choi. Conditional limit theorems under Markov conditioning. *IEEE Trans. Inform. Theory*, IT-33: 788–801, 1987.

[82] I. Csiszár and J. Körner. Towards a general theory of source networks. *IEEE Trans. Inform. Theory*, IT-26: 155–165, 1980.

[83] I. Csiszár and J. Körner. *Information Theory: Coding Theorems for Discrete Memoryless Systems*. Academic Press, New York, 1981.

[84] I. Csiszár and G. Longo. *On the error exponent for source coding and for testing simple statistical hypotheses*. Hungarian Academy of Sciences, Budapest, 1971.

[85] I. Csiszár and G. Tusnády. Information geometry and alternating minimization procedures. *Statistics and Decisions*, Supplement Issue 1: 205–237, 1984.

[86] L. D. Davisson. Universal noiseless coding. *IEEE Trans. Inform. Theory*, IT-19: 783–795, 1973.

[87] A. Dembo. Information inequalities and uncertainty principles. Technical Report, Department of Statistics, Stanford University, 1990.

[88] A. P. Dempster, N. M. Laird, and D. B. Rubin. Maximum likelihood from incomplete data via the EM algorithm. *Journal Royal Stat. Soc., Series B*, 39: 1–38, 1977.

[89] R. L. Dobrushin. General formulation of Shannon's main theorem of information theory. *Usp. Math. Nauk.*, 14: 3–104, 1959. Translated in *Am. Math. Soc. Trans.*, 33: 323–438.

[90] G. Dueck. The capacity region of the two-way channel can exceed the inner bound. *Inform. Contr.*, 40: 258–266, 1979.

[91] G. Dueck. Partial feedback for two-way and broadcast channels. *Inform. Contr.*, 46: 1–15, 1980.

[92] G. Dueck and J. Körner. Reliability function of a discrete memoryless channel at rates above capacity. *IEEE Trans. Inform. Theory*, IT-25: 82–85, 1979.

[93] G. Dueck and L. Wolters. Ergodic theory and encoding of individual sequences. *Problems Contr. Inform. Theory*, 14: 329–345, 1985.

[94] P. M. Ebert. The capacity of the Gaussian channel with feedback. *Bell Sys. Tech. Journal*, 49: 1705–1712, October 1970.

[95] II. G. Eggleston. *Convexity*. Cambridge University Press, Cambridge, UK, 1969.

[96] A. El Gamal. The feedback capacity of degraded broadcast channels. *IEEE Trans. Inform. Theory*, IT-24: 379–381, 1978.

[97] A. El Gamal. The capacity region of a class of broadcast channels. *IEEE Trans. Inform. Theory*, IT-25: 166–169, 1979.

[98] A. El Gamal and T. M. Cover. Multiple user information theory. *Proc. IEEE*, 68: 1466–1483, 1980.

[99] A. El Gamal and T. M. Cover. Achievable rates for multiple descriptions. *IEEE Trans. Inform. Theory*, IT-28: 851–857, 1982.

[100] A. El Gamal and E. C. Van der Meulen. A proof of Marton's coding theorem for the discrete memoryless broadcast channel. *IEEE Trans. Inform. Theory*, IT-27: 120–122, 1981.

[101] P. Elias. Error-free Coding. *IRE Trans. Inform. Theory*, IT-4: 29–37, 1954.

[102] P. Elias. Coding for noisy channels. In *IRE Convention Record, Pt. 4*, pages 37–46, 1955.

[103] Ky Fan. On a Theorem of Weyl concerning the eigenvalues of linear transformations II. *Proc. National Acad. Sci. U.S.*, 36: 31–35, 1950.

[104] Ky Fan. Some inequalities concerning positive-definite matrices. *Proc. Cambridge Phil. Soc.*, 51: 414–421, 1955.

[105] R. M. Fano. Class notes for Transmission of Information, Course 6.574. MIT, Cambridge, MA, 1952.

[106] R. M. Fano. *Transmission of Information: A Statistical Theory of Communication*. Wiley, New York, 1961.

[107] A. Feinstein. A new basic theorem of information theory. *IRE Trans. Inform. Theory*, IT-4: 2–22, 1954.

[108] A. Feinstein. *Foundations of Information Theory*. McGraw-Hill, New York, 1958.

[109] A. Feinstein. On the coding theorem and its converse for finite-memory channels. *Inform. Contr.*, 2: 25–44, 1959.

[110] W. Feller. *An Introduction to Probability Theory and Its Applications*. Wiley, New York, 1957.

[111] R. A. Fisher. On the mathematical foundations of theoretical statistics. *Philos. Trans. Roy. Soc., London, Sec. A*, 222: 309–368, 1922.

[112] R. A. Fisher. Theory of Statistical Estimation. *Proc. Cambridge Phil. Society*, 22: 700–725, 1925.

[113] L. R. Ford and D. R. Fulkerson. *Flows in Networks*. Princeton University Press, Princeton, NJ, 1962.

[114] G. D. Forney. Exponential error bounds for erasure, list and decision feedback schemes. *IEEE Trans. Inform. Theory*, IT-14: 549–557, 1968.

[115] G. D. Forney. Information Theory. Unpublished course notes. Stanford University, 1972.

[116] P. A. Franaszek. On synchronous variable length coding for discrete noiseless channels. *Inform. Contr.*, 15: 155–164, 1969.

[117] T. Gaarder and J. K. Wolf. The capacity region of a multiple-access discrete memoryless channel can increase with feedback. *IEEE Trans. Inform. Theory*, IT-21: 100–102, 1975.

[118] R. G. Gallager. A simple derivation of the coding theorem and some applications. *IEEE Trans. Inform. Theory*, IT-11: 3–18, 1965.

[119] R. G. Gallager. Capacity and coding for degraded broadcast channels. *Problemy Peredaci Informaccii*, 10(3): 3–14, 1974.

[120] R. G. Gallager. *Information Theory and Reliable Communication*. Wiley, New York, 1968.

[121] E. W. Gilbert and E. F. Moore. Variable length binary encodings. *Bell Sys. Tech. Journal*, 38: 933–967, 1959.

[122] S. Goldman. *Information Theory*. Prentice-Hall, Englewood Cliffs, NJ, 1953.

[123] R. M. Gray. Sliding block source coding. *IEEE Trans. Inform. Theory*, IT-21: 357–368, 1975.

[124] R. M. Gray. *Entropy and Information Theory*. Springer-Verlag, New York, 1990.

[125] R. M. Gray and A. Wyner. Source coding for a simple network. *Bell Sys. Tech. Journal*, 58: 1681–1721, 1974.

[126] U. Grenander and G. Szego. *Toeplitz forms and their applications*. University of California Press, Berkeley, 1958.

[127] B. Grünbaum. *Convex Polytopes*. Interscience, New York, 1967.

[128] S. Guiasu. *Information Theory with Applications*. McGraw-Hill, New York, 1976.

[129] R. V. Hamming. Error detecting and error correcting codes. *Bell Sys. Tech. Journal*, 29: 147–160, 1950.

[130] T. S. Han. Nonnegative entropy measures of multivariate symmetric correlations. *Inform. Contr.*, 36: 133–156, 1978.

[131] T. S. Han and M. H. M. Costa. Broadcast channels with arbitrarily correlated sources. *IEEE Trans. Inform. Theory*, IT-33: 641–650, 1987.

[132] T. S. Han and K. Kobayashi. A new achievable rate region for the interference channel. *IEEE Trans. Inform. Theory*, IT-27: 49–60, 1981.

[133] R. V. Hartley. Transmission of information. *Bell Sys. Tech. Journal*, 7: 535, 1928.

[134] P. A. Hocquenghem. Codes correcteurs d'erreurs. *Chiffres*, 2: 147–156, 1959.

[135] J. L. Holsinger. Digital communication over fixed time-continuous channels with memory, with special application to telephone channels. Technical Report, M. I. T., 1964.

[136] J. E. Hopcroft and J. D. Ullman. *Introduction to Automata Theory, Formal Languages and Computation*. Addison Wesley, Reading, MA, 1979.

[137] Y. Horibe. An improved bound for weight-balanced tree. *Inform. Contr.*, 34: 148–151, 1977.

[138] D. A. Huffman. A method for the construction of minimum redundancy codes. *Proc. IRE*, 40: 1098–1101, 1952.

[139] E. T. Jaynes. Information theory and statistical mechanics. *Phys. Rev.*, 106: 620, 1957.

[140] E. T. Jaynes. Information theory and statistical mechanics. *Phys. Rev.*, 108: 171, 1957.

[141] E. T. Jaynes. Information theory and statistical mechanics I. *Phys. Rev.*, 106: 620–630, 1957.

[142] E. T. Jaynes. On the rationale of maximum entropy methods. *Proc. IEEE*, 70: 939–952, 1982.

[143] E. T. Jaynes. *Papers on Probability, Statistics and Statistical Physics* . Reidel, Dordrecht, 1982.

[144] F. Jelinek. Buffer overflow in variable length encoding of fixed rate sources. *IEEE Trans. Inform. Theory*, IT-14: 490–501, 1968.

[145] F. Jelinek. Evaluation of expurgated error bounds. *IEEE Trans. Inform. Theory*, IT-14: 501–505, 1968.

[146] F. Jelinek. *Probabilistic Information Theory*. McGraw-Hill, New York, 1968.

[147] J. Justesen. A class of constructive asymptotically good algebraic codes. *IEEE Trans. Inform. Theory*, IT-18: 652–656, 1972.

[148] T. Kailath and J. P. M. Schwalkwijk. A coding scheme for additive noise channels with feedback—Part I: No bandwidth constraints. *IEEE Trans. Inform. Theory*, IT-12: 172–182, 1966.

[149] J. Karush. A simple proof of an inequality of McMillan. *IRE Trans. Inform. Theory*, IT-7: 118, 1961.

[150] J. Kelly. A new interpretation of information rate. *Bell Sys. Tech. Journal*, 35: 917–926, 1956.

[151] J. H. B. Kemperman. *On the Optimum Rate of Transmitting Information* pp. 126–169. Springer-Verlag, New York, 1967.

[152] M. Kendall and A. Stuart. *The Advanced Theory of Statistics*. MacMillan, New York, 1977.

[153] A. Ya. Khinchin. *Mathematical Foundations of Information Theory*. Dover, New York, 1957.

[154] J. C. Kieffer. A simple proof of the Moy-Perez generalization of the Shannon-McMillan theorem. *Pacific J. Math.*, 51: 203–206, 1974.

[155] D. E. Knuth and A. C. Yao. The complexity of random number generation. In J. F. Traub, editor, *Algorithms and Complexity: Recent Results and New Directions. Proceedings of the Symposium on New Directions and Recent Results in Algorithms and Complexity, Carnegie-Mellon University, 1976*. Academic Press, New York, 1976.

[156] A. N. Kolmogorov. On the Shannon theory of information transmission in the case of continuous signals. *IRE Trans. Inform. Theory*, IT-2: 102–108, 1956.

[157] A. N. Kolmogorov. A new invariant for transitive dynamical systems. *Dokl. An. SSR*, 119: 861–864, 1958.

[158] A. N. Kolmogorov. Three approaches to the quantitative definition of information. *Problems of Information Transmission*, 1: 4–7, 1965.

[159] A. N. Kolmogorov. Logical basis for information theory and probability theory. *IEEE Trans. Inform. Theory*, IT-14: 662–664, 1968.

[160] J. Körner and K. Marton. The comparison of two noisy channels. In Csiszár, I. and Elias, P. , editor, *Topics in Information Theory*. Coll. Math. Soc. J. Bolyai, No. 16, North Holland, Amsterdam, 1977.

[161] J. Körner and K. Marton. General broadcast channels with degraded message sets. *IEEE Trans. Inform. Theory*, IT-23: 60–64, 1977.

[162] J. Körner and K. Marton. How to encode the modulo 2 sum of two binary sources. *IEEE Trans. Inform. Theory*, IT-25: 219–221, 1979.

[163] V. A. Kotel'nikov. *The Theory of Optimum Noise Immunity*. McGraw-Hill, New York, 1959.

[164] L. G. Kraft. A device for quanitizing, grouping and coding amplitude modulated pulses. Master's Thesis, Department of Electrical Engineering, MIT, Cambridge, MA, 1949.

[165] S. Kullback. *Information Theory and Statistics*. Wiley, New York, 1959.

[166] S. Kullback. A lower bound for discrimination in terms of variation. *IEEE Trans. Inform. Theory*, IT-13: 126–127, 1967.

[167] S. Kullback and R. A. Leibler. On information and sufficiency. *Ann. Math. Stat.*, 22: 79–86, 1951.

[168] H. J. Landau and H. O. Pollak. Prolate spheroidal wave functions, Fourier analysis and uncertainty: Part III. *Bell Sys. Tech. Journal*, 41: 1295–1336, 1962.

[169] H. J. Landau and H. O. Pollak. Prolate spheroidal wave functions, Fourier analysis and uncertainty: Part II. *Bell Sys. Tech. Journal*, 40: 65–84, 1961.

[170] G. G. Langdon. An introduction to arithmetic coding. *IBM Journal of Research and Development*, 28: 135–149, 1984.

[171] G. G. Langdon and J. J. Rissanen. A simple general binary source code. *IEEE Trans. Inform. Theory*, IT-28: 800, 1982.

[172] H. A. Latané. Criteria for choice among risky ventures. *Journal of Political Economy*, 38: 145–155, 1959.

[173] H. A. Latané and D. L. Tuttle. Criteria for portfolio building. *Journal of Finance*, 22: 359–373, 1967.

[174] E. L. Lehmann and H. Scheffé. Completeness, similar regions and unbiased estimation. *Sankhya*, 10: 305–340, 1950.

[175] A. Lempel and J. Ziv. On the complexity of finite sequences. *IEEE Trans. Inform. Theory*, IT-22: 75–81, 1976.

[176] L. A. Levin. On the notion of a random sequence. *Soviet Mathematics Doklady*, 14: 1413–1416, 1973.

[177] L. A. Levin and A. K. Zvonkin. The complexity of finite objects and the development of the concepts of information and randomness by means of the theory of algorithms. *Russian Mathematical Surveys*, 25/6: 83–124, 1970.

[178] H. Liao. Multiple access channels. PhD Thesis, Department of Electrical Engineering, University of Hawaii, Honolulu, 1972.

[179] S. Lin and D. J. Costello, Jr. *Error Control Coding: Fundamentals and Applications*. Prentice-Hall, Englewood Cliffs, NJ, 1983.

[180] Y. Linde, A. Buzo. and R. M. Gray. An algorithm for vector quantizer design. *IEEE Transactions on Communications*, COM-28: 84–95, 1980.

[181] S. P. Lloyd. Least squares quantization in PCM. Bell Laboratories Technical Note, 1957.

[182] L. Lovasz. On the Shannon capacity of a graph. *IEEE Trans. Inform. Theory*, IT-25: 1–7, 1979.

[183] R. W. Lucky. *Silicon Dreams: Information, Man and Machine*. St. Martin's Press, New York, 1989.

[184] B. Marcus. Sofic systems and encoding data. *IEEE Trans. Inform. Theory*, IT-31: 366–377, 1985.

[185] A. Marshall and I. Olkin. *Inequalities: Theory of Majorization and Its Applications*. Academic Press, New York, 1979.

[186] A. Marshall and I. Olkin. A convexity proof of Hadamard's inequality. *Am. Math. Monthly*, 89: 687–688, 1982.

[187] P. Martin-Löf. The definition of random sequences. *Inform. Contr.*, 9: 602–619, 1966.

[188] K. Marton. Error exponent for source coding with a fidelity criterion. *IEEE Trans. Inform. Theory*, IT-20: 197–199, 1974.

[189] K. Marton. A coding theorem for the discrete memoryless broadcast channel. *IEEE Trans. Inform. Theory*, IT-25: 306–311, 1979.

[190] R. A. McDonald and P. M. Schultheiss. Information Rates of Gaussian signals under criteria constraining the error spectrum. *Proc. IEEE*, 52: 415–416, 1964.

[191] R. J. McEliece. *The Theory of Information and Coding*. Addison-Wesley, Reading, MA, 1977.

[192] B. McMillan. The basic theorems of information theory. *Ann. Math. Stat.*, 24: 196–219, 1953.

[193] B. McMillan. Two inequalities implied by unique decipherability. *IEEE Trans. Inform. Theory*, IT-2: 115–116, 1956.

[194] R. C. Merton and P. A. Samuelson. Fallacy of the log-normal approximation to optimal portfolio decision-making over many periods. *Journal of
Financial Economics*, 1: 67–94, 1974.

[195] H. Minkowski. Diskontinuitätsbereich für arithmetische Äquivalenz.
Journal für Math., 129: 220–274, 1950.

[196] L. Mirsky. On a generalization of Hadamard's determinantal inequality
due to Szasz. *Arch. Math.*, VIII: 274–275, 1957.

[197] S. C. Moy. Generalizations of the Shannon-McMillan theorem. *Pacific
Journal of Mathematics*, 11: 705–714, 1961.

[198] J. Neyman and E. S. Pearson. On the problem of the most efficient tests
of statistical hypotheses. *Phil. Trans. Roy. Soc., London, Series A*, 231:
289–337, 1933.

[199] H. Nyquist. Certain factors affecting telegraph speed. *Bell Sys. Tech.
Journal*, 3: 324, 1924.

[200] J. Omura. A coding theorem for discrete time sources. *IEEE Trans.
Inform. Theory*, IT-19: 490–498, 1973.

[201] A. Oppenheim. Inequalities connected with definite Hermitian forms. *J.
London Math. Soc.*, 5: 114–119, 1930.

[202] S. Orey. On the Shannon-Perez-Moy theorem. *Contemp. Math.*, 41:
319–327, 1985.

[203] D. S. Ornstein. Bernoulli shifts with the same entropy are isomorphic.
Advances in Math., 4: 337–352, 1970.

[204] L. H. Ozarow. The capacity of the white Gaussian multiple access
channel with feedback. *IEEE Trans. Inform. Theory*, IT-30: 623–629,
1984.

[205] L. H. Ozarow and C. S. K. Leung. An achievable region and an outer
bound for the Gaussian broadcast channel with feedback. *IEEE Trans.
Inform. Theory*, IT-30: 667–671, 1984.

[206] H. Pagels. *The Dreams of Reason: The Computer and the Rise of the
Sciences of Complexity*. Simon and Schuster, New York, 1988.

[207] R. Pasco. Source coding algorithms for fast data compression. PhD
Thesis, Stanford University, 1976.

[208] A. Perez. Extensions of Shannon-McMillan's limit theorem to more
general stochastic processes. In *Trans. Third Prague Conference
on Information Theory, Statistical Decision Functions and Random
Processes*, pages 545–574, Prague, 1964. Czechoslovak Academy of
Sciences.

[209] J. T. Pinkston. An application of rate-distortion theory to a converse to
the coding theorem. *IEEE Trans. Inform. Theory*, IT-15: 66–71, 1969.

[210] M. S. Pinsker. Talk at Soviet Information Theory Meeting, 1969.

[211] M. S. Pinsker. The capacity region of noiseless broadcast channels. *Prob.
Inform. Trans.*, 14: 97–102, 1978.

[212] M. S. Pinsker. *Information and Stability of Random Variables and
Processes*. Izd. Akad. Nauk, 1960.

[213] L. R. Rabiner and R. W. Schafer. *Digital Processing of Speech Signals*. Prentice-Hall, Englewood Cliffs, NJ, 1978.

[214] C. R. Rao. Information and accuracy obtainable in the estimation of statistical parameters. *Bull. Calcutta Math. Soc.*, 37: 81–91, 1945.

[215] F. M. Reza. *An Introduction to Information Theory*. McGraw-Hill, New York, 1961.

[216] S. O. Rice. Communication in the presence of noise—Probability of error for two encoding schemes. *Bell Sys. Tech. Journal*, 29: 60–93, 1950.

[217] J. Rissanen. Generalized Kraft inequality and arithmetic coding. *IBM J. Res. Devel.* 20: 198, 1976.

[218] J. Rissanen. Modelling by shortest data description. *Automatica*, 14: 465–471, 1978.

[219] J. Rissanen. A universal prior for integers and estimation by minimum description length. *Ann. Stat.*, 11: 416–431, 1983.

[220] J. Rissanen. Universal coding, information, prediction and estimation. *IEEE Trans. Inform. Theory*, IT-30: 629–636, 1984.

[221] J. Rissanen. Stochastic complexity and modelling. *Ann. Stat.*, 14: 1080–1100, 1986.

[222] J. Rissanen. Stochastic complexity (with discussions). *Journal of the Royal Statistical Society*, 49: 223–239, 252–265, 1987.

[223] J. Rissanen. *Stochastic Complexity in Statistical Inquiry*. World Scientific, New Jersey, 1989.

[224] P. A. Samuelson. Lifetime portfolio selection by dynamic stochastic programming. *Rev. of Economics and Statistics*, 1: 236–239, 1969.

[225] P. A. Samuelson. The 'fallacy' of maximizing the geometric mean in long sequences of investing or gambling. *Proc. Nat. Acad. Science*, 68: 214–224, 1971.

[226] P. A. Samuelson. Why we should not make mean log of wealth big though years to act are long. *Journal of Banking and Finance*, 3: 305–307, 1979.

[227] I. N. Sanov. On the probability of large deviations of random variables. *Mat. Sbornik*, 42: 11–44, 1957.

[228] A. A. Sardinas and G. W. Patterson. A necessary and sufficient condition for the unique decomposition of coded messages. In *IRE Convention Record, Part 8*, pages 104–108, 1953.

[229] H. Sato. The capacity of the Gaussian interference channel under strong interference. *IEEE Trans. Inform. Theory*, IT-27: 786–788, 1981.

[230] H. Sato, On the capacity region of a discrete two-user channel for strong interference. *IEEE Trans. Inform. Theory*, IT-24: 377–379, 1978.

[231] H. Sato and M. Tanabe. A discrete two-user channel with strong interference. *Trans. IECE Japan*, 61: 880–884, 1978.

[232] J. P. M. Schalkwijk. The binary multiplying channel—a coding scheme that operates beyond Shannon's inner bound. *IEEE Trans. Inform. Theory*, IT-28: 107–110, 1982.

[233] J. P. M. Schalkwijk. On an extension of an achievable rate region for the binary multiplying channel. *IEEE Trans. Inform. Theory*, IT-29: 445–448, 1983.

[234] C. P. Schnorr. Process, complexity and effective random tests. *Journal of Computer and System Sciences*, 7: 376–388, 1973.

[236] C. P. Schnorr. A surview on the theory of random sequences. In Butts, R. and Hinitikka, J. , editor, *Logic, Methodology and Philosophy of Science*. Reidel, Dodrecht, 1977.

[237] G. Schwarz. Estimating the dimension of a model. *Ann. Stat.*, 6: 461–464, 1978.

[238] C. E. Shannon. A mathematical theory of communication. *Bell Sys. Tech. Journal*, 27: 379–423, 623–656, 1948.

[239] C. E. Shannon. The zero-error capacity of a noisy channel. *IRE Trans. Inform. Theory*, IT-2: 8–19, 1956.

[240] C. E. Shannon. Communication in the presence of noise. *Proc. IRE*, 37: 10–21, 1949.

[241] C. E. Shannon. Communication theory of secrecy systems. *Bell Sys. Tech. Journal*, 28: 656–715, 1949.

[242] C. E. Shannon. Prediction and entropy of printed English. *Bell Sys. Tech. Journal*, 30: 50–64, 1951.

[243] C. E. Shannon. Certain results in coding theory for noisy channels. *Inform. Contr.*, 1: 6–25, 1957.

[244] C. E. Shannon. Channels with side information at the transmitter. *IBM J. Res. Develop.*, 2: 289–293, 1958.

[245] C. E. Shannon. Coding theorems for a discrete source with a fidelity criterion. *IRE National Convention Record, Part 4*, pages 142–163, 1959.

[246] C. E. Shannon. Two-way communication channels. In *Proc. 4th Berkeley Symp. Math. Stat. Prob.*, pages 611–644, University of California Press, Berkeley, 1961.

[247] C. E. Shannon, R. G. Gallager, and E. R. Berlekamp. Lower bounds to error probability for coding in discrete memoryless channels. I. *Inform. Contr.*, 10: 65–103, 1967.

[248] C. E. Shannon, R. G. Gallager, and E. R. Berlekamp. Lower bounds to error probability for coding in discrete memoryless channels. II. *Inform. Contr.*, 10: 522–552, 1967.

[249] C. E. Shannon and W. W. Weaver. *The Mathematical Theory of Communication*. University of Illinois Press, Urbana, IL, 1949.

[250] W. F. Sharpe. *Investments*. Prentice-Hall, Englewood Cliffs, NJ, 1985.

[251] J. E. Shore and R. W. Johnson. Axiomatic derivation of the principle of maximum entropy and the principle of minimum cross-entropy. *IEEE Trans. Inform. Theory*, IT-26: 26–37, 1980.

[252] D. Slepian. *Key Papers in the Development of Information Theory*. IEEE Press, New York, 1974.

[253] D. Slepian and H. O. Pollak. Prolate spheroidal wave functions, Fourier

analysis and uncertainty: Part I. *Bell Sys. Tech. Journal*, 40: 43–64, 1961.

[254] D. Slepian and J. K. Wolf. A coding theorem for multiple access channels with correlated sources. *Bell Sys. Tech. Journal*, 52: 1037–1076, 1973.

[255] D. Slepian and J. K. Wolf. Noiseless coding of correlated information sources. *IEEE Trans. Inform. Theory*, IT-19: 471–480, 1973.

[256] R. J. Solomonoff. A formal theory of inductive inference. *Inform. Contr.*, 7: 1–22, 224–254, 1964.

[257] A. Stam. Some inequalities satisfied by the quantities of information of Fisher and Shannon. *Inform. Contr.*, 2: 101–112, 1959.

[258] D. L. Tang and L. R. Bahl. Block codes for a class of constrained noiseless channels. *Inform. Contr.*, 17: 436–461, 1970.

[259] S. C. Tornay. *Ockham: Studies and Selections*. Open Court Publishers, La Salle, IL, 1938.

[260] J. M. Van Campenhout and T. M. Cover. Maximum entropy and conditional probability. *IEEE Trans. Inform. Theory*, IT-27: 483–489, 1981.

[261] E. Van der Meulen. Random coding theorems for the general discrete memoryless broadcast channel. *IEEE Trans. Inform. Theory*, IT-21: 180–190, 1975.

[262] E. C. Van der Meulen. A survey of multi-way channels in information theory. *IEEE Trans. Inform. Theory*, IT-23: 1–37, 1977.

[263] E. C. Van der Meulen. Recent coding theorems and converses for multi-way channels. Part II: The multiple access channel (1976–1985). Department Wiskunde, Katholieke Universiteit Leuven, 1985.

[264] E. C. Van der Meulen. Recent coding theorems for multi-way channels. Part I: The broadcast channel (1976–1980). In J. K. Skwyrzinsky, editor, *New Concepts in Multi-user Communication (NATO Advanced Study Insititute Series)*. Sijthoff & Noordhoff International, 1981.

[265] A. C. G. Verdugo Lazo and P. N. Rathie. On the entropy of continuous probability distributions. *IEEE Trans. Inform. Theory*, IT-24: 120–122, 1978.

[266] A. J. Viterbi and J. K. Omura. *Principles of Digital Communication and Coding*. McGraw-Hill, New York, 1979.

[267] V. V. V'yugin. On the defect of randomness of a finite object with respect to measures with given complexity bounds. *Theory Prob. Appl.*, 32: 508–512, 1987.

[268] A. Wald. *Sequential Analysis*. Wiley, New York, 1947.

[269] T. A. Welch. A technique for high-performance data compression. *Computer*, 17: 8–19, 1984.

[270] N. Wiener. *Cybernetics*. MIT Press, Cambridge MA, and Wiley, New York, 1948.

[271] N. Wiener. *Extrapolation, Interpolation and Smoothing of Stationary Time Series*. MIT Press, Cambridge, MA and Wiley, New York, 1949.

[272] H. J. Wilcox and D. L. Myers. *An introduction to Lebesgue integration and Fourier series*. R. E. Krieger, Huntington, NY, 1978.

[273] F. M. J. Willems. The feedback capacity of a class of discrete memoryless multiple access channels. *IEEE Trans. Inform. Theory*, IT-28: 93–95, 1982.

[274] F. M. J. Willems and A. P. Hekstra. Dependence balance bounds for single-output two-way channels. *IEEE Trans. Inform. Theory*, IT-35: 44–53, 1989.

[275] I. H. Witten, R. M. Neal, and J. G. Cleary. Arithmetic coding for data compression. *Communications of the ACM*, 30: 520–540, 1987.

[276] J. Wolfowitz. The coding of messages subject to chance errors. *Illinois Journal of Mathematics*, 1: 591–606, 1957.

[277] J. Wolfowitz. *Coding Theorems of Information Theory*. Springer-Verlag, Berlin, and Prentice-Hall, Englewood Cliffs, NJ, 1978.

[278] P. M. Woodward. *Probability and Information Theory with Applications to Radar*. McGraw-Hill, New York, 1953.

[279] J. M. Wozencraft and I. M. Jacobs. *Principles of Communication Engineering*. Wiley, New York, 1965.

[280] A. Wyner. A theorem on the entropy of certain binary sequences and applications II. *IEEE Trans. Inform. Theory*, IT-19: 772–777, 1973.

[281] A. Wyner. The common information of two dependent random variables. *IEEE Trans. Inform. Theory*, IT-21: 163–179, 1975.

[282] A. Wyner. On source coding with side information at the decoder. *IEEE Trans. Inform. Theory*, IT-21: 294–300, 1975.

[283] A. Wyner and J. Ziv. A theorem on the entropy of certain binary sequences and applications I. *IEEE Trans. Inform. Theory*, IT-19: 769–771, 1973.

[284] A. Wyner and J. Ziv. The rate distortion function for source coding with side information at the receiver. *IEEE Trans. Inform. Theory*, IT-22: 1–11, 1976.

[285] A. Wyner and J. Ziv. On entropy and data compression. Submitted to *IEEE Trans. Inform. Theory*.

[286] A. D. Wyner. The capacity of the band-limited Gaussian channel. *Bell Sys. Tech. Journal*, 45: 359–371, 1965.

[287] Z. Zhang, T. Berger, and J. P. M. Schalkwijk. New outer bounds to capacity regions of two-way channels. *IEEE Trans. Inform. Theory*, IT-32: 383–386, 1986.

[288] J. Ziv. Coding of sources with unknown statistics—Part II: Distortion relative to a fidelity criterion. *IEEE Trans. Inform. Theory*, IT-18: 389–394, 1972.

[289] J. Ziv. Coding theorems for individual sequences. *IEEE Trans. Inform. Theory*, IT-24: 405–412, 1978.

[290] J. Ziv and A. Lempel. A universal algorithm for sequential data compression. *IEEE Trans. Inform. Theory*, IT-23: 337–343, 1977.

[291] J. Ziv and A. Lempel. Compression of individual sequences by variable rate coding. *IEEE Trans. Inform. Theory*, IT-24: 530–536, 1978.

[292] W. H. Zurek. Algorithmic randomness and physical entropy. *Phys. Rev. A*, 40: 4731–4751, October 15, 1989.

[293] W. H. Zurek. Thermodynamic cost of computation, algorithmic complexity and the information metric. *Nature*, 341: 119–124, September 14, 1989.

[294] W. H. Zurek, editor. *Complexity, Entropy and the Physics of Information. Proceedings of the 1988 Workshop on the Complexity, Entropy and the Physics of Information.* Addison-Wesley, Reading, MA, 1990.

List of Symbols

Index

Page numbers set in **boldface** indicate the primary references.